MARRIAGE AND FAMILY IN A CHANGING SOCIETY

Second Edition

EDITED BY

James M. Henslin

THE FREE PRESS
A Division of Macmillan, Inc.
NEW YORK

The Free Press
A Division of Macmillan, Inc.
866 Third Avenue, New York, N.Y. 10022

Collier Macmillan Canada, Inc.

Printed in the United States of America

printing number

2 3 4 5 6 7 8 9 10

Library of Congress Cataloging in Publication Data

Main entry under title:

Marriage and family in a changing society.

Includes bibliographies and index.
1. Marriage—United States—Addresses, essays, lectures. 2. Family—United States—Addresses, essays, lectures. I. Henslin, James M.
HQ734.M3867 1985 306.8'0973 84-25994
ISBN 0-02-914870-7

Credits and Acknowledgments

Grateful acknowledgment is made to the authors and publishers who have granted permission to reprint the following selections:

1. "The Sociology of Marriage and Family" by James M. Henslin. Copyright © 1985 by James M. Henslin. Written for this volume.
2. "The Family as a Changing Institution" by Harold T. Christensen and Kathryn P. Johnsen from *Marriage and the Family*, pp. 20–30. Copyright © 1971, the Ronald Press Company. Reprinted by permission of John Wiley & Sons, Inc.
3. "The Myth of Family Independence" by Kenneth Keniston. From *All Our Children* by Kenneth Keniston, copyright © 1977 by Carnegie Corporation of New York. Reprinted by permission of Harcourt Brace Jovanovich, Inc.
4. "The American Couple in Historical Perspective" by Philip Blumstein and Pepper Schwartz. From *American Couples* by Philip Blumstein and Pepper Schwartz, pp. 25–34. Reprinted by permission of the authors.
5. "The Stages of the Family Life Cycle" by Monica McGoldrick and Elizabeth A. Carter. Reproduced by permission from *Normal Family Processes*, Froma Walsh Editor. Copyright © 1982, The Guilford Press, New York, NY.
6. "The Paradox of Perfection" by Arlene Skolnick. From the *Wilson Quarterly*, Summer 1980. Copyright © 1980 by the Woodrow Wilson International Center for Scholars. Reprinted by permission.

7. "Equality in North American Marriages" by Leo Zakuta. From *Social Research*, Vol. 30, No. 2 (Summer 1963). Reprinted by permission of the author.

8. "Trends in Fertility" by Sar A. Levitan and Richard S. Belous. From Levitan, Sar A.; Richard S. Belous. *What's Happening to the American Family?* The Johns Hopkins University Press (1981), London/Baltimore. Reprinted by permission.

9. "High-Tech Breeding" by Paul Bagne. Reprinted with permission from *Mother Jones* magazine. Copyright © 1983, Foundation for National Progress.

10. Matilda White Riley, "The Family in an Aging Society," *Journal of Family Issues*, Vol. 4, No. 3 (September 1983), pp. 439–454. Copyright © 1983 by Sage Publications, Inc. Reprinted by permission of Sage Publications, Inc.

11. "Asian-American Families" by Bob H. Suzuki. Adapted from *Parenting in a Multicultural Society*, edited by Mario D. Fantini and Rene Cardenas. Chap. 7, pp. 74–102. Copyright © 1980 by Longman Inc. Reprinted by permission of Longman Inc., New York

12. Paul C. Glick, "Black Families," pp. 106–26. From *Black Families*, Harriett McAdoo, Ed., Beverly Hills, CA: Sage Publications, 1981.

13. "Chicano Families" by Alfredo Mirandé. From *Journal of Marriage and Family*, Vol. 39, No. 4, (November 1977), pp. 747–756. Copyrighted © 1977 by the National Council on Family Relations, Fairview Community School Center, 1910 West County Road B, Suite 147, St. Paul, Minnesota 55113. Reprinted by permission.

14. "The Social Psychology of Sexual Development" by John Gagnon and Bruce Henderson. Excerpts from *Human Sexuality: An Age of Ambiguity* (Westwood, Mass.: The Paperbook Press, 1975), pp. 30–34. Copyright © 1975 by Little, Brown and Company.

15. "Childhood Lessons" by Ann Oakley. From *Subject Women* by Ann Oakley. Copyright © 1981 by Ann Oakley. Reprinted by permission of Pantheon Books, a Division of Random House, Inc.

16. "The Man–Woman Crisis" by Clayton Barbeau. From *Delivering the Male: Out of the Tough Guy Trap Into a Better Marriage* by Clayton Barbeau. Copyright © 1982 Clayton C. Barbeau. Published by Winston Press, Inc., 430 Oak Grove, Minneapolis, MN 55403. All rights reserved. Used with permission.

17. "The Love Research" by Zick Rubin. Copyright © 1977 *Human Behavior* magazine. Reprinted by permission.

18. "The Secret Ranking" by Hans Zetterberg. From *Journal of Marriage and Family*, Vol. 28 (1966). Copyrighted © 1966 by the National Council on Family Relations, Fairview Community School Center, 1910 West Country Road B, Suite 147, St. Paul, MN 55113. Reprinted by permission.

19. "From Strangers to Intimates" by David A. Karp and William C. Yoels. Specified abridgement from pages 128–138 and 149 of *Symbols, Selves and Society: Understanding Interaction* by David A. Karp and William C. Yoels. Copyright © 1979 by David A. Karp and William C. Yoels. Reprinted by permission of Harper & Row, Publishers, Inc.

20. "The Meaning of Love" by Thomas E. Lasswell and Marcia E. Lasswell. Excerpts from *Journal of Marriage and Family Counseling*, Vol. 2, No. 3 (1976), pp. 211–224. Copyright © 1976 by the American Association of Marriage and Family Therapy.

21. "Sexual Revolution, Sexual Evolution—Or Just More of the Same?" by Theodore Caplow, Howard M. Bahr, Bruce A. Chadwick, Reuben Hill, and Margaret Holmes Williamson. Extracts from *Middletown Families: Fifty Years of Change and Continuity* by Theodore Caplow, et al. University of Minnesota Press, Minneapolis. Copyright © 1982 by the University of Minnesota.

22. Pepper Schwartz and Janet Lever, "Fear and Loathing at a College Mixer," *Urban Life*, Vol. 4, No. 4 (January 1976), pp. 413–431. Copyright © 1976 by Sage Publications, Inc. Reprinted by permission of Sage Publications, Inc.

23. "College Dating: Games, Strategies, and Peeves" by Elyce Pike and Stephen Hall. Copyright Elyce Pike and Stephen Hall. Reprinted by permission of the authors.

24. "Theories of Mate Selection" by Bruce K. Eckland. Excerpts from *Eugenics Quarterly* (now *Social Biology*) 15 (1968):17–23. Copyright © 1968 by the American Eugenics Society. Reprinted by permission.

25. "The Voluntary Singles" by Peter J. Stein. Revised by the author for this book from an earlier version that appeared in *Single Life: Unmarried Adults in Social Context*. New York: St. Martin's Press, 1981. Reprinted with permission from the author.

26. Patrick G. Jackson, "On Living Together Unmarried." From *Journal of Family Issues*, Vol. 4, No. 1 (March 1983), pp. 35–59. Copyright © 1983 by Sage Publications, Inc. Reprinted by permission of Sage Publications, Inc.

27. "The World of Singles" by Mimi Rodin. Reprinted by permission of the publisher from "Tuesdays and Saturdays: A Preliminary Study of the Domestic Patterns of Young Urban Singles," in *Urban Anthropology*, Vol. 2 (1973), pp. 93–112. Copyright © 1973 Plenum Publishing Corporation.

28. "American Marriage—Better Than Ever?" by Theodore Caplow, Howard M. Bahr, Bruce A. Chadwick, Reuben Hill, and Margaret Holmes Williamson. Extracts from *Middletown Families: Fifty Years of Change and Continuity* by Theodore Caplow, et al. Copyright © 1982 by the University of Minnesota. Reprinted by permission of the University of Minnesota Press, Minneapolis.

29. "Five Types of Marriage" by John F. Cuber and Peggy Harroff. Excerpts from John F. Cuber and Peggy Harroff, *The Significant Americans*, pp. 43–65. Copyright © 1968 by John F. Cuber and Peggy Harroff.

30. "What Makes Today's Marriages Last?" by Philip Blumstein and Pepper Schwartz. Reprinted by the permission of the authors and Family Weekly, 1515 Broadway, NY, NY 10036.

31. Nicholas Stinnett, "Strong Families," pp. 27–38 in *Prevention in Family Services*, edited by David R. Mace. Copyright © 1983. Reprinted by permission of Sage Publications, Inc.

32. "Working Mothers" by Kenneth Keniston. From *All Our Children* by Kenneth Keniston, copyright © 1977 by Carnegie Corporation of New York. Reprinted by permission of Harcourt Brace Jovanovich, Inc.

33. "Can a Two-Career Family Live Happily Ever After?" From *Tradeoffs: Executive, Family and Organizational Life* by Barrie S. Greiff, M.D. and Preston K. Munter, M.D. Copyright © 1980 by Barrie S. Greiff, M.D. and Preston K. Munter, M.D. Reprinted by arrangement with New American Library, New York, New York.

34. "Role-Sharing Couples" by Linda Haas. From *Family Relations*, July 1980. Copyrighted © 1980 by the National Council on Family Relations, Fairview Community School Center, 1910 West Country Road B, Suite 147, St. Paul, Minnesota, 55113. Reprinted by permission.

35. "The Pleasure Bond: A New Look at Sexuality and Committment" by William H. Masters and Virginia E. Johnson. Copyright © 1970, 1971, 1972, 1973, 1974 by William H. Masters and Virginia E. Johnson in association with Robert Levin. Reprinted by permission of Little, Brown and Company.

36. "Sexuality in the Early Years of Marriage" by Cathy Stein Greenblat. *Journal of Marriage and Family*, May 1983. Copyrighted © 1983 by the National Council on Family Relations, Fairview Community School Center, 1910 West Country Road B, Suite 147, St. Paul, Minnesota 55113. Reprinted by permission.

37. "The Sexual Stages of Marriage" by Ellen Frank and Carol Anderson. Reprinted by permission of the authors.

38. "A Fate Worse Than Death" by Maxine Hong Kingston. From *The Woman Warrior: Memoirs of a Girlhood Among Ghosts*, by Maxine Hong Kingston. Copyright © 1975, 1976 by Maxine Hong Kingston. Reprinted by permission of Alfred A. Knopf, Inc.

39. "Children Out of Wedlock" by Sar A. Levitan and Richard S. Belous. From Levitan, Sar A. and Richard S. Belous, *What's Happening in the American Family?* The Johns Hopkins University Press (1981), London/Baltimore. Reprinted by permission.

40. "Childhood Through the Ages" by Elin McCoy. From *Parents Magazine*, January 1981. Copyright © 1981 by Elin McCoy. Reprinted by permission of Elin McCoy and her agents, Raines & Raines, 71 Park Avenue, New York, NY 10016.

41. "The Transition to Parenthood" by Brent C. Miller and Donna L. Sollie. From Brent C. Miller and Donna L. Sollie, "Normal Stresses During the

Transition to Parenthood" in *Family Relations*, October 1980. Copyrighted © 1980 by the National Council on Family Relations, Fairview Community School Center, 1910 West Country Road B, Suite 147, St. Paul, Minnesota 55113. Reprinted by permission.

42. "Worlds of Pain" by Lillian Breslow Rubin. Excerpts from *Worlds of Pain* by Lillian Breslow Rubin. Copyright © 1976 by Lillian Breslow Rubin. Reprinted by permission of Basic Books, Inc., Publishers.

43. "Permanent Postponement: Childlessness as a Waiting Game" by Jean E. Veevers. Reprinted by permission of Butterworth & Co. (Canada) Ltd. from Jean E. Veevers, *Childless by Choice* (1980), pp. 20–34.

44. "Why So Much Divorce?" by James M. Henslin. Copyright © 1985 by James M. Henslin. Written for this volume.

45. "Uncoupling: The Social Construction of Divorce" by Diane Vaughan. Reprinted from *Uncoupling: The Social Construction of Divorce*, by Diane Vaughan. Commissioned for *Social Interaction: Readings in Sociology*, 2nd Edition, by Howard Robboy and Candace Clark. Copyright © 1983 by St. Martin's Press, Inc. Reprinted with permission of the publisher.

46. "Effects of Parental Divorce" by Judith S. Wallerstein and Joan B. Kelly. From the *American Journal of Orthopsychiatry*, Vol. 46, No. 2, pp. 257–269. Reprinted by permission of the American Journal of Orthopsychiatry.

47. "Part-Time and Single Fathers" by Kristine M. Rosenthal and Harry F. Keshet. From Rosenthal, "Childcare Responsibilities of Part-Time and Single Fathers" in *Alternative Lifestyles*. Reprinted by permission of Human Sciences Press, Inc. 72 Fifth Avenue, NY, NY 10011.

48. "The Current Situation" by Philip Blumstein and Pepper Schwartz. From *American Couples* by Philip Blumstein and Pepper Schwartz. William Morrow, New York, 1981. Reprinted by permission of the authors.

49. "Remarriage and the Family Life Cycle" by Monica McGoldrick and Elizabeth A. Carter. Reproduced by permission from *Normal Family Processes*, Froma Walsh Editor. Copyright © 1982, The Guilford Press, New York, NY.

50. "The Six Stations of Remarriage" by Ann Goetting. From *Family Relations*, April 1982. Copyrighted 1982 by the National Council on Family Relations, Fairview Community School Center, 1910 West Country Road B, Suite 147, St. Paul, Minnesota 55113.

51. "Remarriage as an Incomplete Institution" by Andrew Cherlin. *American Journal of Sociology*, Vol. 84, No. 3, pp. 634–650. Reprinted by permission of the author and The University of Chicago Press.

52. "The Futility of Family Policy" by Gilbert Y. Steiner. Reprinted by permission from the Brookings Institution.

53. David Finkelhor, "Common Features of Family Abuse," pp. 17–23 in *The Dark Side of Families* edited by David Finkelhor. Copyright © 1981 by Sage

Publications, Inc. Reprinted by permission of Sage Publications, Inc., and author.

54. "The Future of the Family" by Edward Cornish. From *The Futurist*, February 1979. Reprinted by permission from *The Futurist*, published by the World Future Society, 4916 St. Elmo Avenue, Washington, D.C. 20014.

For Linda—
with whom I am privileged to share
that life-transforming experience called marriage

Contents

Section 2: Contemporary Issues and Trends

Section 3: Marriage and Family and Minorities

PART II. PATHWAYS

Section 4: Sex Roles

Section 5: Romantic Involvements

Section 6: Dating and Mating

Section 7: Alternatives to Marriage

PART III. MARRIED LIFE

Section 8: Lasting Relationships

Section 9: Work and Marriage

Section 10: Sex and Marriage

Preface

In this second edition readers will find what I hope are welcome changes. Before going into them, however, I would like to address some related issues.

ON VALUES AND OTHER POSITIONS

Over and over one hears that it is necessary for sociologists to specify their value positions. Certainly values do influence the outcome of professional endeavors—as has been amply demonstrated time after time—yet to specify values remains the exception rather than the rule.

As the editor of this volume, I wish to spell out what appear to be relevant value positions, for I am aware that they have been fundamentally instrumental in shaping this book, especially as I chose one article rather than another.

What values, then, helped to shape the contents of this book?

First, I am personally convinced that marriage itself is a remarkably worthwhile social institution. I see marriage as having much to offer individuals as they go through life: a sense of meaning to one's endeavors, solace during periods of crises, the diminution of self-doubts, a challenge to personal growth, a sense of satisfaction in learning to please someone so vital to one's own self, unparalleled emotions as one sees children born and mature, and . . . I could go on and on.

These ideas about marriage—its potential and its role in the individual's life—which may seem obvious to many readers, come from personally held convictions. To be sure, these convictions are based on experience—but are not most convictions? In other words, there is nothing about such a position that is self-evident. They are convictions, firmly held ideas about the nature of social reality. In short, they represent values. And this particular conviction or value has underlain the process of selecting the articles in this book.

That I see marriage as a major part of human development, as a stimulating part of the human experience, does not at all mean that I fail to recognize that marriage is filled with problems and crises. Nor do I view marriage as escapism, a flight from reality into a socially constructed personal haven that offers final solutions to life's problems. On the contrary, what we might call the tough issues of marriage and family emerge strongly in these selections, not some simplistic Pollyannaish point of view.

Second, I am firmly convinced that the sociological perspective is valuable, and that students are better off for taking a course in marriage and family. This means that I view the sociological perspective (or imagination) not simply as a conceptual device divorced from everyday life. Rather, I see the sociological perspective as highly practical, as integrally related to the student's relationships, and even to his or her inner and intimate life.

I tried, then, to select articles that communicate a sociological understanding of marriage and family. If this goal has been met, these selections ought to not only stimulate in-class discussion, but also to be of direct benefit to students by providing a broader contextual understanding of everyday life events.

Because almost all students who take this course will themselves experience marriage, it seems worthwhile, then, to provide them with selections that communicate the potential of marriage. At the same time—and also based on the above value positions—the selections need to communicate the significance of the sociological framework for understanding the potential of marriage, as well as the social barriers that so often prevent that potential from being realized. Making clearer both the potential of marriage, as well as the ease of its failure—and both within the context of its sociological underpinnings—can, I believe, better enable students to overcome those challenges as they grasp the potentials that marriage offers.

Certainly for none will marriage come wholly constructed. Rather, each will be faced with making hard choices in order to work out an individual adjustment to the facts of married life. Part of my values—hopefully explicitly communicated—is that the better one understands the sociological context that constrains people, the better one is equipped to deal with those constraints.

Finally, out of these value positions emerges a theme that runs through the selections in this book: Marriage is not a state, but a process. It is this dynamic of marriage that the selections convey, that marriage is an ongoing, continually developing relationship rather than something attained by a license and vows. By communicating this position, the selections provide a perspective that increases self-awareness, deals with the realities of marriage, and, ultimately, increases the likelihood that one can achieve the potential of marriage.

THE STRUCTURE OF THE BOOK

I have taught the basic course in marriage and family for a good number of years, more, in fact, than I usually care to recall. Desiring to be an effective instructor in this course, which enrolls many students who are not sociology majors, I have tried several approaches in my teaching—some good, some better, and some, unfortunately, at the other end of the evaluative scale.

Of the many things that I have learned in these experiences, the following stands out: Students respond well to a "developmental" approach in the study of marriage and family. By this I mean sequencing the course materials so they begin with early life and then progress through dating and mate selection, marital adjustment, divorce, remarriage, and the like. Consequently, a developmental framework is the organizing device for the selections in this book. Retaining this sequencing also reflects the favorable response with which it was met in the first edition.

The primary value of this organization is that it makes it easier for the instructor to teach and students to learn. This is because it builds on the way students tend to see marriage and family, roughly following the course of events in which students experience the world. For example, most students who take this course are usually at the point in life in which they have already experienced love, are acutely aware of their sex roles, are involved in dating, have at least considered alternatives to marriage, and are now close to marriage in the sense that they are contemplating getting married sometime during the next several years. Following their wedding, they can expect to make the transition to marital sexuality, to parenthood, and so on.

In short, the basic structure of the book roughly parallels the student's life. It matches a framework students already possess for thinking about marriage and family. Consequently, to build on this framework aids students in their learning and, not inconsequentially, teachers in their teaching.

A couple of variations, however, are worth noting. First, not all students who take this class are at the same point in their lives. Especially now that more older students are returning to college, it is not unusual for a student to have already experienced parenting, divorce, and so on. Regardless of the point in life that a particular student has reached, however, the developmental approach allows the student to first look directly at what he or she has already experienced, to attain greater understanding of that personal experience through sociological analysis, and then to anticipate that which is likely to unfold in his or her life.

Second, before moving into the developmental sequence, it seemed good to lay a broad sociological foundation. Consequently, Part I, "Marriage and Family in Sociological Perspective," is new to this edition. Section I of this part lets the student see what a *sociology* of marriage and family is—the interconnections between individual marital and familial experience and the sociohistorical context of marriage and family.

After laying this sociological foundation, we next turn to contemporary issues and trends in marriage and family. This second section also brings the student face-to-face with large-scale influences on marriage and family life—this time by examining specific issues, ones that are likely to provoke a healthy exchange of views among students. Section 3 places the focus on marriage and family and minorities. These selections provide materials not only worth learning in their own right, but also a contrastive context for interpreting the rest of the book.

Following Part I, we turn to the second part, called "Pathways." The selections here turn the focus onto the premarital experiences that are forerunners or pathways to marriage. Section 4 opens this part by highlighting sex roles, a feature of social life that not only underlies our dating and marrying, but is also so far-reaching that it pervades most of our relationships. In Section 5 we focus on romantic involvements, looking at the processes by which people move toward closeness with others (caring, intimacy, love, and romance). The sixth section examines dating and premarital sex, and the seventh follows this up with a look at alternatives to marriage.

"Pathways" will stimulate much in-class discussion. Basic relationships between males and females, love, dating, premarital sex, the world of singles, sex roles, and cohabitation always stimulate lively exchanges among students.

But so it is with the other parts of the book. Part III, for example, focuses on major issues in "Married Life." In Section 8 we look at what makes relationships last, and in Section 9 at the adjustments that couples make to the world of work. In Section 10 we focus on the sexual relationships of married couples, and in Section 11 on major issues in parenting.

In Part IV, "Endings and New Beginnings," we look at divorce and remarriage. Section 12 deals with the question of why the divorce rate in the United States is so high and how people adjust to divorce, while Section 13 looks at major issues in remarriage.

In Part V, "Social Policy and the Future," we examine the controversy that is built into the innocuous-sounding concept of family policy, then apply family policy to family abuse and present scenarios of possible futures of the family.

CHANGES . . . AND MORE CHANGES

Adopters of the first edition will find themselves at home in this edition's basic structure and will, hopefully, welcome the addition of the new Part I. A closer examination will show other changes as well, for this edition also contains new sections on lasting relationships, remarriage, an expanded coverage of divorce, and greater emphasis on social policy. Approximately *90 percent* of the selections are new to this edition! That severe a change merits an explanation.

First, the field of marriage and family is rapidly expanding. Indeed, it is difficult to keep up with the constant stream of research. Consequently, articles tend to be short-lived. Second, much of the materials now appearing is excellent and deserves more widespread circulation among students. Third, and highly significant, an increasing amount of published materials provide a sense of "having been there" as well as solid sociological understanding of what happened "when one was there." I strived for greater emphasis on this approach in this edition.

If this edition is successful, then, it will be because the coverage is broad and the selections communicate well. As we examine essential aspects of the marriage and family experience, the goal is that we do not merely report on facts and figures, which change so rapidly, but share something about the people behind them.

You, of course, are the final judge of whether I have succeeded in the goals of this book.

APPRECIATIONS . . .

I wish to first express my sincere appreciation to my wife, Linda. Her efforts have been instrumental in shaping this second edition, and, in fact, in bringing it into being. Her insight into what is useful to share with students is phenomenal. Because of her efforts on my behalf, this second edition has its new first part and its other new sections. In addition, I owe her public recognition for locating so many articles that ended up being incorporated here. Without her, in fact, this edition would not have become reality this year—and possibly never.

The authors and publishers of these articles also deserve an expression of appreciation for granting permission to use their work in this second edition. It is no exaggeration to say that without it there would be no book. I also wish to thank my students, who have borne with me as I have developed my perspective on the basic materials in marriage and family. From them I have learned much—especially from their frank and enthusiastic (always to be marveled at!) sharing of what is essential in their world. At this point, others will profit from that sharing.

Finally, I would like to add that I would be happy to hear from both students and teachers regarding their experiences, whether positive or negative, in using this book and I welcome your suggestions as aids in making revisions. You may communicate with me by writing to the address given below.

James M. Henslin
Department of Sociology
SIUE
Edwardsville, Illinois 62026

PART I

Marriage and Family in Sociological Perspective

THE SOCIOLOGICAL PERSPECTIVE ON MARRIAGE AND FAMILY is to see marriage and family as social creations, to examine how they take their shape from the society and culture of which they are a part, and the role they then play in the individual's life. For example, molded and shaped by society and culture, marriage and family take different forms in different societies. In one society a man and a woman may have only one spouse at a time, while in another they may have more than one. In one society premarital sex is forbidden and unmarried males and females kept apart, while in another it is tolerated, and in still another encouraged or even required. Similarly, to give birth before marriage is a disgraceful matter in one society, tolerated in another, and in a third it's required as evidence of fertility before a woman is allowed to marry. Again, in one society the disciplining of children is the father's duty, in another the mother's responsibility, and in still another the duty of the mother's eldest brother.

Although the customs and expectations surrounding marriage and family differ markedly from one society to another, in each they come predetermined for the individual. They already exist at the individual's birth, and they become a major part of his or her assumptions of what life is like. What the individual learns about his or her culture's ideas on marriage and family become an essential part of the way he or she sees the world. Learned early, the forms and customs common to one's group are assumed to be natural, and they largely drop from one's consciousness. However, they remain most significant, for they shape the context of the choices available to the individual and provide the basic framework within which the individual makes his or her life choices.

To see how these constraints operate in the individual's life lies at the heart of the sociological perspective of marriage and family: It is to see the boundaries that society sets. It is to make visible how society incorporates its expectations of family life into the individual—how these expectations become the individual's and how they underlie the marital and familial roles the individual assumes. It is to see the social changes unfolding in society as the result of historical forces set in motion long ago and how those changes affect what individuals experience in marriage and family.

The sociological perspective, then, is to unearth the social influences that underlie people's behavior in marriage and family. It is to make visible the social underpinnings of this essential part of life, most of which is ordinarily perceived as simply a matter of personal choice.

The goal of Part I is to introduce the broad social context that influences marriage and family. The chapters are designed to make more visible the sweeping social changes that affect what you yourself have experienced, are now experiencing, and will experience. To gain the sociological perspective is to broaden your vision so you can better see the social forces that affect people's lives—including your own.

To make visible the social constraints within which we all live out our lives is a fascinating challenge that sociology offers and to which this first part of the book invites you. Be fairly warned, however, that after attaining the sociological perspective, nothing may again look the same.

SECTION 1

The Sociology of Marriage and Family

THAT MARRIAGE AND FAMILY DO NOT OCCUR IN A SOCIOCULTURAL VACUUM, but are given shape and are continuously influenced by the society in which they exist, could be taken as the summary of this first section of the book. Stressed throughout these selections is the point that in order to adequately understand marriage and family we need to see the interconnections between them and the other institutions of society. To gain a view of this broad context of marriage and family also provides us invaluable insight into our own personal marital and familial experiences.

In the first chapter James M. Henslin specifies the major dimensions in the sociology of marriage and family. The goal of this introductory chapter is to define for the reader exactly what is a sociology of marriage and family. Because this is sometimes confusing to beginning students, this first chapter should be read with care. It lays the foundation for understanding many of the chapters that follow, both in this section and in the rest of the book.

In the second chapter Harold T. Christensen and Kathryn P. Johnsen focus on the functions of the family. (As with many sociologists, their analysis of marriage is subsumed under the more general term "family.") They attempt to identify *universal* functions of the family, functions that characterize all families everywhere. As they do so, they also stress that the social changes occurring in society are producing corresponding changes in the family's basic functions.

In the third chapter Kenneth Keniston's focus on family functions is somewhat narrower. He examines a myth—the family is somehow an independent unit—that pervades American thought concerning the family. He demonstrates that this assumption has always been a myth, although it did come closer to reality during earlier periods of our history than it does at present. Sweeping social changes in the United States and the Western world have worked together to create a greater dependency of the contemporary American family on other social institutions. At the same time, however, these changes have increased the expectations attached to parenting, making today's parenting tasks a more complicated matter than earlier generations experienced.

In the fourth chapter Philip Blumstein and Pepper Schwartz also focus on the American family as they present a brief overview of how major changes have affected the married couple in American society. Their emphasis is on how husbands and wives have become less of an integrated, cooperative unit—the social changes that have forced husbands and wives apart, have thereby weakened the marital relationship, and have laid the groundwork for increasing divorce.

In the fifth and concluding chapter Monica McGoldrick and Elizabeth A. Carter paint another broad picture of marriage and family. Their focus, however, is not on the effects that broad social change has had on marriage and family, but on the recurring, cyclical features that characterize individual families as they go through life. McGoldrick and Carter first identify the major stages in what they call the "life cycle of the family." They then delineate the major problems that must be solved in each stage if the family members are to move on to the next stage in the cycle. Although their focus is broad, it has a narrowing aspect to it: As they indicate, they are not characterizing all families everywhere, or even all American families, but, rather, the middle-class American family.

It should be apparent that the sociology of marriage and family is not a subject isolated from the rest of one's life, but, rather, is highly integrated with it. Through these opening chapters, you should gain not only a much better idea of what a sociology of marriage and family is, but this broadened perspective should also provide a contextual view on your own experiences in marriage and family.

For example, the Christensen and Johnsen analysis of universal family functions should help provide a context for viewing the family in which you were raised (what sociologists call your "family of orientation"). Keniston's presentation should provide insight into why the family you form by marriage and childbirth (your "family of procreation") is likely to be increasingly dependent on nonfamily institutions, as well as why child-rearing is likely to become even more difficult than it now is. Through the Blumstein and Schwartz overview you should be able to better see some of the social forces that tend to weaken the bonds between a husband and wife, how those forces are continuing to grow, and how they are likely to play a major role in your own marriage. Finally, the McGoldrick and Carter analysis can provide a tool you can use to examine your personal situation. You can look at where you are now in the family life cycle, the major developmental tasks that are involving you, and then glimpse those that still lie ahead.

CHAPTER 1

The Sociology of Marriage and Family

James M. Henslin

ABSTRACT: The sociological approach to understanding marriage and family is to place marriage and family within the social context that shapes people's behavior. It is to examine the social forces that influence what people do in marriage and family—how society molds people's expectations of marriage and family life. The author stresses that through a socialization process that begins with our birth we come to view our own society's expectations concerning marriage and family as "natural." These expectations, however, are arbitrarily established boundaries—a limiting framework within which we live out our married and family lives. Mechanisms of social control (both direct and indirect) influence even the intimate areas of married and family life. The author then uses an extended example to illustrate these points, concluding with the issue of "social forces" versus "individual choice."

To help gain an understanding of what is meant by the term "the sociology of marriage and family," let us first look at the following event:

> The government of China has mobilized an army of party members to enforce its birth control policies. These officials utilize a tempting carrot and a rather brutalizing stick. They offer financial, educational, and health care incentives to couples who limit their reproduction to one child, while they reduce wages and refuse promotions to couples who violate the government's wishes and have a second or third child.
>
> Because the Chinese have a strong preference for sons, this policy has led to a sharp increase in female infanticide.

> A woman who conceives a second or third time is visited by party members who try to convince her to have an abortion for the good of the country. Government officials force abortion on some who refuse, and medical personnel will sometimes inject a woman about to give birth so she delivers a stillborn.
>
> The social control is so exacting and explicit that women must display their sanitary napkins on demand to show they are not pregnant (Vinck, 1981; Mirsky, 1983).

In a similar manner, our society . . . but we shall return to this matter later. First, I wish to stress that the heart of the sociological perspective is that human behavior is not understandable apart from the broader sociocultural context within which that behavior occurs. Human behavior is not determined by instincts; nor do people possess other built-in mechanisms that push them into specific behaviors. Humans are not driven by internal forces that, invariably patterning their lives, make one human group quite like that of another.

Human behavior is quite the contrary. As in the illustration above, patterns of human behavior differ markedly from one human group to another. On the broader level, the customs of a group of primitive people living in Australia differ sharply from the practices of peasants in Southeast Asia. Similarly, both differ markedly from those of people living in industrialized societies. And the customs of one industrialized group can be unlike those of another, just as the way of life of one peasant group differs from another.

It is obvious that to understand these various peoples we must see their behaviors through the lens of their customs, their interrelated ideas of what is right and wrong, and their views of how one ought to go about living life. Only as we apprehend their beliefs and values (as well as their ways of organizing themselves, their environmental and technological constraints) can we make sense out of their way of life.

To interpret an individual's or group's behavior within the broader sociocultural context is also central to the sociology of marriage and family. The sociological approach is to consider the social forces that shape, direct, and otherwise influence what people do in marriage and family.

While this point also seems obvious, and hardly worth stressing—for we all know that wedding customs, for example, differ from one group to another—the implications of this position are anything but obvious. The scope of a society's influence is much more pervasive than is ordinarily visible to us. We are usually unaware of the extent to which society molds us: not only our dating practices, sexual behaviors, sex roles, and modes of child-rearing, but, ultimately, even the most intimate portions of our private lives. Even our thoughts, desires, and expectations, things considered so intimately personal, are molded by the society and broader culture of which we are members.

This shaping process begins as each newborn is ushered into a preformed, ongoing, complex world. One's birth signals membership into a particular culture, one of humanity's thousands of more or less coherent shared ways of thinking and doing. To become socialized—to become a knowing or capable member of society—means that these preestablished ways of thinking and doing become a part of oneself.

Human offspring cannot survive on their own. Babies must be nourished by a caretaker in order for normal physical and emotional development to occur, and they must interact with others so they can develop language and other expected social skills. Culture channels the ways in which the family performs these basic orientational functions. These cultural constraints, this sociocultural context of learning society's basic expectations, also channel sexual expression by providing guidance for viewing one's own self, one's own body, one's spouse, and one's relationships, including rights and responsibilities within the family.

In short, this characteristic of humans not growing up alone or isolated and not depending on instincts to determine their behavior, but becoming members of a family—an ongoing sociocultural unit already embedded within a larger network of social relations—imparts to the individual a sociocultural heritage. Because the family is an intricate part of a larger network of culturally patterned ways of behavior and shared ways of looking at the world, each individual becomes immersed in shaping mechanisms that vitally affect his or her own behaviors, perceptions, and orientations toward all areas of life, including relating to the opposite sex in dating, marriage, and the family.

The focal concern in the sociology of marriage and family flows from this universal fact of cultural heritage. The ways in which human culture and social participation shape the fabric of marriage and family life, then, become basic points of sociological inquiry. For example, in what way does social membership influence how we perceive others as marriageable? As desirable? What are the mechanisms that are brought into play to channel our perception and desires into socially approved and predetermined avenues? While such orientational attitudes are ordinarily deemed a matter of "personal preference," perceptions of marriageability and desirability are, in fact, determined by a myriad of sociocultural factors.

As a quick illustration, ask yourself why you are not (or are, as the case may be) attracted to someone who has colorful scars on his or her face, hair braided in a certain manner, wears very large rings in the ears or a ring through the nose, and so on—for each of these characteristics is a sign of high attractability in some cultures.

To assure continuity over time, each society needs to exercise control over its members. This is a basic fact of social existence. The resulting social control, however, is so pervasive that it affects almost every aspect of life. To accomplish this control, both simple and complex mechanisms are brought into play. In smaller, tribal societies the techniques of social control center around face-to-face relationships, with positive and negative sanctions being given on a direct and fairly immediate basis. In larger societies the direct and face-to-face basis of sanctioning is partially replaced by more formal and sometimes indirect social control mechanisms. Regardless of the type of society into which an individual becomes socialized—whether hunting and gathering, small and agricultural, or large and industrialized—social control mechanisms are utilized to teach the individual to act, think, and believe according to already existing expectations.

In one of his more entertaining and provocative books, Freud (1930) stresses that as civilization develops, greater and greater constraints are placed on the individual. The group attempts to make its members cooperate in activities deemed important, to direct their energies, time, and other resources toward what are considered to be common goals. Even though individuals may be thinking in terms of self-interest, such as their own paycheck, their own glory, or whatever rewards they feel they are receiving from their activities, ordinarily each person comes under the direction of the larger social group.

For resources and efforts to be directed to goals larger than the individual, and in the ideal case for them to become interrelated with the welfare of others, requires restrictions on the individual. Consequently, the actions of large numbers of people become aligned with one another, forming an interrelationship of social institutions. The control that must be exerted over individuals to bring about such large-scale interrelated or cooperative activities includes control over their sex drive, their romantic involvements, and their reproduction. Allowed to operate freely, such individualizing inclinations as love and mating would upset the expected social arrangements, those, presumably, upon which the society's welfare depends (Goode, 1959).

In each society, then, mechanisms of various sorts are put into practice in order to channel dating, marriage, the expression of sexuality, and parenting into acceptable forms. Because the excessive withdrawal of some persons from the activities and interests of the larger sociocultural unit would threaten this collectivization of resources, each society attempts to control the excessiveness of paired involvements. Efforts are made to somehow make certain that people do not so greatly withdraw into dyads that they neglect those activities that ultimately affect the welfare of others. (Cf., Slater, 1963.)

The illustration with which I began this article is a striking example of *direct* social control over matters ordinarily thought quite individual and private. Yet the government of China feels so threatened by population growth that it has instituted family planning this severe.

In contrast, most social control is *indirect*. Most is based on influencing people's expectations that, in turn, affect their actions. In our own country, for example, while no one is forcing women to undergo abortions, officials are not visiting our homes to enforce their reproductive goals on us, and government agents are not inspecting sanitary napkins, we are still immersed in a myriad of sociocultural expectations concerning children. For most of us, these expectations quite effectively limit our desire to reproduce.

These indirect forms of social control, however, are largely invisible to us, yet, immersed in them, we respond unwittingly. Consequently, the sociology of marriage and family attempts to make visible the mechanisms and effects of indirect social control. As we perceive some of the sociocultural influences that act on us, we gain a better understanding of society's influences on marriage and family—and of ourselves.

In each society the mechanisms of social control, perhaps put into effect to reduce the antisocial potential of the sex drive, channel that drive into acceptable forms. This process contributes to the social order by encouraging certain forms of pairing and maximizing the likelihood that procreation will occur within the form of the family idealized within that culture. This centrality to society of the social control of the sex drive becomes apparent when we note that, among other things, marriage and family represent a means of reducing sexual competition, encouraging cooperation, providing a regularized and socially acceptable sexual outlet while reducing erotic outlets deemed unacceptable, defining the responsibilities and privileges of social relationships, and bestowing major role identities such as husband and wife, son and daughter, parent and child. (Cf., Mead, 1949: 183–200; Davis, 1976.)

As other social institutions are so critically significant in the process of determining marital and familial norms and roles, sociologists of marriage and family emphasize how a society's institutions affect family life. What influence, for example, does religion have on marriage? Or how do the economics of society affect the family? Or advances in medical technology? Or war, peace, or other forms of politics?

This institutional focus also leads sociologists to examine other macro (large-scale) determinants on individual's expectations. On the societal level sociologists examine social change, while on the individual level they look at how marital happiness is affected by the forces of social change. This includes such matters as how the macro phenomenon of the state of a society's economic well-being, such as its rate of employment and changes in gross national product, influence such practical micro-level decisions as whether or not a wife goes to work outside the home. And because those economic factors do not exist in isolation, sociologists examine other broad social forces that affect such "simple" marriage and family decision making. For example, they try to decide how changing sex role expectations figure into the picture.

And how these, in turn, are related to education—the wife's, the husband's, or general levels in society. While the issue of a wife taking paid employment outside the home is certainly a private family matter, such individual decisions, and their conflict and resolution, are mitigated by vast, encompasing influences from the larger social system in which the family is embedded.

As they examine such questions as love, sex, and marriage and family, sociologists continually return to the part that membership in a particular culture plays in molding the basic orientations of its members. The institution of marriage and family is an essential consequence of this shaping, while it, in turn, serves to give form to much of the society of which it is a part. Consequently, basic questions include: As a consequence of their membership in a particular group within a particular society how do people view their role in the family? How do such self-views vary cross-culturally? How do they change over time? How do the patterns of marriage and family that characterize a culture reflect broader cultural characteristics—especially how those patterns of behavior are related to the other institutions of that society? In what ways do social institutions and cultural expectations channel people's orientations so they result in those particular forms or patterns of behavior? And in what ways does the playback of cultural learning, as modified by individuals and their unique life experiences in marriage and family life, in turn, affect cultural expectations?

I realize that this analysis, along with the concerns and issues that have been raised, may seem rather abstract, vague, and difficult to grasp. Perhaps the best way of moving from abstract statements about the sociology of marriage and family, in order to make them more real, is to use an extended example. While this example will not illustrate all of the above statements, it will cover the basic points and help to illustrate what is meant by a sociology of marriage and family.

I shall use an example that especially illustrates how society constrains (or channels, molds, or influences) individual choice while at the same time the individual experiences freedoms rather than constraints. To do this, let's look at a common event in our society: one individual dating another and then, eventually, marrying that person. As we focus on this rather prosaic situation, we want to keep asking: From a sociological point of view, what is occurring?

First, it is significant to note that the "choice" of date and eventually of mate takes place within highly constricted boundaries—avenues that, channeling the choice, are largely invisible to the individual. If we look at the matter more closely, we see such things as:

1. The individuals (let's give them typical names and call them Bob and Mary) made the assumption that dating was proper. That is, Bob and Mary assumed dating was a good thing and that they "ought" to

date. In fact, they viewed dating as so proper that they would have thought of themselves as oddballs if they did not date.

Although they experience dating as a personal desire (as something that flows up out of themselves), what is not readily apparent to Bob and Mary is how the society is geared to making them want to date. That dating is merely an artifact of society—an arbitrary practice currently in vogue—and not some activity that spontaneously arises from within individuals, some inevitable expression of human nature, can be illustrated by noting that in many societies dating is unknown. In ours, in contrast, dating is a form of male/female interaction that is highly encouraged—at least among certain people at certain times.

2. Bob and Mary chose each other as dates. They experienced the "choice" as a natural tug from within, a part of personal desire and human freedom.

In point of fact, however, they "chose" one another from within a highly limiting range of choices—limits that were arbitrarily established by their social group membership. For example, Bob and Mary, as typical as they are, did *not* date someone from another race. They did *not* date someone too rich or too poor, or, for that matter, someone too old or too young, too tall or too short, too fat, unhealthy, or ugly. Moreover, the *did* date an unmarried member of the opposite sex.

In other words, not unlike most of us, Bob's and Mary's dating followed certain well-established social lines, demarcations set up before they were born that continue to match basic expectations of society. Growing up in this society, Bob and Mary internalized these expectations (made them a part of their thinking, actually their very being) and, as they followed these internalized expectations, they felt that they were simply "doing what was natural." The constraining effects of their socialization went largely unnoticed by them.

As far as most people are concerned, in fact, following the lines laid out by society is not what needs to be explained, for they seem so "natural." It is violations of these expectations that need to be explained—not why Bob and Mary dated within their own race, for example, but why Joe, a white, dated Ann, a black; or why Elaine, who is twenty-seven, is dating Fred, who is seventeen.

From a sociological point of view, however, both conformity to expectations *and* their violations beg explanation. *Neither* is simply some natural unfolding from within, but *both* are natural outcomes of very human and understandable social processes. Yet, in either case, those processes largely remain invisible to those who are doing the conforming or deviating. It is an essential part of the sociological perspective to make visible that which underlies the social channeling of human choice.

3. After graduating from college, Bob and Mary were married. They had a beautiful wedding—a church, gowns, flowers, music, gifts and

guests, and so on—and each felt that the "choice" of the other as spouse was one "freely" made.

Largely invisible to Bob and Mary were the huge shaping devices put into effect by their society and culture, some of which we have already mentioned. But note some of the strong influences on Bob and Mary:

a. Their culture dictates that monogamy is the only acceptable form of marriage;
b. Society has provided idealized expectations concerning the proper timing of marriage (for example, following specified major life events, such as graduation from high school or college);
c. The peer group exercises remarkable influence, exerting social control over "personal choice" in matters of the height, weight, age, race, intelligence, social class, and popularity and reputational qualities of prospective dates. Accordingly, the peer group wields great influence in channeling people toward prospective spouses;
d. We have not even mentioned a variety of other sources of primary influence on Bob and Mary, such as their parents (whose residence in a social class and racially segregated neighborhood limited their choice), their religion (with its membership typically following social class and racial lines, as well as its highly specific teachings about right and wrong in dating and marriage), and their education (private, public, or parochial schools—with their mix or lack thereof concerning social class and racial backgrounds).

In addition to all these influences are the broad sociohistorical factors that become part of the "choices" that Bob and Mary make after their marriage. For example, these influences, largely determining their basic expectations concerning what Bob is like as a male, Mary as a female, and their expectations of one another as a male or female, become essential in their basic roles of husband and wife. Within those broad frameworks ("What you ought to do because you are a male—and my husband," thinks Mary, and "What you ought to do because you are a female—and my wife," thinks Bob) Bob and Mary will play out their roles as husband and wife.

Again, each largely experiences these roles as a matter of "personal choice," generally remaining blind to the many pervasive cultural, social, and historical factors that shape the "choices" they make. For example, both Bob and Mary have decided to work outside the home. They have also decided that they will share the housework and cooking and child care. Such choices simply were not options for most newlyweds some years back. Now, however, *because society has been under-*

going major modifications and those changes have affected marital roles, Bob and Mary experience that change as a matter of "personal choice."

And in many ways Bob and Mary are right: It is a matter of choice concerning what sex and marital roles they wish to adopt. Several options do lie before them. But largely invisible to Bob and Mary are the constraining forces, those broad social factors, that either make such choices an option for a married couple in the first place or that remove them from even the possibility of consideration.

The sociological perspective on marriage and family, then, is to view the world of marriage and family life in light of the social forces that operate in people's lives. Sometimes this is direct government control, as in the China example, but it usually involves more indirect forms of influence. The specifics on which sociologists focus vary widely. They could be the dynamics of socialization into sex roles, as well as how those roles operate in dating and married life, the influence of peers in mate selection, our expectations concerning sexuality and married life, or even the social factors that underlie our experience of love. Regardless of the specifics, sociologists who specialize in these fascinating activities that we call marriage and family throw the sociological spotlight on the social factors that underlie what people experience as matters of individual taste and choice.

REFERENCES

DAVIS, KINGSLEY. "Sexual Behavior." In *Contemporary Social Problems,* edited by Robert K. Merton and Robert Nisbet, fourth edition, 219–261. New York: Harcourt Brace Jovanovich, 1976.

FREUD, SIGMUND. *Civilization and its Discontents.* Translated by J. Rivière. New York: Cape and Smith, 1930.

GOODE, WILLIAM J. "The Theoretical Importance of Love." *American Sociological Review* 24 (1959): 38–47.

MEAD, MARGARET. *Male and Female: A Study of the Sexes in a Changing World.* New York: William Morrow, 1949.

MIRSKY, JONATHAN. "The Infanticide Tragedy in China." *The Nation,* July 2, 1983.

SLATER, PHILLIP. "On Social Regression." *American Sociological Review* 28 (June 1963): 339–364.

VINCK, MICHELLE. "Abortion and Birth Control in Canton, China." *The Wall Street Journal,* November 30, 1981.

CHAPTER 2

The Family as a Changing Institution

Harold T. Christensen / Kathryn P. Johnsen

ABSTRACT: Every society has some form of marriage and family. The universal functions of the family, that are essential in bringing order to society, are:

1. orderly reproduction (including controlling the sex drive)
2. meeting the biological needs of a society's members (such as food, shelter, and clothing)
3. status placement (bestowing rank or status on people by virtue of their birth and determining their relationship to one another)
4. socialization (training children in appropriate skills, thoughts, feelings, and action)
5. emotional maintenance (providing a sense of security, a feeling of being wanted and cared for)
6. social control (making society stable by keeping people in line)

As society changes, pressure is put on families to meet these changes, and some families do not adapt as well as others.

It is a commonplace to speak of *marriage and family* in the same breath, as if they were synonymous. Actually these terms refer to separate, though closely related, social institutions. Marriage is society's way of sanctioning and controlling adult sexual behavior. It differs from *mating* in that the latter is simply a biological act, largely instinctive and temporary. Marriage is the institutionalization of that act, together with the many psychological and sociological overtones that surround it. Marriage fixes responsibility for sex and makes order out of what otherwise would be chaos. Marriage plus children make a family.

Nearly everyone belongs to at least two families during his lifetime; his *family of orientation* and his *family of procreation*. The first he is born into and the second he establishes through marriage. He is a child in the one and a parent in the other. Thus there is continuity from generation to generation.

UNIFORMITY AND DIVERSITY IN FAMILY FORMS

No society has ever been without marriage and the family. They are what is known as "universal social institutions." Both have antiquity and universality. Societies vary regarding details of custom; but always, in all ages and all cultures, some sort of family life has been the norm. Love and procreation outside of marriage have been exceptions in the history of mankind, never the rule.

There must be a reason. Is it that man is born with the urge to marry, that family life is instinctive? Anthropologists, sociologists, and psychologists say not; for while the drive to mate is a part of one's original nature, the institutions for realizing and controlling this urge are a part of man's culture, and are learned. Why, then, are marriage and family life so ubiquitous? The answer to this question lies in the similarity of needs among men and the apparent tendency of man everywhere to organize similar institutions to meet these common needs. Institutions are promoted and perpetuated for the sake of specific functions they can perform in the light of recognized human needs.

Universal Functions

The long dependency period of the human infant requires some arrangement for his protection and feeding until he is able to care for himself. In every society this recurring need has resulted in the development of a set of norms prescribing how and by whom the infant will be cared for. This set of norms partially forms the family institution of a society. Each activity, however, is closely linked to and has consequences for other activities, resulting in a complex web of interdependent institutions. The consequences which an institution has for the integration between other institutions and the continuity of society are called the *functions* of that institution. Certain family functions appear in every society in some form, no matter how varied the family form. The functions which are recognizable in all known societies are called the *universal functions of the family.*

Some of these are no doubt essential to the perpetuation of a society. Whether they could result equally well from some other type of human grouping rather than one based on kinship is a moot question. Every society *has* grouped people together in terms of the adult sex relationship and blood kin. This arrangement has had universal consequences for other aspects of every society. In order to see clearly the interconnection between various institutions, the universal functions will be examined one by one.[1]

Responsible Reproduction

For a society to continue over one generation there must be some orderly way of replacing aging and dying members. The major portion of this replacement normally comes from reproduction. Reproduction can occur without benefit of a social institution such as marriage. The need, however, is not just for reproduction—the need is for young adults trained to take over as the elders become incapacitated or die. The existence of a family group bound together by blood ties serves to place responsibility for the new infant on an organized group. As the family exercises control over who comes into it through marriage and subsequent reproduction, it has the effect of structuring the choice of marriage mates, ordering the satisfaction of sexual and emotional needs, and legalizing parenthood.

The way this is done gives rise to the family organization considered "right" and "normal" to the individuals reared in that society. The smallest unit or "least common denominator" in family organization, the *nuclear family*, consists of husband, wife, and immediate children. It exists everywhere throughout the world and is the typical pattern in the United States. In many societies, however, nuclear families are clustered together, like atoms in a molecule, to form larger aggregations. Two principles govern the manner in which nuclear families combine. (1) They may be joined at the focus of the marriage relationship, making for plural marriages where one of the spouses is a member of every nuclear family. This is known as *polygamy*, which means that one spouse has two or more mates. If it is a husband with several wives, the technical term is *polygyny*; whereas if it is a wife with several husbands, the technical term is *polyandry*. Though this latter practice is the rarer of the two, there are at least a half-dozen societies in which it has been known to exist. (2) If the blood bond becomes the point at which nuclear families are joined, there develops what is known as an *extended* or *consanguine* family. This is an organization that cuts across several generations. An example is the traditional Chinese family, consisting of the oldest living male, his wife or wives, his unmarried children, his married sons, together with their wives and unmarried children, his married grandsons, together with their wives and unmarried children, and also great-grandsons if there are any. Daughters, on marrying, leave their own families and join those of their husbands. This is an example of an extended family traced by patrilineal descent. Kinship can also be traced by matrilineal descent, in which the family consists of the oldest living female, her husband, unmarried children, married daughters, and so forth. There are variations on these lines of descent but in general extended families represent an expansion of the parent-child relationship; polygamous families represent an expansion of the husband-wife relationship. Both are fairly common in various parts of the world. Most common, however, is the nuclear family founded upon *monogamy* (the marriage of one man to one woman).

Although there is great variation in the structuring of the marriage relationship regarding the number of spouses and place of residence, all family forms result in ordering the satisfaction of sexual and emotional needs, and in placing the offspring from the sexual unions in the midst of a small group which has the responsibility for it. The designation of which individuals are family members also structures the kinds of relationships the child will have as it starts its long journey toward eventual adult participation in the society.

Biological Maintenance

A necessary requirement for the continuance of a society is the meeting of the essential biological needs of its members. They must be fed, clothed, and protected from bodily harm. The gathering together of individuals in family groups results in spreading the responsibility for meeting these individual needs. The family organization determines who is entitled to share in the family's goods, how long he can expect to share, and what he must contribute to the maintenance of other family members.

In some societies the family becomes self-sufficient, meeting all the biological needs of its members. Our own pioneer families approximated this extreme. The great distances between families and the difficulty of transportation made them largely dependent upon their own efforts.

On the other hand, the family may be completely dependent on a societal network of coordinated activities to produce and distribute commodities which must be bought. In this case, typical of present-day America, the survival of the family does not depend on the cooperative efforts of all the members but on the continuation of the economic system which produces the necessities as well as offers the opportunity to earn the money needed to purchase them.

However the raw materials are obtained, some preparation and distribution of goods among family members is necessary. The amount and kind of preparation varies tremendously, but everywhere the meeting of individual biological needs results in some kind of division of labor within the family. Every society has made labor divisions along age and sex lines. Different tasks become differentiated according to whether they are seen to be "man's work," "woman's work," "boy's work," or "girl's work." In the family, these develop into the social roles applying to the positions of husband, wife, son, and daughter.

No matter how extended these roles become, they start from such questions as who takes care of the baby; who provides the food and clothing, whether this means growing raw material or providing money to purchase them; who does the cooking; who feeds the chickens; who mends the clothes; and so on. When these divisions are made, however, they have ramifications which extend to numerous other relationships. Seldom do these sex-based divisions of labor exist without the development of concepts of masculinity and femininity to support them.

Societies, for example, vary within and among themselves from the extreme of making woman the "work-horse" of the family to enshrining her on a throne of fragility. Each of these positions carries with it supporting beliefs about the biological nature of woman and ideals of femininity. In early America, at the same time the pioneer woman was working alongside her husband in the fields, her urban counterpart was swooning in her drawing room at the slightest excitement or exertion.

The degree to which the biological needs of the family are met solely by the cooperative efforts of all members has implications for the internal authority structure of the family. If there are crucial tasks which must be performed for the family to survive, then someone must be responsible for assigning them and seeing that they are carried out. If the failure of one of the members is immediately felt by all the family, that authority structure is reinforced. If the cooperative efforts of all members are not required to meet these crucial needs, there is less necessity for a strong centralized authority structure. Imagine for a moment a strong father in a family dependent upon firewood for cooking and warmth. He assigns to one of his sons the task of filling the firebox by a certain time every day without fail. The boy's failure to do this would probably result not only in a painful response from his father, but he would be as cold and hungry as the rest of the family. Now imagine a strong father in a family living in a modern, centrally heated home. He assigns to his son the task of coming straight home from school every day without fail to bring in wood for the fireplace in the recreation room. This boy's failure to do so may result in the same painful response from his father, but no crucial loss occurs to him or any other family member because of his failure. The action becomes more arbitrary and provides little justification for the need of a strong authority structure.

Some authority structure is present in every family institution. The nature and strength of it will vary, partially, in response to the way the family meets its biological needs. Where the responsibility resides in the father—or eldest male in the extended family—we have the *patriarchal* authority structure so well-known in our past. If the authority is vested in the mother—or eldest female—it is called a *matriarchal* authority structure. Where it is shared between father and mother, it is spoken of as an *equalitarian* authority pattern.

Status Placement

The cooperation necessary for societal survival would not be possible without the ability to predict the behavior of the members in various situations. Part of this predictability comes from an organization of norms guiding the way individuals act toward others in different status positions. Every society has developed some arrangement for ranking individuals in terms of the positions they occupy, characteristics they possess, or tasks they perform. The hierarchical evaluation of individuals is supported by a system of role relationships which emphasizes the legitimacy of the system. The subject bows to the king; the young employee speaks respectfully to his older employer; the tribesman pays homage to the old chief; the "untouchable" crosses the road when a caste Hindu approaches; the Japanese mother bows her infant's head to a person of higher rank. The acting out of the expected behavior may not connote agreement with it, but it does convey a recognition of its legitimacy.

Societies vary drastically in the rigidity of the ranking order—or stratification system—and in the elaborateness of the supporting interactions. Every society, however, supports some differential treatment of individuals, depending upon their positions within it. The prestige awarded the individual occupying the position generally extends to the family members—the prince is treated differently than the pauper. Thus, the infant, by being born into a family, is born into a ready-made place in the society according to his family's position within it. The way he is treated by numerous others outside the family group will be partly ordered because of the existing stratification system. The ordering of these relationships produces the necessary predictability of others' behavior so that the growing child can form a concept of who he is, where he belongs, and where he may hope to go in his society.

Depending upon one's value system, certain stratification systems may be evaluated as fair or unfair; but regardless of the judgment made, they all have the consequence of providing some order in human relationships. This order contributes to the integration of the individual's concept of self, whether the resulting self-concept is evaluated as good or bad.

In some societies, the status placement function of the family extends through adulthood, with the family's class or caste largely determining the occupations the children can aspire to and the field of eligibles from which a mate may be selected. Others, not quite so restrictive, still exert control over the adult status of their children by arranging their marriages. Many of these are economic arrangements uniting families similar in rank, thereby reinforcing the existing stratification system. Some societies, like our own, have freer systems. The individual's adult status is not wholly determined by the family of orientation and marriages are not arranged. Even here, however, potential relationships are ordered through place of residence, school attendance, and social group restrictions. This limiting of the people one may hope to meet shows the continuing effect of the status position of the family on adult occupation and mate selection. A person is much more likely to date and select a marriage partner from his own general social class position than one much higher or much lower. The great attention attracted by the rare Cinderella marriage illustrates the lack of cultural prohibition against them (our value system favoring equality) and the force exerted by the status placement function of the family which almost precludes its occurrence. The status placement function, then, contributes to the continuity over time of predictable individual behavior necessary for societal order, and aids in maintaining the status quo both through the restriction of social groups with which the children have contact and by transmittal to them of the values and expectations expressed in that part of the society to which the family belongs. Although there is great variation among societies, the family in all of them tends to hold its members in well-established class positions, as well as make it seem right and natural to them.

Socialization

As stated earlier, any society must have orderly replacement of its members to exist. This means the young members must be trained in the skills utilized by the society. They must learn how to communicate their thoughts and feelings, how to act. In other words, the biological organism must become a human being, able to participate in the activities of his society. It is this process of transforming the biological organism into a social being that is called socialization. It is the process of acquiring the characteristics, values, attitudes, and behaviors which are associated with being a responsible member of society. This only happens through group interaction within a cultural framework. The family, as it cares for its own offspring, provides the continued interaction for this to take place. As the young child is slowly introduced to the family activities, he learns the expectations held of him in accord with his sex, his age, and his status in the community. Since his family is part of an ongoing society, the tings he learns within it provide the training for participation in the larger community as well.

Societies differ widely in the amount of socialization which occurs within the family. On the whole, the more simple the society the greater the proportion of socialization which takes place informally within the family group. In extremely complex societies, such as our own, the family is not able to socialize the child for full participation. It is aided by other institutions such as the educational and religious institutions. Socialization includes not only the formal acquisition of skills associated with education, but the "taking on" of morals—the internalization of them so that they become a functioning part of the member's personality. This is done *informally* by the family as it transmits the meanings of activities, the beliefs concerning its own place in the scheme of things, and morally "right" and "wrong" behavior; and *formally* through organized religious groupings.

Whether the socialization process is carried out solely by the family or aided by other agencies, the family appears to be the primary influence in developing the personality of the child, which itself is the outcome of the impact of socialization on the unique combination of inherited characteristics in the biological organism. There probably could develop other means of caring for and socializing children, but some continuity of contact with the same individuals over time seems necessary for the acquisition of a stable, integrated personality. A stable family grouping has a consequence of heightening the probability that the necessary contact will occur, thus providing a steady supply of young adults prepared to participate in societal activities and to perpetuate the society by wanting to reproduce the family form in which they were reared.

Emotional Maintenance

Some kind of human interaction appears necessary not only for socialization of the young, but also for the maintenance of stability among adults. Some feeling of belonging somewhere, of being important to someone appears to be a universal human need. The placing of individuals together in terms of kinship at least offers the opportunity for this need to be met. Man's long period of dependency before he is able to care for himself results in the development of some kind of continuing need for dependable, predictable relationships. When this need is met, the individual feels a measure of security. The type of relationship he seeks and interprets as being emotionally secure is probably related to the family structure and kind of nurturing care he received in his family of orientation.

Social Control

All of the foregoing family functions result in a measure of control exerted over individual behavior, thereby contributing to societal order. Not only does the family exert overt control over its members by demanding certain behaviors and restricting others, it lessens the need for overt control by developing internal controls within the individual personality through the socialization process. The amount of social control provided by the family varies with the degree to which the family is the sole agency providing for biological and emotional maintenance, for socialization, and for status placement.

In the days of Rome, long before the beginning of the Empire, there was in existence the archetype of the extended patriarchal family. The ruling patriarch of this family held the power of life and death over the males in the family for life, and over the females until they were transferred to some other family through marriage. The individual family powers were so inclusive that no central government could emerge. Not until they were threatened by invaders was their need for cooperation great enough to force the family patriarchs to relinquish enough power to allow the formation of a loose central government.

At the other extreme, the Israeli kibbutz represents a family form which has been reduced almost entirely to the reproductive function. Biological maintenance, as well as the major portion of emotional maintenance, socialization, and status placement is supplied by the total community. Although the parents and children maintain a certain amount of contact during leisure hours, the basic needs of all are supplied through the cooperative efforts of all members. Here, the social control of the family is at a minimum, being transferred to nurses, teachers, and the informal control of the peer group.

An Adaptive, Conservative Institution

When the universal functions of the family—including responsible reproduction, biological maintenance, status placement, socialization, emotional maintenance, and social control—are viewed together, we see that they result in continuous, ordered interaction which develops individuals capable of participating in the society, places them within it, and maintains them as actively contributing adults. Tied as it is to other institutions, the family is continually mediating between the demands of these other institutions and the demands of its own individual members. The norms forming the institutions are constantly subjected to change as many individual families adapt to changing conditions, thereby presenting to their growing children new models of the correct way to do things.

The Adaptive Aspect

Around the turn of the century, the urban middle-class family in our society was embedded in a relatively stable external world. Transportation and communication systems were, by our standards today, poorly developed. Of necessity, activities tended to be carried out close to home. We have mental images of the punctuality and relative formality of family mealtimes. Children were expected to be gathered around when father returned home from work. Few conflicting interests were present to pull mother and the children away from the schedule geared to father's demands.

Consider the changes which have taken place in this one activity of family meals as millions of individual families have had to adjust to lengthening distances between work and home, demands of the public schools for children's time, church group meetings, civic activities, little league practices, choir rehearsals, and the numerous demands from other groups which require the participation of many individuals in order to exist. Family mealtimes have become informal; time schedules have become flexible. For many, the whole family is gathered together around the table only a few times a week. A father, coming from a family where mealtime schedules were ritualistically observed and valued, may find himself fighting a losing battle as he tries to maintain the customs of his youth. If he insists that his teen-age children be present at dinner regardless of scheduled football practices, play rehearsals, or an extra help session called by the algebra teacher, he is likely to find himself under attack not only by family members but by the school system as well.

It is the formal organization of other groups which puts added pressure on the individual families to adapt. Clark Vincent (1966) sees this adaptive function as one of the important characteristics of our modern families. Since individual families have no formal organization, they are at a disadvantage when pressured by organized groups to give up their members at times when the organized group can attract the greatest number of participants—not when it is convenient for the individual families. Thus, the church choir picks a practice time when the director is available, the rehearsal room is not in use by other church groups, and when competing groups do not have scheduled meetings—not in accord with the schedules of individual families. Thus, if families motivate their members to participate, they must adapt to the demands of the organized groups. As many families adapt to similar external situations new norms begin to develop, and the institution is in the process of adaptation.

The Conservative Aspect

Although the family institution is an adaptive one, it is also conservative. That is, it tends to hold to and promote the status quo. As we grow up in a family we see and interpret the world through that family and that portion of society in which it is embedded. As we obtain emotional support and a feeling of security within it, we have a tendency to want to reproduce it as adults (Kirkpatrick, 1963, pp. 195–99). We gain a measure of security by reproducing the situation in which we felt secure as children. To the extent, then, that the universal family functions are adequately produced by the family institution, the probability is heightened that the individuals will see that way of doing things as "right," "good," and "proper," and will try to reproduce it in the next generation. The father in the previous illustration may be forced to give in somewhat to the demands for flexible mealtime schedules, but he may feel that the family is falling apart and insist on family meals being taken together on certain days—when nothing outside can interfere. The family then becomes a mediating institution: mediating the demands from a changing society through older values and mediating the demands of the society to protect the individual.

Evaluation of the Family

Present day concern about our society's ability to survive is oriented around the functions of the family. The continual concern with strengthening the family can be seen to be organized around securing these family functions. Many social problems are traced to either the failure or extreme success of the family functions. The growing problem of illegitimacy suggests the weakening of the function of *responsible* reproduction. The hurry with which some young people rush into marriage and begin their childbearing period—or the overemphasis on this function—is viewed by others as alarming. The rise of delinquent and criminal behavior brings concern about the failure of the *socialization* and *social control* functions. The increasing number of youths demonstrating for racial equality, peace, and so forth brings concern from some about the failure of the family to transmit values supporting the ongoing system. The same behavior brings praise from other quarters for the successful transmission of the central values of democracy and individual freedom. The problem does not appear to be that families do not transmit values, but that they transmit too well the "wrong" ones. Which ones are seen as wrong varies with the point of view of the observer.

The proportion of hospital beds occupied by the mentally ill questions the adequacy of the family in providing emotional maintenance. The present attempts to combat poverty attack the failure of some families to provide *biological maintenance* while being too successful in their *status placement* and *reproduction* functions. In other words, the successful transmission of the values and skills which provide support for the continuation of the stratification system may be seen as "bad" if there is a desire to upset the system. Recognition of this can be seen in the attempts to counter the early influence of the family by an extension of the educational system through the Head Start program.

The family functions appear to play a crucial part in the survival of a society in its present form. Where the family system is extremely strong, then it becomes a powerful force to combat if wide-scale societal change is attempted, since all of its functions contribute to stability and the continuance of the status quo. Once a change is made, however, the family again begins to function and can as readily transmit the new values. If the family system is extremely weak, then the adaptation to demands for change may be very rapid with little commitment to the preservation of the system. The family appears crucial to societal survival. Whether this is the result of our own socialization within a family system which limits the awareness of other arrangements; or whether it is a *necessary* institution we cannot know at present. No society which has left a history has developed an alternate form with which to compare. The kibbutz comes closest to developing an alternate form, but its history is not yet long enough to give conclusive evidence of its survival over time in its present form.

NOTE AND REFERENCES

1. This discussion of universal functions follows the scheme presented by William J. Goode, "The Sociology of the Family: Horizons in Family Theory," in *Sociology Today: Problems and Prospects*, Robert K. Merton, Leonard Broom, and Leonard S. Cottrell, Jr. (Eds.). New York: Basic Books, 1959, pp. 178–196.

KIRKPATRICK, CLIFFORD. *The Family as Process and Institution*, rev. ed. New York, Ronald Press, 1963.

VINCENT, CLARK E. "The Adaptive Function," *Journal of Marriage and Family*, vol. 28 (February 1966), pp. 29–36.

CHAPTER 3

The Myth of Family Independence

Kenneth Keniston

ABSTRACT: A pervading myth is that the American family is a free-standing, independent unit, a myth that was nourished by the American Revolution and the American frontier. As American society has undergone its various major changes, however, the family has become increasingly dependent. What were once the responsibilities of the family have been taken over by institutions outside the family, such as the schooling of children, the teaching of religion, and the care of the aged, poor, sick, and mentally ill. Yet at the same time that the family's traditional functions have diminished new ones have developed, especially that of more demanding standards of parenting.

"Parents today are selfish and self-centered," one angry parent wrote. "They aren't willing to make sacrifices for their children. But that's what being a parent is all about, so is it any wonder that the children grow up on drugs?" By this logic, everything from working mothers to the rising divorce rate can be blamed on the moral failings of those involved. Families on welfare are lazy, sponging chiselers. Parents who divorce are indulging themselves at the expense of their children. Working mothers neglect their children for a few dollars a day which they waste on clothes and vacations. If children get the outlandish idea from television advertising that there is a box or bottle with a cure for every problem, their parents must not be talking enough, guiding them enough, or supervising them enough. *Parents* are to blame; and if there is a solution, it must lie in reforming them.

Blaming parents and giving them advice both spring from the assumption that . . . families are free-standing, independent, and autonomous units, relatively free from social pressures. If a family proves less than independent, if it is visibly needy, if its members ask for help, then it is by definition not an "adequate" family. Adequate families, the assumption runs, are self-sufficient and insulated from outside pressures. . . .

[T]he American myth of personal self-sufficiency . . . has deep roots in American history, although it did not emerge in its full form until the early 1800's.

The notion of society as a voluntary assembly of independent and self-sufficient individuals who freely contract with each other to form a community or nation was at the heart of the Enlightenment-Age thinking that flourished in the American colonies 200 years ago. The revolution that freed Americans from British rule had a psychological impact that was particularly important in establishing the myth of family independence and self-sufficiency. . . . [F]ree from British rule and isolated from Europe by an ocean that took weeks to traverse, Americans felt truly independent. The expulsion of the Indians to the area west of the Mississippi under Jackson opened vast tracts of forests and prairie for farming and land speculation and helped confirm the view that any American possessed of a minimum of ingenuity and industriousness could become self-sufficient in short order. . . .

The ideal society—and most Americans believed that it was being realized in America—was like an assembly of free atoms: men who came together occasionally to vote and who expected the state to protect their freedoms, but who were otherwise on their own. . . .

Indians, slaves, Mexicans, poor people, immigrants, and growing numbers of factory workers were rarely as self-sufficient and independent as the myth said they should be. The ideal merely defined them as groups to be changed, pitied, condemned, educated, uplifted, reformed, or Americanized. . . .

Even those who could not make [the myth] real in their own lives often subscribed to it and felt guilty about not meeting its standards. The myth determined who was seen as virtuous and who as wanting; it provided, and still provides, the rationale for defining familial adequacy and morality. This moralizing quality is one of its most important features. For this myth tells us that those who need help are ultimately inadequate. And it tells us that for a family to need help—or at least to admit it publicly—is to confess failure. Similarly, to give help, however generously, is to acknowledge the inadequacy of the recipients and indirectly to condemn them, to stigmatize them, and even to weaken what impulse they have toward self-sufficiency.

The myth of self-sufficiency blinds us to the workings of other forces in family life. For families are not now, nor were they ever, the self-sufficient building blocks of society, exclusively responsible, praiseworthy, and blamable for their own destiny. They are deeply influenced by broad social and economic forces over which they have little control.

THE NEW ROLE OF PARENTS

[With increasing frequency over] the last centuries, families have not only been reduced in size but changed in function as well; expectations of what families do for their children have also been reduced. Mothers are no longer automatically expected to spend the whole day with their four-year-olds; fathers are no longer expected to train them in skills for a job. No one imagines that parents will try to manage a child's raging fever without help or teach a ten-year-old set theory in mathematics. As the forms of life have changed, institutions with a great deal of technical expertise have grown up to take over these functions, while parents have gone out to jobs that are less and less comprehensible to their young children. Conversely, children need training and experience to prepare them for a world already strikingly different from that of a generation earlier when their parents were growing up. As a result, families today have drastically changed in their functions and powers, especially in their power to raise children unaided. . . .

CHANGING FAMILY FUNCTIONS

[In the 1600s], almost all families resembled one part of the myth: they were largely self-sufficient agricultural units. They owned and occupied the farms and plantations of seventeenth- and eighteenth-century America. Apart from nails, salt, and a handful of other goods, these family farms produced, sometimes with the help of neighbors, most of what they needed to live: their own houses, their food, bedding, furniture, clothing, and fuel. Barter was more common than purchase for acquiring the goods the family could not produce (except in those regions of the South where cash crops such as tobacco and indigo were introduced early), and working for wages was rare in North and South alike. Family members were "paid" in room and board; most of the extra manpower that family members could not provide was supplied by indentured servants, bound apprentices, trading work between families or, in the South, by slaves.

The most important difference between these early American families and our own is that early families constituted economic units in which all members, from young children on up, played important productive roles within the household. The prosperity of the whole family depended on how well husband, wife, and children could manage and cultivate the land. Children were essential to this family enterprise from age six or so until their twenties, when they left home. (Indeed, in most seventeenth-century American paintings, they are portrayed in the same kind of clothes adults wore—a sign of how much they participated in the world of adult responsibilities.) Families not blessed with children usually faced economic hardship as a result, for boys were necessary to the hard work of cultivating the land and harvesting the crops, while girls were essential to the "homework" of storing and cooking food, caring for domestic animals, spinning, weaving, and sewing.

Children were, in short, economic assets. Early in life, most children began to pay their own way by working with and for their families. Many years later, when the parents were elderly, children paid another economic dividend: in a time when there was no government old-age assistance or social security, grown children were often the chief source of their parents' support.

In the course of the nineteenth century all this began to change. Farm families began to find that raising one crop for sale and using the proceeds of that sale to buy goods produced by others could give them a higher standard of living than could self-sufficient agriculture. The production of cash crops such as grain and cotton replaced agriculture intended chiefly to provide for the family; money became the medium for obtaining necessities the family no longer produced; and families became less self-sufficient. In addition, an influential minority of families ceased entirely to be productive units in which parents and children worked together. Instead, family members (especially fathers) went out to work for wages in factories and businesses. As commerce and factory work became more common, family life and work were sundered: what a worker produced and what he or she consumed were increasingly not the same thing. Money—in the form of wages, salaries, or, for the wealthy, returns on speculation and investments—provided a new and more tenuous link between work and family. . . .

In our time, the family economy has disappeared almost completely. While once almost all American family members worked together at a common economic enterprise on whose success they collectively depended, today most American adult family members work for pay, while children rarely work at all. No common economic task remains. Work and family life are separate enterprises; families consume as a unit, but do not produce as a unit.

The economic "value" of children to families has changed as a result. If weighted in crass economic terms, children were once a boon to the family economy; now they have become an enormous economic liability, [with] costs of housing, feeding, clothing, as well as educating. . . . Moreover, as schooling has lengthened, the financial drain of having children is prolonged to an average of twenty years. . . .

In the past then, the intrinsic pleasures of parenthood for most American families were increased by the extrinsic economic return that children brought. Today, parents have children *despite* their economic cost. This is a major, indeed, a revolutionary, change.

Furthermore, as children more and more have come to be regarded in the economic hierarchy as "dependents" rather than contributors, child rearing itself has come to be seen as a nonproductive job. It yields no wages, and ever since the industrial revolution, people have come to value their work more and more for the cash income it produces.

A second major change in family functions is the removal of education from the family. To be sure, there were schools in colonial America, and a large proportion of boys, at least, especially in New England, attended them for at least a few years, giving the colonies an unprecedented literacy rate as compared to Europe. But over the course of a year children spent less time in schools than they do now, and most of them left school as soon as they learned to read, write, and cipher. And like everything else, most education went on at home, organized either around reading the Scriptures or around learning a trade. In both cases, and whether they were teaching their own children or apprentices, the major responsibility for education fell on parents, with schools playing a distinctly secondary role.

With the creation of the public "common school" in the middle of the nineteenth century under the leadership of Horace Mann, formal education began to replace family education rather than assist it. Compulsory, free public education . . . marked another inroad on traditional family functions. A public institution, armed with the power of legal coercion, was taking over and expanding traditional family prerogatives. . . . We feel its full force only today, with nearly universal institutional attendance now often starting at age four or five and continuing after high school for at least a year or two of college, that is, until age nineteen or twenty. For a total of fourteen to sixteen years, the average American child spends the better part of most weekdays not in the presence of his or her family, but in the presence of day-care workers or teachers and other children the same age. It is hard to imagine a more crucial change in the role of the family.

In addition to economic production and schooling, a long list of other "traditional" family functions has been largely taken over by people and institutions outside the family. Sociologists and historians have pointed to the family's shrinking role in the care of the aged, the "relief" of the poor, the imparting of basic religious attitudes and values, and the care of the mentally ill. We will consider only one of these, the care of the sick, because it illustrates another, broader change: the way rising expectations accompany changing family functions.

Even one century ago, most care of the sick was a family matter. Doctors were rare and their ministrations of dubious benefit; many children survived despite the leeching of their blood by doctors, not because of it. Except for smallpox, preventive inoculations were unavailable; bacterial infections either cured themselves or led to more serious illness and often death. Hospitals did not exist in most localities; where they did, their staffs could do little more than make patients comfortable and wait for an illness to run its course. There were no specialties like pediatrics.

When children fell ill, their families nursed them and, if the children survived, watched over their convalescence. Except for information dispensed in popular magazines, preventive medecine was formally unknown, its informal precursors consisting of little more than keeping a special family watch on children considered frail or sickly. When children died, as they did far more often than today, they died in bed, at home, with their families beside them.

Today the family plays a diminished role in health care. Parents still make the crucial first decision about whether to call the doctor, and in most cases they still give simple care. But for anything complex, the diagnosis is in the hands of experts, not parents, and one crucial role for parents in the complicated business of nursing a sick child is to see that the child "follows the doctor's orders." In part, therefore, it is accurate to speak of health-care specialists assuming yet another traditional family function, but to stop there misses a central point: today we expect far more of health care for children than our forebears could. Most of what we expect of specialists did not exist a century ago: immunization against most life-threatening diseases, effective and accurate diagnosis of even obscure and rare illnesses, safe and hygienic surgery when needed, prompt treatment of bacterial infections, and medical correction of many handicaps. All of these are now considered among the basic rights of children. We are rightly shocked when children suffer or die from any of the host of childhood illnesses or conditions that today can be prevented or cured.

Rising expectations for what we want to give our children are crucial for understanding the transformation of families. Much of what we today consider the birthright of all American children and parents was simply unknown to our forebears. They did not need to rely on social workers to guide them, however tortuously, through welfare bureaucracies, because there were no welfare bureaucracies. They did not complain about inferior school facilities or poor vocational programs or inadequate compensatory education because few of these existed in any form, good or bad.

The point is obvious: at the same time that families have been shorn of many traditional roles with children, new expectations about children's needs have arisen and, along with them, new specialists and institutions to meet the expectations. Part of the change of family functions, which carries with it a new dependence on people and institutions outside the family, rests on the family's needs for forms of help and expert assistance that are the creations of the last century. . . .

The genuine shifts in traditional family functions do not leave families with nothing to do. On the contrary, some needs and tasks appear even more concentrated in families than in the past. Among these is fulfilling the emotional needs of parents and children. With work life highly impersonal, ties with neighbors tenuous, and truly intimate out-of-family friendships rare, husbands and wives tend to put all their emotional hopes for fulfillment into their family life. Expectations of sharing, sexual compatibility, and temperamental harmony in marriage have risen as other family functions have diminished.

Most important, parents today have a demanding new role choosing, meeting, talking with, and coordinating the experts, the technology, and the institutions that help bring up their children. The specific work involved is familiar to any parent: consultations with teachers, finding good health care, trying to monitor television watching, and so on. No longer able to do it all themselves, parents today are in some ways like the executives in a large firm—responsible for the smooth coordination of the many people and processes that must work together to produce the final product. . . .

[W]e must address ourselves less to the criticism and reform of parents themselves than to the criticism and reform of the institutions that sap their self-esteem and power. Recognizing that family self-sufficiency is a false myth, we also need to acknowledge that all today's families need help in raising children. The problem is not so much to reeducate parents but to make available the help they need and to give them enough power so that they can be effective advocates with and coordinators of the other forces that are bringing up their children. . . .

Families were never as self-sufficient or as self-contained as the myth made them out to be, but today they are even less so than they used to be. They are extraordinarily *dependent* on "outside" forces and influences, ranging from the nature of the parents' work to the content of television programming, from the structure of local schools to the organization of health care. All families today need and use support in raising children; to define the "needy" family as the exception is to deny the simplest facts of contemporary family life.

There is nothing to be gained by blaming ourselves and other individuals for family changes. We need to look instead to the broader economic and social forces that shape the experience of children and parents. Parents are not abdicating—they are being dethroned, by forces they cannot influence, much less control. Behind today's uncertainty among parents lies a trend of several centuries toward the transformation and redefinition of family life. We see no possibility—or desirability—of reversing this trend and turning the clock back to the "good old days," for the price then was high in terms of poverty and drudgery, of no education in today's sense at all, and of community interference in what we today consider private life.

CHAPTER 4

The American Couple in Historical Perspective

Philip Blumstein / Pepper Schwartz

ABSTRACT: Characteristics of the American family have traditionally included a small two-generation unit with the position of each member clear and unquestioned, marrying forever and for love, and strong interdependence of the husband and wife. The Industrial Revolution, however, weakened the interdependence of husbands and wives by drawing men away from farm and home. World War II accelerated this trend toward weakened bonds between husbands and wives. The results of these changes include a rise in the divorce rate, a decline in the fertility rate, a lowered marriage rate, and an older age at first marriage. The latter two consequences result largely from increasing education and the "marriage squeeze."

The American family has changed more in the last thirty years than in the previous two hundred and fifty. That is not an exaggeration. We do not have very precise information about personal life in the earliest days of the nation, but beginning with the census of 1790 one fact emerges quite clearly: The American couple—and its family—has been remarkably stable.[1]

Two things can be said about our knowledge of American marriages in the past: As we move farther back in time, the evidence gets sparser and the picture less clear, and in general we know more about the "facts" of marriage—the age at which people married, the size of their households—and less about the internal dynamics of their marriages, the emotional tone of the relationship, how happy people were, who made the decisions, etc. . . ..

Except in times of war and other terrible disruptions of human life, the American couple has been a stable and predictable unit. It is, and has always been, fairly small; even in the 1700's it consisted of a husband, a wife, and approximately three children. The American couple guarded its privacy. This sense of a private, inviolate enclave was respected even by the children in the family as they reached the age of maturity. As soon as they were of age they left the household in which they were raised, either because of their own passionate desire for privacy or because their parents wished to reclaim their household, lands, or adult relationship. Most adult offspring struck out to form new households as soon as they could afford to or as soon as their parents could help them establish themselves.

As families (and the country as a whole) became more wealthy and as land opened up and became available in the West, young people married earlier: Poverty no longer held back the formation of new families. This situation is in sharp contrast to that in nineteenth-century Ireland, where farms were small in comparison to the large number of people they were expected to support. The soil was of poor quality, so it took as much land as the family could jointly afford and the labor of adult children as well as parents to produce enough food to survive. It took a long time for young Irish men to acquire enough money or land to support families of their own. Hence the average age of marriage in Ireland was extremely high, even in comparison to today's standards: middle to late twenties for women and middle to late thirties for men. But such constraints did not operate in rural American to keep young people in the homes where they were born. Land was more plentiful and parents encouraged their young people to form independent households and start their own families.

American families stayed small. There is no strong tradition in this country of the "extended family," where several generations *were expected* to live in the same dwelling. Afro-Americans had a cultural preference for the extended family but this was undermined by slavery and the social disruption after the Civil War. Other ethnic minorities, the Chinese and Japanese for example, occasionally adopted multigenerational living arrangements. But the only major exception among Caucasians is found during the great waves of immigration from eastern and southern Europe toward the end of the nineteenth century. Different cultural traditions combined with economic necessity to encourage larger families with relationships that went beyond the nuclear group (parents and offspring). But for these new arrivals, one of the first goals—and one of the clearest signs that they had become Americans—was surrendering their extended families to create their own households. And as the country developed and the Midwest and the West Coast were settled, children left their families and headed out to farm or to seek other opportunities. If moving from Boston to Philadelphia did not result in liberation, moving to California might. Americans revised the commandment "Honor thy father and mother" to read "Honor thy father and mother—but get away from them."

A small two-generation family is not our only cultural consistency; the American view of the family, and the couple at its core, has remained remarkably constant. In America, the home was a family's castle. What happened there among family members was considered the sole and exclusive province of those involved (usually the husband with advice and consent from the wife) and not of the state. How children or spouses or parents were treated, abusively or lovingly, has traditionally been left to the discretion of adult family members, and was not a legitimate area for interference by the government or the courts.

Moreover, within the family, the duties, expectations, and position of each member were always clearly understood and unquestioned. This held true even if everyday reality differed in some respects (as it did in most farming families where men and women were likely to share the same chores). In American families the husband was expected to be responsible for the economic support of the household, and the wife for all the "interior" considerations, e.g., child rearing, emotional support of the husband, household chores, relations with friends and kin. When the balance between the husband's responsibilities and wife's responsibilities tipped because of illness or economic exigency, it was generally viewed as a temporary departure from the ideal brought on by unavoidable and extraordinary circumstances. The notion of the "good life" was comprised of the hardworking and prosperous husband, the nurturing wife and mother, and the small and happy troop of children for whom she cared while preparing them for an independent future of happiness and achievement.

It was also assumed that the husband-wife relationship, and the entire family structure, was based on, and stabilized by, the affection all the members held for one another. The couple came together and the family stayed together because they all *loved* and respected one another. Because romantic love was the basis for a marriage (rather than money or property), young adults were more or less left alone to choose a partner. But because marriage also entailed the beginning of a lifetime commitment with accompanying responsibilities, parents tried to make sure that their children met only the right kind of potential mate. Falling in love with the wrong person would have a devastating impact on one's offspring's chances in life. It was considered appropriate, therefore, for parents to intervene in courtships they disapproved of. Other institutions (for example, schools and universities) were expected to act *in loco parentis*, which meant that they enforced parental values, as much as possible, especially regarding courtship and sexuality.

A tension developed between unsupervised dating (having a good time while acquiring self-knowledge and social skills) and courtship (dating that could result in marriage). Since what had started out as unsupervised dating might easily turn into courtship, parents feared democratic environments that exposed their child to someone who could be endured as a date but would never be accepted as a son- or daughter-in-law. Thus, sometimes openly, but more often unconsciously, parents supported a double standard that allowed their children to experiment with "exotic" partners, but subtly directed their children's serious romantic commitments toward people who met parental standards. A son who wanted to explore sexuality before marriage (a troublesome, yet expected male pursuit), was encouraged, at least tacitly, as long as his adventures did not jeopardize a "proper" marital alliance in the future. Prostitutes and women from very different social classes were accessible and permitted sexual partners for young men in the middle or upper-middle class. The relationships between these men and women were clearly arranged and understood to be outside the context of romance or extended emotional commitment. Such experimentation was not considered necessary or appropriate for respectable young women. They were to encourage men of "good" family (the definition of "good" depending on one's race, class, religion) and to discourage any sexual relations. Premarital sex, in the woman's case, would not be tolerated. She would be considered "soiled" and her marriageability would be jeopardized.

Thus, romantic love—in the *right* context and with the *right* type of person—is and has been glorified in our country. Marry someone handsome and wealthy and you will be congratulated, but say you are not in love with that person and your cynicism will earn you the censure of all around you. At the same time it is clear that people accrue great benefit (often in terms of an improved standard of living) by the marriages they contract. "Marrying up" is applauded as long as one does not consciously admit to having made this the foundation for choosing a mate. We, as a people, still firmly believe that arranged marriages and marriages of convenience, are un-American.

And Americans have always married "forever." If the marriage contract was abrogated because of desertion, death, or divorce, this was seen as a personal and community tragedy. No one ever thought of marrying for one year or for ten years, and "Till death us do part" is still part of most contemporary marriage ceremonies. This may be no more than a pious hope today in the face of the current divorce statistics, but at the same time that the witnesses to the wedding are feeling a certain cynicism about the couple's future, the couple themselves cling tenaciously to the belief and hope that theirs will be a marriage of permanence. The American tradition is to hope for the best, which means a lifetime of loyalty to and from one's marriage partner.

This partnership was expected to find its ultimate expression in the establishment of a family. But having children required giving up past freedoms and the prospect of making one's way in the world as an independent agent. The decision to have children (and before the widespread use of contraceptives, deciding to have children was synonymous with having sex) was predicated in part on the absolute assurance that the paternity would be acknowledged, that economic support would be guaranteed, and that a paternal presence would be maintained. The family was, consequently, bonded both emotionally and legally; informal expectations were upheld by law and public opinion.

This exceptionally stable ideal of the American family was challenged and changed at two historical periods. Events democratized marriage by giving each member of the couple an opportunity to leave the household and establish a life elsewhere. Traditionally, partners were not allowed the choice of maintaining or terminating their marriage contract. But when the husband "got the vote," the institution of marriage became less stable. When the wife got the vote as well, the institution began to crumble. The institution was no longer larger than the sum of its parts.

What events began the progressive "getting of the vote" for husband and wife? The first was the Industrial Revolution. The latter part of the nineteenth century ushered in new forms of technology that drew men away from the farms and into the cities and factories. The interdependent farm couple (where each partner needed the other for cooperation in the daily survival chores) began to disappear. Husbands left the farm community, and its familiar faces and relationships, and began to see the big, wide world and what it had to offer. The first step in what ultimately was to become the suburbanization and isolation of the American woman had begun.

The second historical event was the Second World War, which accelerated a process that had already been under way during the Depression years. The war made it necessary for hundreds of thousands of women to enter the labor force in order to support their families. They also had to take over jobs, vital to the American economy, that had been vacated when their husbands went into the armed forces. After the war industry worked hard and with some success to "defeminize" the work force: nevertheless, many women remained on the job—or at least recalled what it was like to work for compensation outside the home. Things were never the same again in the American family. Both husbands and wives were out of the home and developed new opportunities, new skills, and new acquaintances. Family life began to change.

The changes were not apparent at the time. On the contrary. While the divorce rate had actually been rising since the turn of the century, it had done so at such a slow and steady pace that few observers were alarmed. Marriage and divorce rates shot up briefly right after World War II, but they fell again sharply and then gradually returned to their previous levels. By the 1950's the United States had entered the most family-oriented period of the century—the generation of the Feminine Mystique and the baby boom—and the couples married at the youngest ages in recorded American history. During the 1950's, 96 percent of people in the childbearing years married.[2] Women's magazines, newspapers, movies, and television were all extolling the perfect family life: zany, if one watched *I Love Lucy*; warm and wise, if it was *I Remember Mama*; or somewhere in between, for *Father Knows Best* or *My Three Sons*. No one recognized that the family was in transition and that couples would never again be the same.

But by the end of the fifties and early sixties, radical changes were becoming evident. The marriage rate began to fall and the divorce rate, which had been fairly level, accelerated its historical trend upward.[3] Now, imagine if you will a movie that takes three hours to unreel the credits, four hours to introduce the characters, and only five minutes to reveal the entire plot. This is an analogy to the history of the modern American couple. Changes that had taken a hundred years to germinate suddenly began to appear at a startling rate, and new family problems were full-blown before we had any idea that they existed.

In the late sixties and early seventies, fertility began to decline. It has stayed low—16.0 live births per 1,000 in 1982.[4] This was not entirely due, as some social scientists have suggested, to the emergence of the Pill on American college campuses, in family clinics, and in private physicians' offices. The Pill did enable women to make childbearing a choice, and after 1974, access to legal abortions became a way for some estimated 13 to 20 percent of the population to terminate unwanted pregnancies. But, in point of fact, the national trend of having fewer children had been developing over the past two hundred years; the baby-boom years were the exception, not the rule. The most profound impact made by the Pill was that it allowed women to have sex without linking it to reproduction, introducing them to the idea that making love could be spontaneous, enjoyable—and above all, an act whose consequences they could control. Accepted views about fertility—how large a family to have and when—had been changing before the Industrial Revolution and the new values were simply enhanced, not created, by the new scientific method of contraception.[5]

In the early seventies, the marriage rate for people under forty-five was as low as it had been at the end of the Depression. By 1974, the average age of marriage was a full year higher than it had been in the

1950's, and the proportion of women who remained unmarried until they reached the ages of twenty to twenty-four had increased by one third since 1960. The divorce rate had soared to the level it had attained only for a moment right after the Second World War, and one out of every three marriages of women at least thirty years old (the rate varies depending on the age group) was ending in divorce.[6] This information is particularly dramatic if one recalls that divorce statistics do not include desertion statistics.

Americans suddenly looked around and saw that social change seemed to have gotten out of hand. The statistics from the early seventies indicate enormous changes in social trends bearing on the meaning of marriage. The statistics of the eighties suggest that while some of the rates of change are slowing down a bit, the direction of change is persistent.

THE PRESENT SITUATION

In 1960, 28 percent of American women between the ages of twenty and twenty-four had not yet married. By 1979, the figure had jumped to 49 percent. (This was a return to pre-1940 levels.[7]) In 1981, 52 percent of women that age were single.[8] This fact alone can have enormous repercussions. First, a woman's fertility (the number of children she will bear over the course of her life) is strongly related to the age at which she marries. The later the marriage, for the most part, the later childbearing begins, and the smaller the family. We are already seeing later childbearing and smaller families. In 1970, 16 percent of the women twenty-five to twenty-nine years old who had ever been married were childless.[9] In 1981, that number rose to 25 percent. The greatest rise in the fertility rate was among women thirty to thirty-four years old. But that is not changing the larger picture. The actual fertility replacement rate in 1981 was about 1.8, well below the level of 2.1 that is needed to replace the present population.[10] There was an increase in 1982 of about 2 percent, but this merely indicates more women of childbearing age, not a change in the size of families.[11] Second, the smaller the family, the less difficult it is for a woman to divorce. Delaying marriage gives a woman more opportunity for advanced education and training, reduces the number of children she will have, and ultimately gives her more independence and flexibility in making life choices. Its secondary effect is to give exactly the same advantages to her husband.

Two explanations are generally offered for the decline in marriage rates and the rise in age of marriage: First, a much higher percentage of the population is going to college and beyond, and extended education tends to delay marriage. Second, men and women are being affected by

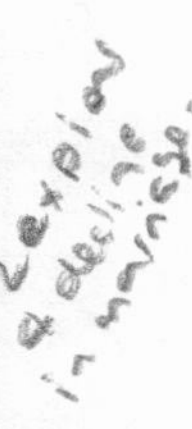

what Paul Glick, formerly senior demographer at the U.S. Bureau of the Census, has referred to as the "marriage squeeze." By this he means that more people want to marry than can be accommodated. For example, women tend to marry men who are two or three years older than themselves. This works out well when the size of the population at each of these ages is approximately the same—for example, if there is an approximately equal number of twenty-year-old women and twenty-three-year-old men.

But that is not how the population took shape in the years following the maturing of the baby-boom children. From 1945 to about 1960, couples were having rather large families. Girls from these families are now women in their twenties and thirties looking for either their first or second husband. They lament—and their comments are echoed in the popular magazines—that a "good man is hard to find." Why? Because there were fewer men born to the generation directly preceding them, and so the ratio of women to men who are a few years older than themselves is unfavorable. In addition, men in their second marriages tend to marry women five or more years their junior, and the statistics show that if a man remarries in his forties, he may choose a partner *ten* years younger than himself. In 1980, 94 percent of all men aged fifty were married! Marriage, even remarriage, is not possible for every woman born in the baby-boom years unless she marries someone younger than herself, or unless there is a great deal of rotation among the available men.[12] The high divorce rate, in an ironic sort of way, is helping these women by "recycling" men into the marriage market. These ratios are even more lopsided for black women. Interracial marriage increases the difference, with black men marrying white women approximately twice as often as black women marry white men.[13]

By the time women are in the forty- to forty-four-year age group, there are 300,000 fewer men than women or 141 single women to every 100 men, and if we include separated and divorced women, it is 213 women to 100 men. If we consider only those who are widowed, it is about 644 widows to 100 widowers. So as people enter their forties there are 233 unattached women for every 100 men.[14]

NOTES

1. Rudy Ray Steward, *The American Family: A Demographic History* (Beverly Hills, Cal.: Sage Publications, 1978).
2. Hugh Carter and Paul C. Glick, *Marriage and Divorce: A Social and Economic Study*, rev. ed. (Cambridge, Mass.: Harvard University Press, 1976).
3. Ibid.

4. U.S. National Center for Health Statistics, *Monthly Vital Statistics Report*, Vol. 31, No. 12 (March 14, 1983).
5. Andrew Cherlin, *Marriage, Divorce and Remarriage* (Cambridge, Mass.: Harvard University Press, 1981).
6. Carter and Glick, *Marriage and Divorce.*
7. Cherlin, *Marriage, Divorce and Remarriage.*
8. U.S. Bureau of the Census, *Current Population Reports*, series P-20 (1981, 1982) and series P-23 (1981, 1982) (Washington, D.C.: U.S. Government Printing Office).
9. Carter and Glick, *Marriage and Divorce.*
10. *Family Planning Perspectives*, Vol. 15, No. 1 (January/February 1983), pp. 38–39.
11. Ibid.
12. Paul C. Glick, "A Demographer Looks at American Families," *Journal of Marriage and the Family*, Vol. 37, No. 1 (February 1975), pp. 15–26. Also, Carter and Glick, *Marriage and Divorce.*
13. Ernest Porterfield, "Black-American Intermarriage in the United States," *Marriage and Family Review*, Vol. 5, No. 1 (Spring 1982), pp. 17–34. See also Graham Spanier and Paul Glick, "Mate Selection Differentials Between Whites and Blacks in the United States," *Social Forces*, Vol. 58, No. 3 (March 1980), pp. 707–725. They state that in 1975 about 4.4 percent of married black men and about 2.4 percent of married black women had partners of a different race (usually white).
14. Andrew Hacker, "Divorce à la Mode," *The New York Review of Books* (May 3, 1979). See also U.S. Bureau of the Census, *Statistical Abstract of the United States* (Washington, D.C.: U.S. Government Printing Office, 1978), tables 114, 118, 119.

CHAPTER 5

The Stages of the Family Life Cycle

Monica McGoldrick / Elizabeth A. Carter

ABSTRACT: A valuable understanding of American middle-class families can be gained by utilizing the "family life cycle." In this model we examine the major stages that occur in family life, delineating the "tasks" that must be adequately completed in each stage in order to successfully move to the next. These stages can be defined as:

1. the unattached young adult
2. the newly married couple
3. the family with young children
4. the family with adolescents
5. launching children
6. the family in later life

All families will be at one stage or another. Each stage offers unique challenges that need to be mastered before a family is able to adequately move on to the next stage.

We now provide a very brief outline of the statistically predictable developmental stages of American middle-class families in the last quarter of the 20th century. Our classification of family life cycle stages highlights our view that the central underlying process to be negotiated is the expansion, contraction, and realignment of the relationship system to support the entry, exit, and development of family members in a functional way. . . .

THE UNATTACHED YOUNG ADULT

In outlining the stages of the family life cycle, we have departed from the traditional sociological depiction of the family life cycle as commencing at courtship or marriage and ending with the death of one spouse. Rather, considering the family to be the operative emotional unit from the cradle to the grave, we see a new family life cycle beginning at the stage of the "unattached young adult," whose completion of the primary task of coming to terms with his or her family of origin will most profoundly influence whom, when and how he or she marries and carries out all succeeding stages of the family life cycle. Adequate completion of this task requires that the young adult separate from the family of origin without cutting off or fleeing reactively to a substitute emotional refuge. Seen in this way, the "unattached young adult" phase is a cornerstone. It is a time to formulate personal life goals and to become a "self" before joining with another to form a new family subsystem. . . . This is the chance for them to sort out emotionally what they will take along from the family of origin and what they will change for themselves. Of great significance is the fact that until the present generation this crucial phase was never considered necessary for women, who were traditionally handed directly from their fathers to their husbands. Obviously, this tradition has had profound impact on the functioning of women in families, as the current attempt to change the tradition is now having. . . .

We have outlined the shifts in status required for successful accomplishment of life cycle transitions in column 2 of [Table 5.1], which outlines the stages and tasks of the life cycle. . . .

In the "unattached young adult" phase, problems usually center on either young adults' or their parents' not recognizing the need for a shift to a less interdependent form of relating, based on their now all being adults complementing each other. Problems in shifting status may take the form of parent's encouraging the dependence of their young adult children, or of young adults' either remaining dependent or breaking away in a pseudoindependent cutoff of their parents and families. It is our view, following Bowen (1978), that cutoffs never resolve emotional relationships and that young adults who cutoff their parents do so reactively and are in fact still emotionally bound to rather than independent of the family "program." The shift toward adult-to-adult status requires a mutually respectful and personal form of relating, in which young adults can appreciate parents as they are, needing neither to make them into what they are not, nor to blame them for what they could not be. . . . An example may clarify the way in which family mem-

TABLE 5.1 The Stages of the Family Life Cycle

Family life cycle stage	Emotional process of transition: Key principles	Changes in family status required to proceed developmentally
1. Between families: The unattached young adult	Accepting parent-offspring separation	a. Differentiation of self in relation to family of origin b. Development of intimate peer relationships c. Establishment of self in work
2. The joining of families through marriage: The newly married couple	Commitment to new system	a. Formation of marital system b. Realignment of relationships with extended families and friends to include spouse
3. The family with young children	Accepting new generation of members into the system	a. Adjusting marital system to make space for child(ren) b. Taking on parenting roles c. Realignment of relationships with extended family to include parenting and grandparenting roles
4. The family with adolescents	Increasing flexibility of family boundaries to include children's independence	a. Shifting of parent-child relationships to permit adolescents to move in and out of system b. Refocus on midlife marital and career issues c. Beginning shift toward concerns for older generation
5. Launching children and moving on	Accepting a multitude of exits from and entries into the family system	a. Renegotiation of marital system as a dyad b. Development of adult to adult relationships between grown children and their parents c. Realignment of relationships to include in-laws and grandchildren d. Dealing with disabilities and death of parents (grandparents)
6. The family in later life	Accepting the shifting of generational roles	a. Maintaining own and/or couple functioning and interests in face of physiological decline; exploration of new familial and social role options b. Support for a more central role for middle generation c. Making room in the system for the wisdom and experience of the elderly; supporting the older generation without overfunctioning for them

TABLE 5.1 (*Continued*)

Family life cycle stage	Emotional process of transition: Key principles	Changes in family status required to proceed developmentally
		d. Dealing with loss of spouse, siblings, and other peers, and preparation for own death. Life review and integration

bers can get stuck in a "more of the same" struggle, where the harder they try, the worse it gets. . . .

> David G., a 24-year-old computer programmer, applied for therapy with vague complaints of depression and the inability to form close relationships. The picture that emerged was of an isolated young man who had trouble keeping himself motivated at work. He also had trouble feeling connected with friends, especially women. When asked about his parents, he said they were not worth discussing. He described them as critical, cynical, having a poor marriage and little to give. Further questioning revealed that he knew very little about his parents as people. They were Jewish immigrants whose families had struggled through the Depression. As we explored the family relationships, it became clear that David saw his parents as wounded people, felt guilty and resentful that they had not given more to him, and sensed their emptiness as he, the younger of two sons, left home. He did not want to reach back for fear that they would pull him into their depression and bitterness and he would never be able to leave. Yet, by cutting off, he had no sense of who he was or how to make other connections. He was not free to move on as an adult. He was reluctant at first to make moves with his family of origin and insisted, "I am an adult and can handle my own problems." Questions about his parents' lives gradually helped him to alter his view of them and to redefine his relationship with them as a relationship of adults. Other relatives were called on for information about the family background, and the details they gave David about his parents' lives helped him in making this shift to a different view of his parents and the nature of their hold on him. As he gave up rigidly resisting his parents, he began to get to know them and became freer to make contacts with peers as well. He also found himself having more energy for his work.

It seems clear in this case that the more David tried to cut himself off from his parents and disassociate himself from traits he identified with in them, the less able he became to get on with his own life and to develop a truly personal identity. By reconnecting with them in a new way and shifting his status in relation to them, he became able to move on developmentally.

THE JOINING OF FAMILIES THROUGH MARRIAGE: THE NEWLY MARRIED COUPLE

Becoming a couple is one of the most complex and difficult transitions of the family life cycle. However, along with the transition to parenthood, which it has long symbolized, it is seen as the easiest and the most joyous. The positive and romanticized view of this transition may add to its difficulty, since everyone wants to see only the happiness of the shift. The problems entailed may thus be pushed underground, only to instensify and surface later on.

Weddings, more than any other rite of passage, are viewed as the solution to a problem, such as loneliness or extended family difficulties. The event is seen as terminating a process instead of beginning one. The myth "And they lived happily ever after" (with no further effort) causes couples and families considerable difficulty. Weddings, far from resolving a "status problem" of young unmarried adults, come in the middle of a complex process of changing family status.

Marriage requires that a couple renegotiate a myriad of personal issues that they have previously defined for themselves or that were defined by their parents, from when to eat, sleep, have sex, or fight, to how to celebrate holidays or where and how to live, work, and spend vacations. The couple must renegotiate their relationships with their parents, siblings, friends, and other relatives in view of the new marriage, and this will to some degree affect all personal relationships. It places no small stress on the family to open itself to an outsider who is now an official member of its inner circle. Frequently no new member has been added for many years. In addition, marriage involves a shifting of family boundaries for the members on both sides to some degree or other. Not only is the new spouse now a factor for each family, but priorities of both systems must now be negotiated in a complex set of arrangements of each system. As mentioned earlier, relationships with the third generation are of utmost importance in understanding the family life cycle, not only because of their historical importance to the system, but because of their direct, ongoing impact on the life of the next generations' family experiences.

In the animal kingdom, mating involves only the two partners. For mankind, it is the joining of two enormously complex systems. In fact, Haley has commented that the fact of having in-laws is the major distinguishing characteristic between man and all other forms of life. In any case, it is surely a complex transition and one that our rituals hardly prepare us for. And, although couples are marrying later and delaying having children more than ever before, the average age of marriage for women in 1975 was 21.3 and men 23.8; the birth of the first child came, on the average, 1½ years later. This means that there is still a relatively short time in which the couple and both families must adjust to this phase of their life cycle, with its accompanying stresses, before moving on. It may also be worth noting that there seems to be an optimum timing for this phase, with those who fall outside it often having more difficulty. Women who marry before the age of 20 (38% of women) are twice as likely to divorce as those who marry in their 20s. Those who marry after 30 (6%) are half again as likely to divorce as those who marry in their 20s (Glick & Norton, 1977). Thus it appears that in our culture there is a time for coupling; while it may be better to marry later than sooner, those who fall too far out of the normative range on either end are more likely to have trouble making the transition. A number of other factors appear to make the adjustment to this life cycle transition more difficult:

1. The couple meets or marries shortly after a significant loss.
2. One or both partners wish to distance from family of origin.
3. The family backgrounds of each spouse are significantly different (religion, education, social class, ethnicity, age, etc.).
4. The couple have incompatible sibling constellations (Toman, 1976).
5. The couple reside either extremely close to or at a great distance from either family of origin.
6. The couple are dependent on either extended family financially, physically, or emotionally.
7. The couple marries before age 20 or after age 30.
8. The couple marries after an acquaintanceship of less than 6 months or after more than 3 years of engagement.
9. The wedding occurs without family or friends present.
10. The wife becomes pregnant before or within the first year of marriage (Christensen, 1963; Bacon, 1974).
11. Either spouse has a poor relationship with his or her siblings or parents.
12. Either spouse considers his or her childhood or adolescence as an unhappy time.
13. Marital patterns in either extended family were unstable. . . .

A number of other factors also add to the difficulty of adjusting to marriage in our time. Changing family patterns as a result of the changing role of women, the frequent marriage of partners from widely different cultural backgrounds, and the increasing physical distances between family members are placing a much greater burden on couples to define their relationship for themselves than was true in traditional and precedent-bound family structures. While any two family systems are always different and have conflicting patterns and expectations, in our present culture couples are less bound by family traditions and freer than ever before to develop male-female relationships unlike those they experienced in their families of origin. This is particularly so because of the changing role of women in families. It appears that the rise in women's status is positively correlated with marital instability (Pearson & Hendrix, 1979) and with the marital dissatisfaction of their husbands (Burke & Weir, 1976). When women used to fall automatically into the adaptive role in marriage, the likelihood of divorce was much lower. In fact, it appears very difficult for two spouses to be equally successful and achieving. There is evidence that either spouse's accomplishments may correlate negatively with the same degree of achievement in the other (Ferber & Huber, 1979). Thus, achieving a successful transition to couplehood in our time, when we are moving toward the equality of the sexes (educationally and occupationally), may be extraordinarily difficult. . . .

THE FAMILY WITH YOUNG CHILDREN

The shift to this stage of the family life cycle requires that adults now move up a generation and become caretakers to the younger generation. Typical problems that occur when parents cannot make this shift are struggles with each other about taking responsibility, or refusal or inability to behave as parents to their children. Often parents find themselves unable to set limits and exert the required authority, or they lack the patience to allow their children to express themselves as they develop. Typically, parents with children who present clinically [appear for counseling] at this phase are somehow not accepting the generation boundary between themselves and their children. They may complain that their 4-year-old is "impossible to control." Given their relative size, the difficulty here relates to the parents' difficulty exerting authority. From this perspective, whether parents placate and spoil their children, or whether they are endlessly critical, they are reflecting a failure to appreciate the new change in family status required in this stage of the family life cycle. . . .

THE FAMILY WITH ADOLESCENTS

While many have broken down the stages of families with young children into different phases, in our view the shifts are incremental until adolescence, which ushers in a new era because it marks a new definition of the children within the family and of the parents' roles in relation to their children. Families with adolescents must establish qualitatively different boundaries than families with younger children. The boundaries must now be permeable. Parents can no longer maintain complete authority. Adolescents can and do open the family to a whole array of new values as they bring friends and new ideas into the family arena. Families that become derailed at this stage are frequently stuck in an earlier view of their children. They may try to control every aspect of their lives at a time when, developmentally, this is impossible to do successfully. Either the adolescent withdraws from the appropriate involvements for this developmental stage, or the parents become increasingly frustrated with what they perceive as their own impotence. For this phase the old Alcoholics Anonymous adage is particularly apt for parents: "May I have the ability to accept the things I cannot change, the strength to change the things I can, and the wisdom to know the difference." Flexible boundaries that allow adolescents to move in and be dependent at times when they cannot handle things alone, and to move out and experiment with increasing degress of independence when they are ready, put special strains on all family members in their new status with one another. This is also a time when adolescents begin to establish their own independent relationships with the extended family, and it requires special adjustments between parents and grandparents to allow and foster these new patterns.

Parents of adolescents often get stuck in attempting to get their children to do what the parents want at a time when this can no longer be done successfully, or they let the children do whatever they want and fail to exert the needed authority. Children may become overly independent and adultlike, or they remain immature and fail to develop sufficient independent functioning to move on developmentally. . . .

LAUNCHING CHILDREN AND MOVING ON

This phase of the family life cycle is the newest and the longest, and for these reasons, it is in many ways the most problematic of all phases. Until about a generation ago, most families were occupied with raising their children for their entire active adult lives until old age. Now, because of the low birth rate and the long life span of most adults, parents launch their children almost 20 years before retirement and must then find other life activities. The difficulties of this transition can lead families to hold on to their children or can lead to parental feelings of emptiness and depression, particularly for women who have focused their main energies on their children and who now feel useless and unprepared to face a new career in the job world. The most significant aspect of this phase is that it is marked by the greatest number of exits and entries of family members. It begins with the launching of grown children and proceeds with the entry of their spouses and children. Meanwhile, it is a time when older parents are often becoming ill or dying; this, in conjunction with the difficulties of finding meaningful life activities during this phase itself, may make it a particularly difficult period. Parents must not only deal with the change in their own status as they make room for the next generation and move up to grandparental positions, but they must deal also with a different type of relationship with their own parents, who may become dependent, giving them considerable caretaking responsibilities.

This can also be a liberating time, in that finances may be easier than during the primary years of family responsibilities and there is the potential for moving into new and unexplored areas—travel, hobbies, new careers. For some families this stage is seen as a time of fruition and completion and as a second opportunity to consolidate or expand by exploring new avenues and new roles. For others it leads to disruption, a sense of emptiness and overwhelming loss, depression, and general disintegration. The phase necessitates a restructuring of the marital relationship now that parenting responsibilities are no longer required. As Solomon (1973) has noted, if the solidification of the marriage has not taken place and reinvestment is not possible, the family often mobilizes itself to hold onto the last child. Where this does not happen the couple may move toward divorce.

The family that fails to appreciate the need for a shift in relationship status at this stage may keep trying to fill their time with the old tasks, or the spouses may begin to blame each other for the emptiness they feel. If they can recognize the new efforts required in this period, they are much more likely to be able to mobilize the energy to deal with them than if they go along on the assumptions of the previous phase. . . .

THE FAMILY IN LATER LIFE

As Walsh (1980) has pointed out, few of the visions we are offered in our culture for old age provide us with positive perspectives for healthy later-life adjustment within a family or social context. Pessimistic views of later life prevail. The current myths are that most elderly people have no families; that those who do have families have little relationship with them and are usually set aside in institutions; or that all family interactions with older family members are minimal. On the contrary, the vast majority of adults over 65 do not live alone but with other family members. Over 80% live within an hour of at least one child (Walsh, 1980).

Another myth about the elderly is that they are sick, senile, and feeble and can be best handled in nursing homes or hospitals. Only 4% of the elderly live in institutions (Streib, 1972), and the average age at admission is 80. There are indications that if others did not foster their dependence or ignore them as functional family members, even this degree of dependence would be less.

Among the tasks of families in later life are adjustments to retirement, which may not only create the obvious vacuum for the retiring person but may put a special strain on a marriage that until then has been balanced in different spheres. Financial insecurity or dependence are also special difficulties, especially for family members who value managing for themselves. And while loss of friends and relatives is a particular difficulty at this phase, the loss of a spouse is the most difficult adjustment, with its problems of reorganizing one's entire life alone after many years as a couple and of having fewer relationships to help replace the loss. Grandparenthood can, however, offer a new lease on life, and opportunities for special close relationships without the responsibilities of parenthood.

Difficulty in making the status changes required for this phase of life are reflected in older family members' refusal to relinquish some of their power, as when a grandfather refuses to turn over the company or make plans for his succession. The inability to shift status is reflected also when older adults give up and become totally dependent on the next generation, or when the next generation does not accept their lessening powers or treats them as totally incompetent or irrelevant.

Even when members of the older generation are quite enfeebled, there is not really a reversal of roles between one generation and the next, because parents always have a great many years of extra experience and remain models to the next generations for the phases of life ahead. Nevertheless, because valuing older age is totally unsupported in our culture, family members of the next generation often do not know how to make the appropriate shift in relational status with their parents. . . .

THE FAMILY LIFE CYCLE OF THE POOR

The adaptation of multiproblem poor families over decades and centuries to a stark political, social, and economic context has produced a family life cycle pattern that varies significantly from the middle-class paradigm so often and so erroneously used to conceptualize their situation. Colon (1980) offers a thought-provoking breakdown of the family life cycle of the poor into three phases: the "unattached young adult" (who may actually be 11 or 12 years old), on his or her own virtually unaccountable to adults; families with children—a phase that occupies most of the life span and commonly includes three- and four-generation households; and the phase of the nonevolved grandmother, still involved in a central role in old age—still actively in charge of the generations below. . . .

CONCLUSION

In concluding this chapter, we direct the reader's thoughts toward the powerful (and preventive) implications of family life cycle celebration: those rituals, religious or secular, that have been designed by families in every culture to ease the passage of its members from one status to the next. As Friedman (1980) points out, all family relationships in the system seem to unlock during the time just before and after such events, and it is often possible to shift things with less effort during these intensive periods than could ordinarily be expended in years of struggle.

REFERENCES

BACON L. Early motherhood, accelerated role transition and social pathologies. *Social Forces*, 1974, 52, 333–341.

BOWEN, M. *Family therapy in clinical practice*. New York: Aronson, 1978.

BURKE, R. J. & WEIR, T. The relationships of wives' employment status to husband, wife and pair satisfaction. *Journal of Marriage and the Family*, 1976, 2, 279–287.

CHRISTENSEN, H. T. The timing of first pregnancy as a factor in divorce: A cross-cultural analysis. *Eugenics Quarterly*, 1963, 10, 119–130.

COLON, F. The family life cycle of the multiproblem poor family. In E. A. Carter & M. McGoldrick (Eds.), *The family life cycle: A framework for family therapy*. New York: Gardner Press, 1980.

FERBER, M., & HUBER, J. Husbands, wives and careers. *Journal of Marriage and the Family*, 1979, 41, 315–325.

FRIEDMAN, E. Systems and ceremonies: A family view of rites of passage. In E. A. Carter & M. McGoldrick (Eds.), *The family life cycle: A framework for family therapy*. New York: Gardner Press, 1980.

GLICK, P., & NORTON, A. J. Marrying, divorcing and living together in the U.S. today. In *Population Bulletin*, 32, No. 5. Washington, D.C.: Population Reference Bureau, 1977.

HETHERINGTON, E. M., COX, M., & COX, R. The aftermath of divorce. In J. J. Stevens, Jr., & M. Matthews (Eds.), *Mother-child, father-child relations*. Washington, D.C.: National Association for the Education of Young Children, 1977.

PEARSON, W., & HENDRIX, L. Divorce and the status of women. *Journal of Marriage and the Family*, 1979, 41, 375–386.

RANSOM, W., SCHLESINGER, S., & DERDEYN, A. P. A stepfamily in formation. *American Journal of Orthopsychiatry*, 1979, 49, 36–43.

SOLOMON, M. A developmental conceptual premise for family therapy. *Family process*, 1973, 12, 179–188.

STREIB, G. Older families and their troubles: Familial and social responses. *The Family Coordinator*, 1972, 21, 5–19.

TOMAN, W. *Family constellation* (3rd ed.). New York: Springr, 1976.

WALSH, F. The family in later life. In E. A. Carter & M. McGoldrick (Eds.), *The family life cycle: A framework for family therapy*. New York: Gardner Press, 1980.

SECTION 2

Contemporary Issues and Trends

THAT THE FAMILY CONTINUOUSLY RESPONDS AND ADAPTS TO SOCIAL CHANGE, the theme of the first section, is continued here. For example, ideas about the "ideal family" change over time, but from where do these ideas come? One source is the mass media, which help to shape the way we think about many aspects of social life, including that of the "ideal" family. Rather than representing reality, however, these ideal families largely exist in the imaginations of the media makers: Few families in real life match the image.

These distorted ideas cause confusion and frustration, for they force people to compare themselves with something that is largely nonexistent. This creates frustration and dissatisfaction—for how can we live up to myths and ideals that have been plucked from the imagination? While they provide good basis for drama (especially tearjerkers in which tragedy strikes to disrupt the ideal) and situation comedies (when the ideal never comes out exactly right, but is nevertheless always in the process of being maintained), they provide only an inadequate picture to which we can compare our own marital and familial experiences. For that, it is useful to turn to the historical record.

The historical record shows that marriage and family have never existed in an idealized state. They have, rather, always experienced all sorts of problems, including a high death rate, poverty, and, in some places, much illegitimacy.

About the time of the Civil War, a far-reaching social change occurred that drove an ongoing wedge between the husband/father and the other family members. This was the industrialization of America. As our country industrialized, work was removed from the home, relocating much of the husband's activities away from his family.

A major consequence of this separation of the husband/father was that he experienced the world differently than did his family. He became more independent of them and felt more alone in the struggle for survival and subsistence. Consequently, he came to look more to his family as a refuge from the trials he experienced in his workaday world. Gradually, the family became for him a "haven from a heartless world."

Over the years, this impetus on meeting the emotional/personality needs of family members has accelerated. Husbands have come to expect increasing amounts of emotional support from their wives, and wives from their husbands. And on both has been placed the expectation that they will produce emotionally well-adjusted children. In short, emotional relationships within the family have taken on increasing importance.

To lodge greater expectations of personal satisfactions on the family made it increasingly difficult for family members to satisfy those expectations. Husbands and wives, however, continued to demand that they be satisfied—having come to see their fulfillment as a legitimate expectation of married life. As people failed to live up to what became ever-expanding needs and expectations, more and more people felt strain in their marriage. As a result, the divorce rate increased, ultimately reaching historical highs.

In the chapter that opens this section, Arlene Skolnick develops some of these ideas. She especially stresses that the American family is enshrined in myths that are impossible to live up to. These myths, presenting a "sentimental model" of the family, increase dissatisfaction with marriage and family life, for the reality that married people face always falls short of the idealized images fostered by the myths.

In the seventh chapter Leo Zakuta takes a somewhat different approach by focusing on the increasing expectations that we have of equality between husbands and wives. He concludes that the rise in our divorce rate has come about because people now demand more personal satisfactions from marriage than they used to. The increase in the number of divorces in the United States, he says, ought not be taken as a sign that people are less committed to marriage and family life today, but, rather, that people's standards and expectations have changed—with the consequence that couples today are placing more of an emotional load on marriage and family than ever before.

Although the analyses by Skolnick and Zakuta may appear quite different from one another, they share certain basic positions and implications.These include:

1. Changes in society (including industrial/economic factors) create changes in images, ideals, and expectations;
2. Changed expectations (including images, ideals, and other social constructs) create changes in the relationships between family members;
3. Social changes have resulted in an increased emotional burden being placed on today's family;
4. The expectations of greater emotional involvements have become so great that it is difficult for husbands and wives to satisfy them;
5. Among the consequences of these increased emotional expectations is a higher divorce rate.

The currents of contemporary social change are many, their effects varied. As people become more mobile, more urban-centered, more away-from-the-home oriented, not only are wedges driven between husbands and wives, but married couples also tend to have fewer children. Children are not only expensive in today's society—and the call for a higher standard of living endless—but ideas of what makes a good parent have become increasingly complicated, making them more difficult to satisfy.

For these and a myriad of other reasons, the American birthrate has declined. This has resulted in huge shifts in the age-balance of the American population, as Sar A. Levitan and Richard S. Belous document in the eighth chapter.

In Chapter 9 Paul Bagne examines a different facet of fertility. Unable to become impregnated by their husbands, many women choose artificial insemination. Although sperm banks offer a solution to their problem, this control over reproduction also poses a potential problem significant not only for our society but perhaps for the entire world. The possibility has now come into being to control reproduction in order to produce someone's idea of what a desirable person is. While such a possibility is yet far from fact, this is one of the ominous implications of what might otherwise be simply an interesting technological development.

In the chapter that closes this section, Matilda White Riley continues the theme of the family changing in response to changes in society. She stresses that for the first time in our history (or that of the world) most people are living to grow old, and increased longevity poses significant implications for marriage and family. Among them, newlyweds (short of divorce or early death) can anticipate living with one another fifty, maybe even seventy-five, years. As people become grandparents they can expect that their own parents—and, increasingly, their own grandparents—will still be alive. As a consequence of this change in longevity, marital and family life will take on new dimensions.

What are those dimensions? Riley indicates some, but this fact of life is so new that they are only now in the process of emerging. At this point we can only try to anticipate them. Whatever they turn out to be, they are a further example of social change and changing family life—returning us once again to the basic position of the intricate interrelationship of society to marriage and family life.

CHAPTER 6

The Paradox of Perfection

Arlene Skolnick

ABSTRACT: The mass media's image of the "ideal family" distorts our concept of what the family is. A more realistic perspective of the family can be gained by a historical view. In early America the bounds between the family and the community merged into one another, marriage was not based on love, and there were high rates of infant mortality and illegitimacy. About the time of the Civil War a major change occurred in the American family: Industrialization separated men's work from the family setting, resulting in changed attitudes. Increasingly, the family came to be considered a haven in a heartless world. As men's and women's worlds continued to become more separate, sentimental ideas of the family increased. Perfectionist ideas of marriage and family emerged, which were difficult to live up to. Not finding this idealistic view in the reality of marriage, Americans became more willing to divorce. Our high divorce rate is a sign that Americans expect more out of marriage and family today then ever before.

The American Family, as even readers of *Popular Mechanics* must know by now, is in what Sean O'Casey would have called "a terrible state of chassis." Yet, there are certain ironies about the much-publicized crisis that give one pause.

True, the statistics seem alarming. The U.S. divorce rate, though it has reached something of a plateau in recent years, remains the highest in American history. The number of births out-of-wedlock among all races and ethnic groups continues to climb. The plight of many elderly Americans subsisting on low fixed incomes is well known.

What puzzles me is an ambiguity, not in the facts, but in what we are asked to make of them. A series of opinion polls conducted in 1978 by Yankelovich, Skelley, and White, for example, found that 38 percent of those surveyed had recently witnessed one or more "destructive activities" (e.g., a divorce, a separation, a custody battle) within their own families or those of their parents or siblings. At the same time, 92 percent of the respondents said the family was highly important to them as a "personal value."

Can the family be at once a cherished "value" and a troubled institution? I am inclined to think, in fact, that they go hand in hand. A recent "Talk of the Town" report in *The New Yorker* illustrates what I mean:

> A few months ago word was heard from Billy Gray, who used to play brother Bud in "Father Knows Best," the 1950s television show about the nice Anderson family who lived in the white frame house on a side street in some mythical Springfield—the house at which the father arrived each night swinging open the front door and singing out "Margaret, I'm home!" Gray said he felt "ashamed" that he had ever had anything to do with the show. It was all "totally false," he said, and had caused many Americans to feel inadequate, because they thought that was the way life was supposed to be and that their own lives failed to measure up.

As Susan Sontag has noted in *On Photography*, mass-produced images have "extraordinary powers to determine our demands upon reality." The family is especially vulnerable to confusion between truth and illusion. What, after all, is "normal"? All of us have a backstairs view of our own families, but we know The Family, in the aggregate, only vicariously.

Like politics or athletics, the family has become a media event. Television offers nightly portrayals of lump-in-throat family "normalcy" ("The Waltons," "Little House on the Prairie") and even humorous "deviance" ("One Day at a Time," "The Odd Couple"). Family advisers sally forth in syndicated newspaper columns to uphold standards, mend relationships, suggest counseling, and otherwise lead their readers back to the True Path. For commercial purposes, advertisers spend millions of dollars to create stirring vignettes of glamorous-but-ordinary families, the kind of family most 11-year-olds wish they had.

All Americans do not, of course, live in such a family, but most share an intuitive sense of what the "ideal" family should be—reflected in the precepts of religion, the conventions of etiquette, and the assumptions of law. And, characteristically, Americans tend to project the ideal back into the past, the time when virtues of all sorts are thought to have flourished.

We do not come off well by comparison with that golden age, nor could we, for it is as elusive and mythical as Brigadoon. If Billy Gray shames too easily, he has a valid point: While Americans view the family as the proper context for their own lives—9 out of 10 people live in one—they have no realistic context in which to view the family. Family history, until recently, was as neglected in academe as it still is in the press. [The summer 1980] White House Conference on Families is "policy-oriented," which means present-minded. The familiar, depressing charts of "leading family indicators"—marriage, divorce, illegitimacy—in newspapers and newsmagazines rarely survey the trends before World War II. The discussion, in short, lacks ballast.

Let us go back to before the American Revolution.

Perhaps what distinguishes the modern family most from its colonial counterpart is its newfound privacy. Throughout the 17th and 18th centuries, well over 90 percent of the American population lived in small rural communities. Unusual behavior rarely went unnoticed, and neighbors often intervened directly in a family's affairs, to help or to chastise.

The most dramatic example was the rural "charivari," prevalent in both Europe and the United States until the early 19th century. The purpose of these noisy gatherings was to censure community members for familial transgressions—unusual sexual behavior, marriages between persons of grossly discrepant ages, or "household disorder," to name but a few. As historian Edward Shorter describes it in *The Making of the Modern Family:*

> Sometimes the demonstration would consist of masked individuals circling somebody's house at night, screaming, beating on pans, and blowing cow horns. . . . [O]n other occasions, the offender would be seized and marched through the streets, seated perhaps backwards on a donkey or forced to wear a placard describing his sins.

The state itself had no qualms about intruding into a family's affairs by statute, if necessary. Consider 17th-century New England's "stubborn child" laws that, though never actually enforced, sanctioned the death penalty for chronic disobedience to one's parents.

If the boundaries between home and society seem blurred during the colonial era, it is because they were. People were neither very emotional nor very self-conscious about family life, and, as historian John Demos points out, family and community were "joined in a relation of profound reciprocity." In his *Of Domestical Duties*, William Gouge, a 17th-century Puritan preacher, called the family "a little community." The home, like the larger community, was as much an economic as a social unit; all members of the family worked, be it on the farm, or in a shop, or in the home.

There was not much to idealize. Love was not considered the basis for marriage but one possible result of it. According to historian Carl Degler, it was easier to obtain a divorce in colonial New England than anywhere else in the Western world, and the divorce rate climbed steadily throughout the 18th century, though it remained low by contemporary standards. Romantic images to the contrary, it was rare for more than two generations (parents and children) to share a household, for the simple reason that very few people lived beyond the age of 60. It is ironic that our nostalgia for the extended family—including grandparents and grandchildren—comes at a time when, thanks to improvements in health care, its existence is less threatened than ever before.

Infant mortality was high in colonial days, though not as high as we are accustomed to believe, since food was plentiful and epidemics, owing to generally low population density, were few. In the mid-1700s, the average age of marriage was about 24 for men, 21 for women—not much different from what it is now. Households, on average, were larger, but not startlingly so: A typical household in 1790 included about 5.6 members, versus about 3.5 today. Illegitimacy was widespread. Premarital pregnancies reached a high in 18th-century America (10 percent of all first births) that was not equalled until the 1950s.

FORM FOLLOWS FUNCTION

In simple demographic terms, then, the differences between the American family in colonial times and today are not all that stark; the similarities are sometimes striking.

The chief contrast is psychological. While Western societies have always idealized the family to some degree, the *most vivid* literary portrayals of family life before the 19th century were negative or, at best, ambivalent. In what might be called the "high tragic" tradition—including Sophocles, Shakespeare, and the Bible, as well as fairy tales and novels—the family was portrayed as a high-voltage emotional setting, laden with dark passion, sibling rivalries, and violence. There was also the "low comic" tradition—the world of henpecked husbands and tyrannical mothers-in-law.

It is unlikely that our 18th-century ancestors ever left the Book of Genesis or *Tom Jones* with the feeling that their own family lives were seriously flawed.

By the time of the Civil War, however, American attitudes toward the family had changed profoundly. The early decades of the 19th century marked the beginnings of America's gradual transformation into an urban, industrial society. In 1820, less than 8 percent of the U.S. population lived in cities; by 1860, the urban concentration approached 20 percent, and by 1900 that proportion had doubled.

Structurally, the American family did not immediately undergo a comparable transformation. Despite the large families of many immigrants and farmers, the size of the *average* family declined—slowly but steadily—as it had been doing since the 17th century. Infant mortality remained about the same and may even have increased somewhat, owing to poor sanitation in crowded cities. Legal divorces were easier to obtain than they had been in colonial times. Indeed, the rise in the divorce rate was a matter of some concern during the 19th century, though death, not divorce, was the prime cause of one-parent families, as it was up to 1965.

Functionally, however, America's industrial revolution had a lasting effect on the family. No longer was the household typically a group of interdependent workers. Now, men went to offices and factories and became breadwinners; wives stayed home to mind the hearth; children went off to the new public schools. The home was set apart from the dog-eat-dog arena of economic life; it came to be viewed as a utopian retreat or, in historian Christopher Lasch's phrase, a "haven in a heartless world." Marriage was now valued primarily for its emotional attractions. Above all, the family became something to worry about.

The earliest and most saccharine "sentimental model" of the family appeared in the new mass media that proliferated during the second quarter of the 19th century. Novels, tracts, newspaper articles, and ladies' magazines—there were variations for each class of society—elaborated a "Cult of True Womanhood" in which piety, submissiveness, and domesticity dominated the pantheon of desirable feminine qualities. This quotation from *The Ladies Book* (1830) is typical:

> See, she sits, she walks, she speaks, she looks—unutterable things! Inspiration springs up in her very paths—it follows her footsteps. A halo of glory encircles her, and illuminates her whole orbit. With her, man not only feels safe, but actually renovated.

In the late 1800s, science came into the picture. The "professionalization" of the housewife took two different forms. One involved motherhood and childrearing, according to the latest scientific understanding of children's special physical and emotional needs. (It is no accident that the publishing of children's books became a major industry during this period.) The other was the domestic science movement—"home economics," basically—which focused on woman as full-time homemaker, applying "scientific" and "industrial" rationality to shopping, making meals, and housework.

The new ideal of the family prompted a cultural split that has endured, one that Tocqueville had glimpsed (and rather liked) in 1835. Society was divided more sharply into man's sphere and woman's sphere. Toughness, competition, and practicality were the masculine values that ruled the outside world. The softer values—affection, tranquility, piety—were worshipped in the home and the church. In contrast to the colonial view, the ideology of the "modern" family implied a critique of everything beyond the front door.

What is striking as one looks at the writings of the 19th-century "experts"—the physicians, clergymen, phrenologists, and "scribbling ladies"—is how little their essential message differs from that of the sociologists, psychiatrists, pediatricians, and women's magazine writers of the 20th century, particularly since World War II.

Instead of men's and women's spheres, of course, sociologists speak of "instrumental" and "expressive" roles. The notion of the family as a retreat from the harsh realities of the outside world crops up as "functional differentiation." And, like the 19th-century utopians who believed society could be regenerated through the perfection of family life, 20th-century social scientists have looked at the failed family as the source of most American social problems.

None of these who promoted the sentimental model of the family—neither the popular writers nor the academics—considered the paradox of perfectionism: the ironic possibility that it would lead to trouble. Yet it has. The image of the perfect, happy family makes ordinary families seem like failures. Small problems loom as big problems if the "normal" family is thought to be one where there are no real problems at all.

One sees this phenomenon at work on the generation of Americans born and reared during the late 19th century, the first generation reared on the mother's milk of sentimental imagery. Between 1900 and 1920, the U.S. divorce rate doubled, from four to eight divorces annually per 1,000 married couples. The jump—comparable to the 100 percent increase in the divorce rate between 1960 and 1980—is not attributable to changes in divorce laws, which were not greatly liberalized. Rather, it would appear that, as historian Thomas O'Neill believes, Americans were simply more willing to dissolve marriages that did not conform to their idea of domestic bliss—and perhaps try again.

A "FUN" MORALITY

If anything, family standards became even more demanding as the 20th century progressed. The new fields of psychology and sociology opened up whole new definitions of familial perfection. "Feelings"—fun, love, warmth, good orgasm—acquired heightened popular significance as the invisible glue of successful families.

Psychologist Martha Wolfenstein, in an analysis of several decades of government-sponsored infant care manuals, has documented the emergence of a "fun morality." In former days, being a good parent meant carrying out certain tasks with punctilio; if your child was clean and reasonably obedient, you had no cause to probe his psyche. Now, we are told, parents must commune with their own feelings and those of their children—an edict which has seeped into the ethos of education as well. The distinction is rather like that between religions of deed and religions of faith. It is one thing to make your child brush his teeth; it is quite another to transform the whole process into a joyous "learning experience."

The task of 20th-century parents has been further complicated by the advice offered them. The experts disagree with each other and often contradict themselves. The kindly Dr. Benjamin Spock, for example, is full of contradictions. In a detailed analysis of *Baby and Child Care*, historian Michael Zuckerman observes that Spock tells mothers to relax ("trust yourself") yet warns them that they have an "ominous power" to destroy their children's innocence and make them discontented "for years" or even "forever."

As we enter the 1980s, both family images and family realities are in a state of transition. After a century and a half, the web of attitudes and nostrums comprising the "sentimental model" is beginning to unravel. Since the mid-1960s, there has been a youth rebellion of sorts, a new "sexual revolution," a revival of feminism, and the emergence of the two-worker family. The huge postwar Baby-Boom generation is pairing off, accounting in part for the upsurge in the divorce rate (half of all divorces occur within seven years of a first marriage). Media images of the family have become more "realistic," reflecting new patterns of family life that are emerging (and old patterns that are re-emerging).

Among social scientists, "realism" is becoming something of an ideal in itself. For some of them, realism translates as pluralism: All forms of the family, by virtue of the fact that they happen to exist, are equally acceptable—from communes and cohabitation to one-parent households, homosexual marriages, and, come to think of it, the nuclear family. What was once labeled "deviant" is now merely "variant." In some college texts, "the family" has been replaced by "family systems." Yet, this new approach does not seem to have squelched perfectionist standards. Indeed, a palpable strain of perfectionism runs through the pop literature on "alternative" family lifestyles.

For the majority of scholars, realism means a more down-to-earth view of the American household. Rather than seeing the family as a haven of peace and tranquility, they have begun to recognize that even "normal" families are less than ideal, that intimate relations of any sort inevitably involve antagonism as well as love. Conflict and change are inherent in social life. If the family is now in a state of flux, such is the nature of resilient institutions; if it is beset by problems, so is life. The family will survive.

CHAPTER 7

Equality in North American Marriages

Leo Zakuta

ABSTRACT: Just as our society has changed (such as the growth of democratic ideology, cities, industry, and mobility), so have our expectations of relationships between husbands and wives. More equality is now expected, leading to more intense emotional relationships. Although romance or feelings of affection is one possible outcome, the association of husbands and wives on a more equal basis can also intensify clashes, antagonisms, and even hatred. The changed expectations attached to today's marriages (greater equality accompanied by emotional closeness) have several outcomes: Among them is an increased difficulty in meeting what spouses expect of one another, coinciding with less "breathing room" (or escape) from one another. Our higher divorce rate is not a sign that marriage means less to people today, but that it means something different—that its expectations of emotional involvement are higher than ever.

During the past several generations there have been important changes in North American family relationships. While this essay emphasizes the husband-wife relation, its main perspectives also apply to the relations between parents and children. . . .

My central point is that certain changes in the behavior of family members toward each other stem from alterations in their mutual sentiments—or feelings toward one another; these feelings, in turn, are closely linked to shifts in their standards and forms of family organization. For the sake of economy, these standards and forms will be taken as given, as will be the general conditions out of which they arise: namely, the growth of democratic ideology, cities, and industry; the mobility and mixture of people; and the development of an essentially new society. . . .

IDEOLOGICAL CHANGES AND ROMANTIC MARRIAGE

I have been trying in vain to recall from whom I first heard the suggestion that our fiction—popular as well as "serious"—provides an intriguing symptom of how significantly the married relation has changed in our society. The argument, which is perhaps familiar, goes as follows: In the past, love stories were ordinarily about courtship, and they usually concluded with marriage. The emotional relations of the married were of much less consuming interest, presumably on the assumption that they contained little of comparable fascination. In contrast, today's fiction, drama, and movies frequently center on the emotional relation between husband and wife; typically, they are already married when the story begins. The inference obviously is that those intense feelings which we think of as romance now occur much more often within marriage than they once did. If this inference is valid, why does contemporary marriage produce feelings of romantic involvement or such distress at their departure that the couple may dissolve or seriously consider dissolving their marriage? To pursue this question one must find the structural and ideological conditions which seem most closely associated with romance in general first, then those with its growing importance in contemporary marriage.

In general, romance seems to occur where the partners feel that they choose each other freely rather than where others, usually the parents, do the choosing. (Whether the choice is really "free" is not only beyond proof but, from the perspective of the social scientists, as totally irrelevant as whether man's will is really "free." It is the actor's sense or feeling of being free to choose that matters, just as a man's view of whether another's will is free or not governs his feelings and behavior toward him.) . . .

[H]ow does the sense of free choice affect romance in marriage? Many obvious circumstances make divorce or separation seem much more feasible to a contemporary couple than to their grandparents and thus give them a greater feeling of choice than was once the case. The argument, however, that ideological and structural changes are responsible for the development of, or concern about, romance in marriage must rest on some distinctive grounds. These are more easily seen if we compare those two familiar models—the "patriarchal" and "contemporary" family types.

Three structural changes from the first type to the second seem to be closely linked to the growing importance of romantic feelings within marriage. They are, in ascending order of importance: the family's smaller size, the greater mobility of the family, and the equality of the married couple. . .

The family's contraction results from fewer children and fewer relatives in the household. As a result, the child may become more deeply involved with the fewer remaining adults so that in his subsequent marriage he seeks the intensity of emotional involvement which he has already experienced. Framed in this way—the more adults in the family, the greater the dispersal of emotional involvement—this argument does not seem very convincing. The reduction in family size may not be important in itself. But it has been accompanied by another, though somewhat unrelated, change, which has made it important—the growing equality between parents and children which tends to intensify their mutual involvement by lowering the barriers that authority usually creates. Once the generations can become closer, numbers become important because the typical family contains fewer adults to serve as the focus for the children's involvement.

The family's greater mobility also tends to intensify the mutual involvement of its members by throwing them together more than would a more stable existence. If the unit which moves is usually the nuclear family, then it cuts itself off from its closest relatives as well as from its whole network of friends and acquaintances. Weakened ties with outsiders increase the members' mutual dependence and reduce their avenues of escape from one another. Although many families may not move, the growth of so many large organizations, including government, with their numerous branches probably means that increasing numbers regard relocation as a distinct possibility. If so, it need not be actually moving, but merely the prospect that heightens the married couple's feeling of how much their happiness hinges on the "success" of this one tie which not only endures when all others are severed but which, by the very breaking of other ties, becomes all the more important. Under these circumstances, would they not count somewhat more heavily on the congeniality of this relation?

It is the third condition of equality that merits the most serious consideration. Its general effect is similar to that of the other two—it brings people together more often and more intimately. Status differences everywhere seem to inhibit free and easy association, and the more pronounced they are, the more separate are the parties, except where their association is formally specified. This principle is built into the official military structure in the form of separate messes that limit extracurricular association and therefore presumably personal involvement across hierarchical levels. We see it arise somewhat more spontaneously in the cafeterias of work organizations and in relations between racial and ethnic groups—in the latter cases, it is called segregation.

Consequences of Inequality

In an apparent paradox, the barriers to ease and intimacy are often less where the status differences are very great, so that a man may have a much freer and easier relation with his slave or servant than he does with his employee or even with his children, or, in some family systems, with his mistress than with his wife. . . .

What permits ease and intimacy in these various instances is, of course, that status differences are so large and clear that a more relaxed relation brings no suggestion of fundamental equality between the parties. Furthermore, the relaxation of formalities in relations of this type is ostensibly subject to the pleasure of the superior, and the parties do not associate as equals in any of the situations in which friends ordinarily meet. These considerations indicate that the links between friendship, sociability, and equality deserve a comprehensive examination.

The main point, however, is that if separate activities and restrained relations arise out of status differences, then separation and restraint should be much more prominent in the "patriarchal" than in the "contemporary" family. A casual glance at Toronto's large, post-war, Italian immigrant district shows how obviously they are more prominent. True to the traditions of their Italian patriarchal rural society, males congregate sociably in exclusively masculine groups in the streets and restaurants and the women presumably stay home. If the customers in the restaurants are couples, it is fairly certain that they are not first generation Italians. That the present Toronto pattern is not unusual is clear from William F. Whyte's portrait of comparable Italian groups in Boston in the 1930s.[1]

If status differences lead to segregation because people usually seek the companionship of their "equals," then the marital relation in the patriarchal family should display the same kind of separation in matters of sex and companionship as it does in most other activities. And, by all accounts, it does. Allowing for whatever exaggeration is introduced to achieve humor or drama, the stories, movies, and literature of continental Europe in the Victorian age or of contemporary rural society in France, Italy, and elsewhere indicate both the prevalence and the rela-

[1]*Street Corner Society* (Chicago: University of Chicago, 1943).

tive openness—the two are obviously interdependent—of extra-marital affairs for men. The relatively open acceptance of prostitution and of having a mistress on the grounds that "boys will be boys" or, less indulgently perhaps, "men are like that," coupled with the clear understanding that girls should be "lady-like," suggests once more the link with status differences. Again, it is the higher status category that is permitted freedom; who can roam, perhaps symbolically; and who at least feel that they have a choice that is less readily available to the lower status group.

One test of this general argument would involve looking at family systems with varying degrees of status difference between the spouses in order to examine the accompanying patterns of sexual fidelity. Thus, in the traditional Chinese family, in which the husband's standing was especially lofty, concubinage was apparently much more acceptable than was its counterpart in Europe, and the concubine's position was correspondingly higher. In the Chinese family, though below the level of a wife, the concubine was often brought into the household and, significantly, her children were considered legitimate. Wifely infidelity, as one would expect, was regarded as more outrageous and disastrous than it was in the European family. The elevated status of the Japanese *geisha* is another case in point. (It would be interesting to know how the occupation of the *geisha* has been affected by the reported rapid "Westernization" of the Japanese family.) Whether polygyny is a further point along this same continuum should be relatively easy to determine by determining whether it is always associated with even greater male dominance.

The contemporary "American" pattern, in which husband and wife are much closer in standing, fits neatly into this scheme on the other side of this argument. Whether extra-marital affairs are less frequent in this system is impossible to say because of their more clandestine nature, but the secrecy itself is the best evidence of its greater unacceptability to all concerned. Were it possible to know, one would expect that infidelity is also more evenly distributed between the sexes in this system than in the patriarchal.

I have pursued this theme in order to show both the extent of separation between wives and husbands in the patriarchal system as well as the link between separateness and relative rank. Relations between the sexes, married or unmarried, between the old and young, and between countless other groups all display essentially the same pattern. Our assumptions about what it is natural for people to do together obviously involve assumptions about their relative status. In most parts of the world, as introductory sociology students soon learn, men and women do not ordinarily dance, walk, or spend their leisure time together. Frequently, they do not even eat together—that seemingly universal expression of equality—and, in the more patriarchal homes in the North American society, parents and children eat separately much more regularly. Finally, our conventional assumption that sex relations, at least in marriage, are highly personal hardly corresponds to that of many males in the more patriarchal societies who make the distinction between duty and pleasure or between work and play that so often differentiates the formal from the informal.

Consequences of Equality

The extended remarks about the consequences of inequality are a background against which we can see more clearly the consequences, in sentiment and behavior, of greater equality. For various reasons, the status of women and wives in Western and Westernized societies has increased considerably while that of men and husbands has dropped somewhat so that a woman's relationship to them in marriage has become much closer to equal. By reducing the distance which inequality imposes, both the range of association and of reciprocal emotional involvement increase. By emotional involvement, I refer not only to feelings of affection but also to their opposite. Both are likely to grow within the same relation. The central argument is that since mutual involvement increases and becomes more complex, feelings of antagonism and hatred are also likely to become intensified. . . .

As their positions become more equal, the prospect of informal or sociable association seems more natural and appealing to husbands and wives. In effect, they now view their prospective relation in terms of something like friendship, the main requisite of which is, of course, status equality. As a result, wives and husbands tend to leave their sexually compartmentalized worlds and to do many things together which their grandparents did not. Ideologically, this change is expressed in such phrases as "partnership, companionship," and even "togetherness." Their companionship, we have seen, is fostered not only by their greater equality but also by being more cut off from relatives and friends, including the adult kin who have disappeared from the household. The possibilities of friendship—perhaps it had better be called companionship—are further augmented by some blurring of their former distinctive roles and activities. Not only is the wife freer to venture from the home to work for pay, or on behalf of "worthy causes," or simply to play—all, incidentally, formerly reserved for higher status groups, either men or women of the wealthy leisure class—but her husband is also more likely to participate in the formerly exclusively wifely tasks—in the kitchen, nursery, or even in public by sharing the shopping. Thus, like friends and equals, they do numerous similar things, many of them together.

The combination of these conditions—a smaller, more mobile, and more equalitarian family—leads not only to a more informal, intimate, and complex marital relation; it also leads to a new conception of what that relation ought to be, that is, to new standards of what constitutes a successful marriage. Both partners are likely to expect and to want the more intense mutual involvement that the altered structure of the marriage relation facilitates and to judge the success of their marriage in terms of the extent and the character of that involvement. Under these circumstances, the sense of personal congeniality or, in the more usual phrase, "compatibility," becomes a, or perhaps the, central criterion on which the partners assess the success of their marriage and decide on its future.

Those who regard these developments with dismay or distaste usually conclude that marriage has come to mean less to the contemporary couple since so many do decide to terminate it. The advocates of the new often argue, on the other hand, that these decisions indicate the very opposite; namely, that people now expect more from their marriage and are unwilling to settle for the unhappy relations that previous generations endured. But this argument, like any evaluative one, is insoluble and beside the point. It is not a matter of greater or lesser expectations but of different ones. And the heavy emphasis placed on personal congeniality means that many of the relations that do not measure up to the expectations of at least one of the partners will be terminated.

Furthermore, the new marital structure and expectations create additional hazards to the permanence of the relation. By facilitating very strong involvement, they are likely to lead, at least on occasion, to more intense antagonism and bitter clashes. Feelings of equality contribute to this possibility by removing or threatening to remove ultimate authority from the husband and thereby open the way to struggle for power, since the right to decide is no longer vested in a position but in each individual's conviction of what should be done. Finally, if their relation "goes sour" chronically, both partners are likely to feel the consequences as more devastating than did their grandparents. Unlike the latter, they have fewer avenues of escape from each other, they face the agonies of decision about the formal status of their marriage, and their deeper mutual involvement tends to produce stronger friction and animosity. It is therefore hardly surprising that, under these conditions, so many contemporary couples find their marriages too intolerable to endure. (In addition, if equality tends to reduce or conceal the incidence of husbands' infidelity, it simultaneously increases its seriousness as an offence and thus its threat to the continuation of the marriage.)

Thus instead of regarding a "high" rate of divorce and separation as a somewhat alien virus which has managed to infect the North American marriage system, we may, perhaps more profitably, view it as an inevitable outcome of the distinctive ideology, structure, and sentiments of that system.

I have suggested previously that the sense of free choice seems a necessary condition for romance—whether before or within marriage. Several obvious conditions provide this sense to the contemporary married couple. Among them are, of course, the greater prevalence and acceptability of divorce, one further instance of how an effect is also a cause, as well as the greater earning power of women, that facilitates the step for both partners. If I seem to have underemphasized this last condition, it was mainly out of reluctance to overempahsize it. While it seems extremely important, its exact significance is very difficult to determine since divorce and women's earning power have both risen considerably over the long run. Unless one can somehow separate these variables, precise statements about their relation seem impossible. These considerations naturally lead to speculation about Hollywood, where both divorce and the earning power of women seem to have reached unprecedented heights. Here is the community in which the status and income of women is least dependent on their husbands and where equality between the married partners and the sense of free choice about continuing the marriage are at a peak. It is under these circumstances, I would guess, that the concern about romance in marriage is most intense since the feeling of great freedom makes the continuity of the marriage contingent on little else. And despite all of the tongue-clucking about Hollywood, it seems clear that marriage still rates very highly there. How else can we account for Hollywood's apparently endless optimism about marriage in the face of such seemingly overwhelming odds?

The shifts in the standards and structure within the family, and more generally between the sexes, and between adults and children have several other effects on sentiments and behavior that seem worthy of note. As a result of the diminishing status distance between the sexes, in general, and between the various age levels, males and females seem increasingly at ease with each other and so do the young with their elders, though the reverse is not necessarily as true.

More specifically, greater equality seems to reduce the fear, deference, and perhaps even awe that children once had toward their parents and possibly wives toward their husbands. The contemporary father who lectures his son, "I would never have dared speak to *my* father as you do to me," may be doing something more than repeating a universal and timeless lament of fathers; he may, for a change in this endless litany, be uttering a simple truth. Correspondingly, husbands are more likely to be attentive and sensitive to the wishes, tastes, and viewpoints of their wives and children than they have been in the past, one example of which is the new ideology of sex relations in the twentieth century.[2] Status equality seems to be the central condition for reciprocal sensitivity to the wishes and feelings of others. And this is a point that warrants fuller examination than is possible in this short essay. . . .

In the older family type, cohesion or integration depended more heavily on specialized and physically interdependent roles with a fairly clear, if elaborate, chain of command, as well as, of course, considerable emotional involvement and interdependence. In the contemporary family, specialized roles, physical interdependence, and authority are all still of central importance, but the balance has been shifting away from these aspects toward the emotional involvement on which the cohesion of more informal groups depends. In brief, the family has been moving away from the elaborate, formal, and involuntary structure characteristic of large and stable organizations toward the smaller, more intense, and more volatile association composed of freely consenting equals which is characteristic of more informal groups.

CONCLUSION

I will conclude with a venture into the more fanciful, where the sociologist can treat more easily then he can test. If changes in the relations between the sexes can affect their conscious sentiments toward each other, then why can they not similarly affect those feelings that are more buried and which are manifested only indirectly in overt behavior? If males have experienced a loss of status relative to females, then one should expect that at least some—like any group which has suffered a loss of status—would exhibit various forms of compensation for the loss and resentment toward the usurpers, and that these forms would be perhaps partly in the realm of fantasy.

Possibly the popularity of magazines of the *Playboy* type represents such a reaction. After all, the central themes of these magazines can be interpreted easily enough in terms of both compensation and resentment. There is self-enhancement through the vicarious association with the habits and objects of the rich and lofty. But the outstanding "plaything" of the "playboy" is women. His sure and easy "way with women" is perhaps his chief qualification for solid standing as a "play-

[2]Significantly, that ideology emphasizes "sensitivity" for the male, "freedom" for the woman, and reduction of the traditional or stereotyped differences in their sexual roles and responses. And, as might be expected, the evidence of Alfred Kinsey and his associates strongly suggests that these modes of behavior are much more prevalent in the middle class, especially among the more highly educated.

boy." The growing discrepancy between the fantasy—the smooth, self-assured, sophisticated, and uninvolved male mastery of uniformly devoted and eager women—and the increasingly free and equal relations between the sexes may be the source of the apparent popularity of these periodicals. Another branch of this type of periodical—a "lower" one by popular repute—expresses the male's resentment much more directly, sexual "sadism" permitting him to participate vicariously in a more vigorous revenge on those who have robbed him of his glorious patrimony.

CHAPTER 8

Trends in Fertility

Sar A. Levitan / Richard S. Belous

ABSTRACT: Shifts and uneven swings in the U.S. birthrate are part of our history: We have had baby "booms" and "busts" before. Contributing to the lowered birthrate we are now experiencing are: a rising age at first marriage, an increased interval between marriage and first birth, and an expectation of fewer children. Our lowered birthrate is creating a fundamental change in America's age distribution (population pyramid). This has far-reaching ramifications for our lives because it creates various strains and imbalances in American society.

As more women receive longer education and enter the labor force, motherhood increasingly must vie with their other options or aspirations. Following the post–World War II baby boom, fertility rates have plummeted to historic lows. Many Western countries already have zero population growth, and they are starting to record fertility rates that portend significant population declines. . . .

Beyond decisions on whether to bring children into this world, there remains the problem of who will provide for, and socialize, them once they are born. Under traditional social mores and legal sanctions, the answer to these questions was the family. However, as the number of separations, divorces, and out-of-wedlock births has increased, the answers have been changing. These changes have had a dramatic impact not only on the structure of the family, but also on the role of the state in modern society. The ways in which American society and families cope with these changes could well determine the future viability of the family and the direction of the modern welfare state.

FERTILITY PATTERNS

Demographers have developed several different ways to measure annual fertility rates. The *crude birth rate* records the number of births per 1,000 population, while the *general fertility rate* considers only the childbearing portion of the population by counting the number of births per 1,000 women between 15 and 44 years old. Finally, the *total fertility rate* measures the annual fertility of 1,000 women over the course of their reproductive lives based on the rates characteristic of various age groups, In order to maintain zero population growth, females must sustain a total fertility rate of 2.1—rather than 2—because not all of them survive to the reproduction ages or are fertile.

In its early years, the United States had a higher total fertility rate than many European nations.[1] While early data are fragmentary, the crude birth rate in the United States appears to have been about 50 per 1,000 population in 1800.[2] Thereafter, the American birthrate declined fairly steadily until World War II. The postwar "baby boom" lasted until the early 1960s, when the birth rate resumed its secular decline, plummeting to 15 per 1,000 by the close of the 1970s.

Not only have women tended to postpone marriage, reducing the number of years available for legitimate births—which is still the prevailing, if old-fashioned, standard—but they also have deferred becoming mothers after they do marry. The median interval between a first marriage and the birth of the first child rose from about 15 months in the early 1960s to over 2 years during the late 1970s. By the third year of marriage only about one of five women in their first marriage was still childless during the early 1960s, compared with roughly three of seven by the end of the succeeding decade. The number of births expected or desired by women also fell sharply, from 3.1 in 1965 to 2.3 in 1978 among wives 18 to 34 years old, and by the latter year the average for wives 18 to 24 years of age was only 2.1, or roughly the zero population growth level.[3]

As analysts tend to base their predictions of fertility rates on historic trends, it is important to consider both the long-run and short-term fluctuations of these statistics [Figure 8.1]. Current fertility rates take on more meaning when they are placed in historical perspective.

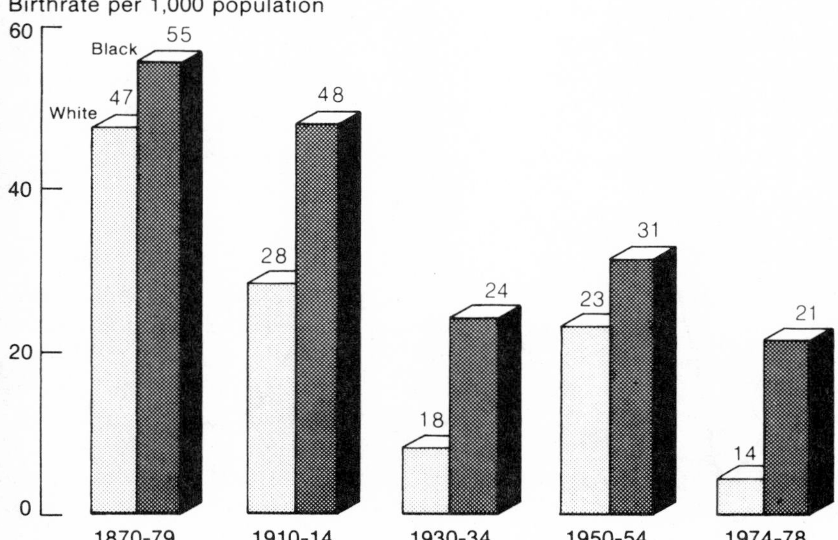

Figure 8.1 Following the post–World War II baby boom, the American birthrate for both whites and blacks has resumed its historic decline.

Source: U.S. Department of Commerce, Bureau of the Census.

BABY BOOMS AND BUSTS

The Great Depression of the 1930s brought a major reduction in American fertility levels. With the nation in dire economic circumstances, many adults put off marriage, and many of those who did marry decided that they could not afford as many extra mouths to feed as in the past. Given these conditions, the birth rate plummeted to about 18 per 1,000 by 1933, and it remained under 23 per 1,000 during World War II.

At the end of the war, many American adults decided to make up for lost time, and a new baby boom was on at full speed. From a low of 2.4 million births in the depth of the depression and 2.9 million in the final year of World War II, births in the United States rose to a peak of 4.3 million in 1957. Since then, the annual number of births has declined almost continuously, reaching a low of 3.1 million in 1975, but then rising slowly to 3.3 million three years later. . . .

Women of all ages have shown a marked decline in fertility since the baby boom [Figure 8.2]. Women in the older childbearing years have recently shown a slight increase in their fertility rate, indicating that many females who postponed motherhood are deciding that it is either now or never.

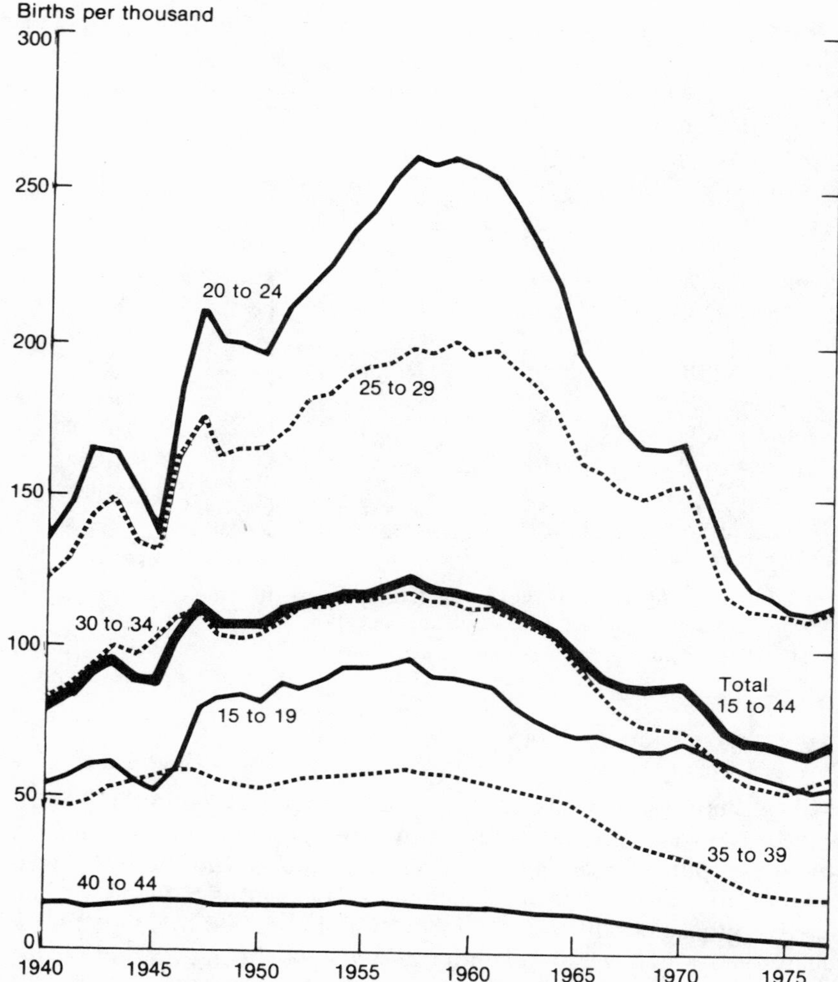

Figure 8.2 Women of all ages have shown a marked decline in fertility since the baby boom.

Source: National Center for Health Statistics.

While the U.S. total fertility rate closed the 1970s at about 1.8 and was well under the 2.1 zero population growth level, the size of the total American population will not decline in the twentieth century. Despite birth rate declines, births still out numbered deaths by 1.5 million during 1979. Also, the United States continued to serve as a haven for immigrants fleeing either persecution or poverty in their native countries. Most of these immigrants have been young adults. Population bulges, like the post–World War II baby boom, are like a boa constrictor digesting its prey. The age-cohort bulges can be tracked as their ramifications are evolving. The postwar baby boom resulted in a surfeit of women whose childbearing years span the period from about 1960 to about 2000—long enough to sustain a growth in the native American population for several decades. It will take about 65 years for the American population to stabilize at zero population growth even if current rates hold firm.[4] If one assumes that the total fertility rate will nudge down to 1.7, the American population would not stop growing until about the year 2015, when it would reach approximately 250 million people—an 11 percent growth in 35 years. If the total fertility rate would jump back to 2.1, the American population would be about 260 million in the year 2000 and 283 million in 2015. Both levels are considerably lower than the 300 million population prediction for the year 2000, which until quite recently was the ballpark estimate given by many reputable demographers.[5]

The United States is far from unique in these fertility rate trends, and a reduced birth rate seems to be shared by most industrialized nations regardless of whether their economic and social structure is a capitalistic welfare state or a communist regime. While international comparisons can be misleading, it appears that in the 1970s the United

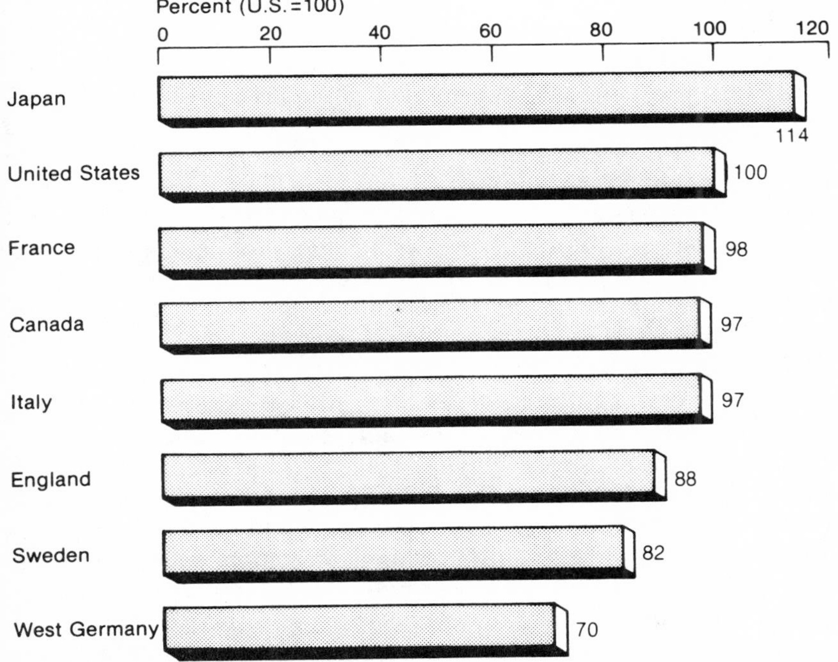

Figure 8.3 U.S. fertility has exceeded that of most other major industrial countries.
Source: U.S. Department of Commerce, Bureau of the Census.

States continued to experience a higher birth rate than many other industrialized countries [Figure 8.3].

Lower birth rates seem to have caused far more public concern in European countries than in the United States.[6] For example, West Germany's native population has been falling steadily since 1972, with annual deaths exceeding births. Given the present course, the German native population will fall to 52 million by the year 2000, a 9 percent decline in less than one generation. In several Eastern European nations, abortion laws have been made stricter.

The uneven swings in the U.S. birth rate since the 1930s have already affected the age distribution of the American population [Figure 8.4]. In 1920 the age configuration of the population looked very much like a pyramid. The largest group of the population was children under 10 years of age, who formed the base of the population pyramid. At that time, each successive age group was smaller than the one preceding it.

However, with steep fertility declines during the 1930s—followed by continued low birth rates during World War II—the percentage of children under age 10 declined. Then came the baby boom, which was succeeded by the renewed birth rate declines. By the end of the 1970s, the profile was far from the simple triangular shape depicted half a century earlier. Several relatively small birth cohorts are now sandwiched in between far larger groups, so the profile resembles a tiered cake put together by an amateur. If current fertility trends continue—coupled with a longer life expectancy—the American population profile could look more like an inverted pyramid. Smaller and younger birth cohorts would be supporting a far larger and topheavy structure represented by an increasing number of older Americans. The changing relative composition of the age cohorts has created wide variations and imbalances between the demands of successive birth cohorts for educational facilities, health care, and provisions for the aged. It also has placed uneven strains on American labor markets as birth cohorts reach successive stages in their work lives. . . .

A declining population growth rate requires diverse social and economic adjustments. Shifting American fertility rates have altered the age profile of the nation's population, and, combined with changes in mortality rates, the average family life cycle now shows a different pattern from the past. The size of the U.S. population is going to grow, albeit at a slower rate, for many years before the annual number of deaths exceeds the yearly number of births and net migration gains. Moreover, fertility patterns do not appear to be immune from active governmental human resource policies, and there appears to be sufficient lead time to adjust and formulate "pronatalist" programs if the need arises and if public policy deems it wise. However, given the current state of the art and social scientists' knowledge about fertility decisions, policymakers

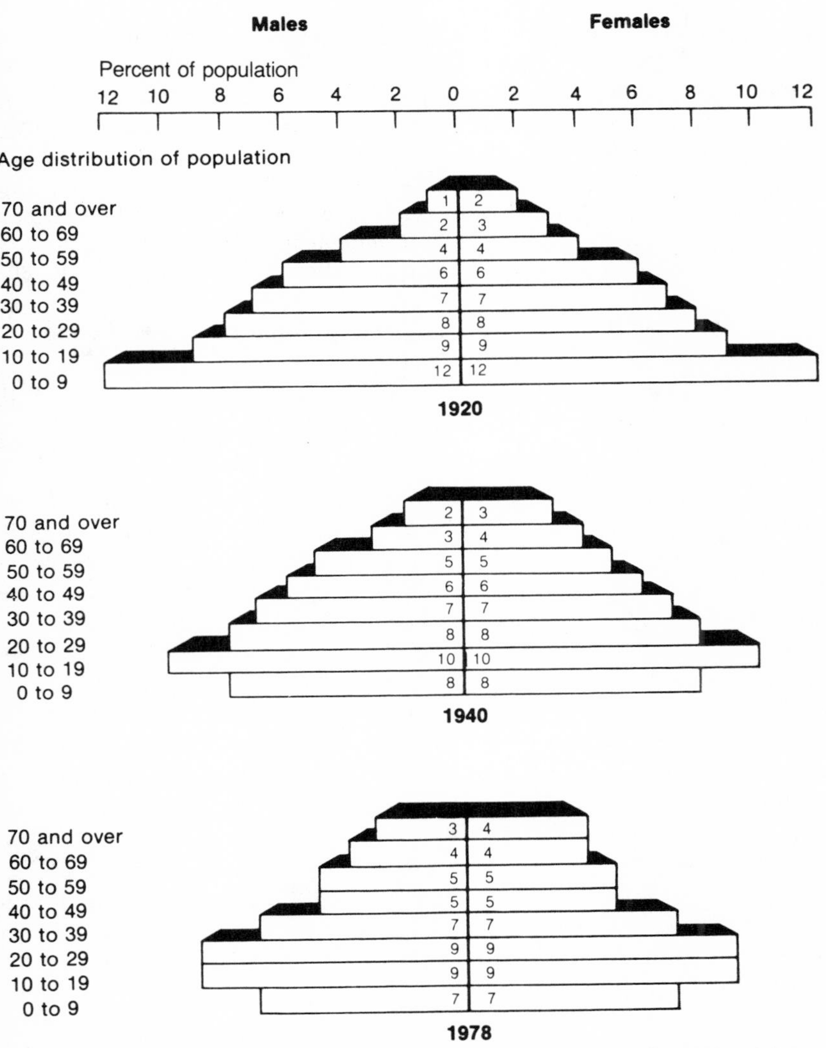

Figure 8.4 Wide variations in the birthrate have changed the age profile of the American population.
Source: U.S. Department of Commerce, Bureau of the Census.

are a long way from being able to "fine tune" the birth rate, and it is to be hoped that they will not attempt to achieve such a questionable goal.

REFERENCES

1. Ansley Coale and Melvin Zelnick, *New Estimates of Fertility and Population in the United States* (Princeton, N.J.: Princeton University Press, 1963), p. 36.

2. Richard A. Easterlin, "The American Population," in *American Economic Growth: An Economist's History of the United States,* ed. Lance E. Davis et al. (New York: Harper & Row, 1972), pp. 123–27.
3. U.S. Department of Commerce, Bureau of the Census, *Fertility of American Women: June 1978* (Washington, D.C.: Government Printing Office, 1979), Current Population Reports, series P-20, no. 341, pp. 5, 66.
4. U.S. Department of Commerce, Bureau of the Census, *Estimates of the Population of the United States and the Components of Change: 1940 to 1978* (Washington, D.C.: Government Printing Office, 1979), series P-25, no. 802, pp. 2, 8.
5. Charles F. Westoff, "Marriage and Fertility in the Developed Countries," *Scientific American* (December 1978), p. 51.
6. Maurice J. Moore and Martin O'Connell, *Perspectives on American Fertility* (Washington, D.C.: Government Printing Office, 1978), series P-23, no. 70, p. 9.

CHAPTER 9

High-Tech Breeding

Paul Bagne

ABSTRACT: Artificial insemination, now a highly developed technology, is becoming increasingly significant for our lives. With long-term preservation of sperm, coupled with a capitalist market, specialized sperm banks have come into existence. Competitive clinics, some specializing in sperm from specific types of donors, make it possible for a customer to specify what she wants in a donor—and to then make the purchase. The current situation raises serious questions concerning the role of science in social biogenics: We could create a population along predetermined, select biological lines.

Sensing she had ovulated, Afton Blake reached for the phone and called Paul Smith. He agreed to meet her that evening after work.

As he left his office, Smith took with him a tiny vial, which he carefully placed in an insulated tank stowed in the back seat of his Volkswagen Rabbit. The vial contained the frozen sperm of an anonymous Nobel laureate who Afton Blake hoped would become the father of her first child.

When Smith arrived, he thawed the semen and placed a small sample under a microscope. Most of the spermatozoa he saw were dead. A few pathetically wagged their tails but were clearly going nowhere. Blake was deeply disappointed. She had seen a photo of the donor when he was young, and "he seemed to have such character."

Smith stayed late into the night. Together he and Blake pored over a catalog from the Repository for Germinal Choice, where Smith works. After studying traits, values and characteristics of these anonymous men, Blake selected a new donor, not a Nobel Prize winner. She conceived but miscarried. Several more months of insemination followed before she conceived again. A year ago Afton Blake gave birth to a healthy boy she named Doron.

Doron Blake's father is a computer scientist and an accomplished classical musician—the kind of man Afton says she "might have married." She calls him "28." Doron is the second of five children produced by the Repository for Germinal Choice, in Escondido, California, a relatively small, specialty sperm bank dedicated to the improvement of the human species. Its founder, retired lensmaker and millionaire Robert Graham, told *Mother Jones*, "We provide the finest germinal material we can get our hands on." Paul Smith is Graham's employee. He travels around the country by bus and plane to fetch the sperm of the six men Graham has decided are superior. He delivers specimens to women who hope that the seed of an accomplished man will help them give birth to a brilliant and talented child.

The five Germinal Choice offspring join 300,000 other children conceived in the United States since 1960 by artificial insemination. The number of such births is expected to rise dramatically in the coming years as more and more gynecologists begin to perform artificial insemination regularly: several sources estimate that 1.5 million more Americans will be created this way by the year 2000. As the practice grows more popular and the demand for sperm increases, sperm bankers are refining the methods of selecting, concentrating, freezing and even genetically altering the samples. Along the way, artificial insemination—with its accompanying technology—has come to mean different things to different people.

- To infertile couples it simply means babies.
- To single women it means children without having to find Mr. Right.
- To lesbians it means conception without being sexually intimate with men.
- To geneticists it means control of inherited disorders such as diabetes and cystic fibrosis.
- To clinical ecologists it provides an opportunity to preserve the sperm of young men who are likely to be exposed to chemical and radioactive mutagens in the environment and the workplace.
- To advocates of selective breeding, like Graham and Smith, insemination is the method that has been sought since it was first proposed to improve the human race by encouraging the fit to multiply.

- And to genetic engineers, who each day get closer to restructuring the DNA molecule, artificial insemination is just about the simplest of many procedures that will create people designed by science rather than nature.

SHOPPING FOR DADDY

Doron Blake lives in a quiet neighborhood in a house crammed with books and art. He is a robust and happy child. His mother, Afton, rushes through ideas with contagious energy. "It was time to have a child," she says. "I was secure emotionally and not in a steady relationship with a man." She thought first of asking a friend to coparent with her, but she feared that such a setup could turn into an awkward triangle. That left insemination.

Donor No. 28: Doron Blake's Father

Summary: Good intellectual and musical ability, charismatic personality and very good looks, with cataract risk.
Ancestry: Northwest European. Born: 1950s.
Eye color: Hazel. Skin color: Fair.
Hair: Blond (straight but thinning).
Height: 1.8 m. (6′0″).
Weight at 24: 77 kg. (170 lb).
General appearance: Normal with narrow face. Very handsome.
Personality: Good presence, very charismatic, friendly and highly creative. Interests include swimming, bicycle riding and hiking.
Achievements: He teaches a hard science at a major university. He has won many prizes and fellowships.
I.Q.: Not known; scored 800 in Math on SAT.
Music: He has won prizes performing classical music.
Athletics: No achievement, but two first-degree relatives were track champions.
Manual dexterity: Excellent.
General health: Excellent.
Defects: Impacted wisdom teeth. Slight hemorrhoids. Two grandparents developed cataracts in their 60s.
Blood type: O+. Pressure: 122/80.
Comment: The estimated recurrence risk is 30 percent for hemorrhoids, 40 percent for impacted wisdom teeth and 22 percent for cataracts developing after age 60.

Each donor to the Repository for Germinal Choice is given a random number. Children must remember their father's number to keep from marrying their own siblings.

She went first to the Tyler Medical Clinic in nearby Westwood. "It was huge and commercial and took so much away from the wonders of conception," she says. "They were more interested in assuring me the donor was Caucasian than in telling me what kind of person he was." To Blake, who had once considered having an interracial child, the Tyler pitch was repulsive. She then contacted Southern California Cryobank, a firm she found much more appealing and personal, but she felt it offered too little information about its donors. She finally turned to the Repository for Germinal Choice. "From the first day they were just what I had hoped for. They were extremely involved and obviously dedicated to helping in every way."

Blake, a psychologist interested in child development, believes that intelligence is both acquired and inherited. She chose a donor described as "brilliant." But it was not only intellect she sought. "It's something beyond that," she says. "More like soul. And I think genes play a part in this too." In the catalog, she found the kind of person she wanted to father her child: "someone who treasures the world and everything in it."

The psychologist who tested No. 28 as part of the repository screening process said the donor was creative in all directions, suggesting that in another age he might have been a painter or composer. Professionally, the man works in computers, but he has won acclaim as a pianist.

"Music is very important to me," Blake says. Just after bringing her infant home from the hospital, she placed him between the speakers of her stereo for a quick test of his musical aptitude. "I put Chopin on, and he started to go like this." She swayed and moved her hands in gentle circles, fingers open. "When I turned it off, his hands went down. Turn it on, he'd do this again. It never ceased to amaze me and everybody else."

The sperm bank that begat Doron the musician was inspired by the late American geneticist Hermann Muller, who suspected that traits like brotherliness, loving kindness and humility were linked to genes. He proposed gathering and freezing "copious reserves of the most precious of all treasures: the germinal material that has formed the biological basis of those human values that we hold in highest regard." Donors would be outstanding men with such values: they would be healthy, vigorous and bright. Couples would have a choice of "material [sperm] likely to embody" the traits they personally admired, such as "infectious sociability," "physical agility" or "the gift of song."

Muller won a Nobel Prize for research that proved that X-rays cause mutations. In 1961, he proposed that men likely to confront the unassessed hazards of modern life should store their semen in underground repositories. Future generations, he wrote, would regard our failure to take this precaution as gross negligence. He envisioned great banks of human semen containing "stocks [which] might become recognized as especially worthy." He predicted that widespread procreation by "conscious selection of germ cells" would begin after the sperm of superior men was available. He even dreamed of a democratic, eugenic republic, where all would be born genetically improved.

In 1964, Muller began recruiting some 40 colleagues and sympathizers to promote genetic improvement through sperm-banking. Respected biologists, physicians and psychologists were contacted, as were famed British biologist Julian Huxley and two self-described disciples of Muller: Robert Graham and Paul Smith, who later founded the Repository for Germinal Choice. The repository has "changed the face of sperm-banking forever," says Dr. Charles Sims, codirector of the Southern California Cryobank. Recipients are no longer satisfied with terse donor descriptions listing favorite sport, academic achievements and other interests. Women who used to go to sperm banks and say "I just want a baby" are now more likely to say "I want a baby and it had better be the best." . . .

Chemists made the long-term preservation of sperm possible in the early 1960s, when they turned to liquid gases. The temperatures of some liquid gases can be more than a hundred degrees colder than dry ice—solid carbon dioxide—which had been used in previous experiments in cryobiology, the study of how living matter responds to low temperatures. Liquid nitrogen, at −196°C, will vitrify sperm (hold it in a glasslike state:) biochemical reactions cease and molecules stop moving. "We are in the dark ages of cryobiology," said [Dr. Cappy] Rothman [a specialist in male fertility]. "It's a whole new science that we are just now getting familiar with."

One of the country's leading cryobiologists is Armand Karow, Ph.D., director of Xytex, a sperm bank in Augusta, Georgia. "Theoretically, when you lower sperm to this temperature, assuming the cell is not damaged, there is no reason it will not remain viable indefinitely," he says. Although with current techniques, many cells are killed in freezing, a recent study calculated that sperm, if properly frozen, could be thawed and used in 10,000 years—a figure Karow regards with skepticism. But as research progresses, he says, the recovery rate, now about 50 percent, will improve dramatically. Red blood cells can be frozen and thawed with a 95 percent recovery, Karow says. "There is no reason this cannot be done with sperm cells."

Some sperm banks, however, attempt to improve marginal semen samples by concentrating and freezing the best swimmers of several ejaculates. At Gametrics Ltd., a biotech research firm in Sausalito, California, Dr. Ronald Ericsson has developed ways to separate good sperm from bad. He can even separate X-chromosome sperm from Y, so that his clients can choose the sex of their baby. He has licensed this technique to physicians in the United States, Egypt, Italy, Taiwan, Singapore, Malaysia and Korea. The sex selection process is especially popular in Asia, Ericsson says, where boy babies are much preferred.

Medical science is also making rapid advances in understanding conception, says Cappy Rothman optimistically. "With better technology, we'll be able to use very few sperm and get conception," he says. "If you freeze two ejaculates—800 million sperm—that's all a man will need to store for the rest of his life." Other researchers may take the same technology and use it for more nefarious purposes, Rothman says, but "what we are doing in clinical medicine is simply helping people have babies."

THE DOCTOR AS DONOR

The sperm count of the average American male has dropped to what some believe is an all-time low. Men who have not contributed to this decline, some of whom can deliver an ejaculate twice as potent as others, are popular at sperm banks. One of them, No. 17, visits a doctor's office once or twice each week to impregnate women he will never meet. He arrives just before the patient, slips into a bathroom with a copy of *Penthouse* or *Playboy*, locks the door and exits a few minutes later with a small cup of semen. "If there is a way to help women have babies, I don't think they should be denied it," he told *Mother Jones* anonymously over the phone. "I saw the look on my wife's face after she had given birth. I know how much it meant to her." No. 17's wife approves of what he does, even though to keep his sperm count high they must abstain from sex for two days before he contributes.

For every five donors who apply to sperm banks, four are rejected after genetic screening and physical exams. Others are rejected because of poor semen quality or a bad attitude. "A donor must be able to drop a sample into a black box and never care what happens to it," says one physician. Of the sperm banks surveyed for this article, at only one, the Repository for Germinal Choice, can donors restrict the use of their semen in any way. Just as money bankers decide what will be done with your cash, so will sperm bankers decide what will be done with your seed.

One Saturday morning I visited an insemination clinic—part of a fertility study—at a medical school; two donors, who avoided making eye contact with me, waited at the door of a storage closet to do their duty for science (and a $50 fee). In a small lab near exam rooms down the hall, five little cups of semen sat in a row on a stainless steel table, awaiting the ovulating women who were scheduled to arrive, 15 minutes apart.

Despite advances in techniques of freezing sperm, most doctors still use the fresh stuff, and most of their donors are medical students or hospital residents. A 1979 study by University of Wisconsin researchers found that 62 percent of doctors used men training to be physicians as donors. That computes to some 186,000 pre-med tots born in the past two decades. "They are selecting what they consider superior genes and they have chosen to reproduce themselves," said George Annas, professor of health law at Boston University School of Medicine.

But the director of the medical school insemination clinic said that getting fresh semen to a woman at the right time would be an "impossible logistics problem" without students as donors.

They do it for convenience, I told Annas on the phone.

"Seems like it would be just as handy to use the janitor," he responded.

Do you think it's a plot to spread their genes? I asked.

"I don't think it's a conscious thing, but given the choice, doctors choose doctors. If law professors were doing it, they would pick attorneys. If the military were doing it, they'd pick their favorite generals."

THE CHASE MANHATTAN

"You need a Malaysian donor?" asks Joseph Feldschuh, director of Idant Fertility Laboratories in New York City. "We have several." Idant is the Chase Manhattan of American sperm banks.

Feldschuh is proud of the ethnic diversity of his bank, which has so far produced 11,000 babies. Idant sends catalogs and ships semen to physicians across the United States, as well as in South America, Canada and Europe. In Idant's tanks are 40,000 specimens. Some were stored by men who have since had vasectomies; others by cancer patients who were later made sterile by chemotherapy. Some are reserved by mothers who want another child by the same donor. About half are for sale.

Idant, a commercial venture, was set up in 1971 to store the ejaculates of men about to have vasectomies or undergo chemotherapy. By 1974, investors had put $1.2 million into its facilities, but only a small percentage of vasectomy patients were storing their sperm. Feldschuh, who by that time had begun working at Idant, arranged a merger with Daxor, a New York corporation that designs and sells electronic medical equipment. Feldschuh expanded the donor program with an eye on the growing market for artificial insemination—half of the estimated three million American couples who are trying and failing to conceive a child, each couple needing an average of half a dozen inseminations at $40 per specimen. Feldschuh predicts steady growth for Idant, particularly as the technology of freezing semen improves and as more and more doctors give up the notion that for specimens, fresh is best.

The Idant people say they go to great lengths to recruit donors of above-average intelligence. "Anybody who thinks intelligence is not partly inherited is just silly," says Feldschuh. They also offer donors with specific desired traits. Women are asked to list the characteristics they are seeking in descending order of importance. Ask for a medium-built Mediterranean type with math skills and a love of the outdoors, and chances are Idant will find one for you. Feldschuh is developing computer software to track the permutations. . . .

Scientist as Creator

Insemination by frozen sperm is the most primitive of the new reproductive technologies. Down the road are far more exotic practices: transplanting fresh and frozen embryos, bringing the human fetus to term in artificial wombs and redesigning the DNA of human cells.

"Mankind is on the verge of modifying life," says Dr. Richard Seed, a specialist in embryo transplants at Chicago's Reproduction and Fertility Clinic. "You'll be able to sit down and specify a DNA sequence associated with intelligence and put that in the embryo. We're talking about manipulation. We're talking about control."

When I spoke with Seed, he had just transplanted a fertilized embryo into a human uterus. He was waiting to see if it would take. The procedure would soon be routine, he said.

Will you have a few hundred embryos frozen in liquid nitrogen to sell someday? I asked.

"Maybe in five or ten years. Just as semen is for sale today."

Somewhere on this trek through the Brave New World of high-tech procreation, near this milepost of the frozen embryo, distinctions begin to blur between physician as healer and scientist as creator.

What happens when something goes wrong in the course of transplanting genes into an embryo?

"That's where we are, my friend," answered medical ethicist Paul Ramsey, professor of religion emeritus at Princeton University. "In a quiet moment you can get a scientist to admit they may have to practice infanticide. The child may be regarded as not human enough; just a mishap—something which falls below the standard for entering the world."

Gifts for the Führer

In December 1935, in Nazi Germany, S.S. Commander Heinrich Himmler launched a selective breeding program called Lebensborn. Pornographic films and military decrees encouraged elite German troops to impregnate carefully selected Aryan women both in Germany and in occupied countries. The women, once they had been certified as racially pure, were placed in special homes so that they could give birth under the most advantageous conditions. The Lebensborn children were to become the first-generation leaders of Hitler's Thousand-Year Reich. Before the end of World War II, the Lebensborn project created 12,000 blond, blue-eyed babies. Himmler called them "gifts to the Führer."

One architect of Nazi race policies, Dr. Hans Endres, predicted that one day the young German male would be the most desired in Europe. "He will make the women shiveringly submissive wherever he appears. Radiant, tall and vigorous, he will conquer and embrace them." Women, he said, would consider his sexual advances an honor—helping to "procreate men of his kind."

Lebensborn ("Well of Life") was only part of the Nazi program of eugenics (human improvement through genetic control). Cash grants and loans were awarded to acceptable couples who wanted children. Laws prohibited intercourse between Jews and Aryans. Anyone who was "hereditarily ailing" was sterilized. Later, certain undesirables were put to death and, finally, Jews were exterminated.

Before Lebensborn and the Holocaust, eugenic ideas had gained a large measure of acceptance here in the United States. By 1932, laws in 27 states permitted public health officials to sterilize institutionalized "defectives and subnormals," in some cases without consent. In 1935, Dr. Clarence Campbell, the only American speaker at the Berlin Population Congress, endorsed the concept of Nordic supremacy. In February 1937, Earnest Hooton, a Harvard University anthropologist, proposed that "morons, criminals and social ineffectuals" be purged through compulsory sterilization. And in December of that year, the National Education Association formally proposed "the improvement of the national stock" through government subsidies that would encourage the intellectually superior to procreate.

—P.B.

CHAPTER 10

The Family in an Aging Society

Matilda White Riley

ABSTRACT: For the first time in history most people live to be old. This changed historical condition is more than simply a new fact of life, for it has far-reaching effects on family relationships. These effects include: (1) family relationships are prolonged; (2) the stability and number of generations are increased; and (3) a shifting kinship network gives individuals more control over which relationships they wish to activate. It is too early to tell what effects the increasing number of fourth generations is going to have on people's lives and on society, but they are likely to be considerable.

I am going to talk about families and the revolution in longevity. This revolution has produced configurations in kinship structure and in the internal dynamics of family life at every age that have never existed before.

Over two-thirds of the total improvement in longevity from prehistoric times until the present has taken place in the brief period since 1900 (Preston, 1976). In the United States, life expectancy at birth has risen from less than 50 in 1900 to well over 70 today. Whereas at the start of the century most deaths occurred in infancy and young adult-

Master Lecture delivered at the annual meeting of the National Council on Family Relations, 14 October 1982, Washington, D.C. The following persons have been kind enough to read and comment on earlier versions of this manuscript: Kathleen Bond, Anne Foner, Marcia Ory, John W. Riley, Jr., and Joan Waring.

hood, today the vast majority of deaths are postponed to old age. . . . [F]ew die before the end of the full life span. For the first time in all history, we are living in a society in which people live to be old.

Though many facts of life extension are familiar, their meanings for the personal lives of family members are elusive. Just how is increasing longevity transforming the kinship structure? Most problematic of all, how is the impact of longevity affecting those sorely needed close relationships that provide emotional support and socialization for family members? To answer such questions, . . . we need a whole new way of looking at the family. . . .

Indeed, an exciting new family literature is beginning to map and interpret these unparalleled changes; it is beginning to probe beneath the surface for the subjective implications of the protracted and intricate interplay of family relationships. . . .

From this developing literature, [three] topics emerge as particularly thought-provoking: (1) the dramatic extension of the kinship structure; (2) the new opportunities this extension brings for close family relationships; . . . and (3) the still unknown family relationships of older people in the future. I shall touch briefly on each of these topics. . . . Perhaps they will aid our understanding of increasing longevity and the concomitant changes about us. . . .

THE CHANGING CONFIGURATIONS OF THE KINSHIP STRUCTURE

I shall begin with the kinship structure as influenced by longevity. The extent and configurations of this structure have been so altered that we must rethink our traditional view of kinship. As four (even five) generations of many families are now alive at the same time, we can no longer concentrate primary attention on nuclear families of young parents and their children who occasionally visit or provide material assistance to grandparents or other relatives. I have come to think of today's large and complex kinship structure as a matrix of latent relationships—father with son, child with great-grandparent, sister with sister-in-law, ex-husband with ex-wife, and so on—relationships that are latent because they might or might not become close and significant during a lifetime. Thus I am proposing a definition of the kinship structure as a latent web of continually shifting linkages that provide the *potential* for activating and intensifying close family relationships.

The family literature describes two kinds of transformations in this structure that result from increasing longevity: (1) The linkages among family members have been prolonged, and (2) the surviving generations in a family have increased in number and complexity.

Prolongation of Family Relationships

Consider how longevity has prolonged family relationships. For example, in married couples a century ago, one or both partners were likely to have died before the children were reared. Today, though it may seem surprising, couples marrying at the customary ages can anticipate surviving together (apart from divorce) as long as 40 or 50 years on the average (Uhlenberg, 1969, 1980). As Glick and Norton (1977: 14) have shown, one out of every five married couples can expect to celebrate their fiftieth wedding anniversary. . . . As marital partners, my husband and I have so far survived together for over 50 years. What can be said about the form (as distinct from the content) of such a prolonged relationship?

For one thing, we share over half a century of experience. Because we are similar in age, we have shared the experience of aging—biologically, psychologically, and socially—from young adulthood to old age. Because we were born at approximately the same time (and thus belong to the same cohort), we have shared much the same historical experiences—the same fluctuations between economic prosperity and depression, between periods of pacifism and of war, between political liberalism and reactionism, and between low and high rates of fertility. We have also shared our own personal family experiences. We shared the bearing and raising of young children during our first quarter century together; during our second quarter century we adjusted our couplehood to our added roles as parents-in-law and grandparents. The third quarter century of our married life, by the laws of probability, should convert us additionally into grandparents-in-law and great-grandparents as well. In sum, prolonged marriages like ours afford extensive common experiences with aging, with historical change, and with changing family relationships. . . .

The very extension of marriage may increase the likelihood of divorce, as Samuel Preston (1976: 176–177) has shown. Returning to my personal experience, I was the only one of four sisters who did not divorce and remarry. But as long as their ex-husbands were alive none of my sisters could ever entirely discount the remaining potential linkages between them. These were not only ceremonial or instrumental linkages, but also affective linkages that could be hostile and vindictive, or (as time passes and need arises) could renew concern for one another's well-being. Whatever the nature of the relationship, latent linkages to ex-spouses persist. Thus, a prolonged marriage (even an ex-marriage) provides a continuing potential for a close relationship that can be activated in manifold ways.

The traditional match-making question—"Will this marriage succeed or fail?"—must be replaced and oft-repeated as the couple grows older by a different question: "Regardless of our past, can we—do we want to—make the fresh effort to succeed, or shall we fail in this marriage?"

Here I will state as my first proposition: *Family relationships are never fixed*; they change as the self and the significant other family members grow older, and as the changing society influences their respective lives. Clearly, the longer the relationship endures (because of longevity) the greater the opportunity for relational changes.

If, as lives are prolonged, marital relationships extend far beyond the original nuclear household, parent-offspring relationships also take on entirely new forms. For example, my daughter and I have survived together so far for 45 years of which only 18 were in the traditional relationship of parent and child. Unlike our shorter-lived forebearers, my daughter and I have been able to share many common experiences although at different stages of our respective lives. She shares a major portion of the historical changes that I have experienced. She also shares my earlier experience of sending a daughter off to college, and will perhaps share my experience of having a daughter marry and raise children. . . . Although the relational age between me and my daughter—the 26 years that separate us—remains the same throughout our lives, the implications of this difference change drastically from her infancy to my old age.

Number and Stability of Generations

I have dwelt at length on the prolongation of particular relationships to suggest the consequent dramatic changes in the family structure. Longevity has, in addition, increased the stability and the number of generations in a family. A poignant example of this instability (Imhof, n.d.) can be found in an eighteenth-century parish where a father could spawn 24 offspring of whom only 3 survived to adulthood—a time in which "it took two babies to make one adult." With increased longevity each generation becomes more stable because more of its members survive. For the young nuclear family in the United States, for example, though the number of children born in each family has been declining over this century, increased longevity has produced a new stability in the family structure. In an important quantitative analysis, Peter Uhlenberg (1980) has shown how the probability of losing a parent or a sibling through death before a child reaches age 15 have decreased from .51 in 1900 to .09 in 1976. Compared with children born a century ago, children born today are almost entirely protected against death of close family members (except for elderly relatives). To be sure, while mortality has been declining, divorce rates have been increasing but less rapidly. Thus, perhaps surprisingly, Uhlenberg demonstrates that disruptions of marriage up through the completion of child rearing have been declining since 1900. In other words, many marriages have been broken by divorce, but overall more have remained intact because of fewer deaths! Thus the young family as well as each of the older generations becomes more stable through survival. . . .

CHANGING DYNAMICS OF CLOSE FAMILY RELATIONSHIPS

What, then, are the implications of this greatly expanded kinship structure for the dynamics of close family relationships? How does the matrix of latent kinship linkages provide for close ties between particular individual lives, as these lives weave in and out of the intricate and continually shifting kinship network? Under what conditions do some family members provide (or fail to provide) recognition, advice, esteem, love, and tension release for other family members?

The answer, it seems to me, lies in the enlarged kinship structure: It provides many new opportunities for people at different points in their lives to select and activate the relationships they deem most significant. That is, the options for close family bonds have multiplied. Over the century, increased longevity has given flexibility to the kinship structure, relaxing both the temporal and the spatial boundaries of optional relationships.

Temporally, new options have arisen over the course of people's lives because, as we have seen, particular relationships have become more enduring. Particular relationships (even following divorce) are bounded only by the birth and death of the members. Now that the experience of losing family members by death is no longer a pervasive aspect of the full life course (and is in fact rare except in old age), people have greater opportunity to plan their family lives. They have time to make mutual adjustments to personal crises or to external threats such as unemployment or the fear of nuclear war. Here we are reminded of my first proposition: Family relationships are never fixed, but are continually in process and subject to change. As family members grow older, they move across time—across history and through their own lives—and they also move upward through the generations in their own families and the age strata of society. As individual family members who each pursue a separate life course, thoughts and feelings for one another are developed; their lives weave together or apart so as to activate, intensify, disregard, or disrupt particular close relationships. Thus the relationship between a mother and daughter can, for example, become close in the daughter's early childhood, her first years of marriage, and again after her children have left home although there may be interim lapses. . . .

Just as such new options for close ties have emerged from the prolongation of family relationships, other options have arisen because the number and variety of latent linkages have multiplied across the entire kinship structure. Spatially, close relationships are not bounded by the nuclear households that family members share during their younger lives. Given the intricacy of current kin networks, a wide range of linkages can be activated—between grandchild and grandparent, between distantly related cousins, between the ex-husbands of sisters, or between a child and his or her new step-parent. (Only in Grimm's fairy tales, which reflected the earlier frequency of maternal deaths and successive remarriages, were step-mothers always "wicked.") Aided by modern communication and transportation, affection and interaction can persist even during long periods of separation. . . .

Given these options, let me now state a second general proposition: As active agents in directing the course of their own lives, *individuals have a degree of control over their close family relationships.* This control, I submit, has been enhanced because longevity has widened the opportunities for selecting and activating relationships that can provide emotional support and advice when needed.

This part of my discussion suggests a new view of the family. Perhaps we need now to think of a family less as the members of one household with incidental linkages to kin in other households and more as a continuing interplay among intertwined lives within the entire changing kinship structure. The closeness of these intertwined lives and the mutual support they provide depend on many factors (including the predispositions of each individual and the continuing motivation to negotiate and renegotiate their joint lives) but the enlarged kinship structure provides the potential. . . .

OLDER GENERATIONS OF THE FUTURE

About the fourth generation (great-grandparents) that is being contributed by longevity, I want to make three final points.

First, it is too early to tell how an enlarged great-grandparent generation will fit into the kinship structure, or what close family relationships it may form. It is too early because the marked increases in longevity among the old began only in recent decades and are still continuing at a rate far-exceeding earlier predictions (Preston, 1976; Manton, 1982; Brody and Brock, n.d.). Will this added generation be regarded as the more familiar generation of grandparents has been regarded—either as a threat to the young adult generation's independence, or as a "social problem" for family and community, requiring care from the mid-generation that is "squeezed" between caring for both young children and aging parents? Or will an added fourth generation mean new coalitions and new forms of personal relationships? And what of five-generation families in which a grandmother can be also a granddaughter (see Hagestad, 1981)? It is still too early to tell what new family norms will develop (see Riley, 1978).

Second, while we do not know how a fourth or even a fifth generation may fit in, we do know that most older family members are not dependent or disabled (some 5% of those 65 and over are in nursing homes). For those requiring care or instrumental support, families generally make extraordinary efforts to provide it (see Shanas, 1979). Yet most of the elderly, and especially those who are better educated and more active, are stronger, wiser, more competent, and more independent than is generally supposed. Public stereotypes of old people are far more negative than old people's assessments of themselves (National Council on the Aging, 1981). Healthy members of this generation, like their descendants, must earn their own places in the family and create their own personal ties. They cannot expect obligatory warmth or emotional support.

Third, at the close of their lives, however, old people will need advice and emotional support from kin. This need is not new in the annals of family history. What is new is the fact that terminal illness and death are no longer scattered across all generations but are concentrated in the oldest one. Today two-thirds of all deaths occur after age 65, and 30% after age 80 (Brody and Brock, n.d.). And, although most deaths occur outside the home, programs such as the hospice movement are being developed for care of the dying in the home where the family can take part (see M. W. Riley, forthcoming).

In conclusion, I have attempted to trace the impact of the unprecedented increases in longevity on the family and its relationships. In our own time the kinship structure has become more extensive and more complex, the temporal and spatial boundaries of the family have been altered, and the opportunities for close family relationships have proliferated. These relationships are no longer prescribed as strict obligations. They must rather be earned—created and re-created by family members throughout their long lives. Each of us is in continuing need of advice and emotional support from one another, as we contend with personal challenges and troubles, and with the compelling effects of societal changes in the economy, in technology, in culture, and in values. We all must agree with Mary Jo Bane (1976) that the family is here to stay, but in forms that we are beginning to comprehend only now. . . .

REFERENCES

BANE, M. J., 1976. *Here to Stay: American Families in the 20th Century.* New York: Basic Books.

Brody, J. A., and D. B. Brock, n.d. "Epidemiologic and Statistical Characteristics of the United States Elderly Population." (Unpublished)

Glick, P. C., and A. J. Norton, 1977. "Marrying, Divorcing, and Living Together in the U.S. Today." *Population Bulletin*, 32. Washington, D.C. Population Reference Bureau.

Hagestad, G. O., 1981. "Problems and promises in the Social Psychology of Intergenerational Relations" pp. 11–46 in R. W. Fogel et al. (eds.) *Aging: Stability and Change in the Family*. New York: Academic Press.

Imhof, A. E., 1982. "Life Course Patterns of Women and Their Husbands—16th to 20th Century." Presented at the International Conference on Life Course Research on Human Development, September 17, Berlin, Germany.

Manton, K. G., 1982. "Changing Concepts of Morbidity and Mortality in the Elderly Population." Milbank Memorial Fund Q. 60:183–244.

National Council on the Aging, 1981. *Aging in the Eighties: America in Transition*. Washington, D.C.: Author.

Preston, S. H., 1976. *Mortality Patterns in National Population: With Special References to Recorded Causes of Death*. New York: Academic Press.

Riley, M. W., 1978. "Aging, social change, and the power of ideas." *Daedalus*, 107, 4:39–52.

______. Forthcoming "Age Strata in Social Systems," in, R. H. Binstock and E. Shanas (eds.) *The New Handbook of Aging and the Social Sciences*.

Shanas, E., 1979. "Social Myth as Hypothesis: The Case of the Family Relations of Old People." *The Gerontologist*, 19:3–9.

Uhlenberg, P. R., 1969. "A Study of Cohort Life Cycles: Cohorts of Native Born Massachusetts Women, 1830–1920." *Population Studies*, 23, 3:407–420.

______, 1980. "Death and the Family," *J. of Family History* (Fall):313–320.

SECTION 3

Marriage and Family and Minorities

A SUBCULTURE IS A GROUP that shares in the overall culture of a society but is set apart by its distinctive values, norms, beliefs, and life-style. A large society such as ours has thousands of subcultures; some are based around unique occupational experiences—such as those of cabdrivers, construction workers, and physicians—while others are based around specific activities and interests—such as swimming, race car driving, and stamp collecting. Still others are based on the stage of life in which people are classified, such as teenager and retiree.

Regardless of the basis of the subculture (and the bases are almost endless), each has features or characteristics that set it apart from most other members of the society. Subcultures differ in what the members hold dear in life (their values), their rules for living and getting along (their norms), the ways in which they view reality or what they think is true about the world (their beliefs), the ways in which they evaluate life's experiences (their attitudinal orientations), and the general approach they take to living out life in society (their life-style). These differences include their appearance, manner, and conduct, characteristics that not only set them apart in some way, but also provide a basis for group membership, for personal identification, for bonding with others, and for orientating themselves toward the world.

Some subcultures are distinct only in highly specific ways. Stamp collectors or swimmers, for example, are likely to be similar in most ways to most people. That is, in general, their values, norms, beliefs, attitudinal orientations, and life-style match the dominant culture of the United States. Consequently, one would ordinarily be hard pressed to identify the stamp collectors or swimmers in a crowd of people. Their differences are highly focused, centering on some specific activity or interest. Apart from the values, norms, beliefs, and attitudes (and, to a much lesser extent, a resulting life-style) that center on stamp collecting or swimming, they are similar to other members of the dominant culture.

In contrast, some subcultures are more highly developed and much more encompassing. They can be so encompassing, in fact, that they include almost all aspects of life, leaving only some general ways in which its members share in the broader culture in which they are embedded. The authors of the following three chapters focus on such groups: Asian–Americans, Blacks, and Chicanos.

Each of these groups has experienced a unique history, one that sets it apart from others. These shared group experiences provide a basis for approaching the world in a distinct way; that is, they provide general orientations to life, directions for how to adjust to the life contingencies its members face. On the basis of their common history, and of being raised and living within their specific group, members identify with one another. Consequently, we can say that these three groups share a highly developed, broad, encompassing subculture.

A major way in which these groups are set apart from others is by their family customs—their values, beliefs, and norms concerning marriage and family. It is to the identification of what is unique about family life in these three racial/ethnic/cultural groups that the authors address themselves.

The value of focusing on differing groups is that such an examination can help us attain a sociological perspective, the goal of this first part of the book. Looking at marriage and family among distinct groups in American society can lead us out of the narrow focus that our own individuating experiences in marriage and family provide. From them we can gain a contrastive, comparative base from which to view and understand our own experiences, as well as an appreciation of the diversity of marriage and family in our pluralistic society.

CHAPTER 11

Asian-American Families

Bob H. Suzuki

ABSTRACT: The term "Asian-Americans" as used in this chapter refers only to Chinese-Americans and Japanese-Americans. After briefly recounting the discrimination these groups have suffered in the United States, Suzuki identifies their major values. Their traditional emphasis has been placed on education, hard work, Confucianistic values, and a strongly integrated patriarchical family. But because of acculturation, less emphasis is now given to these value orientations, and in addition, the family structure is changing. Nevertheless, these characteristics continue to set these groups apart from most of the American population. Their families are still more extended, more strongly bonded in close networks, and they have less divorce and less premarital sex than the majority of the American population. The families of recent immigrants, however, are undergoing a high amount of strain.

Relevant terms for understanding this chapter are:

Issei: the immigrants
Nisei: first generation born in America
Sansei: second generation born in America
Yonsei: third generation born in America

INTRODUCTION [AND BACKGROUND]

[D]ue to their seemingly phenomenal success in American society, Asian-Americans have been hailed by many as the "model minority" that other minority groups might do well to emulate (Peterson, 1966; Anonymous, 1966; Alsop, 1971). Their widely extolled success appears remarkable considering their long history as an oppressed racial minority, and has been attributed largely to the unity, stability, and strength of the Asian family. . . .

Since it will not be possible to present a comprehensive picture of all Asian-American families within the scope of this [chapter], only the families of the two largest Asian-American ethnic groups, the Chinese and Japanese, will be treated. The term, Asian-American, will be used to refer to only those two groups, and not to other groups, such as the Koreans, Filipinos, Pacific Islanders, East Indians, and Indochinese that are often included in the generic use of the term. . . .

Immigration

The first of the Asian immigrants, the Chinese, began arriving in the 1850's, lured initially by the discovery of gold in California and later by recruiters seeking cheap labor for the sugar plantations in Hawaii and for railroad construction, mining, and agriculture in the western states. The vast majority were poor peasants, nearly all men, from the Canton area of southeastern China. Most of them came to earn money, hoping to return home reasonably prosperous after a few years. Those who were married left their wives at home, while single men hoped to marry when they returned. Only a few realized their hopes. The rest ultimately resigned themselves to remaining in the United States (Coolidge, 1909; Sung, 1967; Chinn, 1969).

By 1880, some 105,000 Chinese were living in the western states and another 12,000 in Hawaii. Men outnumbered women by more than twenty to one. In 1882, as a result of a virulent anti-Chinese movement, Chinese immigration was brought to a halt by an exclusion act passed by the United States Congress (Lyman, 1970).

The major proportion of the Japanese immigrants arrived in Hawaii and on the United States mainland between 1890 and 1920. They were brought in to work as cheap laborers in many of the same areas in which the earlier Chinese immigrants had worked. . . .

As in the case of the Chinese, males, predominantly unmarried, far outnumbered females. While most of them hoped to marry upon returning to Japan, they later realized, like the Chinese before them, that such a goal would be nearly impossible to achieve. Their hopes further faded in 1908 when, under pressure from the United States, Japan began restricting emigration.

It was at this time that the practice of "picture-bride" marriages, arranged through photographs, became popular. These marriages redressed the male-female imbalance considerably among the Japanese immigrants. Nevertheless, thousands of Japanese men were still unmarried in 1924 when Japanese immigration was halted by the United States Congress, this time as a result of intense anti-Japanese agitation. . . .

The culmination of the anti-Japanese movement, however, was reached during World War II when most of the mainland Japanese, over 110,000 people, two-thirds of whom were American-born citizens, were removed from the West Coast and incarcerated in concentration camps. . . . While the Japanese in Hawaii were not incarcerated *en masse* (except for about 1,000 supposedly "high risk" community leaders), they were viewed with great distrust and subjected to many abuses and restrictions during the wartime period (Fuchs, 1961; Daws, 1968). . . .

[D]uring the decade of the 1950's, the job market improved measurably for Asian-Americans. This was due in large part to the unparalleled expansion in the technological/bureaucratic sectors of the American economy during this period. A high demand was created for appropriately trained technical-scientific workers. Since many Asian-Americans had gone on to college, despite the bleak outlook for jobs, and had been educated in these fields, they were in a good position to meet this demand when it arose (Lyman, 1974; Suzuki, 1977). As a result, by 1960 the census showed that Asian-Americans had the highest median family income of any minority group and a higher educational level than whites (United States Bureau of the Census, 1963).

In order to achieve this rise in socioeconomic status, Asian-Americans on the United States mainland generally adopted a low-profile strategy for advancement that would not attract too much attention nor elicit adverse reaction. They became known as quiet, hardworking, dependable, and accommodating—attributes that were viewed favorably by employers (Caudill, 1952). On the other hand, Asian-Americans in Hawaii, mainly the Japanese, chose quite a different strategy for gaining upward mobility. Since the Japanese constituted over one-third the state's population, Nisei leaders could clearly see the potential for gaining political power and decided to aggressively enter the political arena. By 1959, when Hawaii was granted statehood, the Japanese had succeeded in becoming a powerful political force in the Islands. Their success in politics was paralleled by their success in many other fields (Fuchs, 1961; Gray, 1972). . . .

Cultural Values

[W]e will now describe the major traditional cultural values common to both China and Japan. . . .

Humanism

This concept, which is central to Confucianism, is based on the optimistic belief that human nature is basically good and that the inherent tendency of man is toward virtuous and benevolent behavior. Man is thought to have the potential within himself to achieve fulfillment and happiness during his earthly existence. However, satisfaction in life is to be gained not through the acquisition of power, wealth, or prestige, but through an individual's diligent and sincere efforts to conduct himself morally and to develop his full potentialities as a person.

Collectivity

This concept arises from the altruistic nature of Confucianism and its emphasis on kinship ties and mutual dependence. An individual is expected to subordinate or even sacrifice his personal interests for the greater collective good of his family, kinship group, village, or country. Since egocentricity is not compatible with such a value system, modesty and humility are considered important virtues.

Self-Discipline

Confucianism teaches that a person should learn to control his emotions in order to think logically and make objective judgments. Control over both emotions and psychological and material gratification is thought to be necessary for cultivating the mind and self-improvement. A person is also expected to make every effort to utilize his own capabilities and resources to solve his personal problems and improve his life. Failure is attributed to either the lack of resolve or the result of fate beyond an individual's control.

Order and Hierarchy

Since Confucius's goal was to establish a stable and harmonious social order, Confucianism placed great emphasis on the proper relationships between man in all aspects of life. Since he believed that the cornerstone of these relationships was that between a child and his parents, he placed major emphasis on the virtue of filial piety. A child was expected to pay homage and give unquestioning obedience to his parents and be concerned and understanding of their needs and wishes. This expectation, in turn, was extended to all subordinates in their relationships with persons of authority above them. However, all of these relationships were supposed to be mutually dependent, entailing two-way obligations.

Wisdom of the Elderly

The pursuit of knowledge was highly stressed by Confucianism since knowledge was considered essential for wisdom and goodness. Learned scholars, especially the elderly sages, were highly respected because of their experience, knowledge, and wisdom. For the same reasons, the elderly in general were accorded much respect. These value orientations were reflected in the practice of ancestor worship, the high value placed on education, the respect given to tradition, and the emphasis on the past rather than the future. While these precepts insured social stability and cultural continuity, they also tended to make traditional Asian societies rigid and difficult to change.

Moderation and Harmony

This concept is based on the idea that man should seek to maintain a balance and pursue a middle course between extremes of theory and practice, action and inaction. Thus, a flexible mode of thinking is promoted that values relativity and gradualism and prohibits rigid absolutes. Interactions between persons are generally characterized by politeness and restraint and by sensitive consideration for the position and feelings of others. Open confrontations and conflicts between persons are discouraged and tend to be avoided. Thus, Asians appear to be humble, modest, nonaggressive, and unemotional to many Westerners, who, therefore, often mischaracterize them as inscrutable.

Obligation

We have already mentioned the mutuality of obligations involved in the concept of filial piety. The Japanese have extended these obligatory relations through a category of obligations known as *giri*, for which there is no equivalent in Chinese culture. They include gift-giving, mutual assistance, and other considerations (Benedict, 1946). Another type of obligation stems from the concept of collectivity. As part of his obligation to his group, an individual is obliged not to bring dishonor or shame to his family by socially unacceptable behavior. Consequently, Asians face considerable pressure to conform to social norms.

Family Structure and Relationships

To Westerners, perhaps the best-known characteristic of the traditional Asian family has been its patriarchical structure. True to Confucian precepts, the father was the dominant authority figure in the family, while other members were in clearly prescribed, subordinate roles. . . .

The eldest son was accorded the next highest position in the family hierarchy, followed by his younger brothers. Females were considered inferior to males, and accordingly, daughters were relegated to lower-status roles. As Wong (1974) has noted, however, the position of females in Asian societies was probably not too different from that of women in traditional Western societies.

The grandparents occupied a special position of honor in the family. As its most elderly members, their wisdom was respected and their advice often sought on important family matters.

While the children were expected to show filial piety to both the father and mother, their relationships with each were distinctly different. In order to command their respect and obedience, the father tended to establish a rather distant and formal relationship with his children, especially the older sons who often viewed him with trepidation. In contrast, the relationship of the children to the mother was generally one of greater intimacy, affection, and informality. Especially close, affective ties tended to develop between the mother and her sons, particularly the eldest son.

Due to the custom of arranged marriages and the hierarchical structure of the family, the husband-wife relationship was neither the strongest nor the most intense one within the family, and was usually overshadowed by father-son and mother-son relationships (Hsu, 1975).

Finally, the relationship between the mother and daughter-in-law has received much attention in Asian folklore. Stories about the suffering of new brides under the domination of a despotic mother-in-law are well known not only in Asia but also in the West. However, due to the strong tradition of extended families and the dictates of filial piety, the burden of the role in Asian societies was much less avoidable and probably more onerous (Lang, 1946; Benedict, 1946).

Child-Rearing

In both China and Japan, the early years of childhood were characterized by the permissiveness of parents toward their children. By American standards, young children were indulged, receiving close attention, much soothing care, and little discipline. Close intimate contacts with the mother were continual during this stage of early childhood. The child was seldom left alone or to cry, and was almost always being fed, carried, soothed, or played with. Children usually slept with their mothers until weaning, which usually occurred at one or two years of age, but sometimes continued for years. Mothers seldom left their children alone. Thus, the infant was quiet and content most of the time, and came to relate the physical presence of the mother with emotional security (Hsu, 1949; Benedict, 1946).

At the age of five or six, children were assumed to have reached the age of reason and to be ready to begin their entry into the world of adulthood. Discipline was rather suddenly imposed at this age by both the father and mother as they began to more strictly control the conduct and behavior of the child. Minor infractions, such as boastful or selfish behavior, were controlled by ridicule or teasing. More serious misbehavior, such as emotional tantrums or fighting, was more sternly handled, usually by scolding or through the inculcation of shame and, in rare instances, by corporeal punishment.

In more direct ways, parents taught their children the ethics of good conduct, their obligations to the family, and the virtues of filial piety and self-control. They also soon learned that acts of serious social deviance such as stealing would greatly stigmatize the entire family; whereas, outstanding achievements such as success in school would be a source of much collective pride. Through this process, the child was gradually socialized from an egocentic to a family-centered orientation (Lang, 1946; Wolf, 1970; Embree, 1939). . . .

THE CONTEMPORARY ASIAN-AMERICAN FAMILY

Sociohistorical Changes

Because of the exclusion act of 1882 and the resulting shortage of women, families were practically nonexistent among the early Chinese immigrants. The few Chinese wives present were married to the wealthier merchants. Although many of the immigrants had left families behind in China, most of them, together with their unmarried compatriots, were destined to live out their lives as homeless bachelors (Lyman, 1974).

It was not until the 1920's that the bachelor-society character of the Chinatowns began to change as families became increasingly visible (Nee and Nee, 1972). Many of these families were started by former laborers who achieved merchant status and were finally eligible to bring wives over from China. Others were started by marriages between immigrants and the few American-born Chinese women. Because wives were prized, they had more status than their counterparts in China, and indeed, sometimes assumed more authority than their husbands. Since grandparents were usually absent they also did not have to contend with the dictates of mothers-in-law. Moreover, the traditional extended patrifocal family was generally replaced by the nuclear family (Sung, 1967).

Many of the children in these early families grew up in the familiar surroundings of their parents' small shop, laundry, or restaurant, where they lived and helped in the family business. While most of them were subjected to strict, traditional upbringing, their early childhoods were generally secure and family-centered. However, when they began school and were exposed to Western ideas and values, cultural conflicts with parents frequently broke out and led to strained relations (Lowe, 1943; Wong, 1950). Parents were inevitably forced to make some concessions to this Americanization process, but still managed to inculcate their children with many traditional values and norms. . . .

Perhaps no event had a greater impact on Japanese-American families than the internment experience of World War II (Broom and Kitsuse, 1956; Thomas and Nishimoto, 1946). The sudden uprooting of families and the oppressive conditions in the concentration camps had traumatic, long-lasting effects on the family which even today have not been fully assessed (Morishima, 1973).

Many Japanese-Americans, especially the Nisei, felt deeply stigmatized by their internment experience. After their release from the camps many of them undoubtedly decided, consciously or unconsciously, to reject all vestiges of Japanese culture and to acculturate as quickly as possible into the American mainstream (Okimoto, 1971). . . .

The traditional Asian cultural values described earlier appear to have been modified, often significantly, through the process of acculturation. Generally speaking, third-generation Asian-Americans have acculturated to a greater degree than second-generation Asian-Americans, with Japanese showing greater acculturation than their Chinese counterparts (Sue and Kirk, 1973). Certain values, such as filial piety and respect for the wisdom of the elderly, appear to have depreciated more than others. Parents can no longer expect unquestioning obedience from their children, and relationships within the family have become more democratic. Furthermore, the knowledge and experience of grandparents no longer carry the weight they did in the past.

Despite such acculturative trends, both generations of Asian-Americans are still found to subscribe to many traditional values, though to a lesser degree than first-generation Asian-Americans. In particular, they believe more strongly than their Anglo counterparts in such values as respect for ethical behavior, duty and obligation to family, restraint of strong feelings, respect for authority, and modesty and politeness toward others (Kitano, 1969; Schwartz, 1971; Fong, 1973; Sue, 1973). . . .

The 1970 census showed that the average size of Asian-American families was somewhat larger than that of white families; namely, 4.0 for Chinese, 3.7 for Japanese, and 3.5 for whites (United States Bureau of the Census, 1973). The larger size of Asian-American families is mainly due to extended family relationships, that is, the presence of grandparents, aunts, uncles, and so forth. In fact, 18 percent of all Chinese and 16 percent of all Japanese families were found to be of the extended type, compared to 12 percent of families in the total population (Urban Associates, 1974).

While the 1970 census showed that a high percentage (80 to 90 percent) of Asian-Americans were married within their groups, recent studies (Omatsu, 1972; Kikumura and Kitano, 1973: Sung, 1974) indicate that the rate of outmarriage has sharply increased in the past decade among the younger Chinese and Japanese, approaching 50 percent in many areas. A notable exception are the Japanese in Hawaii, whose outmarriage rates remain relatively low.

In 1970, the proportion of divorced to married men was about 3 percent for both Chinese and Japanese, compared to about 4 percent for the total population. Correspondingly, the proportion of divorced to married women was about 3 percent for Chinese and 4 percent for Japanese, compared to about 6 percent for the total population. Again, these proportions were lower for the Japanese in Hawaii (United States Bureau of the Census, 1973).

Family Structure and Relationships

It has become almost axiomatic to describe the Asian-American family as patriarchal that is, as vertically structured with the father as undisputed head and all others in subordinate roles (Kitano, 1969; Sung, 1967). While this traditional structure may have prevailed in many first-generation families, it has almost certainly been modified in second- and third-generation families. In fact, as mentioned earlier, even in first-generation families the mother frequently assumed much more authority than her counterpart in Asia. . . .

Relationships between Asian-American parents and their children have also become more egalitarian. While they are still differentially socialized, boys enjoy little, if any, preferential treatment or status over girls with regard to the allocation of family resources. Furthermore, the duties and obligations expected of children are less demanding and restrictive than in the past. However, they are still generally subjected to stricter limits and constraints than their Anglo peers (Kriger and Kroes, 1972).

Verbal communication within Asian-American families is relatively restrained compared to that in Anglo families. This verbal reticence is not only rooted in traditional cultural norms but may also have been strongly reinforced by racial discrimination (Watanabe, 1973). On the other hand, there appears to be much greater utilization of nonverbal and indirect modes of communication. Family members generally become quite sensitive to using nonverbal cues and to reading between the lines of indirect statements.

Unlike traditional Asian families, contemporary Asian-American families are not dominated by parent-son relationships. The strongest relationships appear to be those between husband and wife and between the mother and her children. Husbands and wives appear to enjoy much closer companionship today than in previous years. Since mothers continue to assume most of the responsibility for child-rearing they develop the closest relationships with their children. Fathers still tend to maintain some distance from their children in order to engender respect and obedience. While fathers play with the children, they do not try to become close companions in the way that Anglo fathers do. Parents are more likely to show affection for their children in indirect ways (for instance, by sacrificing their own needs for their children's), rather than with words or overt displays of affection, such as hugging or kissing.

These relationships have served to make the Asian-American family a close-knit social unit. This cohesiveness is reflected in the social activities of Asian-American families, which tend to be more family-centered than those of Anglo families. Children are more likely to be included in Asian-American social gatherings since parents appear less comfortable about leaving them at home with babysitters (Hsu, 1971; Kitano, 1969).

Child-Rearing

While acculturation toward Anglo middle-class patterns has taken place, many aspects of traditional Asian child-rearing practices appear to be continued among contemporary Asian-American families (Young, 1972; Sollenberger, 1968; Johnson, 1972; Kitano, 1969). The early years of childhood are still characterized by close, nurturant care by the mother, who tends to be more permissive with the young infant than her Anglo counterpart. Infants are seldom allowed to cry for prolonged periods before they are picked up by their mothers. Mothers tend to feed their infants on demand rather than by scheduling. On the average, weaning takes place at a later age than for Anglo infants. Toilet training is also more gradual. Parents often allow the young child to sleep with them, occasionally tolerating such behavior even after the child begins school.

Such indulgences would very likely be viewed by middle-class Anglo parents as a sure way of spoiling the child and retarding his/her development into a mature, independent, and autonomous adult. However, such an approach to child-rearing develops close, affective ties within the family and the child's sense of belonging to the family. It also results in the child's becoming strongly dependent on the mother to satisfy his/her needs and, in turn, enables the mother to use various depriviation techniques to control the child's behavior. Moreover, even as the Asian-American mother caters to the needs of her child, she inculcates the child with a sense of obligation, which she continues to reinforce as the child grows older. Consequently, she is able to use shame and guilt to control behavior by appealing to this sense of obligation whenever the child deviates from her expectations.

Despite their seemingly permissive child-rearing methods, Asian-American mothers are able to use the nonphysical disciplinary techniques described above together with limited amounts of physical punishment very effectively to control their children's behavior. Although much childish behavior is tolerated, aggression, especially fighting, is strongly disapproved of and quickly admonished. Mothers maintain close supervision over all of their children's activities, carefully selecting their playmates and rarely leaving them alone or on their own. This protective care is reflected in the low childhood accident rates suffered by Asian-American children (Kurokawa, 1966).

Although their role appears to be increasing, most Asian-American fathers still play a relatively minor role in the rearing of children during their years of infancy. Since the time the father spends with his children usually is quite limited, he tends to take a rather tolerant attitude toward them, leaving most of the disciplining to the mother. However, when the children reach school age they are no longer indulged and begin to assume duties and responsibilities in the household. They also are subjected to stricter discipline and taught in various ways that their actions will reflect not only on themselves but on the entire family. In cases of serious misbehavior by older children, the disciplining often is done by the father since his authority evokes greater fear and respect. He also spends more time with the older children, particularly if they are boys, joining them in recreational activities and having them assist with household chores.

As Asian-American children reach adolescence, many of them join peer groups and begin showing interest in the opposite sex. Their friends are now even more carefully screened by the parents. Dating among Asian-American teenagers is often on a group basis, whereby girls and boys go out as a group without necessarily pairing off. Dating on an individual basis generally does not start until later; in fact, group dating patterns sometimes persist even into college.

Parental attitudes toward pre-marital sexual exploration are still relatively strict but are becoming more tolerant. In fact, it is not uncommon to find unmarried couples living together among Asian-American college students. However, while marriages among Asian-Americans today are based on romantic love and free choice, parents still exert considerable influence on their children in this matter.

Kinship and Community

The nuclear family consisting of the parents and their children is the norm today among Asian-American families. However, close ties are still maintained with many relatives outside the immediate residential family through frequent visits and telephone calls, mutual assistance, reciprocal gift-giving, and various social gettogethers. The bonds appear particularly strong between married sisters and between a mother and her married daughters. While grandparents generally do not live with their married children, they often live nearby and become quite involved with their children's families. . . .

Strongly complementing these family ties are the extensive networks of affiliations and communications that exist in the Asian-American communities. These include both informal networks, such as family friends and social groups, and formal networks, such as ethnic newspapers, churches, family and business associations, recreational clubs, and various other community organizations (Hsu, 1971; Kiefer, 1974). . . .

It is these networks that made the Asian-American communities very close-knit social entities. They strongly reinforce the sanctioning techniques of the family for controlling behavior by serving as very effective channels for gossip and news about both misdeeds and achievements of individuals in the community. Through such communications, the "good families" and "bad families" are readily identified. Thus, community members are quite aware that their actions will become widely known and ultimately reflect on their families' reputations. . . .

Recent Immigrant Families

Since 1965 when discriminatory immigration quotas were finally eliminated, well over 200,000 Chinese immigrants have entered the United

States, principally from Hong Kong and Taiwan. Most of them have crowded into the Chinatowns of San Francisco, New York City, Boston, and other major cities. These Chinatowns are stricken with some of the worst conditions to be found in any of the inner-city ghettoes, including increasing crime and delinquency, grossly inadequate health care, overcrowded and substandard housing, chronic underemployment, and a multitude of other pressing social problems (Chin, 1971; Wong, 1971; Lyman, 1974).

The families of these immigrants must contend with circumstances quite different from those faced by earlier Asian immigrant families. Parents no longer work and live with their children in small business establishments, but are now generally wage workers in restaurants, garment factories, and other large enterprises. Both parents usually must work, often ten hours a day, seven days a week, for subsistence-level wages. Consequently, they have little time to spend with their children and must live under poverty conditions (Chao, 1977).

Parents also no longer can rely on traditional techniques for controlling the behavior of their children. Unlike earlier Asian immigrants, most of the recent immigrants have come frm urban areas, which have experienced major changes under the impact of modernization and Western influences. Values and lifestyles have undergone corresponding changes. Furthermore, the youth are far more sophisticated in their perceptions about the society in which they live.

All of these factors have subjected recent Chinese immigrant families to severe strains. Due to the absence of their parents and traditional constraints, the teenage youth of these families have been especially prone to acts of rebellion and social deviance. Since many of them cannot speak English and experience traumatic family/school discontinuities, they frequently become alienated from school, drop out, and join their peers in street gangs (Sung, 1977). A large number of such gangs have formed over the past few years in all of the major Chinatowns and have been increasingly involved in crime and acts of violence, including an estimated forty-five killings attributed to intergang warfare (Wu, 1977). . . .

Deculturalization

[In the United States, despite] their high achievement levels, Asian-American students face many subtle forms of discrimination in education due to the Anglo-centric orientation of most schools. The curriculum usually omits or badly distorts the experience and contributions of Asian-Americans. Teachers often stereotype Asian-American students as quiet, hard-working, and docile, and tend to reinforce conformity and stifle creativity. Therefore, Asian-American students frequently do not develop the ability to assert and express themselves verbally, and are channeled mainly into technical/scientific fields (Watanabe, 1973). As a consequence of these influences, many Asian-American students suffer from low self-esteem, are overly conforming, and have their academic and social development narrowly circumscribed.

Subtle forms of discrimination against Asian-Americans also appear widespread in employment. Although they have gained access to many professional occupations because of their high educational attainment levels, most Asian-Americans appear to be relegated to lower-echelon, white-collar jobs having little or no decision-making authority and low mobility. They are consistently passed over by Anglos for most supervisory and administrative positions, apparently because they are viewed as not having the requisite personality traits, such as aggressiveness, verbal fluency, and self-confidence, for such positions (Suzuki, 1977). . . .

[T]he emergence of the Asian-American movement . . . has played a major role in raising the ethnic consciousness and social awareness of Asian-Americans. As a consequence, Asian-Americans are having second thoughts about the merits of acculturating further into the mainstream of American society, and are becoming concerned about preserving important traditional aspects of their own cultures. Many of them are also currently seeking to redefine their identity and role in American society on their own terms and can be expected to take a far less accommodating approach in this quest than in the past. . . .

BIBLIOGRAPHY

ALSOP, JOSEPH. 1971. "New American Success Story." *Los Angeles Times*, January 12.

Anonymous. 1966. "Success Story of One Minority Group in U.S." *United States News and World Report*, December 26:73–76.

BENEDICT, RUTH. 1946. *The Chrysanthemum and the Sword*. Boston: Houghton Mifflin.

BROOM, LEONARD and KITSUSE, JOHN I. 1956. *The Managed Casuality: The Japanese-American Family in World War II*. Berkeley: University of California Press Reprint, 1973.

CAUDILL, WILLIAM, 1952. "Japanese-American Personality and Acculturation." *Genetic Psychology Monographs*, 45 (February):3–102.

CHAO, ROSE. 1977. *Chinese Immigrant Children*. Preliminary Report, Betty L. Sung (Ed.). New York: Department of Asian Studies, City University of New York.

CHIN, ROCKY. 1971. "New York Chinatown Today." *Amerasia Journal*, 1 (March):1–24.

CHINN, THOMAS (Ed.). 1969. *A History of the Chinese in California: A Syllabus*. San Francisco: Chinese Historical Society of America.

Coolidge, Mary R. 1909. *Chinese Immigration*. New York: Arno Press Reprint, 1969.

Daws, Gavin. 1968. *Shoal of Time; A History of the Hawaiian Islands*. New York: Macmillan.

Embree, John F. 1939. *Suye Mura: A Japanese Village*. Chicago: University of Chicago Press.

Fong, Stanley L. M. 1973. "Assimilation and Changing Roles of Chinese Americans." *Journal of Social Issues*, 29:2:115–127.

Fuchs, Lawrence. 1961. *Hawaii Pono: A Social History*. New York: Harcourt, Brace and Jovanovich.

Gray, Francine du Plessix. 1972. *Hawaii: The Sugar-coated Fortress*. New York: Random House.

Hsu, Francis L. K. 1949. *Under the Ancestor's Shadow*. London: Routledge and Kegan Paul.

______. 1971. *The Challenge of the American Dream: The Chinese in the United States*. Belmont, CA: Wadşworth.

______. 1975. *Iemoto: The Heart of Japan*. Cambridge, MA: Schenkman.

Johnson, Colleen L. 1972. *The Japanese-American Family and Community in Honolulu: Generational Continuities in Ethnic Affiliation*. Ph.D. Dissertation in Anthropology. Syracuse: Syracuse University.

Kiefer, Christie W. 1974. *Changing Cultures, Changing Lives: An Ethnographic Study of Three Generations of Japanese Americans*. San Francisco: Jossey-Bass.

Kikumura, Akemi, and Kitano, Harry H. L. 1973. "Interracial Marriage: A Picture of the Japanese Americans." *Journal of Social Issues*, 29:2:67–81.

Kitano, Harry H. L. 1969. *Japanese Americans: The Evolution of a Subculture*. Englewood Cliffs, N.J.: Prentice-Hall.

Kriger, Sara F., and Kroes, William H. 1972. "Child-rearing Attitudes of Chinese, Jewish, and Protestant Mothers." *Journal of Social Psychology*, 86:205–210.

Kung, S. W. 1962. *Chinese in American Life*. Seattle: University of Washington Press.

Lang, Olga. 1946. *Chinese Family and Society*. New Haven, CT: Yale University Press.

Lowe, Pardee. 1943. *Father and Glorious Descendant* Boston: Little Brown and Company.

Lyman, Stanford. 1970. *The Asian in the West*. Social Science and Humanities Publication No. 4. Reno: Western Studies Center, Desert Research Institute. University of Nevada System.

______. 1974. *Chinese Americans*. New York: Random House.

Morishima, James K. 1973. "The Evacuation: Impact on the Family." In *Asian Americans: Psychological Perspectives*, Stanley Sue and Nathaniel N. Wagner (Eds.). Palo Alto, CA: Science and Behavior Books.

Nee, Victor, and Nee, Brett D. 1972. *Longtime Californ': A Documentary History of an American Chinatown*. New York: Pantheon Books.

Okimoto, Daniel I. 1971. *American in Disguise*. New York: Walker/Weatherhill.

Omatsu, Glenn. 1972. "Nihonmachi Beat." *Hokubei Mainichi*, January 12.

Peterson, William. 1966. "Success Story, Japanese-American Style" *New York Times Magazine*, January 9.

Schwartz, Audrey J. 1971. "The Culturally Advantaged: A Study of Japanese American Pupils." *Sociology and Social Research*, 55 (April): 341–353.

Sollenberger, Richard T. 1968. "Chinese-American Child-rearing Practices and Juvenile Delinquency." *Journal of Social Psychology*, 74:13–23.

Sue, Derald W. 1973. "Ethnic Identity: The Impact of Two Cultures on the Psychological Development of Asians in America." In *Asian-Americans: Psychological Perspectives*, Stanley Sue and Nathaniel N. Wagner (Eds.). Palo Alto, CA.: Science and Behavior Books.

Sue, Derald W., and Kirk, B. A. 1973. "Differential Characteristics of Japanese and Chinese American College Students." *Journal of Counseling Psychology*, 20:142–148.

Sung, Betty L. 1967. *The Story of the Chinese in America*. New York: Collier Books.

______. 1974. "It Figures: Chinese Interracial Marriage." *Bridge*, 3 (April): 40–41.

______. 1977. *Gangs in New York's Chinatown*. New York: Department of Asian Studies, City University of New York.

Suzuki, Bob H. 1977. "The Education and Socialization of Asian Americans: A Revisionist Analysis of the 'Model-Minority' Thesis." *Amerasia Journal*, 4:2:23–51.

Thomas, D. S., and Nishimoto, R. 1946. *The Spoilage: Japanese-American Evacuation and Resettlement During World War II*. Berkeley: University of California Press.

United States Bureau of the Census. 1963. United States Census of Populations: 1960. Subject Reports. Nonwhite Population by Race. Final Report PC(2)–1C. Washington, D.C.: United States Government Printing Office.

______. 1973. Census of the Population: 1970. Subject Reports. Japanese, Chinese and Filipinos in the United States. Final report PC(2)–1G. Washington, D.C.: United States Government Printing Office.

Urban Associates, Inc. 1974. *A Study of Selected Socio-Economic Characteristics of Ethnic Minorities Based on the 1970 Census*. Vol. 2: Asian Americans, Washington, D.C.: Office of Special Concerns, Department of Health, Education and Welfare (July).

Watanabe, Colin. 1973. "Self-Expression and the Asian American Experience." *Personnel and Guidance Journal*, 51 (Feb.):390–396.

Wolf, Margery. 1970. "Child Training and the Chinese Family." In *Family and Kinship in Chinese Society*, Maurice Freedman (Ed.). Stanford, CA.: Stanford University Press.

Wong, Aline K. 1974. "Women in China: Past and Present." In *Many Sisters: Women in Cross-Cultural Perspective*, Carolyn J. Matthiasson (Ed.). New York: Free Press.

Wong, Buck. 1971. "Need for Awareness: An Essay on Chinatown San Francisco." In *Roots: An Asian American Reader*, Amy Tachiki, Eddie Wong, and Franklin Odo (Eds.). Los Angeles: Continental Graphics.

Wong, Jade S. 1950. *Fifth Chinese Daughter*. New York: Harper Brothers.

Wu, Robin. 1977. "Front Page Chinatown: What the *** is Going on?" *Bridge*, 5 (Fall):4–7.

Young, Nancy F. 1972. "Socialization Patterns among the Chinese in Hawaii," *Amerasia*, 1(Feb.):31–51.

CHAPTER 12

Black Families

Paul C. Glick

ABSTRACT: Compared with the American average, Black families are more likely to have children present, to be one-parent households, to postpone marriage, to experience a "marriage squeeze," to separate or divorce, to have fewer intact marriages, and to be less likely to remarry after divorce. In addition, married Black women are more likely to be in the work force than married White women. As with other groups, birthrates vary by education: Poorly educated Black women have higher than average birth rates, and the more highly educated have lower than average birthrates. The rate of intermarriage is increasing and, compared with either all-Black or all-White marriages, such marriages are more likely to end in divorce.

Among the many well-recognized differences between Black and other families, some have been converging, some diverging, and others simply persist. These differences can be overemphasized, however, because all families tend to share in the periodic changes that occur in economic opportunities and in other aspects of the cultural environment, although the sharing is not always equal. During periods of economic expansion, Black families have tended to improve their well-being especially rapidly because a larger proportion of their adults were available

Author's Note: I wish to thank my colleagues Arthur J. Norton, James A. Weed, and Steve W. Rawlings for their helpful comments on this chapter.

to fill expanding vacancies. But during the last few decades, the pursuit of greater personal freedom has been on the increase, even if it results in the diminished economic well-being that is usually associated with marital dissolution.

This chapter will throw light on changes in the diversity of family life in the United States during the 1970s, with special reference to comparisons between the family patterns of the Black population and the population of all races combined. The presentation will confirm that "'the' Negro family is itself a fiction. Different family forms prevail at different class and income levels throughout our society" (Willie, 1970). The treatment is organized around three major demographic areas: family composition, marriage and divorce, and employment and income. . . .

FAMILY COMPOSITION

According to the traditional norm, families are formed through marriage, and those who marry remain married until one spouse dies. The extent to which current marital behavior differs from this norm will be examined in this section, along with some of the implications for the living arrangement of children [and] when children leave home and establish new families. . . .

Variety of Family Types

Most of the families in the United States are maintained by a married couple or by one parent and one or more of the parent's sons and/or daughters. Fully 86 percent of Black families in 1980 were of these two types, and the corresponding proportion for all families without regard to race was 93 percent [Table 12.1]. Thus, although the vast majority of families consist of one of these types, twice as large a proportion of Black families as other families (as defined by the Census Bureau) were not of these types (14 versus 7 percent). Many of the families of the latter type consist of grandparents providing homes for grandchildren whose parents live elsewhere or have died, or consist of such combinations as brothers and sisters living together apart from their parents.

One distinguishing feature of Black families is that they continue to be more likely than other families to include young children. By 1980, 62 percent of the Black families, as compared with 52 percent of the families of all races, included one or more sons and/or daughters under 18 in the home. The larger proportion of Black families with young chil-

TABLE 12.1 Families by Type, Race and Presence of Own Children Under 18 Years Old: United States, 1980 and 1970

Type of Family and Presence of Own Children under 18	1980		1970		Percent Change 1970 to 1980	
	All Races	Black	All Races	Black	All Races	Black
All families						
(thousands)	58,426	6,042	51,586	4,887	13.2	23.6
Percent	100.0	100.0	100.0	100.0	—	—
With own children	52.2	61.8	55.9	61.1	5.8	25.0
Not with own children	47.8	38.2	44.1	38.9	22.5	21.4
Married-couple families	82.5	55.5	86.7	68.0	7.6	0.9
With own children	42.0	31.2	49.5	40.9	−3.9	−5.9
Not with own children	40.5	24.3	37.2	27.1	22.9	11.1
Parent-child families	10.2	30.6	6.4	20.2	81.7	87.7
Mother and own children	9.2	28.9	5.7	18.7	82.4	91.6
Father and own children	1.0	1.7	0.7	1.5	76.5	39.7
Other families	7.3	13.9	6.9	11.8	20.5	44.9
Female householder	5.4	11.3	5.2	9.6	19.8	45.3
Male householder	1.9	2.6	1.7	2.2	22.5	43.1

SOURCES: U.S. Bureau of the Census, 1980a, 1980b, and unpublished Current Population Survey data.

dren reflects, among other things, the higher birth rate of Black women and the shorter joint survival of Black marriages after the children leave home. There was little change during the 1970s in the proportion of Black families with young children present because the substantial increase in one-parent families was nearly offset by a decrease in married-couple families with children.

In 1980, one-half of the Black families with children present were one-parent families (31 percent), and one-half were married-couple families (31 percent). At the same time, less than one-fifth of the families of all races with children were maintained by one parent. As far back as 1950, 9 percent of the Black families were one-parent families, but at that time only 4 percent of the families of all races were one-parent families. Therefore, this is one aspect of family life in which the gap between Black families and other families has persisted. . . .

Children Leaving Home

The departure of young adults from their parental home is generally a critical period for all persons involved and most often occurs in the early 20s. The proportion of Black persons 20 to 24 years of age who were still living with their parents (or had returned to their parental home) declined from 45 percent in 1940, near the end of the Depression, to 39 percent by 1960, after a couple of decades of more prosperous times. Nevertheless, by 1970, the direction had changed; at that time 42 percent were living with their parents. Although statistics are not available from the 1980 census on this subject, they are expected to show further increases in this proportion during the latter part of the 1970s because of the relatively high unemployment rates and divorce rates and because more young adults during recent years have been able to remain in their parental homes while they delay marriage and attend the growing number of community colleges.

Childbearing

Most of the young adults who leave their parental homes rather soon establish separate households at the time of marriage and before childbearing. Historically, Black families have had more children than other families as a whole, but there are some signs that the average number of children born to mothers in the two racial groups may be currently in a phase of convergence. This impression is based partly on answers to questions the Census Bureau asked in 1979 about how many children they had borne and how many more they expected to have. Among women 18 to 34 years of age regardless of marital status, Black women had already had an average number of children that was 32 percent above that for women of all races combined. However, the average number of "lifetime births expected" by Black women was only 8 percent higher than that for all women. Recent studies have shown that married women during the 1970s tended to overestimate the total number of children they will have.

Childlessness is another measure of fertility, which generally varies inversely with the average number of children per woman and which is often analyzed for women 45 to 49 years of age because almost all of them have ended their childbearing. Women of this age in 1960 had been at the height of childbearing during the Depression of the 1930s, and fully 28 percent of the Black women of this age had borne no children; for all races the figure was 18 percent. During the two following decades, these childlessness rates declined dramatically, so that by 1979 only 9 percent of the Black women and 7 percent of the women of all races 45 to 49 reported they had had no children. These women had been at the crest of childbearing during the baby boom period of the 1950s. When the women in 1979 were asked how many children they expected to have during their lifetime, 9 percent of the Black women 30 to 34 years of age reported they expected to have none; this level was actually lower than that—11 percent—for women of all races. Here, the trend for the two racial groups not only converged but crossed.

Poorly educated Black women tend to have especially high birth rates, and highly educated Black women tend to have especially low birth rates. For example, Black women age 35 to 44 in 1979 with less than 8 years of school had borne 4.6 children, on the average, as compared to 3.8 children for women of all races of this age and educational level. But corresponding rates for women with some college education were 2.4 children for Black women and 2.3 for all women. Still sharper contrasts at the upper educational level are available from the 1970 census, which revealed that Black women 35 to 39 years old with graduate school training had even lower fertility than women of all races of the same age and education—1.9 children versus 2.2 children ever born, on the average.

These differentials suggest, among other things, that Black women with little education may be more inclined than other women to have several children as a primary source of personal and family enjoyment, or that they tend to use less effective means of family limitation, or both. The differentials also suggest that Black women with advanced college education may tend to find it necessary to limit their family size especially severely in order to be competitive in the world of work. . . .

MARRIAGE AND DIVORCE

The most meaningful analysis of marital status depends strongly on classification by age. Yet attention cannot be given to the full distribution of marital status by age in the space to which the subject must be limited in this chapter. Consequently, the following treatment of each marital status category focuses on the age range that is most relevant.

Delay of Marriage

During the 1960s and 1970s, young adult Blacks had a consistent pattern of postponing marriage longer than their White counterparts [Table 12.2]. However, this difference became much more apparent by 1980 than it had been in either 1970 or 1960 among those 20 to 24 years of age, the period of life when the median ages for first marriage occur for both men and women. Contributing factors were the higher unem-

TABLE 12.2 Marital Status of the Noninstitutional Population in Selected Age Groups by Race and Sex: United States, 1980, 1970, and 1960

Marital Status, Age, and Race	Men			Women		
	1980	1970	1960[a]	1980	1970	1960[a]
Percent never married, 20 to 24 years old						
All races	69	56	53	50	36	29
Black	79	57	56	69	43	36
Percent separated or divorced 25 to 34 years old						
All races	9	5	4	14	8	6
Black	13	9	8	28	20	17
Percent in intact marriage, 35 to 44 years old						
All races	81	84	84	84	79	80
Black	61	69	71	49	58	62
Percent widowed, 55 years old and over						
All races	9	11	12	37	38	38
Black	14	16	16	45	44	47

[a]Races other than White for 1960.
SOURCES: U.S. Bureau of the Census, 1972, 1966, and unpublished Current Population Survey data.

ployment rates and more rapidly increasing college enrollment rates among Blacks.

A strictly demographic factor in the large amount of marriage postponement during the last two decades has been the "marriage squeeze." In the context that women are usually two or three years younger than men at marriage, the marriage squeeze developed as a consequence of the upward trend of births during the baby boom. Thus, a woman born in 1947 when the birth rate had risen was likely to expect to marry a man born in 1944 or 1945 when the birth rate was still low. The result, about 20 years later, was an excess of women in the primary ages for marriage, and this phenomenon continued for the length of time that the baby boom lasted. Therefore, by 1970, the number of Black men 20 to 26 years of age was only 82 percent of the number of women 18 to 24. The corresponding figure for persons of all races was 93 percent.

Thus, by 1970, for young adults regardless of race, there was a shortage of men in the primary marriageable ages for women. By 1980, these percentages had risen somewhat, to 89 percent for Blacks and 98 percent for all races. And by 1995, the corresponding figures are expected to rise to 96 percent and 108 percent, respectively, as the declining birth rates of the 1960s and early 1970s cause a reversal of the marriage squeeze phenomenon. Incidentally, the consistently lower figures for Blacks is a consequence of both a smaller proportion of boys among Blacks than others at birth and to the larger undercount of young Black men than of other young men in the census.

Separation and Divorce

An acceleration in marital disruption (separation and divorce), as well as in the delay of marriage, occurred during the 1970s among Blacks as well as others [Table 12.2]. The racial difference in the level of disrupted marriages is more marked among women than men, primarily because of the especially large minority of Black women who are reported as separated. To some extent this discrepancy may be the result of many never-married mothers incorrectly reporting themselves as separated. Another consideration is the greater tendency for persons in the lower economic strata to use separation as the "poor person's divorce." An alternate hypothesis is that Black women are more likely than other women to experience a period of married life before deciding to maintain themselves in an unmarried state.

Among adults of all races combined, currently divorced persons in 1980 were about 10 percent as numerous as persons in intact marriages. The corresponding proportion has doubled since 1970 for Blacks as well as those of other races. By 1980, there were 15 percent as many Black divorced men as Black married men and 26 percent as many Black divorced women as Black married women.

Divorced and income tend to be negatively correlated for men of all races 35 to 44 years old, according to 1970 census data for this age group, by which most marriages and divorces have occurred. But for Black men, the smallest proportion of divorces occurs among those in the middle income range, above which the proportion increases. An explanation for the deviation of Black men from the general pattern does not readily occur to this writer. However, the proportion of Black men in the upper income range where the anomaly occurs is relatively small.

Women college graduates with no graduate school training tend to have the most stable first marriages, regardless of race. Black women with an incomplete college education have the greatest likelihood of divorce; and those with graduate school education also have relatively high divorce probabilities, as do women of other races. Women with advanced college degrees, regardless of race, are probably the most likely to have career interests that compete with the desire to maintain a permanent marriage.

Intact Marriages

As first marriages have been delayed and marital disruption has become more frequent, the proportion of persons in the middle adult years who are in intact marriages has been declining. Again, both the general trend and the race differential were accelerated during the 1970s, as is evident from the data on persons age 35 to 54 shown in [Table 12.2]. During both the 1960s and the 1970s, the extent to which marital stability was affected by changes in the proportion widowed was very slight; widowhood continues to be far more prevalent among women than men above the mid-50s, partly because of lower death rates among women and higher remarriage rates among men, regardless of race.

As the income level of men increases, the proportion of men with intact first marriages tends to increase, among both Black men and men of other races, according to 1970 census data. Evidently for men there is a positive relation, on the average, between their degree of success in their field of work and in the continuation of their experience as a partner in an intact marriage, but this relationship is strongest at the lower end of the income distribution. This fact suggests that marital permanence for men depends less on being well-to-do than it does on not being poor.

The pattern for women is generally in the opposite direction: The more income women earn, the less likely they are to remain in their first marriage. Women with high incomes often find that the demands of their work interfere with their marital adjustment, and such a situation has a likelihood of being made worse if the wife earns more than her husband. . . .

Remarriage

The most recent information available from Census Bureau surveys on remarriage is that collected in June 1975. At that time 20 percent of the Black men and 19 percent of all Black women who had ever married were reported as remarried (Glick, 1980). The corresponding proportion of divorced persons who remarry is higher among Whites than among Blacks at each interval since divorce (Eckhardt et al., 1980). This apparent contradiction is a result of the different socioeconomic levels of Blacks and Whites on the average. There has been a historic tendency for Black couples to have lower average incomes than White couples, for their divorce rates to be relatively high, and yet for remarriage rates after divorce to be relatively low among men of low income.

Among divorced women, however, remarriage rates are higher for those with less than a full high school education than they are for those with more education, regardless of race. This generalization suggests that poorly educated women tend to remarry rather quickly because they have more difficulty in finding employment that would sustain them and their children, especially in view of the comparatively high fertility and dependency rates among women without a high school education.

Early marriage, regardless of race, is associated with twice as much likelihood of divorce and remarriage within three to five years after first marriage as marriage at more "preferred" or intermediate ages, according to 1970 census data. Early marriage refers to persons 14 to 17 years of age for women and 14 to 19 years for men. Intermediate ages refers to women 20 to 24 years and to men 25 to 29; these are the ages at which college graduates are most likely to marry. The 1975 study mentioned previously demonstrated that remarriage is more likely to be followed by redivorce among Black women age 35 to 44 than among other women of the same age. It also showed that Black women 35 to 44 with no children were more likely to become redivorced than those with children, especially those with preschool-age children; this result no doubt reflects the greater ease of childless women than mothers to be self-sustaining.

Intermarriage

A special tabulation of 1977 data from the Current Population Survey showed that there were 421,000 interracial married couples in the United States, or about one-third more than the number in 1970 (U.S. Bureau of the Census, 1980d). The reported number had approximately doubled during the 1960s; some of the increase may have resulted from more willingness to report accurately. The 125,000 Black/White couples in 1977 were close to twice the number in 1970: 65,000. Three-fourths (74 percent) of the Black/White couples in 1977, as compared to close to two-thirds (63 percent) in 1970, had a Black husband and a White wife. Altogether, the Black/White married couples in 1977 represented about 3.6 percent of all Black couples and 0.3 percent of all White couples. Thus, the number of interracial married couples has continued to grow, and the predominant proportion of Black/White couples that include a Black husband and a White wife is evidently increasing.

Interracial married couples have a greater probability of having a short marriage than married couples with the husband and wife of the same race, whether both are Black or both are White. Perhaps the best evidence is found in census data reported by Heer (1974) concerning first marriages contracted in the 1950s that were still intact in 1970. The results show that 90 percent of the couples with a White husband and wife, both in their first marriage, were still living together and that 78 percent of the couples with a Black husband and wife were also still together; however, smaller proportions—63 percent—of the couples with a Black husband and a White wife and only 47 percent of those with a White husband and a Black wife had continuing first marriages. Presumably the current proportion of couples with a Black husband and a White wife is larger than that for couples with a White husband and a Black wife, not only because more couples of the former type become married but also because the former type tend to have a longer duration of marriage than the latter type.

Unmarried couples are more likely than married couples to be interracial. Although the numbers involved are quite small, the 1975 survey mentioned previously shows that 2 percent of unmarried couples, but only about 0.5 percent of married couples, were combinations of a Black adult and a White adult of opposite sex (Glick and Spanier, 1980).

EMPLOYMENT AND INCOME

Working Wives and Mothers

Most of the Black husbands as well as husbands of other races are in the labor force, but the proportion of men in the labor force has been declining as the population has been aging and as more men choose to retire at an earlier age. Thus, 84 percent of the Black husbands were in the labor force in 1970, but the percentage decreased to 80 percent in 1979 (U.S. Bureau of the Census, 1973b; U.S. Bureau of Labor Statistics, 1981). The corresponding change for husbands of all races was from 86 percent to 81 percent. By contrast, the worker rate for wives rose sharply during the 1970s.

The labor force participation rate for Black wives as well as other wives rose by 9 percentage points between 1969 and 1979. However, at both dates the rate for Black wives was about 11 percentage points higher than that for wives of all races. Specifically, 51 percent of Black wives in 1969 and 60 percent in 1979 were in the labor force, as compared to 40 percent and 49 percent, respectively, for wives of all races. This growth in the proportion of wives in the labor market reflects many other social and economic changes, including the extensive increase in education and therefore the employability of young women and the expansion of employment opportunities for the performance of clerical and professional work.

Young wives with no children have continued to include a relatively high and increasing proportion in the labor force. Childless Black wives

16 to 34 years of age in 1970 had a worker rate of 64 percent, and by 1979 the rate had risen to 72 percent, a few percentage points below the rates for women of all races—68 percent and 82 percent, respectively. A more detailed analysis of the differences by race would show, among other related things, that the Black wives have higher unemployment rates and a somewhat lower average educational level than other wives; both of these factors must discourage some other women from even looking for work.

By contrast, Black wives under 35 years of age with one or more of their children under 18 in their home have had worker rates 16 percentages points higher than the corresponding rates for wives under 35 of all races in both 1970 and 1979. For Black wives the respective rates were 49 percent in 1970 rising to 65 percent in 1979, whereas for wives of other races the rates were 33 percent rising to 49 percent. These shared increases in the worker rates for young mothers are no doubt related to both the falling birth rate and the increasing proportion of children in the home who are of school age.

In 1979, more than half (57 percent) of the Black married couples had both the husband and wife in the labor force. This compares with 51 percent for all married couples. But between 1970 and 1979, the increase in this type of two-worker family was twice as large for Black couples as for all couples (up 11 percentage points versus 5 percentage points). . . .

Per Capita Income

This measure provides a basis for assessing the comparative income standing of the Black population independent of differences in family structure that change from one time to another. Recent information from the Current Population Survey shows that the average annual income per Black person in 1979 was $4,414, and that the average for persons of all races was $7,061; thus, per capita income for Blacks in 1979 was 63 percent of that for persons of all races. In 1970, per capita income for Blacks had compared somewhat less favorably, when it was 60 percent of that for persons of all races ($1,922 as compared to $3,183 in terms of 1970 dollars). . . .

DISCUSSION

This chapter represents the author's attempt to add to the growing number of "works on Black families that tend to view them from a positive rather than a negative perspective" (Wilkinson, 1978). From a balanced viewpoint, Black families are regarded as "an important subculture of American society, different in many ways from White families, but possessing a value system, patterns of behavior, and institutions which can be described, understood, and appreciated for their own strengths and characteristics" (Peters, 1978).

A strength, as well as a liability, that is prominent among Black families is "the centrality of children," to borrow an apt expression from Cazenave (1980). As [Table 12.1] demonstrated, a larger proportion of Black families than families of other races include young children among their members. Another distinguishing feature of Black families has been the large and continually growing proportion maintained by women. These prevailing Black family lifestyles have been interpreted, in part, as adaptations to the special circumstances in which many Black persons find themselves and, in part, as preferences for certain values that often differ from those of members of other races. Yet Black families vary widely in the personal and social characteristics of their members; moreover, Black family members tend to be concentrated somewhat more in selected parts of the range of these characteristics than family members of other races because of differing circumstances or matters of choice. . . .

REFERENCES

Cazenave, N. A. (1980). "Alternate Intimacy, Marriage, and Family Lifestyles among Low-Income Black Americans." *Alternative Lifestyles*, 3 (November): 425–444.

Eckhardt, K. W., W. R. Grady, and G. E. Hendershot (1980). "Expectations and Probabilities of Remarriage: Findings from the National Survey of Family Growth, Cycle III." Unpublished manuscript.

Glick, P. C. (1980). "Remarriage: Some Recent Changes and Variations." *Journal of Family Issues*, 1 (December): 455–478.

______ and G. B. Spanier (1980). "Married and Unmarried Cohabitation in the United States." *Journal of Marriage and the Family*, 42 (February): 19–30.

Heer, D. M. (1974). "The Prevalence of Black-White Marriage in the United States, 1960 and 1970," *Journal of Marriage and the Family*, 36 (May): 246–258.

Peters, M. F. (1978). "Black Families: Notes from the Guest Editor." *Journal of Marriage and the Family*, 40 (November): 655–658.

U.S. Bureau of the Census (1966). *Marital Status*. 1960 Census, II; 4E. Washington, D.C.: Government Printing Office.

______ (1970). "Income in 1969 of Families and Persons in the United States." Current Population Reports, Series P-60, No. 75. Washington, D.C.: Government Printing Office.

______ (1972). *Marital Status*. 1970 Census, II: 4C. Washington, D.C.: Government Printing Office.

______ (1973a). *Persons by Family Characteristics*. 1970 Census, II: 4B. Washington, D.C.: Government Printing Office.

——— (1973b). *Employment and Work Experience.*1970 Census, II: 6A. Washington, D.C.: Government Printing Office.

——— (1978). "Perspectives on American Husbands and Wives." Current Population Reports, Series P-23, No. 77. Washington, D.C.: Government Printing Office.

——— (1980a). "Population Profile of the United States: 1979." Current Population Reports, Series P-20, No. 350. Washington, D.C.: Government Printing Office.

——— (1980b). "Households and Families, by Type: March 1980." Current Population Reports, Series P-20, No. 357. Washington, D.C.: Government Printing Office.

——— (1980c). "Child-Support and Alimony." Current Population Reports, Series P-23, No. 106. Washington, D.C.: Government Printing Office.

——— (1980d). "Money Income and Poverty Status of Families and Persons in the United States: 1979," Current Population Reports, Series P-60, No. 125. Washington, D.C.: Government Printing Office.

——— (1980e). *Social Indicators III.* Washington, D.C.: Government Printing Office. U.S. Bureau of Labor Statistics (1981), "Marital and Family Characteristics of the Labor Force, March 1979." Special Labor Force Report 237. Washington, D.C.: Government Printing Office.

WILLIE, C. V. (1970). *The Family Life of Black People.* Columbus, OH: Charles E. Merrill.

WILKINSON, D. Y. (1978). "Toward a Positive Frame of Reference for Analysis of Black Families: A Selected Bibliography." *Journal of Marriage and the Family*, 40 (November): 707–708.

CHAPTER 13

Chicano Families

Alfredo Mirandé

ABSTRACT: Chicanos place a strong emphasis on the importance of the family (familism). Closely knit, relatives are frequently considered to be friends. In general, families tend to be patriarchical, with the father close to the younger children and more remote with the older ones. The mother is more family-centered, warm, and affectionate. The double standard persists, but families are now finding it more difficult to maintain control over their daughters.

Relevant terms for understanding this chapter are:

barrio: neighborhood, ghetto
Chicanita: a young female of Mexican descent
Chicano: American of Mexican descent
compadrazgo: a special relationship of obligations and privileges that characterize godparents and godchildren
la palomilla: the peer or friendship group
la raza: Chicano (literally, "the race")
macho: male-dominated, extreme masculinity, with an emphasis on strength, dominance, and freedom

[Studies by both supporters and detractors tend to agree] that the Chicano family is characterized by:

1. male dominance;
2. rigid sex-age grading so that the older order the younger, and the men order the women;

3. clearly established patterns of help and mutual aid among family members; and
4. a strong familistic orientation whereby individual needs are subordinated to collective needs.

The basic difference between the two views [of the Chicano family as developed by critics and supporters] then, is not to be found in their substantive characterization of the family, since there is much overlap between them, but in their interpretation and evaluation of these characteristics. While the familistic orientation of Chicanos is universally recognized, critics see it as undemocratic, un-American, and impeding individual achievement and advancement; supporters see it as a source of emotional and material support in a hostile and unrewarding world. These polar depictions of the family are important not so much for what they reveal about the family, but for what they reveal about those who study the family. . . .

The task at hand is to present a balanced and objective view that captures the reality of Chicano family life without exaggerating or distorting that reality. It is therefore important to note that the family system as it is depicted is an ideal type that may not correspond to any real family. Just as there is no one uniform Anglo-American family, there is no one Chicano family but a number of family types that vary according to region, recentness of migration to the United States, education, social class, age, and urban-rural locale. Given this internal diversity it is necessary to extrapolate key features found among Chicano families across various settings and situations. The traits attributed to the Chicano family are not true of all families, but they are more likely to characterize the Chicano than the Anglo family.

Probably the most significant characteristic of the Chicano family is its strong emphasis on familism. While the impact of the family may have been eroded somewhat by urbanization and acculturation, it is still a central institution for the individual. The family is a basic source of emotional support for the child as he develops close bonds not only with members of the immediate family but with grandparents, aunts and uncles, cousins and family friends. A study of young children, age seven to thirteen, in a Houston *barrio* concluded that "in the child's-eye-view the central feature is home, and the people at home" (Goodman and Beman, 1971:111). Significantly, in response to the question, "Who do you love?" none of the *barrio* children included anyone but relatives in their responses, whereas Anglo children and black children included many nonfamily members, and friends also played a prominent part in their listing of persons loved (Goodman and Beman, 1971:112). Grandparents are also important in the lives of children but they are likely to be seen as warm and affectionate rather than as authority figures. "Grandparents appear to be highly influential, as distinguished from being powerful" (Goodman and Beman, 1971:111). Similar to parents in the kibbutz, they are free of the responsibilities of parenthood and their relationships with grandchildren can be warm and nurturing (Talmon, 1961). In addition to being loved, however, grandparents are respected because they are considered to be older and wiser.

The familistic orientation of Chicanos is such that relatives are frequently included as friends. There is no sharp distinction made between relatives and friends as they are often one and the same. Not only are relatives included as friends, but friends are symbolically incorporated into the family. The institution of *compadrazgo* dates back to the early post-Conquest period in Mexico. This Spanish custom was apparently adopted by the Indians during the Colonial Period (1550–1650) as widespread epidemics led to massive native depopulation leaving many orphaned children (Gibson, 1966:142). Godparents thus originally functioned as parent substitutes. Over the centuries the original meaning of *compadrazgo* has been modified so that *compadres* have more of a social function that one as parent substitutes. Nonetheless, the custom remains intact. A recent study found that nearly all of the adult respondents reported at least one such relationship and, in many instances, two, three, or more (Goodman and Beman, 1971:111).

Both pejorative and positive accounts of the Chicano family see the male as the ultimate and unquestioned authority in the family. Such characterizations have focused on the formal aspects of Chicano culture, neglecting its more subtle and informal nuances. The father is formally accorded much deference and respect but he is not the all-powerful lord and master of the household, as has been suggested. There is, in fact, an implicit contradiction in the stereotypical view of the *macho* who comes and goes as he pleases and the view of him as the all-powerful authority and arbitrator in the family. The male may officially be the ultimate authority but he is frequently aloof or uninvolved in family matters. The father tends to be warm and affectionate when children are little, but as they enter puberty, relations between him and children become more tenuous (Rubel, 1966:66). The expectation of women, on the other hand, is one of almost total devotion to the family (Murillo, 1971:104). A woman should be warm, nurturing, and minister to the needs of her husband and children. Ministering mothers are respected, revered, and recognized as important figures, despite their alleged low status in the family. Indeed, for children, their importance appears to take precedence over the father. A study of Chicano children found that the father is seen as a somewhat distant authority figure, and is frequently slighted, especially by boys. "Few say they go to him with questions, either for information or for permission to do something" (Goodman and Beman, 1971:112). Significantly, few children want to be "like father when they grow up" or to have a job like his. This remoteness may result from his frequent absence from home. He may leave home before the children are awake and not return until late in the evening (Goodman and Beman, 1971:112). Mothers, however, play a critical part in the lives of children. They perform many domestic tasks such as preparing breakfast, fixing lunches, cooking dinner, doing dishes, and various other household chores. Mothers are also responsible for setting parameters on the children's behavior. They determine when one gets up or goes to bed and when one comes in from playing (Goodman and Beman, 1971:112). "She scolds, she sometimes slaps or spanks for disobeying small rules, and she stops sibling squabbles" (Goodman and Beman 1971:112). Thus, while the woman does not have the formal prestige or status of the man, she has great informal influence in the home.

The strong familistic orientation of the Chicano family has led some observers to conclude that it is an extended family system much like the traditional Chinese family system. While Chicanos are familistic, the Chicano family is not a functioning extended system identical to that of the Chinese. The father is formally head of the household but, as has been noted, much of his authority is more apparent than real. The concept that the oldest surviving male should be recognized as the patriarchal head of the household is also not found in Chicano culture. Grandparents are more important as sources of warmth and support than as authority figures. While patterns of mutual aid and support are clearly established, nuclear families should ideally function as relatively autonomous and independent units. One may choose to live near parents and other relatives, or perhaps even with them, out of economic necessity, but the norm is that the nuclear family remains autonomous and in a separate residence.

Although the mother has been depicted as a lowly and insignificant figure, she is extremely important in intrafamily relationships. Her relationships with children are characterized by warmth and affection. Whereas the father-son relationship is somewhat distant, the mother's relation with her daughter is more intimate. Early participation in the domestic realm produces identification with the mother and her maternal role. "Little girls learn early to assume responsibilities and tasks, especially those that are particularly maternal in character, such as taking care of smaller siblings" (Peñalosa, 1968:687). In addition, "the confinement of females within the home gives rise to a closely knit group of a mother and her daughters, a relationship which endures throughout the lifetime of the individuals" (Rubel, 1966:100). The same close environment gives rise to enduring relationships between sisters.

Although the mother-son relationship does not appear to be as strong as the mother-daughter relationship, it is nonetheless a close bond. During childhood the mother is more likely to be pampering and indulgent with her son than with her daughter. During adolescence especially, mothers are permissive with their sons. These socialization practices are indicative of a dualistic conception of appropriate behavior for males and females. The boy is a fledgling *macho* who must be allowed to venture out of the home so he may "test his wings" and establish a masculine identity. Peers contribute significantly to the process of socialization into manhood. He begins to hang out with other boys, or *la palomilla*, and peer relations may begin to rival family ties in importance. These associations are prominent for the man and are retained even after marriage.

Adolescent girls are much more restricted and sheltered than adolescent boys. Throughout her life, a female is prepared for her role as a virtuous mother of *la raza*:

> The girl has been brought up in such a manner that she represents herself as a paragon of virtue, a woman fit to mother the children of a respectable male of *la raza*. Early in her life she was made aware that she represented her household group fully as much as she represented herself, an individual. In all instances her claims to enjoyment were made secondary to the claim of propriety. In other words, hers was a road carefully planned from girlhood to womanhood within the tight restraint of family discipline [Rubel, 1966:77].

Premarital chastity is the culmination of feminine virtue. The norm of premarital virginity prevails, although its enforcement may prove more difficult today than in the past. Thus, the behavior and character of the contemporary Chicana, like that of her ancient forebears, is severely circumscribed by rigid role expectations which limit her activities to the domestic sphere. . . .

Many women, [however,] especially the younger generation, are challenging their traditional roles. In urban areas *Chicanitas* are venturing beyond the protective confines of the home and joining social clubs or gangs. Thus, the *palomilla* is no longer the exclusive domain of the male. "There are fewer and fewer women who are willing to accept the traditional role assigned to them according to traditional values. Chicanas are struggling for greater equality not only in the Anglo society but also in comparison to the Mexican American male" (Murillo, 1971:106). Traditional male-female relations are undergoing change, particularly among younger and better-educated urban Chicanos. Many Chicanas are advocating changes that incorporate positive cultural values and permit "more flexibility in carrying out a greater variety of activites that traditionally have been denied her" (Murillo, 1971:106).

The Chicano family has thus been subjected to many of the same forces of change as the Anglo-American family. It has had to adapt to changes resulting from increasing urbanization, industrialization, and acculturation. Middle-class urban Chicano families appear to be more equalitarian and to have discarded some of the more traditional features of the family. Similarly, as the influence of the Church declines, so has the importance of the institution of *compadrazgo*. These changes, however, are [forms of] Americanization, for many Chicanos are self-consciously seeking to modify sexual and familial roles without rejecting their cultural heritage or assimilating into mainstream Anglo-American society. . . .

REFERENCES

GIBSON, CHARLES (1966). Spain in America. New York: Harper and Row.

GOODMAN, MARY ELLEN, and ALMA BEMAN (1971). "Child's-eye-views of life in an urban barrio." Pp. 109–122 in Nathaniel N. Wagner and Marsha J. Haug (Eds.), Chicanos: Social and Psychological Perspectives. Saint Louis: C. V. Mosby.

MURILLO, NATHAN (1971). "The Mexican American family." Pp. 97–108 in Nathaniel N. Wagner and Marsha J. Haug (Eds.), Chicanos: Social and Psychological Perspectives. Saint Louis: C. V. Mosby.

PEÑALOSA, FERNANDO (1968). "Mexican family roles." Journal of Marriage and the Family 30 (November): 680–689.

RUBEL, ARTHUR J. (1966). Across the Tracks: Mexican Americans in a Texas City. Austin: University of Texas Press.

TALMON, YONINA (1961). "Aging in Israel, a planned society." American Journal of Sociology 67 (November): 284–295.

PART II

Pathways

IN THIS SECOND PART OF THE BOOK, the focus is on our experiences prior to marriage. In looking at the premarital world we examine major aspects of our society that are significant in preparing us for marrying and for forming a family of our own.

As I stressed in the introduction to Part I, no one creates his or her own world. (Those who do experience such a unique form of reality are usually labeled mentally ill—generally called schizophrenic—and put away in institutions.) Rather, we all enter a preformed social world, and a good part of our socialization centers around learning to get along in that world. Part of this learning involves specialized skills for making a living, but most of it centers on mastering the rules for getting along in social life—that is, learning the expected manners, ways of speech (conversational etiquette), and other basic social expectations of what is deemed appropriate in our society for presenting ourselves to others.

Significantly, a major part of this basic socialization (or we might look at it as a major consequence of this socialization) is learning to think "correctly;" that is, to adopt ways deemed appropriate for conceptualizing objects, people, and events. As we learn to apply the proper categories of thought (for example, "good," "bad," "safe," "dangerous," "desirable," "undesirable," and so on), we come to think and feel about things as we "should" (that is, as fully socialized members of the society are expected to).

If our socialization is successful, most of us will think in roughly the same terms (or along the same lines) when it comes to such varied aspects of social life as "good" and "bad" words and when they should and should not be used, war and peace, money, cars, taxes, education, and so on. In fact, such views tend to make us distinctly American.

But by no means does this imply that we all think alike or that we are all little robots. (There is, as one example among many, the matter of subcultural differences that I dealt with at length in the introduction to Section 3.) Rather, as we grow up in American society we inevitably learn to think "like an American." Specifics of our American-like thinking that are among the most easily recognizable include our ideas about independence; the value we place on individuality; the power of what we, in American fashion, refer to as the "almighty dollar"; and so on.

Yet beyond these more easily identifiable characteristics of American thought is a whole array of Americanized thinking that belongs in large part to the Western world. These basic ideas and related behavioral patterns within which we are immersed from birth and which constantly influence us include the ways in which we conceptualize and use space, time, money, work, property, leisure, sex, and the behaviors considered proper among people due to their designated relationships to one another.

This latter idea—that of proper relationships among people—becomes part and parcel of our basic orientation to life. This includes not only our ideas about what is right for bosses and employees, teachers and students, customers and clerks, but also—and especially significant for our purposes in this book—friends with friends, husbands with wives, and parents with children. Our basic ideas of what is right and wrong, of what one *ought* to be able to expect because of people's basic relationships to one another, are an essential aspect of our socialization into American society. Although the specifics of this socialization are ordinarily difficult for us to pinpoint as uniquely American, and they do have ample cultural antecedents elsewhere and are similar in many ways to basic expectations in other societies, our basic ideas of these fundamental areas of social life carry their own unique American "flavor."

As I mentioned in the introduction to Part I, most such ideas are so basic to our culture, are learned at such a young age, and are so consistently taught and reinforced that we seldom question them. In fact, they are so basic to our orientation to social life that not only do they ordinarily go questioned, they are also invisible to us: We simply assume that this is how people do and ought to experience life.

The chapters in this part of the book focus on some of those basic, taken-for-granted, and ordinarily unquestioned assumptions of male/female relationships. In this part, called "Pathways," we look at the social context that inexorably directs us toward marriage. As members of American society, we cannot escape these social influences, although they do take somewhat different forms or expressions among different social groups. These social influences shape our expectations of life—not only how we ought to act toward others, but also our fundamental assumptions about who we are and therefore how others ought to regard and act toward us. We might say that these assumptions of relationships become rooted into our social being, that they become a major part of what goes into making us social creatures.

There are four sections in Part II. In the first, Section 4, we focus on socialization into sex roles. To become a member of society is to learn one's sex role—to be able to carry out the behaviors (and thinking) associated with one's gender. On the basis of a biological characteristic we are given a social identifier that influences almost every aspect of our lives. This identification tag, in fact, forms our basic orientation to life, for the sex roles we learn as children become the major axis around which our activities in life revolve. Not incidentally, this includes the roles we play in marriage and family life.

In Section 5 we look at how this early (and ongoing) learning of sex roles is played out in romantic involvements. The emphasis here is love and its different meanings to different people, including how people "know" when they are "in love."

In Section 6 we place the emphasis on dating, looking primarily at dating among college students. The chapters in the seventh and concluding section deal with alternatives to marriage. In these last two sections the focus remains on sex roles, for whether the situation is dating, the world of singles in general, or unmarrieds living together, basic sex roles are vital to those relationships.

Whether desired or undesired—and even though individuals feel they have freed themselves from them—the presence of basic sex roles continues to be felt. In spite of many preferences to the contrary, as these chapters show, traditional sex roles remain an essential part of intimate relationships.

SECTION 4

Sex Roles

In this section we focus on sex roles, perhaps the single major factor that determines what the world means to us—what we think about things (including ourselves), what we see when we look at others, as well as what we feel and how we act in the presence of others.

Social scientists have studied many characteristics of social life that are important for determining how people look at the world and how they interact with one another. They have examined such factors as social class (education, occupation, and income), religion, race, age, marital status, and number of children in one's family. Although social scientists disagree concerning the relative importance of such social characteristics and how they work to affect our lives—and there is room for healthy debate in this area—certainly no single factor works by itself, but only in combination with others.

The factor that in *every* society cuts across *all* others is that of masculinity or femininity. This characteristic that sociologists call sex role is a *master trait*: No matter what else one is, one is always that *plus* a male or a female. One might be rich, for example, but one is always seen as a rich man or a rich woman. One might be a priest or doctor, but one is reacted to as a male or female priest or a male or female physician. One might be old or young, but one is perceived as an old or young man or woman. This social status of masculinity or femininity cuts across all social class, religious, age, racial, cultural, and occupational lines.

In talking about this vastly important watershed identifier, we are not referring to whether an individual has the anatomical characteristics of a male or whether biology has imparted the physical endowment of a female. While the physiological base underlies the various social distinctions people make, we are talking about *sex role*, that is, what it *means* in one's society to be male or female. As John Gagnon and Bruce Henderson emphasize in the first chapter in this section, what is important are the expectations of masculinity or femininity that prevail in one's group and in one's society, for it is these expectations that largely shape what a person becomes. And it is especially significant, as Ann Oakley stresses in Chapter 15, that it is through the socialization process in childhood that boys and girls learn that males are powerful and woman are to play a support role to them.

At birth we receive the genitalia of one gender or another. Although the role of these biological characteristics in determining what we become is at present only inadequately and partially understood, the prevailing view in sociology is that it is small. It functions in some way, but it is overridden by cultural learning. Particular ideas of what a male or female *ought* to be like dominate in each society, and a good part of each person's socialization is getting him or her to match those idealized images. Because these ideas, images, and ideals differ among societies and cultures, people in different societies and cultures both learn different concepts and end up exhibiting different behaviors. In some societies the idealized imagery stand in sharp contrast to one another, and their sex–role behaviors are similarly highly contrastive—while other societies are so similarly oriented that in going from one society to another one perceives little difference in either their sex–role expectations or behaviors.

Our sex role pervades our interactions. In some situations, such as dating, our sex is highly relevant to the interaction. In most situations in life, however, our sex is probably irrelevant to what we are doing, as, for example, being a student, a mechanic, or a checkout clerk in a supermarket. Yet others react to us as a student, mechanic, or male or female checkout clerk, and we ourselves fulfill such specific roles within the broader context of our sex roles. In short, we never cease being masculine or feminine even when we are doing something that, in and of itself, is neither masculine nor feminine.

Our sex role is far from limited to external behaviors. It penetrates our very being. This definition of male or female that is so proudly proclaimed by our parents at our births, and then is so carefully constructed during our formative years, becomes the essential ingredient by which we define ourselves. No matter what we may be doing or what may happen to us, we know that above all else we are male or female.

Although the origin of our masculinity or femininity was originally external to us, we internalize the social expectations of our group. They become an essential part of our internal world of meaning. They become that standard by which we consciously, subconsciously, and unconsciously judge our own attitudes and behaviors. To our very core, we become male or female sexual beings.

Each child, then, is given a sex role based on gender, one that totally divides males and females from one another. As we are assigned characteristics, we find ourselves on one side or the other of this demarcation. A stringent social division forces us into two separate worlds. This sexual division, as Clayton Barbeau stresses in Chapter 16, leads to difficulties between men and women, to basic antagonisms that bode ill for marriage.

Several major purposes underlie such a stringent division of people into watershed roles, two of which I shall comment on. The first is to assure that each of us will identify with "our own kind." That is, we all are taught to take a particular stance toward the world—one that matches the basic perspective shared by our own sexual grouping. This perspective takes on its reality by being sharply opposed to that held by "the other group," members of the opposite sex.

This "defining in" and "defining out" provided by sex-role socialization underlies a good part of the basic structure of society. Through our sex-role socialization each of us is primed to take his or her "proper" place in society, vis-à-vis members of the opposite sex. It is this fundamental reality that feminists have grasped so clearly and against which they have aligned themselves.

The second major purpose of sex-role socialization is distinctly related to the first. It is preparation for the marital role. As we learn our basic sexuality, we are learning how to react "appropriately" toward our future husband or wife. Thousands of future encounters in marriage will be but a replay of this basic learning. Our script becomes locked into us, and although there is room for variation in the personal playing out of the script, play it we do—within the basic framework of the sexuality we have learned so thoroughly.

In applying these ideas it would be constructive for you to think about the various ways that you learned your sex role. What major factors were brought into play in your life to shape your perceptions of how a man or a woman "really" is? What events in your life were significant in channeling your behavior along the lines generally laid down by your culture? How have you felt the winds of change affecting traditional sex-role expectations? What conflicts have you experienced? What steps do you think you can take to try to overcome sex-role stereotyping in order to make certain that you and your husband or wife relate together on a more intimate, individual, meaningful, and creative level? Do you think it is possible to remove sex roles? If so, how? And, if possible, is it desirable? Desirable or undesirable from what perspective or point of view?

CHAPTER 14

The Social Psychology of Sexual Development

John Gagnon / Bruce Henderson

ABSTRACT: Anatomy does *not* equal destiny. Rather, at birth males and females are assigned a sexual identity and sorted into separate social groups. What we become as sexual beings is therefore the result of this sorting process, not our biology. A good part of this sorting is verbal, the application of labels to define behavior as appropriate or inappropriate to our assigned sexual identity. We also learn sexual scripts, the organization (by ideas, words, and gestures) of our behavior, by which we define—and then respond to—a situation as either sexual or nonsexual.

The largely social-psychological approach to the explanation of how human sexuality develops is supported by a growing body of knowledge which suggests that:

1. Quite apart from the anatomical and hormonal equipment with which we are born, our psychological gender identity—whether we consider ourselves man or woman, boy or girl—is acquired separately. . . . [O]ur gender identity can be of one sex even though our sexual organs may be of the other. In short, the old formula that A = D—anatomy equals destiny—is not supported by recent evidence.

2. We become sexual not as the outcome of an inborn biological plan or drive but from a complex body of learned impressions. These experiences create in each of us culturally defined sexual commit-

ments—what we think of as being sexual, what turns us off or on, even the belief that we are horny because we are sexually deprived.

3. As a result, the physiological signs of the sexual, such as arousal and orgasm, are triggered not by biologically determined sexual needs but largely by responses to learned symbols and meanings. Even the physical sexual acts that we perform are possible only because they are part of social scripts that permit and set the stage for them.

4. Psychosexual development is not, as has been widely thought, the history of a "sex drive" being repressed or molded. Instead, it is the creation of a world of meanings and activities most of which are learned in nonsexual circumstances. We assemble our sexuality beginning with gender identity, and we build upon the activities that we come to think of as fitting to ourselves. Our belief in what is correct and proper results more from our social class, religion, style of family life, and concepts of masculinity and femininity than from the specifically sexual things that we learn.

GENDER

Traditional views of psychosexual development have translated human anatomical arrangements into socio-cultural commands. If we are born with a penis we must feel and act like a boy, if with a vagina we must feel and act like a girl. By these equations, an infant with a penis means to parents that the child must turn into whatever is thought to be a normal boy, and ultimately a man, in a given society. A similar process must occur to a baby having a vagina; this organ equals girl and woman.

As a result, parents begin to create a child with a specific gender identity ("I am a boy or a girl") and gender-role performances ("I should play with a football or dolls, have a chemistry set or stove")—and ultimately create an adult with specific kinds of sexual orientations that are considered to be normal.

The doctor looks at the newborn infant's external sexual organs and tells the parents "It's a boy," or "It's a girl." From this moment, limits are set upon the child's course of development by everyone who comes in contact with "him" or "her." This original label releases a particular program of treatment which seems to be the basis for our ultimate gender identity. The power of this social response to shape one's identity has been demonstrated in research on children who, for a variety of reasons, are born with ambiguous external genitalia and who are socially identified as being of the sex opposite to their genetic make-up. In many such cases, genetic males have been reared as social females, and genetic females as social males. The work of many researchers in the field of gender identity suggests that the social-psychological gender that emerges in these situations is usually final. When the error is discovered (usually at puberty) the best course of action in most cases is to change the biological characteristics (through surgery and hormonal treatments) to conform to the psychological gender identity.

The clear conclusion is that there must be factors other than the biological that are responsible for one's gender identity. Exactly what those factors are is still not completely known. But they surely involve symbols and influences that, taken together, make us think of ourselves in terms of what our society believes to be a man or woman, boy or girl. There may be potential biological influences; hormonal effects prior to birth may make us lean toward some degree of gender identification. However, the major forces are social.

Permanent Consequences

The decision whether to rear a child as male or female is probably the most significant labeling experience that the youngster will receive. At that point, the separate cultural combinations that are related to the rearing of male or female children are released.

Many of these inputs of gender-forming information to the child occur without intent on the part of the parent. Nonetheless, the parents' belief that their infant is either male or female has permanent consequences for the child. The vigor of play, the frequency of mother-child as opposed to father-child interaction, and the tolerance of aggression in the male but not the female infant and child all contribute to the development of the self, defined as masculine or feminine. During the years after the child learns to talk, the build-up of gender identity continues.

Moreover, the social forces behind the formation of one's sense of gender are basic to other aspects of human sexuality.

BECOMING SEXUAL

Rarely do we shift our attention from the sexual organs themselves to the meanings that are attached to them. In fact, the mind can be said to be our most erogenous zone—most sensitive to sexual stimulation. We are not born sexual, nor do we become sexual all at once at puberty. Rather, we become "sexual"—that is, have an awareness of and are able to respond to stimuli conventionally deemed erotic—by means of a long and involved process. The very experience of sexual excitement, often considered to originate from mysterious hidden sources, is the result of an educational process. Sexuality is learned and, in various ways, fitted into particular moments of life.

To understand how one becomes sexual, we must start with the child. The observer of what is termed "children's sexual behavior" frequently assumes that the child has the same set of motives that accompanies adult sexual behavior. Nevertheless children cannot be sexual in the same way as adults. Children lack the language, the symbols, the complex set of meanings that give a physical act the psychological significance that the same act has for older persons.

The infant who fondles his or her genitalia cannot be sexual in the same sense as the adult who masturbates, but experiences instead a general pleasurable sensation. Only through maturing and learning the adult labels for this experience can the child come to masturbate in the adult sense of the word. Adult masturbation is complex rather than simple, requiring the close coordination of physical, psychological, and social resources.

Ability to Relate

In infancy, prior to the acquiring of language, experiences occur that will influence the development of sexuality. In the interactions that happen during child care, there take place (1) much of the preparation for verbal skills that will bind the child to the social world; (2) some experiences—perhaps only sensations—that will help bring about a sense of the body and its capacity for pleasure and comfort; and (3) those experiences that will influence the child's ability to relate to other bodies.

As Freud suggested in one of his most convincing contributions, to experience pleasure and comfort, even on the most primitive levels, is to create the unavoidable experience of a denial of pleasure and of discomfort. To experience attachment, the beginnings of love and identification, is also to create the inevitability of separation, the experience of frustration, anger, and even rage. In this relationship, which gives rise to guilt and anxiety, the groundwork for the potential complexity of the sexual is laid.

The important word for such experiences is "potentiation"—they make us potentially able to respond to the new experiences that will ultimately be part of adult sexuality.

Structure of Needs

It is after infancy, when the child begins to acquire language, that one can begin to recognize the processes of awareness and verbal understanding that go beyond a world of unnamed gestures. During this period the role of language in locating and creating meaning begins to emerge. And in translating and organizing experience into names, and ultimately scripts, children begin to make their plans for dealing with the world.

Through this system of transforming external labels into internal capacities for naming, sexual activities become more precisely defined as such. They are then linked to a structure of socio-cultural expectations and needs that define what we regard as sexual.

With the beginning of adolescence—and the increasing acknowledgment by the surrounding social world of an individual's sexual potential—many new factors come into play. As a result, adolescence may represent more of a break with than a continuing of previous "sexual experience." Although hormonal shifts in the body occur, they find their real meaning in the way in which a society greets the new adolescent. In the United States, it is with the arrival of adolescence that one is first given the status of a sexual being. This provides youngsters with ways of interpreting their new internal experiences, as well as the new physical profile that they present to the world around them.

The early years around puberty are of major significance in the development of a sexual element in the character structure. Only a few years earlier, kissing was seen by most boys as sissified; for most girls it was asexual. But during adolescent dating, the same physical act is defined as sexually important and is accompanied by physical excitement. There has been no change in the physical act, only in the meaning attached to it.

RESPONDING SEXUALLY

Where do the meanings come from that touch off sexual response?

Human sexual activities become possible only because they are, figuratively speaking, written into our social scripts. Those are mental programs or stories through which we view a given stage of life, take part in it, and react to it. Scripts are the outcome of a complex psychosocial process of development, and change as we move through the life cycle.

Suitable Script

The term "script" can be used to describe the mental organization and motivation of virtually all human behavior, since in fact very little happens that can be called totally spontaneous. Ironically, the current vogue of organizing "encounter groups" to bring about "spontaneous" behavior can be defined as learning the appropriate script for spontaneous behavior. Indeed, the widely accepted theory of "internal rehearsal"—gearing up our responses to events before actually responding—suggests just such scripting of all but the most routine behavior.

In the arena of sex, if an actor does not possess the proper elements of a script that defines a situation as potentially sexual, that makes other persons potentially erotic, and that plots the appropriate behavior, nothing sexual will happen. One can think of many situations in which all of the physical ingredients of a sexual event are present, but that remain nonsexual. Therefore, even if one combines such elements as desire, privacy, and a physically attractive person of the appropriate sex, the chances of something sexual happening will normally be exceedingly small—until either one or both of the persons organize these factors into a suitable script.

For instance, two office workers, male and female, who have long been unspokenly attracted to each other, find themselves working alone together after hours. Here are desire, privacy, and physical attraction. Still, the two are hardly apt to take to the office couch until one or the other confesses his or her feelings, establishes a sense of personal relationship, and persuasively justifies further action.

External and Internal

The sexual script has two key dimensions. One deals with the external, that which is outside us, which relates us to other persons. This part of the script organizes shared ideas that allow two or more actors to take part in a complex act involving mutual dependence. The external includes all of those words and gestures that are understood by both. Saying the right things, petting in an effective sequence, removing the clothing deftly—these and other conventional styles are elements of what our culture agrees is sexual.

The second dimension of the sexual script has to do with the internal, that which is inside us, the motivating elements that produce arousal. A vast number of physiological events are reported to the central nervous system, but we are aware of only a small proportion in any single moment. These are the ones heavy with meaning; they are the internal counterparts of external "meanings" of experience. Because of the meaning attached to certain outside stimuli, biological reactions get translated into significant psychological experiences. It is through scripting that psychological and bodily activities are organized in such a way as to release internal biological states.

Thus the script that we possess for sexuality is the go-between for our internal processes—this is what is inside of me and this is what it means—and the external world of persons and situations—this is who I am with, this is our relationship, and this is what it means. As a result, we come to identify our rapid heartbeat as evidence of physical attraction, penile erection or vaginal lubrication as a sign of sexual excitement; and we come to have sexual thoughts associated with these events rather than think about the weather.

At the same time we define other persons as appropriate sexual partners (by age, gender, attractiveness, social status). We also have a set of sexual activities that we think are morally correct and technically proper; and we have motives that we think are right for these activities with these persons in given situations. When we are adults we lose our awareness of how problematic all of this behavior was when we were learning it, and how little of it was clearly "sexual" to us at the time.

Society still has much to learn about the processes of psychosexual development and the ways in which what humans do sexually as adults is influenced and shaped. What is increasingly evident is that adult sexual experience is in no way programmed either by a biological plan or by only the earliest experiences of childhood as Freud argued. The developmental process does not have a fixed sexual outcome, and adults are not merely the completed and unchanging product of that process.

The important dimensions of human sexuality—the Who, What, When, Where, and Why—are assembled in the developmental process, but not completed by it, since most of these elements of our sexual scripts are extremely changeable throughout our entire life cycle.

CHAPTER 15

Childhood Lessons

Ann Oakley

ABSTRACT: At birth each of us is assigned a gender identity, and on the basis of that identity people treat us one way or another. That treatment is the basis for our internalizing a gender identity. The cognitive-developmental, social-learning, and psychoanalytic theories of gender development assume that identification with the same-sexed parent is essential to this process. Essential to our gender identity is the lesson that males are powerful, females are not. This childhood lesson is buttressed by children's parents, toys, home, teachers, schoolbooks, fairy tales, and television programs. This division into power and support roles is entirely arbitrary.

> DOCTOR: Come on junior. Only a lady could cause so much trouble. Come on, little one [baby is delivered].
> MOTHER: A girl.
> DOCTOR: Well, it's got the right plumbing.
> MOTHER: Oh, I'm sorry, darling.
> FATHER (laughs)
> DOCTOR: What are you sorry about?
> MOTHER: He wanted a boy.
>
> —Macfarlane (1977, p. 63)

Conversations of this kind set the scene for a lifetime's lesson. Gender is in most situations the most salient social fact about an individual, both because of its presumed relationship to eroticism and because in the culture of capitalist societies social differences between females and males are a basic structural theme.

Gender is assigned at birth when parents and medical staff view a baby's external genitals. They bring to this occasion all their own preconceptions about the social content and psychic meaning of boyhood/girlhood and manhood/womanhood, matching their categorization of the newborn's genitals with this determination of gender. It is therefore long before she reaches adulthood that a female experiences the full extent of her cultural definition as a secondary feminine being. . . .

Let us look at some of those factors known to be responsible for the development of gender identity. Few parents, in the first place, are indifferent to the sex of their child. In my own study of London women having their first babies in 1975–76, three-quarters said in pregnancy they had a definite sex preference and many of those who said they 'didn't mind' added after the child was born that they had minded, but hadn't wanted to voice a preference for fear of being disappointed, or because to do so is regarded superstitiously as bringing bad luck. [Table 15.1] shows how many women wanted boys and girls and what their reactions were: 93 per cent of those who had boys were pleased; 44 per cent who had daughters were not (as in the delivery room scene above). Whatever treatment girls receive in childhood to point them in the direction of femininity, it is clear that they are more likely to start off as a disappointment to their parents. Dana Breen (1975) found more cases of postnatal depression occurring among mothers of girls than mothers of boys. . . .

Sex preferences are conscious; gender-differentiated treatment of children often is not. Lake (1975) gave five young mothers Beth, a six-month old in a pink frilly dress for a period of observed interaction; five others were given Adam, a six-month old in blue overalls. Compared to Adam Beth was smiled at more, offered a doll to play with more often and described as "sweet" with a "soft cry." Adam and Beth were the same child.

TABLE 15.1 Sex Preferences and Reactions

Wanted girl	22%
Wanted boy	54%
Didn't mind	25%
Had girl: pleased	56%
Had boy: pleased	93%
Had girl: disappointed	44%
Had boy: disappointed	7%

Sources: Oakley (1979) p. 118.

CONCEIVING GENDER

[Still] . . . the question is how do women come to think of themselves as feminine people?

Money and Ehrhardt (1972) have suggested that a relevant analogy for the development of gender identity is that of bilingualism. A child growing up in a bilingual environment is presented with two languages that require two different sets of behavioural responses. So with gender: there are two sets of stimuli to be programmed by the brain into two different complexes of behaviour. The child's task is to identify with one and reject the other; the parents' conscious or unconscious duty is to provide the means whereby little girls identify with the feminine model and little boys with the masculine one.

"Identification" is the key concept. Most theories of gender-identity development reserve an important place for it. Because it implies the idea of a 'model' with whom identification can take place, most theories also stress the importance of parents as the primary teachers of gender. The three main theories are the cognitive-developmental, the social learning and the psychoanalytic.

The first of these builds on the work of Piaget (1952) and says that gender is based on genital sex and so is a physical property of people that has to be learnt in the same way as other unchanging physical properties. Children below the age of 4 or 5 years cannot appreciate the unchangeable character of physical objects: cats can become dogs at will, water poured into different-sized glasses has changed its volume; girls can become boys. Thus a little girl first of all develops the idea that she is a girl and later (by the age 5 or 6) appreciates that gender is invariant, that everyone has a gender and that gender is primarily a question of physical sex differences. Once the idea of a stable feminine gender identity is developed, she begins actively to prefer feminine activities and objects. The thinking is: I am a girl; therefore I like girl things; therefore doing girl things is rewarding (Kohlberg, 1967; Kohlberg and Ullian, 1974).

The second theory, that of social learning, contends that the development of gender identity involves a learning process that is essentially the same as other learning processes. A little girl observes her parents performing feminine and masculine roles, but when she imitates the various behaviours she sees, she is only rewarded for those considered appropriate to her gender. Through such differential reinforcement, feminine behaviours come to be positively evaluated and masculine ones rejected: I want rewards; I am rewarded for doing girl things; therefore I want to be (am) a girl. The result is a generalized tendency to imitate all same-gendered "models" (Mischel, 1967, 1970).

Thirdly, we have the psychoanalytic view of gender-identity development. . . . In this, awareness of genital difference comes first and paves the way for an identification with the parent who has a similar set of genitals. The formula runs: I do not have a penis; therefore I am a girl. . . . Because women rear children, the love of both girls and boys is originally centred on the mother. This, combined with an early unawareness in small children of the genital difference, means that at first the psychological development of females and males is the same. But when the girl discovers that she has no penis she also recognizes that her mother shares the same fate and blames her for her disadvantaged condition. This leads to a rejection of the mother as a love object; the girl turns to her father instead, a move that lays the foundation for her adult sexual attraction to males and her desire to bear male children. When she realizes the futility of seeing her father as a love object and its threat to her mother's attitude towards her, she is again inclined to a maternal identification. The discovery of the missing penis is thus the event that, in a complex series of stages, determines the feminine character with its three special qualities of masochism (a permanent sense of being castrated), passivity (the reluctant acceptance of the clitoris as an inadequate analogue of the penis) and narcissism (women's overvaluation of their superficial physical charms as compensation for their inferior genital equipment).

All three theories—the cognitive-developmental, the social-learning and the psychoanalytic—take the actual processes that are involved in the emergence of adult femininity and masculinity as in need of explanation. All assume that some identification with the same-sexed parent has to take place and is the main precursor of the desire to be seen as feminine or masculine. This "motivational consequence" is not only a necessary element in the continuing gender socialization of children ("self-socialization"), but is, of course, an absolutely central means for the cultural transmission of gender concepts from one generation to another. Lessons learnt in childhood become the lessons that parents want their own children to learn. . . .

PENIS AND OTHER ENVIES

It is significant that feminist descriptions of the imprisonment of women in a feminine mould blame "society" in general for their captivity. Particular individuals are not usually identified as the teachers of femininity; it is the wide range of cultural pressures all acting in the same direction—the "overdetermination" of gender—that is implicated. In Simone de Beauvoir's words,

> One is not born, but rather becomes, a woman. No biological, psychological, or economic fate determines the figure that the human female presents in society; it is *civilisation as a whole* that produces this creature, intermediate between male and eunuch, which is described as feminine. [De Beauvoir, 1960, p. 8; italics added]

"Civilization" is not feminine; it is "a man's world." Of all the lessons girls learn, this is the most important one. Freud, from his enviable position of masculine hegemony, called it penis envy, but it is not the penis that women want. Clara Thompson, one of the small band of female analysts who challenged Freud's thinking, wrote

> one can say the term penis envy is a symbolic representation of the attitude of women in this culture . . . the penis is the sign of the person in power in one particular competitive set-up in this culture, that between man and woman. The attitude of the woman in this situation is not qualitatively different from that found in any minority group in a competitive culture. So, the attitude called penis envy is similar to the attitude of any underprivileged group toward those in power. . . . [Thompson, 1974, pp. 53–4]

Women envy men their power. Small children learn effortlessly about masculine power within the asymmetrical nuclear family. Father leaves the house each day as the family's representitive in the public world and returns with proof (money) of the valuation of his labour; his status in the household and in society is clearly different from that of mother. But in fact, and paradoxically, dominance and nurturance are the two adult qualities that most attract children to identify with parents (Bandura and Huston, 1961; Hetherington, 1965; Hetherington and Frankie, 1967). Such an inherent contradiction throws light on many of the difficulties men and women have in adjusting their identities to fit the standard gender formulae.

When Florence Nightingale was born, she was the second daughter, intended to be a son, of ill-matched parents. Fanny Nightingale was six years older than her husband, a dedicated hostess married to an indolent and charming dilettante. Florence's biographer, Cecil Woodham-Smith, comments:

> She did not attach herself to her mother. The companion of her childhood was W.E.N. [as her father was known]. . . .
>
> W.E.N. was a man to enchant a child. He loved the curious and the odd, and he loved jokes; he had a mind stored with information and the leisure to impart it. He had great patience, and he was never patronising. Partly as a result of marrying Fanny, partly by temperament, he was a lonely man, and it was with intense pleasure he discovered intellectual companionship in his daughters. Both were quick; both were unusually responsive; both learned easily, but the more intelligent, just as she was the prettier, was Flo. [Woodham-Smith, 1952 pp. 7–8]

He educated both Florence and her elder sister Parthenope (Parthe) himself, teaching them Greek, Latin, German, French, Italian, history and philosophy. Parthe rebelled and joined her mother in domestic activities. Florence and her father "were deeply in sympathy. Both had the same regard for accuracy, the same cast of mind at once humorous and gloomy, the same passion for abstract speculation." Affection for her father and resentment of her mother (and her sister) were the dominating passions of her life.

Florence found the life of a Victorian lady boring, debilitating and depressing; her two havens were her father, who had some understanding of his daughter's need to find an outlet for her energy, and her father's sister, with whom she conspired to learn mathematics "instead of doing worsted work and practising quadrilles." Her difficulties were multiplied by the fact that she was evidently a success at the feminine role: "very gay. . . . Her demure exterior concealed wit. She danced beautifully. . . ." For this success she reproached herself: "All I do is done to win admiration" she wrote in a private note. When she was 16, Florence received her first call from God. "On February 7, 1837, God spoke to me and called me to His service." The voice reappeared three more times: in 1853, just before she took up her first post at the Hospital for Poor Gentlewomen in Harley Street; before the Crimean War in 1854; and after the death of her friend and "Master," Lord Sidney Herbert in 1861. Seven years after the first call, and after an intense inner struggle, Florence became certain that her vocation was to nurse the sick. It took nine more years to convince her family that this was what she should be allowed to do. Her mother was "terrified" and "angry," her sister "hysterical." Her father was disappointed that his education of Florence had led to this unsuitable wilfulness, but he did eventually grant her an allowance of £500 a year, and later bought her a house. In his last years, they were completely reconciled and had "long talks on metaphysics" together.

Such closeness between father and daughter allows the model of a masculine life-style to filter through the barrier of feminine socialization pressures. A study of women enrolled in the Harvard Business school in the mid-1960s picked up this theme in the childhood histories of "managerial" women. Most were first children, and "All had extremely close relationships with their fathers and had been involved in an unusually wide range of traditionally masculine activities in the company of their fathers, beginning when they were very young" (Hennig and Jardim, 1978, p. 99). While the *absence* of a father appears to endanger the learning of masculinity in boys (Tiller, 1967), his presence would therefore seem to encourage androgynous development in girls.

The role played by fathers as powerful and affectionate representatives of non-domestic culture can, of course, be taken by mothers as well. Daughters of working mothers have less rigid conceptions of gender roles than daughters of "non-working" mothers (Morantz and Mansfield, 1977; Hansson *et al.*, 1977). They tend to have less "feminine" identities, stressing such masculine qualities as independence and self-reliance (Hoffman and Nye, 1974).

In a very different society, that of the !Kung bush people of the Kalahari desert, the same general importance of women's socially valued productivity is seen. Among the !Kung, women's agricultural work is crucial to everyone's physical survival. Women have a great deal of autonomy and influence over the economic resources of the community as well as its ceremonial and power relations:

> A common sight in the late afternoon is clusters of children standing on the edge of camp, scanning the bush with shaded eyes to see if the returning women are visible. When the slow-moving file of women is finally discerned in the distance, the children leap and exclaim. As the women draw closer, the children speculate as to which figure is whose mother and what the women are carrying in their karosses. [Draper, 1975, p. 82]

Women's work is part of their childhood games, of female socialization:

> We . . . played at being hunters and we went out tracking animals and when we saw one we struck it with our make-believe arrows. We took some leaves and hung them over a stick and pretended it was meat. Then we carried it back to our village. When we got back, we stayed there and ate the meat and then the meat was gone. We went out again, found another animal and killed it. We again threw leaves over a stick, put other leaves in our karosses, and brought it back. We played at living in the bush like that. [Interview with !Kung woman, *Spare Rib*, October 1975, pp. 15–16]

In a society where small children of both sexes are brought up by women but expected to learn to be different genders, it is also true to say that girls have an obvious built-in advantage. There is no room for doubt as to who they are expected to be like—whereas boys have the problem of working out what masculinity is and switching from an early identification with their mothers to a later and more enduring one with their fathers. . . .

ARTIFACTS OF GENDER

Parental work in the area of teaching gender also takes place within the broad context of cultural artifacts that separate the world of girls from the world of boys.

Gender-appropriate toys are both the cause and the proof of correct gender identification. In the case of the boy whose penis was accidentally removed and who was reassigned as a girl at the age of 17 months. . . .

> The mother reported: "I started dressing her not in dresses but, you know, in little pink slacks and frilly blouses . . . and letting her hair grow." A year and six months later, the mother wrote that she had made a special effort at keeping her girl in dresses, almost exclusively, changing any item of clothes into something that was clearly feminine. "I even made all her nightwear into granny gowns and she wears bracelets and hair ribbons." The effects of emphasizing feminine clothing became clearly noticeable in the girl's attitude towards clothes and hairdo another year later, when she was observed to have a clear preference for dresses over slacks. . . . [Money and Ehrhardt, 1972, p. 119]

The girl asked for dolls, a dolls' house and a dolls' pram for Christmas; her [twin] brother, a toy garage with cars.

Walum (1977, p. 49) did analysis of the 1972 edition of the Sears Roebuck Christmas toy catalogue. Her base unit was each half page of the catalogue showing a different toy with a picture of the child (female, male, both genders) for whom it was promoted. She found that 84 per cent of the toys portrayed as suitable for girls fell under the heading of "preparatory for spousehood and parenthood," whereas none of those portrayed for males did so; 75 per cent of male toys were "manipulatory" in character, and 25 per cent related to male occupational roles. As Alice Rossi once remarked, a girl may spend more time playing with her dolls than a mother will ever spend with her children (Rossi, 1964, p. 105), and the message is clearly that girls play house and do not play the kinds of games with the kinds of toys that would prepare them for other occupational roles. . . .

The child's own space within the home is full of gender signals. In a middle-class area of a university community, "a locale that would presumably be on the less differentiated end of the sex role socialization spectrum" (Weitz, 1977, p. 61), the bedrooms of boys and girls were instantly identifiable. Boys' rooms "contained more animal furnishings, more educational art materials, more spatial-temporal toys, more sports equipment and more toy animals. The rooms of girls contained more dolls, more floral furnishings and more 'ruffles'" (Rheingold and Cook, 1975, p. 461). The 48 girls' rooms boasted 17 toy vehicles—the 48 boys', 375; 26 of the girls' rooms had dolls, compared with 3 of the boys'. . . .

Another potent source of gender messages is children's literature. . . . Weitzman *et al.*'s survey of [pre-school picture books] begins by noting the fact that women are barely visible in most of them. In their sample of prizewinning books, the male:female sex ratio in pictures of people was 11:1 (for animals it was 95:1). Most of the plots centered on some form of male adventure and females figured chiefly in their traditional service function or in the more imaginative, but ultimately no less restrictive, roles of fairy, fairy godmother and underwater maiden. In the duo *What Girls Can Be* and *What Boys Can Be* (Walley, n.d.), the pinnacle of achievement for a boy is to be President of the nation and for a girl it is motherhood. . . .

Although much of the early analysis of sexism in children's literature was done in the United States, similar studies in Britain have shown no substantive differences, except perhaps that British material lags behind American in revising the stereotypes it presents to children. Glenys Lobban (1976) looked at six popular British reading schemes: *Janet and John, Happy Venture, Ready to Read, Ladybird, Nipper* and *Breakthrough to Literacy*. [Table 15.2] gives some of her findings. It shows the same definition of girls and women as relatively passive, indoor creatures, the same glorification of masculine adventurousness as the American research. . . .

[As] Belotti observes in her retelling of some traditional fables, [women are often portrayed as pervasively stupid]:

> "Little Red Riding Hood" is the story of a girl, bordering on mental deficiency, who is sent out by an irresponsible mother through dark wolf-infested woods to take a little basket full to the brim with cakes, to her sick grandmother. Given these circumstances her end is hardly surprising. But such foolishness, which would never have been attributed to a male, depends on the assurance that one will always find at the right moment and in the right place a brave huntsman ready to save grandmother and granddaughter from the wolf. [Belotti, 1975, p. 102]

It is sadly true that female figures in fairy tales and in children's fiction generally belong to two alternative categories: the good but useless, and the wicked. It has been calculated that 80 per cent of the negative characters in comics and fairy tales are female (d'Ascia, 1971), and the myth of feminine evil is a pervasive cultural theme with which women still have to contend.

Lastly, children's television provides no relief from the relentless feminine message. Even such "liberal" programmes as Sesame Street do not place girls and women in prominent or seriously powerful positions. It is relevant to observe that most of the controversy about the effects of television on children is about the prevalence of male aggression in programmes directed at children. It is also important that children spend more of their lives watching television than they do at school, and that much of what they watch from an early age is adult television: they are thus exposed to the general range and effect of media representations of women.

All cultures have a division of labour by gender, but some are more divided than others. The need to differentiate children's roles and identities by sex is therefore immensely variable. Such variation must be borne in mind when viewing our own arrangements, which are one, not the only, way of grouping children in readiness for their adult life. . . .

TABLE 15.2 Sex Roles Occurring in Three or More of Six British Reading Schemes*

Sex for Which Role Prescribed	Content of Children's Roles				
	Toys and Pets	Activities	Taking Lead in Both-sex Activities	Learning New Skill	Adult Roles Presented
Girls only	Doll Skipping rope Doll's pram	Preparing tea Playing with dolls Taking care of younger siblings	Hopping Shopping with parents Skipping	Taking care of younger siblings	Mother Aunt Grandmother
Boys only	Car Train Aeroplane Boat Football	Playing with cars Playing with trains Playing football Lifting/pulling heavy objects Playing cricket Watching adult males in occupational roles Heavy gardening	Going exploring alone Climbing trees Building things Taking care of pets Flying kites Washing and polishing Dad's car	Taking care of pets Making/building Saving/rescuing people or pets Playing sport	Father Uncle Grandfather Postman Farmer Fisherman Shop or business owner Policeman Builder Bus driver Bus conductor Train driver Railway porter
Both sexes	Book Ball Paints Bucket & spade Dog Cat Shop	Playing with pets Writing Reading Going to seaside Going on family outing			Teacher Shop assistant

**Janet and John, Happy Venture, Ready to Read, Ladybird, Nipper, Breakthrough to Literacy. [The term "reading schemes" refers to a programmed series of reading lessons—Ed.]*

SOURCE: Lobban (1976) p. 40.

REFERENCES

BANDURA, A., and HUSTON, A.C. "Identification as a process of incidental learning." *Journal of Abnormal and Social Psychology* 63 (1971):311–318.

BELOTTI, E.G. *Little Girls.* London: Writers and Readers Publishing Co-operative, 1975.

BREEN, D. *The Birth of a First Child.* London: Tavistock, 1975.

D'ASCIA, U. "Onorevolmente Cative," *Noi Donne* no. 50, December 19, 1971: Cited in Belotti (1975).

DE BEAUVOIR, S. *The Second Sex.* London: Four Square Books, 1960.

DRAPER, P. "!Kung women: contrasts in sexual egalitarianism in foraging and sedentary contexts" (1975). In Reiter (ed.).

FRIEDMAN, R.C.; RICHART, R.M.; VAN DE WEILE, R.L. (eds.). *Sex Differences in Behavior.* New York: John Wiley, 1978.

HANSSON, R.E.; CHERNOVETZ, M.E.; and JONES, H. "Maternal employment and androgyny." *Psychology of Women Quarterly* 2 (1977): 76–78.

HENNIG, M., and JARDIM, A. *The Managerial Woman.* New York: Pocket Books, 1978.

HETHERINGTON, E.M. (1965) "A developmental study of the effects of sex of the dominant parent on sex-role preference, identification and imitation in children." *Journal of Personality and Social Psychology* 2 (1965):188–194.

HETHERINGTON, E.M., and FRANKIE, G. "Effects of parental dominance, warmth and conflict on imitation in children;" *Journal of Personality and Social Psychology* 6 (1967):119–125.

HOFFMAN, L.W., and NYE, F.I. eds. *Working Mothers: An Evaluative Review of the Consequences for Wife, Husband and Child.* San Francisco: Jossey-Bass, 1974.

KOHLBERG, L. "A cognitive-developmental analysis of children's sex-role concepts and attitudes" (1967). In Maccoby (ed.).

KOHLBERG, L., and ULLIAN, D.Z. "Stages in the development of psychosexual concepts and attitudes" (1974). In Friedman et al. (eds.).

LAKE, A. "Are we born into our sex roles or programmed into them?" *Woman's Day* January 1975: 24–25.

LOBBAN, G. "Sex roles in reading schemes" (1976). In Children's Rights Workshop.

MACCOBY, E.E. (ed.). *The Development of Sex Differences.* London: Tavistock, 1967.

MACFARLANE, A. *The Psychology of Childbirth.* London: Fontana, 1977.

MISCHEL, W. "A social-learning view of sex differences in behaviour" (1967). In Maccoby (ed.).

———. "Sex-typing and socialization" (1970). In Mussen (ed.).

MONEY, J. and EHRHARDT, A.E. *Man and Woman, Boy and Girl.* Baltimore: Johns Hopkins Press, 1972.

MORANTZ, S., and MANSFIELD, A. "Maternal employment and the development of sex role stereotyping in five to eleven year olds." *Child Development* 48 (1977): 668–673.

Mussen, P.H. (ed.). *Carmichael's Manual of Child Psychology*. New York: John Wiley, 1970.

Oakley, A. *Becoming a Mother*. Oxford: Martin Robertson, 1979.

Piaget, J. *The Origins of Intelligence in Children*. New York: International Universities Press, 1952.

Reiter, R.R. (ed.). *Toward an Anthropology of Women*. New York, Monthly Review Press, 1975.

Rheingold, H.L. and Cook. K.V. (1975) "The content of boys' and girls' rooms

Rossi, A. "Equality between the sexes" (1964). In *The Woman in America*, edited by R.F. Lifton. Boston: Houghton Mifflin.

Thompson, C. "Penis envy in women" (1974). In *Psychoanalysis and Women*, edited by J.B. Miller. Harmondsworth: Penguin. (First published 1943.)

Tiller, P.O. "Parental role division and the child's personality development" (1967). In E. Dahlstrom (ed.), *The Changing Roles of Men and Women*. London: Duckworth, 1967.

Walley, D. *What Boys Can Be* and *What Girls Can Be*. Kansas City: Hallmark, n.d.

Walum, C.R. *The Dynamics of Sex and Gender: A Sociological Perspective*. Chicago: Rand McNally, 1977.

Weitz, S. *Sex Roles: Biological, Psychological and Social Foundations*. Oxford: Oxford University Press, 1977.

Weitzman, L.J.; Eifler, D.; Hokada, E.; and Ross, C. (1976) "Sex-role socialization in picture books for pre-school children" (1976). In Children's Rights Workshop.

Woodham-Smith, C. *Florence Nightingale 1820–1910*. London: The Reprint Society, 1952.

CHAPTER 16

The Man–Woman Crisis

Clayton Barbeau

ABSTRACT: Although the traditional man-woman relationship has been rendered obsolete by technology, our socialization perpetuates male–female inequality. Men's basic feelings of superiority, combined with their economic power, create resentment in women. Because our obsolete sex roles continue to dominate male–female relationships, they continue to engender resentment. Consequently, in marriage men and women struggle against one another—with one result being incompatible approaches to sex. To solve this basic man–woman crisis requires that individuals break out of the stereotypical roles into which they have been thrust—not an easy thing to do, but not impossible either.

[F]or most of human history and for most of humankind, the respective roles of men and women have been determined by the needs for maintenance and survival of the family and tribe or nation. Whatever we may think of such roles as they were worked out in different cultures in different eras, the fact is that they were usually clearly defined. In times previous to ours, most men and women conformed to patterns of behavior toward each other that were taught by their society. It was left to our current century—with its newborn industrialism, its rapid shift of population from farms to cities, its sudden access to cross-cultural information, its universal education, its advances in communication and personal mobility—to shatter the old functional roles. Add to the list the new demands of a technological society, the enormous increment of scientific research, the advances in knowledge of human behavior, the provision of means of having sexual pleasure without fear of pregnancy, and we have the elements that dramatically render obsolete previously hallowed patterns of the man-woman relationship.

Despite this, much of our acculturation of boys and girls for their adult man-woman roles persists in educating them for patterns of sexual relating that are no longer functional. This cultural lag appears to be a major factor in the current almost palpable tension between men and women in our society. . . . [W]e still tend to educate the majority of boys in modes of behavior that place the masculine label upon toughness, the suppression of tender emotions, the notion of masculine dominance over women. . . .

Often enough, the only area in which a particular man can feel or assert his power over women is in the economic sphere. Many men define their roles in family life solely in terms of being the "breadwinner." Thus they are threatened when their wives decide to earn an income of their own, and even some of the most "liberated" men are unwilling to see their wives earn an income larger than their own. More than one professional woman has turned down a job promotion with increased income because it would mean that she would be making more money than her husband and she didn't think he would be able to adjust to that. At the same time, some women who are totally economically dependent upon their husbands have very negative feelings about their own situation. A former client has written me about this:

> I remember the freedom I felt when I got my first paycheck for a part-time job. I had earned this money. I could buy those things (a new lamp, fix the kitchen floor, etc.) that Peter said we couldn't afford. He was making $34,000 a year. I never could understand why we couldn't afford nicer furniture, etc. It was two months after I took the part-time job that he said he was leaving me to marry another woman (or should I say "mother"?). All I cared about, he said, was a career. He told people I wasn't satisfied with my home life; that it was obvious I was really messed up.
>
> My earning power was very subtly sabotaged. All counseling fees were to be paid by me—"You're the one who wanted this!" Any time we had dinner out other than for social or business reasons, I paid. After all, if I didn't have that job, I wouldn't be too tired on Friday night to make dinner, right?

For many men, not only does economic power continue a superior-inferior notion of the male-female relationship; many men expect it to be understood as an expression of their love. "I don't know what in hell more she can want from me," one client shouted. "She can write a check for any damned thing she needs." His wife was asking for intimacy. She phrased it as "consideration for my feelings," "a willingness to listen to me," "sharing his feelings with me." He countered such declarations with angry assertions of his economic strength, flexing his money muscles. "You ought to see the home I've bought her. And she's got her own car."

The male mystique works in other ways to destroy healthy relationships between men and women. One man had ignored his wife's feelings for years. He had had more than one affair, which, while not overtly boasting about, he made little attempt to conceal from his male friends. His wife confronted him one day with the news that she was getting a divorce in order to marry a man to whom she had turned for intimacy. The husband went on a furniture-breaking rampage, threatened murder, stormed out for a three-week binge, flirted with suicide, then sobered up and promptly moved into the apartment of one of his former bedpartners. He incorporated into that behavior much of the male mystique: He subscribed to the double standard; he threatened aggression against others and himself as a solution to his problem; he then sought out another woman to be dependent upon him, thereby reassuring himself of his masculine power. Informative as is his reaction to the crisis, it is a reaction rooted in the same male mystique that led to his marital breakup. . . .

The symptom of adultery on the part of wives has been, in my counseling experience, most often caused by a searching for intimacy with a man who cares and who demonstrates his caring, for a personal relationship that the husband is not supplying. One woman having an affair with an impotent man stated, "My husband is a stud in bed, but my lover is just that, a romantic lover who listens to me, who shares with me." Adultery on the part of a husband, on the other hand, is often a flight from the very demands of intimacy his wife is making. "She wants too much. I can't take all that closeness," one wandering husband disclosed. Particularly in one-night stands, he finds he can have some sexual activity without love, without self-revelation. And therein he hopes to find reassurance of his masculinity. The very fact that he needs such constant reassurance signals the location of his personal difficulties. The misnamed "great lovers" Don Juan and Casanova were likewise afflicted: Because their last conquest had not proved to them that they were adequate, they had to find another.

In reality, the sexual act itself—and the male orgasmic response—is closely tied to these problems. It is not uncommon for both husbands and wives to express dissatisfaction with their sexual lovemaking: she because of the lack of positive emotional content, of tenderness or true intimacy in their relationship; he because he finds her basic dissatisfaction, or her demands, a hindrance to his sense of "good performance." Her lack of response and his sense of failure often lead to a diminishing, even disappearance, of sexual lovemaking in marriage.

One client, separated for over a year, said, "Initially I begged him for some understanding. He simply tossed a sex manual at me. When I suggested counseling he said no. He said the problem was mine, not his. For the last ten years of our marriage, we lived like good friends, brother and sister, good parents. To the outside world, we were a lovely couple. Then I decided life must offer something more. Our separation was amicable. Then I met a man. He courted me, paid attention, listened, understood, responded to me as a person. When we finally, months later, made love, I discovered there was nothing wrong with me; I loved it. I think it was because he touched me emotionally, spiritually, personally, long before he ever touched me physically."

Because the male tends to think of the sexual act as an adequacy test, a performance equivalent to the strong swing of the hammer that will ring the gong at the state fair, he may not understand the causes of his wife's dissatisfaction. If he is one of those who is focused on "providing" an orgasm for his wife as a means of showing his prowess, he may himself get little pleasure from the activity. And if he fails to "provide" an orgasm, he too is dissatisfied. . . .

I have been present in group therapy sessions where . . . I've heard a veritable chorus of voices saying, "I'm tired of being his mother. I want a husband. I want a man to husband me, not a big boy who alternates between boasting to his friends, getting into angry rages with me or the kids and then coming with whimpering requests for sex, like it was some sort of candy I dole out when he's been a good boy for the last hour."

Coupled with complaints that "he's the oldest boy in the family" and "he won't talk to me of anything that really matters" (i.e., won't talk of their relationship or what's really happening with him or them) is the plaint that "he's more in love with television sports than with me." The television program "Love American Style" once had a skit which illustrated this syndrome. The husband was totally caught up in watching a football game, while the wife tried every seductive wile she knew to distract him from the ongoing competition to her presence. Failing every effort, she finally shouted, "You love football more than you love me!" He turned for the moment to announce, "Yes, but I love you more than I love baseball," and returned to watching the game.

Humorous as the sketch was, it is less than humorous when seen in the life of the women who know its truth. . . . In such cases it seems apparent that sports are being used merely to avoid intimate contact with the spouse. One athlete whose wife had left him wept over his loss. "I sent her two dozen roses. She refused them, saying, 'Last year a single rose might have done. It's too late now.' She smashed the television set one day with a beer bottle, during a game I was watching. I said she was crazy and went to a buddy's house to watch the game." Significantly, he admitted to neglecting his daughter also, while he devoted full attention to his "jock" son and to the boy's progress as a young athlete.

These examples of typical problems in the man-woman relationship are directly related to the miseducation of the American male. They are outcroppings, on the adult level, of the masculine mystique inculcated from birth. Another example is the astonishing level of drug addiction, especially alcoholism, among males. In adolescence, drinking is seen as a sign of manliness. One of the rites of initiation into the cult of the big-boys peer group when I was growing up was the ability to chugalug a pint or so of hard liquor. . . .

Because drinking hard liquor is touted as masculine, many men in our society promptly run for the bottle when they feel their adequacy threatened. They prefer it as a form of escape from women who demand that they meet them on a more adult ground. . . .

"What does woman want?" Freud plaintively asked, and left us without the hint of an answer, having his own problems with women. It is a question on the minds of many men today. Surely everyone knows what women do not want: They do not want to be considered as receptacles for male sperm; they do not want to be servants to men; they do not want less pay for the same work that some man is doing; they do not want discrimination in job promotions; they do not want. . . . But what *do* they want? More specifically, what do they want from the men or the man in their life? Perhaps as a man I am being terribly presumptuous in even offering the question to myself. And surely I risk being more than presumptuous when I essay some possible responses to the question. Yet I sally forth like Don Quixote because I'm afraid we've had all too many explorations of what's wrong in the man-woman relationship, where the problems originate, and how dreadful things are, with too few people offering even a hint of positive steps that might be taken to turn this crisis into a moment of true growth in understanding between men and women. . . .

What they really want, if I hear them at all correctly, is that their men grow up. Single or married, the articulate, self-possesed, self-supporting woman finds herself too often confronting the tender ego of the male who wants a woman who will look up to him (which implies his elevated status and her genuflection at his shrine), and who will be, or appear to be, dependent upon him in those ways (emotionally or financially or intellectually) that will make him feel strong. If she doesn't play this game, he may feel uncomfortable with her, threatened by her, ill at ease in her company. Or, he may want her to meet all his needs—emotional, physical, nurturing, supportive—as his mother did, without his paying much attention to any of her needs. In either case, then, what she wants of the man in her life is that he be a grown-up person.

But what do we mean by grown-up? . . . If the men of our time are to live up to the women of our time, then I think that they must take a long, hard look at their upbringing and their assumptions as men. How much of my life is lived as a role I am playing, trying to "be a man" in the eyes of other men rather than having the courage to be myself? Consider for a moment a simple, tiny example of this sort of thing. One of my favorite before-dinner drinks is a sweet vermouth with a twist of lemon. Yet, on more than one occasion when ordering this, I've had men who were ordering a scotch or "double martini, very dry" exclaim, "Why don't you have a man's drink?" I've often wondered how many men really would have preferred a daiquiri, or even a soft drink, but were afraid of losing esteem as "real men" for ordering less than hard liquor. . . . Sometimes the assertion of oneself takes such simple forms as rejecting pressures of that sort.

The courage to be myself and not play roles implies, of course, the courage to examine myself and find out who I am. If the criteria for manliness are uncertain in our time, it is because too few men have had the courage to reexamine the attitudes inculcated in them in their early years and to question the validity of such conditioning today. While many men are ready to pay lip service to the notion of women's equality as persons, even to agree on the important aspects of man-woman relationships, men continue to lag behind women in doing the hard work of digging into themselves and seeing what historical baggage they can jettison, what chains from the past they can saw off, to bring themselves greater emotional freedom.

That introspective look into ourselves to confront what we consider masculinity to be for us is the first task for any man who wishes to begin the process of growth. . . .

Freud left the popular impression that we are unfree creatures, victims of our unconscious drives and instincts. Marx claimed we were economically determined creatures, victims of the system. Darwin argued, as did Spencer, that we were biologically determined. Too many of us men today seem to have accepted this status of victimhood; but we do that at our own peril. The fact is that we are responsible creatures, free to choose our own course. No one need remain a victim of his or her upbringing or of unexamined assumptions. We really can open ourselves up to the questioning that leads to growth. . . . Furthermore, we men might begin to pay attention to what the women in our lives are trying to tell us. . . .

I personally do not hear my female clients telling their husbands to define themselves only in terms of wifely needs or to dedicate their lives simply to serving their wives' desires. I do hear them calling for us to have the courage to drop our masks and our role-playing and to begin to search for new and more authentic ways of treating ourselves and of relating to them.

Perhaps most crucial to our growth as men is that we learn to take the risks of disclosing ourselves to those we love. For there can be no authentic loving that does not involve self-revelation. It is only in authentic love relationships—ones in which we are openly listening to one another, in which we are touching one another on everdeepening levels of personal awareness—that we begin to gain a sense of personal fulfillment. . . .

Women who complain of the men in their lives as "not caring for my feelings, not listening, always walking all over me, talking down, treating me like a child, not giving a damn about me" are describing a male victim of the masculine mystique. If we have heard those remarks directed at us, we ought to examine ourselves carefully for the cause. Usually, in my own case, the cause was the same: a lack of respect for the woman's personhood. The comment was a warning signal that I was not living up to my own ideals. The mature man, in touch with his own personhood, has the ground for appreciating and reverencing the personhood of others. The basic sign of this lack of respect is not paying attention to the other. Paying attention is a profound sign of love for another. My attentiveness to you tells you that you are important to me. The fact that I am truly listening to you, not interrupting or discounting what you say, but seeking to hear it, to empathize with it, tells you that you are as important to me as my own self—perhaps even more important, for I've laid down my preoccupations in order to let your thoughts, your feelings, enter into me. . . .

Manliness, the sort of manliness that may enable men to cope more effectively with the man-woman crisis in our times, is not a set of trophies to be won and put on a shelf. There is no classroom in which it can be learned. Most men and women today find manliness difficult to define, for many of the qualities found admirable in men are equally admirable in women. Yet I do think that the beginning of a definition of masculinity can be found in those men who listen to their own feelings and to those of the women in their lives. In both sets of feelings we have sources of insight into what we might do to rid ourselves of the oppression of the male-female stereotypes that are so often the source of conflict between men and women today. . . .

SECTION 5

Romantic Involvements

BECAUSE LOVE IS CONSIDERED BY AMERICANS TO BE THE ESSENTIAL ELEMENT OF MARRIAGE, it is appropriate for us to also focus on this significant experience. From childhood we learn the romantic ideal. We are taught to expect to "fall" in love at some point in our lives. We learn that love is the eventual outcome of dating and the appropriate basis for establishing marriage and having children. We come to expect the experience of love, and most of us do experience it.

But what is love? Beyond being one of the most talked-about and longed-for of human experiences in the Western world, what is it? We all speak and act as though we know exactly what love is, but when one attempts to pin it down love turns out to be fantastically elusive. It is almost impossible to put into words. Although we all "know" what love is, our "knowing" fails when it comes to defining the specifics of love.

It is bound to be that way, for we are dealing with a basic and encompassing human emotion. Any definition of love must fall short of the deep experience that it attempts to describe. To define love can only disappoint; for definitions are attempts to be dispassionately objective—in this instance, about the most passionately subjective of human experiences.

To experience love is certainly one thing, but an understanding of love is what we are after. So it is with a dispassionate look at love that we begin.

Why have sociologists and other social scientists been interested in the topic of love? The major reason is because in societies where love is a significant experience, its understanding is important for comprehending how men and women relate to one another. That which at first appearance may seem to belong to the realm of the poets and lyricists, upon deeper reflection turns out to have deep sociological significance.

When we look at the situation cross-culturally we find that expectations concerning love vary tremendously. In some societies love is considered to be the *essential* ingredient that should underlie each and every marriage. It is the sine qua non of marriage. Why would anyone ever get married if he or she were not "in love"? For it to be otherwise strikes people as bordering on the immoral—if not already having crossed the boundary.

In contrast with such a society (which ought to strike the reader as highly familiar), others disassociate marriage and love. In these societies not only to they not teach their children that love and marriage go together like a horse and carriage, but they teach them that love and marriage are irrelevant to one another. Some other element, commonly respect or duty, is considered the essential that underlies a good marriage. Above all, a husband and wife should respect each other and perform their respective duties. If love develops after a couple is married, that is fine, but love is only a possible plus in marriage; respect is essential. If respect is not present, then something is fundamentally wrong—again, something bordering on immorality.

No matter what is considered to be the essential basis underlying marriage, in all societies marriage means a changed set of relationships. Through marriage one becomes "related" not only to husband or wife but also to a group of other persons, in our society called "in-laws." In one sense, then, one not only marries a spouse, but also the spouse's family. Marriage also means a changed set of relationships between families (or sometimes clans or tribes). Depending upon the specific rules of each society, one group of people is placed in a different relationship with another set of people, namely the family of the person who married their son or daughter.

For both bride and groom and their families, these new relationships bring with them interrelated sets of rights, duties, and privileges. How the obligations entailed by these relationships are calculated can be very complicated, depending on how the particular society is set up. They can involve property ownership and use, the right to be supported, the duty of supporting, the need of visiting, the obligation to refrain from visiting, informal rules concerning the showing of respect, and rules of law specifying who must inherit what.

Consequently, because in one way or another their welfare may be at stake, many people other than the bride and groom are interested in who marries whom. It is in their own best interest to make certain that the "right" people marry. In all societies, however, even those in which love between a man and a woman is considered irrelevant, passionate love that makes people violate the fundamental expectations into which they have been so studiously socialized, and propels them to one another in spite of the consequences, can and does occur.

Sociologists are vitally interested in what keeps societies together. In their attempt to understand what they call social control, sociologists analyze factors that support and maintain the social structure, the usual or patterned arrangements among the members of a society. This characteristic of love—that of leading people to disregard the expectations of others, propelling them into relationships that are not considered "right" or "proper" or "wise" by others—makes love an important sociological topic; if love can upset expected relationships, it is important for the members of a society to control it—and for sociologists to understand it.

In applying the idea of the social control of love, think about the ways in which love is channeled toward desired outcomes in our own society. It should be obvious that people in our society do not randomly fall in love with one another. Rather, in the average case love follows certain broad, predictable lines, such as those of social class, race, age, religion—and even height. How does this happen? If love is not "by chance," then what "control or guidance devices" are used by parents, relatives, peer groups, and socializing institutions such as school and church to "help" people "fall in love" with the "right type" of person, and thus to upset as few people as possible?

It is even better to apply this idea to your personal experiences. Do not let the word "control" bother you when it is applied to love. It simply means that parents and friends help "guide" someone into making particular "kinds" of choice. Try to think of examples of how your love has been "given direction" by others. Have you not perhaps done the same type of "guiding," "directing," or "channeling" when it came to your own friends and brothers and sisters?

When it comes to understanding who selects whom in love and marriage, some people think almost exclusively in terms of personality traits. But personality traits are themselves dependent on larger societal influences. An individual's personality traits do not develop in a social void, but are the result of many years of exposure to particular people and specific situations. As I stressed in previous introductions, it is within a particular culture and subculture that one learns basic orientations to life and the particular expectations that are attached to myriad social situations. One learns to define certain experiences and people as pleasing or displeasing. Consequently, we each develop characteristic ways of acting toward others. In sum, out of our social experiences develop our characteristic predispositions in preferences and behavior.

Consequently, if we find that some (type of) person matches our needs better than another (type of) person, we are not dealing with inborn personality but with the end result of complex and extensive social learning. It is socialization within a particular group and adaptation to their expectations that make us feel more at ease with some people than with others. Feeling comfortable around someone makes us more inclined to share intimate aspects of the self. This allows two persons to become dependent on one another, persons who then develop the capacity to satisfy each other's personality needs. This, in short, underlies the development of love.

In applying these ideas, think back on some love/attraction relationship that you have experienced. Did your initial attraction turn into love? Why? Or why not? Try to analyze the factors that increased (or impeded) feelings of mutuality or rapport, the desire to share deep aspects of your self, feelings of mutual dependence, and mutual satisfaction of personality needs. Once you have located these factors in that relationship, you will have found the keys to why love did or did not develop between you.

CHAPTER 17

The Love Research

Zick Rubin

ABSTRACT: As significant as love is to people, scientifically we have only recently begun to research love; the main findings of these studies are herein summarized. Studies of fear or anxiety-producing situations indicate that love is preceded by an increase in emotion—a physiological arousal of some sort (which can be anger or fear)—to which people attach the label "love" (or "sexual arousal" or "passion"). Further, contrary to popular stereotypes, men are quicker to attach the label "love" to a situation of emotional arousal than are women (that is, men "fall in love" more easily). Men also "fall out of love" more slowly and with more difficulty than women. Finally, unequal emotional involvement makes a love relationship unstable.

Love has always been one thing, maybe the only thing that seemed safely beyond the research scientist's ever-extending grasp. With an assist from Masters and Johnson, behavioral scientists have, to be sure, dug rather heavily into the topic of human sexual behavior. But whereas sex might now be explored scientifically, love remained sacrosanct.

Or so we thought. . . .

Over the past dozen years, and at a positively accelerating pace, behavioral scientists have begun to study love. They have done so on their own terms, with the help of such tools of the trade as laboratory experiments, questionnaires, interviews and systematic behavioral observation. And although the new love research is still in its early stages, it has already made substantial progress. The research has proceeded on several fronts, including explorations of the psychological origins of love, its links to social and cultural factors and the ways in which it deepens—or dies—over time.

Recent studies of falling in love have indicated that there is a sense in which love is like a Brooks Brothers suit or a Bonwit dress. For one person's feelings toward another to be experienced as "love," they must not only feel good and fit well, they must also have the appropriate label. Sometimes a sexual experience contributes to such labeling. One college student told an interviewer that she was surprised to discover that she enjoyed having sex with her boyfriend, because until that time she had not been sure that she loved him. The pleasant surprise helped to convince her that she was actually "in love."

Paradoxically, however, people sometimes label as "love" experiences that seem to be negative rather than positive. Consider the rather interesting case of fear. Ovid noted in *The Art of Love*, written in first-century Rome, that an excellent time for a man to arouse passion in a woman is while watching gladiators disembowel one another in the arena. Presumably the emotions of fear and repulsion stirred up by the grisly scene would somehow be converted into romantic interest.

Ovid himself did not conduct any controlled experiments to check the validity of the fear-breeds-love principle; but two psychologists at the University of British Columbia, Drs. Donald L. Dutton and Arthur P. Aron, recently did so. They conducted their experiment on two footbridges that cross the Capilano river in North Vancouver. One of the bridges is a narrow, rickety structure that sways in the wind 230 feet above the rocky canyon; the other is a solid structure, built only 10 feet above a shallow stream. An attractive female experimenter approached men who were crossing one or the other bridge and asked if they would take part in her study of "the effects of exposure to scenic attractions on creative expression." All they had to do was to write down their associations to a picture she showed them. The researchers found that the men accosted on the fear-arousing bridge were more sexually aroused than the men on the solid bridge, as measured by the amount of sexual imagery in the stories they wrote. The men on the high-fear bridge were also much more likely to telephone the young woman afterward, ostensibly to get more information about the study.

The best available explanation for these results comes from a general theory of emotion put forth by Dr. Stanley Schachter of Columbia University. Schachter's experiments suggested that the experience of emotion has two necessary elements. The first is physiological arousal—a racing heart, heightened breathing, sweating and the like. These symptoms tend to be more or less identical for any intense emotion, whether it be anger, fear or love. The second necessary element, therefore, is the person's subjective labeling of his or her arousal. In order to determine which emotion he or she is experiencing, the person must look around and determine what external stimulus is causing the inner upheaval.

This labeling is a complicated process, and (as Ovid apparently knew some 2,000 years ago) mistakes can happen. In the Capilano Canyon study, subjects apparently relabeled their inner stirrings of fear, at least in part, as sexual arousal and romantic attraction. This sort of relabeling is undoubtedly encouraged by the fact that the popular stereotype of falling in love—a pounding heart, shortness of breath, trembling hands—all bear an uncanny resemblance to the physical symptoms of fear. . . .

In the case of the Capilano Canyon study, of course, one cannot say that the subjects actually "fell in love" with the woman on the bridge. But the same sort of labeling process takes place in more enduring romantic attachments. In the process, social pressures also come crashing into the picture. Young men and women are taught repeatedly that love and marriage inevitably go together, and in the large majority of cases they proceed to act accordingly on this assumption.

Americans are more likely than ever to get married (well over 90 percent do so at least once), and all but a minuscule proportion of people applying for marriage licenses will tell you that they are in love. It is not simply that people who are in love decide to follow their hearts' dictates and get married. It also works the other way around. People who are planning to get married, perhaps for economic reasons or in order to raise a family, invariably follow their culture's dictates and decide that they are "in love."

The pressure to label a promising relationship as "love" seems especially strong for women. Sociologist William Kephart of the University of Pennsylvania asked over a thousand Philadelphia college students the following question: "If a boy (girl) had all the other qualities you desired, would you marry this person even if you were not in love with him (her)?" Very few of the respondents (4 percent of the women and 12 percent of the men) were so unromantic as to say yes. But fully 72 percent of the women (compared with only 24 percent of the men) were too practical to answer with a flat no and, instead, pleaded uncertainty.

One of Dr. Kephart's female respondents put her finger on the dilemma, and also on the resolution of it. She wrote in on her questionnaire, "If a boy had all the other qualities I desired, and I was not in love with him—well, I think I could talk myself into falling in love."

Whereas women may be more highly motivated than men to fall in love with a potential spouse, men tend to fall in love more quickly and less deliberately than women. In a study of couples who had been computer-matched for a dance at Iowa State University, men were more satisfied than women with their dates, reported feeling more "romantic attraction" toward them and even were more optimistic about the possibility of a happy marriage with their machine-matched partners. In a study of dating couples at the University of Michigan, I found that among couples who had been dating briefly—up to three months—boyfriends scored significantly higher than their girlfriends did on a self-report "love scale." These men were more likely than their partners to agree with such statements as "It would be hard for me to get along without ———," "One of my primary concerns is———'s welfare" and "I would do almost anything for———." Among couples who had been together for longer periods of time the male-female difference disappeared.

The idea of measuring love on a paper-and-pencil scale is, incidentally, not an entirely new one. When Elizabeth Barrett Browning wrote, "How do I love thee? Let me count the ways," she was, as any mathematician can tell you, referring to the most basic form of measurement. Six years ago, when I was searching for an unspoiled topic for my doctoral dissertation, I decided to take Browning's advice. ("Why do you want to measure *that*?" my dissertation committee asked me. "Why not measure something more conventional like cognitive dissonance or identity diffusion?" I looked down at the rocky canyon 230 feet below and answered, voice trembling. "Because it's there.") The items on the scale that emerged refer to elements of attachment (the desire to be near the other), caring (the concern for the other's well-being) and intimacy (the desire for close and confidential communication with the other). The ancient Greeks had a similar conception of love. Where they went wrong was in never asking the masses to put their *eros* and *agape* for one another on nine-point scales.

Skeptics may point out, of course, that a paper-and-pencil love scale does not really measure how much people love each other, but simply how much they *say* they love each other. But there is some corroborating behavioral evidence for the scale's validity. For example, scores on the scale checked out with the well-known folk wisdom that lovers spend a great deal of their time gazing into each other's eyes. Surreptitious laboratory observation through a one-way mirror confirmed that "strong lovers" (couples whose members received above-average scores on the love scale) made significantly more eye contact than "weak lovers" (couples whose scores on the love scale were below average). Or, as the popular song puts it, "I only have eyes for you."

Whereas men seem to fall in love more quickly and easily than women, women seem to fall out of love more quickly and with less difficulty than men, at least in the premarital stages. For the past several years, my coworkers and I have been conducting an extensive study of student dating couples in the Boston area. We found, to our initial surprise, that women were somewhat more likely to be "breaker-uppers" than men were, that they saw more problems in the relationship and that they were better able to disengage themselves emotionally when a breakup was coming. Men, on the other hand, tended to react to breakups with greater grief and despair.

These tendencies run counter to the popular stereotypes of women as starstruck romantics and men as aloof exploiters. In fact, women may learn to be more practical and discriminating about love than men for simple economic reasons. In most marriages, the wife's status, income and life chances are far more dependent on the husband's than vice versa. As a result, the woman must be discriminating. She cannot allow herself to fall in love too quickly, nor can she afford to stay in love too long with "the wrong person." The fact that a woman's years of marriageability tend to be more limited than a man's may also contribute to her need to be selective. Men, on the other hand, can better afford the luxury of being "romantic."

Sociologist Willard Waller put the matter most bluntly when he wrote, some 40 years ago. "There is this difference between the man and the woman in the pattern of bourgeois family life: a man, when he marries, chooses a companion and perhaps a helpmate, but a woman chooses a companion and at the same time a standard of living. It is necessary for a woman to be mercenary." As more women enter business and professional careers, and as more men make major commitments to homemaking and child-rearing, it is likely that this difference will diminish.

In spite of these culturally based sex differences, the usual course of love is probably pretty much the same for human beings of both sexes. . . . My study of Boston couples, conducted in collaboration with Drs. Letitia Anne Peplau and Charles T. Hill has [shown that] love is most likely to flourish when the two partners are *equally involved* in their relationship. In our study of 231 dating couples, 77 percent of the couples in which both partners reported that they were equally involved . . . were still going together (or, in some cases married) [two years later], as compared with only 45 percent of unequally involved couples.

The importance of equal degrees of involvement makes it clear that love, like water, seeks its own level. As Columbia University sociologist Peter M. Blau explains, "If one lover is considerably more involved than the other, his greater commitment invites exploitation and provokes feelings of entrapment, both of which obliterate love. . . . Only when two lovers' affection for and commitment to one another expand at roughly the same pace do they mutually tend to reinforce their love."

Because of this mutual reinforcement, love will sometimes beget love—provided that the first person's love is communicated to the second. To help make the point, Dr. Paul Rosenblatt of the University of Minnesota sifted through anthropologists' reports of "love magic" in 23 primitive societies, from the Chaga of East Africa to the Kwoma of New Guinea. He came to the conclusion that although love magic often works, it isn't really magic. Instead, such exotic practices as giving one's "victim" a charmed coconut, flashing a mirror at her or blowing ashes in her face all serve to heighten the woman's love by indirectly communicating the man's love for her. When love magic is practiced without the victim's knowledge, it is not nearly so effective. (Other studies have made it clear, however, that expressions of love must also be well-timed. If too much affection is expressed too soon, equity is undermined and the tactic will backfire.)

Dr. Rosenblatt's study illustrates quite directly what some observers fear most about the new love research—that it will rob love of its magic and mystery. Sen. William Proxmire is one of those who takes this point of view. In a much-publicized statement, Sen. Proxmire identified a study of romantic love sponsored by the National Science Foundation as "my choice for the biggest waste of the taxpayer's money for the month of March. I believe that 200 million Americans want to leave some things in life a mystery, and right at the top of the things we don't want to know is why a man falls in love with a woman and vice versa."

Dr. Ellen Berscheid, the University of Minnesota researcher whose work was singled out by the senator, responded vigorously to the attack: "I assume the senator has some knowledge of the divorce rate in this country and understands that the absence of love is the basis on which many divorces are instigated. I believe he has been divorced and recently was reconciled with his second wife (in February, 1975). He ought to realize better than most people why we should know all we can about the determinants of affection."

Writing in the *New York Times*, columnist James Reston also defended the love researchers. "Mr. Proxmire is a modern man," Reston wrote, "who believes that government should help people with their problems. He is a land-grant college man and will vote any amount of money for basic research on the dangers of natural selection in animals, and on how to get the best bulls and cows together on the farms of Wisconsin, but he is against basic research on the alarming divorce rate or breakup of the human family in America. You have to assume he was kidding."

But, of course, the senator was not kidding, and his sentiments are undoubtedly shared by a large number of Americans, even if not by the entire 200 million claimed in his statement. Even some psychologists themselves share his viewpoint. At a symposium sponsored by the American Psychological Association Convention several years ago, one panelist declared that "the scientist in even attempting to interject love into a laboratory situation is by the very nature of the proposition dehumanizing the state we call love."

My view of the matter, and that of other love researchers, is rather different. We are quite aware of the difficulties inherent in the attempt to study love, and we have no illusion that we will ever unlock all of love's mysteries. But we also believe that especially at a time when many people are terribly confused about what love is or should be, the scientific study of love can make a positive contribution to the quality of life. To shun this task is no more justified than the taboo until several centuries ago against scientific study of the human body, on the grounds that such research would somehow defile it. In the words of one of the most humane of modern psychologists, the late Dr. Abraham H. Maslow, "We *must* study love; we must be able to teach it, to understand it, to predict it, or else the world is lost to hostility and to suspicion."

CHAPTER 18

The Secret Ranking

Hans L. Zetterberg

ABSTRACT: Highly significant for social life is what we might term "erotic ranking"—that is, a person's capacity to create infatuations or "emotional overcomeness" in others. This informal, hidden ("secret") ordering of emotional involvement guides much of our interactions, even to the point of overriding a corporation's formal organization chart. A high visible status is sometimes confused with a high erotic ranking, and often leads to disappointments in intimacy. Erotic ranking can also propel us into situations of anomie—that is, they can move us outside our usual boundaries so that we lose our bearings. Norms exist in society to protect people from erotic involvements that are considered unwise or degrading.

In a business enterprise the president wanted to fire his obvious crown prince. The board of directors objected, because they liked the up-and-coming man, had invested company funds in his training, and had gladly met the offers he had received from competitors by paying him a very high salary; in fact, they had done all this at the suggestion of the president who now wanted him fired. A look into the situation showed that the president's private secretary had fallen in love with the young man. As far as one could tell, it was a purely emotional surrender and involved no sex relations nor any proven attempts by the young man to get access to information that should remain confidential with the secretary and her boss. Nor was there any indication that the president and the secretary were or had been lovers. Yet the behavior of the parties resembled the triangle of a love story in which an older rival attempted to remove a younger one with aggressive unreason. . . .

In helping boards of directors to tackle problems such as major reorganizations or firing of the big executive, there is always a need to know the actual hierarchy and communication flow within the organizations. Because the organizational chart is too rough an approximation of these patterns, a consultant pursues other ways to establish who has power and prestige and who can talk effectively with whom. In the course of establishing the real hierarchy and the real communication pattern, he repeatedly encounters a latent but considerably significant rank order which, for want of a better term, might be called the *erotic ranking*. The young man in our illustration had bypassed his boss in the erotic ranking of the company.

OVERCOMENESS

Erotic rankings enter into the "rating-dating complex" observed on some American campuses[1] as well as in other patterns of courtship. Its operation, however, is usually intermingled with and obscured by other more conventional rankings. The hero of the football field, the owner of the flashy sports car, the president of the fraternity, and the senior student, are ranking persons on campus not primarily because of their position in an erotic stratification, but because of their position in the hierarchies of athletics, publicity, consumption, power, and occasionally education. The rating-dating complex is highly visible; one advertises one's rank by being seen with a ranking figure in public. The point of the rating-dating game is to catch a high-ranking partner and be seen together. . . .

Erotic rankings are particularly significant among teen-agers, who have not yet grown into the ordinary community ranks that dominate adult life. One may surmise that teen-aging will forever remain puzzling unless we learn to understand interaction in erotic hierarchies. It also makes sense to assume that the erotic hierarchy is more salient in coeducational organizations, such as hospitals, laboratories, and offices, than in settings where one sex prevails. . . . The question in what settings this ranking becomes dominant remains puzzling. In some occupational communities, e.g., filmdom and advertising, the erotic hierarchy is part of the folklore, but in others it is not, as in publishing and banking. Variations seem great also between otherwise similar organizational structures. In one university department the erotic stratification may be so emphasized that the female graduate student who is offered an assistantship does not know whether her academic or erotic competence has brought her the job. In the same university there may be other departments in which academic competence rules supreme. . . .

We all have seen instances in which students fall for their teachers, airline stewardesses for their pilots, theatre-going gentlemen for a ballerina or actress, men for the rich belle at the ball, nurses for their doctors, secretaries for their bosses, bobby socksers for a pop idol, laboratory assistants for a scientist, the females in the congregation for the minister, et cetera. In such instances they may be attracted to an assumed high erotic rank: ranks in the world of money, power, academic competence, sacredness, and artistic taste provide cues for assumed erotic ranks. Of course, the high community rank need not be real; it is enough if it appears high to start this process.

Many novels describe a seduction process that makes use of the likelihood of falling for visible ranks. The plot may show an ambitious but poor family banding together in an attempt to appear blue-blooded and honorable. They sacrifice to dress up one of the daughters to attract desired suitors. The prospect falls for the visible and is then stuck with the privately kept truth. . . .

If a surrender to visible status is pursued into the private world of the object of infatuation, the actual erotic rank may end up very differently from the one inferred from visible status characteristics: the famous doctor may turn out to be a narrow-minded bore, the rich girl a drab lover, the celebrated actor or popular singer an insecure mother's boy, et cetera. That "disappointment in love" should be a prevailing theme is thus quite predictable.

The constellation of a high visible rank in the larger community but a modest erotic rank leads to a pattern of attracting partners all the time but soon finding that they are either dissatisfied and leave or, that they hang on for reasons other than erotic ones. Persons with this constellation of ranks are thus changing partners quite often. One mistakenly speaks of "their high sex drive" or their "nymphomania" or "philandering." The truth is probably that they cut a painfully modest erotic rank. Perhaps the most stable relation or marriage they can have is with a "gigolo," that is, a person who uses and comforts the unhappy, lowly erotic state of another in return for money or the other advantages of his victim's high community rank.

The frequent failures of marriages formed after brief courtships may also be seen in this context. Both lay and professional marriage counselling holds that one should not make lasting commitments on the basis of a first love-impulse. We can perhaps refine this and say that love is fine as a basis for immediate commitment, but since it consists of rather private qualities, invisible to the outside, it takes time to cut through the visible misleading paraphernalia. "Love is blind," one says. Its blindness can be of two entirely different kinds: one can fail to see things that are there, and one can see things that are not there. The person who is falling in love is usually blind in the second sense: the presence of more visible desired things leads us to believe that the less visible desired quality is there. Great love can be blind in the other sense: our erotic rank exalts us so that no other consideration matters, concern over one's worldly station and the pursuit of ordinary goals become totally unimportant by comparison. As Antony says to Cleopatra, "We have kissed away kingdoms and provinces." . . .

[W]e may take as a worthwhile assumption that equals in erotic rank get along best. They surrender to each other in equal shares and seem to have a wide range of conversation and fun. The matchmaker is probably most successful when pairing off equals. Yet minor assymetries in erotic ranks are as common as in other kinds of status; one person usually outranks another, and one usually surrenders more than the other. When the assymetries are large, the problems may be great; for there is immeasurable agony in loving without being loved in return. . . .

ANOMIE IN EROTIC RANKS

The most interesting insights into the conception of the erotic hierarchy come from its confrontation with the theory of anomie. Anomie as Durkheim used the term is what prevails outside our customary range of ranks. To suddenly lose all one's money would place a person outside his accustomed rewards. Likewise, to quickly come into a huge amount of money places him outside the security of the familiar range. Such sudden changes up or down leave a person without his bearings and are dangerous; in extreme cases they may result in suicide.

The secret nature of the erotic hierarchy implies that people in general have a very limited accustomed range of erotic scale. Breakouts into anomie territories are therefore possible for most. Feelings of, "Where have I been? I never knew anything like it," are thus predictable as new experiences are encountered. In love one discovers letters before *a* and others after z, and life translates into new languages. The sudden great falls into anomie, when the comfort of the familiar no longer embraces us, may of course be desperate. To be totally bereaved of erotic rank causes despair and in extreme cases, suicide. To suddenly gain rank beyond all imagination is also frightening and, in extreme cases, as we have heard, the great lovers seek death together.

Anomie, here as elsewhere, is countered by norms and social controls. Durkheim noted this in one of his striking insights into the sociology of marriage.

> It [marriage] completely regulates the life of passion, and monogamic marriage more strictly than any other. For by forcing man to attach himself for-

> ever to the same woman it assigns a strictly definite object to the need for love, and closes the horizon.[2]

The horizon of the erotic hierarchy closes, restricting men to whatever have become their customary ranges. This Durkheim sees as a gain.

> Thus we reach a conclusion quite different from the current idea of marriage and its role. It is supposed to have originated for the wife to protect her weakness against masculine caprice. Monogamy, especially, is often represented as a sacrifice made by man of his polygamous instincts, to raise and improve woman's condition in marriage. Actually, whatever historical causes may have made him accept this restriction, he benefits more by it. The liberty he thus renounces could only be a source of torment to him.[3]

His argument that the restriction to a customary range is beneficial becomes more eloquent in an article written several years later.

> In assigning a certain object to desires, definite and unvariable, it prevents men from exasperating themselves in the pursuit of the ever new, the ever changing. . . . It prevents the heart from becoming agitated and from tormenting itself in a vain search for happiness . . . it renders more easily peace of heart, that inner equilibrium which is an essential condition for mental health and happiness.[4]

The phrase that "marriage kills love" can now be appreciated as an important half-truth: marriage restricts the pursuit of erotic rank to a customary range. Upon marriage, the spouses become members of castes, be they high or low, prohibited from leaving their accustomed territories. . . .

THE SOCIAL NORMS OF SEX

All this talk of an erotic hierarchy may have lead some learned colleagues to visualize a sociometric ranking of who sleeps with whom within a community. Of course, every coeducational office, hospital, laboratory, or college has more or less appealing men and women; and the issue of who has access to whose bed is not an idle one. However, as we have seen, what is at stake in the erotic hierarchy, namely, emotional overcomeness, is different from sexual intercourse. This emotional surrender may, of course, lead to, be achieved with, or be confirmed in sexual intercourse. But the latter is not necessarily involved; and, as is well known, there are many sexual relations that do not involve any emotional surrender of either party. . . .

It is known that society regulates whatever places persons in any one of its dimensions of stratification. In all societies, norms govern the acquisition and assignment of economic, political, academic, and religious ranks. It seems entirely reasonable to assume that norms emerge to govern erotic ranks as well. If sexual relations produce ranks, that fact in itself will generate a set of social norms. . . .

Such considerations lead us, first, to an explanation of the incest taboo. From the varying and sometimes fantastic explanations offered for this set of norms, we can now select the one that implicitly assumes an erotic hierarchy as the one deserving special attention. In other words, we follow Kingsley Davis.

> Suppose that brothers and sisters were allowed to violate the incest taboos. Consider first the effect of the sexual rivalry which would develop between brothers and between sisters. If, for example, there were two brothers and only one sister in the family, sexual jealousy would probably destroy the brotherly attitudes. . . . Moreover, since the number and sex distribution of the siblings in different families is impossible to control, no standard institutional pattern could be worked out so that jealousy would be a support rather than a menace. . . . If sexual relations between parent and child were permitted, sexual rivalry between mother and daughter and between father and son would almost surely arise, and this rivalry would be incompatible with the sentiments necessary between the two.[5]

The family is only one of the primary groups in which insurance against erotic degradation emerges. Other groups in which we are also much involved, such as friendships, neighborhoods, and work groups, develop similar prohibitions. A social norm that, in addition to the ordinary incest taboo, is irremovable from any society is, thus, a prohibition to steal a friend's, workmate's, or neighbour's spouse. In other words, the minimum sexual morality is an extension of the incest taboo to cover not only close relatives as before, but friends of the family, workmates, and neighbors. For sexual license in groups in which people are so intimately engaged makes for shifts in erotic hierarchies that cause too much agony to be tolerated. . . .

REFERENCES

1. Willard Waller, "The Rating and Dating Complex," *American Sociological Review* 2 (1937), pp. 727–735.
2. Emile Durkheim, *Suicide*, (1897). Cited from English translation, Glencoe, Ill.: Free Press, 1951, p. 270.
3. *Ibid.*, pp. 273–274.
4. Emile Durkheim, "Le divorce par consentement mutuel," *Revue Bleue*, 5 (1906), p. 552.
5. Kingsley, Davis, *Human Society*, New York: Macmillan, 1949, pp. 402–403.

CHAPTER 19

From Strangers to Intimates

David A. Karp / William C. Yoels

ABSTRACT: How do strangers become intimates? Before we even begin to answer this question, we need to note that society provides guides for its members in this area of life—for example, in some societies people learn that they "ought" to "fall in love," as well as when is the most appropriate time to experience love. Like a slowly turning wheel, love gradually develops as people become involved in rapport and self-revelation, mutual dependency, and need fulfillment. Rapport and self-revelation involve meeting one another, physical attractiveness, continued interaction, idealized images, and self-disclosure in an information game. Mutual dependency and commitment involve the development of intertwined lives, a public identity as a couple, and a commitment to the relationship.

We want to explore the process through which strangers become intimates. Such persons must meet, typically date one another, gradually become committed to each other, experience falling in love, and usually marry. So, while the specifics of the process through which strangers are transformed into intimates may vary widely, the socially prescribed benchmarks or stages of our respective relationships look much alike. In the following pages we will examine some of the available literature describing the central points in the intimacy process. . . .

We expect to "fall in love," have sex, and get married within well-recognized time frames. Adults typically define teenagers' first attempts at establishing an intimate relationship as infatuation or "puppy love." Teenagers are, after all, too young to experience the "real thing." At the other extreme, persons who remain unmarried past their late twenties may be considered "problems" by parents, relatives, and friends. . . .

In America the completion of formal education seems to be a key point in our intimacy time conceptions. High school students who do not go on to college frequently marry soon after graduation. For many others the college years are thought an appropriate time to fall in love. Indeed, because college students constitute a readily accessible sample of persons for researchers, most of the generalizations concerning the process through which persons fall in love come from studies of college students. To understand this process, we must first appreciate the conception of love that guides the construction of our intimate relations.

THE ROMANTIC IDEAL

Some years ago one of the authors had as a friend a Korean graduate student who became visibly distressed and depressed as she neared the completion of her master's degree work. When questioned about it, she answered that she had been receiving letters from her parents indicating that she would be married upon her return to Korea. Throughout her several years of undergraduate and graduate education in the United States she knew that she would eventually be expected to marry the person her parents had chosen for her. At this point, she did not want to return to Korea and she certainly did not want to marry someone she had never met. She knew, however, that it would be a breach of cultural tradition to refuse her parents' wishes. Had she not adopted American values which hold the idea of arranged marriages as archaic and silly, she probably would not have experienced strain or tension. She would have considered her arranged marriage as inevitable and reasonable as we consider "love" the inevitable basis for marriage.

The tenets of the romantic love ideal, first formulated in France and Germany during the twelfth century, gradually filtered down from the nobility to the lower classes. Today, the elements of the romantic love ideal are captured in the lyrics of popular songs and in greeting card verses. In its pure form the ideal of romantic love involves the notion that there is only one person in all the world that we are meant to love; that, although "love is blind" we will recognize our "true love" at first sight. The role of *fate* is an important strong feature of the romantic ideal. We are, after all, expected to "fall" in love, and the lyrics of songs have us believing that "you were meant for me." Don't we all wait from adolescence on for that moment when "That old black magic [has us] in its spell?" While we celebrate the pure romantic ideal in movies, literature, and song, we interpret it liberally in our own lives. Kierkegaard points this out when he says:

> The proposition that the first love is the true love is very accommodating and can come to the aid of mankind in various ways. If a man is not fortunate enough to get possession of what he desires, then he still has the sweetness of the first love. If a man is so unfortunate as to love many times, each time is still the first love. . . . One loves many times, and each time one denies the validity of the preceding times, and one still maintains the correctness of the proposition that one loves only once. [Kierkegaard, 1959:252]

[It is of significant import here that there] are studies indicating differences between men and women in the weight given to love as a condition for marriage. Contrary to popular belief, men are more likely than women to hold to the romantic ideal. In other words, women are *less* romantic than men (Waller, 1938:243). Women's traditional dependence on men has made the process of mate selection of much greater consequence to women, and, for this reason, women have been less idealistic and more rational and cautious than men. In one study, many of the female respondents made such comments as the following: "I don't think I ever felt romantic about David—I felt practical. I had the feeling that I'd better make the most of it" (Hill, Rubin, and Peplau, 1977).

You all no doubt know someone who claims to have fallen in love "at first sight." For most couples, however, the development of a love relationship is a gradual process. One researcher, Ira Reiss (1960), has described the steps in what he calls the "wheel theory of love." The four central stages of a relationship are represented by the spokes of the wheel [see Figure 19.1]. They are: rapport, self-revelation, mutual dependency, and need fulfillment. According to Reiss, persons must proceed through these stages one at a time and in order. The theory suggests that, before we are willing to reveal deep identity information about ourselves to others, we must first have achieved a certain level of rapport with them. Self-revelation, in turn, sets the stage for persons' sense of mutual dependency. The final stage in this process is the belief that another person fulfills our basic needs.

Much research (see Davis, 1973; Rubin, 1973) has been conducted on various aspects of the process leading to mate selection and marriage. This literature suggests that there is, indeed, considerable regularity and rationality to the process. Using Reiss' wheel theory as a general guide, we can more fully analyze the movement from rapport to self-revelation to commitment and marriage as well as the factors that sometimes hinder such movement.

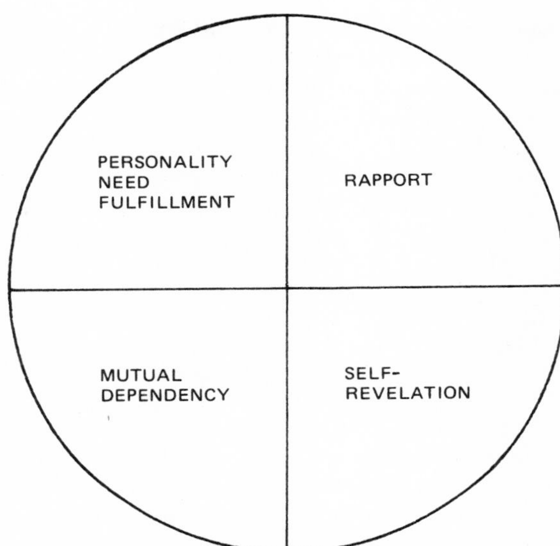

Figure 19.1 Graphic Presentation of the Wheel Theory of the Development of Love. *Source:* Ira Reiss, "Toward a Sociology of the Heterosexual Love Relationship," *Marriage and Family Living* 22 (May) 1960, p. 143.

RAPPORT AND SELF-REVELATION
("You think you know me, but you don't know me.")

We all have had the experience of meeting a stranger at a party, through the introduction of mutual friends, at bars, and the like. Such meetings typically begin with casual conversation and the exchange of superficial biographical information. College students meeting at a party engage in fairly ritualistic conversation: "What year are you in? What is your major? Where are you from? If one of the persons has no desire to continue the conversation, this incipient relationship is easily ended. If, however, the individuals wish to pursue the relationship, the conversation will necessarily become progressively less superficial and more far-reaching, as each person seeks to learn more about the other.

[Most people are aware that] physical attractiveness is a critically important factor determining whether persons will want to see each other again after an initial meeting. Additional studies support the importance of physical attractiveness, but these studies also note the differential significance attached to it by men and women. In one study (Byrne, 1970) persons wsere asked to rank a variety of factors concerning their attraction to others, and 90 percent of the male respondents ranked physical attractiveness as most important. This was not true for women. Although they certainly ranked attractiveness high, they considered it more important that the males with whom they develop an ongoing relationship share their attitudes and values. Ninety-two percent of the female respondents ranked value and attitudinal similarity as more important than physical attractiveness. Such a finding supports Bertrand Rusell's contention that "On the whole, women tend to love men for their character, while men tend to love women for their appearance."

Typically, once persons have begun to interact, their primary goal is to determine the issues on which they agree and disagree and to assess the significance of their similarities and differences. . . . One of the factors inevitably complicating the information assessment process during the initial stage of a relationship is the purposive impression-management engaged in by both parties. Individuals may be so intent on establishing a relationship that they systematically present attitudes and values that they believe accord well with the others' values and attitudes. Each will be careful early in a relationship to "feel out" the other person before expressing an opinion that he or she might dislike enough to end the relationship. All of us manipulate identity information to present the proper first impression. Let us acknowledge that deliberate identity manipulation early in a relationship frequently leads at some point to the declaration: "I thought I knew him/her, but I didn't." In their book *Pairing*, Bach and Deutsch (1970) offer several examples of couples who learn later in their relationship that the other had deliberately manipulated original presentations of self. Many of you are likely to find parallels in your own relationships to the following exchange:

> DOUG: I don't understand why you don't want to take the weekend backpack trip with Hal and Gwen. You know it's been three months since we've been in the woods or the mountains? I really miss it.
>
> HELEN: Well, I was never that much of an outdoor woman after all. I mean, I love the scenery, but camping out is pretty hard on a woman. It's different for a man.
>
> DOUG: But don't you remember what you said when we met on that Sierra Club Hike?
>
> HELEN: What did I say? That I loved the scenery? That I loved nature? Of course, I do. But carrying a pack is really exhausting for me.
>
> DOUG: It seems so much like part of us—being alone in the wilderness. Remember how we slipped away, the two of us? Cooked our meals together?
>
> HELEN: Well, what do you want me to say?

> DOUG: I don't know. You seem different now, somehow. It just isn't the same. That's why I want to get into the mountains with you again, bring it back, bring you back. [Bach and Deutsch, 1970:175]

Throughout the whole period of courtship persons tend to offer idealized images of themselves and largely to accept the idealized image others offer. An interesting study (Knafl, 1975) related to the idea of information control during the early stages of a relationship suggests that one of the best predictors of eventual marital success is the extent of conflict and its management by couples as they plan for their weddings. The author contends that this is the first time during the idyllic and fantasy-like period of courtship that the couple must make some of the practical social and economic decisions that will later typify their married life.

> With regard to the experience of preparing for the wedding, without exception, the couples interviewed reported difficulties surrounding the planning and execution of this event. They associated the staging of the wedding with an explicit shift in the nature of their relationship. While respondents typically described courtship as an essentially carefree time characterized by numerous shared, pleasurable experiences, questions concerning their wedding plans elicited a very different kind of response. Typically the respondent's tone of voice changed and comments focused on the multitude of problems being faced. [Knafl, 1975:8]

We have been suggesting that during the early stages of a relationship the participants engage in what might be termed an "information game." Persons manage impressions of themselves by systematically concealing information they consider potentially damaging in the encounter. At the same time, they seek out information about the other. Our examples indicate that it is relatively easy for persons to manipulate information about their attitudes and values. Other items of identity information, however, are difficult to hide or conceal, such as the ascribed attributes of ethnicity, race, religion, and social class. These "master attributes" also serve as relationship "filters." If persons discover that another's ethnic, religious, or class affiliation is very different from their own, they are likely to end the relationship at an early stage.

Whatever might be the unique elements involved, we can say that during the early stages of a relationship, individuals make presentations of themselves and the symbols defining their worlds. Supplied with this information, individuals decide whether the social worlds they respectively inhabit are close enough that they will eventually be able to produce and sustain a common reality as a couple. The literature that stresses class, value, and attitudinal similarity as initial filtering mechanisms implies that if persons' biographies are too dissimilar they will likely be unable to produce a viable joint reality. As an illustration of this point, we may see that it is the obvious disparity in biography that forms the substance of such fairy tales as *Cinderella*. *Cinderella* is a fairy tale precisely because it expresses the highly unlikely story of an ongoing relationship forged between persons with widely different biographies. It is the success of the relationship despite the incongruity of the individuals' biographies that gives the story its fairy-tale quality.

If a relationship endures beyond the point of self-disclosure and individuals have begun to date each other "seriously," they begin to interpret seriously their level of commitment to the relationship. "Intimates, like college professors, want tenure. And in order to guarantee that their relationship will continue, they must make a commitment to each other. After [a] probationary period, intimates, again like academics, go 'up or out'" (Davis, 1973:192). As one single friend has put it, "You reach a crossroads in the relationship where you either have to break it off or continue it and probably get married."

MUTUAL DEPENDENCY AND COMMITMENT ("All I ever need is you.")

You may be involved or know others who are involved in a relationship that has reached the point where persons' everyday lives are much intertwined. Most significant at this juncture in the relationship—the stage of mutual dependency—is that the couple's relationship has ceased to be their private affair. At this point, the individuals have likely been *publicly defined* as a couple. This public definition is critically important because, once it occurs, the exclusivity of their relationship becomes more inevitable. The couple now finds itself embedded in a complex and constraining system of expectations. Not only do the participants in the relationship have new expectations of each other, so also do their friends and family. The couple is now issued joint invitations, each person is expected to accompany the other to social gatherings, and when they are apart, each partner is expected to be able to account for the other's ideas, attitudes, and whereabouts. The partners signal the seriousness of their relationship to each other, family, and friends by engaging in a variety of activities generally understood to indicate a growing level of commitment. Such symbolic gestures may include: spending time together every day rather than just on weekends, introducing the partner to relatives, bringing the other to such important family events as weddings and annual gatherings, and the purchase of expensive gifts for each other.

As those of you who have seen your relationship with another progress to the point of mutual dependency know, it is a time when the relationship may undergo severe tensions and stresses. These difficulties are often related to the growing intensity of commitment that is occurring. Given the set of expectations described above, one or another of the partners may feel smothered by the pressure to make a permanent commitment. We should mention here that the meaning attached to commitment has, in the past, been different for men and women. Traditionally, males have viewed the acceptance of a long-term relationship as a surrender of their freedom and independence. Women, on the other hand, have been socialized to seek the security of a permanent commitment. More and more, however, women also are becoming wary of losing their identity in a relationship. Many women today refuse to subordinate their interests to those of their male friends and are increasingly willing to dissolve a relationship in which they are treated as "appendage" to the male.

Another threat to a relationship at this stage may be the negative evaluation of an individual's dating partner by parents and friends. If, for example, a woman's friends, upon meeting her companion, demand to know what she sees in him, she may be inspired to reconsider and possibly end the relationship. In college, as in high school, students turn to their friends for advice on personal and academic matters. Many college students form friendships with slightly older persons such as seniors, graduate students, or young faculty members who frequently offer guidance in loco parentis. Students may also experience conflicts with parents that threaten a developing relationship. Consider the father who has dreamed of sending his son to medical school. If the father perceives his son's intimate relationship as a potential threat to this plan, he may demand: "Stop seeing her or I will stop paying for your education." Parents' control over students' financial welfare can extend as well to control over their love lives.

For many students, graduation from college precipitates a "commitment crisis." Time and again students come to our offices with much the same problem:

> I think that I am in love with him, but he has been accepted to graduate school and I don't want to go there. I have my own career to think about. But I am pretty sure that if we go our separate ways now, it will in all likelihood spell the end of our relationship. This whole situation is driving me crazy and I don't know what to do."

In years past, many women in this situation would have subordinated their own career plans in order to sustain the relationship. Today, many relationships founder at this point unless arrangements can be made for both persons to pursue their own career goals in the same geographic area.

In their study of breakups before marriage, Hill, Rubin, and Peplau (1977) find it useful to speak of "his breakup" and "her breakup." Contrary to commonly accepted stereotypes, these investigators found that breakups are much harder on men. Men find it more difficult to believe that they are no longer loved. As we have noted, this sex difference might be explained by women's greater practicality in love relationships. In general, these investigators found support for the view that the partners in a lasting relationship are likely to share equal commitments to it. Their data indicate that only 23 percent of equally involved couples broke up compared to 54 percent of those relationships in which one person was more committed than the other.

Because the couples they studied were college students, Hill, Rubin, and Peplau found that relationships tended to break up at clear demarcations in the school year: May-June, September, December-January. Understandably, the person interested in terminating the relationship found it easier to suggest just before vacation that "It might not be a bad idea for us to date others while we are apart." Also, as might be expected, individuals' conception of the relationship differed according to whether they acted in the role of "breaker-upper" or "broken-up-with." Both women and men felt considerably "less depressed, less lonely, freer, happier, but more guilty when they were the breaker-uppers than when they were the broken-up-with" (Hill, Rubin, and Peplau, 1977:324). Moreover, there is a tendency for each partner to claim that he or she initiated the breakup. It is obviously preferable to define the situation as one in which you have exercised power and, therefore, largely controlled another's behavior.

Many relationships end in the face of the kinds of pressures we have described. Alternatively, it does frequently happen that persons develop a commitment to a relationship because it has continued over a long time period. Intimate relationships often develop a momentum as a result of sheer endurance. Investing time and energy in their own relationship while foregoing others commits people; often they remain in the relationship even when it becomes a painful one (see Becker, 1960). . . .

Relationships are not static, thing-like entities. Rather, they are continually being interpreted and reevaluated by the participants. Such interpretation and evaluation does not occur randomly. We described the process through which strangers are transformed into intimates as constituting a "career" with discernible stages. Relying on current literature, we analyzed the "typical" movement of a relationship from the participants' achievement of rapport to self-revelation to mutual demonstration of commitment. . . .

REFERENCES

BACH, G., and DEUTSCH, R. *Pairing: How to achieve genuine intimacy.* New York: Avon Books, 1970.

BECKER, H. "Notes on the Concept of Commitment." *American Journal of Sociology,* 1960, 66, 32–40.

BYRNE, D. "Continuity between the Experimental Study of Attracton and Real-Life Computer Dating." *Journal of Personality and Social Psychology,* 1970, 16, 157–165.

DAVIS, M. *Intimate relations.* New York: The Free Press, 1973.

HILL, C., RUBIN, Z., and PEPLAU, I. "Breakups Before Marriage: The End of 103 Affairs." In A. Skolnick and J. Skolnick (Eds.), *Family in transition,* Boston: Little, Brown, 1977.

KIERKEGAARD, S. *Either/or.* Garden City, N.Y.: Doubleday Anchor, 1959.

KNAFL, K. "Preparing for Marriage: A Case of Misrepresentation." Paper presented at the *American Sociological Association Annual Meetings.* San Francisco, California, 1975.

REISS, IRA. "Toward a Sociology of the Heterosexual Love Relationship." *Marriage and Family Living,* May 1960, 22, p. 143.

RUBIN, Z. *Liking and loving.* New York: Holt, Rinehart & Winston, 1973.

WALLER, W. *The family: A dynamic interpretation.* Hinsdale, Ill.: Dryden Press, 1938.

CHAPTER 20

The Meaning of Love

Thomas E. Lasswell / Marcia E. Lasswell

ABSTRACT: The term "love" has many meanings. Six types of love have been identified: storge (life-long friends), agapic (totally "thou" centered), mania (possessiveness and intense dependency), pragma (logical-sensible), ludus (self-centered game player), and eros (romantic). Having unique characteristics, these types represent highly contrasting styles of loving (or ways of approaching emotional involvements).

[Among both clinicians and clients] there seems to be a popular belief that there *is* such a phenomenon as love. It is also commonly believed that there is *one* "true" or "perfect" kind of love that *ought* to be achieved before two people marry or otherwise commit themselves to each other. The suggestion that there may be other kinds of love is usually met with the reply that if there are, they must be "infatuations," "puppy-love," or they are labeled with some other apparently negative judgmental term which implies that it is not "real love."

The term "love" appears frequently in the sociological literature on marriage and the family as well as in questionnaires and interview schedules used to gather basic research data; yet attempts made to define love are confusing at best.

Even in this scientific age, many people feel that love should or must remain a mystery. Thousands of years ago, Solomon said: "Three things are too wonderful for me; four I do not understand: the way of an eagle in the sky, the way of a serpent on a rock, the way of a ship on the high seas, and the way of a man with a maiden" (Proverbs 30:18, 19).

More recently, others (e.g., Senator Proxmire) have suggested that analyzing or defining love may destroy it. We differ from both of these categories of critics in that we believe that there is perhaps as much to be gained from studying the way of a man with a maiden as has been gained from studying the way of an eagle in the air or the way of a ship on the high seas.

In our initial examination of the idea that love means different things to different people, we constructed definitions of six hypothetical types of love, defined them operationally, tested the operational definitions for their distinctness and exclusivity of meaning, and then constructed profiles of the six scales which measured the six types of love for 188 subjects. As expected, we found both individual and categorical differences among the profiles of the subjects. . . .

A personal profile was computed to show the extent to which each subject conceptualized "love" as each of the six types. This profile is called the SAMPLE profile, so named by using the initial letter of each of the six scales. . . .

CONSTRUCTED TYPES OF LOVE

A description of the constructed types follows:

Storge (Life-Long Friends)

The constructed type of storgic love is characterized by rapport, self-revelation, interdependency, and mutual need fulfillment (Reiss, 1960). Storgic lovers are essentially good friends who have grown in intimacy through close association, with an unquestioned assumption that their relationship will be permanent and that they will find a way to deal with their problems that causes them minimum pain. A storgic lover does not fantasize finding some other—perhaps unknown but ideal—lover in the future and abandoning the storgic partner. It never occurs to extreme storgic types that a romantic "knight on a white horse" or "femme fatale" will appear at some future time to solve their problems. It is more likely that even if this should occur to the storgic lover, he/she would need the storgic partner around to discuss the romantic lover, to give advice, and to share the joys of discovery.

The storgic lover is not a person bored by routine home activity, but is more likely to find it comfortable and relaxing. Storgic lovers are not constantly on the search for new love experiences; rather they enjoy the security of being able to predict each other's responses to their behaviors.

If storgic lovers should break up, they would probably remain close and caring friends, perhaps continue corresponding with one another and actively caring about one another.

Physical intimacy, coitus, and the appreciation of their partners as sexual persons usually come relatively late in a storgic relationship, are accepted comfortably and joyously when they do appear on the scene, and are thus satisfying. Pure storgic types are extremely unlikely to "keep an eye out" for new or more romantic sexual partners.

Temporary separations are not great problems to storgic persons. Their mutual trust is such that separations are viewed as necessary inconveniences, needed diversions, or opportunities for personal growth which will either improve or at least not damage their relationship.

The storgic lover does not "fall in love" in the way that other types of lovers do. The storgic type is more likely to recognize that he/she has been in love for some time without realizing it earlier. As a result, anniversaries, birthdays, Valentine's Day, and like occasions are not important to them and may even be forgotten or overshadowed by other matters.

In many ways storgic lovers resemble siblings in their understanding of the love relationship. If they fight and argue, it is not an indication that they do not love each other. They are likely to feel that when their love has matured it will be permanent and that they cannot replace their relationship with each other any more than they can replace those that they have with siblings or with parents.

Agapic (Totally "Thou" Centered)

An agapic lover is forgiving. This kind of lover typically assumes that when the loved one causes pain to himself or herself or to someone else, that he or she is acting in ignorance, innocent error, or is the victim of forces not originating in the love-object's personality. A male agapic lover might, for example help his female love object arrange an abortion if she became pregnant by someone else during their love affair. Or he might easily love and accept a child conceived by some other man with deep concern for the anguish caused to his loved one and with tender affection for the child. An agapic lover would be more likely to help his or her love object to get medical attention for a venereal disease contracted from someone else during their love affair than to be angry or punitive toward the love object for having a sexual relationship with another.

Agapic persons never "fall in love." Their love for others is always available and they are simply given the opportunity by some of their love objects to show their love to a greater extent than they are by others. An agapic lover cares enough about his/her love object's happiness to understand and give up the loved one if that would seem to give him or her a greater chance for happiness elsewhere.

An agapic lover is patient with the behaviors of his or her love object to an extent that seems to border on masochism. The ideal agapic lover would wait indefinitely for a love object to be released from prison or from a mental hospital, would tolerate the behaviors of an alcoholic or drug-addicted spouse, and would be willing to live with a partner who was engaging in illegal or immoral activities, even though he/she personally disapproved of such behaviors. The agapic lover is always supportive of his/her partner.

Mania (Possessiveness and Intense Dependency)

The constructed ideal of this type of lover is obsessed with his or her love object. A manic lover may be unable to sleep, eat, or even think logically around the loved one. The manic lover has peaks of excitement, but also depths of depression, with very few periods without a high or low.

This type of lover is jealous to an extent that might be described as irrational. A manic lover cannot tolerate loss of contact with a love object, even for short periods of time, and is distressed by a lack of the lover's presence or anticipated interaction. A manic lover is typically crushed by either real or fancied rejection, possibly to the point of suicidal ideation.

The manic lover often tries to manipulate the behaviors or feelings of the loved one, but because he or she seems to be bereft of logic, often succeeds only in looking foolish in his or her own eyes. For example, a manic lover may tell the loved one that they should spend a few days apart to think objectively about their relationship, and then go into a state of panic because the partner cannot be located during that period. Manic lovers do not tolerate separation at all well. . . .

Mania is probably associated with low self-esteem and a poor self-concept. Because of this, manic persons are typically not attractive to persons who have good self-concepts and high self-esteem. They become burdensome to more self-sufficient others. If they are rejected by them, their anxieties intensify, making them even less attractive.

Pragma (Logical-Sensible)

The ideal constructed type identified as pragma is that of a person who is unable to invest love in "unworthy" love objects. The pragmatic lover is keenly aware of the comparison level for alternatives that he or she has. Pragmatic lovers are inclined to look realistically at their own assets, decide on their "market value" and set off to get the best possible "deal" in their partners. Once the "deal" is made, the pragmatic lover remains loyal and faithful and defines his or her status as "in love" because the loved one is a "good bargain." Should the assets of either partner change, the pragmatic lover may feel her or his contract has been violated, and may begin to search for another partner.

A pragmatic lover typically assists the loved one to fulfill his or her potentials; for example, such a lover might make sure the love object finishes school, asks for deserved promotions, gets the attention that he or she "deserves" from physicians, stockbrokers, or employers.

Typically, a pragmatic lover maximizes his or her own assets before "putting them on the market." A male pragma may decide not to become involved with any females until he has $10,000 in the bank, or has gone through psychoanalysis, or has a secure job, or has assured himself by reading enough or consulting experts to be sure that he is sexually skillful, or the like. A sterile or impotent pragmatic lover may deliberately seek out a widow or widower with children if he or she wants a family.

Once a prospect is in sight, the prototypical pragmatic lover might check out future in-laws and friends systematically, find out if the couple's Rh factors are compatible, and obtain assurance that there is a minimal probability of hereditary defects showing up in their mutual children, and so forth.

Pragmatic persons break up or divorce or stay married for practical reasons. Divorce may actually be planned for some future date. For example, pragmatic partners may decide to finish school, to get a different job at another location, to put their youngest child through high school, or to reach some other such goal or state before they get divorced.

Pragma always looks at things *in context* and knows his or her basic values, scaling everything by them. (E.g., if sex life is mediocre, pragma may consult a sex counselor, but is more likely to assign sexual activity a low value in his or her value system and simply accept its mediocrity. "After all, he *is* a good provider, and being orgasmic isn't all that important." "She *is* a good mother, and I can get by on coitus once a week without getting too tense.") . . .

Pragma thinks ahead about family size (and probably even about what sex the children will be). If pragma is a schoolteacher, he or she may plan an October/November conception so the baby will arrive during vacation.

Ludus (Self-Centered Game Player)

The ideal constructed type of a ludic lover is that of a person who "plays" love affairs as he or she plays games or puzzles—to win, to get the greatest rewards for the least cost. A ludic lover hates dependency, either in himself/herself or in others. This type shies away from commitment of any sort (does not like lovers to take him or her for granted). The ludic lover enjoys strategies, and may keep two or three or even four lovers "on the string" at one time. A ludic person may even create a fictional lover to discourage a real one's hopes for a permanent relationship. He or she avoids long-range plans, is careful not to date the same person often enough to create the illusion of a stable relationship. A ludic lover would rather find a new sex partner than to work out sexual problems with an old one. And yet, he or she may suddenly show up for a replay, even years later, with birthday flowers, a bottle of a favorite wine, a sentimental Valentine, or a record of a favorite song, and vanish just as suddenly. A ludic person usually enjoys love affairs, and hence rarely regrets them unless the threat of commitment or dependency becomes too great.

Dates with a ludic person are never dull, even though they may not happen with great regularity. He or she is never possessive or jealous. The ludic lover usually has good self-concept, usually is assured of current success in love as well as most other areas. Unlike a pragmatic lover, a ludic lover never reveals all of himself or herself nor demands such revelation by partners.

Ludic lovers are not likely to be very sophisticated sexually. As a rule, they have only one sexual routine; if the sex partner is not pleased by the ludic lover's sexual pattern, then the ludic one simply finds another partner rather than attempting to improve an unsatisfying relationship. . . . Sex is self-centered and may be exploitative rather than symbolic of a relationship. A ludic lover does not listen to (or take time for) feedback; that suggests commitment, which is "scary." A ludic lover may not even *want* to be his or her partner's best sex partner because that might necessitate commitment or dependency that would be "awful." Physical appearance of the partners is less important than other qualities, such as self-sufficiency and lack of demanding behavior, to ludic persons.

Eros (Romantic)

The constructed type of Eros is *romantic* love. Erotic lovers believe that love at first sight is possible if not mandatory. Falling in love is highly desirable, it is believed to produce an optimum state in the whole mind-body; persons in love feel ten years younger, sleep well, wake up rested and refreshed. Impotent persons become potent; inorgasmic persons become orgasmic. Every gland and organ is believed to be operating at maximum efficiency.

Eros is monogamous although often serially. Erotic lovers remember exactly how their partners looked when they met; they remember exactly the day they met, the time they first touched, the time they first kissed, the day, hour, minute, place, smell, lighting effects of their first sex; and they expect their partners to remember and celebrate the anniversaries of such occasions.

An erotic lover is certain he or she is in love because the beloved has *exactly* the skin, fragrance, hair, voice, body build, eye color, and style he or she likes the most. If that is not objectively true, it becomes easy to *believe* it is true.

The romantic lover must always have his or her best foot forward. Risks of losing the beloved cannot be afforded. On the other hand, erotic lovers constantly search for new ways to please their beloveds with ever-increasing delights—presents, new foods, new sexual techniques, and so on.

An erotic lover wants to know *everything* about the beloved from the first moment of their meeting, all of his or her experiences, joys and sorrows, who else he or she has loved in the past, how much and in what ways. At the same time, an erotic lover want to *reveal* everything to the loved one—what she or he dreamed about last night, what happened on the bus today, how a second-grade teacher embarrassed him or her.

Erotic lovers may like to wear matching T-shirts, identical bracelets, matching colors, order the same foods when dining out, find out that their blood types are the same; they typically want to be identified with each other as totally as possible.

Erotic lovers usually report having had a secure and happy childhood and believe that their parents were happily married.

If erotic lovers do not get jealous it is because they are rarely apart. There is thorough commitment. An erotic type can go quite comfortably without falling in love, sometimes for a long time, but when cupid strikes, it is hard, fast, and total. Break-ups are explosive and painful.

Erotic lovers initiate sex early in their relationship. It is always perceived as perfect, or becoming so, as indeed are all qualities of and experiences with the partner.

These six types are ideal constructs. Rarely is anyone a "pure" type. Rather, persons have varying degrees of each quality. They may be high in two or even three scales or they may have only moderate elevation in some categories and be very low in all of the rest. The cognitive component of each person's sentiment of love is best shown by the profile which shows the degree to which the subject fits each ideal type.

REFERENCES

Holy Bible, Revised Standard Version, Catholic Edition. Camden, N.J.: Thomas Nelson & Sons, 1966.

LEE, J. A. "The Styles of Loving." *Psychology Today,* October 1974, 44–51.

REISS, I. L. "Toward a Sociology of the Heterosexual Love Relationship." *Marriage and Family Living,* 1960, 22, 139–145.

SECTION 6

Dating and Mating

As I HAVE STRESSED EARLIER, each of us is socialized into both dominant ideas of masculinity or femininity and the idea that we will fall in love. Matching this cultural expectation of romance and love is the belief that dating is the means by which love will come about. Dating, an essential part of romance, will somehow provide the framework within which each of us finds love, and, ultimately, the right marriage partner.

Within this commonly held "romance-love-dating" complex the sex role into which each of us has been so carefully socialized takes on new meaning. Not without a great deal of trepidation and uncertainty, we begin through dating to see ourselves as true sexual beings. We learn to relate to members of the opposite sex in a form that marks the watershed between "childhood" and "not-childhood." In our culture we do not award adulthood because people date, but we do acknowledge that they are no longer children. This in-between status of being a "not child" and a "not adult," this sort of literal no man's land, brings with it severe identity problems that are carried into the dating situation.

First-time daters have been learning their basic masculinity and femininity for an average of fourteen years. For the last couple of years of this "training period," these same individuals have been growing in sexual interest and have been painfully learning expectations of proper interaction with members of the opposite sex. They have begun to discover themselves tentatively as sexual beings. Now they are expected to date in order to: (1) enjoy themselves (but not sexually); (2) develop their sex-role capabilities (but, again, not sexually); and (3) begin the process that will result in finding their future, lifelong mate (with whom sexual interaction will be desired, expected, and eventually required).

In our cultural dictate of wisdom, then, young and inexperienced daters are sent out alone, at night, into situations that maximize "close encounters of the real kind." They are expected to follow the adults' slightly jaundiced but highly hopeful expectations to enjoy themselves, develop socially, and not become involved with sex. Any Martian who might be dispassionately examining the American scene and who knows anything about humans could predict what this contradictory framework will lead to. It cannot possibly accomplish only what it is supposed to and not result in what it is not supposed to. It does not take much sociological expertise to predict that these circumstances will result in sex—and a lot of it.

People who have been told for years that they should "grow up" and "act like an adult" are, indeed, going to act like adults when the adult action is something that pleases them. For years they have yearned to be adults, and all along there was this one area that was reserved exclusively for adults, an area that the adults were somewhat secretive about. This activity has become equivalent both to being adult and to having intense fun—from the stories they have heard, the workings of their imagination, and their knowledge of their own bodies it comes to be thought of as perhaps the most pleasurable experience available in life.

As has been emphasized in previous introductions, from our social experiences we develop ideas of how the world is, and we then act according to these ideas. With this highly charged view of sexual relations, along with the context of American dating customs (mostly alone and at night), it is no wonder that premarital sexual relations are a frequent result.

Contradictory influences are at work, however, and each has some effect. Preteenagers and teenagers learn from both adults and their peers. From adults they generally learn they should not have sexual relations until they are married. But the message often comes out fuzzy. It usually begins clearly enough, but when probed it becomes surrounded with many "excepts," "in the case of," "unless," "Well, certainly not if . . .," and "Definitely not until. . . ." Through this muddled mess that represents the adults' confusion about social change, the cryptic message is deciphered. "Sex is ok if . . .," with the *if* being filled in with particulars from the individual's unique environment.

During the same time that adults are offering their cryptic communication, the individual is hearing a much clearer message from his or her own peer group. Specific information is filtering down from the older teens at school, and from these conversations are ordinarily developed expectations of sexual intimacy that differ radically from those typically held by parents. The direction, or course, is not toward greater sexual stringency, but greater sexual latitude. More is approved by peers than most parents would ever dream of—much, much more.

The "message" is never uniform, however. There is neither blanket approval on the part of peers, nor is there blanket disapproval on the part of parents and other adults. Some approve in general, while others generally disapprove. Some disapprove under a particular set of circumstances, while others approve under that same set of circumstances while disapproving under another set, and so on. Cultural change does not affect everyone, or every group of people, in the same way. Consequently, there is a great deal of confusion over this highly volatile issue.

Dating, appearing at first glance to be a private interaction between two people, is really a playing out by individuals of roles (or expectations) that have been developed for them by others and accepted for the self. In one sense, the whole society goes along on a "private" date. In this sociological sense, the two persons are playing out in their own lives the various contradictory forces in which they are immersed.

No one, then, is really alone. Each of us has been socialized for so many years into our sex role that we can never leave the role and "be ourselves." For where is the self apart from the role? The role that has been constructed so carefully for us becomes us. We ultimately become persons who have accepted a sex role and who play out its expectations within the general framework laid down for us.

It is apparent, then, that the particular framework into which we have been socialized is highly influential in determining what we will do—even during the "privacy" of a date. No researcher, however, has adequately grasped the dynamics of how conflicting expectations are worked out in actual situations. But to your own experiences, which have led you to some point of understanding how this occurs, you can add these general features. Norms will be followed that: (1) were learned the earliest; (2) were learned with the greatest intensity; (3) were learned with the greatest consistency; (4) were learned over the longest period of time; (5) are supported by a set of strongly held related norms; and (6) for which there is the least exposure to contradictory norms.

From these general principles it becomes apparent that making moral choices is extremely complicated. It is most difficult to know what "intensity" is. And how does one measure "consistency"? What was learned earliest may have been superseded by recent contradictory learning. It is especially the sixth item that gives trouble. When it comes to premarital sex, for example, contradictory norms are certainly present. "Pro-sex" norms, though only recently learned, may have been learned under compelling situations of highly valued peer expectations ("high intensity") and thus be the significant factor in determining behavior.

Certainly the norms governing sexual behavior have undergone major modification in recent years—so much so that some analysts refer to a "sexual revolution" in the United States and the western world. Just how much of a "revolution," however, has really occurred in our midst? In the opening chapter to this section Theodore Caplow et al. look at the changes in sexual behaviors of adolescents during the past sixty years. They conclude that there has not been so much of a revolution as a gradual, continuous evolution in sexual standards among American youth.

In the next two chapters, we swing the sociological spotlight to college dating. Pepper Schwartz and Janet Lever examine what happens at a college mixer; then Elyce Pike and Stephen Hall analyze the problems that college students experience when they go on a first date. Keep in mind the participants' early socialization into sex roles as you attempt to understand their behaviors and feelings in these dating situations.

In spite of the changing sexual standards, the game playing, and the playing out of sex roles, in almost all cases it is through dating that Americans choose their mates. In the midst of what often are contradictory and conflicting expectations, more than 90 percent eventually make a decision concerning the choice of a mate. How does this happen? Of all the people there are in this world, how does someone decide to marry a particular person? The broadly explanatory concepts of "true love" and "the one and only" are very handy at a time like this—but they really explain little or nothing. The scientist, however, searches for answers, and in this section's concluding chapter Bruce K. Eckland reviews the wide-ranging theories of mate selection.

The final answers to these questions, though, are far from clear, and if you are married you probably can identify many reasons why you married your spouse. Accident, circumstance, socialization, timing, choice—they all carry a part of the answer. If you are not married, you probably can identify several reasons for your current desire to get married some day—or not get married, as the case may be.

CHAPTER 21

Sexual Revolution, Sexual Evolution—Or Just More of the Same?

Theodore Caplow / Howard M. Bahr / Bruce A. Chadwick / Reuben Hill / Margaret Holmes Williamson

ABSTRACT: In the 1920s Muncie, Indiana, was the subject of a classic sociological study by Robert and Helen Lynd (*Middletown*). The authors of this chapter replicated that study in the late 1970s. From that encompassing study of an entire community we present some of their materials on the sexual behaviors of the town's adolescents.

Already in the 1920s Middletown's adolescents were undergoing extensive change in their sexual behaviors. During this time petting became common, a sort of compromise between sexual desire and the value of sexual purity. Petting patterns persisted into the late 1950s. The incidence of premarital sex climbed during the 1950s and continued to increase during the 1960s and 1970s. Most of the change was on the part of females, who became more willing to go beyond petting. In general, the change among Middletown's adolescents has not been revolutionary, but is best seen as a gradual liberalizing in their sexual behavior: Middletown youth have remained strong believers in monogamy, and most of their premarital sex is brief, infrequent, and limited to one partner.

In describing apparent changes in Middletown's sexual behavior, it is easy to compare today's Middletown with the Middletown of the 1950s, before the sexual revolution. Most of the information communicated to us by local people relates to changes that have occurred during the past two decades. It is much harder to make comparisons with the Middletown of the 1920s, as described by the Lynds; we are hampered by the sketchiness of their material on sex. Their only reliable data about sexual activity came from the high school survey. Paradoxically, we found the schools less permissive in the 1970s and were unable to replicate their surveys; we were warned by school officials that questions about sexual behavior would be defined as invasions of privacy and would present difficulties to the legal counsel and school administrators who had to approve our questionnaires before they could be used.

The Middletown studied by the Lynds during the 1920s was in the throes of sexual revolution as far-reaching as the one we have experienced during the past two decades. The earlier revolution's components were the change from courtship to dating that came with the advent of the automobile; the initiation of dating by girls; the use of feminine clothing for erotic display instead of erotic concealment; and the development of sex, especially illicit sex, as the dominant theme in popular literature and movies.

The automobile freed young people from adult surveillance and greatly enhanced their opportunities for intimacy. Before the era of the automobile, courting had been home-centered. Dating in automobiles meant that teenagers and young adults selected their own partners and spent their evenings outside the range of parental disapproval, often in the backseats of parked cars. The circulation among high school students of magazines like *True Story*, which told tales of sexual adventure, and the "constant witnessing of 'sex films'" also heightened young people's interest in sex, according to the Lynds (1929, 138).

As for changing fashions in clothing and in the initiation of dates, Middletown mothers in the 1920s had these comments to make.

> It's the girls' clothing; we can't keep our boys decent when girls dress that way.
>
> Girls have more nerve nowadays—look at their clothes!
>
> Girls are far more aggressive today. They call the boys up to try to make dates with them as they never would have when I was a girl.
>
> Last summer six girls organized a party and invited six boys and they never got home until three in the morning. Girls are always calling my boys up trying to make dates with them [Lynd and Lynd 1929, 140].

There was also some corroboration from the young people themselves. Half of the junior and senior high school students the Lynds interviewed agreed that "nine out of every ten boys and girls of high school age have 'petting parties,'" and, among the entire high school population, 44 percent of the boys and 34 percent of the girls indicated that they had taken part in a "petting party" (Lynd and Lynd 1929, 138–39).

We have only fragmentary evidence from which to reconstruct the patterns of sexual behavior common in the 1920s, since no general studies of American sexuality were undertaken until Kinsey's studies in the 1940s. According to Morton Hunt, who has pieced together a description of sexual change in America, the 1920s were the era when petting became popular. The dating pattern that emerged in the twenties provided the opportunity to engage in premarital intercourse. But traditional values proscribing such behavior were slow to fade, and Hunt argued that petting emerged as a compromise between new opportunities and old values. Although petting included most of the sexual activities that often precede intercourse, it stopped short of actual intercourse and allowed sexually active girls to preserve their virginity technically. In Hunt's words, petting was the compromise between "desire and purity."

> In 20th-Century America, however, petting came to occupy a most significant position in terms not only of the number of persons involved but of the number of years involved. Even in its "game" aspect, it was serious business: The boy tried to see how much he could get—and the girl how little she could give—by way of recompense for the time and money he had spent on her, and the better he "made out," the higher was his status among his fellows, while the less she gave in, the more desirable she was deemed. But petting was also expressing erotic and emotional feelings before marriage. The more deeply a boy and girl cared about each other, the "further" they considered it all right to go. The standard enforced by the girls and grudgingly accepted by the boys held, in a general way, that kissing was all right if the two merely liked each other; "deep" or "French" kissing if they felt romantic about each other; breast touching through the clothing if they were halfway "serious" about each other, and with the bra off if they were somewhat more serious than that; and explorations "below the waist" . . . only if the couple considered themselves really in love [Hunt 1974, 132–33].

The emergence of petting as acceptable sexual expression between dating partners did not preclude entirely premarital intercourse. But the fragmentary evidence suggests that, although the incidence of premarital intercourse had increased between the turn of the century and the 1920s, it was much less common than petting.

Kinsey (Kinsey, Pomeroy, and Martin 1948 and 1953), writing 25 years after the Lynds, reported substantial differences in the incidence of premarital sexual behavior by sex and class. Twice as many young men as young women reported having premarital sexual intercourse. Working-class men reported having more premarital intercourse and less petting than business-class men. The double standard kept most young girls from having intercourse with their boyfriends, many of whom experienced their sexual initiation with prostitutes.

A pioneer study of premarital sexual behavior was conducted in the mid-1930s by Louis Terman. Although Terman's sample was not representative of the entire nation, his findings did suggest that some remarkable changes had occurred in sexual behavior during the first decades of the century. Of his male subjects born before 1890, 51 percent had been virgins when they married; the corresponding proportion for men born after 1910 was only 14 percent (Terman 1938, 321–23). Of his female subjects born before 1890, 87 percent said that they had been virgins when they married, compared to only 32 percent of those born after 1910. Terman predicted that premarital coitus would become increasingly common to the point that practically all men born after 1930 and all women born after 1940 would be sexually experienced at marriage.

Surprisingly, Terman's prediction was wrong. The petting pattern seems to have stabilized in the mid-1930's and persisted through the 1950s. . . .

The incidence of premarital intercourse began to increase again in the late 1960s and continued to increase during the 1970s. Most studies agree that the change in male behavior has been rather modest, with the exception of a significant increase in the sexual activity of college men. Hunt surveyed a national sample of men over 18 years old in 1972 and found that by the age of 17 half of the college-bound young men had premarital coital experience, which is more than double the rate reported by Kinsey in the late 1940s. The increase for males not attending college was much smaller, only 5 or 6 percentage points (Hunt 1974, 149). Thus, for men as a group the increase in premarital sex during the past decades has not been particularly startling. Although unmarried men are having more premarital sex, the increase certainly does not warrant the term "revolution."

Much more change apparently has occurred in the sexual activities of young women. [Table 21.1] illustrates changes in the percentage of women who reported that they had premarital coital experience during their teen years. The change from the Kinsey era (1938–1949) to 1971 is impressive. The rates of premarital sex in 1971 are more than double the 1940s rates for each age category. But the increase during the subse-

TABLE 21.1 Percentages of White American Teenage Girls Who Have Ever Had Premarital Intercourse, by Age, 1938–1949, 1971, and 1976

Age	1938–1949	1971	1976
14		2.1	2.6
15	1.0	4.3	7.0
16	2.0	8.8	16.4
17	8.0	18.1	29.1
18	14.0	28.7	42.2
19	18.0	42.6	55.8

SOURCES: Kinsey, Pomeroy, and Martin 1953, 286 (the data are taken from a figure, which limits the preciseness of the percentages); Zelnik, Young, and Kantner 1979.

quent five years (1971–1976) was nearly as great. By 1976, over half of the unmarried 19-year-old girls in the United States had engaged in intercourse. The liberation of women and the consequent demise of the double standard brought men and women to virtual equality in premarital sexual experience.

That more than half of all men and women are sexually experienced when they marry for the first time does not mean that most young Americans are promiscuous. The premarital sexual experience of most of them is brief, infrequent, and limited to one partner (or a few) whom they hope to marry. One exhaustive analysis of the studies of premarital sexual behavior conducted since 1965 concluded that, while there has been a gradual liberalizing of premarital sexual behavior, "the available data suggest a gradual evolution in sexual behavior of adolescents; there is little support for the notion of a sexual revolution" (Diepold and Young 1979, 45).

We do not wish to minimize the changes in premarital sexual behavior that have occurred in the United States during recent decades, whether we call them an evolution or a revolution. They have been important, and often they have been startling. But surely the mass media have exaggerated the scope of the changes. Monogamic heterosexual marriage is still the nearly universal norm, and most nonmarital sexual behavior involves the possibility of eventual marriage.

The national trend toward increased tolerance of premarital sex and increased rates of sexual activity among the young is clearly evident in Middletown. Every indicator, from the perceptions of local observers to the statistics assembled by Planned Parenthood, from the percentage of out-of-wedlock births to teenagers to the percentage of abortions that involve pregnant teenagers, suggests that there had been a substantial increase in the amount of premarital sexual activity. . . .

Planned Parenthood has come to play an increasingly important role as a provider of contraceptive information and supplies for teenagers in Middletown. In 1976, 6 percent of Middletown's teenage girls were clients of Planned Parenthood. By 1979 [as noted elsewhere], more than a third used that service. Planned Parenthood estimates that 42 percent of Middletown's teenage girls were sexually active in 1978. The abortion rate for teenage girls in Middletown's county increased from 29.5 per 1,000 in 1974 to 41.1 in 1977 and then declined to 36.5 in 1978. Figures from the National Center for Health Statistics show that in 1975 Middletown had an illegitimacy rate of 146 (i.e., 146 out-of-wedlock births per 1,000 live births) compared to 90 in 1970 and 58 in 1957. (See [Table 21.2].)

Some of the change in the sexual attitudes and activity of teenagers may be attributable to a long-term decline in the age of sexual maturity. Today's youngsters achieve sexual maturity about two years earlier than their grandparents did. The average age for the onset of menstrua-

TABLE 21.2 Out-of-Wedlock Births per 1,000 Live Births, Middletown, 1957–1975

Year	Out-of-Wedlock Births	Total Live Births	Out-of-Wedlock Births per 1,000 Live Births
1957	106	1,838	57.7
1960	104	1,752	59.4
1962	98	1,667	58.8
1964	110	1,671	65.8
1966	132	1,644	80.3
1968	112	1,615	69.3
1970	156	1,733	90.0
1972	174	1,468	118.5
1974	204	1,379	147.9
1975	178	1,221	145.8

SOURCES: Figures for out-of-wedlock births are from U.S. Census data; total live births are from Indiana State Board of Health 1976, 90, and 1966–1975.

tion today is about 12 (Tanner 1973), and 14-year-old high school girls can and do pass as full-grown women. This influence, however, is difficult to assess. . . .

REFERENCES

DIEPOLD, JOHN, JR., and RICHARD DAVID YOUNG. "Empirical Studies of Adolescent Sexual Behavior: A Critical Review," *Adolescence* 14 (Spring 1979), 45.

HUNT, MORTON. *Sexual Behavior in the 1970's*. Chicago: Playboy Press, 1974.

Indiana State Board of Health. *Annual Statistical Reports*. Indianapolis: Division of Public Health Statistics, 1966–1975.

______. *Marriages by County of Marriage and Month of Occurrence*. Indianapolis: Division of Public Health Statistics, 1976.

KINSEY, ALFRED, WARDELL B. POMEROY, and CLYDE E. MARTIN. *Sexual Behavior in the Human Male*. Philadelphia: W. Saunders Company, 1948.

______. *Sexual Behavior in the Human Female*. Philadelphia: W. B. Saunders Company, 1953.

LYND, ROBERT S., and HELEN MERRELL LYND. *Middletown: A Study in American Culture*. New York: Harcourt and Brace, 1929.

TANNER, J. M. "Growing Up," pp. 17–25 in *Life and Death and Medicine* (a Scientific American Book). San Francisco: W. H. Freeman and Company, 1973.

TERMAN, LOUIS H. *Psychological Factors in Marital Happiness*. New York: McGraw-Hill, 1938.

ZELNIK, MELVIN, KIM J. YOUNG, and JOHN F. KANTNER. "Probabilities of Intercourse and Conception among U.S. Teenage Women: 1971 and 1976," *Family Planning Perspectives* 11 (1979), 177–83.

CHAPTER 22

Fear and Loathing at a College Mixer

Pepper Schwartz / Janet Lever

ABSTRACT: In a study of a Yale "college mixer," a form of structured dating common at many universities, the authors found that the participants felt pressured to meet someone. During the mixer, males and females make hurried appraisals of one another on the basis of looks while at the same time feeling uncomfortable making such frank evaluations—as well as having such evaluations made about them. To avoid rejection, and to save "face," the participants utilize three protective devices: eye messages, ritualistic brush-offs, and an offensive-defensive tactic. Among its effects, the college mixer encourages males and females to perceive and treat one another as sexual commodities.

The predominant view expressed in the sociological literature on dating is that the social events and interactions are "fun" for the participants. An adult observer of adolescents at a social gathering would see them dressed up for the occasion, flirting with one another, dancing to loud music, engaging in light conversation, and generally seeming to be enjoying themselves. . . .

Our study of social patterns on a college campus leads us to believe

Author's Note: The authors are grateful to Wendell Bell, Philip Blumstein, Louis Wolf Goodman, R. Stephen Warner, and Stanton Wheeler for their helpful comments on an earlier draft of this paper. We also wish to thank J. A. Gilboy and Erving Goffman for the constructive criticism they offered at the 66th Annual Meeting of the American Sociological Association.

that the moves and countermoves of dating carry great meaning for the individual and for the group and that the process of finding a balance between self-protection and self-exposure is anything but pure play. The participant, while supposedly in a "light" environment of introduction to peers, is at the same time in a situation where his or her desirability as a partner is being tested. The rating and ranking of the individual may be apparent and stressful. As the individual seeks to be both vulnerable (open to meeting an attractive other) and self-protective (invulnerable to rejection), the social world becomes fraught with tension, anxiety, and implications for the individual's sense of self. . . .

The [college] mixer is a dance sponsored for the express purpose of meeting members of the opposite sex. Mixers have always been an integral part of the formal social system in most high schools, colleges, and universities. The ideal-type is represented by the schoolwide dance which ends freshman orientation week each fall. But graduate student "happy hours," sorority-fraternity exchanges, and dorm dances are variations on the same theme. . . .

These data were collected as part of a larger study chronicling the first year of coeducation at Yale (Lever and Schwartz, 1971). We conducted 96 in-depth interviews with Yale undergraduates.[1] Sixty-five percent of the women in our sample had transferred to Yale from Eastern women's colleges and had been long acquainted with the mixer system. Ninety percent of the men and women in the sample had attended at least one mixer during their college career. In addition, the authors were participant observers at five mixer dances during the academic year.

THE MIXER

Heterosexual encounters are universal features of the social world, but their forms vary according to the structural constraints of the environment. The physical location of monosexual schools place severe strains on the natural development of heterosexual relationships.[2] Yale is approximately 80 miles from Vassar, Smith, and Mt. Holyoke—the closest of the prestigious Seven Sister schools. The scheduling of classes forces monosexual institutions to endorse a weekend dating system, encouraging their students to study for five days and play for the remaining two. Even with the beginning of coeducation at Yale, the sex ratio remained weighted with eight men to every woman. Clearly, the men were forced to take steps to increase the recruitment pool of available women if they wanted to participate in heterosexual dating activities.

The mixer has long been the solution to this structural problem. Each of Yale's twelve residential colleges sponsors its own dances several times during the year. The social committees at the women's colleges charter buses for the trip and sell low-cost tickets on a first-come-first-serve basis. The less prestigious schools from the immediate vicinity also send small envoys, but the pain purpose of mixers is to attract women of comparable social status and educational attainment, i.e., potential future mates, not just sex partners for an evening. In this sense, mixers perform the same endogamous screening services of the sorority-fraternity system described by Scott (1965: 12).[3] Although the monosexual mixer bears important similarities to institutions on coeducational campuses, it also has special properties that cause strained relations between the sexes that we wish to explore.

Before the women arrive, the men take their positions in the college dining hall where the dance will take place. The dining room, like high school gymnasiums decked out for a prom, is suitably changed. The tables have been cleared away, the lights are low, and a stage has been marked off at one end of the room for the band. A beer table is set up, usually in the common room outside the dancing hall. Here the lights are brighter and groups of men stand around talking. This beer table will serve as a prop for them throughout the dance. Getting a beer gives people something to do when they need to look busy, provides an avenue of escape ("Pardon me, I think I'll go get a beer"), and allows people to get drunk to loosen inhibitions and numb sensitivities for the personal tests that are to come.

The typical mixer at Yale starts around 8:30 p.m., when the buses from surrounding women's colleges begin to arrive. These same buses leave promptly at midnight. So time pressure exists. In fact, the element of time points to one major difference between the mixer and other kinds of formal dating. The mixer is not like a Saturday night dance on a coeducated campus. The girl will not be there throughout the week. Both male and female are aware that they have approximately two hours to find out if they want to get to know each other better.

People must quickly evaluate each other and attempt to make contact with those they have decided are desirable partners for the evening. Some are mutually attracted, but many more get rebuffed or end up with someone they do not really care for. All night long people are being approved or discarded on the basis of one characteristic that is hard, or at least painful, to discount—their appearance.

When persons are asked to dance, their names are exchanged and often some light conversation occurs but the rating and ranking that goes on is still primarily by personal appearance. The music level is deafening. As one woman said, "How can you expect to really meet anyone at 400 decibels?" Since conversation is difficult and people have just met one another, physical appearance is the only criterion of selection. There is little chance to talk, to be clever or interesting or simply flattering. Therefore, if the other person is not interested, that fact cannot be rationalized as a lack of things in common, a fundamental difference in world views, or dissimilar kinds of temperament. Only one criterion exists, so the situation is bound to be more tense. When rejection is obvious and even recurrent within the same four-hour period, it makes inroads on one's self-image. Students reported feelings of "ugliness," "fatness," "clumsiness," and so forth during and after the mixer situation.[4]

Thus, there is a strong approach-avoidance tension in the air. Some women stand slightly apart so that they are more approachable; some stand close together and look indifferent. The general strategy of both sexes seems to be a question of how to achieve the maximum exposure with the least possible risk. That is, one wants to be seen and appreciated and asked for a dance (or be given the cue that someone would like you to ask her for a dance) without being seen as alone and needing someone. Erving Goffman (1967: 43) maintains that social life is orderly because people voluntarily stay away from places where they might be disparaged for going. The monosexual arena is different from the coeducated one precisely because the opportunities to meet others of the opposite sex in "safer" situations where one can protect his or her "face" have been minimized. Defensive maneuvers available in the mixer are few, difficult to manage, and, as we shall, see, can be self-defeating.

The men first ask pretty women or those with good figures to dance; women usually prefer handsome men or men with some sort of "cool." Being "cool" is not necessarily based on looks for a man. It means that somebody "puts himself together" well, that he walks or talks with some authority, or that he looks "interesting" or at ease. The participants know that the appearance criterion is inadequate and demeaning, but they use it. People are very conscious about how their partner will reflect on their own desirability. A male junior was very frank about the situation:

> There have been times when I've seen a girl and, you know, I imagined I might not get along too well with her just from talking with her, but she was so good-looking that I just wanted to be seen walking into the dining hall with her or something like that, something prestigious.

Since there is only one "prestigious" criterion, meeting the standard becomes more and more consuming. You try to better your own game. One man put it this way:

> It's such a superficial thing. You judge a girl there strictly by her looks. So you talk to a pretty girl while your eyes scan the floor for another pretty girl. . . . It's like looking at an object in the window. It's probably mutual.

Women *are* under the same sort of pressures. Besides appearance, a man's age influences his overall rating. A sophomore man testified to this fact bitterly:

> Sophomore and freshman girls really have a thing. It's very important to them that they be dating an upperclassman. Like last year when I would be at a dance and it would come out that I was a freshman, that was it.

[N]one of the women we interviewed, and only one of the men, claimed personally to like mixers. They referred to mixers as "body exchanges" and "meat markets." The women reacted most strongly against the mixer system. A junior transfer described her feelings:

> I generally think mixers are grotesque. There you are, a piece of meat lined up along a wall in this herd of ugly females. You try to stand casually as guys walk back and forth and you know you're on display. You just want to crawl up the wall. Then you're asked to dance by these really gross creatures. I'm so revolted by the whole thing. . . .

Throughout the evening men and women are conscious of being constantly evaluated, desired, or disregarded. But they don't leave the mixer even though they feel uncomfortable there. The women are captive until their buses leave at midnight; the men stay because the mixer is the place to secure names for the year's dating events. Because everyone's ego is threatened, people devise ways to protect themselves. Verbal patter and social maneuvering are used in this instance to avoid being too vulnerable. Fear of ridicule and rejection is so great that methods of ego preservation (be they cruel, clever, even ultimately self-defeating) are seen as essential. . . .

The three protective devices we saw and heard about most frequently were "eye messages," the "ritualistic brush-off," and the "offensive-defensive" tactic.

"Eye messages" are part of the more general category of body language. If someone undesirable is approaching, the uninterested party allows her eyes to glaze over; she looks past the individual and concentrates on some other direction. Or the person finds "something to do." A man becomes engrossed in the beer stand; a woman can be totally preoccupied in a hitherto trivial conversation with a friend. The eyes are straight—locked into the diversion—never once glancing in the direction of the person to be avoided. The intent is usually obvious: by denying eye contact, one is refusing to acknowledge the other's presence or claim on one's attentions. If eye contact is achieved, then the individuals are forced to interact, if only to the extent that now they must acknowledge ignoring one another.

On the other hand, eye contact can be used for the opposite effect. If the individual wishes to engage someone in an encounter, eye contact is used to grab attention. A really aggressive person may lock eyes with someone, but many just glance at one another. The meaning is clear, that is "I consider you very attractive. Come over," (Or, "Can I come over?") One senior described the technique which had served him well during his four years at Yale:

> You try to meet eyes with a girl who doesn't look happy with the person she's with, in the hope that she'll say she has to go to the bathroom. Then you pick her up on the return trip. It's a big game, obviously.

The woman who changes partners in the manner described above is employing what we call the "ritualistic brush-off." Excuses and lines that would be embarrassing to use elsewhere are used with great frequency during a mixer to get out of an unpleasant mismatch with the least amount of trauma and embarrassment for all concerned. Unfortunately, because they have become ritualized, they only mute the surface blow. Everyone recognizes them for what they are, and the rejection still hurts. The favorite line used by men, as we have mentioned, is "Pardon me, I think I'll go get a beer." At a mixer the ladies' room is to women what the beer table is to men. Leaving for the bathroom, as indicated in the quotation above, serves as an excuse for the woman to get out of an uncomfortable match and to reenter the room in a different area and meet new partners. Of course, she is bound to see the man she has "temporarily" left, but they usually avert eyes. It is an effective "good-bye."

Sometimes the rituals are only recognizable to one partner in the interaction. This way of ending further contact is even less benign. One woman related common practices among her friends at Wellesley:

> At Wellesley, I heard stories about how to brush off a guy you don't like. Like one thing you do is give him your phone number and when he calls he gets "Dial-A-Prayer." Or you tell him it's your number and it's really a guy's.

Instead of lines, some people merely say "thank you" with a final-sounding air. After the dance is over there are a couple of seconds of undefined meaning. The girl is undecided whether she is going to be asked to dance again, and the boy may be unsure whether the girl would like to stay with him. A "thank you" and exit often end the suspense—sometimes precipitously. Afraid to be the one who is turned down, people protect themselves by terminating the interaction first. We call this the "offensive-defensive" tactic. No matter what the original likelihood was that the couple would not get along, by "jumping the gun" the individual has made the outcome virtually guaranteed. This protective device often condemns the innocent before any act has been committed and nurtures the type of interaction that the individuals say they are trying to escape. . . .

People at a mixer, or in a mixer-like situation, describe members of the opposite sex as the "enemy." They act as though their chosen roles are conflicting, not complementary. They assess the risks of "winning" and "losing," net outcomes, and maintenance of face. Winning means a date, self-enhancement, status in the eyes of others. Losing means letting someone feel superior to you and perhaps accepting their definition of your unworthy status. It means being seen as less attractive than you had previously thought and having that verified in front of your peers. It means for some very vulnerable people, taking on an identity as a social maladept or Unattractive Person. This identity is one that most people will avoid even if avoidance means "cutting off one's nose to spite one's face."

Thus, a situation forces these kinds of choices [see Figure 22.1]: if the person terminates the encounter quickly, s/he has saved face, but s/he loses the opportunity to establish a new relationship. On the other hand, if the initiator (always the male) waits and tries to engage his partner for another dance, the woman may terminate the encounter and the man will consequently lose face. Again, the opportunity for a successful relationship—which is one's motive for risking "face" in the first place—is lost. Or if both the man and woman trust each other, there is a possibility that both will win what they are seeking. Unfortunately, since both have been to a mixer or similar event before, or heard about mixer norms, they do not expect that the other person will "cooperate" and openly court their attention; therefore, they minimize risk-taking by showing a low level of affect. The individuals have saved face, but in so doing they have undermined their initial goals.

Of course, some do play the game cooperatively, and risk face while allowing the other person to decide whether to continue the relationship or break it off. If the other person takes a similar risk, the couple will most likely remain together for the duration of the evening. Sometimes such unions are immediately romanticized by both persons as part of what we call the "pit or the pedestal" syndrome. That is, the boy then treats the girl as a "one-nighter" or as a "dream girl," and the girl makes a similar judgment. Because the mixer is experienced as unpleasant, both men and women are searching for someone they can date so that they minimize the number of mixers they must attend during the year. Because they live so far apart, there is encouragement for an immediate, intense experience that will justify a weekend together in the future.

For the majority, however, it is clear that the effects of the mixer are seen as personally destructive. To take a symbolic interactionist perspective, one's image of self grows out of interaction with significant others. Repeated failures can cause people to doubt their attractiveness to the opposite sex. A junior transfer reflected back on her three years in the mixer system:

		MALE	
		Continues	*Terminates*
FEMALE	*Continues*	opportunity for new relationship	loss of face for female
	Terminates	loss of face for male	no loss of face but loss of opportunity for relationship

Figure 22.1 [The Gaming Strategies to Minimize Risk-Taking.]

> I always ended up with someone I was very unhappy with. I used to wonder why I attracted that type. Very few people ever found anyone decent. Most people came back from those things feeling negatively about the experience and feeling negatively about themselves.

Mixers had long-term effects on the self-images of the successful as well; many of those individuals had come to see their worth mostly in terms of their surface qualities. For everyone involved, the mixer situation encourages a calculating approach to heterosexual contact that is more starkly visible than in settings which do not limit such encounters to specific times and places.

NOTES

1. We drew a stratified sample which included an equal number of males and females, randomly selected from the student body of approximately 4,000 men and 500 women. According to all available indicators, the sample well represented the Yale undergraduate population, except for the deliberate over-representation of females. All grade levels were represented equally, as were all twelve residential colleges. The percentage of students in our sample (1) from public high schools versus private schools; (2) from the Eastern seaboard versus other regions of the country; and (3) from alumni families, mirrored the percentages for the entire student population.
2. We are primarily speaking of those institutions not affiliated with a coordinate college for the opposite sex.
3. Although the singles' bar and the mixer share structural similarities they are functionally distinct in that the former does not perform the endogamous screening services of the latter. The customers in a singles' bar will vary with respect to age, educational attainment, and social class background (and often marital status as well).
4. During participant observation at mixers, the authors never grew accustomed to the role of "coeds." Considering that we as "researchers" had little personally at stake, we found that our egos were, nevertheless, involved. No

matter how peripheral one is to this kind of situation, it is never easy to disregard completely someone else's estimation of one's attractiveness.

REFERENCES

Goffman, E., 1967. *Interaction Ritual: Essays on Face-to-Face Behavior*. New York: Anchor.

Lever, J., and P. Schwartz, 1971. *Women at Yale: Liberating a College Campus*. Indianapolis: Bobbs-Merrill.

Scott, J. R., 1965. "Sororities and husbands." *Transaction*, 2 (Sept./Oct.): 10–14.

CHAPTER 23

College Dating: Games, Strategies, and Peeves

Elyce Pike / Stephen Hall

ABSTRACT: The dating customs of college students often come into conflict with their beliefs about the equality that should characterize the relationships of males and females. Based on interviews concerning "first dates" only, the authors found: (1) first dates resemble buying and selling relationships, with males paying for the date but expecting sexual favors in return; (2) this market relationship creates resentment in males concerning the cost of the date and in females for being expected to provide sexual returns; (3) first dates are filled with distrust as each doubts the motive of the other; (4) to overcome the ambiguity of first dates, males and females draw upon traditional sex–role behavior, which in turn creates its own problems; and (5) each participant in the date utilizes gaming strategies to combat the gaming strategies of the other.

The authors have been teaching marriage and the family classes for a number of years and have become aware of the fact that the contradictions and dynamics of dating norms intrigue university students. Few other topics provoke as much interest. From class discussions it became apparent that norm conflicts exist in the dating process, and that these conflicts appear to be out of step with current beliefs that suggest that males and females are relating to one another more equally than in the past.

In this paper we will explore the possibility that dating relationships, particularly "first-dates," are still based on an "exchange system" and not an equalitarian relationship. Within this context, we will consider the following questions: (1) Do males still expect a return for paying (i.e., that females "put-out") or has this type of dating norm faded away in light of the women's movement? (2) Do males and females still try to live up to traditional norms (i.e., gentlemanly versus ladylike behavior) or has there been a breakdown in such norms making them irrelevant? and (3) What are the implications of strategies or game-playing behavior in dating for interpersonal relationships?

METHODOLOGY

Since the present study was exploratory in nature, responses to open-ended questions were synthesized from among 130 male and female freshmen and sophomore students at a southern state university. The data were examined for dominant themes in dating norms. The following kinds of questions were asked: (1) What do you dislike about your dates (e.g., bad experiences you have had on dates, including problems with parents, curfews, money, sex, or any other barriers)? (2) What would you say you most resent about the dates you have had? (3) Is there anything you can think of that you particularly resent being expected to do on a date?

While respondents were asked to evaluate their dating behavior, questions were limited to "first dates" only. Consequently, conclusions drawn about dating norms from the present study cannot be generalized to continuous dating with the same person.

RESULTS: "PAYING VERSUS PUTTING-OUT"

Males and females differed in their response patterns. It appears from the data that both the women's movement and economic inflation have combined to affect dating norms. For example, when asked what they resent most about their dates, males most often said they resent having to "pay." The following comment reflects this sentiment:

> I hate having to blow my entire paycheck on my date just because girls think we can't have fun by doing something that doesn't cost a whole lot of money.

The anguish males mentioned in having to wine and dine often (what they perceive to be) ungrateful females, in order not to be thought of as cheap, suggests that the male sex-role is straining under the effects of economic inflation. Males resent it, but continue to try and be good providers early in a dating relationship, much like they do later in marriage. However, there was evidence in the data that though males are still doing this, they do not enjoy it. Consequently, males who may not agree with the principles of the women's movement (e.g., women should pay their own way) find themselves strangely aligned with its ideology, again, as a consequence of economic inflation.

It may or may not be true that females actually expect males to take them to expensive places. It may or may not, in fact, be true that males expect females to "put-out" for either a good or bad date. Nevertheless, the data reflect acceptance of each of these themes. A typical female comment suggests that females often feel men expect them to "pay" socially (i.e., in terms of social prostitution; hence, putting-out):

> I resent being expected to go to bed with my date especially after somewhere like Hardee's, and always feel like kissing him even when I don't.

Perhaps it is the nature of our buying and selling behavior in the market place that we extend such behavior to the dating relationship. Males seem to support females' suggestions that they are expected to reward their buyers. One male simply said: "It's still true that most guys, *me* included, still expect girls to 'put-out or get-out'." One can only speculate as to how dating norms would change if both parties were expected to pay their own way. Would the rewards of the date become "just having a good time?" Would going "dutch treat" increase the couple's enjoyment of each other, relieved of the emphasis on the "free meal" or the "easy lay" of the traditional date?

IMMEDIATE VERSUS DELAYED GRATIFICATION

The paying versus putting-out behavior superficially suggests that females are holding-out and males will have sex with anyone for whom they can buy a dinner. However, our data suggest that there is more to it than this. Females are not simply holding-out for the sake of holding-out. Sex to females, before marriage in particular, still means sex with someone for whom one cares—perhaps even someone one might consider as a marital partner. Consequently, having sex before marriage for women has to be meaningful. It is not the meal per se but the meaning of the date, the total situation. If a female does not have much to go on (or has to wonder: Does he like me? Is he just using me?) she will use external criteria (e.g., the date, the meal, the male's behavior) to determine if in fact he is sincere or an exploiter. Some males interpret such scrutiny as cruel and unusual punishment given today's inflationary situation. They cannot relate to women's fears of exploitation or the feeling of being sexually vulnerable. The inability to raise to the female's dilemma may be a result of the males' being exempt from labels such as "slut," "nympho," or "whore" (ever hear of a male slut?). It appears from the data that if females do not like putting-out it is because they are dealing with the knowledge of these negative stigmas.

In addition to stigmas, females still feel they have to "save" themselves for the last buyer, the last sale. However, there is no way of telling if the first date is leading to the last sale or if both parties are just browsing. Consequently, the data indicate that compounding the fears experienced by both males and females of being "ripped-off," and cheated, is the fact that first dates are not based on feelings of trust.

GENTLEMANLY VERSUS LADYLIKE BEHAVIOR

The data also suggest that if males and females do not like paying and putting-out, they like some of the traditional male-female sex-role behaviors even less. Consider for instance comments by the following male respondents as to what they resent most:

> Having to open doors.
>
> Having to go all the way around to the other side of the car just because she's too helpless to do it herself and if she's not because she'll think I don't like her.
>
> Always expecting me to pull her chair out, light her cigarette, decide where we should go, what we should do.

By contrast, women reflected resentment but in terms of "waiting." Women resent:

> Waiting for males to open doors for me. Knowing that my date will think I am a women's libber if I want to open my own door. I usually have to wait for him to pull my chair out. Why should I have to do that? Why should *he* have to do that?

It is perhaps a function of the first date being such a market-type arrangement that males and females engage in expected behavior rather than in behaviors they simply might want to do out of courtesy for their dating partner. Also, males were understandably confused in these times when they are not certain if they are being "male chauvinist pigs" by opening doors, lighting cigarettes, or pulling out chairs for their dates. Males wonder: Does she expect me to open the door? What will she think if I *don't* open her door? It would appear, therefore, that because first dates are often ambiguous in terms of expectations, males and females do not draw on more relaxed norms that might apply later if a couple continues to date. Rather, on first dates, males and females draw upon what is familiar: traditional norms.

The authors do not feel that there is anything inherently wrong with tradition. However, the data reflect that out of the awkwardness of relying on tradition, males and females engage in a great deal of "pretending" behavior. For instance, females mentioned that they *resent*: "pretending they were having a good time," "always having to build up a guy's ego—especially when he may not have one to begin with," "making certain not to disagree too much." "having to ask him *in* even if you've had a rotten time," and finally "being certain not to drink too much, or eat too much, so as to avoid appearing unladylike."

Males, on the other hand, pointed out that they resent having to compliment their dates "even when they look lousy," or having to say "it was fun—when it wasn't." Neither males nor females in our study liked engaging in the psychological game of stroking versus being stroked. Although male and female respondents mentioned that they engaged in such games, very few mentioned that they enjoyed playing. The obvious question then becomes: "Why do something you hate and that you know is, after all, only a game?" Apparently, even if one does not want to "win" the game or play more than one game with the same dating partner, it is far worse to feel that one has totally lost the game. This feeling of not wanting to be a "loser" may be a function of trying to get some "return" (psychological or otherwise) back for one's "investment" of time.

TECHNIQUES AND STRATEGIES

In order to deal with the ambiguity of expectations and norms of the first date, males and females pointed out that they developed certain "strategies" and/or "techniques" to handle the situation. Consider, for instance, the following comments by one female respondent.

> It always helps a woman to get what she wants if she lets the man feel (think) he dominates. Another way to achieve your goal is for a woman to boost the male ego. Tell him he is handsome, he is sexy, etc. Try not to use crying too much, it works best when not overdone. Maybe it isn't right, but if a woman is really being taken for granted, the best strategy is to make the man jealous. If done properly, this works very well. It never hurts to flirt with your boyfriend or husband. This is not the same as teasing. Dress up, roll your eyes at him, roll your hair, but just do *something* to make yourself more attractive. If you are just going to be at home alone this is even more special. Have a good fight when it's necessary, and then be sure to spend more time making up than you did fighting. You should always take the advantage in making up right after a fight.

It may be a function of the initial game played on the first date that fosters the development of such strategies. Although many of the respondents pointed out that games broke down with continuous dating, the existence of strategies suggests that games continue to be played.

One of the games females played, for which males developed a strategy, was: "wanting the male to make a pass, but resenting it when the male *did* make a pass." Apparently, "timing" is the key to understanding this approach-avoidance behavior. For example, if a "pass" was made, or interpreted by the female as being "too fast" (e.g., on the first date), no matter how much she "wanted it," she still resented it and felt uncomfortable about it. Some might ask: "Isn't it rather shallow to feel that one set of behaviors is appropriate on the third date and not on the first?" Such behavior could be interpreted as superficial if one did not understand that females do not resent "the pass" itself, so much as what it means symbolically. Being too hasty is likely to be interpreted by females as: "not caring about them as individuals," "no desire to establish a relationship," "a desire for only a sexual relationship rather than a person-oriented one." Apparently females associate continuous dating with the feeling that one is being asked out because the other person is interested in them as whole persons rather than only as sexual partners. Hence, a pass on a third or fourth date would be interpreted differently from a pass on the first date, as a function of the definition of the dating situation changing over time.

The opposite of this type of behavior is feeling bad that the male does not make a pass after a prolonged dating period. Females worry that such "waiting" is reflective of the fact that they might not be attractive or that the male does not like them. We are not going to second guess the motives of males who do not make advances on subsequent dates. However, one strategy that has been known to pertain to such behavior is the "ripe-fruit" strategy. Here, the male simply waits out the female until he knows definitely she is ready (i.e., "over-ready") in his estimation. Thus in her eagerness to accept his pass and her consequent boosted ego he may "get more" than he would have otherwise.

DISCUSSION AND CONCLUSION

The present paper has attempted to examine the status of dating norms as they apply to first dates. It was discovered from analyzing the responses of 130 male and female college students that (1) first dates resemble buying and selling relationships in that males still pay for their dates but also expect females to "put-out"; (2) females do not hold-out simply for the sake of holding-out. Their motives appear to be related to the fact that they still perceive sex as being permissible before marriage only with those for whom they care. Nevertheless, first dates are replete with distrust, often because each is not certain of the other's motives;

(3) because first dates are often ambiguous in terms of norms, males and females still draw on traditional norms (e.g., gentlemanly versus ladylike behavior) to guide them. Pretending behavior (i.e., lying about having a good time, the appearance of one's date, and so on) appears to develop out of the use of traditional norms; and (4) both males and females develop strategies and techniques in order to combat the "games" that each plays in dating relationships.

The literature on dating behavior has not taken the "game-playing" aspect into account. Much of what has been written tends to focus on the dating process in terms of long-term relationships. There is no way of telling from the present data what the implications of this first-date type of behavior are for subsequent dates. Hence, we cannot make definite statements as to long-term effects. However, we suspect that this buying and selling relationship does have effects for the dating relationship that evolves into courtship behavior. Although some of the games may break down, it is important to remember that males and females initially "relate" to one another as if in a market place. Much of what is written about power relationships in marriage and the family may be nothing more than extensions of different aspects of the buying and selling techniques on the "exchange" relationship that exists at all stages of dating and courtship between males and females. Perhaps such effort would better explain how it is that males and females appear to have so little understanding of what the other's perspective is in a variety of relationships.

It should be remembered that while the data on this article might well be interpreted as too negative to some people, it reflects only the *complaints* about dating. "Complaint analysis," while it neglects the positive side of dating, reveals very well many of the social psychological stresses underlying the dating process. The data in this paper should not be interpreted as revealing the total picture of dating relationships.

CHAPTER 24

Theories of Mate Selection

Bruce K. Eckland

ABSTRACT: Marriage is a conservative social institution that binds two individuals not only to one another, but also to others and even to other social institutions. Two types of theories have been developed to explain who marries whom. "Individualistic" theories stress characteristics of the individual. They include the unconscious archetype, the parent image, like attracts like, and the principle of complementary needs. "Sociocultural" theories, in contrast, stress aspects of the larger human group, or society, that sorts people into selected avenues of marriage. They include propinquity and interaction, exchange theory, values and belief patterns, social stratification and class endogamy, and ethnic solidarities.

The following discussion involves a search for those psychological and structural features which best show how assortative mating operates in contemporary societies.

INDIVIDUALISTIC THEORIES

The disappearance of unilineal kinship systems in Western societies has led to a decline of kinship control over mate selection. The resulting freedom which young people now enjoy has brought about an enormously complex system. No doubt, the selection process actually begins long before the adolescent's first "date." Moreover, under conditions of serial monogamy where it is possible to have many wives but only one at a time, the process for some probably never ends. Determining the "choice" are a myriad of emotional experiences and it is these experiences, along with a variety of subconscious drives and needs, upon which most psychological and other "individualistic" theories are based.

The Unconscious Archetype

Some of the earliest and perhaps most radical theories of mate selection suggested that what guides a man to choose a woman (it was seldom thought to be the other way around) is instinct. Scholars believed that there must be for each particular man a particular woman who, for reasons involving the survival of the species, corresponded most perfectly with him. A modern rendition of the same idea is Carl Jung's belief that falling in love is being caught by one's "anima." That is, every man inherits an anima which is an "archetypal form" expressing a particular female image he carries within his genes. When the right woman comes along, the one who corresponds to the archetype, he instantly is "seized" (Evans, 1964). However, no one, as far as we know, has actually discovered any pure biologically determined tendencies to assortative mating.

The Parent Image

A psychoanalytic view, based on the Oedipus configuration, has been that in terms of temperament and physical appearance one's ideal mate is a parent substitute. The boy, thus, seeks someone like his mother and the girl seeks someone like her father. While it admittedly would seem reasonable to expect parent images to either encourage or discourage a person marrying someone like his parent, no clear evidence has been produced to support the hypothesis. Sometimes striking resemblances between a man's wife and his mother, or a woman's husband and her father, have been noted. Apparently, however, these are only "accidents," occurring hardly more frequently than expected by chance.

Like Attracts Like

Another generally unproven assumption, at least with respect to any well-known personality traits, involves the notion that "likes attract."

Cattell and Nesselroade (1967) recently found significant correlations between husband and wife on a number of personality traits among both stably and unstably married couples. The correlations, moreover, were substantially higher (and more often in the predicted direction) among the "normal" than among the unstably married couples. As the authors admit, however, it was not possible to determine whether the tendency of these couples to resemble each other was the basis for their initial attraction ("birds of a feather flock together") or whether the correlations were simply an outgrowth of the marital experience. Although the ordering of the variables is not clear, the evidence does tend to suggest that the stability of marriage, and thus the number of progeny of any particular set of parents, may depend to some extent on degrees of likeness.

The Principle of Complementary Needs

Probably as old as any other is the notion that "opposites attract"; for example, little men love big women, or a masochistic male desiring punishment seeks out a sadistic female who hungers to give it. Only in the past twenty years has a definitive theory along these lines been formulated and put to empirical test. This is Winch's theory of complementary needs which hypothesizes that each individual seeks that person who will provide him with maximum need gratification. The specific need pattern and personality of each partner will be "complementary" (Winch, 1958). Accordingly, dominant women, for example, would tend to choose submissive men as mates rather than similarly dominant or aggressive ones. The results of a dozen or so investigations, however, are inconclusive, at best. More often than not, researchers have been unable to find a pattern of complementary differences. No less significant than other difficulties inherent in the problem is the discouraging fact that the correlation between what an individual thinks is the personality of his mate and the actual personality of his mate is quite small (Udry, 1966). Nevertheless, the theory that either mate selection or marital stability involves an exchange of interdependent behaviors resulting from complementary rather than similar needs and personalities is a compelling idea and perhaps deserves more attention.

No firm conclusions can yet be reached about the reasons for similarity (or complementariness) or personality and physical traits in assortative mating. (Even the degree of association or disassociation on most personality characteristics is largely unknown.) To state that "like attracts like" or "opposites attract," we know are oversimplifications. Moreover, few attempts to provide the kinds of explanations we seek have thus far stood up to empirical tests.

SOCIOCULTURAL THEORIES

In a very general way, social homogamy is a critical point in the integration or continuity of the family and other social institutions. It is a mechanism which serves to maintain the status quo and conserve traditional values and beliefs. And, because marriage itself is such a vital institution, it is not too difficult to understand why so many of the social characteristics which are important variables generally in society, such as race, religion, or class, are also the important variables in mate selection. Thus, most studies in the United States report a very high rate, over 99%, for racial endogamy, an overall rate perhaps as high as 90% for religious homogamy, and moderately high rates, 50% to 80%, for class homogamy, the exact figures depending on the nature of the index used and the methods employed to calculate the rate.

One possible way of illustrating the conserving or maintenance function of social homogamy in mate selection is to try to visualize momentarily how a contemporary society would operate under conditions of *random* mating. Considering their proportions in the population, Negroes actually would be more likely to marry whites than other Negroes, Catholics more often than not would marry Protestants, and a college graduate would be more apt to marry a high school dropout than to marry another college graduate. In a like manner, about as often as not, dull would marry bright, old would marry young, Democrats would marry Republicans, and teetotalers would marry drinkers. What would be the end result of this kind of social heterogamy? A new melting pot, or chaos?

It seems that, in the absence of "arranged marriages," a variety of controls govern mate selection and, in the process, substantially reduce the availability of certain individuals as potential mates. Many structures in society undoubtedly carry out these functions, sometimes in quite indirect ways, such as, the subtle manner in which the promotion of an "organization man" may be based, in part, on how well his mate's characteristics meet the qualifications of a "company wife." Thus, despite the "liberation" of mate selection and the romantic ideals of lovers who are convinced that social differences must not be allowed to stand in their way, probably one of the most important functions of both the elaborate "rating and dating" complex and the ceremonial "engagement" is to allow a society to make apparent who may "marry upward" and under what conditions exogamy is permitted. We are referring here, then, not merely to a society's control over the orderly replacement of personnel, but to its integration and the transmission of culture as well.

Rather than reviewing any very well-formulated theories (since there may be none) in the remaining discussion, I have attempted to touch upon a fairly broad range of conditions under which homogamy, as a social fact, relates to other aspects of contemporary societies.

Propinquity and Interaction

Whether we are speaking about place of residence, school, work, or such abstruse features of human ecology as the bus or streetcar routes along which people travel, propinquity obviously plays a major part in mate selection since, in nearly all cases, it is a precondition for engaging in interaction. (The mail-order bride, for instance, is one of several exceptions.) A person usually "selects" a mate from the group of people he knows. Findings which illustrate the function of distance have been duplicated in dozens of studies. In Columbus, Ohio, it was once found that more than half of the adults who had been married in that city had actually lived within sixteen blocks of one another at the time of their first date (Clarke, 1952). Cherished notions about romantic love notwithstanding, the chances are about 50–50 that the "one and only" lives within walking distance (Kephart, 1961).

Exchange Theory

An explanation often cited in the literature on mate selection, as well as in that on the more general topic of interpersonal attraction, deals in one form or another with the principle of exchange. A Marxian view, marriage is an exchange involving both the assets and liabilities which each partner brings to the relationship. Thus, a college-educated woman seldom brings any special earning power to the marriage, but rather she typically enters into contract with a male college graduate for whom her diploma is a social asset which may benefit his own career and possibly those of his children. In exchange, he offers her, with a fair degree of confidence, middle-class respectability. Norms of reciprocity might also help to explain the finding that most borderline mentally retarded women successfully marry and even, in some cases, marry upward, if they are physically attractive. This particular theory, however, has not been well-developed in regard to mate selection, despite its repeated usage. Also, it may be a more appropriate explanation of deviations from assortative mating or instances of negative mate selection than of positive selection.

Values and Belief Patterns

In contrast to the inconclusive evidence regarding assortative mating in terms of personality characteristics, numerous studies do indicate that married couples (and engaged couples) show far more consensus on various matters than do randomly matched couples. Even on some rather generalized values, as in the area of aesthetics or economics, social homogamy occurs. Apparently, our perception that other persons share with us the same or similar value orientations and beliefs facilitates considerably our attraction to them (Burgess and Wallin, 1943).

The importance of norms and values in mate selection, part of the social fabric of every society, also can be illustrated in a more direct way of looking at some of the specific sanctions that we pass along from generation to generation. Without really asking why, children quite routinely are brought up to believe that gentlemen prefer blondes (which may be only a myth perpetuated by the cosmetic industry), that girls should marry someone older rather than younger than themselves (which leaves most of them widows later on), and that a man should be at least a little taller than the woman whom he marries (which places the conspicuously tall girl at an enormous disadvantage). Simple folkways as such beliefs presently are, they nevertheless influence in predictable ways the "choice" of many individuals.

Social Stratification and Class Endogamy

We have already noted that the field of eligible mates is largely confined to the same social stratum to which an individual's family of orientation belongs. Social-class endogamy not only plays a significant part in the process of mate selection, it may also help to explain other forms of assortative mating. For example, part of the reason why marriage partners or engaged couples share many of the same values and beliefs no doubt is because they come from the same social backgrounds.

There are at least five explanations which can be offered for the persistence of class endogamy, each of which sounds reasonable enough and probably has a hold on some part of the truth.

First, simply to turn the next to last statement around, persons from the same class tend to marry *because* they share the same values (which reflect class differences) and not because they are otherwise aware or especially concerned about each other's background.

Second, during the period of dating and courtship most young people reside at the home of their parents. (Excluded here, of course, are the large minority in residential colleges and those who have left both school and home to take an apartment near their place of work.) The location of parental homes reflects the socioeconomic status of the family and is the general basis for residential segregation. With respect to both within and between communities, the pattern of segregation places potential mates with different backgrounds at greater distances than those with similar backgrounds. Thus, to the extent that the function of distance (or propinquity) limits the field of eligibles, it also encourages class endogamy by restricting class exogamy.

Third, class endogamy in some cases is simply a function of the interlocking nature of class and ethnicity. A middle-class Negro, for example, probably is prevented from an exogamous marriage with member of the upper-class not so much because class barriers block it but because he (or she) is Negro. The majority of the eligible mates in the class above are whites and, in this instance, what appears to be class endogamy is really racial endogamy.

Fourth, ascriptive norms of the family exert a great deal of pressure on persons, especially in the higher strata, to marry someone of their "own kind," meaning the same social level. The pressures that parents exert in this regard sometimes are thought to have more than anything else to do with the process and certainly are visible at nearly every point at which young people come into meaningful contact with one another. Norms of kinship regarding the future status of a child may be involved, for example, in the parent's move to the right community, sending a child to a prep school, or seeing that he gets into the proper college.

Fifth, and an increasingly convincing argument, even as the structure of opportunities for social mobility open through direct competition within the educational system, class endogamy persists owing to the educational advantages (or disadvantages) accrued from one's family of orientation. Most colleges, whether commuter or residential, are matrimonial agencies. As suggested earlier, despite whatever else a woman may gain from her (or, more often, her parents') investment in higher education, often the most important thing she gets out of college is the proper husband or at least the credentials that would increase her bargaining power in an exchange later on.* Given the fact that men generally confer their status (whether achieved or ascribed) upon women and not the other way around (female proclamations to the contrary notwithstanding), marriage as a product of higher education on the average still has far more functional value for women than vocational or other more intrinsic rewards.

To carry this argument a bit further, access to college depends in large measure on the academic aptitude (or intelligence) of the applicants. Moreover, the hierarchical ordering of colleges which is based on this selectivity has led to a system of higher education which, in many ways, replicates the essential elements of the class structure. Differentiating those who go to college from those who do not, as well as where one goes to college, are *both* aptitude and social class. These two variables correspond so closely that despite the most stringent policies

*In recent years, as careers have become increasingly important for larger numbers of American women, this factor has declined in significance. The principle of "bargaining power" in mate selection increasing with a college education—for both men and women—continues to be highly significant, however.—Ed.

at some universities where academic aptitude and performance are the central criteria for admissions and where economic aid is no longer a major factor, students still come predominately from the higher socio-economic classes. For whatever the reason, genetic and environmental, this correspondence facilitates the intermarriage of individuals with similar social backgrounds, especially on American campuses where the sex ratio has been declining. It is interesting to note in this context that Warren's study of a representative sample of adults showed that roughly half of the similarity in class background of mates was due to assortative mating by education (Warren, 1966).

Ethnic Solidarities

While intermarriage is both a cause and consequence in the assimilation of the descendants of different ethnic origin, various writers claim that the American "melting pot" has failed to materialize. Religious and racial lines, in particular, are far from being obliterated. In fact, the very low frequency of exogamous marriages across these lines itself underscores the strength of the cleavages. Most authors also agree that nationality is not as binding as either race or religion as a factor in mate selection. Nation-type solidarities are still found among some urban groups (Italian and Poles) and rural groups (Swedes and Finns), but our public school system and open class structure have softened considerably what were once rather rigid boundaries. There is some evidence, too, that religious cleavages have been softening somewhat, and perhaps are continuing to soften as the functions of this institution become increasingly secular and social-problem oriented. On the other hand, racial boundaries, from the view of mate selection, appear to be as binding today as at any previous point in history; at least I have found no evidence to the contrary. The gains that Negroes have made in the schools and at the polls during the past ten years apparently have not softened the color line with respect to intermarriage.

Explanations of racial endogamy in America, some of which would take us back several centuries in time, are too varied to discuss here. It might be well to point out, however, that cultural and even legal prohibitions, probably have relatively little to do with the present low rate of interracial marriage. As one author has stated, "the whole structure of social relationships between whites and Negroes in the United States has been organized in such a way as to prevent whites and Negroes from meeting, especially under circumstances which would lead to identifying each other as eligible partners. . . . Under these circumstances, the few interracial marriages which do occur are the ones which need explaining" (Udry, 1966).

PRECAUTIONARY NOTES

In conclusion, five brief comments may be made upon the present state of research and theories of mate selection as revealed in the foregoing discussion.

First, there is a great deal of evidence of homogamous or assortative mating but relatively few theories to explain it and no satisfactory way of classifying its many forms.

Second, nearly all facts and theories regarding mate selection deal with engaged or married couples and hardly any attention has been given to illegitimacy (including adultery) and its relationship to assortative mating. It may be, such as in the case of miscegenation, that some of the most important aspects of mate selection occur outside the bonds of matrimony.

Third, our heavy emphasis upon courtship and marriage has obscured the fact that people often separate, divorce, and remarry. Mate selection may be a more or less continuous process for some individuals, affecting the character of the progeny of each new set of partners.

Fourth, the relationships between fertility and assortative mating still must be specified. Are there, for example, any patterns of assortative mating on certain traits, like education, which affect the number of children a couple will have?

Fifth, most of the factors in mate selection appear to covary. We discussed some of the more obvious problems in this regard, such as the relationship between residential segregation (propinquity) and class endogamy. It would appear that much more work of this sort will need to be done.

In regard to the last point, it would also appear that it is precisely here that social scientists, and sociologists in particular, may best serve the needs of population geneticists. Through the application of causal (chain) models and multivariate techniques, it may eventually be possible to sort out the relevant from the irrelevant and to specify in fairly precise terms not only the distribution of assortative mating in the social structure with regard to any particular trait, but also the ordering of variables and processes which restrict the field of eligibles.

REFERENCES

BURGESS, ERNEST W., and PAUL WALLIN. 1943. Homogamy in social characteristics. *Amer. J. Sociol.* 49:109–124.

CATTELL, RAYMOND B., and JOHN R. NESSELROADE. "Likeness" and "completeness" theories examined by 16 personality factor measures on stably and unstably married couples. (Advance Publication No. 7.) The Laboratory of Personality and Group Analysis, University of Illinois.

CLARKE, ALFRED C. 1952. An examination of the operation of residential propinquity as a factor in mate selection. *Amer. Sociol. Rev.* 17:17–22.

EVANS, RICHARD I. 1964. *Conversations with Carl Jung*. Van Nostrand. Princeton.

KEPHART, WILLIAM M. 1961. *The Family, Society and the Individual*. Houghton Mifflin, Boston.

UDRY, J. RICHARD. 1966. *The Social Context of Marriage*. J. B. Lippincott, Philadelphia and New York.

WARREN, BRUCE L. 1966. A multiple variable approach to the assortative mating phenomenon. *Eugen. Quart.* 13:285–290.

WINCH, ROBERT. 1958. *Mate Selection*. Harper & Row, New York.

SECTION 7

Alternatives to Marriage

THE THRUST OF OUR PREMARITAL LEARNING is that we should take our place as conforming members of society. Therefore, the bulk of our premarital social experiences—our countless experiences with social institutions, with our parents, peers, and the mass media—are part of a grand scheme of exacting, finely tuned social mechanisms designed to motivate us to become full-fledged members of society. In short, our experiences are designed to make us "good citizens." *And the fully conforming, contributing member of society is married.*

We cannot lose sight of this basic assumption, for around it is based most of social life. Sex roles, for example, do not exist merely for the sake of sex roles. They do not exist in the abstract. They are not something theoretical. They are meant to be played out as a basic part of social relations. And it is especially in marriage that they find their fulfillment, which is why we focused so strongly on them earlier. All else is part of the preliminaries to the play, so to speak.

We are destined, predetermined, and carefully molded to become husbands and wives—and, eventually, fathers and mothers. And sex roles are intended to help us fulfill those expectations.

Similarly, dating does not exist simply for the sake of dating. It, too, is an experience intended to play its part in the continuing drama: to narrow down the marital choices, and, one day, to result in marriage—and, of course, after that, in the birth and care of children.

In other words, in one way or another the bulk of our social experiences can be analyzed in terms of the contributory part they play in preparing and nudging, or, if necessary, pushing and shoving, us into marriage and parenthood. Almost all of us accept the normalcy of this assumption, and most of us even become willing participants in both the process and the outcome. Consequently, between 90 and 95 percent of Americans marry.

Most go directly from the process of dating to the outcome of marriage. But increasing numbers are first taking a sort of detour and living together for a period of time. With the easing of the double standard in our society, combined with the general increasing acceptance of premarital sex, cohabitation has become more of an acceptable option for the unmarried.

When they begin to cohabit, the couple feels they have the best of two worlds: they retain much of the independence that they value and that being single allows, and yet they have access to frequent sex with a caring partner. Almost all cohabiters, however, experience pressures to marry, and, since they were not opposed to marriage in principle but only for themselves at that particular time, most eventually give in. So, though they may have resisted marriage at first, most end up at the same place as their more conventional friends.

There are still some, however, who are determined to remain single. They have chosen singlehood as an alternative life-style—not as something temporary, but as a designated way of life, an alternative to marriage itself. They gladly adapt themselves to being single, usually choosing to live in an urban environment, and there search for personal satisfactions and meaning for life within an extended, rather amorphous network of singles.

As singles, they generally find many satisfactions, but not enough it seems, for over time they see marriage as comparatively more attractive. Year by year their numbers dwindle, as marriage claims even them.

To sum up, cohabitation is usually a temporary living/sexual arrangement, one that in the ordinary case eventuates in marriage (although not necessarily to the cohabiting partner); for most, being single is also a temporary situation, with most singles looking to get married. It is on these two alternatives (more factually termed postponements) to marriage that we focus in this section. Peter J. Stein first presents an overview of singles, analyzing them by age and sex groups, and looking at the pushes and pulls they experience. Patrick G. Jackson then reports on his study of unmarried cohabiters. He looks especially at how they get along with one another and how they try to maintain fronts of respectability. In the concluding chapter, Mimi Rodin looks at a group of singles in an urban area, analyzing their life-style and relationships with one another.

As I have stressed, both living together unmarried and being single are almost always experienced as temporary situations prior to adopting a conforming life-style of marriage. Yet, there are some for whom singlehood and/or cohabitation are not simply detours or temporary situations. For some, they represent a permanent way of life. About these people we know almost nothing, and if you are interested in becoming a sociologist this may be a highly fruitful area for you to pursue.

CHAPTER 25

The Voluntary Singles

Peter J. Stein

ABSTRACT: In the past quarter century the proportion of Americans in their twenties who have never married has markedly increased. These young singles have not forsworn marriage, just postponed it. They seek meaningful work, living arrangements, and friends, moving in disproportionate numbers to large urban areas. To these singles age thirty appears to mark a transition point, a time for reevaluating their life-styles and life goals. In contrast to married women, who report more frustration and negative feelings than do their husbands, single women are better adjusted than are single men. All singles experience the pushes and pulls toward marriage, but for a variety of reasons some remain single, even in their elderly years.

THE LIFE CYCLE OF SINGLE ADULTS

The concept of the life cycle, initially proposed by Erik Erikson (1959), adds a dynamic aspect to this otherwise static continuum. The stage of the life cycle is also related to issues of life style and life chances and the need and availability of social support systems.

Levinson (1978) has suggested a model for the various stages of adult life. He compares these stages to the seasons of a single year and sug-

Revised by the author for this book from an earlier version that appeared in *Single Life: Unmarried Adults in Social Context*, New York: St. Martin's Press, 1981.

gests that development occurs in predictable segments which follow each other in chronological order. His model, developed from studies of married men, is useful when applied to the lives of single people, but it is limited.

The stage model assumes that development is hierarchical, sequenced in time, and cumulative. The implications of life stages are that (1) every "normal" adult must pass through the stages; (2) each stage has distinctive qualities which are tasks that must be accomplished during that stage; (3) an individual is more or less successful in negotiating these crises; (4) successful resolution of a prior stage is necessary for the successful resolution of subsequent stages; and (5) each stage is tied to chronological age (Brim, 1977). According to Levinson, "although important changes go on within it, each season or era has its own distinctive and unifying qualities, which have to do with the character of living" (Levinson et al., 1978, p. 18).

Etzkowitz and Stein (1978) suggest that life has many seasons and that a spiral more accurately represents life's configuration. Development is not necessarily related to chronological age, and themes of development may be resolved at one age only to need reevaluation later on. Developmental stages may overlap; one may never resolve certain issues. Life is an ongoing process with themes and patterns which repeat. It is less like the seasons of a single year than like a panorama of seasons.

These two contrasting models may be seen as representing a continuum. For adults whose lives follow fairly traditional patterns of development, the cycle, with its stages, may accurately represent their lives. Less traditional lives may be more accurately described by the spiral model. There may be changes over the span of one's life: The spiral may be more accurate at one period, the cycle more accurate at another.

THE YOUNG NEVER-MARRIEDS

We can identify various stages of the adult life cycle. The years from the early twenties to about twenty-eight are the period of "getting into the adult world," when the focus of one's life shifts from the "family of origin to a new home base in an effort to form an adult life of one's own" (Levinson et al., 1974, p. 246). It is a time of "exploratory searching and provisional choices" (p. 247). It is also a time of assessing the correctness of such initial choices and increasing the commitment to choices.

The twenty-three-year period from 1960 to 1983 saw a large increase in the percentage of women and men between the ages of twenty and twenty-nine who have remained single (see Table 25.1). Among twenty- to twenty-four-year-olds 55 percent of the women and 73 percent of the men remained single; the corresponding figures for the twenty-five- to twenty-nine-year-olds were 25 percent and 38 percent. The median age at first marriage has increased for women from 20.3 in 1960 to 22.8 in 1983 and for men from 22.8 in 1960 to 25.4 in 1983. While most Americans continue to marry and while most young Americans expect to marry—more than 90 percent according to a 1980 study—they do so somewhat later in their lives than did earlier cohorts (Thornton and Freedman, 1983). As the legitimacy of remaining single has come to be increasingly accepted by both young people and their parents (Thornton and Freedman, 1983) and as more singles are postponing their own marriages, the percentage who will never marry is expected to increase. Thornton and Freedman conclude that "it now appears that about 10 percent, and possibly more, [of current singles] will never marry" (1983:5).

Single people are leaving their parents' homes in record numbers, between the completion of school and the beginning of marriage, and establishing their own households—either alone or with friends of the same or opposite sex. Between 1960 and 1982 the percentage of never-marrieds between the ages of twenty-five and thirty-four maintaining their own households almost tripled. In 1982, 53 percent of never-married women and 43 percent of never-married men had their own households. (*Current Population Reports*, 1982). A majority of such singles are concentrated in large cities and specific areas of such cities. Over 60 percent of all single persons, compared to 40 percent of the total adult population, live in large cities. The major concerns of single adults are with finding meaningful work, satisfying living arrangements, and congenial friends. Large cities are more likely to offer the occupational opportunities and social networks to satisfy these concerns. Adjustments to the world of work and patterns of forming friendships provide crucial connections and a positive sense of self (Starr and Carns, 1972; Stein, 1981).

TABLE 25.1 Women and Men Remaining Single (1960–1983)

	1960	1970	1980	1983	Change from 1970 to 1983
Women remaining single:					
Ages 20–24	28.4%	35.8%	50.2%	55.5%	+19.7%
Ages 25–29	10.5	10.5	20.8	24.8	+14.3%
Men remaining single:					
Ages 20–24	53.1	54.7	68.6	73.2	+18.5%
Ages 25–29	20.8	19.1	32.4	38.2	+19.1%

SOURCE: U.S. Bureau of the Census, Marital Status and Living Arrangements: March 1983. *Current Population Reports*, Series P-20, No. 389. Washington, D.C.: U.S. Government Printing Office, 1984.

THE AGE THIRTY TRANSITION

Levinson further suggests that for many the years between twenty-eight and thirty-two involve considerable turmoil, confusion, and struggle with societal pressures, with family, and with oneself. For others these years involve a quieter reevaluation of goals and values and an intensification of efforts to achieve such goals. Many men and women who remain single into their thirties report that the late twenties and early thirties was a period of great difficulty (Adams, 1976; Kurth, 1975; Schwartz, 1976).

During these years the number of singles decreased dramatically. Among thirty- to thirty-four-year-olds only 19.6 percent of the men and 13 percent of the women have never married. A majority of these men and women experienced intense societal and parental pressures to marry, and some of them worked hard at finding prospective spouses. Yet many derived little intrinsic satisfaction from the search for a mate and some reported negative experiences and decline in self-esteem.

A major source of difficulty during these years was work-related. This transitional period marked a deeper commitment to an occupation for some, but for others it involved a rejection of earlier occupational choices as too constricting and not meeting initial expectations of satisfaction (Starr and Carns, 1972; Stein, 1976). More women than men had no clear occupational goals upon graduation from college, and a substantial number of women viewed their occupations as temporary, unsatisfactory, and noninvolving. Similarly, living arrangements were seen as temporary, often with a same-sex roommate, to be changed with marriage. "As these singles approached 30, many became critical of those patterns and began to reevaluate their lives . . . [recognizing] the possibility that they might never marry and that they themselves had the responsibility for designing meaningful lives" (Schwartz, 1976). They reexamined earlier occupational decisions, weighed possibilities of starting or returning to graduate or professional schools, reevaluated living situations and improved living places, developed new interests, started new activities, and expanded and reinforced circles of friends.

THE MIDDLE YEARS: HIS AND HERS SINGLEHOOD

By 1980, in the thirty-five to forty-four age group only 8 percent of men and 6 percent of women had never married. (These percentages of never-married decrease to 6.0 percent and 4.5 percent respectively in the forty-five to fifty-four age group.)

In a summary of studies of marriage, Bernard (1982) concluded that while "his" marriage is physically, socially, and psychologically good, "her" marriage is filled with frustration, dissatisfaction, negative feelings, unhappiness, and other problems. The situation with respect to singlehood is quite the opposite—long-term singlehood tends to be experienced as a more positive state for women and a more negative state for men. This is particularly true of the older never-married singles.

Bernard reports that women who remain single are superior to single men in terms of education, occupation, and income. These women are often more upwardly mobile than married women, educationally and professionally. By 1970 one in every five women around the age of forty with some graduate school education, or with an income of $20,000 or more, had not married—compared to only one in every twenty women with no college education.

In contrast, a number of studies have reported that older never-married men are likely to show mental health problems, including depression, severe neurotic symptoms, phobic tendencies, and passivity. In summarizing more than a dozen mental health studies, Gove (1972) reports that among the unmarried, including the never-marrieds, the divorced, and the widowed, men have mental health problems more frequently than women.

How can these findings be explained? Is the experience of singlehood more stressful and more contradictory for men than for women? Or do the men who remain single have more psychological and interpersonal problems to begin with?

ELEMENTS OF CHOICE: PUSHES AND PULLS

My study of voluntary singles reveals the complex factors that enter into the decision to remain single, to live with a lover, to marry, or to separate (Stein, 1976). These factors can be seen as a series of pushes and pulls and are so presented in Table 25.2.

Pushes represent negative factors in a situation; pulls represent attractions to a potential situation. The strength of these pushes and pulls varies according to a number of other variables, including stage of the life cycle, sexual identification, extent of involvement with parents and family, availability of friends and peers, and perception of choice. For some, dating patterns, pressures from parents, and acceptance of the cultural script led to early marriage. At a later time in their lives, these same people found greater pulls toward satisfying careers, work colleagues, and developing friendships, all of which seemed more possible outside of marriage.

Others never married and found the single state satisfying. These men and women offered many positive reasons, or pulls, for remaining

TABLE 25.2 Pushes and Pulls toward Marriage and Singlehood

Marriage	
Pushes (Negatives in Present Situations)	Pulls (Attractions in Potential Situations)
Pressure from parents	Approval of parents
Desire to leave home	Desire for children and own family
Fear of independence	Example of peers
Loneliness and isolation	Romanticization of marriage
No knowledge or perception of alternatives	Physical attraction
Cultural and social discrimination against singles	Love, emotional attachment
	Security, social status, social prestige
	Legitimation of sexual experiences
	Socialization
	Job availability, wage structure, and promotions
	Social policies favoring the married and the responses of social institutions
Singlehood	
Pushes (To Leave Permanent Relationships)	Pulls (To Remain Single or Return to Singlehood)
Lack of friends, isolation, loneliness	Career opportunities and development
Restricted availability of new experiences	Availability of sexual experiences
Suffocating one-to-one relationship, feeling trapped	Exciting life style, variety of experiences, freedom to change
Obstacles to self-development	Psychological and social autonomy, self-sufficiency
Boredom, unhappiness, and anger	Support structures: sustaining friendships, women's and men's groups, political groups, therapeutic groups, collegial groups
Poor communication with mate	
Sexual frustration	

SOURCE: Stein, 1976.

single. They spoke of freedom, enjoyment, career opportunities, developing friendships, economic self-sufficiency, enjoyable sexual experiences, and personal development. They experienced the factors Adams (1976) cites as making singleness a viable life style: economic independence, social and psychological autonomy, and a clear intent to remain single by preference.

The interview data suggest that singlehood contributes to a developed personality. Singles are highly adaptive. Without the clarity of role models or the support of society as a whole, they shape their lives by taking risks and forging into uncharted territory. Without the support of a partner and with varying social and cultural support, adults who choose singlehood can be understood as pioneers of an emergent cultural life style.

REFERENCES

ADAMS, M. *Single Blessedness*. New York: Basic Books, 1976.

BERNARD, J. *The Future of Marriage*. New Haven, Conn.: Yale Univ. Press, 1982.

BRIM, O., JR. Remarks on life span development. Presented to the American Institute on Research, 1977. Mimeographed.

CARTER, H., and P. C. GLICK. *Marriage and Divorce: A Social and Economic Study*. Cambridge, Mass.: Harvard University Press, 1976.

ERIKSON, E. H. *Identity and the Life Cycle*. New York: International Universities Press, 1959.

ETZKOWITZ, H., and P. STEIN. The life spiral: Human needs and adult roles. *Alternative Lifestyles*, 1978, 1, 4, 434–446.

GOVE, W. R. The relationship between sex roles, marital status and mental illness. *Social Forces*, 1972, 51, 34–44.

KURTH, S. A process of identity transformation for non-marrieds. Paper presented at the annual meeting of the Society for the Study of Social Problems, 1975, San Francisco.

LEVINSON, D. J., C. M. DARROW, E. B. KLEIN, M. H. LEVINSON, and B. MCKEE. The psychosocial development of men in early adulthood and the mid-life transition. In D. F. Ricks, A. Thomas, and M. Roff (Eds.), *Life History Research in Psychopathology* (Vol. 3). Minneapolis: University of Minnesota Press, 1974.

LEVINSON, D., et al. *Seasons of a Man's Life*. New York: Knopf, 1978.

SCHWARTZ, M. A. Career strategies of the never married. Paper presented at the annual meeting of the American Sociological Association, August 1976, New York City.

STARR, J., and D. CARNS. Singles in the city. *Society*, 1972, 9, 43–48.

STEIN, P. J. *Single*. Englewood Cliffs, N.J.: Prentice-Hall, 1976.

______ (Ed.). *Single Life: Unmarried Adults in Social Context*. New York: St. Martin's Press, 1981.

THORNTON, A., and D. FREEDMAN. The Changing American Family. *Population Bulletin*, October 1983, 38, 4.

U.S. Bureau of the Census. Marital status and living arrangements: March 1983. *Current Population Reports*, Series P-20, no. 389. Washington, D.C.: U.S. Government Printing Office, 1984.

CHAPTER 26

On Living Together Unmarried

Patrick G. Jackson

ABSTRACT: The author reports on a study of unmarried and unrelated persons of the opposite sex who are living together in a sexually intimate relationship (cohabiters). He found that cohabiters usually "drift" into living together, and that males and females give different meanings to their living arrangements. Three styles of relating with others (especially with parents) are: concealment, pretense, and open relationships. Cohabiters generally experience pressures, usually from their families, to adopt a more conventional life-style (to marry).

[As to the frequency of cohabitation, census] data indicate that the number of unmarried couples who reported living together in the same house or apartment in 1978 has more than doubled since 1970, from 523,000 to 1,137,000 (Glick and Spanier, 1980: 20); . . . Glick and Spanier note that "there have been few developments relating to marriage and family life which have been as dramatic as the rapid increase in unmarried cohabitation" (p. 20). And it is likely that the incidence of cohabitation is underreported due in part to its nonlegal status in the majority of states.

Researchers have asked what implications the apparent increase in cohabitation may have for the family, courtship, and marriage. Does

I wish to thank William Goode and Lenore Weitzman for comments on an earlier draft of this article. Edwin Lemert also made some helpful editorial suggestions.

cohabitation represent a rejection of or competition to conventional marriage? Do cohabiters practice a more equitable sex role division of labor? Does prior theory about conventional courtship and marriage also apply to cohabiters? . . .

Evidence supports the argument that cohabitation is a slight variation of the classical pattern of courtship in the United States, that is, one in which mate choice is formally free, grounded in a love relationship, but nonetheless controlled to some extent by both family and an autonomous peer group (see Goode, 1966: 44–45). To begin with, cohabitation does not appear to represent a rejection of marriage. Over 90% of college student cohabiters desire to marry (Bower and Christopherson, 1977; Macklin, 1972). . . . As one would expect, the most frequently cited reason for cohabitation is the desire for a close, affectionate, and largely exclusive relationship (Macklin, 1972).

What differentiates cohabitation from conventional courtship within the United States, however, is the lesser degree of legitimacy it is accorded by the family. Although there appears to be greater toleration of the relationship in some segments of society (e.g., Liebow, 1967), among the largely middle- and upper-class youth studied by researchers there is considerable disapproval by parents upon learning of the relationship. . . .

METHODS

[To obtain respondents for this study,] cohabiters were solicited by an ad placed in a local newspaper, notices on bulletin boards, and included a few referred from other cohabiters. At the time of the interview the average age of the 14 males was 25, and of the 10 females, 23. Most had no current religious preference and only 1 attended church. Their parents' education, occupation, and income were roughly middle- and upper-middle class; fathers were generally college educated, managerial or professional—in a few cases blue collar in occupation—with incomes ranging from $11,000 to over $60,000 a year. . . .

For present purposes cohabitation is defined as two unrelated persons of the opposite sex who share common living arrangements in a sexually intimate relationship without legal or religious sanction. All of the respondents had cohabited at least four months.

ENTRY INTO COHABITATION

The first stage of what may loosely be called the career of a cohabiting couple is the exclusion of other intimate or potentially intimate relations (Davis, 1972: 192). . . .

> [Central to the couple's move was their] gradual merging of daily rounds. The most adequate metaphor to describe this movement is drift (e.g., Matza, 1964), in which couples spend an increasing amount of time in the mundane activities of everyday life: eating, entertainment, sleeping, studying, and occasionally visiting with friends. . . .
>
> Financial and living conditions, roommates who suddenly decided to part, squabbles with other living companions, departures from parents' home with no place to reside, loneliness, and other life circumstances opened the way for living together. Viewed in this light, living together was a pragmatic alternative that resolved problems and tensions of daily living and the need for human companionship. . . .

A Disparity of Meanings

The meaning of entry into the cohabiting relationship differed significantly for males and females: the former viewed it as pragmatic, while females defined it as a step toward a stable, long-term relationship, if not marriage (see Lyness et al., 1972; Arafat and Yorburg, 1973).

One male who asked his partner to move in commented on the mutual awareness of this differential involvement:

> When I first asked her she looked at me like I was asking her a momentous thing. And I scratched my head, because it wasn't momentous to me. . . . I think we discussed that once, and she said, "You don't attach much importance to this," "No" (he said), "it's just that you can come and stay with me, that's all."

Many females at this point spoke of permanence, stability, or even marriage. The woman in the following case was aware of her mate's lack of commitment, as well as her own acceptance of this as a fait accompli in which she left the future of the relationship up to him.

> INTERVIEWER (I): Did you talk about marriage when you moved in together?
>
> RESPONDENT (R): Yeah. When we first moved in together I told him that I would never bring marriage up, that it would be up to him when he was ready to get married, and it was. . . . I went into that relationship as if it were a marriage, a commitment. I never had any desire to date anybody else. . . .

LIVING TOGETHER UNMARRIED

The second stage in the career of a cohabiting couple emerges with the sharing of common space (Davis, 1972: 102–194). . . .

Change and Continuity in Household Form

Moving into and setting up a common household was a piecemeal operation, and reflected the equivocal nature of the decision to do so. Eventually couples affirmed the awareness of their living arrangement, as shown by one male's rhetorical question to his partner, "Well, I guess we're living together, aren't we?" By this time all books, clothes, and other belongings had been moved.

Usually there was little money to begin with, and rent, food costs, and bills were often divided. Keeping most of their resources separate, though, was often inconvenient and took constant effort, so most couples pooled them. Household duties were most often split along traditional sex-role lines: Females typically shopped and cooked, while males sometimes washed or dried the dishes, but usually took out the garbage (see Stafford et al., 1977). . . . Finances were not usually pooled until couples moved. . . . [I]n the majority of cases phones were put in the man's name; likewise for bills and leases.

But some exceptions should be noted. In two cases couples kept their finances completely separate and attempted to guard against falling into traditional sex-role segregation of tasks. In four other relationships though, the woman took a traditional approach to setting up and maintaining the household. This meant cooking all the man's meals, doing all the housework, laundry, and other domestic tasks, and in one instance even refusing offers of assistance from her partner. The most common explanation for this was to please her companion, if not to demonstrate her domestic competence.

> I wanted to show him that I was a good cook and that I knew how to keep care of the house. . . . He never asked me to. It's just that I really liked him and felt that it was important he knew I was competent in doing those things.

As time passed, however, these women, like some others, reported regret over having assumed such responsibilities, but found it was too late or too difficult to do anything about it:

> I finally figured out that I blew it when we first started living together because it's really hard to break out of old habits. If I quit doing most of the things I do, who knows what might happen? I don't want him to leave, although I don't think he'd go that far. He might even do some of the housework, but he does such a shitty job I'd have to do it over again, and he knows that. He really has a good thing going.

These statements substantiate Whitehurst's (1974: 3) earlier conclusion that "one cannot make the assumption that because people violate conventional norms and engage in cohabitation that they are therefore 'liberated' and striving for sex-role equality." At best the present study suggests wide variation in sex-role equality.

Relations with Others

Most relationships were hidden from others in the beginning, a stage here called *concealment*. The concealed relationship often evolved into one of *pretense*, where cohabiters' perceived others knew of the relationship but neither party admitted it to the other. Eventually, they entered the public domain and their relationships become *open* (see Glaser and Strauss, 1964). . . .

Concealment

In anticipation of parental disapproval, most couples concealed their relationships. . . . Separate communication was important, particularly with families; separate phones were a "must," and with them a rule that each answer only his or her phone. One couple actually had six phones in their home, two in each kitchen, bedroom, and loft, largely for their (separate) convenience. Separate mail boxes were also sometimes used, and because most apartment complexes provided one mailbox, one cohabiter sometimes rented a post office box; otherwise one name was removed from the apartment box.

The extremes of segregation were shown in one case in which the couple drove separate cars to work for six months, went home for lunch separately, and kept their relationship a closely guarded secret from workmates because they worked in the same agency, which had a nepotism rule. . . .

Another problem of concealment was dealing with visits by family or, less frequently, "uptight" friends, which ordinarily required much time and effort to make the apartment look as though it were occupied singly. Otherwise the couple parted while one or the other went to a friend's residence to meet visitors. But this in time created strain because friends—who hadn't been seen so much as before—were not happy to be used as part of the concealment tactics and in one case told a cohabiter to "get your act together."

For these reasons and others noted below, a concealed relationship moved toward pretense or openness. A sharing of common space (Davis, 1972: 192) is a way of increasing intimacy and commitment, which was difficult to hide. For example, some cohabiters were less likely to lean on parents during times of personal troubles, and parents asked if things were going okay. In other instances the plural possessive "we" rather than "I" was used in talking with parents, a natural outgrowth of a merging of selves as the relationship grew. This meant inevitable curiosity of parents when a son or daughter supposedly living alone or with same-sex roommates proceeded to talk—usually inadvertently—in plural possessives about his or her fellow cohabiter. Passage of time also tended to reveal the nature of the relationship inasmuch as both partners always seemed to be with each other, despite such rules as having the female answer the phone.

The most problematic situation for a concealed relationship was the unexpected visit. The "case of the curious father" shows how a conjoint front quickly dissolved into panic and movement toward marriage:

> Her folks didn't know that we were living together, but they started to get the idea. (How was unknown.) Her dad started dropping by and my stuff would be in the living room and I would always be there. So then he started dropping by more and more. Like right before we got married he dropped by three times in three months, which was pretty often. . . .

Pretense

Parents [usually] denied or pretended to ignore that the cohabitation actually existed, but left little question that they disapproved. One woman spoke eloquently of this phenomenon of denial, and the resultant sense of depersonalization that went with it:

> Jeff and I went to visit his parents for the first time—his parents are fairly conservative people—and Jeff had already hinted to them that we were living together. They didn't believe him when he told them and didn't act like they knew it when we were there.
>
> I: What do you mean "they didn't act like it"?
>
> R: It was about two days before Christmas when we got there. From the time we walked into the house it was like I was a nobody. All they could do was say, "Oh, it's nice to meet you," and then (they) completely ignored me. It was as though they wouldn't admit it to themselves, much less to me, and it was strange because I felt prepared to deal with the whole issue. . . .

While in open relationships, discussed below, women were the object of attention, within a pretense context it took the form of inattention or conspicuous omission from letters, cool treatment in family gatherings, or near complete disregard on the part of family for feelings she had. Such situations were on occasion a point of hidden friction between the cohabiters. In discussing the reasons for the lack of her willingness to marry her partner, the following woman (who had left her partner six months earlier) mentioned his family:

> His family was very cold. Like he went through this whole scene of *not* telling his family that we were living together for a really long time and I really resented that. But I figured that was his decision and there wasn't really much I could do about that. . . .

Open Relationships

[In most cases] women were put on the spot by family and called upon to account for their conduct. In contrast, the men did not feel they had to justify their behavior to others, nor were they pressured by circumstances. Parents were perceived to adapt a "boys will be boys" attitude toward the relationship where a male was involved, suggesting that the so-called double standard of sex morality still survives.

Women in some cases resisted this and sought to change the parental definition of what they were doing:

> One of the things I told him that I thought we should do was tell his parents that we were going to live together. We were honest with my mother and it would only be fair to be honest with them. He kept putting it off and putting if off, but I kept saying "You've got to tell her, you've got to tell her." . . .

[Yet in] other cases, the women were questioned about the moral propriety of the move by family members and (less frequently) friends, who expressed concern that the female was being "used." . . .

Parents who became aware of the relationship *after* the couple already had moved in together were generally nonsupportive of the woman's behavior. This was true of the man's parents as well as her own. This apparently came as a surprise to one female cohabiter who paraphrased their statements that

> I would be the one who would be hurt financially, socially, and so far as emotional security was involved. . . .

THE DECISION TO MARRY

[In general, females] experienced a strong emotional bond in the earlier stages of the relationship, while males reported similar feelings later, around the time of marriage. The decision to marry was based much more on intrusive factors, especially the pressure of parents and relatives, than what might otherwise have been the case. Marriage was in many cases simply seen as an easier path to travel. The general pattern here was one in which life crises or turning points of major or minor consequences disposed the couple to a redefinition of the relationship in terms of marriage.

The importance of the family in the decision to marry is exemplified by a previously cited case of a couple in a concealed relationship in which the woman's father dropped by their home three times in three months. The man described the situation as follows:

> She was starting to get nervous at the time, and upset because she was afraid her folks were going to find out. She was always making jokes every

> time we'd pass the sign to Reno. She'd say, "Gee, it's only 100 more miles," stuff like that. So I said, "If she's saying that, then maybe she wants to get married."

Intentionally or otherwise, the family made couples aware of their unmarried status even when it was partially accepted in open form. One female cohabiter's parents refused to help them purchase a house together. When they announced they would marry, the down payment came almost immediately. Another woman said she was not allowed to discuss intimate family concerns with his family because that was restricted to those who were married. When asked if she spoke about this persistent problem with her fellow cohabiter, she replied:

> Oh, yeah. I remember one night at his place I was absolutely sick and tired of it all. His sister-in-law started saying things about his other sister-in-law calling me a slut. It caused a lot of conflicts. . . . I was really pissed off and tired of the whole scene. Then Dean goes, "Well, I know what I'm getting you for graduation." Then I kinda thought it might be a ring (which it was). . . .

[At other times the] possibility of separation due to external claims in some cases resolved the issue of marriage. One woman prefaced her statement by saying she "always wanted to get married," then went on to say:

> He [her partner] had been back to school for three months and said he was considering moving up to San Francisco. He asked if I would live with him there, and I told him that I wanted to be married, like I wouldn't move that far away [from home] and not be married. I think he knew the condition. And he said he had thought about it and said, "I'd really like to get married." . . .

DISCUSSION

Entry into cohabitation is a gradual movement characterized by drift and choice-making in a situation of opportunity largely divorced from immediate familial and peer controls. As an adaptation to the anticipated, perceived, or actual negative reactions to the relationship, most couples concealed their relationship, which eventually evolved into situations of pretense and/or openness.

The overall consequence of pretense and open awareness contexts, respectively, was indirect and direct moral questioning of the relationship—largely through the woman. . . . The modal pattern for the present respondents was one in which the enactment of traditional role obligations or marriage was called forth by actual or perceived reactions of others.

The findings clearly betray the differing expectations of women and men—that women are responsible for the maintenance and course of a heterosexual relationship. For a significant number of couples this occurred in the context of an interpersonal relationship in which the decision to marry was either statedly or impliedly the male's. . . . One can speculate that the male's decision to marry was, in turn, simply more contingent upon various turning points or crises attendant to life changes. In general, however, marriage appeared to represent an attempt to prevent the attribution of spurious negative imputations to the cohabitation in the context of uncertainty and turning points or life changes in the lives of the cohabiters. . . .

REFERENCES

Arafat, I., and B. Yorburg, 1973. "On living together without marriage." J. of Sex Research 9: 97–106.

Bower, D. W., and V. A. Christopherson, 1977. "University student cohabitation: a regional comparison of selected attitudes and behavior." J. of Marriage and the Family 39: 447–452.

Davis, M. S. 1972. Intimate Relations. New York: Macmillan.

Glaser, B. G., and A. L. Strauss, 1964. "Awareness contexts and social interaction." Amer. Soc. Rev. 29: 15–26.

Glick, P. C., and G. B. Spanier, 1980. "Married and unmarried cohabitation in the United States." J. of Marriage and the Family 42: 19–30.

Goode, W. J. 1966. "The theoretical importance of love." Amer. Soc. Rev. 24: 38–47.

Liebow, E., 1967. Tally's Corner. Boston: Little, Brown.

Lyness, J. L., M. Lipetz, and K. E. Davis, 1972. "Living together: an alternative to marriage." J. of Marriage and the Family 34: 305–311.

Macklin, E., 1972. "Heterosexual cohabitation among unmarried college students." Family Coordinator 21: 463–472.

Matza, D., 1964. Delinquency and Drift. New York: John Wiley.

Stafford, R., E. Beckman, and P. Dibona, 1977. "The division of labor among cohabiting and married couples." J. of Marriage and the Family 39: 43–57.

Whitehurst, R. N., 1974. "Sex role equality and changing meaning in cohabitation." University of Windsor (unpublished).

CHAPTER 27

The World of Singles

Mimi Rodin

ABSTRACT: After closely associating with urban singles, Rodin reports her observations (warning that she is analyzing one group in one city and this cannot represent singles across America). She found that singles develop personal relationships almost exclusively with other singles. They adopt a life-style satisfying to them, within the framework of their situation in life and present orientations. Singles have an air of impermanence: They move often, and their possessions are casually piled about their apartments. At least from time to time singles live with members of the opposite sex, being careful, however, (especially the men) to preserve their independence. Women tend to play traditional female roles, even in quasi-conjugal households.

The purpose of this study is to provide a description of the social and domestic organization of young, never-married, urban, American apartment dwellers, whose lifestyles have never been studied by anthropologists or sociologists. . . .

Gatherings are often occasioned by culturally determined holiday seasons. Over the last Christmas–New Year holiday, one person organized a reunion of his high-school graduating class. Another attempted to organize a week-end reunion of several college friends, now married, in their old college town. Both reunions failed. A third donated his apartment for a highly successful office Christmas party.

Two examples illustrate the consequences of violating the discreteness of sectors of one's networks. One woman stated that whenever she had invited her boyfriend, whom she had met at work, to gatherings of her college friends, he sulked in a corner. Another told of inviting friends from work and friends from a voluntary association to a party. The party broke up into two groups along the lines of prior acquaintance, and she spent the evening moving back and forth between them.

Membership in any of the above categories differentially calls into play informal social pressures to communicate with others. As greater social and geographical distances arise between members, due to marriage and job changes, the pressures on people to reaffirm these relationships decreases. This is especially true of some relatives, old friends and college friends. Ultimately, the relationships are terminated or reduced to networks of letters, occasional telephone calls, or symbolic exchanges of Christmas cards. . . .

Members of "the gang" were predominantly single, and predominantly male, although the office employed about equal numbers of men and women. Several women carried the burden of entertaining. When informants were asked who had been present at parties, they noted that several people had dropped out of the party circuit after marriage. These married individuals no longer give parties for "the gang," although they occasionally invited individuals from it home to dinner. Subsequently, two informants observed that acquaintances from their college and voluntary association sectors also became socially detached from them after marriage.

I have labeled this phenomenon the "dropping out through marriage phenomenon." It effectively functions to keep social networks distinct on the basis of married status. It is interpreted as a sign of marital problems for a married man to appear on the single's party circuit.

Perhaps the least easily explainable feature of singles' networks is the predominantly male composition, although it appears to be related to the "dropping out through marriage phenomenon." When women were asked to account for how they met people, they included in their list of acquaintances that the connecting individuals were usually men. I was not able to confirm this for men, but the following generalizations appear to be true. Single men meet single women at work and through other men in their job and voluntary association networks. Women meet men through the same sectors of their networks, which are predominantly male by actual count. Same-sex acquaintances are recruited the same way. This would appear to indicate that men have more acquaintances than women and that men are the active links through which both men and women extend their networks.

The discussion suggests a process by which singles prune their networks of past associations based on kinship and childhood, propelling themselves into a world rooted firmly in the present. After marriage, former singles drift away from their single acquaintances. The remaining singles operate, as they grow older, in a world that is progressively more oriented around their place of work and more masculine in composition. . . .

In the personal networks I studied, the men were usually several years older than the women with whom they associated. This is consistent with census data that shows that the median age at marriage for men is slightly higher than for women. Only a small percentage of adults over the age of thirty-four have never married. Functionally this means that men are marrying women who are several years their juniors. There are indications then that singles' networks function to bring potentially marriageable people into contact with each other. . . .

Singles move often. During the period of study, I documented four moving parties demonstrating how sectors of personal networks can become cooperative labor groups. "Saturday at my place. Free beer for anyone who helps load the van. Bring a muscle-bound friend." There are apartment-painting parties, "booze and brushes provided by the management." Another singles-set mailed out engraved invitations to "a gala fete in honour of D.D., on his natal date." Friends look in on each other when they are ill. They stay up all night with emotionally distressed friends and call in sick at work while bringing a friend down from a bad drug experience.

The following example illustrates the extent to which singles' networks provide support for their members:

> Nan moved to Chicago, found an apartment on the near-north side and a job at the firm. She met Sara at work and they found they both lived in the same apartment building. Every now and then they had dinner together at home or went out. A couple of times a week they went singly or together to Mother's. Mother's is a bar, one of about two dozen such establishments located within three blocks of each other on North Lincoln Avenue. Like the others, it caters to singles. Nan says: "I don't like bars, but I like Mother's. If you've gotta get out, there's always someone there you know. And if some guy starts hassling you, Andy throws them out." Andy is the bartender and part-owner of Mother's. He is a former roommate of Sara's boyfriend. Meredith was one of Sara's friends from Mother's. She was out of work for two months until Sara and Nan found an opening for her at the firm. During those two months she crashed with Sara. Andy gave Meredith a free steak sandwich and fries every night at Mother's until her first paycheck. "He says it's good for business." After that, Nan loaned Meredith her car to go apartment hunting.

ORGANIZATION OF TIME, SPACE, AND PROPERTY

The diaries [that the author had her informants keep on their personal relationships—Ed.] indicated that people who live alone actually spend very little time alone. Time alone was always punctuated by telephon calls from others who lived alone. Informants said that if they felt lonel or were suffering from "cabin fever" that they phoned friends to talk o to arrange to meet them. Women met other women for a drink, shop ping, or a movie. Men went to bars, played pool or golf, visited femal friends, or found card games. If none of these activities were possible all resorted to television or going to sleep. Most of the time that single spent alone at home was accompanied by noisemaking devices such a radio, stereo, or television.

There was a noticeable tendency for men to spend less time alone a home or even at home than women. Men were less likely to answer th telephone than women when they were alone. This is apparently re lated to several of the findings previously discussed under social net works. Men are the active links in arranging social meetings. It appear that women will remain alone rather than violate that norm. It has als been suggested that women simply have a greater tolerance for soli tude, which may or may not be biologically based, but it is not my pur pose here to discuss such notions. It is clear, however, that single mer and women do structure their solitude in ways that are generally char acteristic of their sex, as it is socially defined.

"Cabin fever" was mentioned only by women and was brought or not so much by being alone as by self-imposed solitary confinemen during periods of nervousness, depression, or embarrassment. Suck feelings were termed "the blue funk." Women were also more likely than men to mediate solitude with nonhuman companionship (such as pets) or by using the telephone.

Singles' time is relatively loosely scheduled, and this characteristic is carried over into the way they organize their living space. American houses are designed to provide for the privacy of their residents by par titioning of internal space by function. Living rooms and dining rooms are public and social gathering places. Bedrooms and bathrooms are private.

Although singles differ from members of family households in their organization of property and time, their usage of space maintains many of the same features. They have few possessions, but, as one woman observed, these possessions spread out to fill the available space, besides, "Why buy it? I'd only have to move it." After a moment's reflection, she observed that her activities also spread out to fill the available space.

All of the singles lived in at least two- or three-room apartments. Several had four or more rooms. Though they felt free about states of undress and rarely closed doors, even to the bathroom, they observed a discreteness of function for the areas of their apartments.

There was an air of impermanence to their apartments, a lack of investment in time or money. Furniture was sparse, provided by the landlord, obviously secondhand or collapsible. Steamer trunks were left packed. Luggage was shoved in a corner not stowed out of sight in a closet. Laundry in its wrapping paper lay on, not in, chests of drawers. Dishes, silverware, and linens were rarely of matched sets. A few maintained office addresses or post office boxes in lieu of home mail delivery.

This pattern is rather different from that of older singles who were less eager or likely to marry or remarry. Their residence histories indicated that they moved less often. The older singles to whom I talked placed their first purchases of furniture soon after their decisions to remain single, at least for the time being. Older singles (over thirty) had acquired matched sets of linens, dishes and silverware, draperies, carpets, life insurance and annuity policies, and home mortgages.

This is especially instructive if we notice that in American society a permanent home, furniture, and matching housewares are expectably acquired by newlyweds. These things are a material representation of the stability of married life. The distinction seems to be the difference between "my place" of the young single, who regards himself as going through a stage of independence before settling into marriage, and "my home" of the older single whose complete residence expresses his personal completeness. . . .

QUASI-CONJUGAL HOUSEHOLDS

Earlier in the discussion, it was shown that singles can mobilize sectors of their social networks as cooperative labor groups to assist for special purposes, such as moving and house-painting. Individuals exchange domestic services as well. Such a reciprocal relationship can become routinized between a single man and a single woman, while each continues to maintain a separate residence. I have termed this a quasi-conjugal household.

All eight of the original group of informants are currently, or have recently been, members of one or more quasi-conjugal households. Some of the households were regarded as preliminary to living together in a marriagelike joint household, either as a preface to marriage or not. Other households were regarded as satisfactory without the likelihood of eventual marriage.

Although all of the singles in the original sample expressed the desire to marry "sometime" in the future, they had many reservations about immediate marriage, even with the people they planned to marry "eventually." The following passage is quite typical in giving reasons for not marrying, and for maintaining separate residences.

> Right after college I got very uptight about not being married. But then I decided I had my own life to lead. No, I'm not in any rush to get married. Children seem like an awfully heavy responsibility. After that (getting together again after breaking up) Mike decided we should live together anyway. But I decided not to because if we broke up then I would be the one to move out and there wouldn't be anywhere to go home to. It's security. (Anne, age twenty-five)

The division of labor in quasi-conjugal households is nearly identical to that described by Blood and Wolfe for nuclear families. Women provided shopping, cooking, and housekeeping services for their boyfriends. Men sometimes assisted them in this, and usually offered to share expenses for the running of both households. This kind of division of labor developed after the establishment of a sexual relationship in all cases.

One woman said that she regularly kept house for her boyfriend but never initiated such activities until he asked her to or offered some sort of trade in the form of a "heavy date." She said that once he had offered cash payment for a particularly thorough job, which she accepted rather than be "pushy." She felt that if she kept house for free, that the man might "take her for granted" or suspect that she was escalating the relationship to marriage. By not permitting him to reciprocate immediately, she felt she would have endangered the relationship.

Some tasks are highly indicative markers of the degree of commitment by partners to a relationship. Men and women agreed that washing dishes was not a loaded service. But one man added, "You've got to watch out when they start wanting to do your laundry." Sometimes women will attempt to force reciprocation on men who are not willing.

> I'd just like to find a nice girl to call up and go out for a beer. Just to have fun. But the first thing they do when you bring them home, like the first thing they do when they come in, is start picking up your socks. (Hal, age twenty-six)

The degree of commitment to a quasi-conjugal household and the relationship it symbolizes is measurable along two axes: the number and kind of domestic services traded and shared and the degree of routinization and coordination of scheduling between members. Scheduling increases with the intensity of the relationship. Activities, especially meals, become increasingly routinized into predictable time slots. . . .

In more fragile relationships, the exchange of services is carefully negotiated and casually scheduled. Several stable couples in the sample, both during and prior to the study, reciprocated services easily and spent three or more evenings a week together. Because they spent so much time in each others' apartments, they frequently kept toothbrushes, changes of clothing, and other personal items in both apartments, thus symbolically staking out a joint territory.

In each of the quasi-conjugal households I found, there seemed to be no routinized pattern of sleeping arrangements. The sexual business of the household was conducted about equally under both roofs. Singles felt that if they stayed away from their own apartments too regularly that their independence would be challenged. Men especially felt that women should not spend "too much" time in their apartments. . . .

[I]n American culture, kinship is traced through the children of the married couples. Some social scientists consider marriage as no more than legitimate sexual relations. They do not take into account the legal standing of such relations and especially the prescriptions in law pertaining to the maintenance of a joint-residence by married couples. In some states joint-residence acquires jural standing in definitions of common-law marriages and provisions for the legitimation of the children of couples who have not legally married.

The conjugal nature of quasi-conjugal households derives from the fact that the sexual aspect of the relationship is routinely conducted within the homes of its members. Sexual encounters of brief duration, such as "one-night stands" or encounters situated in borrowed apartments, hotels, and motels, are not accorded the same aura of legitimacy.

It is important to recognize that quasi-conjugal relationships are further routinized to the degree that partners reciprocate domestic services. The relationship has no jural content, however. There are no enforceable sanctions for failure to reciprocate. The relationship is based rather on mutual expectations. When expectations on the part of either or both parties no longer coincide and negotiation fails to restore agreement on the content of the relationship, the quasi-conjugal household is dissolved.

> Anne told me that Laura's boyfriend, Jack, was a real SOB because he had started seeing Carol even though Laura continued to do his laundry, as she had for nearly six months. Anne said that Laura was being a real idiot for letting Jack "use" her that way. But Laura kept on doing Jack's wash. Later Jack defended his actions to Don, who worked in the same office as Jack, Laura, and Anne. Jack said that he had no intention of marrying her. But despite his protests, Laura insisted on helping him.

As single men and women form intense, personal relationships, women extend their housekeeping to more than one residence. To a much lesser degree, men extend domestic services to women. Since most of these services are given by women and taken by men, we may say that a woman establishes sexual rights in a man to the degree to which she keeps his house. A single man validates her claim to the extent that he permits and publicly encourages her in this.

Sexual relationships between single men and women are mediated through this exchange of domestic services. Either party can symbolically assert the right to other sexual partners by refusing to accept or to perform domestic services. The giving and taking of some services are more obligating than others.

Not every quasi-conjugal household leads to marriage, but an individual's willingness to escalate its conjugal nature indicates a willingness to marry. By following the career of a quasi-conjugal household, and by seeing whether reciprocity is increasing or decreasing, it is possible to tell whether it is a transitional stage to living together or marriage. A quasi-conjugal household can also be a steady and ambiguous state in which each member remains self-sufficient and nominally head of his or her own household.

SUMMARY

This study is not intended to account for all possible singles' lifestyles. Thus, such subjects as "the singles's bar complex" and the "swinging-singles" lifestyle have not been considered here. Instead, I have focused on a limited sample of semiprofessional singles in a small midwestern city, where the possibility of developing the kind of lifestyle that is alleged to be characteristic of big-city singles' life is less likely to develop because of the lack of the appropriate facilities (such as singles' bars) and conditions (such as the anonymity of urban housing and settings). For these reasons it would be inappropriate to draw broad general conclusions from this research. Thus, the following statements are offered more as tentative hypotheses for further testing than as conclusions.

Urban singles operate as autonomous individuals in a social milieu devoid of kin or conjugal ties. Few of their interpersonal relationships are invested with jural rights and duties. That is to say, their personal relationships are not formed or sanctioned in terms of extrapersonal rules or norms other than those applicable throughout the society. Concomitantly, singles are free of enforceable obligations to others. Their freedom from such restriction is expressed in their high degree of job and residence mobility. Thus, the majority of personal relationships among singles lack the time depth and the complexity of overlapping identities that are characteristic of married people.

Young urban singles, however, develop strategies for building a modicum of stability and predictable reciprocity into their relationships. Through processes of social selection, singles form personal relationships primarily with other singles. The resulting personal networks provide the basis for various kinds of cooperative and supportive activities and exchanges. The shared knowledge that they all lack other sorts of support groups draws them together. . . .

As the personal relationship between a man and a woman approaches the conjugal form and becomes more or less stable, the man begins to perform the traditionally male tasks involved in maintaining both of their residences, thus approximating the form of the conjugal family in terms of the division of labor. An alternate pattern may also develop as the man assumes or shares some of the traditionally female tasks, such as shopping or laundry, creating a division of domestic labor in which men and women are structurally and functionally equivalent.

PART III

Married Life

WHEN TWO PEOPLE DECIDE TO MARRY, they anticipate a welcome change in their lives. The typical couple eagerly looks forward to a ceremony that marks their transition from singlehood to married life. In spite of their anticipations, however, most couples appear rather surprised and somewhat confused by how extensive the changes are that they encounter. The world of marriage is so unlike the premarital milieu in which they have lived, and usually grown comfortable, that the newlyweds discover that they have moved into an entirely different world.

A married couple usually finds that nothing is quite the same as it was before marriage. Sociologically we can expect this, for marriage is not only (1) the public bestowal of a new identity, and (2) the creation of a new legal unit, but marriage also brings changes in (3) the couple's social relationships, (4) their relationships with one another, (5) their behavior, (6) their perception and evaluation of their spouse, and (7) their perception and evaluation of the self.

I shall briefly discuss each of these changes.

1. Around the world, marriage is the bestowal by the community of a new public identity. In fact, one can look at marriage ceremonies as ritualistic, dramatic displays that serve as public announcements that the individuals involved have formally taken on a new identity. This new identity can be bestowed only by the community, and the community does this selectively. On the basis of having followed its particular rules (usually age and sex, in some cases social class, race, and property, and in all societies the avoidance of what they view as incest), the community proclaims that the couple is now married.

According to ordinary perception, this analysis places matters backward. Most people believe it is the individuals themselves who are announcing to the community that they are married. And, in one sense, of course, the couple is indeed making such an announcement. But sociologically it is just the opposite. The *community* establishes the rules about who is eligible to marry whom; the *community* bestows the public identity of married on those who have met these qualifications, while it withholds that status from those who fail to meet its standards.

2. As the wedding ceremony marks the individual's transition from singlehood to the marital state, it simultaneously creates a legal unit. The two individuals have been wed or, as the literal sense of this verb applies directly to their situation, they have been joined together. For many practical purposes in our society, others react to them as a single legal unit. They are, for example, now one when it comes to bank loans. (In spite of various changes in this area, bank officials invariably insist on obtaining both spouses' signatures on a loan application.) The couple is also one when it comes to the Internal Revenue Service: At their discretion, the couple may file singly or jointly, an option not offered to the unmarried.

3. The couple also undergoes major changes in their social relationships. When it comes to most friends and relatives, the two are considered one. Seldom are invitations for parties, dinners, and other social gatherings extended only to the husband or wife. Similarly, cards are usually addressed to Mr. *and* Mrs., while gift exchanges usually follow the same lines. They are now seen as a unit, and it is as a pair that the married couple is reacted to in myriad social situations.

4. The couple's relationship to one another also changes. For example, they no longer see one another on an optional basis. No matter how committed to each other they were before marriage, there was always an option underlying their relationship. At any given time it was their decision whether or not they were going to see each other; if they so wished, they could dispense with their agreements and understandings and break up.

While it is true that in our current society marriages are easily broken (in some places, such as Illinois, one can file for divorce one week and be divorced the next), the critical difference is that *because the community has bestowed this public identity, a married couple's relationship is no longer a private matter*. Before marriage, a couple can separate and be done with it. But marriage occurs within the assumption of permanence, and after marriage a couple must take into account their changed legal status and public identity and, at a minimum, fill out papers and have an official add his or her stamp of agreement that the *community* grants the termination of their relationship.

5. These changes in legal and social relationships lead to changes in the way the couple act toward one another. Marriage entails obligations of support and nurturance that must be fulfilled—whether or not one wishes to fulfill them. For most, for example, it is no longer an option whether or not one will

come home at night, cook a meal, share money, visit relatives, or even talk to the other. The changed relationship demands these activities, turning them from options into responsibilities, and those who refuse to follow such expectations are usually married but a short time.

6. Marriage also leads to changes in how each perceives and evaluates the other. Each no longer sees the other as the man or woman "I'm going to marry," but the man or woman who is now "my husband" or "my wife." Each has undergone a major change in status and has entered a role whose dictates are largely determined by others. The responsibilities and rewards of this role certainly are not constant throughout society, as the individual's understanding of them is always filtered through membership and participation in smaller social groups. Each individual, however, has a set of expectations about how a husband or wife ought to act. (Presumably, the better the husband's and wife's expectations match, the better their marital adjustment.) Newlyweds now see their martial partner through the lens of these expectations. Each evaluates the other, noting the degree to which the other's performance matches these expectations. As this evaluative judgmental process occurs, each receives different ideas of the other.

7. Finally, marriage also leads to changes in the way each perceives and evaluates the self. The ideas that each has of idealized marital roles also apply to one's own role in marriage, i.e., the wife has specific ideas about how a wife ought to act, and the husband ideas about a husband's ideal behavior. Each evaluates his or her own self according to how one feels one is fulfilling these expectations. As this self-reflective process continues, it leads to changes in self-evaluation.

Nothing, then, can be the same after marriage. A newly married couple does not simply make superficial changes in their lives. They do not merely enter a new social status; rather, they enter an entirely different world, a world filled with the unexpected.

New experiences are usually demanding, and a new world of experiences demands major adjustments. It radically challenges fundamental and taken-for-granted aspects of one's existence. Consequently, adapting to a world that alters basic assumptions involves making changes in fundamental aspects of the self and in one's significant relationships in life.

While the wedding ceremony officially marks the beginning of marriage, being married is not something attained by having words spoken over the couple. Being married is not so much a state as an activity. Being married is a dynamic relationship worked out by each couple as they make their own transition to the new reality they have entered.

It is on life following the marriage ceremony, then, on which we focus in this third part of the book. To examine ways by which couples forge bonds during marriage, we first look at lasting relationships (Section 8), then work and marriage (Section 9), sexual relations over the course of marriage (Section 10) and parenting (Section 11).

To apply this material to your own life, think first about past adjustments you have made in your relationship with someone of the opposite sex. If you have ever gone with someone for any length of time, whether you went steady, were engaged, or were married, you experienced change in various directions and to different degrees. What changes took place? How did you come to see things differently because of your relationship? What things did you see differently? Why those things? Of the differences between your expectations and your actual behaviors toward one another, which were based primarily on your gender? What did you think about these expectations and behaviors? When this relationship ceased, how did the world look different to you? Why did it appear different?

By thinking along these lines you can discover how your own reality was rooted in a heterosexual relationship. As you mentally examine past relationships, look especially for changes in the way you thought about yourself. Did your view of who you are change? How? In what ways was this change based on the ways you were treated by the one you were going with? In what ways was it based on the ways others treated you because you were going with that person? In what ways was it based on your evaluations of how your behavior matched some set of idealized expectations about how you should act? And, finally, what were the origins of those expectations?

SECTION 8

Lasting Relationships

PEOPLE ARE CONSTANTLY ASKING what is wrong with marriages today. They see divorce all around them—their friends and relatives, their neighbors and associates—and they know this is but a reflection of national statistics.

If I were to try to pinpoint the reason for our high divorce rate, one that hit at the very heart of the matter, I would pick incompatible expectations. This choice encompasses the major problems couples experience in the primary areas of money and sex, as well as most other basic disturbances in married life. I am comfortable with this choice because these incompatible expectations largely arise from people's basic socialization into sex roles. (As was discussed earlier, our sex roles have built into them contrasting and conflicting approaches to life.) This emphasis would also allow me to focus on the structural features of American society that maintain these basic male-female patterns, differences that ultimately show up in the marital relationship.

The fact is, though, that *most marriages last*. Although our divorce rate is high, most American marriages last until the death of either the husband or the wife. In other words, most marriages, even today, last throughout the married person's lifetime. The heavy concentration on marital problems and divorce in American society, however, tends to obscure this significant fact.

It seems worthwhile, then, to pose the question of what is *right* about marriage today. Consequently, this section focuses on lasting relationships. The first chapter here is from the Middletown study that was introduced in Section 6. In this portion Caplow et al. contrast today's marriages in Muncie, Indiana, with those of the 1920s and 1930s In what may be a surprising finding, they report that the basic relationship between husbands and wives has *improved* during the past half century.

Could this finding, which so flies in the face of common assumptions about American marriage, be true? Is this true just in Muncie, Indiana? Certainly the researchers' findings are limited to Muncie, for that is where they did their study—they did not look at Roseau, Minnesota, or Chino, California, or Selma, Alabama, or Boston, Massachusetts. In fact, the researchers cannot make comparisons with the past in those places because there is no similar original study against which to compare.

Is Muncie an exception to the United States in general? We cannot say for certain, but there are indications that it is not an unusual situation: Divorce, for example, has also markedly risen in Muncie. However, it is *not* incompatible to find basic relationships between husbands and wives improving while divorce is simultaneously increasing: We are not talking about the same marriages. As Theodore Caplow and his team report, husbands and wives generally find marriage more satisfying today because they spend more time with one another and their communications have improved; they talk to each other more about a wider variety of things. Most, then, find greater satisfactions with one another.

At the same time, however, husbands and wives have come to expect more out of marriage in the sense of greater personal fulfillment. With their expectations having increased, and in light of divorce carrying less stigma, those who do not find these satisfactions are more likely to abandon their marriages. Marriage simply has fewer other functions to hold discontent people together. (Remember the material in Section 1 on the changing functions of marriage?)

How do husbands and wives in lasting marriages relate to one another? Does some single pattern distinguish them from the husbands and wives who give up? As John F. Cuber and Peggy B. Harroff found, lasting marriages show no single or overriding marital style. Rather, lasting relationships show remarkable diversity—there are basically five fundamentally different approaches to marriage. While some of these marital styles may represent considerably less than the ideals that you and I might hold, for the couples involved, they work. This does not mean that you or I would be satisfied with these marital patterns (although there is one or two to which we are likely to wholeheartedly subscribe), but they do provide enough satisfactions to those husbands and wives that they maintain their commitment to one another.

In the third chapter sociological researchers look at the areas of most common disagreement between husbands and wives—money, work, and sex. Philip Blumstein and Pepper Schwartz (whose work was introduced in Section 1) find that the successful couples have more conciliatory and less demanding approaches to one another. Those who are demanding or who quarrel a lot about these matters so central to married life are less likely to remain together. In addition, engaging in extramarital sex, rather than focusing one's sexual desires on one's spouse, also increases the likelihood of a couple breaking up.

There is a significant difference, of course, between marriages that are merely lasting and those in which the husband and wife are satisfied with one another, content about the relationship, and actually feel happy about their marriage and one another. Why are some marriages not only long-lasting but also happy? Do such couples have any characteristics in common? Can we learn from them so we can improve our own chances of marital success?

It is on this topic that we conclude this section. Nicholas Stinnett uses the term "strong family" to refer to a family in which the husband and wife and children are highly satisfied with one another, families in which there is a great deal of happiness and a feeling of marital success. After interviewing such families, Stinnett found that they do indeed have major features in common. He identifies those features and suggests that they can provide the bases around which we can build strong, positive marriages and families.

As you read these selections, then, you might ask yourself what is *right* about these relationships. What can I learn from these findings? How can I improve my own marriage to make it stronger, more secure, and more satisfying? Are there keys here that I can use to unlock my own marriage in order to make it come closer to what I expect out of it?

CHAPTER 28

American Marriage—Better Than Ever?

Theodore Caplow / Howard M. Bahr / Bruce A. Chadwick / Reuben Hill / Margaret Holmes Williamson

ABSTRACT: The picture that the Lynds painted of marriages in the Middletown of the 1920s was fairly dreary by today's standards: tiredness, disappointment, pressures, lack of communication, quarrels, sexual maladjustment, and male dominance. By the 1930s husbands and wives were spending more time together, but they also experienced mounting tensions. In general, today's marriage relationships have improved. Husbands and wives communicate more, spend more leisure time together, and generally report being satisfied with their marriage. This stands in sharp contrast to the common view that marriage in America has gone to hell in a handbasket.

MARRIAGE IN THE 1920s

The Lynds' portrait of the average marriage in the Middletown of the 1920s was a dreary one, especially for the working class. Marriage for many husbands meant weariness from trying to provide for their families, numerous children, and wives weary from doing other people's washing (Lynd and Lynd 1929, 129). For many wives, marriage meant poverty, cruelty, adultery, and abandonment. The Lynds did observe a few happy marriages. "There are some homes in Middletown among both working- and business-class families which one cannot enter without being aware of a constant undercurrent of sheer delight of fresh, spontaneous interest between husband and wife (Lynd and Lynd 1929,

130). But they noted that such marriages stood out because of their rarity and that the majority of Middletown's couples seemed to lead a depressing existence. Though disappointment and depression did not dominate the family's daily life, they lurked in the background, occasionally resulting in a domestic fight or a drinking spree. It appeared to the Lynds that most families, although less than happy, were held together by community values discouraging divorce and by the husband and wife's focusing on "the plans for today and tomorrow," "the pleasures of this half-hour," and their "share in the joint undertaking of children, paying off the mortgage, and generally 'getting on'" (1929, 130). Married life was disappointing, but the prospect of a divorce was even more painful. They forgot their discouragement by focusing on day-to-day living and by ignoring the question of whether it was worth the effort.

Companionship

Observations of husbands and wives revealed that most of them developed a relationship with limited companionship. In the social and recreational activities of the 1920s, the sexes were separated more often than not. At dinners, parties, and other social gatherings, men and women seemed to form separate groups so that the men could talk about business, sports, and politics and the women could discuss children, dress styles, and local gossip. Men's leisure activities generally excluded women. Business-class husbands played golf or cards at their clubs without their wives, while no self-respecting working-class wife would join her husband for an evening in the local cigar store. The one recreational activity that husbands and wives shared was card playing with friends in their homes.

Because of the harsh demands of work in the factories, working-class families had less time, energy, and money to spend on family leisure. According to the Lynds, "Not infrequently, husband and wife would meet each other at the end of a day's work too tired or inert to play or go anywhere together" (1929, 119). Compounding the problem was the economic pressure of the times that left few dollars to spend on entertainment.

The time couples did spend at home does not appear to have been filled with pleasant or stimulating conversation. Decisions about the children, the house payment, and the food budget were quickly dealt with in a bickering fashion, and with those problems disposed of, couples often lapsed into "apathetic silence." The Lynds reported that many times during their survey of wives, the interviewer had a difficult time terminating the interview. The women seemed hungry for someone to talk to.

"I wish you could come often. I never have anyone to talk to," or "My husband never goes anyplace and never does anything. In the evenings he comes home and sits down and says nothing. I like to talk and be sociable, but I can hardly ever get anything out of him" [Lynd and Lynd 1929, 120].

The limited communication between husbands and wives and the trivial nature of their conversation left many of them isolated in their separate worlds, his pertaining to work and friends and hers to the children and the home. In many marriages, they shared a house, each other's bodies, and little else.

Even their sexual relations seemed troubled. Lack of information about birth control and the prejudice against its use made babies the inevitable consequence of physical intimacy for most working-class couples. The uncertainty of employment often made another child an unwanted burden. The conflict between not wanting more children and needing the physical pleasures of marriage, and the resulting stress placed on the marriage, were evident in the comments of Middletown wives.

One wife hopes to heaven she'll have no more children. She said that people talked to her about contraceptives sometimes, and she told "him" what they said, but he said it was none of their business. She had never dared ask him what he thought about birth control, but thought he disapproved of it. She would "die" if she had any more children, but is doing nothing to prevent it [Lynd and Lynd 1929, 124].

A wife of twenty-two replied to the question about number of children: "We haven't any. Gracious, no! We mustn't have any till we get steady work. No, we don't use anything to prevent children. I just keep away from my husband. He don't care—only at times. He's discouraged because he's out of work. I went to work but had to quit because I was so nervous" [Lynd and Lynd 1929, 125].

Such comments provide considerable insight into Middletown's working-class marriages of the 1920s. The fact that a wife might not dare ask her husband what he thought about birth control, let alone what he felt about practicing it, shows how shallow some of the relationships were. In some cases, the threat of unwanted children made wives resentful; they felt that their husbands were insensitive and selfish to expose them to the risk of conception. In other cases, the fear of an unwanted pregnancy forced a wife to "keep away" from her husband, which certainly did not strengthen their marital relationship. On the other hand, husbands felt rejected by their wives' avoidance of physical contact.

It may have been that limited marital sex contributed to the flourishing prostitution in Middletown during the 1920s. Husbands whose wives were sexually unresponsive, perhaps because of their fear of pregnancy, may have sought sexual satisfaction outside of marriage. Although a husband's visits to prostitutes probably did not strengthen his marriage, they were not a sure indicator of marital dissatisfaction. Some men sought commercial sex out of consideration for their wives' fear of unwanted pregnancy. And, of course, we do not know what proportion of the clients of Middletown's brothels were unmarried. Moreover, the effects of changing laws and policies on prostitution make its prevalence a very unsure indicator of marital happiness. The number of whorehouses in Middletown fluctuated dramatically over the years, before beginning a permanent decline in the 1940s.

Another glimpse of the shallowness of husband-wife relationships in the 1920s is provided by the responses of 69 working-class wives to the question "What are the thoughts and plans that give you courage to go on when thoroughly discouraged?" Not one of them mentioned her husband as a source of emotional support! . . .

MARRIAGE IN THE 1930s

The Great Depression was thought by Middletown people to have mixed effects on marital happiness. On the one hand, they spoke of how married couples spent more time together and became more dependent on each other, and this enforced togetherness was perceived as strengthening the quality of Middletown's marriages. The Lynds quoted an editorial in a local newspaper in the spring of 1933 that remarked that

> All of us are hoping for a quick return of the prosperity we once knew, or thought we knew, but in the meantime, some millions of Americans already have a kind of prosperity that includes the strengthening of family ties, better health, and the luxury of simple pleasures and quiet surroundings, although of this they may not be aware [Lynd and Lynd 1937, 147].

On the other hand, the economic chaos of the depression created problems in many marriages, including those of the business class. *Middletown in Transition* suggests that the depression did increase the amount of time husbands and wives spent together by making outside activities unaffordable. Although couples spent more time together, they often reacted to economic pressures by mutual recrimination. The wives were quick to reproach their husbands for failing to provide for the family's needs, and the husbands were equally quick to defend their wounded egos by lashing out at wives and children. Despite these mounting tensions, the typical marital relationship during the depression was similar to that of the 1920s. According to the Lynds, in the 1930s Middletown's homes still housed somewhat impersonal, tolerant couples, in the same rooms, with the same pictures looking down on them, planning together the big and little immensities of personal living by which people in families in this culture seek to ameliorate the essential loneliness and confusion of life. These homes seem to give the lie to the ricocheting process of social change outside [Lynd and Lynd 1937, 145]. . . .

MARRIAGE IN THE 1970s

During the years between 1920 and the late 1970s, the family institution faced a great deal of criticism. It has been argued by some that the family has not changed as rapidly as other social institutions and thus it has become obsolete. The death of the nuclear family has also been widely heralded.

> Depending upon whether one regards oneself as an attacker or defender of the institution, the final death scene may be viewed in different terms. The attackers seem to see the family's death as being hastened by natural causes—that is, hardening of the institutional arteries or something akin to inability to make the evolutionary adjustment to a changed social and economic climate. In this latter view, something has caused the family, like some ancient dinosaur, to breathe its last. Some ardent defenders regard the family's demise as having been engineered by a devilish army of debauched sociologists, radical psychiatrists, "Commie perverts," bra-burning feminists, "knee-jerk liberals," and assorted libertines of predictable intent [Pickett 1975, 7].

Those who would celebrate the death of the family feel that, because the family is not in step with modern society, it stifles human potential, creativity, and freedom. Their conclusion is that most people would be happier free of family ties (Crosby 1975, 12). On the other hand, some claim that many of society's current problems—crime, alcoholism, and drug abuse, for instance—stem from the weakening of the family and that a return to the "old-fashioned family" would alleviate such problems.

Some writers (Libby and Whitehurst 1975) contend that, as American society has adjusted to rapid technological development, new forms of the family have emerged even though they have not been accepted by the vast majority of the population. Some of the alternative forms of the family that have appeared are *cohabitation*, in which couples live together without being married; *group marriage*, which involves the marriage of three or more people; *part-time marriage*, in which the couple is married only for certain family activities for a specified time period; *open marriage*, which allows each partner to establish relationships, including sexual relationships, with other people; and *mate swap-*

ping, or *swinging*, which organizes extramarital sexual behavior. The more radical family forms have usually appeared in some type of communal setting, since they require extensive group support to endure.

Except for a few cases of discreetly practiced cohabitation and mate swapping, alternative forms of the family are rare in Middletown. This situation is not a function of ignorance about alternative family styles. Middletown people are very much aware of family innovations because of their exposure to the mass media. Middletown's newspapers showed an interest when the members of Synanon began dissolving their marriages and entering into three-year love matches (Middletown's evening newspaper, January 2, 1978). Synanon is an organization of approximately 1,600 individuals that was founded in 1958 to rehabilitate "drug addicts, alcoholics and other social misfits." When the wife of Chuck Dederich, the 65-year-old founder and leader of Synanon, died, he married a much younger woman, and the experience started him thinking about how other people would react to a similar experience. He decided that most would enjoy it as much as he had. Besides, according to Dederich, "Most of these people [members of Synanon] were going to divorce anyway, eventually." He persuaded nearly all the married couples in Synanon to divorce and enter into three-year love matches with other people. Husbands and wives helped each other draw up lists of potential love-match partners, and within a few weeks, 230 couples had made love matches. Dederich felt that he had demonstrated a viable alternative to the traditional family. He concluded that "what happened is what I thought would happen. People fell madly in love with their new partners." Although the love matches were only for three years, Dederich predicted that many would last much longer. Although this experiment in family style occurred within a mini-society isolated in the mountains of northern California, it was noted and discussed in Middletown. But there was no rush of Middletown couples to involve themselves in love matches.

The consequences, both good and bad, of couples living together before marriage have been continually debated in the mass media. Some social scientists have been reported as favoring cohabitation as a way of determining a couple's compatibility before marriage. This practice, according to them, should reduce the frequency of divorce, ". . . since the subtleties of a marriage relationship are not taught in school and not learned in courtship, living together provides the only proving ground" (Snider 1975, 12). Other "behavior experts" take up the opposing position and claim that trial marriages place too much pressure on the partners and make it more difficult to develop a close, stable relationship.

> . . . a truly successful marriage and sexual relationship need time to grow and to mature and must be measured in years rather than weeks or months.

> To be successful . . . marriage needs the security of an unconditional future. Living together doesn't provide sufficient time for thought about the future. Partners in a trial marriage do not live in a marriage environment while each must be on guard to pass the examinations of the other [Snider 1975, 12].

Contradicting both positions, research has indicated that cohabitation has little effect on the quality of subsequent marriage. A recent study of a sample of college students in a southern state reported that "persons with a history of premarital cohabitation do not describe their marriages differently from persons without a history of cohabitation" (Jacques and Chason 1979, 36). Although living together has received considerable media coverage, very few Middletown couples have adopted this family style. Less than 2 percent of the adult respondents in the various surveys indicated that they were living together. . . .

Companionship

The last 15 years have witnessed a major change in the style of communication between husbands and wives. Numerous books and magazine articles have appeared, encouraging wives to make their needs and preferences known to their husbands (and vice versa to a lesser degree). Assertiveness-training programs have blossomed across the country. They attempt to teach people, primarily women, to communicate their feelings and opinions to others and, as the term "assertiveness" implies, to do so forcefully. Marriage-enrichment programs, including recorded lessons, weekend training sessions, and month-long retreats, have purported to teach thousands of American couples how to communicate with each other more effectively. The women's rights movement, as well as other forces in American society, have fostered a more equal marriage relationship in which the needs and wishes of the wife are considered to be at least as important as those of the husband.

It is difficult to imagine many contemporary wives who would be afraid to discuss birth control with their husbands, particularly after the couple has had several children. The taboo on discussing financial matters observed in the 1920s has almost disappeared, and today nearly all wives play an active role in the management of family finances, especially when they work and contribute to the family income. The open communication between spouses in most Middletown families today was evident in some of the comments housewives made during our interviews. A typical example from one wife who emphasized the oneness between her husband and herself was this: "I feel there is nothing I couldn't go to him and ask. . . . I mostly talk to one of my best friends, but I feel that you should look to your own husband for basic communication."

Free communication between spouses apparently has permitted many contemporary couples to increase the happiness they derive from their marriages; at the same time, it has helped other couples to identify their irreconcilable differences. The process of identifying and solving a marital crisis has occasionally been reported in Middletown newspapers and probably has encouraged couples to improve family communication. An example is an account of a working wife who had been married eight years and who resented the fact that her husband did not do a greater share of the housekeeping chores (Middletown's evening newspaper, January 17, 1978). She attacked the problem by using a communication technique called the "contract method," whereby she negotiated the assignment of household tasks with her husband. She remarked after tne initial session that, "for the first time, I could see his side. I didn't agree, but I [did at least] understand how he felt." This couple then drew up a list of housekeeping chores and "listened, negotiated, and compromised" about who would do what. The young wife credited improved communication with resolving a serious marital problem and preserving an otherwise good marriage.

This does not mean that all couples in Middletown communicate openly. Interviews with both husbands and wives about their marriages revealed cases of lack of communication, too. An example was one husband, who admitted, "She tries to tell me what she does all day but I don't like to hear it. . . . We don't really talk a lot. She talks about things at work. But I don't really like to talk about it. . . . We eat together every night, but don't spend much time together." A working-class wife said, "I would try to talk to him about the other women he was seeing or money problems we were having, but whatever it was he would refuse to talk about it." She reported that, when she persisted in her complaints, her husband shouted and cursed at her until she stopped. Occasionally, her insistence angered her husband to the point that he "shut her up" with a severe beating. But such cases were relatively uncommon, and the evidence is overwhelming that husband-wife communication has improved during the past 50 years.

Not only are contemporary husbands and wives talking to each other, they are engaging in a great deal of leisure activity together. Shopping; eating out; going for drives and to movies, sporting events, fairs, and musical presentations; and taking part in physical fitness activities are frequently shared by husbands and wives. This conclusion is based on the observations of married couples in the malls, shops, theaters, parks, and playing fields of Middletown made by the research staff over a three-year period. The people we interviewed referred again and again to the voluntary activities and interests they shared with their spouses.

In contemporary American society, television has become an integral part of daily life, a source of news as well as of recreation. The sample of wives interviewed in 1978 was asked how often they watched television with their husbands alone. The majority of both business- and working-class couples spent an average of more than five hours each week watching television together. The time spent watching television may not involve much direct interaction between husband and wife when the attention of both is focused on the screen, but they *are* together and can comment on the program or share a snack. It is interesting that both working- and business-class couples report almost identical patterns of joint television viewing. The pervasive class differences in marital behavior observed during the early part of this century are not apparent in this contemporary behavior.

So that we could assess marital satisfaction, the married respondents in the samples of men and women were asked to describe how they felt about their marital relationships [Table 28.1]. Our results indicate a high level of satisfaction; 57 percent were "very satisfied" with their relationships, and another 36 percent were "satisfied." Barely 5 percent said they felt "neutral" or were "dissatisfied." Many couples said that their relationships had been satisfactory since their honeymoon, and others reported that they had had to work out an agreeable arrangement. One working-class wife told us that the adjustment was harder than she had expected but that a meaningful relationship eventually developed. "In marriage, there is always an adjustment period. During this time you learn your mate's strengths and weaknesses which you must understand. I expected it would be easier than it was." She said that, although it took them six years to achieve, she and her husband "have a total marriage, . . . [we have] really adjusted to each other."

Although there were some slight differences between the average satisfaction reported by working- and business-class couples, none was statistically significant. Working-class couples were as satisfied with

TABLE 28.1 Satisfaction with Marital Relationships in Middletown, by Social Class, 1978 (in Percentages)

	Husbands		Wives	
Level of Satisfaction	Business Class (*N* = 87)	Working Class (*N* = 80)	Business Class (*N* = 159)	Working Class (*N* = 159)
Very satisfied	62%	68%	57%	49%
Satisfied	31	28	36	41
Neutral	2	4	4	9
Dissatisfied	5	1	3	1
Total	100%	101%	100%	100%

SOURCE: Middletown III housewives' survey.
QUESTION: How do you feel about your relationship to your wife/husband?

their marital relationships as business-class couples. Husbands in both social classes felt somewhat more satisfied with marriage than wives, although the differences were not extreme. . . .

The claims in the mass media that modern marriage is an oppressive yoke borne by many because they do not know how to unburden themselves appear absurd in Middletown, where a happy marriage is the common experience. These findings are consistent with recent studies of other communities and of the nation as a whole (Chadwick, Albrecht, and Kunz 1976; *The Playboy Report on American Men* 1979).

There is additional evidence suggesting that the quality of the average marital relationship has improved over the past 50 years—the number of wives who mentioned their husbands as a source of strength during difficult times. As noted earlier, when a 1924 sample of Middletown housewives was asked the question "What are the thoughts and plans that give you courage to go on when thoroughly discouraged?" not a single wife mentioned her husband as a source of reassurance. In response to the same question in the 1978 survey, 7 percent of the wives mentioned their husbands as a source of strength and comfort, and another 16 percent referred to their families, which, in most cases, included husbands as well as children. The question was asked in the context of religious beliefs, and most responded in such terms; if it had been set in a different context (in terms of "who" rather than "what"), the number of responses mentioning husbands might have been even higher. The data suggest again that the marital relationship has deepened since the 1920s and that husbands and wives share each other's burdens and provide emotional support to a greater degree now than then. Despair about the family is as fashionable in Middletown as it is elsewhere in the United States, so it comes as something of a surprise to learn that 95 percent of Middletown's husbands and wives are satisfied with their marital relationships.

The influence of the media's portrayal of marital conflict is apparent in people's evaluations of their marriages compared to those of their friends. Almost *all* respondents rated their own marriages as happier than those of their friends ("I wish everyone got along as well as we have"). One business-class woman described her third and current marriage as "incredibly better" than those of her friends. Even those who confessed to having problems were likely to describe their marriages as "better than most." Many couples compare their marriages to what they see of their friends' marriages, what their friends tell them about their marriages, and what they observe of marriages in the media, and they are pleasantly surprised that their own marriages seem so satisfying.

We often heard in the in-depth interviews that a satisfying marriage takes time, even years, to develop. "It took us a long time to kind of get things worked out so that we can work together. . . . We now have things worked out and have a good marriage." "It's lasted four years and gotten better each year." This finding is not inconsistent with studies of marital happiness over the life cycle (Rollins and Feldman 1970; Burr 1970). Such studies have discovered that, on the average, marriages are the happiest during the early years but not necessarily at the very outset.

REFERENCES

BURR, WESLEY. "Satisfaction and Various Aspects of Marriage Over the Life Cycle: A Random Middleclass Sample," *Journal of Marriage and the Family* 32 (1970), 29–37.

CHADWICK, BRUCE A., STAN L. ALBRECHT, and PHILLIP R. KUNZ. "Marriage and Family Role Satisfaction," *Journal of Marriage and the Family* 38 (1976), 431–42.

CROSBY, JOHN F. "The Death of the Family—Revisited," *The Humanist* 35 (May/June, 1975), 12–14.

JACQUES, JEFFREY M., and KAREN J. CHASON. "Cohabitation: Its Impact on Marital Success," *Family Coordinator* 28 (January 1979), 32–39.

LIBBY, ROBERT W., and ROBERT N. WHITEHURST. *Renovating Marriage.* Danville, Calif.: Consensus Publisher, 1975.

LYND, ROBERT S., and HELEN MERRELL LYND. *Middletown: A Study in American Culture.* New York: Harcourt and Brace, 1929.

———. *Middletown in Transition: A Study in Cultural Conflicts.* New York: Harcourt and Brace, 1937.

PICKETT, ROBERT S. "The American Family: An Embattled Institution," *The Humanist* 35 (May/June 1975), 5–8.

The Playboy Report on American Men. Survey conducted for Playboy Enterprises, by Louis Harris and Associates. New York: Playboy, 1979.

ROLLINS, BOYD, and HAROLD FELDMAN. "Marital Satisfaction over the Family Life Cycle," *Journal of Marriage and the Family* 32 (1970), 20–28.

SNIDER, ARTHUR J. "Learn First, Marry Later: One Way to Reduce Divorces?" *Salt Lake Tribune* (February 5, 1975).

CHAPTER 29

Five Types of Marriage

John F. Cuber / Peggy B. Harroff

ABSTRACT: The authors examine enduring relationships: 211 couples who had been married ten or more years who felt committed to one another. They discovered five basic marital styles: (1) conflict-habituated; (2) devitalized; (3) passive-congenial; (4) vital; and (5) total. These types illustrate that lasting relationships differ markedly from one another in the basic approaches that couples take to marriage and in their overall satisfactions and expectations.

The qualitative aspects of enduring marital relationships vary enormously. The variations described to us were by no means random or clearly individualized, however. Five distinct life styles showed up repeatedly and the pairs within each of them were remarkably similar in the ways in which they lived together, found sexual expression, reared children, and made their way in the outside world.

The following classification is based on the interview materials of those people whose marriages had already lasted ten years or more and who said that they had never seriously considered divorce or separation. While 360 of the men and women had been married ten or more years to the same spouse, exclusion of those who reported that they had considered divorce reduced the number to 211. The discussion in this chapter is, then, based on 211 interviews; 107 men and 104 women.

The descriptions which our interviewees gave us took into account how they had behaved and also how they felt about their actions past and present. Examination of the important features of their lives revealed five recurring configurations of male-female life, each with a central theme—some prominent distinguishing psychological feature which gave each type its singularity. It is these preeminent characteristics which suggested the names for the relationship; the *Conflict-Habituated*, the *Devitalized*, the *Passive-Congenial*, the *Vital*, and the *Total*.

THE CONFLICT-HABITUATED

We begin with the conflict-habituated not because it is the most prevalent, but because the overt behavior patterns in it are so readily observed and because it presents some arresting contradictions. In this association there is much tension and conflict—although it is largely controlled. At worst, there is some private quarreling, nagging, and "throwing up the past" of which members of the immediate family, and more rarely close friends and relatives, have some awareness. At best, the couple is discreet and polite, genteel about it in the company of others—but after a few drinks at the cocktail party the verbal barbs begin to fly. The intermittent conflict is rarely concealed from the children, though we were often assured otherwise. "Oh, they're at it again—but they always are," says the high-school son. There is private acknowledgement by both husband and wife as a rule that incompatibility is pervasive, that conflict is ever-potential, and that an atmosphere of tension permeates the togetherness.

An illustrative case concerns a physician of fifty, married for twenty-five years to the same woman, with two college-graduate children promisingly established in their own professions.

> You know, it's funny; we have fought from the time we were in high school together. As I look back at it, I can't remember specific quarrels; it's more like a running guerrilla fight with intermediate periods, sometimes quite long, of pretty good fun and some damn good sex. In fact, if it hadn't been for the sex, we wouldn't have been married so quickly. Well, anyway, this has been going on ever since. . . . It's hard to know what it is we fight about most of the time. You name it and we'll fight about it. It's sometimes something I've said that she remembers differently, sometimes a decision—like what kind of car to buy or what to give the kids for Christmas. With regard to politics, and religion, and morals—oh, boy! You know, outside of the welfare of the kids—too much and that's just abstract— we don't really agree about anything. . . . At different times we take opposite sides—not deliberately; it just comes out that way.
>
> Now these fights get pretty damned colorful. You called them arguments a little while ago—I have to correct you—they're brawls. There's never a bit of physical violence—at least not directed to each other—but the verbal gunfire gets pretty thick. Why, we've said things to each other that neither of us would think of saying in the hearing of anybody else. . . .

> Of course we don't settle any of the issues. It's sort of a matter of principle *not* to. Because somebody would have to give in then and lose face for the next encounter. . . .

There is a subtle valence in these conflict-habituated relationships. It is easily missed in casual observation. So central is the necessity for channeling conflict and bridling hostility that these considerations come to preoccupy much of the interaction. Some psychiatrists have gone so far as to suggest that it is precisely the deep need to do psychological battle with one another which constitutes the cohesive factor insuring continuity of the marriage. Possibly so. But even from a surface point of view, the overt and manifest fact of habituated attention to handling tension, keeping it chained, and concealing it, is clearly seen as a dominant life force. And it can, and does for some, last for a whole lifetime.

THE DEVITALIZED

The key to the devitalized mode is the clear discrepancy between middle-aged reality and the earlier years. These people usually characterized themselves as having been "deeply in love" during the early years, as having spent a great deal of time together, having enjoyed sex, and most importantly of all, having had a close identification with one another. The present picture, with some variation from case to case, is in clear contrast—little time is spent together, sexual relationships are far less satisfying qualitatively or quantitatively, and interests and activities are not shared, at least not in the deeper and meaningful way they once were. Most of their time together now is "duty time"—entertaining together, planning and sharing activities with children, and participating in various kinds of required community responsibilities. They do as a rule retain, in addition to a genuine and mutual interest in the welfare of their children, a shared attention to their joint property and the husband's career. But even in the latter case the interest is contrasting. Despite a common dependency on his success and the benefits which flow therefrom, there is typically very little sharing of the intrinsic aspects of career—simply an acknowledgment of their mutual dependency on the fruits. . . .

> Judging by the way it was when we were first married—say the first five years or so—things are pretty matter-of-fact now—even dull. They're dull between us, I mean. The children are a lot of fun, keep us pretty busy, and there are lots of outside things—you know, like Little League and the P.T.A. and the Swim Club, and even the company parties aren't always so bad. But I mean where Bob and I are concerned—if you followed us around, you'd wonder why we ever got *married*. We take each other for granted. We laugh at the same things sometimes, but we don't really laugh together—the way

> we used to. But, as he said to me the other night—with one or two under the belt, I think—"You know, you're still a little fun now and then." . . .
>
> Now, I don't say this to complain, not in the least. There's a cycle to life. There are things you do in high school. And different things you do in college. Then you're a young adult. And then you're middle-aged. That's where we are now. . . . I'll admit that I do yearn for the old days when sex was a big thing and going out was fun and I hung on to everything he said about his work and his ideas as if they were coming from a genius or something. But then you get the children and other responsibilities. I have the home and Bob has a tremendous burden of responsibility at the office. . . . He's completely responsible for setting up the new branch now. . . . You have to adjust to these things and we both try to gracefully. . . . Anniversaries though do remind you kind of hard. . . .

Regardless of the gracefulness of the acceptance, or lack thereof, the common plight prevails: on the subjective, emotional dimension, the relationship has become a void. The original zest is gone. There is typically little overt tension or conflict, but the interplay between the pair has become apathetic, lifeless. No serious threat to the continuity of the marriage is generally acknowledged, however. It is intended, usually by both, that it continue indefinitely despite its numbness. Continuity and relative freedom from open conflict are fostered in part because of the comforts of the "habit cage." Continuity is further insured by the absence of any engaging alternative, "all things considered." It is also reinforced, sometimes rather decisively, by legal and ecclesiastical requirements and expectations. These people quickly explain that "there are other things in life" which are worthy of sustained human effort.

This kind of relationship is exceedingly common. Persons in this circumstance frequently make comparisons with other pairs they know, many of whom are similar to themselves. This fosters the comforting judgment that "marriage is like this—except for a few oddballs or pretenders who claim otherwise." . . .

THE PASSIVE-CONGENIAL

The passive-congenial mode has a great deal in common with the devitalized, the essential difference being that the passivity which pervades the association has been there from the start. The devitalized have a more exciting set of memories; the passive-congenials give little evidence that they had ever hoped for anything much different from what they are currently experiencing.

There is therefore little suggestion of disillusionment or compulsion to make believe to anyone. Existing modes of association are comfortably adequate—no stronger words fit the facts as they related them to us. There is little conflict, although some admit that they tiptoe rather gingerly over and around a residue of subtle resentments and frustrations. In their better moods they remind themselves (and each other) that "there are many common interests" which they both enjoy. "We both like classical music." "We agree completely on religious and political matters." "We both love the country and our quaint exurban neighbors." "We are both lawyers."

The wife of a prominent attorney, who has been living in the passive-congenial mode for thirty years, put her description this way:

> We have both always tried to be calm and sensible about major life decisions, to think things out thoroughly and in perspective. Len and I knew each other since high school but didn't start to date until college. When he asked me to marry him, I took a long time to decide whether he was the right man for me and I went into his family background, because I wasn't just marrying him; I was choosing a father for my children. We decided together not to get married until he was established, so that we would not have to live in dingy little apartments like some of our friends who got married right out of college. This prudence has stood us in good stead too. Life has moved ahead for us with remarkable orderliness and we are deeply grateful for the foresight we had. . . .
>
> I don't like all this discussion about sex—even in the better magazines. I hope your study will help to put it in its proper perspective. I expected to perform sex in marriage, but both before and since, I'm willing to admit that it's a much overrated activity. Now and then, perhaps it's better. I am fortunate, I guess, because my husband has never been demanding about it, before marriage or since. It's just not that important to either of us. . . .

People make their way into the passive-congenial mode by two quite different routes—by default and by intention. Perhaps in most instances they arrive at this way of living and feeling by drift. There is so little which they have cared about deeply in each other that a passive-congenial mode is a deliberately intended arrangement for two people whose interests and creative energies are directed elsewhere than toward the pairing—into careers, or in the case of women, into children or community activities. They say they know this and want it this way. These people simply do not wish to invest their total emotional involvement and creative effort in the male-female relationship. . . .

The passive-congenial mode . . . enables people who desire a considerable amount of personal independence and freedom to realize it with a minimum of inconvenience from or to the spouse. And it certainly spares the participants in it from the need to give a great deal of personal attention to "adjusting to the spouse's needs." The passive-congenial menage is thus a mood as well as a mode.

Our descriptions of the devitalized and the passive-congenials have been similar because these two modes are much alike in their overt characteristics. The participants' evaluations of their *present situations* are likewise largely the same—the accent on "other things," the emphasis on civic and professional responsibilities, the importance of property, children, and reputation. The essential difference lies in their diverse histories and often in their feelings of contentment with their current lives. The passive-congenials had from the start a life pattern and a set of expectations essentially consistent with what they are now experiencing. When the devitalized reflect, however, when they juxtapose history against present reality, they often see the barren gullies in their lives left by the erosions of earlier satisfactions. . . .

THE VITAL

In extreme contrast to the three foregoing is the vital relationship. The vital pair can easily be overlooked as they move through their worlds of work, recreation, and family activities. They do the same things, publicly at least; and when talking for public consumption say the same things—they are proud of their homes, love their children, gripe about their jobs, while being quite proud of their career accomplishments. But when the close, intimate, confidential, empathic look is taken, the essence of the vital relationship becomes clear: the mates are intensely bound together psychologically in important life matters. Their sharing and their togetherness is genuine. It provides the life essence for both man and woman.

> The things we do together aren't fun intrinsically—the ecstasy comes from being *together in the doing*. Take her out of the picture and I wouldn't give a damn for the boat, the lake, or any of the fun that goes on out there.

The presence of the mate is indispensable to the feelings of satisfaction which the activity provides. The activities shared by the vital pairs may involve almost anything: hobbies, careers, community service. Anything—so long as it is closely shared.

It is hard to escape the word *vitality*—exciting mutuality of feelings and participation together in important life segments. The clue that the relationship is vital (rather than merely expressing the joint activity) derives from the feeling that it is important. An activity is flat and uninteresting if the spouse is not a part of it.

Other valued things are readily sacrificed in order to enhance life within the vital relationship.

> I cheerfully, and that's putting it mildly, passed up two good promotions because one of them would have required some traveling and the other would have taken evening and weekend time—and that's when Pat and I *live*. The hours with her (after twenty-two years of marriage) are what I live for. You should meet her. . . .

People in the vital relationship . . . find their central satisfaction in the life they live with and through each other. It consumes their interest and dominates their thoughts and actions. All else is subordinate and secondary.

This does not mean that people in vital relationships lose their separate identities, that they may not upon occasion be rivalrous or competitive with one another, or that conflict may not occur. They differ fundamentally from the conflict-habituated, however, in that when conflict does occur, it results from matters that are important to them, such as which college a daughter or son is to attend; it is devoid of the trivial "who said what first and when" and "I can't forget when you. . . ." A further difference is that people to whom the relationship is vital tend to settle disagreements quickly and seek to avoid conflict, whereas the conflict-habituated look forward to conflict and appear to operate by a tacit rule that no conflict is ever to be truly terminated and that the spouse must never be considered right. The two kinds of conflict are thus radically different. To confuse them is to miss an important differentiation.

THE TOTAL

The total relationship is like the vital relationship with the important addition that it is more multifaceted. The points of vital meshing are more numerous—in some cases all of the important life foci are vitally shared. In one such marriage the husband is an internationally known scientist. For thirty years his wife has been "his friend, mistress, and partner." He still goes home at noon whenever possible, at considerable inconvenience, to have a quiet lunch and spend a conversational hour or so with his wife. They refer to these conversations as "our little seminars." They feel comfortable with each other and with their four grown children. The children (now in their late twenties) say that they enjoy visits with their parents as much as they do with friends of their own age.

There is practically no pretense between persons in the total relationship or between them and the world outside. There are few areas of tension, because the items of difference which have arisen over the years have been settled as they arose. There often *were* serious differences of opinion but they were handled, sometimes by compromise, sometimes by one or the other yielding; but these outcomes were of secondary importance because the primary consideration was not who was right or who was wrong, only how the problem could be resolved without tarnishing the relationship. When faced with differences, they can and do dispose of the difficulties without losing their feeling of unity or their sense of vitality and centrality of their relationship. This is the mainspring.

The various parts of the total relationship are reinforcing, as we learned from this consulting engineer who is frequently sent abroad by his corporation.

> She keeps my files and scrapbooks up to date. . . . I invariably take her with me to conferences around the world. Her femininity, easy charm and wit are invaluable assets to me. I know it's conventional to say that a man's wife is responsible for his success and I also know that it's often not true. But in my case I gladly acknowledge that it's not only true, but she's indispensable to me. But she'd go along with me even if there was nothing for her to do because we just enjoy each other's company—deeply. You know, the best part of a vacation is not *what* we do, but that we do it together. We plan it and reminisce about it and weave it into our work and other play all the time.

The wife's account is substantially the same except that her testimony demonstrates more clearly the genuineness of her "help."

> It seems to me that Bert exaggerates my help. It's not so much that I only want to help him; it's more that I want to do those things anyway. We do them together, even though we may not be in each other's presence at the time. I don't really know what I do for him and what I do for me.

This kind of relationship is rare, in marriage or out, but it does exist and can endure. We occasionally found relationships so total that all aspects of life were mutually shared and enthusiastically participated in. It is as if neither spouse has, or has had, a truly private existence. . . .

[T]he five types [are not] to be interpreted as *degrees* of marital happiness or adjustment. Persons in all five are currently adjusted and most say that they are content, if not happy. Rather, the five types represent *different kinds of adjustment* and *different conceptions of marriage*. This is an important concept which must be emphasized if one is to understand the personal meanings which these people attach to the conditions of their marital experience.

Neither are the five types necessarily stages in a cycle of initial bliss and later disillusionment. Many pairings started in the passive-congenial stage; in fact, quite often people intentionally enter into a marriage for the acknowledged purpose of living this kind of relationship. To many the simple amenities of the "habit cage" are not disillusionments or even disappointments, but rather are sensible life expectations which provide an altogether comfortable and rational way of having a "home base" for their lives. And many of the conflict-habituated told of courtship histories essentially like their marriages.

While each of these types tends to persist, there *may* be movement from one type to another as circumstances and life perspectives change. This movement may go in any direction from any point, and a given couple may change categories more than once. Such changes are relatively *in*frequent however, and the important point is that relationship types tend to persist over relatively long periods. . . .

Whether examining marriages for the satisfactions and fulfillments they have brought or for the frustrations and pain, the overriding influence of life style—or as we have here called it, relationship type—is of the essence. Such a viewpoint helps the observer, and probably the participant, to understand some of the apparent enigmas about men and women in marriage—why infidelities destroy some marriages and not others; why conflict plays so large a role for some couples and is so negligible for others; why some seemingly well-suited and harmoniously adjusted spouses seek divorce while others with provocations galore remain solidly together; why affections, sexual expression, recreation, almost everything observable about men and women are so radically different from pair to pair. All of these are not merely different objectively; they are perceived differently by the pairs, are differently reacted to, and differently attended to. . . .

CHAPTER 30

What Makes Today's Marriages Last?

Philip Blumstein / Pepper Schwartz

ABSTRACT: Based on a national sample, the authors looked at money, work, and sex among American couples. Money shows up as a regular source of disagreements, especially on conflicting approaches to managing it. In general, couples who argue a lot about money are dissatisfied with their marriages and tend to break up. Major differences about work center on ideas about the wife working and how to divide up the housework. A marriage needs a caretaker, and if both are work-centered, problems tend to persist. Spending time together helps couples stay together. Finally, in general, the more sex a couple has, the higher their satisfaction with the marriage, and those who have sex outside the marriage are more likely to break up. These findings can help to provide bases around which to build a lasting relationship.

American marriage is in trouble. The divorce rate has tripled since 1960, and 41 percent of all presently married couples will see their marriages end by decree rather than by death. For those who take comfort in recent statistics showing a drop in the number of divorces, the fact that lifetime marriage is no longer guaranteed is still sobering. It is a particularly unhappy fact when we realize that second marriages have a slightly higher divorce rate than first marriages, indicating that we don't learn from experience.

To better understand the complexity of modern-day relationships, we decided to do a large national study. In the first phase of our study, we asked each member of a couple (our sample included married, cohabitating and homosexual couples) to fill out separately a 38-page questionnaire. Twelve thousand people did so. From this group we selected 600 people (balancing those in short-, medium- and long-term relationships) whom we interviewed for several hours in order to ask more intimate questions. Approximately 18 months later we recontacted about one half of the people who had sent in the original questionnaires to see if they were still together as a couple, and if they had broken up, what the reasons were.

We present the results of our investigation in our book, *American Couples*. We concentrate on three specific areas: money, work and sex. Here we reveal how these three factors affect married couples and what makes some marriages work and others falter.

MONEY

In our culture, money is a more taboo topic of conversation than sex. Couples in particular tend to be reticent with each other when talking about money, and this is unfortunate, because if a man and woman don't know each other's financial philosophies, they probably won't discover that they have different values until they are well into the marriage. Indeed, we found that couples fought more about how to spend money than about whether they had enough. If one person's financial philosophy was based on spending while the other's was based on saving, then regular confrontations tended to occur.

Furthermore, when couples told us they argued a lot about how to spend money, they were less likely to be together when we contacted them 18 months later, particularly if they fought in the early years of marriage. The inability to respect each other's financial values opened up the whole question of how well suited the two people were to each other.

Of course, how much money the couple had also was an important element of the relationship. Husbands and wives dissatisfied with the amount of money they had found the entire marriage less pleasing than couples who felt comfortable about income. But having little money did not break them up. It is possible to have a good marriage when a couple is poor—so long as the couple agrees on how to manage the money it has.

There was one area of managing money that often emerged as a problem area for married individuals. When the husband was the only wage earner, or when he earned more money than his wife, he often thought of himself as the provider and his wife as the budgeter. As the budgeter, one of her jobs was to buy the things needed to run the household smoothly. We found that if a husband delegated authority to his wife to act as the "purchasing agent" for the couple but really didn't trust her competence, conflict arose.

Interestingly, wives with incomes of their own sometimes did not want to pool all their money with their husbands' because they did not want to be watched over or grilled on personal expenses. Wives with no source of personal income, or with no money to spend as they wanted, often became so frustrated that they resorted to a kind of "guerrilla warfare." For example, one wife said, "I skim a little off the top. Oh, I'll tell him the groceries cost more than they did, or something like that. Nothing spectacular, but it gives me a little breathing room."

Deciding jointly how money should be managed may be tedious, and working out an economic plan may bring up unpleasant issues, but shared control and shared values do seem to predict a happier, calmer, longer-lasting marriage.

WORK

The world of paid work used to be a male domain, but today, while the traditional male provider still exists, the two-paycheck family is becoming more and more common. We discovered that either life style could work well: Some couples were very happy with the wife staying home; others were happy when she was out in the work force. But if a wife wants to work and her husband will not let her or gripes about the fact the she works, the marriage becomes less stable.

Disagreement could become especially heated if the husband and wife began their marriage with the understanding that the wife would stay home, but she ended up going to work. Even if she did so out of financial necessity or because she needed a new outlet once her children were grown, her husband may have seen this as a disastrous turn of events. Said one man who'd been married for 19 years: "I find it odd that she wants to go out and do somebody else's dirty work when she could stay at home and enjoy the life we worked hard to put together. We argue over this about once a month, especially when she is grouchy because of something someone in the office did or said. I'll tell her again to quit and let me provide, and she'll get huffy and unreasonable."

Our study also showed that when a wife worked, the couple fought more about how the children were being raised. The majority of men and women in our study felt that mothers should be at home during a child's preschool years. Many of the mothers with young children could not, or did not, want to stay at home, and this caused feelings of guilt in both working and nonworking mothers and quarrels between husband and wife.

We did find, however, more wives who wanted to work than husbands who wanted to let them. Husbands were more likely to believe it was unnecessary, because they felt it was the man's duty to provide for the household. When the wives wanted to work despite their husbands' wishes, they sometimes cited the need for the extra income. But just as commonly they indicated that money was not the only—or even the main—reason. Even though many of them spoke of the frustrations of an unwelcoming job market and low pay, they still wanted to work. But when wives were employed outside the home, husbands were more likely to say that they respected their wives' decision-making abilities and were more likely to listen to their opinions. In fact, a man whose wife was successful in the working world was more likely to say she should not have to do housework!

This did not mean, however, that *he* was doing the housework. Rather it meant that she did somewhat less than wives who were not employed, and that the couple learned to tolerate more dirt. It was extremely rare for husbands to do the majority of the housework and uncommon for them to do half. Even unemployed husbands did much less housework than wives who worked 40-hour weeks. To be blunt, men hated housework and really wanted women to relieve them of that responsibility, in whatever manner they managed to do it. Husbands' aversion to work was so intense, our study showed, that the more housework a husband did, the more the couple fought about household duties.

This is not just a harmless disagreement: We found that new marriages are more likely to fail when husbands feel their wives don't do their "fair share" of housework. And her "fair share" is usually well over half. This is clearly a sensitive problem for women who want equal responsibility for tasks in their marriage.

In a healthy marriage there is also a balance of home and work. Marriages need a caretaker, someone who makes sure that the relationship is in good shape, who notices if it's not, who tends to its needs. This caretaker may suggest they have a "date" away from the children or the routine, or that they take the time to discuss a point of contention that has been festering beneath the surface of their daily life. Marriages are best served if both partners take on the caretaker responsibility, but having at least one such person seems essential.

If, however, both partners are "work-centered"—very much bound up in their work and its issues—the marriage may wither from lack of attention. Such couples have a tendency to be less satisfied and less committed to their relationship. While initially they may have been attracted to each other because they admired each other's ambition and commitment to a career, their similarity of outlook, which places their relationship second to their work, tends to undermine their marriage.

Spending enough time together is important. We found that it was not only work that competed with marriage for the individuals' allegiance. If a husband and wife spend too much time apart, for *any* reason—attending to relatives, friends, hobbies, etc.—they're more likely to break up. Some couples told us that they loved each other but had many diverse interests or responsibilities and therefore had to spend a lot of time away from each other. They insisted they were still very happy and committed, precisely because their outside activities gave them rich experiences which made them more interesting spouses.

Nonetheless, people who maintained such a life style were more likely to break up than couples who spent a lot of time together. In some cases having "separate" lives may have been just a symptom of a husband and wife who didn't enjoy each other's company. But we think it is also true that couples may love each other deeply, yet spend more and more time doing things with other people because they believe their marriage to be so solid that it needs very little constant care to support it. It seems to us that couples should not be too smug. Spending too much time away from each other may make the couple forget what it was that drew them together in the first place.

SEX

Both the quantity and quality of sex are important for the well-being of a marriage. Couples who have sex frequently are more pleased with their sex life. However, frequent sex seems to mean more to men than to women. Married men feel so strongly about having sex regularly that those who told us that sex was infrequent were more likely to be dissatisfied with their entire relationship. Married women may have been unhappy when sex was infrequent, but it was less likely to affect their assessment of the entire marriage. When husbands or wives felt their sex life was not satisfying or was a source of fighting between them, they were more likely to have broken up when we contacted them 18 months later.

How much sex is enough?

We found that the majority of our married couples had sex at least once a week. And even after 10 or more years of marriage, 63 percent had sex at least that often. We found a low sexual frequency in very few couples: Of those married 10 years or more, fewer than 15 percent had sex once a month or less. Thus, while we would say that "enough" sex is a very subjective and personal evaluation, most couples in our study maintained sex as a continuous part of married life. Sex did decline over the length of the marriage and it is less frequent among older people (older people in a new marriage, however, have more sex than those in a long-term marriage).

Couples were more likely to tell us they have a good sex life when they shared responsibility for making it happen. While initiation of sex was generally still the husband's prerogative, couples were particularly pleased when suggesting was shared 50–50. What was disturbing in the couple's relationship was when the wife was the more aggressive initiator and the husband more inclined to veto sex.

Another American tradition that seems firmly in place is monogamy. Or perhaps we should say the *belief* in monogamy. The following statement by a wife of 10 years was a typical opinion:

> Before marriage we discussed monogamy and we both wholeheartedly agree about how important it is. I don't believe in cheating and he doesn't believe in cheating. And that's what it would be—cheating someone out of love and trust. It would make a mockery of marriage.

Nonetheless, more people believed in monogamy than always practiced it. Approximately 26 percent of our husbands and 21 percent of our wives had had sex outside of their marriage (this varied, depending on how long the couple was married). These percentages did not mean changing values about monogamy; most people were quiet about it, and many did it only once, felt guilty and did not wish to repeat the experience.

We didn't find that married people who had extramarital sex were any less satisfied with their sex life together or had sex any less often with their spouse than those who had never had sex outside their marriage. And husbands who were non-monogamous were not any less committed to the future of their marriage. But wives who had had sex recently with someone else were more inclined to feel their marriage was not going to last. Ultimately, we found that couples in our study were less likely to survive if they had sex outside their relationship in the preceding year.

This is not a complete list of all the things we discovered that can threaten happiness in a marriage and its longevity, but these things are important. These are problems that can gnaw at a marriage. Something like disagreeing about how to spend money may seem just an annoying difference of opinion—until it starts to dismantle the trust and security of the entire relationship. Today's marriages require a new level of awareness and more commitment to problem solving. When marriage was *forever*, issues could be left alone because there was the understanding that the couple had a lifetime together to work them out. Because this is no longer the case, we hope that a little information can help people to spot vulnerabilities and give their marriage the best chance it has to be a satisfying lifetime experience.

CHAPTER 31

Strong Families

Nicholas Stinnett

ABSTRACT: To improve family life it is helpful to look at what makes families strong, not at what is wrong with families. Strong families are defined as families that are intact and have a high degree of marital happiness, of parent-child satisfactions, and of meeting each other's needs. Studies of strong families consistently show six qualities: (1) appreciation; (2) time spent together; (3) commitment; (4) good communication; (5) very religious; and (6) a constructive approach to crises. Based on these qualities, the author suggests recommendations designed to help strengthen families.

The quest for self-fulfillment during the twentieth century has developed into a major goal in American culture (Yankelovich, 1981). However, in our preoccupation with this objective we have neglected the family and lost sight of the fact that so much of the foundation necessary to facilitate the life-long process of individual self-fulfillment (such as the development of interpersonal competence, self-confidence, self-esteem, respect for self and others, and the vision and knowledge that life can be enriched) is developed within strong, healthy families.

We have considerable evidence that the quality of family life is extremely important to our emotional well-being, our happiness, and our mental health as individuals. We know that poor relationships within the family are very closely related to many problems in society (such as juvenile delinquency and domestic abuse).

As we look back in history we see that the quality of family life is very important to the strength of nations. There is a pattern in the rise and fall of great societies such as ancient Rome, Greece, and Egypt. When these societies were at the peak of their power and prosperity, the family was strong and highly valued. When family life became weak in these societies, when the family was not valued—when goals became extremely individualistic—the society began to deteriorate and eventually fell.

Obviously, it is to our benefit to do what we can to strengthen family life; this should be one of our nation's top priorities, but unfortunately it has not been.

So much of what is written about families has focused on problems and pathology. On the newsstand we see many books and magazine articles about what's wrong with families and the problems that families have. There are those who like to predict that the family will soon disappear and that it no longer meets our needs.

Certainly we need information about positive family models and what strong families are like. We need to learn how to strengthen families. We don't learn how to do anything by looking only at what *shouldn't* be done. We learn most effectively by examining how to do something correctly and studying a positive model. We have not had this positive model as much as we need it in the area of family life. Understanding what a strong family is provides educators, counselors, and families with a positive model. Getting this knowledge first-hand from those who have created a successful family situation gives us a good picture of how families become strong.

We have many strong families throughout this nation and the world. There has been little written about them because there has been very little research focusing on family strengths. It was with this in mind that we launched the Family Strengths Research Project, a search that has taken us throughout our nation as well as to other parts of the world. This research was inspired in part by the pioneer work in family strengths of Otto (1962, 1964).

Our search began in Oklahoma where we studied 130 families identified as strong. More recently we have completed a national study of strong families representing all regions of the nation, an investigation of strong Russian immigrant families, a study of strong black families, and an examination of strong families from various countries in South America.

The research method varied. For example, one approach was represented by the Oklahoma study. In this project we had the assistance of the Cooperative Extension Service to help identify the strong families. We asked the Home Economics Extension Agent in each of the counties of Oklahoma to recommend a few families that the agent considered particularly strong. The Home Economics Extension Agents were suited to this task for three reasons—their background training in family life, their concern for improving family life as part of their work, and the great amount of contact they have with families in the community. Also, we gave the agents some guidelines for selecting the families. The guidelines were that the families demonstrated a high degree of marital happiness, a high degree of parent-child satisfaction as perceived by the Extension Agent, and that the family members appeared to meet each other's needs to a high degree.

For purposes of this study, all the families were intact with husband, wife, and at least one child living at home. The first requirement for inclusion in this sample of strong families was the recommendation of the Extension Agent. The second requirement was that the families rate themselves very high in terms of marriage satisfaction and parent-child relationship satisfaction. The 130 families that met these two conditions were included in the sample. Both urban and rural families were represented in the sample, although there were more families from small cities, towns, and rural areas than from large urban areas. In most instances, we found very little difference between the urban and rural families.

A second research technique was demonstrated by the national study. The strong families in this study responded to an article sent to various daily and weekly papers across the nation. The 41 newspapers asked to run the article were selected to ensure a sample from all regions of the country, and from both rural and urban areas. The news release described the national study and asked families who felt they qualified as strong families to send their names and addresses to the researchers. The philosophy behind this approach can be debated almost endlessly. In short, we believed that rather than we as professionals defining what a strong family is, we would let families make the decision themselves.

The response to the news release was tremendous. Each family that responded was sent copies of the Family Strengths Inventory for the husband and wife. Many families also sent elaborate stories describing their family and its characteristics and activities in detail. The inventory focused on both the husband-wife and parent-child relationships and collected demographic information. Only families that rated themselves very high on marriage happiness and parent-child satisfaction were included in the final sample. This was similar to the screening procedure used in the Oklahoma study. The final sample size for the national study was 350 families.

In summary, we researched 130 families in the Oklahoma study, 350 families in the National Project, and 180 families in the South American study. In addition, smaller studies of Russian immigrant families and black families have been completed. In all of these research projects the families completed questionnaires and later a few of them were interviewed. Our questions covered a broad range of factors concerning their relationship patterns. For example, we asked how they deal with conflict, about communication patterns, and about power structure. When we analyzed the vast quantity of information, we found six qualities that stood out among these strong families. Six qualities they had in common seemed to play a very important role in their strength and their happiness. It is interesting that the same six qualities were found to characterize strong families in all of the research studies we conducted.

THE SIX QUALITIES OF THE STRONG FAMILIES

Appreciation

The first quality of the strong families was certainly one of the most important. It emerged from many different questions and in many ways that we were not expecting. The results were permeated by this characteristic. That quality is appreciation. The members of these families expressed a great deal of appreciation for each other. They built each other up psychologically, they gave each other many positive psychological strokes; everyone was made to feel good about themselves.

All of us like to be with people who make us feel good about ourselves; we don't like to be with people who make us feel bad. One of the tasks of family counselors who are working with family members who make each other feel terrible is to get them out of that pattern of interaction and into a pattern where they can make each other feel good. William James, considered by many people to be the greatest psychologist our country has ever produced, wrote a book on human needs. Some years after that book was published he remarked that he had forgotten to include the most important need of all—the need to be appreciated. There are so many things that we do for which we receive no reward other than appreciation; perhaps we all need to work on our ability to express appreciation. One difficulty in this is that we sometimes fear that people will think we're not sincere or that it's empty flattery. This need not be a concern. We *can* be sincere. Every person has many good qualities, many strengths. All we have to do is look for them, and be aware of them.

There are many ways in which we can develop the ability to express appreciation and thus make our human relationships better and certainly improve the quality of our family life. One widely used technique is one that Dr. Herbert Otto, Chairman of the National Center for Exploration of Human Potential, has used and written about a great deal. It has also been a tool for many counselors and is now being used by families on their own. This is called the "strength bombardment" technique. Here is the way it operates: The entire family comes together. There may be a group leader or counselor, or some member of the family can act as a leader. One person in the family is designated as the target person. For example, the mother may begin as target person. She is asked to list the strengths that she feels she has as a person. If she lists only two or three because she's modest, the leader can urge her to list others. After she has finished the list, her husband is asked to add to her list of strengths. Or he may elaborate on the strengths that she has already listed. When he has finished, each of the children is asked to add to mother's list of strengths. When this process is finished, the husband becomes the target person. The same procedure is repeated for him. Then each of the children becomes the target person.

The "strengths bombardment" technique is very simple, but the results have been amazing. When families do this exercise, they become more aware of each other's strengths, and more aware of their strengths as a family. They get into a pattern of looking for each other's good qualities and they also get into the habit of expressing appreciation. The result of this with so many families is that it makes their interaction with each other more positive. Some follow-up studies done with families who have gone through this activity show that the increased level of positive interaction is maintained for a period of time after the exercise has been completed. Many families are now using this technique periodically on their own.

Spending Time Together

A second quality found among strong families is that they did a lot of things together. It was not a "false" togetherness; nor a "smothering" type of togetherness—they genuinely enjoyed being together. Another important point here is that these families structured their life-styles so that they could spend time together. It did not "just happen," they *made* it happen. And this togetherness was in all areas of their lives—eating meals, recreation, and work.

One interesting pattern which has emerged from our research is the high frequency with which the strong families participate in outdoor activities together such as walking, jogging, bird watching, camping, canoeing, horseback riding, and outdoor games. While there are many strong families who are not particularly fond of outdoor activities, the finding in our research that so many strong families employed this as an important source of enjoyment and of their strength as a family raises the question of how the participation in outdoor activities as a family might contribute to family strengths. One logical possibility is that when families are participating in outdoor activities together they have fewer distractions—the family members are away from the telephone and the never-ending array of household tasks—and can concentrate more upon each other, thus encouraging a good communication experience. Another possibility is that physical exercise is often one benefit of participation in outdoor activities and the exercise itself contributes to personal feelings of well-being, health, and vitality.

Commitment

A third quality of these strong families was a high degree of commitment. These families were deeply committed to promoting each other's happiness and welfare. They were also very committed to the family group, as we reflected by the fact that they invested much of their time and energies in it. We have not had very much research on commitment, and perhaps in recent years it has not been fashionable to talk about it. Yet, Yankelovich (1981) observes that our society is now in the process of leaving behind an excessive self-centered orientation and moving toward a new "ethic of commitment" with emphasis upon new rules of living that support self-fulfillment through deeper personal relationships. Also, as David and Vera Mace (1980) have noted, only if you have produced a commitment to behavior change have you done anything to improve the life of a person or the life of a marriage or family.

Some of the best research on commitment has been done in communes. Some communes have been successful and others have not. One of the main differences found between the two groups is commitment. Those communes that are the most successful, that last the longest, and that are the most satisfying in terms of the relationships, are those in which there is a great deal of commitment—among individuals and to the group. Again, commitment in the communes was reflected in the amount of time the members spent together. The same was true with the strong families.

All of us are busy and we sometimes feel that we have so many things to do that we are pulled in a thousand different directions at the same time. Strong families experience the same problem. One interesting action that these families expressed was that when life got too hectic—to the extent that they were not spending as much time with their families as they wanted—they would sit down and make a list of the different activites in which they were involved. They would go over that list critically and inevitably there were some things that they really did not want to be doing, or that did not give much happiness, or that really were not very important to them. So they would scratch those activities and involvements off their lists. This would free time for their families and would relieve some of the pressure. As a result they were happier with their lives in general and more satisfied with their family relationships.

This sounds very simple, but how many of us do it? We get involved too often and it's not always because we want to be. We act so often as if we cannot change the situation. We *do* have a choice. An important point about these families is that they took the initiative in structuring their life style in a way that enhanced the quality of their family relationships and their satisfaction. They were on the "offensive." We may have talked too much about families as simply reactors in society, being at the mercy of the environment. In fact, there is a great deal that families can do to make life more enjoyable. These strong families exercised that ability.

Good Communication Patterns

The fourth quality was not a surprise. Strong families have very good communication patterns. They spend time talking with each other. This is closely related to the fact that they spend a lot of time together. It's hard for people to communicate unless they spend time with each other. One of the big problems facing families today is not spending enough time together. Dr. Virginia Satir, a prominent family therapist, has stated that often families are so fragmented, so busy, and spend so little time together that they only communicate with each other through rumor. Unfortunately, too often that is exactly what happens.

Another important aspect of communication is that these families also listen well. They reported that their family members were good listeners and that this was important to them. The fact that family members listen to one another communicates a very important message—respect. They are saying to one another, "You respect me enough to listen to what I have to say. I'm interested enough to listen too."

Another factor related to communication is that these families do fight. They get mad at each other, but they get conflict out in the open and they are able to talk it over, to discuss the problem. They share their feeling about alternative ways to deal with the problem and in selecting a solution that is best for everybody. These strong families have learned to do what David and Vera Mace (1980) have reported to be essential for a successful marriage—making creative use of conflict.

High Degree of Religious Orientation

The fifth quality that these families expressed was a high degree of religious orientation. This agrees with research from the past 40 years that shows a positive relationship of religion to marriage happiness and successful family relationships. Of course, we know that there are persons who are not religious who have very happy marriages and good family relationships. Nevertheless a positive relationship between marriage happiness and religion exists according to the research of many years. These strong families went to church together often and they participated in religious activities together. Most of them, although not all of them, were members of organized churches. All of them were very religious.

There are indications that this religious quality went deeper than going to church or participating in religious activities together. It could most appropriately be called a commitment to a spiritual life style. Words are inadequate to communicate this, but what many of these families said was that they had an awareness of God or a higher power that gave them a sense of purpose and gave their family a sense of support and strength. The awareness of this higher power in their lives helped them to be more patient with each other, more forgiving, quicker to get over anger, more positive, and more supportive in their relationships. Many of the values emphasized by religion, when put into action, can certainly enhance the quality of human relationships. Dr. Herbert Otto has observed that we could spend more time looking at the spiritual aspect of developing human potential, and perhaps we could benefit by exploring more about the spiritual aspects of developing family strengths. For these strong families, religion played a major role.

Ability to Deal with Crises in a Positive Manner

The final quality that these families had was the ability to deal with crises and problems in a positive way. Not that they enjoyed crises, but they were able to deal with them constructively. They managed, even in the darkest of situations, to see some positive element, no matter how tiny, and to focus on it. It may have been, for example, that in a particular crisis they simply had to rely to a greater extent on each other and a developed trust that they had in each other. They were able to unite in dealing with the crisis instead of being fragmented by it. They dealt with the problem and were supportive of each other.

CONCLUSIONS AND RECOMMENDATIONS

The qualities that characterized the strong families in our research coincide with what other researchers examining healthy families have reported (Otto, 1964; Lewis et al., 1976; Lewis, 1979; Nelson and Banonis,

1981). It is interesting that most of these qualities that we found to characterize strong families have been found to be lacking in families that are having severe relationship problems and in families broken by divorce. This fact supports the validity of the finding and suggests the importance of these qualities in building family strength. How can we translate this information into practical help to strengthen families? What kind of recommendations can we make? What can we do?

1. One recommendation is that we help families develop some of these skills, such as the ability to express appreciation and good communication patterns. If we were able to do that, relationships and the quality of family life could be improved. This can be done—in fact, it is being done. One example is the research project we instituted at the University of Nebraska, the Family Strengths Enrichment Program. This was an eight-week program in which couples were assisted in developing skills and competencies found to be characteristic of strong families. Pre- and post-tests were administered to the couples. The results indicated significant, positive increases in marriage and family satisfaction. Substantial positive change was found in the ability of the couples to communicate, to deal effectively with conflict, and to express genuine appreciation.

Also, considering the emphasis by these strong families on outdoor activities, recreational ares could be expanded and developed more for family units. For example, having special family days and outdoor seminars specifically for families might encourage them to do more as a unit.

2. Communities, in order to be strong and healthy, must have strong and healthy families. Therefore, we need to devise more research projects which relate family strengths to community needs. We then need to follow through to help the communities use the information we obtain through the research. An example can be found in Lincoln, Nebraska, where a very interesting demonstration project called the Willard Community Family Strengths Project was established. The project was developed in response to a pressing community need. This particular section of Lincoln—the old Willard School District—had a disturbingly high vandalism and delinquency rate. It was the imaginative thesis of Lela Watts, a Ph.D. student at the University of Nebraska, that the most effective way to meet the delinquency problem was a total family approach. So a program, beginning in 1980, was conducted to build the strengths and skills of the families of the youth in the neighborhood. Building self-esteem, communication skills, and expanding the scope of activities which the entire family enjoyed were among the areas of focus for the Willard Family Strengths Program. Some excellent research data were collected, but most importantly the delinquency and vandalism rates were reduced by 83% within a six-month period. This pro-

gram is ongoing and at the time of this writing the delinquency and vandalism rates had been reduced almost to the point of elimination.

3. Another recommendation that we could make is to have a comprehensive human relationships education program incorporated at the preschool, elementary, secondary, and college levels. Isn't it amazing that we have not already done that? Good human relationships are basic and vital to our happiness, our well-being, and our mental health.

4. Also, if we are truly serious about strengthening family life, we might make more of a concerted effort to improve the image of family life. Perhaps we need to make commitment more fashionable as we are so much influenced by it. Some psychologists have stated that if we are really serious about strengthening family life, we are going to have to build much more prestige into being a family member, in being a good father, mother, wife, or husband. We are influenced tremendously by what we think we are rewarded for.

Perhaps we could improve the image of family life through some television spots like public service announcements. The Mormon Church, for example, has done an excellent job of this. They have some very effective television spots. These short announcements could communicate messages about the importance of expressing appreciation or the importance of parents listening to their children for example.

5. Another thing that we are going to have to do is reorder our values and priorities. We will have to make family life and human relationships a top priority, and apply this commitment in terms of the way we spend our time and our energy.

6. Finally, in order to build stronger families in the future we must match our remedial services, as David and Vera Mace (1980) have urged. We must turn from our preoccupation with pathology and the commonly accepted practice of spending all our energies doing "patchwork" and "picking up the wrecks." This approach is more expensive—both financially and in terms of human suffering. In order to be most effective we must make preventive services and programs available early in the lives of individuals and families to provide them with skills, knowledge, motivation, and positive models that can help develop family strengths. Just one example of how this might be done is through more family life education and enrichment programs in the community, which could be organized through such groups as churches, schools, YMCA, YWCA, and local Family Service Association Organizations. Secondary and primary schools could place more emphasis on family life education in the curriculum and encourage, if not require, all students to participate. College curriculum could also be improved by placing more emphasis on family strength in marriage and family classes and designing whole courses specifically for teaching ways to develop family strengths.

Strong families are the roots of our well-being as individuals and as a society. The dream of facilitating strong families that produce emotionally and socially healthy individuals can be realized. The positive potential for the family is great.

Editor's Note:

Stinnett's findings also contain the basis for additional "conclusions and recommendations." To further apply the empirical findings that he reports concerning what makes families strong, we ought to also pay attention to the role of religion. One of the main characteristics of strong families that Stinnett reports in this chapter is their high degree of religious orientation. In fact, he found that *all* the strong families were "very religious." Highly concerned with the spiritual aspects of life, they expressed "an awareness of God or a higher power that gave them a sense of purpose," that provided these families with "a sense of support and strength."

To use this finding as a basis for recommendations for strengthening families would be to encourage the spiritual development and religious participation of entire families. If Stinnett's findings are generalizable, as they appear to be, to encourage the religious involvement of families would not only strengthen families, but also the communities in which they live.

—J.M.H.

REFERENCES

LEWIS, J. M. (1979) How's Your Family? New York: Brunner/Mazel.

———, R. W. BEAVERS, J. T. GOSSET, and V. A. PHILLIPS (1976) No Single Thread: Psychological Health in Family Systems, New York: Brunner/Mazel.

MACE, D., and V. MACE (1980) "Enriching marriages: the foundation stone of family strength," in N. Stinnett et al. (eds.) Family Strengths: Positive Models for Family Life. Lincoln: Univ. of Nebraska Press.

NELSON, P. T., and B. BANONIS (1981) "Family concerns and strengths identified in Delaware's While House Conference on families," in N. Stinnett et al. (eds.) Family Strengths 3: Roots of Well-Being, Lincoln: Univ. of Nebraska Press.

OTTO, H. A. (1964) "The personal and family strength research projects: some implications for the therapist." Mental Hygiene 48:439–450.

———. (1962) "The personal and family resource development programs: a preliminary report." Int. J. of Social Psychiatry 8: 185–195.

YANKELOVICH, D. (1981) New Rules: Searching for Fulfillment in a World Turned Upside Down. New York: Random House.

SECTION 9

Work and Marriage

IN THIS SECTION WE TURN TO AN AREA that touches the lives of every married couple, drastically affecting the well-being of each family. The occupational world always impinges on marital partners, but in the past generation or two a new twist has been added to this occupational factor. More and more, both the husband and the wife work outside the home. In many ways dual employment helps a couple adjust to married life. Their increased income makes it easier to provide for basic needs, for example, as well as to meet many of their highly developed wants. But in addition, because each is participating in the world of paid employment, they share more mutual experiences. To the degree that the work world brings with it a common perceptual base, it should help each understand the other.

At the same time, however, although both husband and wife are employed outside the home and it seems that they are both participating in the same world of experiences, in fact they are not. Their work experiences are separated by three major differences. The first is that, at least in the typical case, the husband has a job that brings with it more responsibility than does his wife's. He is more likely, for example, to be directing the activities of others or to be in a position of making decisions that affect others. The wife, on the other hand, is more likely to be found in a support position, performing tasks that are designed to help others—primarily men. For example, she is much more likely than her husband to be performing secretarial tasks in an office or doing nurturing tasks in a hospital.

The second major difference that separates the occupational worlds of men and women is income. On the average, women make less money than do men. This is true even though they both are employed full time and do the same type of work. In every occupation for which I have seen salary figures, men average higher pay than women. And the average difference is not small. Overall, considering full-time, year-round employees, women make only about two-thirds of what men make.

The third major difference is that the continued employment of a married woman outside the home is often an optional matter. This is a difference of utmost importance, since it contributes so greatly to further separating the male and female occupational worlds. In spite of far-reaching changes in our society concerning growing expectations of a wife's employment, to work outside the home is largely a choice for a wife. The choice of not working may indeed bring with it complex difficulties as the employment of both husband and wife has become increasingly common, and now is often mandatory for maintaining an above-average standard of living.

The difference is that no similar option is available for the husband. In very few cases would a husband be taken seriously if he were to tell his wife that he no longer wishes to work outside the home, that he wants to quit work and devote himself to taking care of the family's needs at home. Seldom would he be able to survive the storm of criticism that such an announcement would elicit. Not only his wife would protest in shocked disbelief, but so would his friends. And his mother-in-law, too, would remain anything but silent. The reactions to a wife expressing that same desire would be quite different. Even if her marital contingencies make her desire impractical and she finds that she must continue her employment outside the home, unlike her husband she would be unlikely to run the risk of being ostracized from "polite society" for expressing deviant desires. Such intentions on her part, rather, would ordinarily find broad cultural support.

These three major factors make a husband's and wife's occupational worlds quite different places. Consequently, husbands and wives who are both employed experience different worlds, and their disjointed experiences greatly affect their orientations. The differences are even greater when only the husband (or, in the extremely rare case, only the wife) works outside the home. Whether only one or both are employed, however, their occupational experiences tend to create differences in their ideas and values. These changes become a major factor in maintaining basic men/women divisions in evaluating life and in taking a general stance toward the world.

As I have emphasized in other introductions, each married couple must work out their own adjustment in marriage, face their own contingencies, and struggle to gain a foothold on a reality that makes sense for their situation. If the wife works outside the home, they must make one sort of adjustment; if she does not, they must make another. In either case the occupational world requires adaptation on the part of both husband and wife.

If their marriage is going to be successful, to thrive or to at least endure, each couple must work out ways of dealing with one another that are satisfactory to them. The employment or nonemployment of the wife and husband outside the home drastically affects the reality that the married couple faces and to which they must adjust. It involves how they treat one another, and what tasks, responsibilities, and duties are shared in what way, such as how children are taken care of, who does the cooking, cleaning, shopping, washing, lawn care, car maintenance, pet care, bill paying, checkbook balancing, gift wrapping, thank-you card writing, and the myriad other tasks in which the modern couple is involved.

Work always brings with it both problems and challenges, troubles and rewards, each of which has its effect on marriage. When both husband and wife are employed outside the home, the contingencies facing the couple become even more complicated, and it is on these that we focus in this section. Emphasized are the disruptions that dual employment presents for traditional marital roles and the trade-offs that husbands and wives make as they attempt to satisfy their own needs and yet be fair to each other.

Why are so many wives, including mothers, joining the paid labor force today? What are the effects of work on marriage? What adjustments do couples make? These are some of the issues that the chapters in this section examine. Kenneth Keniston first presents a brief overview of the major factors that are sending increasing numbers of mothers into employment outside the home. Economic considerations underlie the employment of most wives, but this does not characterize all of them. Barrie S. Greiff and Preston K. Munter consider the motivations and consequences of wives who do not need the money but who choose to work outside the home. In the concluding chapter Linda Haas reports on the attempts that some couples have made to combine the requirements of work and home in egalitarian marriages.

To apply this material, keep in mind that dealing with the occupational world will not be an option for you. Rather, it is a question of how you will deal with it, that is, in what ways you will adjust, adapt, and cope. Whether you are male or female, in one way or another you must come face to face with the realities of the world of work. For almost all male readers, and for the majority of female readers, this will mean direct participation in that world. How do you think work experiences will affect your marriage? What adjustments do you think you will have to make in order to be simultaneously successful at both? How will you divide tasks and responsibilities? What pitfalls to marital happiness does the occupational world pose? What opportunities does it offer? If both you and your spouse are employed and one of you is given an offer of a promotion with a sizable salary increase if you move to another state, will it make a difference in your deliberations whether that offer was made to the husband or to the wife? How would you go about making the decision? How would you react if the husband of a friend announced his intention to quit work and become a "househusband?" Can you see the role of "househusband" in your own marriage?

CHAPTER 32

Working Mothers

Kenneth Keniston

ABSTRACT: Why do so many mothers work outside the home today? First, we must keep in mind that mothers have traditionally helped the family economically, though without leaving home. Today, mothers experience a combination of "pushes" and "pulls" to work outside the home. These include a sense of self-worth, financial stress (especially the expense of raising children), an inflated standard of living, schools providing child care, an expanded job market, and greater acceptance of the employment of mothers, combined with feelings of independence, smaller families, and increased longevity.

The entry [of mothers] into the labor force is not a product of selfish eagerness to earn pin money but is related to the disappearance of the family as an economically productive unit. Mothers on traditional farms played too vital a role in keeping the farm afloat to work for wages anywhere else. Stay-at-home mothers with wage-earning husbands, in contrast, are important to their families and indeed work hard at housekeeping and child rearing, but many find it hard to maintain the sense of self-worth that can come from doing work society values and pays for, and they do not contribute directly to the family cash flow.

The economic drain children now represent adds to the new economic pressures on families. Since most children now use family income for seventeen to twenty-five years and few yield significant income in return, the years of child rearing are the years of greatest financial stress on families; that stress helps push women out into paid jobs to maintain the family standard of living. This is particularly true of single-parent families headed by a woman; her work is a necessity if the family is to avoid welfare and the stigmas that accompany it. . . . Many families are above the poverty line not because wages have kept abreast of needs and inflation, but because wives have gone to work to make up the difference. Mothers work outside the home for many reasons, but one of them is almost always because their families need their income to live up to their standards for their children.

At the same time, rising expectations have inflated most Americans' definition of a reasonable standard of living. A private home, labor-saving appliances, time and money for entertainment and vacations have all become part of normal expectations. Some of these components of a good life in turn make work outside the home more possible for those who can afford them: freezers can reduce shopping to once a week; automatic washers and dryers have eliminated long, hard hours at the washboard and clothesline, store-bought bread eliminates the need to bake. All of these add up to a greater opportunity to work yet in a circular fashion make the income from work more necessary.

We see the same circle connecting mothers' employment to schools. If a mother must work, having children in school for 200 days a year leaves her many childless hours during which she can work without neglecting them. School thus permits mothers to enter the paid labor force by indirectly providing the equivalent of "free" baby-sitting, making working possible without expensive child-care arrangements.

Finally, the changing nature of the job market has opened up millions of jobs to women. What sociologists call the "service sector"—jobs that consist primarily in providing personal services, help, and assistance such as nursing, social work, waiting on tables in restaurants, teaching, and secretarial work—is growing more rapidly than any other sector of the American economy. Many jobs in this sector have traditionally been held by women. In a number of service jobs, qualities such as physical strength that favor men are irrelevant, and stereotypically "female" qualities such as helpfulness, nurturance, or interpersonal sensitivity are thought necessary and therefore employable. These jobs pay less than those usually taken by men—one reason for the poverty of female-headed households—but they are all that is available to most women, who have taken them for lack of anything else. . . .

[O]ther factors are important as well: for example, greater cultural acceptance of women being gainfully employed, and the new insistence on women's right to independence, security, and fulfillment in work. Birth control and increased longevity also play a role that is often overlooked. Whereas formerly many women kept on having children as long as they were fertile, women now have fewer children and space them closer together, so that on the average their last child is in school by the time they are in their late twenties or early thirties. Faced with the prospect of living to seventy-five instead of, say, sixty-five, a woman in her twenties today knows that the days are gone when her role as mother would occupy most of her adult years. A job, even when children are at home, is, among other things, a way of preparing for the decades when the nest is empty.

Over time, however, economic pressures and the way we define economic well-being have had the most pervasive—and most often ignored—influence on mothers working for wages. . . .

CHAPTER 33

Can a Two-Career Family Live Happily Ever After?

Barrie S. Greiff / Preston K. Munter

ABSTRACT: The concept of "dual-career marriage" (or "two-career family") refers to a husband and wife both being executives (or professionals). While the occurrence of such families has been on the rise, increased income is not the prime motivator for the wife's employment. Some of the reasons behind this change include a general push toward women working, financial security, greater career opportunities for women, inflation, the commonality of divorce, and the higher status assigned paid employment.

We don't yet know the consequences of this change—but they might include a division of women into those with and without careers and the deterioration of the health of women—nor do we know the effects on children. But some problems include those uniquely faced by pregnant executives, as well as conflicts between family and career, competition between husbands and wives, and the problem of maintaining intimacy.

A businessman is aggressive; a businesswoman is pushy.
He is careful about details; she is picky.
He loses his temper because he's so involved in his job; she's bitchy.
He's depressed (or hung over), so everyone tiptoes past his office; she's moody, so it must be her time of the month.
He follows through; she doesn't know when to quit.
He's firm; she's stubborn.
He makes wise judgments; she reveals her prejudices.
He is a man of the world; she's been around.
He isn't afraid to say what he thinks; she's opinionated.
He exercises authority; she's tyrannical.

He's discreet; she's secretive.
He's a stern taskmaster; she's difficult to work for.

—*Family Circle*, May 1976

Recent changes in men's and women's roles have created dramatic tradeoffs in executives' lives at home and at work. Between 1947 and 1975 the number of working husbands increased 27 percent while the number of working wives increased 205 percent. Although it is true that only a small proportion of working wives occupy major executive positions, the trend suggests that more and more women will become executives. There are many consequences of this trend already. None is more obvious than the necessity of developing a new language that eliminates long outdated, sex-linked phrases. Another is the need to deal with those new tradeoffs in executive marriages.

Lest we get carried away about the burgeoning role of women in industry, there is another point of view and it's an equally important one. There are some women, after all, who have not been swept along and find themselves more comfortable in the traditional role of wife and mother. They trade the satisfaction of having a business career for the excitement of raising a family. Yet this group has been devalued to a significant extent. These women find it gratifying to be wives and mothers but are often subject to pressure from competitive and achievement-oriented women who work outside the home. Perhaps these women who feel the need to exert such pressure may really be expressing their own guilt for not being as involved at home as "they should be." Those who do "home" work feel incapable of defending themselves adequately, as though the traditional role of women has in some way or other become of lesser value in our society. "I feel what I do is worthwhile. But I have no benchmarks and no bonuses or other perks, like my husband gets all the time, that tell me and everybody else that what I do at home is worthwhile. There aren't any five- or ten-year pins or any award nights for women who run their homes efficiently and profitably." Some women stay home angry; others enter the work force out of guilt. Both are vulnerable.

More and more executives and their spouses can and do make the *choice* of dual careers quite apart from the need to augment family income. Their reasons are deep and personal and reflect their changing values and a reassessment of their goals in life, in particular, the priority they now assign to the legitimate need each partner has for fulfillment outside the home and family.

Dual-career families have significantly altered not only the personal and professional lives of individuals but also the ways in which their organizations conduct business and make their tradeoffs.

What exactly is a dual-career family? It is a marriage in which husband and wife each has a *career* as opposed to a *job*. Both take "line" (decision-making) and "staff" (implementing) positions that are open-ended as to time and commitment. Both may travel, both may relocate, both are on tight schedules, and both earn better-than-average incomes. While increased economic benefits play a major part in their career choice, that is only part of their motivation. Self-fulfillment is one of their dominant goals and it is at least as important to them as money. Each career requires a separate major commitment outside the marriage and that dictates crucial tradeoffs in the marriage as well as in the kind of family life that is then possible.

Dual-career marriages are likely to continue and even to increase. Why? As technology has altered organizational life it has also affected our personal and family lives. The dual-career arrangement is an outgrowth of those changes. Critical factors responsible for dual careers are:

• The desire of both men and women to achieve a better way of life. This requires more capital because they want here-and-now benefits as well as healthy bank accounts for their future. The luxuries of the past have become the necessities of the present and somebody has to pay for them. They feel deeply entitled to whatever they prescribe for themselves as essential to their pleasure, comfort, and security. The expectations of executives, as of so many others, are apparently boundless. Executives live an affluent life-style. They don't believe it's ever going to change, except to get better.

• The feminist movement has provided peer reinforcement for women, particularly those who have felt ambivalent about pursuing careers outside their marriages. It has persuaded some women to search out careers who otherwise might not have done so. Thus, it has forced women to consider very specific tradeoffs—whether to pursue a career at all or to remain at home; whether to pursue a career first and postpone having a family; or whether to have a family first and postpone a career. In the long run the movement may or may not help women to decide one way or another. But there can be no question that it has confronted all of us with the simple fact that most women now have a number of possible choices they didn't have previously.

• Equal opportunity laws and community programs have smoothed the way for women to develop independent careers. Aggressive recruitment programs by schools in business, law, and medicine have underscored the professional opportunities available to them.

• Modern technology has freed women from many of the constraints of running the home. Contemporary contraceptive methods permit people to plan their families more effectively.

• Careers have higher status than families for some executives. Therefore, they make the tradeoff of postponing having children in favor of both partners having careers. Furthermore, many women feel that the only way they can keep pace with their executive husbands is to have their own careers.

• Dual careers protect the family as a unit against the disruptive limitations sometimes imposed by corporate life. Some women and their husbands see the dual-career situation as a way of making their personal and family lives more flexible because they are not so dependent on a single corporate paycheck. The loss of a single job becomes much less damaging to the family. The paradox is that dual careers may impose twice the limitations that single careers impose, even though they provide more economic security and flexibility. For these couples the dual career provides a buffer against job loss and indiscriminate relocation.

• The rising divorce rate among executives has stimulated executives' wives to think about supporting themselves independently, if need be. This is underscored by the new ethic in executive families, one expression of which is the reluctance of some wives to accept alimony as a part of a divorce settlement. Instead, they develop their own careers and their own incomes. In addition, some women find at work the consistency in personal relationships that they may not have found in their family. The company becomes their family and they look to it to provide stability in their lives.

• Older couples, faced with the burdens of an inflationary economy, also need to augment their incomes if they are to sustain their life-styles and prepare adequately for retirement.

Many women are convinced that they can do the jobs they see their husbands doing just as well and see no reason why they shouldn't try. They recognize the satisfactions and the rewards; and they are convinced that they should be equally satisfied and equally rewarded. But they are also aware of the challenges and problems, the fatigue and frustration of executive careers.

> You will be working with men and women without family commitments who will expect you to work long hours with them. You will *want* to work those hours. If you cannot, you may not be hired, or you may lose a promotion or be fired. If you *do* work the long hours, you will have guilt feelings. You *should* have guilt feelings. The professions are filled with men who do not see enough of their children; to imitate them is no solution.
>
> . . . I am pessimistic. Also, I see an increased acceptance of women's rights to their own careers. I see little corresponding desire on the part of men to raise their children and little encouragement to do so from our social institutions.
>
> . . . What I fear is that, like our mothers and our grandmothers, we will become two kinds of women—*women with children and women with careers*. The women's movement, it is true, has increased the career options for women, so childless women can now be lawyers and welders, as well as

school teachers. If women *only* must choose, however, we have not come s far at all.

. . . Child-raising is important work but it is not a respected professior If it were, men as well as women would want to do it. The corollary is tha by taking a few years out to raise your children you will inevitably hurt you career. Having those years on your résumé, explicitly or by omission, wi put you at a competitive disadvantage with anyone who has been "work ing," studying, or traveling during those years. That you are a mother ma also hurt because of the stereotype to which, I think, we are all susceptible that mommies are dumb.

. . . If my own experience means anything, I cannot overstate how diffi cult it is to do justice to both children and a career. It is a constant battle. I does have its rewards—some day, some time, you too may need to fight. hope that you will do so.*

—Marilyn Smit

To better cope with the tradeoffs of dual careers, each partner has to have a very clear sense of his or her own identity.

• Both must be able to specify what their goals are—planning anc delegation are key factors. Bear in mind, however, that it is easy to be come entrapped by the people and facilities to whom one delegates re sponsibility and authority.

• Both have to have enormous reserves of energy to be able to handle schedules that are frequently overloaded.

• Both have to be able to make decisions and choices effectively anc quickly and both must be flexible. This means that, among other things they both must be able to handle timetables, missed planes, no-show baby-sitters, and late meetings.

• Both must be able to manage guilt feelings in themselves and each other because they often are not available to each other.

• Both must be able to manage themselves effectively so pressures demands, and contingencies do not make them feel depersonalized or out of control of their own lives. When that happens they feel a loss of mutual support and reinforcement, simply because the demands of their schedules disrupt the ordinary day-to-day exchanges that are more readily accessible to single-career couples.

• Dual-career couples must carve out some segment of their schedules that remains inviolate and allows them to catch up with themselves.

HEALTH OF CAREER WOMEN

The issue of women's energy and health, often overlooked, becomes increasingly important for dual-career women. So much has been written

*"Parents and Professionals," Harvard Law School graduation address, June 1976. Reprinted from *Harvard Gazette*, June 17, 1976.

about heart attacks and ulcers in executive men; are we to assume that executive women are naturally immune to the wear and tear that careers may have on their health? The dual-career woman now finds herself hardly able to catch her breath in order to fulfill all of her obligations—work, husband, children, home, social arrangements, and, somewhere down the list, herself.

What effect will the heavy demands of work have on her health? What effect will a career have on women's sickness and death rates as they become involved in a more competitive, aggressive working life? In 1920 the life expectancy of women was 56 years and for men it was 54 years. In 1970, women's life expectancy was 75, men's 65. Men seem to have a higher rate of suicide, fatal motor vehicle accidents, cirrhosis of the liver, respiratory cancer, and emphysema. Each of these causes of death appears to be linked to behaviors that are encouraged or accepted for males—the use of guns, drinking alcohol, smoking, and working at hazardous jobs in which they are expected to be competitive and fearless. Thus, the behavior expected of males in our society appears to have a relationship to their sickness and death rates. Will the role of the career woman in the future become more like that of the male? Will she then be more subject to illnesses that so far have afflicted men predominantly? In a recent article in *The New England Journal of Medicine*, "Sexual Equality and Health" the following statements were made:

> At a time when society's expectations of women and men are changing—although slowly—it will be fascinating to observe the future health-related behavior of the female of the species. . . . As sex roles change, will those health-related behaviors that seem highly linked to sex also change, i.e., will women demonstrate a pattern of decreased use of services? Will they experience, as younger women physicians do, a relative increase in mortality as compared to men? Will they gain equity in death rates for most diseases as they already have done for cancer of the lung? . . .

The authors add a fascinating conclusion to the article:

> What is the better measure of equality, for women to die like men, or for men to live a little bit like women?

It appears that the protective immunity that women once enjoyed may be changing. They may become subject to the whole range of stress-related disturbances that are so familiar to male executives. Female executives are going to need to learn early in the game how to pace themselves, to have periodic physical examinations, to moderate their use of alcohol and drugs, to make appropriate tradeoffs as they actively juggle their personal, family, and corporate lives. And male executives are going to have to learn to be more caretaking in their relationships with their working wives.

Some dual-career couples find it difficult to meet the demands of a dual-career life. They can't acknowledge or even recognize conflict within the family or between the family and their jobs. They take o more and more activity outside the home and in business and pay les and less attention to each other. As a result their personal relationship tend to become superficial. In the end they feel less and less involved i more and more of their life. And they derive little pleasure from any o it, inevitably facing the dilemma: "I'm working my tail off—what's it al for?"

In dual-career relationships one result of ineptly managed tradeoff is guilt. Guilt about not having time for one another, guilt about no spending adequate time with their children, guilt about cheating th corporation to meet their other needs, and even guilt about not havin enough time for themselves.

After getting her MBA, Betty Thornton thought she had resolve this dilemma:

> I have decided not to work right away, and I thought I had my husband' support in this decision. I'd like to raise our family while we're young an while we can live comfortably on Steve's salary. But I have to admit I fee kind of guilty that we will miss certain luxuries my salary would have pro vided. Right now I prefer being a housewife to working. I enjoy caring fo our children, cooking, cleaning, etc., and hardly even consider these as be ing work, at least at this point in my life.
>
> Interestingly enough, my parents and my in-laws feel that I shoul work. After all, they helped pay for my MBA and they want me to use it And I really feel my husband wants me to do both—have a career and no change in any way how I run our home. I feel like I'm in a revolving door.
>
> I don't know whether I've made the right choice or not. I'm happy wit my kids but my husband is having some career problems and we sure coul use the added income. Maybe I've made the wrong decision after all.

Initially, Betty's decision appeared to be right for her since there ha been reasonable discussion and thought beforehand. In fact, however Steve had a hidden agenda. Part of what he really wanted was openly expressed, but part was withheld. He wanted it both ways—the advantage of a double income as well as a full-time wife and mother. For him the decision was clear. For her it wasn't merely either/or; it seemed impossible to make any tradeoff without disappointing someone and leaving herself with unresolved guilt. . . .

DUAL-CAREER FAMILY LIFE

In the dual-career family the nature and quality of family life has changed for both partners and especially for children. It may be better or worse, we don't know yet. But it is surely different from the traditional pattern. When both parents are outside the home in full-time careers, they can be only in intermittent contact with each other and with their children. That is a basic change.

It's unrealistic for women to justify their career by arguing that it won't have any effect on their children. That's nonsense. It has to have an effect, just as absent fathers have an effect on their children. The question is, What is the effect and how can both parents make it a positive one?

Dual-career parents must recognize the increased vulnerability of their children to separation and loss. Children aren't "little adults," but like adults they have difficulty dealing with separation. They may not show disappointment readily but they react to separation and loss, and parents have to help them deal with the anger, hostility, rebellion, and feelings of being abandoned that their absence can evoke. It's important to provide continuous communication with their children while they're away, recognizing that logical explanations about the priorities of their careers, however clear and realistic, are not adequate substitutes for their presence at home. They shouldn't burden their children with inappropriate responsibility for themselves, or for their siblings, or for running the household. That only cheats them out of their childhood and confuses them about parental roles. Nor should their children be made to feel they must compete with their parents' careers for adequate time and attention.

The dual career may be the contraceptive of the future. The time and effort and continuity that are necessary to establish a career cause some dual-career couples to consider how appropriate it is to have children at all. For similar reasons, others delay having them until later in the marriage, or adopt them. Other couples decide to have children at the start of their careers and place them in day-care centers or other community resources or use surrogate parents. But they can't avoid worrying that their children have appropriate role models and the kind of care, discipline, and training "only biological parents can provide." That's a sensitive tradeoff that doesn't let parents off the hook no matter what their choice turns out to be. If parents delegate "caring" to an extreme, children may feel guilty, sensing that somehow they have become obstacles to their parents' careers. They may also feel angry at being rejected and retaliate against their parents, making them feel guilty for abandoning them. . . .

By itself pregnancy would seem to be a very happy and exciting event in a woman's life. But for some women executives pregnancy is fraught with ambivalence, concern, anxiety, and fear. After struggling to establish themselves in roles equivalent to those of men, pregnancy defines women unmistakably, once again, as different. It requires them to live and work a little differently because for months they have to monitor their activities in special ways. Despite their desire not to be treated as being special or different, in a practical way it becomes very difficult for their male colleagues not to do so. After all, there are certain physical aspects of pregnancy that often do require altered schedules. Just the simple matter of increased fatigability as the pregnancy goes on may dictate certain changes in the way a woman paces herself and the kind of schedule she undertakes. Generally, however, there is no reason why in attitudes and behavior men need to alter significantly their relationships with pregnant female colleagues. But the fact that they often do so places a special pressure on the pregnant executive. . . .

Part of the problem for the pregnant executive is that the delivery of her baby takes her away from her active work responsibilities. She may feel guilt that she is letting other people down for not carrying her share of the load. This concern is similar to that of a male colleague who may have had a heart attack, an accident, or elective surgery and was forced to be out of action for a while. When both are taken out of active duty, whatever the reason, they develop a certain amount of anxiety about letting the troops down, about whether their rightful place will be open to them when they return.

Medical technology has in many ways become the ally of women executives. More sophisticated obstetrical care reduces the risk of late childbearing by emphasizing good general health during pregnancy and delivery. These measures do not altogether eliminate the risks to mother and child but they do, in effect, extend the childbearing years into the late thirties or even the early forties. In other words, it is no longer altogether true that having children late in the childbearing years presents inescapable risks to mother or child. As for the option of adopting children, in recent years it has become increasingly difficult to adopt healthy children without elaborate negotiations or great expense. . . .

Many people are antagonistic toward dual-career marriage because they perceive it as inimical to the healthy growth and development of children. There is insufficient evidence to determine precisely what the effects of dual-career families are on children. Dual-career parents are acutely sensitive to this issue. If anything, many bend over backward to make sure their careers do not, in and of themselves, place special stress on their children or create special disadvantages for them. As a matter of fact, family relationships in dual-career families may be better, if anything, than in many families where only one spouse is the breadwinner. A father and mother who both find deep satisfaction in their work lives may offer an especially nurturant and creative family life to children.

The successful dual-career couple share home tasks on an equitable basis because they genuinely understand and respect each other's needs. They accept the reality that all of their individual and combined activities at home are not separable but rather part and parcel of the total fabric of their life together. Each partner reinforces the other, performing whatever task needs doing, whether it be cooking, taking care of the children, or keeping the house clean, each according to what needs to be done, not according to who is "supposed" to do it.

There are some obstacles to dual-career marriages, of course, simply in the nature of our social customs and historical roles. For one thing, it is still true that even in dual-career families certain tasks—most notably care of the children—tend to fall to the partner who has the less prestigious title and who earns less money. Such responsibilities almost always fall on the wife. She most typically earns less money and is perceived as carrying less responsibility at work. As a result she has less leverage in the marital relationship if leverage is based on bottom-line finances. Even in the current social context the burden of child care generally falls on the mother because the basic social expectation is still that she will be at home caring for "their" children. So if she should be away when something dire happens to a child, the automatic response is that it's the mother's fault. The guilt is real and directly conditioned by her background, her husband, and society. A woman who feels ambivalent, sensitive, or unsure about pursuing a career is especially vulnerable to this kind of censure and to the guilt it provokes.

A profound change is occurring that challenges the traditional separation of jobs and family. When a man stays home from work to take care of family responsibilities, as, for example, when his wife is traveling and a child becomes ill, as some men are now doing, he admits that his family is as important to him as his work. And he spells out that changed reality not just in words but in making a specific tradeoff—family for job. That has consequences; being viewed as not being fully committed; potentially limiting his growth in the organization; being perceived as a maverick, an oddball, with the implication that he may influence others to do the same; and finally, his career may plateau, and the irony is that his wife may lose her respect for him. But there are positive results from such a tradeoff: he isn't just talking about being a sharing person, he is doing it. That gives him an authentic and enhanced sense of self-respect.

The new ground rules in dual-career marriage of sharing tasks and interchanging roles do not eliminate the ordinary competitiveness between husband and wife. More particularly, competitiveness could become heightened between a husband and wife, each of whom has a separate career. Competitive issues concerning who makes more money, who has the more important title, whose progress is more rapid in the organization, who appears to be more aggressive can become quite overt between dual-career husbands and wives. Great flexibility, endless coordination, and again, a clear sense of self and goals are essentia[l] in order that home life be comfortable and rewarding for both parties. Even for individuals who appear to be quite secure and who practic[e] and openly profess a desire for equality, there can be threatening under currents.

> Bob Wilson is a highly competitive entrepreneur who has amassed a large amount of capital. He is held in high esteem by his colleagues and is considered to be one of the "big men in the community."
>
> His wife is equally competent and also has an important job. He sees himself as very liberal in *allowing* his wife "to do whatever she has to do to pursue her career." Privately, however, he believes that she can never top him, no matter how successful she becomes.
>
> On one occasion she was considered for a major job in another city. He requested that she not accept the job because he felt it would "interfere with our quality of life." She subsequently rejected the position because she recognized, among other factors, that he could not handle his loss of identity in a new city and the move would negatively affect their relationship.

Her decision is essentially a tradeoff between her own career aspirations and her reluctance to surrender the traditional values of her marriage that she respects and needs.

The problem of sustaining the intimate, tender, and romantic side of a dual-career relationship is a particularly sensitive one. Many couples who shift from traditional to dual-career marriages aren't prepared for critical changes in that side of their relationship. Some young couples, especially, who start out with dual careers may be caught off guard here. They have to learn to accommodate each other's absences and distractions, at times unpredictable, and conflicting work schedules and priorities. Even when they are actually at home, their separate job responsibilities may affect their personal lives. Talking, eating, sleeping, playing, and especially sexual activity may be disrupted. Special awareness and effort about each other's needs and responses must be built into the relationship in order to preserve, and enhance, the essence of the relationship.

CHAPTER 34

Role-Sharing Couples

Linda Haas

ABSTRACT: The author reports on a rare type of marriage: couples who try to share equally the tasks and responsibilities that are traditionally sex-segregated. Motives for this egalitarian approach to marriage are that the couple might pursue a variety of interests, gain relief from overload, distribute the anxiety of the provider role, and increase independence. The benefits they report are lessened resentment, increased satisfaction with the relationship, and improvements in communication, parent-child relationships, and finances. They also encountered problems: how to divide the domestic tasks, difficulties in breaking their traditional sex–role patterns, differing standards of housework, and the reluctance of wives to give up authority over housework.

[This chapter reports the] results of a detailed empirical study of couples who have attempted role-sharing and generally succeeded in putting it into practice. The goals of the study were to discover the reasons couples adopted this alternative family lifestyle, the problems they had adjusting to it, and the solutions they developed to combat the problems encountered.

The author wishes to thank Sally Weiler and Rose Gartner for help with interviewing, and Ain Haas, Russell Middleton, Bert Adams, Bill Strahle, and Colin Williams for comments on an earlier version of this paper. This research was partially supported by a traineeship and a small research grant from the NIMH Social Organization Training Program, University of Wisconsin-Madison, 1975–76.

A marriage style based on the equal sharing of traditionally sex-segregated roles is very rarely found in practice and subsequently has been generally unstudied by social scientists. There have been several studies of dual-career families, but these families generally do not practice role-sharing. While the wife is committed to a career, her basic family responsibilities typically remain intact and her husband's career has precedence over hers. . . .

[F]ully developed role-sharing can be defined as the sharing by husband and wife of each of the traditionally segregated family roles, including:

The breadwinner role. The husband and wife are equally responsible for earning family income; the wife's employment is not considered more optional or less desirable than the husband's. Consequently, the spouses' occupations are equally important and receive equal status, or at least the occupation which has more status is not determined by notions of the intrinsic supremacy of one sex over the other.

The domestic role. The husband and wife are equally responsible for performing housekeeping chores such as cooking, cleaning, and laundry.

The handyman role. The husband and wife are equally responsible for performing traditionally masculine tasks such as yardwork and repairs.

The kinship role. The husband and wife are equally responsible for meeting kinship obligations, like buying gifts and writing letters, which have traditionally been the wife's responsibility.

The childcare role. The husband and wife are equally responsible for doing routine childcare tasks and for rearing and disciplining of children.

The major/minor decision-maker roles. The spouses have generally equal influence on the making of major decisions which males have traditionally dominated and the minor decisions traditionally designated to the female.

Specialization within any of these roles (e.g., husband cooks, wife launders) would be compatible with role-sharing, as long as specific tasks are not assigned to a spouse *on the basis of sex* (i.e., because they are deemed more appropriate for someone of his/her gender) and as long as the over-all responsibility for the duties of *each* role is evenly shared.

STUDY DESIGN

Since past studies of the family imply that role-sharing couples make up a very tiny proportion of the general population, a random sampling design could not be employed in this study without a great amount of expense and time. Therefore, a type of purposive or strategic sampling technique was employed (cf. Glaser & Strauss, 1967). In the liberal university community of Madison, Wisconsin . . . names were obtained through contacts in various local institutions and associations (e.g., a daycare center, a chapter of the National Organization for Women, a liberal religious group, university organizations) and through announcements published in local newsletters and newspapers.

Each of these couples was contacted by telephone during January, 1976. Whoever answered the phone was asked several questions designed to ascertain in a rough fashion whether or not his or her relationship was characterized by role-sharing, as reputed. To be included for further study, both spouses had to be engaged in, looking for, or preparing for work and spending roughly the same number of hours per week on work or school-related pursuits. The wife's employment could not be seen as something less permanent than the husband's, and an unequivocally affirmative answer had to be given to the question, "Would you say that each of you has roughly the same amount of influence over family decisions?" When asked, "What percent of all the housework that's done in your household do you think you do?", the answer had to be in the 40–60% range, as did the answer to a similar question about childcare. . . .

[Thirty-one couples] qualified on the various criteria and were willing to participate in the study. The sample was fairly homogeneous, despite efforts to recruit a variety of types for the study. For the most part, the people in the sample were training themselves for or engaged in jobs in professional fields, usually in social service or the humanities. The sample couples tended to be young, with a majority of them being 26 to 30 years old. The mean number of years they had been married was six. Nearly half of them had children, most of which were not yet old enough to go to school.

Both the husband and wife in each of the 31 couples were interviewed three times from January through June of 1976. Averaging 1½ hours each, these interviews usually took place in the couples' homes and were tape-recorded. The spouses were interviewed separately during most of the questioning. After the interviews, written forms were left with the individuals to be filled out and returned by mail. These included a time-budget and an attitudinal questionnaire. . . .

RESULTS AND DISCUSSION

Motivations for Role-Sharing Behavior

In replies to open-ended questions about why they shared the responsibilities of breadwinning, decision-making, and domestic chores, each couple gave several motives for role-sharing. In the results which follow, couples are listed as giving a certain reason if either spouse reported it, but spouses usually answered the same way. Almost all of the couples in the sample revealed that they adopted role-sharing not as a result of an ideological commitment to sexual equality, but rather as a practical way of obtaining certain benefits which they perceived could not be realized in a traditional marriage with segregated husband-wife roles. The vast majority of couples said they became pessimistic about traditional marriage roles after trying a traditional pattern in their marriage in its early years. Over one-third of the individuals said they were also predisposed to attempt a non-traditional role pattern because they felt their parents had been constrained by the traditional familial division of labor. Finally, a handful of the respondents had been married previously and complained that conflict over sex-role expectations had been a major factor in their divorces.

The benefits attainable through role-sharing usually occurred to the wife first and more often aided her than the husband. However, a considerable part of the motivation to try a non-traditional pattern also involved a desire to liberate the husband from the confines of his traditional family role.

Benefits for the Individual

One anticipated benefit for both spouses was a greater opportunity to develop their abilities and pursue personal interests without being limited by traditional role expectations. Over four-fifths of the sample adopted role-sharing so the wife could satisfy her desire to work outside the home for personal fulfillment. One-fifth of the couples reported picking the role-sharing lifestyle so that each spouse would have the freedom to quit outside employment for a time and pursue other interests.

Another motive for role-sharing was relief from the stress and overwork that results from having primary responsibility for a broad area of family life. Almost three-fourths of the couples wanted to eliminate the overload dilemmas faced by working women who remain primarily responsible for housework and childcare. This benefit of rolesharing did seem to have been realized, according to time-budget data collected in individual diaries for a week between the first and second interviews. Wives in the sample averaged 16.0 hours per week at housework, while men averaged 16.2

Mothers in the study averaged 12.2 hours per week at specific childcare tasks, while father spent 10.4. The general equality of the workload was also evident in the finding that the women spent 26.8 hours per week at hobbies, watching television, socializing, organizational meetings, etc., compared to the men's average of 26.2 hours of leisure activities. In contrast, time-budget studies of the general population show employed husbands averaging about 6½ more hours of free-time activities a week than employed wives (Szalai, 1972).

Over half of the couples mentioned that the role-sharing lifestyle was adopted so that the husband would not be burdened more than the wife with the provider responsibility and its concomitant anxiety and stress. While this benefit was fully achieved by the majority of couples in the study, at least one partner in one-third (ten) of the couples (usually the male) reported a little difficulty in completely letting go of the traditional idea that the man is more responsible for earning income than the wife, or that the wife was less obligated to work to provide family income. In most of these cases, it was the wife's newer or lesser interest in a career that was used as an explanation for the partial retention of this traditional sex-role expectation for men. These ten couples said, however, that this was an idea they no longer wanted to believe in and certainly would not act on.

Another major motive for role-sharing cited by these couples was greater independence of the husband and wife. While the role-sharers in the study neither desired nor actually led completely independent lives within marriage, over one-fourth of them initiated role-sharing to avoid the economic dependence wives traditionally have had on husbands, while one-sixth wanted to avoid the dependence most husbands experience when it comes to getting domestic chores done—e.g., cooking, laundry, mending.

Benefits for the Family

Several people who were happier because of new opportunities for self-fulfillment and relief from one-sided burdens reported themselves to be better marriage partners as a side benefit; however, there were other ways in which couples tried to improve their family life directly through role-sharing. For instance, almost two-thirds of the couples cited a desire to cut down on the resentment and conflict that they saw resulting from husbands having more power in marriage. Generally, a shared decision-making pattern was the first aspect of role-sharing to be tried, and the one aspect that was relatively easy to establish. Several individuals commented that a positive but unanticipated consequence of a shared decision-making pattern was that it called for a considerable amount of discussion and this communicating in turn brought greater intimacy between husband and wife.

Another way couples thought role-sharing would improve husband-wife relations, reported by one-fifth of the couples, was in giving them more in common—with both spouses working and both having domestic responsibilities. Several individuals reported that having so much in common caused them to appreciate and sympathize with each other more. Each could appreciate problems the other had at work or school because they came up against the same things, and they were less likely to nag at each other if a task went undone because they personally knew how hard it was to get around to doing an undesirable chore. Several people also said the role-sharing gave them the opportunity to do more things together, increasing interaction and thus enhancing husband-wife closeness. A few couples were in the same occupational field, so they could profitably discuss their work and occasionally work on projects together. The spouses also had occasion to be together while domestic chores were being performed. Since the work hours of husbands and wives were approximately even and their work schedules were often similar, the couples had occasion to spend a lot of their free time together.

Besides an improvement in husband-wife relations, another major benefit of role-sharing cited for the family was improvement in parent-child relations. This was not a factor in the initial decision to adopt role-sharing, but it became a reason for continuing the arrangement. Five of the 12 women with children at home felt they had become better mothers because they worked outside the home and shared childcare with their husbands. They felt they were less bored, less hassled with managing two roles, and not resentful about shouldering the entire burden of childcare. Three of the 24 parents mentioned that sharing childcare meant that the children got to know their father better than they would in a traditional family, and three parents thought children benefited by being exposed to more than just the mother's outlook on things.

The final major benefit for the family that couples wanted to achieve with role-sharing was greater financial security. One-fourth of the couples said they chose a dual-earner arrangement to provide the family with more income on a permanent basis. Incidentally, the vast majority of couples pooled their incomes, and in all of the couples the wife's income was not saved for extras but was used for family expenses as much as was the husband's.

Problems with Role-Sharing

While these couples' efforts to implement role-sharing brought the benefits they anticipated, several difficulties with this arrangement were reported in responses to questions about problems with role-sharing. Some of these problems appeared to result from certain personal obstacles related to vestiges of traditional sex roles in the family. Others seemed to come from trying to transcend sex roles within family units in the context of a larger more traditional society. Still other problems seemed to be inherent in the role-sharing lifestyle itself.

Problems Sharing the Domestic Role

Of all the areas of role-sharing, couples reported problems most often in the establishment of an egalitarian division of domestic chores. These problems can be grouped into four types, listed here in order of their frequency: disinclination to do non-traditional tasks, discrepancies in housekeeping standards, wife's reluctance to delegate domestic responsibility, and lack of non-traditional domestic skills.

The most common type of problem in sharing domestic chores, reported by over half of the couples, was that one or both spouses lacked the inclination to do some non-traditional tasks for which they had skills or for which no special skill was required. About one-third of the couples with this problem mentioned that it was hard to break with the traditional pattern they had observed in their parents' households. Over one-third claimed that it often seemed more efficient to let the traditional spouse perform the chore in the face of the other partner's inexperience, busy schedule, or laziness.

Couples had different solutions for this problem. Most often, the spouse who felt overworked (usually the wife) complained and threatened to stop doing the chore or some other task until the lazy spouse resolved to do better. Sometimes a temporary system of rotation was agreed upon to get the recalcitrant spouse into the right habit. Occasionally the lazy spouse would develop more of a liking or tolerance for the chore or become so experienced at it that the problem would be solved. Some couples ended up agreeing to some specialization in order to avoid further conflict, especially if each spouse wanted to avoid certain non-traditional chores that the other spouse did not mind doing.

Another frequent problem in overcoming the traditional chore pattern involved the standards spouses had for housekeeping. Over half of the couples reported that at an earlier time in their marriage the wives had generally advocated a much higher standard of orderliness and cleanliness in the household than their husbands. This did not produce any conflict as long as the woman was in charge of getting the chores done, but when the decision to share responsibility for chores was reached, wives pushed for chores to be done as often as they wanted to see them done and in the manner they preferred. They fretted about the condition of the house all the time and experienced embarrassment if someone dropped in unexpectedly. Husbands, on the other hand, wanted to do the chores according to their own ideas on how often they needed to be done and in the manner (often unconventional) that appealed most to them. Husbands consistently felt wives were too finicky and wives regarded husbands as too sloppy.

Most of the couples coped with this discrepancy in standards by simultaneously having wives lower their expectations and husbands raise theirs. This change was usually precipitated by wives being busy with their jobs or schoolwork and it was accompanied by many heated discussions and practical experiments. Both spouses generally professed to be happier with the new standard, but the wives still tended to believe in a somewhat higher standard than their husbands. When asked, "Do you think that housework is done as often and as well as you want it to be?" almost one-half of the wives (but less than one-third of the husbands) expressed discontent with the level or orderliness and cleanliness of their homes. . . .

Since both the husband and wife were busy with jobs or schoolwork, it is not surprising that many individuals felt anxious about their housekeeping standard. On the other hand, there was little evidence that their homes were in fact being neglected, for their homes generally seemed neat and clean to the interviewers. . . .

A third problem, mentioned by half the couples, was the wife's reluctance to give up her traditional authority over many domestic chores. For all but one of these couples, this problem had been overcome by the time of the study. One-third of the women in the study reported that they expected to do all the traditionally female domestic chores when they got married because of socialization—their mothers had done them and they had learned it was the women's duty to do those chores. Some of the women in the sample mentioned that they had actually enjoyed the challenge of trying to be simultaneously a great housewife and a successful professional.

The change to a more even sharing of domestic chores was not easy. Not only did the wives have to contend with the husband's disinclination to do chores, they also had to cope with guilt feelings about abandoning their traditional role and with the mixed feelings they had seeing their husbands do non-traditional tasks. As their strong interest in a profession consumed more and more of their mental and physical energy over the years, however, housework seemed increasingly tedious rather than challenging. In addition, the women's movement led them to believe that doing double work is unfair and made them feel better about sharing domestic chores with their husbands.

The last type of problem couples had in sharing domestic chores was a lack of skills on the part of one or the other of the spouses. Over one-third of the couples cited this as an impediment to the realization of equality. For half of these couples it was the husband's lack of expertise in areas such as cooking or sewing which had caused problems, and in the other half of the cases it was the wife's inability to do things like make repairs or handle the car which had inhibited an equal sharing of responsibility.

Couples sought to cope with this type of problem by having the more knowledgeable spouse teach the other one the new skill, or by having the incapable spouse develop the necessary ability on his or her own. This solution often failed to work out, for the spouse without a certain skill often lacked a desire to persist through the frustration and disappointment accompanying the learning experience. Other individuals claimed they were too busy with their careers or hesitated giving up valuable leisure time to learn a new skill and it seemed more efficient to let the expert spouse do the task. Many tasks also came up only in a crisis (stopped-up drain, faulty car brakes, popped-off button) and many individuals felt that this was not a good time to learn. Normalcy would be restored quicker if the expert fixed things up. Finally, in cases such as wives trying to learn car maintenance and home repairs, they had to interact with skeptical and hostile outsiders in the pursuit of these skills (e.g., hardware store personnel, garage mechanics). As a result, wives tended to shrink away from this type of contact and avoid learning the task.

Wives were generally less successful at acquiring the skills required for the husband's traditional chores than vice versa. Husbands on the average spent the same amount of hours doing traditionally feminine domestic chores as wives but wives spent less time on the average than husbands on "male" chores such as interior home repairs and yardwork (1.3 hours per week vs. 2.9, according to time-budget data). The figures are small, but they do suggest that the wives, who typically were the instigators of role-sharing, hadn't put much effort into sharing all of the husband's traditional family responsibilities. Interestingly, most of the couples did not perceive this difference to be a problem, perhaps because masculine domestic chores take up so little time compared to other types of domestic chores. . . .

Conflicts Involving Jobs

Besides problems in sharing domestic responsibilities, couples also described several difficulties associated with having two jobs in the [same] family. One serious problem was conflict between the spouses' jobs or studies. All but three of the couples felt that conflicts between jobs could be a problem in the future, when asked about a hypothetical situation where one spouse would be offered a job in a city different from that in which his or her spouse already worked. Most couples had already settled on strategies for dealing with this situation. A strategy most of them planned to employ was to give the spouse who had the *less* marketable skills or the poorer job opportunities their choice when a conflict arose. (Husbands' jobs were not any more likely to be given priority in the total sample than were wives'.) The next most common plan was establishing a long-distance marriage—that is, both spouses accepting their job offers, living in different cities, and visiting each other regularly. This possibility was mentioned by over half of the couples, most of whom did not yet have children. For the most part, couples did not like the idea of separating but were willing to consider it as a way to maintain a dual-career marriage. Another solution mentioned by some couples was for husband and wife to take turns holding the job of their choice. Finally, a few couples mentioned that one spouse's job offer in another city might be regarded as an opportunity for the other to do free-lance work, engage in independent research, or start a business. Several couples hoped to avoid making a decision about job priority by only looking for jobs at the same time in the same geographic area. This solution was only available to couples in which the husband and wife were at comparable stages in their careers, which was not common, since husbands tended to be older than wives.

Another common problem was conflict between jobs and family responsibilities. This was reported by over half of the total sample, by husbands a little more often than wives (in contrast to typical dual-career couples, where the wife usually reports job-family conflicts). Most of those individuals reporting job-family conflicts mentioned that their jobs interfered with family responsibilities in various ways: housework didn't get done, they lacked energy and patience to interact well with their children, or they did not have enough leisure time to spend with their families. About one-third of those reporting conflicts mentioned that family duties interfered with their job performance: they had to cut down on overtime work, had trouble doing job-related work at home, had to rearrange their schedules when children became ill, or had little time to attend job-related meetings in the evenings and on weekends.

The couples' strategies for dealing with job-family conflicts usually involved adjusting housework. The most common strategy, employed by over one-third of the couples, was to cut down on housework or at least to give it a very low priority—after meeting job or school responsibilities and after spending free time with family members. Next most common was for couples to maintain a regular schedule of housekeeping so it never got out of hand. Several couples mentioned that almost daily they engaged in negotiation and discussion regarding who would assume responsibility for the various family chores that would come up that day. By careful planning they were able to save considerable time while also assuring that chores got done. The two couples with the oldest children had encouraged their offspring to take care of themselves to a great extent (e.g., wash their own clothes) and to assume regular responsibility for some household chores.

Several couples mentioned that they tried to cut down on their jobs' interference with family life by segregating the two as much as possible. Both husbands and wives tried not to bring work home and tried to reserve weekends and evenings for family activities. It was not clear whether role-sharing put these individuals at a real career disadvantage, although some observers have suggested that it would (Hunt & Hunt, 1977). Many of the role-sharers in the study were noticeably productive in their fields, so perhaps a role-sharing lifestyle contains some compensations that allow an individual to do well at a career (e.g., interaction with spouse on professional matters, more efficient time-use).

CONCLUSION

The problems and pitfalls experienced by the role-sharers in this study suggest that role-sharing is a lifestyle demanding the wholeheartedly and enthusiastic willingness of both spouses to participate. Both partners have to take into account each other's job and leisure activities when planning things that impinge on each other. For these couples, this kind of commitment to role-sharing seemed to derive from the expectation that the arrangement would produce benefits for both spouses which would outweigh the costs of implementing a new style of marriage.

REFERENCES

Glaser, B.G., and A.L. Strauss. *The Discovery of Grounded Theory: Strategies for Qualitative Research*. Chicago: Aldine, 1967.

Hunt, J., and L. Hunt. Dilemmas and contradictions of status: The case of the dual-career family. *Social Problems*, 1977, **24**, 404–416.

Szalai, A. *The Use of Time*. Paris: Mouton, 1972.

SECTION 10

Sex and Marriage

AN ESSENTIAL PART OF MARRIAGE is marital sex. Before marriage, sexual relations may have been tabooed, slightly approved, highly approved, or any combination of the preceding, depending on who was reacting to the fact of premarital sex. It may or may not have been part of the individual's life before marriage, depending upon choices the person made based upon his or her morality and the circumstances he or she confronted. But after marriage there is no choice. Marriage, by the definition imposed upon it and by common assumptions around the world regarding its meaning, entails sexual relations. (To be technically correct, there are groups that do not connect sex and marriage, such as the Nayars of Malabar, who marry their prepubic daughters to a stranger, have a divorce ceremony a few days after the wedding ceremony, allow the divorced women to have lovers, by whom they give birth to children, but never allow the husband to touch the wife, neither before nor after the wedding.)

In almost all cultures, however, marriage and sex are connected, and adjusting to the world of marriage includes coming to grips with marital sexuality. One of the major reasons people marry centers around sex. Not many people marry only for sex but, at the same time, not many people marry without expecting sexual relations to be a part of their lives.

In one form or another our sex-role learning centers around sexuality. Through our association with peers and other groups important to us, each of us learns basic orientations toward the opposite sex. What we learn during our premarital life may help ease our marital adjustment, or it may create difficulties for us. In any event, when it comes time for marriage, what we have learned from our reference groups must be modified in the light of our marital experience.

A major component in the background of each individual is social class. "Social class" is a shorthand term used by social scientists to refer to a combination of factors: the amount of education one has, one's income, and the prestige of the job at which one works. The significance of this term is that it represents contrasting worlds of social experiences.

Social class is an important factor in marriage. First of all, it provides different constraints for people. Material situations differ radically among social classes, and this either closes or opens certain opportunities. For example, if marital stress becomes too great the rich can fly to Acapulco and "get away from it for a while," but in a similar situation the poor cannot afford even their local Hotel Fleabag for a night.

Besides such gross differences, social class also affects basic orientations toward life. How one thinks, perceives, and evaluates what is good and worthwhile are dependent to a great degree upon one's social class. Included in this orientational and evaluative function of social class are basic ideas of what one can reasonably expect from people.

Since they are quite different in the various social classes, these backgrounds also provide contrasting roles for the husband and wife. As such, they greatly determine what someone will expect from his or her marital partner. These expectations, in turn, help determine how one will act toward one's own spouse.

As we covered in previous introductions, one's sex role is also vitally significant in determining one's orientations and actions. We need not repeat the particulars here, but we now can build on those ideas. It is especially useful to tie sex role socialization in with social class.

It is first of all very important to keep in mind that what a married (or unmarried for that matter) couple does sexually is not so much biologically determined as it is the consequence of years and years of socialization. Consequently, both gender and social class play a significant role in human sexual behavior, including marital sexuality.

Indeed, socialization into social class and sex roles creates contrasting approaches to marital sexuality. For example, in general, middle-class females are more open sexually (such as being willing to experiment with sexual variations) and expect to receive more satisfaction from sex than lower-class females, who tend to be less demanding of sexual satisfaction for themselves and more resigned to sex as a duty rather than a pleasure. In contrast, lower- and middle-class men . . . perhaps a table might illustrate this and related ideas better. (See Table 1.)

Orientation to Marital Sex on the Basis of Social Class and Gender

Orientation	Females		Males	
	Lower Class	Middle Class	Lower Class	Middle Class
Open to sexual experimentation	Low	Medium	High	High
Demands own satisfaction first	Low	Medium	High	Medium
Idea that sex is a woman's duty	High	Medium	High	Medium
Idea that sex is for pleasure	Medium	High	High	High
Expects the self to experience orgasm	Low	Medium	High	High
Expects the spouse to experience orgasm	High	High	Medium	High

The terms "high," "medium," and "low" are admittedly vague, but they are not meant to fix hard and fast lines, simply to represent differing orientations. Such basic orientations as shown on this table (and many, many other differences) do differ by social class and gender, and that is the point. While not all sociologists would agree with all the classifications I have made—for what "high," "medium," or "low" is in a given case is quite subjective—these classifications are based on fairly consistent findings over the years by researchers in the sociology of sex.

From this table it should be apparent that males and females reflect differing basic orientations on fundamental assumptions about sexual behavior. Consequently, marital sexuality, a source of physical and emotional pleasure, can also present frustrations and dashed hopes. More positively put, the differences in orientation present challenges around which to work out a mutual adjustment. And that, in fact, is what a good deal of marital sexuality actually is—an ongoing, mutual adaptation to one another's needs and feelings.

From the table you can also note that the differences are greater between lower-class males and females than they are between middle-class males and females. This may be one additional reason (among the many, including especially their greater financial stress) that marriages are more likely to break up among lower-class Americans.

The chapters in this section, then, place the focus on marital sexuality. William H. Masters and Virginia E. Johnson look at marital sex as a bonding that occurs between a husband and wife because of their mutual commitment to give the other physical and emotional pleasure within the context of commitment, caring, and appreciation. Cathy Stein Greenblat then documents the frequency of marital sex, as well as its general decline after the first year of marriage. Ellen Frank and Carol Anderson conclude this section by looking at sexuality in the early, middle, and later stages of marriage.

To apply this material, think about your own expectations of sexual relations in marriage. From where did you get them? To what degree do you think they are related to your social class? To your sex? How might these expectations have differed if you had been raised in a different social class? How do you think they would differ if you were a member of the opposite sex? How might they have differed if you had been brought up in a different culture? To what degree do you think your expectations are similar to or dissimilar from those of your same-sexed friends? How do you think your expectations of marital sexuality might differ from those held by your husband or wife? To what do you attribute these differences and similarities?

CHAPTER 35

The Pleasure Bond: A New Look at Sexuality

William H. Masters / Virginia E. Johnson

ABSTRACT: The bond of marriage is the giving of pleasure within the framework of commitment and caring. The circle of commitment is: being together provides mutual pleasure, which leads the couple to want to stay together and to guard their relationship as a source of pleasure. In short, the couple becomes committed to one another on the basis of the pleasure they provide each other, and the bases of that pleasure are appreciation of the other as a unique individual and a validation of the sexual self. A couple's commitment to mutual concern—appreciation, understanding, caring, and pleasure—however, often changes to a commitment of obligation, the achieving of goals. This causes emotional "disinvolvement." To keep marriage emotionally rewarding requires total commitment of each to the other, in which feelings of loving concern provide the bond that overcomes the commitment of obligation.

DONNA ROSS: In this marriage I feel that I am a totally free human being. I am me all the way. In my first marriage . . . I didn't really know myself and I couldn't even express my feelings. . . .

BILL MASTERS: How is your second marriage different, sexually, from your first?

DONNA ROSS: [In] my first marriage . . . even though sex wasn't satisfying, I didn't know anything else was possible. Or I just felt that maybe it was me, that I was inadequate. But our marriage [now] is a whole new different kind of thing. . . . I'm much less inhibited than I was because I'm much more trustful. . . .

TONY ROSS: We've gone through terrible emotional crises together, and sometimes—maybe because we felt the need to be close or to reassure each other—it leads to sex.

DONNA ROSS: A comforting, a closeness, an intimacy kind of thing.

A commitment is a pledge to do something. One person tells another, "I promise," and the promise is kept, the obligation fulfilled. Trust has been asked for; trust has been given; and trust has been repaid.

This is the basic meaning of commitment. It is the cement that binds individuals and groups together. Without the ability of one person to rely upon another, the social bond could not exist. Even a legal contract depends, in the final analysis, on the keeping of a pledge. For if a contract is broken, the commitment not kept, the law can penalize the person who failed to perform as he had promised, but penalizing him leaves the obligation unfulfilled, the job undone, the need unmet.

That is all there is to commitment insofar as it relates to associations that exist for practical purposes. When the association is for emotional reasons, however, the meaning of commitment changes. It can still be defined as a pledge to do something, but the pledge possesses a radically different dimension. "I promise," one person tells another, "because I care about you."

Caring—which is defined as paying attention, being concerned, solicitous and protective—flows from two related but different kinds of feelings. One is a feeling of being *responsive to* someone, of *caring for* that person; the other is a feeling of being *responsible for* someone, of wanting to *take care of* him or her. These feelings are generated in entirely different ways. Responsiveness occurs spontaneously, before the mind is consciously aware of what is happening—a sudden surge of interest and attraction, triggered by another person's physical presence. Responsibility is consciously, though often unwillingly, invoked by the mind—an acknowledgment of obligation.

Most human beings experience these elemental feelings when holding an infant. This combination of emotions, this interaction in which each caring impulse reinforces the other—a wish to take care of someone for whom one cares—creates an overpowering sense of involvement and identification, of oneness. Some people call it love, and it is the original source of commitment.

As such, however, it is still a one-sided commitment, one person pledging himself to another, who may not even realize that a commitment has been made. Obviously this is true of the infant and its parents; there is nothing mutual about the bond. The responsiveness and sense of responsibility exist entirely within the parents. They are committed; the baby is dependent.

Before too long, however, emotionally mature parents stop identifying with their child in such a total way. Gradually they accept it as a separate human being whose needs are not only different from their own but often in conflict with their immediate desires. Thus long before parent and child are equals in any sense of the word, each needs something of the other: acceptance, appreciation, affection. And the smallest child soon learns that his parents hope to receive from him precisely what he expects from them—pleasure. *Mutual pleasure sets a seal on emotional commitment.*

This is the foundation on which all future affectionate relationships will be constructed. The search for pleasure—and pleasure is an infinitely deeper and more complex emotional matter than simply sensual gratification—continues throughout life. The quality of marriage is determined by whether the pleasure derived exceeds the inevitable portion of displeasure that human beings must experience in all their associations. When there is more displeasure than pleasure in a marriage, a husband and wife are more aware of the obligations of marriage than they are of its rewards. It may clarify the subject if their bond is characterized as a commitment of obligation.

In contrast, there is the commitment of concern, a bond in which a man and a woman mutually meet their obligations not because they feel *compelled* to but because they feel *impelled* to do so. They do so in response to impulses, desires and convictions that are deeply rooted within themselves, not all of which do they fully understand. When they act in each other's best interests, even though this may at the time be in conflict with their own immediate wishes, they are saying to each other, in effect: "I care very much about your feelings—because your feelings affect mine. Your happiness adds to mine, your unhappiness takes away from my happiness, and I want to be happy."

So obvious does all this seem to most young couples that they believe that they know all that there is to know—or certainly all that they need to know—about how and why being committed to each other is linked to sexual pleasure. They met as two strangers and eventually became lovers, and because this is how life is expected to move, they accept it as a natural sequence of events. They do not reflect on how it actually happened; to them, it seems a matter of elementary logic: love leads to sex, which leads to greater love, which in turn leads to better sex—and so it goes. This, at least, is how they expect it to be, and if it turns out otherwise, they have convenient explanations: insufficient love, inadequate sex. It is as simple as a-b-c. Like the alphabet, however, it does not mean much by itself.

In a more reflective mood, they might say: "Since we enjoy being together, the greater our enjoyment, the more reason we have to stay together." They are describing the circle of commitment. Being together gives them satisfactions, including sex, that reinforce their decision to live together as a couple; these satisfactions, which are highly valued, must be safeguarded. Each partner, to protect his or her own happiness, tries to sustain the other partner's happiness so that their relationship will flourish; and these reciprocal efforts intensify the satisfactions they find in living together—which further strengthen their wish to remain a couple. *They live according to the commitment of mutual concern, and pleasure is the bond between them.*

They expect to be faithful because they want to be. Furthermore they realize that if either or both of them must seek sexual satisfaction with other partners, the circle of commitment will have been broken. The more satisfactions they find with other people, the fewer satisfactions do they need from each other; and the less they need from each other, the easier it is for them to go their separate ways. Beyond all rationalization, extramarital affairs would demonstrate two things: first, that they were incapable of meeting each other's most basic physical and emotional needs, and second, that they did not consider each other unique, and therefore irreplaceable, sources of satisfaction and pleasure.

Just as no one stops to think about what is required for him to breathe until he has trouble breathing, so couples give little thought to what is needed for their happiness to continue—until the day they discover that theirs is no longer a happy marriage. Unaware of what nurtured their relationship in the first place, they have unwittingly deprived it of precisely the emotional rewards that were necessary for it to flourish. Then, to the extent that they never really understood what united them as lovers, they find it difficult to understand what has made them strangers once again. It seems as though the movie of their life has been put in reverse.

If their life together had actually been filmed and could now be reviewed, they might better appreciate some things that, in the beginning of their relationship, greatly contributed to their satisfaction in being in each other's company. There was, for example, the simple fact of acceptance. The need to be recognized and accepted as a unique individual, to have an emotional identity as specific and singular as one's fingerprints, is crucial to an intimate relationship. Its contribution to self-esteem is well established, and it plays a significant part in sexual responsiveness. The more confident a man and woman become that each perceives and values the uniqueness of the other, the more likely they are to be drawn together.

This is particularly important in the beginning of a sexual relationship. What is needed is not simply to be admired or desired, vitally important though that is, but to be confirmed as a sexual person. It is comparatively simple, after all, for anyone to establish the extent to which his personality seems to appeal to other people; there is ample opportunity in the normal course of daily events to observe how people respond. But a person's sexuality, which is just one dimension of personality, is more difficult to assay. It finds its fullest expression in a mutually appreciated physical relationship, which, even among emancipated men and women, doesn't happen often.

In one lifetime, therefore, most men and women will have few reflections of themselves as sexual beings. Consequently, each relationship carries the potentiality of exerting a powerful emotional effect, for better or for worse. In every encounter, no matter how absorbed both partners may be in their own physical and emotional responses, they remain distinctly conscious of the other person's reactions. In part, this reflects concern for the partner: was it good? And in part, it reflects uncertainty about one's self: was I good?

This is one of the satisfactions that all couples seek in their relationships—a validation of their sexual selves. Each hopes to find mirrored in the eyes of the other an image of himself or of herself as a sexually desirable person. This appreciation that they seek—which will free them to appreciate themselves with some security—is paradoxical in nature. On one level, a man wants to be reassured that he is like other men; the woman, that she is like other women. There is a sense of sexual universality that they want to share, and this can come to them only through cross-sex appreciation, a comparatively nonspecific response by which males and females mutually confirm each other's biological nature.

Beyond that, however, lies a need to differentiate themselves from the others of their sex, a wish to be appreciated in an entirely specific way as unique individuals. The lasting satisfaction that comes from having one's individuality recognized and esteemed can hardly be overestimated. It is among the most powerful of all human motivations and it figures significantly in every aspect of life. Such recognition of individuality for most people comes best from a successfully sustained sexual relationship. In the intimacy of a sustained sexual relationship, few things matter more to both partners than to be perceived as the individuals they are. Indeed, it is perception that makes mutual, sustained pleasure possible.

To make an emotional commitment to someone is to be on his or her side, a steadfast ally; it is essentially an expression of loyalty. This is what most people have in mind when they speak of commitments; to some extent, commitments involve obligations and responsibilities but they are obligations that have been voluntarily chosen.

When a man and woman marry, they do so believing that as a couple they can improve their chances of increasing the satisfactions that make life worth living. They are confident that the pleasures they have experienced in the past will increase as a consequence of their formal commitment. Unfortunately, what usually happens, through no fault of their own, is that they begin to think of themselves not as two individuals who have the capacity to enhance each other's joy in being alive and who therefore feel committed to each other, but as a couple mutually committed to tasks they must complete. They feel that they must establish a new life pattern, and they find themselves with new needs, facing new problems, and obliged to establish new priorities. They want to make money, to advance in their careers, to set up a home or become socially established, and, sooner or later, to have children. These are all reasonable and praiseworthy goals—but secondary in importance to their original commitment: the mutual need to flourish as individuals in the climate of pleasure that each afforded the other.

Of course, it is true that there are people who marry in order to accomplish specific objectives, and for them it is not too important if their personal relationship also becomes businesslike in character. But they are surely in the minority. Generally, when couples discover, after a period of time, that they are acting more as business partners than married lovers, it comes as a bit of a shock and usually with considerable regret. Rarely do they understand what is happening. They have forgotten that before their marriage they were two people who tried to be together as much as they could because they found comfort and security in each other's acceptance, appreciation, and understanding. This was the commitment of mutual concern. With marriage, however, they became husbands and wives, individuals who expected to take care of specialized responsibilities and who increasingly followed separate paths if their day's work was to be done. They slowly became emotionally uncommitted—and were left with the commitment of obligation.

Commitment to goals of achievement preempted the commitment to one another. All the forces that brought them together as a man and a woman were now losing intensity. Instead of being joined as a male and a female who could give each other support and pleasure, they now played the roles of husband and wife, or mother and father, who must separately struggle with onerous obligations. And because they were less directly involved in each other's lives, each partner experienced the "disinvolvement" as being less cared for, less valued, less desired.

This is one of the main reasons why sex grows unsatisfactory. In the early years of their relationship, both before marriage and probably for some time afterward, their lovemaking would occur at the end of a day during which, for a few hours at least, they had been closely involved. Intercourse then expressed the feelings that had been accumulating all the while they were enjoying other aspects of their life together. Thus they were prepared to give each other pleasure and to find pleasure in each other's embrace; it was the culmination of all their prior emotional interaction.

But after years of marriage, sex becomes a postscript tacked on at the end of the day. Having had little opportunity to spend time together and little to say beyond discussing their separate obligations, they meet in bed and expect to turn on passion as though with an electric switch. It is hardly surprising, under these circumstances, that sex, which earlier in marriage was one of the strongest forces drawing them together may later be experienced as an obligation that, at least to one of them, seems close to being an imposition. Instead of uniting them, sex separates them.

Such changes are not always attributable to the fact that a husband and wife have devoted their energies to other goals that they consider more important than their intimate relationship. Frequently the deterioration of the sexual bond stems from the couple's lack of a secure sense of themselves as sexual beings. The insecurity may stem from negative sexual attitudes and early repressions, from unfortunate sexual experiences, or simply from a lack of sexual information. They remain insecure with their own sexuality.

In the beginning of their relationship, this inadequacy may go unremarked because the earliest sexual encounters generally—although certainly not always—prove stimulating enough to propel them into a sexual union. One naked body touching another is, after all, sufficient to generate a powerful drive that can carry both individuals past inhibitions that might otherwise deprive sex of any real satisfaction.

Even if this were not the case, however, some lack of satisfaction in their early encounters would be what any two inexperienced individuals might anticipate. If they do have problems, they would consider this only natural since either one, or both, may have had little chance to learn what sex is all about. They believe that time alone will overcome their difficulties and allowances are made for their lack of responsiveness. Of course, the concept that time together will increase low levels of sexual response frequently proves correct, particularly for committed couples.

There is no particular reason for a newly committed couple to doubt that in time, and with each of them fully supporting the other in a commitment that is secure enough to allow them to be vulnerable without fear, they will become fully functional sexual beings. They usually will become responsive *if* they have some concept of what it means to be a sexual person. It means more than just the acceptance of male or female identity.

Being a sexual person means being responsive to one's sexual feelings—that is, being conscious of spontaneous sexual impulses generated within the body, accepting them as natural, healthy, and "good," enjoying them without shame or guilt and permitting them to build up into the tensions that then require some sort of release. It means being responsible for the satisfaction of one's sexual feelings—that is, actively reaching out for ways to achieve that release, whether through masturbation, intercourse, or any mutually acceptable caress that couples exchange. And, finally, it means deriving pleasure not only from released tension and from sensual gratification but from the total experience as an affirmation of one's sexual nature. Only with security in these feelings about one's self, is it possible to pursue sexual pleasure as an active goal with one's partner, to be committed to sex as a couple.

Just as the willingness of a man and a woman to reveal themselves to each other and to become vulnerable brings them closer together, so their unwillingness to be vulnerable leads them *not* to reveal themselves and to become uncommitted. A natural sense of self-protection takes over. In learning not to be vulnerable with each other, a married couple is usually reenacting a scenario that was originally written during childhood years. When these individuals marry, they frequently find it all too easy to react to conflict by what might be described as a conditioned emotional reflex—the deadening of feelings. With their marriage partners, as they probably did with their parents, they hide behind defensive barriers. In time, their partners, too, become guarded, if not equally defensive. In such cases, the husband has not committed himself to his wife and she has not committed herself to him. Neither is willing to be emotionally vulnerable. They may depend on each other but they do not entrust themselves to each other. They are partners, not mates, in a mutual venture in which both are willing to invest time and effort and from which both hope to profit. Thus, for the sake of clarity, their marriage might more appropriately be described as an investment that they share—in truth, a relatively sterile form of mutual commitment.

In successful marriages of this kind, the husband and wife manage to accommodate each other in what amounts to a working partnership, an arrangement that allows them to get the major jobs done without too much emotional stress. Because their commitment is governed by reason and practical considerations rather than by emotion, their feelings are generally low-keyed. The bond between them may be primarily one of toleration, each respecting what the other contributes to their common enterprise rather than exploring and enjoying the nature of their personalities. Or they may even appreicate each other's individuality and share the kind of affection that reflects a sense of comfort with familiar things.

Either way, they relate to each other much as they do to the telephone company. They pay whatever price is required for service to continue—for the house to be cleaned, meals prepared, children cared for, bills paid, possessions purchased, entertainment provided, and, when either partner chooses, for sexual relations. They attend to each other's needs to the best of their ability but passion is something they must go to the movies to see.

To the extent that each fulfills his or her obligations, their marriage survives. Sexual pleasure, if it ever existed, does not survive for long. Sex becomes perfunctory at best; more often it is either dull, dormant or dead. In many such cases the husband and wife live essentially celibate lives—at least, within the marriage.

The ability of a man and woman to become sexually committed stands or falls primarily on their willingness to give and receive pleasure in all its forms. But this is not the willingness that reflects an application of will power, which says more of deliberation, discipline, and obligation than of desire. It is the willingness that flows from wishing or wanting something, of caring for someone, when the mind serves only as a catalyst and the body asserts itself in ways that the mind may not have anticipated.

Giving and getting pleasure does not mean bartering favors. It involves a mutuality, a flow of excitement and gratification that shuttles back and forth between the partners who frequently find it impossible to draw a line between the pleasure they are receiving and the pleasure they are giving. It is the same as it is with a kiss—only if a man and woman are *not* caught up in the kiss will either one be aware of the physical separateness of their lips.

If a man and woman are committed to the enjoyment of their own sexual natures and to each other as sexual persons, intercourse allows them to express their emotions in whatever ways seem desirable and appropriate at the moment, revealing themselves not only to each other—but to themselves. By responding freely to the urgencies of their own bodies as well as to the urgings of their partner, their actions embody their feelings. Liberated from the domination of reason and discipline, they are able to communicate spontaneous wishes that need no justification.

This does not mean that every sexual embrace is a transcendent experience. On the contrary, precisely because both partners are under no pressure to perform or pretend, any sexual embrace can be as casual as a good-night kiss, if that is what both partners want or if it is what one of them needs and the other is pleased and privileged to provide. Moreover, in such a relaxed atmosphere, each has earned emotional credit in the other's bank. If, as it occasionally must, sex proves unsatisfactory or disappointing or even frustrating to either husband or wife, their security as a committed couple lies in knowing that there is always a tomorrow.

Total commitment, in which all sense of obligation is linked to mutual feelings of loving concern, sustains a couple sexually over the years. In the beginning, it frees them to explore the hidden dimensions of their sexual natures, playing with sex as pastime and passion, seeking the erotic pleasures that give life much of its meaning. Then, when carrying the inescapable burdens that come with a family and maturity, they can turn to each other for the physical comforting and emotional sustenance they need to withstand economic and social pressures that often threaten to drain life of all joy. Finally, in their later years, it is in the enduring satisfactions of their sexual and emotional bond that committed husbands and wives find reason enough to be glad that they still have another day together.

CHAPTER 36

Sexuality in the Early Years of Marriage

Cathy Stein Greenblat

Abstract: When asked how often they have sexual intercourse during their marriages, both in the early and the later years, the numbers the couples reported showed a wide range of frequency. Consequently, averages are misleading. Most couples (69 percent) report a decline in frequency after the first year of marriage, while only 6 percent report an increase. The decline appears to be related to pressing factors in life, including children, jobs, commuting, housework, finances, and familiarity.

[We] know every little about how [the frequency of sexual intercourse is] set in the early years of marriage or what the meaning and importance of sex is in those early years. In addition, it is unclear why the decline in frequency with age takes place. In particular, we do not know if it is really an *age-related* phenomenon or an example of a confounding of age effects and duration-of-marriage effects. That is, it may be that what is really evidenced is an outcome not of increased age but rather of longer times with the same partner. If people marry or remarry at "later ages," for example, are their rates similar to those of their age peers or duration-of-marriage peers? . . . The material presented here represents one . . . attempt to explicate the processes of rate-setting in the early years of marriage and to suggest how and why the decline is set in motion.

METHODS

Troubled by some of the anomalies discussed above, I included some questions about sex in a larger study of emotional relationships in the early years of marriage. The study was exploratory rather than hypothesis-testing, and sexual activity and attitudes were examined only insofar as they shed light on the more general questions of interest in the factors that shape and are shaped by the expressive dimensions of marriage.

A subcontract was let to Opinion Research Corporation of Princeton, New Jersey, for the random-digit dialing (cf., Dillman, 1978) of telephone numbers in the telephone area of New Brunswick, New Jersey—an eight-community area. With this procedure, names, addresses, and telephone numbers for 97 persons (41 males and 56 females) who were married five years or less were obtained. . . .

In-depth, structured interviews with open-ended questions were conducted with 30 males and 50 females (not married to one another). They ranged from two hours to five hours in length, averaging about two hours and 45 minutes, and were tape-recorded. Most interviews were conducted in the respondents' homes when the spouses were not present; a few were done at our offices at the university. . . .

FREQUENCY AND CHANGE IN FREQUENCY

The most striking finding concerning the frequency of intercourse during the first year of marriage is the wide *range* of responses. The men reported monthly frequencies from 1 to 43, while the women's reports ranged from 2 to 45. This is not an instance of a few aberrant cases creating a picture belied by the bulk of the cases; rather, the responses are widely scattered through the range. The two sets of reports are fairly similar: wide ranges, similar means, high standard deviations, and similar medians, as seen in [Table 36.1].

No differences in first-year marital coitus rates were reported by those married different amounts of time at the moment the interview was conducted. That is, there appear to be no serious errors of inflation or deflation in the retrospective reports when these are compared to reports of those still in the first year and thus giving current rates. . . .

In examining the intercourse rates after the first year, the striking finding is the degree of decline in frequency of intercourse. . . . [Table 36.2] summarizes the decline. . . .

Both first-year and current rates were available for 62 persons who had been married for more than one year. The current frequency was

TABLE 36.1 Frequency of Intercourse in the First Year of Marriage

Distributions	Men	Women
1–4 times/month	2	4
5–8 times/month	5	10
9–12 times/month	9	10
13–16 times/month	3	9
17–20 times/month	6	8
21–24 times/month	0	4
25–29 times/month	0	1
30 or more times/month	3	2

	Range	Mean	SD	Median
Men's reports (*N* = 28)	1–43	14.43	8.96	12.0
Women's reports (*N* = 48)	2–45	13.81	8.44	12.5

divided by the first-year frequency for each of them, yielding a percentage. This revealed that: (a) 6% reported current rates *higher* than their first-year rates; (b) 24% reported current rates *the same* as their first-year rates; (c) 32% reported rates from *60%–99%* of their first-year rates; and (d) 37% reported rates of *less than 60%* of their first-year rates (including 6% for whom the rates were less than 30% of the first-year rates). Men's and women's distributions were similar. . . .

Interpretation and Discussion

[Findings show] that the frequency of intercourse in the first year of marriage is highly variable, ranging from once a month for some couples to 45 times a month for others. Furthermore, there appears to be little relationship between the frequency of early marital coitus and other social characteristics of the respondent or couple. Knowing such things about a newlywed as age, education, whether he or she has been married before, religious preference, and degree of prior sexual experience

TABLE 36.2 Frequency of Intercourse Per Month, by Years Married

Years Married	*N*	Mean Frequency	Range
1	12	14.8	4–45
2	10	12.2	3–20
3	19	11.9	2–18
4	7	9.0	4–23
5	18	9.7	5–18
6	8	6.3	2–15

does not help much to predict the frequency of marital intercourse in the first year.

In some ways this is not surprising. Indeed, while the premarital sexual world is replete with proscriptions and prescriptions, there is little to guide the newlywed couple in how to develop a sexual pattern. Few people are aware of the findings of that handful of research studies that describe what is the "typical" frequency. Bridal magazines and guides, premarital counseling, and sex manuals may endorse the idea that marital sex is important and may offer suggestions about good sexual technique and/or etiquette, but none of them say anything about how *often* to do it! Finally, few people talk with others to obtain the personal advice that on other topics is so abundant (or overabundant) as the nuptials approach (Greenblat and Cottle, 1981). In short, the marital sex domain has few cultural norms.

Furthermore, most people experience considerable difficulty *discussing* their sexual desires, preferences, and behaviors, even with those persons with whom they are most intimate, emotionally and physically (Gagnon, 1977). What these data suggest, then, is that the initial rates are set fairly idiosyncratically by each couple, through a relatively mute or, at least, indirect communication/negotiation process.

While there was not a steady, clear pattern of decline from year to year, far fewer persons, male or female, reported that they were having intercourse with their spouses more than twice a week at the present time. While approximately 75% had reported such rates for the first year, only 40% reported such current frequencies. Once more, there is considerable variation in the reports, which ranged from once a month to 20–25 times a month; again, little of the variance is explained by respondents' social characteristics. Rather, the best predictor of frequency in years 2–6 proved to be frequency in the first year.

It appears, then, that a pattern (or habit) is set in the first year. From then on almost everything—children, jobs, commuting, housework, financial worries—that happens to a couple conspires to *reduce* the degree of sexual interaction, while almost nothing leads to increasing it. Thus, some couples with children have high rates while others have low rates; but most couples who have children will experience a *decline* in the frequency of intercourse. They are not likely to know whether their initial rates or their current rates are high or low in comparison to others, nor are they likely to realize that others *without* children are also experiencing a decline in the frequency of intercourse. Instead, for them as for most persons, their own prior experience represents the only known and relevant comparison. Even if they might fall into the "high" category compared to others, they are unlikely to know this; they do know that sex between them is less frequent than it used to be. A self-explanation is required; and in this case, an explanation to an outsider also was requested, as seen in the next section.

ACCOUNTS OF CHANGES IN MARITAL COITAL RATES

Respondents' Accounts

What do the respondents themselves report about the changes (or lack of changes) in coital frequency? As indicated, there were only four cases in which respondents indicated that the frequency of intercourse had *increased* from the first year. In one case the couple had decided that they now wanted to have children, and the procreative character of the act changed its meaning to the wife. Another respondent who reported an increase was very unhappy in his marriage from its start, having married someone his family approved of rather than a woman he loved. He reported intercourse once a month in the first year. Now, feeling even more trapped in the marriage, he drinks a great deal, comes home drunk a few times a week, and reports intercourse about twice a week. The other two respondents indicated they now had *fewer* external obligations and more relaxed time together; this permitted more frequent sexual relations.

Fifteen respondents reported that the current frequency was the same as that of the first year. In response to the question of why there had been no decline, four types of reasons were offered: habit; deliberate effort to maintain the frequency; the absence of negative factors in their lives which would decrease it; and finally, the positive values they see in their sexual relationship. . . .

Those responses considered to represent "habit" were offered largely by those who had lived together prior to marriage. Their statements included: "It declined before we were married" (F); "it declined while we were living together" (F); "we settled into a routine" (M); and "we established a pattern before we were married, and marriage didn't change much of our lives" (M).

One respondent spoke of the couple's deliberate efforts to maintain the early rates, inspired by the sickness of a friend:

> We went through a couple of months where it was lower, about once a week; and then one of Dave's friends went into shock after having her third child. Her pituitary gland collapsed and she had no desire for sex at all. It was a one in a million type thing that happened and I don't know if it's temporary or not—she's still having tests. But it's been hard on her husband because it's a once a month thing now. And that made Dave and me definitely more aware of each other and about showing our love physically.

Several people saw their constant rates as being the result of the absence of those elements that they believe lead to declines: "There's been no friction between us" (M); "we eased into marriage and things have been smooth since then" (M); "in the beginning we had so many pressures from life, and if anything they've eased up in the last few years."

The most frequent type of response dealt with positive elements of their sex lives: "It's a way of expressing your love" (F); "we have a relaxed feeling about it" (F); he's a good man with a lot of sexual needs; he's a good lover, and I enjoy it" (F); . . . and "we still have a need for each other--it's a way of expressing our love—it's fun and we enjoy it" (M).

One additional response must be noted here. Although it was the lone one of its sort from someone whose rates had stayed the same, it is strongly echoed in the interpretations of those whose rates have declined. This woman noted that their rates had stayed the same because "we didn't start as sex maniacs!" In other words, by not having "overdone it" at first, they were able to avoid the typical decline!

Far more common, of course, were responses to the question about decline. . . . Again, the responses fell into four major categories: birth-control and pregnancy-related reasons; children; work; and familiarity (including settling into a routine). A few responses did not fit into one of these categories, including three persons who reported medical problems or medication which affected sexual desire or behavior, one person whose husband's views of sex and religion became more powerful in the intervening years; and one person who reported that phone interruptions were now more common and prevented spontaneity!

The birth-control and pregnancy-related responses were given almost exclusively by the women. Two men referred to their wives' current pregnancies as reasons current rates were low, and two women reported the same thing. In general, however, the women's responses in this category were more varied: "The pill ruined my desire"; "I wasn't interested for a while after the pregnancy, and he got used to it less often"; "I had an undesired pregnancy and froze after that; first we abstained for six months, and then we did it a little—and I got pregnant *again*!"; "I was afraid of getting pregnant and couldn't discuss it"; "I had an abortion, and that lowered my trust in him in general."

Children were reported as directly responsible for declines in coital frequency by several men and women. Some just said "the kids!" assuming that was self-explanatory. Others who said "fatigue" connected that statement to child-care tasks (while others connected it to labor-force work); and some pointed to particular elements of the parental role: "Our kid hasn't slept through the night for 16 months . . . " (F); "our child doesn't take naps anymore" (M). One woman explained why the presence of children affected their sex lives as follows:

> Our sex life is still good because for me it's the same as for him—we enjoy sex together and we can express ourselves without any inhibitions, and we're comfortable. There's no problem there. Also, it's not just that we're going to bed, you know—it's that we're making love, and that's a big thing. But we don't like to just jump into it, and we don't just do it and that's it, go to sleep—we'll watch TV and take our time saying good night after. But it's

hard because with kids you have to get up a lot and you can't just relax and enjoy it. . . .

Work responsibilities, long hours, and the resulting fatigue were also common responses. People reported that one or both had new jobs with heavy work schedules; some couples had opposite work hours (i.e., he works a night shift, and she works days); some men were working two jobs to pay for child-related or housing expenses; some people had long commutes or traveled extensively, reducing the amount of time they had together. In general, these respondents reported that their schedules were far busier now than when they were first married, with both being active at home, at work, on in a range of activities. Thus, many others, having earlier described these enterprises just said "fatigue" or "not enough energy when everything I have to do is done" or "exhaustion," clearly tying this state to work-related demands. Some were more specific, making it clear that it was work that caused the reduction, as in the case of the woman who said:

> Tiredness. When he comes home he's exhausted. He just goes from 8:00 in the morning till 10:00 at night, and it's not fair for me to say "All right, let's go!" He needs his sleep. . . .

The male who reported the highest first-year rates (40-45 times a month) said his current frequency was 20-25—about half—but then explained:

> It's because of my job. As far as an overall picture, as far as whether it's still satisfying or still exciting, it pretty much is. I know what you're talking about—I have friends, and these guys tell me, "Forget it—after the first year the honeymoon's over," But it's really not like that for us. It's pretty good. I'm only going by what I know, but I have friends who tell me they go home and they're tough out of luck, whereas with me, even if my wife is tired and she doesn't want to, she still will to keep me happy. It's that kind of a deal. So it's job related, or we wouldn't be too far off the first year. And she likes it better now, too, because she's gotten over her hesitation; and before I was getting the best part of the deal, but now it's improved for her. . . .

The most common responses, however, were those that referred in one way or another to familiarity and availability. Sometimes these were said with a negative cast, sometimes neutral, and sometimes positive. The negative tones were found almost exclusively in the men's responses. For example: "We're not together as much, so our moods aren't as similar, as synchronized"; "we've gotten into a routine with each other and it's not as exciting any more"; "it's like a routine"; "that's as much as she wants and will give now"; "familiarity—the spark isn't as big." A woman gave a similar reason: "He spends a lot of nights at the lab and I have more activities, too, like dancing lessons twice a week and what not. We're just busy I guess. When you're first married it's something unique—now it's not."

One man and several women suggested more neutral reasons: "It's easier to admit if you're tired or don't feel like it" (M); "we have options now—he's home every night, so we're together a lot and, thus, we don't have that now-or-never sense" (F); "we're available to each other now—so we can say, if not tonight, tomorrow—and sometimes we do the same thing tomorrow!"(F)

Another set of persons stressed that the decline represented something *positive*. Comments included: "It's better because it's more relaxed" (F); "it's more the quality now than the quantity" (F); "not having it regularly or daily makes it more interesting" (M); "I get a good feeling just being with her in bed, so it's not as important now" (M); "there are other things that satisfy us besides sex: reading to each other, listening to music together . . ." (M). One woman explained it as follows:

> Maybe it's not a necessity anymore. We have other ways of expressing our feelings, and intercourse is one of the ways. When we first got married we thought it was the only way, and now we realize it's not. And the *quality* of our sex life has improved. Now it gives us so much satisfaction, it's not really necessary that we have it every single night. . . .

Finally, one set of these responses must be singled out. A number of people suggested that the reason for the decline was that the first-year rates were artificial—they didn't represent what these people would "normally" do; for at that time sex had a "novelty" element, or they felt pressure to have frequent sex. They responded with such statements as . . .:

> The quantity is probably related to familiarity. It's really nothing new now. I think when you find new things, different things, it tends to be more interesting, and sometimes we do that. But it really depends on the time of the month. Sometimes I feel like I'm horny all the time and twice a day just wouldn't be enough. Other times I think, "Do we really have to do it now? Couldn't we do something else? I'm sure there's something more interesting around!"—that type of feeling. I think, all in all, it's okay the way it is. . . .
>
> Looking back at it now, it seems like it was kind of silly. It was, ah, I don't know, not silly, but it was just like a new toy in a way. The present figure is the more real one. . . .

CONCLUSION: THE RELATIVE IMPORTANCE OF MARITAL SEX

Examining data on frequency of marital intercourse, we have seen that marital sex does not appear to be very important to many people. Despite the highly sex-oriented media and social environment, the frequency of intercourse in these couples, all in the early years of marriage, is not very high. Furthermore, first-year rates are not maintained by most persons, particularly in the face of increased work and parenthood pressures. Others discount the first-year rates as inflations, temporary phenomena.

One might ask, however, do these respondents consider sex to be important? Surely there are other measures of importance than the frequency of intercourse. Near the end of the interviews, respondents were queried about what they thought marriage *should* be like. One question in this section asked how important they thought the sexual aspect of a marital relationship is. A few respondents (15%) indicated that "it depended." The rest of the responses were almost equally split between those that could be classified as "important" and those that could be classified as "very important." Once again, these responses were not related to the frequencies.

People who describe sex as important stressed that there are *other* ways to show love or stressed that closeness, tenderness, love, companionship or affection are more important. Some said they had found that just cuddling or lying together was rewarding and they didn't require the specifically sexual interaction much of the time. [This] sort of sentiment [is] shown in the following quotation:

> I think it's very important, but I don't think its number one or even number three on the list. On my list it would come fourth. Marriage, as far as I'm concerned, is friendship and companionship: that ranks first. Then there's consideration for one another, and then trust and then fourth I'd say your physical relationship. And those three that come before hopefully enhance what you experience in your physical relationship. [F] . . .

Those who said it was "very important" stressed the special character of sex as a form of intimacy or bonding for a husband and wife, as in the following cases:

> I think it's really important. You don't have to do it constantly all the time and hanging from the mirror. You don't have to have that kind of sex life, but you need that physical contact—it brings you closer together. Like when the baby is first born, having his mother holding him is very important; in that way I think that a husband and wife need that contact. They get out their frustrations, and it does bring them closer. [F]

> I think it's very important. It's a form of assurance; it's a form of communication, aside from language. You can communicate with your bodies better than verbally, I believe. It's very important. It's communicating an inner feeling of oneness, I guess, of something shared, of giving, and a willingness to be totally open with each other. [M] . . .

REFERENCES

Dillman, D. A., 1978. Mail and Telephone Surveys: Total Design Method, New York: Wiley.

Gagnon, J. H., 1977. Human Sexualities. Glenview, IL: Scott Foresman.

Greenblat, C. and Cottle, T. J., 1981. Getting Married. New York: McGraw Hill.

CHAPTER 37

The Sexual Stages of Marriage

Ellen Frank / Carol Anderson

ABSTRACT: The authors report on the sexual adjustment of a hundred couples who classify themselves as happily married. During the *early* years of marriage (first five years) sex is frequent and generally satisfying; each spouse feels he or she can please the other. During the *middle* years of marriage (up to twenty years) other parts of life take priority over the sexual relationship, there are problems in maintaining sexual interest in the spouse as well as an increase in sexual dissatisfactions. During the *later* years (twenty or more years) the frequency of intercourse decreases, husbands report a general satisfaction with their sex lives while most wives report dissatisfaction. In general, in all stages of marriage about half of the wives have difficulty achieving orgasm; also in all stages runs the theme that men and women experience sex differently.

Last month two of our good friends got married. It was an ideal type of wedding in many ways—a small knot of close friends huddled expectantly in an imposing Gothic chapel; the bride, serene and lovely in a short chiffon dress; the groom glowing; the minister—a woman—offering sage advice about love, marriage, sexuality, commitment and how all of those fit together.

At the warm, informal reception, when the last glass of champagne had been downed, conversation turned to what sort of life our two friends would have together.

*The authors would like to thank Barbara Duffy Stewart for her research assistance.

Since we've recently been involved in research on marriage sexuality, we wondered what to predict about the sexual relationship of these newlyweds. What would happen to their attraction, interest and performance over the years?

If most of us predicted what would happen to a man's and a woman's sexual adjustment over the course of their marriage, we would probably say that sex would be frequent, fun, but somewhat awkward and unsatisfying in the beginning. Then it would gradually increase in satisfaction over the years as each partner became more aware of the other's needs and more skilled at communicating their own desires. Also, interactional difficulties, such as finding the best kind of foreplay or choosing the right time for sex, would decrease as the couple got to know one another more intimately and learned to read each other's signals. We would also think that, since sex takes two, spouses' periods of dissatisfaction would probably correspond. But it turns out that things are *not* quite so "logical."

When we asked 100 relatively well-educated, middle-class couples whose marriages were "working" to describe their relationships in a number of areas, we were surprised by many of their responses about sexual adjustment.* Here are three findings:

- First, it is clear that men and women are indeed different. Husbands and wives appear to have different sexual attitudes and behaviors that change in different ways during the course of their marriage.
- Second, there is neither a *coordinated* increase nor decrease in the overall satisfaction of a couple over the years of their marriage.
- Third, while sex may be symbolically important throughout a marriage, performance factors are not as important as we once believed.

Now, let's look more closely at the different stages of marriage and the sexual attitudes unique to them, and see as well how the crises of adult life have their impact in the master bedroom.

EARLY MARRIAGE—YEARS OF SATISFACTION

Almost all newlyweds like sex in the beginning. Ninety-one percent of the women and 95% of the men married less than five years describe their sex lives as either satisfying or very satisfying, using words like "excitement," "pleasurable anticipation" and "confidence" when talk-

*The researchers interviewed a hundred couples who consider themselves to be happily married. The couples were predominately white (95 percent), Christian (32 percent Catholic and 47 percent Protestant), and well educated (73 percent of the women and 97 percent of the men had attended college).—Ed.

ing about their sexual relationships. No male in this early-marriage group reports difficulty with erections, and only 24% report premature ejaculation, compared with over 40% of those men married five years or longer. Despite the fact that in most of these new marriages both partners work (78% of the women have a full-time job), they have a relatively high frequency of intercourse. Approximately 18% report a frequency of four to five times a week, over a third report a frequency of two to three times a week, and another third report a frequency of once a week. The major sexual complaint of these couples revolves around the arousal and orgasmic difficulties of the women. But although women in this early period of marriage have as many difficulties becoming excited or reaching orgasm as women married longer (50% of the women in each marriage stage seem to have this problem), the newlyweds are more optimistic, believing that these problems will dissipate with time.

Another interesting finding is that among those newly married, 97% of the women and 90% of the men feel they *know* what pleases their spouses sexually. Fewer individuals in the middle and late periods of marriage express the same confidence. Either a spouse's sexuality becomes a greater enigma over time, or communication becomes more difficult as novelty lessens and other priorities compete for attention. Interestingly, recently married women are likely to report that they feel their [spouses do] not know what pleases *them* sexually. Recently married men (93%), in contrast, feel that their [spouses do] know what pleases *them*. Later on, these trends reverse: More women feel understood while more men do not.

THE MIDDLE YEARS—THE ERA OF DISTRACTIONS

Things seem to fall apart a bit in the middle years, when more husbands and wives report that they are distracted from their sexual relationship with one another. But men and women express this distraction in different ways. Men maintain an interest in sex, but are troubled by attractions to women other than their wives. Women seem to lose interest in sex itself and report that it is more difficult to relax prior to intercourse. Many studies have indicated that women may reach their "sexual peak" in their 30's in terms of their capacity to respond sexually. Yet it does not appear that their life circumstances necessarily foster their enjoyment of that capacity.

At first this seems surprising, since these women apparently have more time to devote to husband and family. Only 39% of them have a full-time job. But these middle years of marriage are also years of child-rearing. The never-ending responsibilities and interruptions of child-caring may be a much greater distraction from sexual pleasure than holding a full-time job.

Also, a woman's working outside the home may contribute to sexual stimulation. Certainly, this stimulation could be related to the increased self-esteem many women derive from a rewarding job. People who feel good about themselves invariably experience greater sexual pleasure.

These middle years are certainly a time in which nonsexual priorities are likely to be higher. The honeymoon is over: Women are devoting their time to child-rearing and men are interested in career advancement. This concentration on children and career also helps explain why, during the middle years of marriage, foreplay becomes more important for both women and men. Yet more than one-third of the men and 40% of the women in this phase of marriage report that there is too little foreplay in their sexual relationship.

Still, like their younger counterparts, individuals in this middle period of marriage are more satisfied than dissatisfied sexually. They, too, use "excitement," "pleasurable anticipation," and confidence" in describing their sexual relationships. However, while only 9% of women in the early phase of marriage and only 4% in the late period report anxiety about their sexual lives, approximately 20% of those in the middle period report such feelings. Women in this group are also more likely than their more recently married counterparts to report fears about their own sexual inadequacy. This worry prevails among the men as well. These fears, however, apparently grow stronger still in the later period of marriage, when age may well contribute to self-doubts for those who view sexual adequacy in terms of performance.

THE LATER YEARS—A TIME FOR TENDERNESS

The couples in our study who have been married 20 years or more tend to include husbands settled professionally and wives working outside the home (79% or more). Most of their children are about to leave home or have already left. Although these couples give their marriages high marks in terms of satisfaction and compatibility, the picture they paint of their sex lives is less glowing. For instance, although the men report less trouble with premature ejaculation, they have more difficulty in both getting and maintaining erections. Intercourse becomes less frequent: Only 20% of those married 20 years or longer report a frequency of intercourse greater than once a week (as compared to 59% of those married less than 10 years).

But despite this decrease in potency *and* frequency, older males do not report decreased satisfaction with their sex lives. Apparently these men find alternate sources of pleasure in marriage or simply accept the inevitability of change with age.

Women, on the other hand, tell another story: They agree with their husbands about the decreasing frequency of intercourse but report more dissatisfaction. They more often describe themselves as less exconfident and more resigned. In fact, over half the women in use the word "resignation" to describe their feelings about al relationship. This may be because about 50% of women in oup still report difficulty in getting excited and in having orgasms. This, combined with their husbands' becoming less potent, may cause the couple to discontinue a sexual encounter in which erection is elusive, leaving the woman unsatisfied.

Some decline in frequency of intercourse is normal, and while those who are unhappily married may be very upset by it, happily married couples are less so. For more content couples, the issue seems to become tenderness in this later phase of marriage. It is sought by both the men and women in our study who have been married 20 years or more.

HAS THERE BEEN A SEXUAL REVOLUTION?

If the much-discussed sexual revolution really has occurred, we would expect the sexual experience of our younger couples to differ dramatically from those who are older. This does *not* seem to be the case. In fact, the young marrieds have almost as many anxieties and not that much more pleasure than those who have been together for years.

What does seem to be affected by the increased sexual freedom in our culture is premarital experience. Seventy-five percent of women in their 20's had an ongoing sexual relationship with their partner before marriage. This compares with 50% of those in their 30's, only 25% of those in their 40's and 19% of those in their 50's and 60's. Eighty-two percent of the men in their 20's, 56% of those in their 30's, 35% of those in their 40's and 25% of those in their 50's and beyond reported an ongoing sexual relationship with their partner prior to marriage.

Does premarital sex contribute to sexual adjustment when one marries? Apparently not. Those groups with a higher percentage of premarital activity do not appear to have fewer sexual complaints or more sexual fulfillment in their marriages. Practice, in this case, does not make perfect.

WHAT DOES ALL THIS MEAN?

What do we conclude from our study of the sexual stages of our couples?

In an earlier study we found that it is not so much the quality of *sexual performance* that counts within a relationship, but rather the quality of *feeling* that goes with it. This appears to hold across all periods of marriage.

Also, there appears to be a kind of curvilinear sexual relationship in marriage, implying that if couples can weather the middle years, then sexual intimacy, if not performance, can improve even after years of marriage.

What advice might the couples we studied pass on to our young friends whose marriage we toasted? They can tell them that there will be some phases in which sex will be extremely important, other phases when it will not matter so much. And that all of these sexual stages are "normal" and do not mean that the total relationship they have together is not special indeed. . . .

TION 11

Parenting

The next area of adjustment to married life that we shall examine concerns children. If a couple is contemplating the possibility of marriage, they focus at some point on this question: Shall we have children? If so, when and how many? (If our biological engineering developments continue, they will soon be adding, "And what sex shall they be?")

In one way or another, married couples continually face this issue of parenthood. If they have no children, they are still trying to avoid them, frenetically trying to have them, or "letting nature take its course" with little concern one way or the other. If they have children, they are wishing they could have more or wishing they had fewer or even none at all. In the later years of marriage they are happy about the number they had, wistfully regretful they did not have more, or bitter about the fact that they had any, granted the way they are now being treated by those they did bring into the world.

The question of children is central to each marriage and to each marital couple: Shall we? Shouldn't we? When? Why? Why not? If the husband and wife agree on both the number and the timing, the tension is tremendously eased between them. If they do not, fireworks are likely to fly, feelings to be hurt, and bitterness and resentment to set in. While the issue must be resolved, it is one of the thorniest that the married couple faces. Unlike some of the issues between husbands and wives that we have already discussed—such as differences in orientations, sexuality, and dual careers—parenting has a key ingredient that distinguishes it from these. This is its irrevocable element. Once the child is born, one cannot wish it away. Regardless of their feelings, the parents face the outcome for eighteen or twenty-five years or so.

Our society has grown increasingly tolerant about many things, including divorce. Within broad limits it allows a couple to change their minds about their marriage and to have it declared null and void. In contrast, the arrival of a child is not an event about which a couple is allowed the luxury of changing their minds if "things don't work out." They are not permitted to go before a judge and have the birth declared null and void so they can be free of all responsibilities toward an undesired factor in their lives.

Certainly there are unusual situations in which a father or mother is allowed to disclaim the parental role. For example, if a marriage terminates it is permissible within our culture for either the father or mother to allow the one who has filled his or her place to adopt the child or children. The state agrees and makes provision for this eventuality. Relatives and friends, however, often do not acquiesce so easily to such an agreement.

But the approved circumstances of giving up children are highly narrow and circumscribed by tight legal rules and social expectations. In almost all instances within marriage, when one has taken on the role of parent one has no option as to whether or not to see it to its completion. And this advent of parenthood marks one of the most significant changes in the couple's life.

When a child is born, the couple is no longer just husband and wife. In addition they are now father and mother, terms bringing with them whole new sets of expectations. The change in roles and relationships is so qualitatively different that social scientists change their descriptive terms for defining the unit. Before children, the couple is a couple. They are a married couple, a husband and wife, and so on. But, technically, *they are not considered a family*. While for governmental statistical purposes they might be called a family, the term "family" is technically reserved for the marital unit that contains children. One can quarrel with this position, for such things are only a matter of arbitrary definition. Before my wife and I had our first child, for example, I thought of us as being a family. I have an anthropologist friend, however, who took seemingly perverse pleasure in reminding me that we really were not a family. Now that we have our first child, any doubt as to whether or not we are a family has been removed.

Nothing is the same after the arrival of the first child. As I discussed in the introduction to this third part of the book, the couple making the transition from single to married undergoes modification of almost all aspects of their lives. Similarly, with parenthood comes a transition that now forces modifications in almost all these adjustments that have been so precariously worked out.

Not much is known, however, about the process by which prospective parents adjust to the impending event. This is an open area for research. A study could be built around interviews that focus on the couple as they consider the possibility that the wife might be pregnant, then followed up when the couple finds out for certain. Ideally, the study would be longitudinal and follow the parents through pregnancy and the arrival of their child. Certainly the transition process is different in the social classes, and a cursory examination of individual concerns will readily show a particular social class orientation. The process is also different depending on whether it is the "transition to parenthood" or the "transition to more parenthood."

Parenting, then is the focus of the following six chapters. The authors provide cross-cultural, historical, and contemporary materials—all designed to broaden our perspective and enhance our understanding of our own situation.

Maxine Hong Kingston begins this section by recounting a morality story told by her mother. The point of its inclusion is that each human group has its own ideas about morality, its way of computing right and wrong, and central to those views is proper parenting. The next chapter, by Sar A. Levitan and Richard S. Belous, presents a sharp contrast with Kingston's as they discuss the increasing rate of illegitimacy in American society and some of the implications of that change. For further contrast, Elin McCoy next presents a brief overview of how child-raising practices used to be startlingly different than they are today. With child-rearing generally taken seriously today, Brent C. Miller and Donna L. Sollie look at how middle-class couples cope with the stresses that they experience during their transition to parenthood. This is followed by Lillian Breslow Rubin's analysis of the more difficult adjustment of working-class parents to the arrival of their first child. Jean E. Veevers then closes this section with an analysis of the process by which some couples choose to remain permanently childless.

To apply this material, consider the following questions. If you were to have your first child about a year after you were married, what adjustments do you think you would have to make? How would you go about planning for the birth? In what ways might the arrival of this child affect your educational and occupational aspirations? The way you feel about yourself? The way you feel about your spouse? Your feelings about the purpose of your marriage? How might this birth affect the way you act toward your spouse? How might the transition to parenthood be different if the birth of your firstborn were to occur five years after your marriage? Ten years?

Then, concerning child-raising, think first about your ideas of the "ideal" parent, then about your ideas of the "ideal" child. What are those "ideals"? From where did you get them? In what ways are these "ideals" likely to affect your behavior? In what specific ways would you be likely to act differently if you had different ideas of parenthood?

Finally, consider this set of interrelated issues. Why do people choose to have or not to have children? Is life better as a consequence of one choice rather than the other? In what ways is it better or worse? According to what criteria? And could you consider the possibility of being married and purposely choosing never to have children? Why or why not? Could you consider the possibility of being married and choosing to have six or eight children? Why or why not?

CHAPTER 38

A Fate Worse Than Death

Maxine Hong Kingston

ABSTRACT: Most families have favorite stories that they use to teach the young the great lessons of life. These morality stories are often effective in "pointing the way." Here Kingston shares the one her mother told about her aunt.

"You must not tell anyone," my mother said, "what I am about to tell you. In China your father had a sister who killed herself. She jumped into the family well. We say that your father has all brothers because it is as if she had never been born.

"In 1924 just a few days after our village celebrated seventeen hurry-up weddings—to make sure that every young man who went 'out on the road' would responsibly come home—your father and his brothers and your grandfather and his brothers and your aunt's new husband sailed for America, the Gold Mountain. It was your grandfather's last trip. Those lucky enough to get contracts waved good-by from the decks. They fed and guarded the stowaways and helped them off in Cuba, New York, Bali, Hawaii. 'We'll meet in California next year,' they said. All of them sent money home.

"I remember looking at your aunt one day when she and I were dressing; I had not noticed before that she had such a protruding melon of a stomach. But I did not think, 'She's pregnant,' until she began to look like other pregnant women, her shirt pulling and the white tops of her black pants showing. She could not have been pregnant, you see, because her husband had been gone for years. No one said anything. We did not discuss it. In early summer she was ready to have the child, long after the time when it could have been possible.

"The village had also been counting. On the night the baby was to be born the villagers raided our house. Some were crying. Like a great saw, teeth strung with lights, files of people walked zigzag across our land, tearing the rice. Their lanterns doubled in the disturbed black water, which drained away through the broken bunds. As the villagers closed in, we could see that some of them, probably men and women we knew well, wore white masks. The people with long hair hung it over their faces. Women with short hair made it stand up on end. Some had tied white bands around their foreheads, arms, and legs.

"At first they threw mud and rocks at the house. Then they threw eggs and began slaughtering our stock. We could hear the animals scream their deaths—the roosters, the pigs, a last great roar from the ox. Familiar wild heads flared in our night windows; the villagers encircled us. Some of the faces stopped to peer at us, their eyes rushing like searchlights. The hands flattened against the panes, framed heads, and left red prints.

"The villagers broke in the front and the back doors at the same time, even though we had not locked the doors against them. Their knives dripped with the blood of our animals. They smeared blood on the doors and walls. One woman swung a chicken, whose throat she had slit, splattering blood in red arcs about her. We stood together in the middle of our house, in the family hall with the pictures and tables of the ancestors around us, and looked straight ahead.

"At that time the house had only two wings. When the men came back, we would build two more to enclose our courtyard. The villagers pushed through both wings, even your grandparents' rooms, to find your aunt's, which was also mine until the men returned. From this room a new wing for one of the younger families would grow. They ripped up her clothes and shoes and broke her combs, grinding them underfoot. They tore her work from the loom. They scattered the cooking fire and rolled the new weaving in it. We could hear them in the kitchen breaking our bowls and banging the pots. They overturned the great waist-high earthenware jugs; duck eggs, pickled fruits, vegetables burst out and mixed in acrid torrents. The old woman from the next field swept a broom through the air and loosed the spirits-of-the-broom over our heads. 'Pig.' 'Ghost.' 'Pig,' they sobbed and scolded while they ruined our house.

"When they left, they took sugar and oranges to bless themselves. They cut pieces from the dead animals. Some of them took bowls that were not broken and clothes that were not torn. Afterward we swept up the rice and sewed it back up into sacks. But the smells from the spilled preserves lasted. Your aunt gave birth in the pigsty that night. The next morning when I went for the water, I found her and the baby plugging up the family well.

"Don't let your father know that I told you. He denies her. Now that you have started to menstruate, what happened to her could happen to you. Don't humiliate us. You wouldn't like to be forgotten as if you had never been born. The villagers are watchful."

Whenever she had to warn us about life, my mother told stories that ran like this one, a story to grow up on.

CHAPTER 39

Children Out of Wedlock

Sar A. Levitan / Richard S. Belous

ABSTRACT: As the American birthrate has declined, our rate of illegitimacy has increased sharply. Each year about 10 percent of all fifteen- to nineteen-year-old females in the United States become pregnant. How these pregnancies are handled shows broad differences along racial lines: Black teenagers are more likely to give birth, white teenagers more likely to seek abortion. In many instances, unwed mothers drop out of school, and, if they marry, they rather quickly separate or divorce. Children born out of wedlock, then, are often raised in unstable homes and in poverty.

One of the main functions of a family has been to produce, nurture, and socialize the next generation. While the family does not have to be child oriented, the needs of the young have played a primary role in the evolution of this institution. An old nursery rhyme summed up the traditional mores quite succinctly: "First comes love; then comes marriage; then come children in a baby carriage."

However, in a growing number of cases this conventional order has not been followed. Love often results in just living together—not in marriage. Even if marriage does follow love, the need for the proverbial baby carriage may be long postponed—the result of advanced birth control practices. And since the 1973 Supreme Court ruling, which struck down restrictive state laws regarding abortion—especially during the first three months of pregnancy—legal abortions increasingly have been used as a means of fertility control. In some cases, the baby carriage is never needed. For many adults, the word crib more often is associated with cheating on tests than with a child's bed. With a rise in illegitimate births, the baby carriage—if it can be afforded—has often preceded marriage. In many cases, nuptial vows have not followed the birth. . . .

[A]bout one in seven children in the United States [was] born out of wedlock in 1978—triple the comparable rate in the mid-1960s. While the number of total births and of legitimate births have declined in recent years, the number of children born to unwed mothers has continued to climb. Currently, over half of all black births and 8 percent of white births are out of wedlock [Figure 39.1].

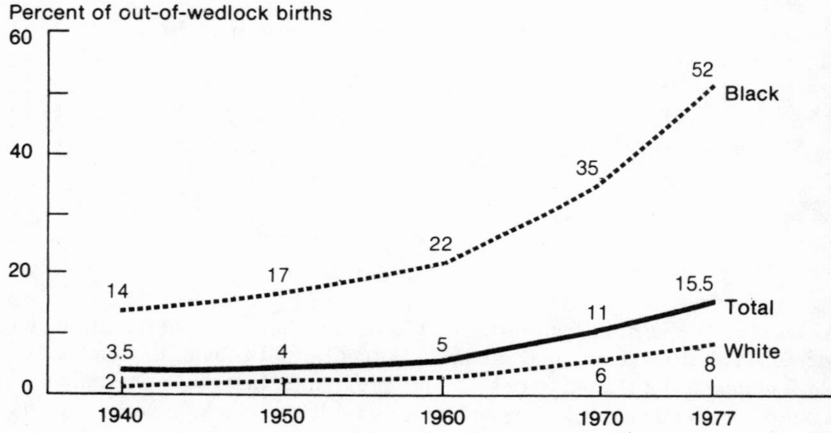

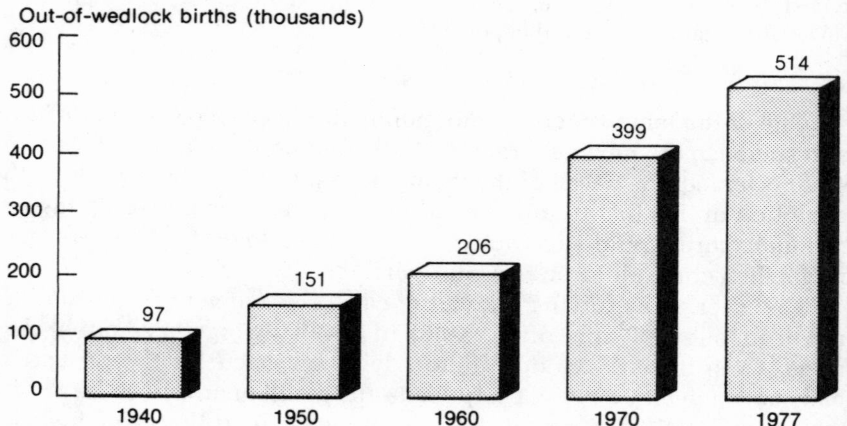

Figure 39.1 The proportion and number of out-of-wedlock births have grown rapidly.

Source: National Center for Health Statistics.

Teenage girls are the mothers of more than half of the children born out of wedlock each year. Illegitimacy rates for women 20 years and older have declined somewhat due to wider availability and greater acceptance of better contraceptive devices. However, the benefits of modern bedroom technology have not filtered down to many teenage girls. Limited knowledge and use of contraceptive devices, as well as restricted accessibility and the failure to use the devices when they are available, have kept teenage illegitimacy rates at their high level. About 45 percent of premarital pregnancies by white teenage girls in metropolitan areas are aborted compared with 20 percent of those of black teenage girls.[1]

About 10 percent of all females between the ages of 15 and 19 become pregnant annually, accounting for about 600,000 births—including some 250,000 born out of wedlock. After giving birth, the teenage mother—even if she is married—faces the difficult challenge of raising the child. In almost nine of ten cases, the teenage mother decides to keep the child; 8 percent are put up for adoption while the rest are sent to live with other relatives or families.[2] Black teenage mothers on average show a higher propensity to keep their children born out of wedlock than do white teenagers. During pregnancy, almost all of these unmarried teenage mothers live with their families, and nearly half are still living with their families five years after the birth.[3]

Being an unmarried teenage mother has many negative economic and social impacts on the young female as well as the child. These mothers are three times more likely to drop out of school than are teenage girls who are not mothers. Even when family background and other variables that attempt to measure motivation and ability are considered, being an unmarried teenage mother has the statistically significant impact of cutting short a young woman's educational chances. While they may make up part of this educational gap later in life, most of these women will never catch up with those who did not become unwed mothers during their teenage years. Also, becoming an unwed teenage mother increases the chances that a young woman will be living in a poverty household for many years.[4]

As sociologist Arthur Campbell noted, "The girl who has an illegitimate child at the age of 16 suddenly has 90 percent of life's script written for her."[5] In most cases it is a bleak scenario. It will be difficult for her to provide for and raise the child. Her lack of education and other difficulties will make it hard to find and hold a steady, well-paying job. She may feel compelled to marry a man she might not have chosen in different circumstances, and the chances are far greater than average that this marriage will not last.

In fact, there appears to be a direct link between out-of-wedlock births and future divorces leading to broken homes. Four out of five women who have premarital births will eventually marry. In many cases of premarital conception, the couple will—voluntarily or under shotgun—marry, and the child will be born after marriage. About one-quarter of the women who entered their first marriage during the period 1970–74 had a first child who was premaritally conceived. Of these women, roughly one-third had the child before marriage, while the remaining two-thirds gave birth during the first eight months following the nuptial vows.[6]

Premarital conception is not new. Historian Richard Lingeman estimated that one-third of the recorded births in Concord, Massachusetts, during the two decades prior to the Revolution were conceived out of wedlock. This is roughly the same proportion as in recent years.[7] Whatever the consequence of premarital conceptions in the past, the problem today is that the marriages of women who have a child before the wedding bells sound are far more likely than other marriages to end in early separation or divorce.

Hence, while there is a high probability that a woman who either conceives or bears a child before marriage will wind up with a husband at some time, the probability is also great that she will become a single parent. For the child born prior to the marriage, these circumstances may mean a series of traumatic experiences. The child may first face the world of a one-parent family. If the mother marries, the child for a while may live in a two-parent but unstable household that is likely to be shattered, thus returning the youngster to life in a single-parent household. Next to divorce, out-of-wedlock births have contributed most to the decline in the proportion of children who are living in two-parent families.

NOTES

1. Melvin Zelnik and John F. Kantner, "Unprotected Intercourse Among Unwed Teenagers," *Family Planning Perspective* (January/February 1975), p. 39; idem, "Sexual Activity, Contraceptive Use and Pregnancy Among Metropolitan Area Teenagers: 1971–1979," *Family Planning Perspective* (September/October 1980), p. 234.
2. Audrey E. Jones and Paul J. Placek, "Teenage Women in the U.S.A.: Sex, Contraception, Pregnancy, Fertility, and Maternal and Infant Health," in *Teenage Pregnancy and Family Impact: New Perspectives on Policy*, ed. Theodora Ooms et al. (Washington, D.C.: Family Impact Seminar of the George Washington University, 1979), p. 14.
3. Frank Furstenberg, Jr., "Burdens and Benefits: The Impact of Early Childbearing on the Family," in Ooms, *Teenage Pregnancy and Family Impact*, p. 21.
4. Kristin A. Moore et al., *Teenage Motherhood: Social and Economic Consequences* (Washington, D.C.: Urban Institute, 1979), pp. 9, 38, 43.

5. Arthur Campbell, "The Role of Family Planning in the Reduction of Poverty," *Journal of Marriage and the Family* (May 1968), p. 236.
6. Maurice J. Moore and Martin O'Connell, *Perspective on American Fertility* (Washington, D.C.: Government Printing Office, 1978), series P-23, no. 70, p. 46.
7. Richard Lingeman, *Small Town America* (New York: Putnam, 1980) as cited by Walter Clemons, "Of Sleepers and Swings," *Newsweek* 28 July 1980, p. 65.

CHAPTER 40

Childhood Through the Ages

Elin McCoy

Abstract: Historical evidence indicates that attitudes toward children varied widely. Life was generally oppressive, and child care reflected that harsh reality: a high proportion of unwanted children, high death rates, wet-nursing for the upper class, lack of supervision, swaddling, and harsh discipline. The particular practices, however, varied from country to country and, within countries, by social class. Considering children's welfare, today's child-rearing practices appear to be a decided improvement.

A gentleman-in-waiting and the nurse of little Comte de Marle often amused themselves tossing the swaddled infant back and forth across the sill of an open window. One day one of them failed to catch him, and the infant landed on a stone step and died.

The surgeon of the newborn Louis XIII cut the "fiber" under his tongue a few days after he was born, believing that if it remained uncut, Louis would be unable to suck properly and would eventually stutter.

These aren't atypical examples of child rearing in the past. Recent historical research indicates that for most of the past 2,500 years, childhood was a brief, grim period in most people's lives, especially when judged against contemporary views of child rearing.

A NEW FIELD—FAMILY HISTORY

Through a new field of historical research, known as family history, we now know that family life and childhood in the previous centuries were startlingly different from what most people, including historians, had imagined them to be. Scores of historians are currently probing such questions as: How were children treated in the past? What concept of childhood did people have in different centuries? How important were children to their parents? Is there such a thing as "instinctual" parental behavior? What do the prevailing child-rearing beliefs and practices of the past tell us about the political, social, and psychological ideals of society? And what kind of adults resulted from such child-rearing practices?

"Family history is the most explosive field of history today," says Professor Lawrence Stone—director of Princeton University's Shelby Cullom Davis Center for Historical Studies—whose 1977 book, *The Family, Sex and Marriage in England 1500–1800*, came out in an abridged paperback last year. "In the 1930s only about 10 scholarly books and articles on the family and childhood in history were published each year, but, incredibly, between 1971 and 1976 over 900 important books and articles were published on that subject, just covering America, England, and France." Two scholarly journals devoted to the subject were also started in the 1970s.

Why, suddenly, have so many historians focused on the family? "A whole series of contemporary anxieties has contributed to this new interest," explains Professor Stone. "General anxiety about the state of the family and whether it's breaking down, concern about the rising divorce rate, anxieties about current permissiveness in raising children, and concern about what effects women's liberation will have on children, the family, and society. And underlying all of these anxieties are two questions: Are we really doing so badly? Was it better in the past?"

In addition, two other trends in historical research have focused attention on childhood and the family. The first is social historians' growing interest in the daily lives of ordinary people in history, which has meant a greater concern with children, parenting, marriage, disease, death, and aging. The second is historians' recent efforts to employ psychological concepts as a research tool in order to understand human motivations and experiences in the past.

Although all family historians agree that child-rearing patterns influence what happens in history, they disagree about how much and in what precise ways the treatment of children shapes history. Some researchers in the field, like Lloyd deMause, founder of *The Journal of*

Psychohistory: A Quarterly Journal of Childhood and Psychohistory, go so far as to say that, in deMause's words, "child-rearing practices have been *the* central force for change in history." Along with some other psychohistorians, deMause believes that "if you want to understand the causes of historical events like the growth of Nazism, you have to look at how the children who became Nazis as adults were treated as children." But many scholars have reservations about attributing the character of a society solely to the relations between parents and children, pointing out that these relations must be understood in the context of the society as a whole and that such factors as economics must also be taken into account.

SURPRISING DISCOVERIES

Family historians have recently exploded many long-standing myths about childhood and the nature of the family throughout history. It's now clear that the functions and structure of the family have changed continuously over the years and that a variety of family types coexisted in each historical period in different regions and classes. Scholars have found, surprisingly, that the prevailing family mode in America today (the small nuclear family of parents and children living apart from other relatives)—a structure that is under much attack—is not as new to our culture as they had previously thought. Even as long ago as thirteenth-century England, as many as half of all families consisted of only a mother and/or father and two to three children. In fact, the large, loving extended families we tend to picture, with eight to ten children and several generations of relatives living under the same roof, were more the exception than the rule, even in Colonial America.

According to Professor Tamara Hareven—founder and head of the first History of the Family program in the country, at Clark University in Worcester, Massachusetts, and founding editor of the *Journal of Family History*—one of the great surprises for today's historians was "finding out that in the past, the concept of childhood and children was not the same in all centuries, classes, and countries. While the middle classes were 'discovering' childhood and becoming interested in children," she explains, "the working classes still regarded children as small adults with the same responsibilities. And in the past, childhood as we know it lasted for a much shorter time." In medieval England, for example, children as young as seven were sent to live in other households as apprentices, and for peasant children, childhood was even briefer—they joined their parents to work in the fields as soon as they could.

Infants were regarded in medieval times as unimportant, unformed animals, in the sixteenth century as "exasperating parasites," and even as late as the seventeenth century they were not seen as individuals with their own identities. Children were considered interchangeable, and frequently were given the same name as an older sibling who had died. Small children were not even viewed as interesting; Montaigne, the French essayist, summed up the prevailing attitudes of a few hundred years ago when he dismissed infants as having "neither movement in the soul, nor recognizable form in the body by which they could render themselves lovable."

Scholars tell us that infants and small children were important only insofar as they could benefit their parents. Considered possessions with no individual rights, they were used to further adult aims, and they ended up as security for debts, as ways of increasing property holdings through arranged marriages, as political hostages, and even as slaves sold for profit.

INFANCY IN THE PAST

Throughout history, parents' treatment of infants and very small children has been characterized by psychological coldness and physical brutality that horrify most of us today. But this behavior becomes at least comprehensible when we realize some of the conditions of people's lives. The physical realities of life were oppressive. And there were severe parental limitations as well: in addition to being influenced by unscientific medical knowledge and religious views about the nature of man, most adults had to concentrate so much of their energy on mere survival that they had little time to care for or worry about infants and small children. Abusive and violent behavior was common among adults and, therefore, not looked on with disapproval when it appeared in the treatment of children.

In view of the following facts, consider what your experience as a parent and your child's experience as an infant would have been if you had lived prior to the eighteenth century.

Your child probably wouldn't have been wanted. Lack of birth control meant that having children was not a choice. For poverty-stricken peasants, an infant meant another mouth to feed—and food was precious—as well as interference with the mother's role as a worker whose contribution was necessary to the family's ability to survive. In all classes, the high risk of maternal mortality made the birth of a child a traumatic event. Even in the relatively healthy conditions enjoyed by the inhabitants of Plymouth Colony, 20 percent of women died from causes related to childbirth (compared with under 1 percent today), and in seventeenth-century England and France, the rates were much higher. It's no wonder that most children were probably unwanted. In fact, Professor Stone suggests that the availability of birth control was probably one of the necessary conditions for the increase in affection for children that began in England and America in the eighteenth century.

Your infant would have had a good chance of dying before his or her first birthday. In medieval England and seventeenth-century France, for example, between 20 and 50 percent of all infants died within the first year after birth. Complications of childbirth, prematurity, diseases such as smallpox and the plague, and generally unsanitary living conditions, as well as such customs as baptism in icy water in freezing churches, took a heavy toll among vulnerable newborns. America was healthier for infants—in Plymouth Colony, infant mortality was only 10 to 15 percent (which is still ten times higher than it is in America today). The likelihood that one's infants would die discouraged parents from investing much affection or interest in them and from regarding them as special, unique individuals until it appeared more certain that they might live to adulthood.

Illegitimate infants and infants of poverty-stricken parents (and parents who felt they already had enough children) were often the victims of infanticide through deliberate murder, abandonment, or neglect. In ancient Greece, for example, infants who seemed sickly or didn't have a perfect shape or cried too much or too little were "exposed," or abandoned to die, a decision that was made by the father shortly after birth. In mid-eighteenth-century England, so many babies—both legitimate and illegitimate—were abandoned to die in the streets of cities and towns that the first foundling home established in London received several thousand babies a year. In early America, infanticide seems to have affected only illegitimate children.

If you were well-off, your baby probably would have been breast-fed by someone else. In spite of the fact that all medical advice since Roman times had stressed that babies breast-fed by their own mothers had a better chance of survival, for eighteen centuries any woman who could afford it sent her infant to a wet nurse.

Recuperation from a difficult childbirth prevented some women from breast-feeding, but many others thought it too demanding, especially since it was customary for infants to breast-feed for as long as two years. Also, many husbands would not allow their wives to breast-feed, partly because medical opinion held that women who were breast-feeding should not engage in sexual intercourse.

Underlying these reasons may have been parents' desire to distance themselves emotionally from their infants.

In Renaissance Italy, middle-class infants were delivered to the *bália*, or wet nurse, immediately after baptism—two or three days after birth—and, if they survived, remained there for two years. Rarely did mothers visit their infants, and thus a baby was returned home at the end of that time to a stranger.

Although some wet nurses moved in with the family, most women left their babies at the wet nurse's home, where the child was often neglected and starved because wet nurses commonly took on too many babies in order to make more money. Frequently wet nurses ran out of milk, and infants had to be sent to a series of different nurses and thus were deprived even of a single surrogate mother.

The first groups of middle-class women to change this 1,800-year-old pattern on a large scale were the Puritans in the seventeenth century. Eventually, in the eighteenth century, there was a widespread cult of maternal breast-feeding in both America and England. Scholars have suggested that this shift may have contributed substantially to the shift in parental feelings for infants that began in the eighteenth century; certainly it reduced infant mortality.

Your infant would have spent little time with you. In the past, parents spent much less time with their children than even working parents do today and clearly did not feel the need to arrange supervision for them. Peasant women commonly left their infants and toddlers alone all day at home while they worked elsewhere. In one area of England during the thirteenth century, for example, half the infant deaths involved infants in cradles being burned while no one was home. Unsupervised toddlers frequently wandered off and drowned. In the middle and upper classes, parental neglect took the form of turning toddlers over to the servants to raise.

Your infant would have been swaddled in tightly bound cloths from birth to as old as eight months. Emotional distancing, economic necessity, and faulty medical knowledge are also evident in another common practice—swaddling. In England this practice continued up to the eighteenth century; in France, the nineteenth century; and in Russia, into the twentieth century. Kept in tightly bound bandages, swaddled infants were totally isolated from their surroundings for the first four months or so. After that, only their legs were bound. They couldn't turn their heads, suck their own thumbs for comfort, or crawl. Swaddling that was too tight occasionally caused suffocation. Although doctors advocated changing the infant two or three times a day, this apparently was uncommon, and even Louis XIII developed severe rashes because of his swaddling bands.

Medical reasons for the practice included the beliefs that if free, the infant might tear off his ears or scratch out his eyes, that swaddling was necessary to keep infants warm in cold, draughty cottages, houses, and castles, and that it ensured that the infant's pliable limbs would grow straight so he would be able to stand erect. Even when the swaddlin bands were removed from their legs, children were not allowed t crawl "like an animal," but were forced to stand with the help of b zarre contraptions. Convenience was another reason for swaddling: i caused infants to sleep more and cry less, so they could be left for lon periods of time while mothers worked. Also, swaddled infants wer easier to carry and could even be hung on a peg on the wall out of th way.

Your infant or child would probably have received harsh beatings reg ularly—from you or a servant—even for such "normal" behavior as cry ing or wanting to play. For many centuries, discipline and teaching o the infant and young child concentrated on "breaking the child's will, which meant crushing all assertiveness and instilling complete obed ence. This was accomplished through physical and psychological ma treatment that today we would consider "child abuse." Susanna We ley, mother of John Wesley, the founder of the Methodist Church records her treatment of her children: "When turned a year old, an some before, they were taught to fear the rod and cry softly." Louis XII was whipped every morning, starting at the age of two, simply for bein "obstinate," and was even whipped on the day of his coronation at th age of nine. The Puritans believed that "the newborn babe is full of th stains and pollutions of sin" and saw the first strivings of a one- an two-year-old to independence—which we now recognize as essential t a child's growing mastery of himself and understanding of the world— as a clear manifestation of that original sin. It was considered the dut of parents to use physical harshness and psychological terrorization— locking children in dark closets for an entire day or frightening then with tales of death and hellfire, for example—to wipe this sin out.

These child-rearing practices, as well as the difficult realities of lif in the past, had important psychological effects on children's develop ment. According to Professor Stone, the isolation, sensory deprivation and lack of physical closeness that resulted from swaddling; the ab sence of a mother because of death in childbirth or the practice of wet nursing; the common experience for small children of losing parent and siblings; and the suppression of self-assertion through whippin and other fear-producing techniques all resulted in an "adult world o emotional cripples."

A CHANGE FOR THE BETTER

In the late seventeenth and eighteenth centuries, many of thes childrearing practices began to change among wealthy merchants an other groups in the upper middle classes of England and America. Some changes can be traced to the Puritans, who, even though they advocated harsh disciplinary measures, focused a new attention on children and the importance of their upbringing. By the late eighteenth century, among some groups, methods of contraception were available, swaddling had been abandoned, maternal breast-feeding had become the fashion, and "breaking the will" had given way to affection and a degree of permissiveness that seems extraordinary even by today's standards. In England the indulgent Lord Holland, for example, intent on gratifying his little son Charles's every whim, allowed him to jump and splash in the large bowl of cream intended for dessert at a grand dinner while the guests, a group of foreign ministers, looked on. Many adults feared the effect on society when these spoiled children reached maturity. And in fact, many of them did spend their lives in lifelong dissipation and often became followers of evangelical religions. While the Victorian era varied from harsh to permissive in the treatment of children, by the end of the nineteenth century the child-oriented family became a reality for all classes in Western society.

WHAT IT ALL MEANS FOR US

Were childhood and family life better in the past? The answer—obviously—is a resounding no. One is tempted to agree with Lloyd deMause that "the history of childhood is a nightmare from which we have only recently begun to awaken."

Nevertheless, Professor Hareven feels that there *were* some good aspects to childhood in the past, which we can learn from today. "Children were not so segregated from adults and responsibility," she points out. "The historical record shows children grew up in households that included servants, other workers employed by the family, lodgers, visiting relatives, and siblings of widely differing ages, as well as parents. They were exposed to a greater variety of adult roles than children usually are today and they interacted with a greater variety of people of all ages. They also knew more about their parents' work. And unlike today, children were working, contributing members of families and the society from an early age—as they are in contemporary China. Today's child-oriented family and the postponement of responsibility and work limit children's experience. The models are there in history for us to borrow and shape to today's ideals."

Historical research on childhood helps us view our own ideas about parenthood from a perspective in which it is clear that there are no absolutes. The new facts that are available to us show that assumptions behind child rearing change and that what we think of as parents' "instincts" actually depend on the beliefs and experiences of their society. The possessiveness and affection toward infants, which we take for granted, is a recent development. Even the "maternal instinct" to breast-feed one's own child was not instinctive for many women for over 1,800 years.

Family history also gives us an informative view of family structure. Those who are worried about the high divorce rate and the effect of parental separation on children, for example, should realize that in the past, approximately the same percentage of families were separated—only it was by the death of one of the parents instead of by divorce.

Although problems with child rearing will probably always be with us, the very existence of family history means that we have come to the point where we are much more self-conscious about how we raise children, and, in turn, this may help us to be more thoughtful about the way we treat them. By examining childhood in the past, we become aware that our own attempts to do things differently—"nonsexist" child rearing, co-parenting, and different mixes of permissiveness and discipline—may have profound effects on society. If we can avoid the mistakes of the past, borrow what was good, and continue to examine our own aims and practices, the society our children make may be a better one than ours.

CHAPTER 41

The Transition to Parenthood

Brent C. Miller / Donna L. Sollie

ABSTRACT: The birth of a child ushers in changes in the marital relationship. How do new parents cope with those changes? Based on this study of middle-class parents, the authors identify the following coping strategies: being adaptable; integration, that is sharing responsibilities and trying to continue their usual nonparenting activities; utilizing social supports; and looking to the future. The arrival of a baby can create marital stress—or it can lead to a sense of fulfillment and add new meaning and strength to the bonds between husband and wife.

Some events in life are fairly predictable; they occur at about the same time and in the same order for most people. This is not to say that everyone goes through precisely the same sequence of life events, but there is a series of normative expereinces. Such normal or developmental events, and their attendant problems, can be anticipated.

For a large majority of married adults one of the sharpest expected changes is the transition to parenthood. Although pregnancy is a harbinger, the roles and tasks of parenting are acquired abruptly. As soon as the first infant is born, and certainly by the time parents go home from the hospital, they *have* parental roles—there are social expecta-

Appreciation is expressed to the office of Graduate Studies and Research at the University of Tennessee, Knoxville, for supporting the larger study on which this paper is based, and to the College of Family Life at Utah State University for supporting the analyses.

tions about what they should do. By comparison, later normative changes during the parental career occur much more gradually as children become toddlers, school children, teenagers, and then leave home. There is, then, a point in time when parental roles are abruptly acquired, but there is also a more gradual transition into the skills and routines of parenting. Although the transition to parenthood is considered a "critical role transition *point*," it is also a *phase* or span of time (Aldous, 1978). . . .

SAMPLE AND DESIGN

The 120 couples who began the present study were recruited from one of three different hospital-based parenthood preparation classes in Knoxville, Tennessee. Couples volunteered to participate after hearing a brief overview of what would be required; they were not randomly selected. The majority of couples had middle-class occupations, incomes, and lifestyles. Both husband and wife in 109 couples completed and returned questionnaires at three points in time: first, when the wife was in midpregnancy; second, when the baby was about five to six weeks old; and finally, when the baby was between six and eight months old. Eleven couples were lost from the sample because of such diverse reasons as divorce, disinterest, and moving without forwarding addresses. . . .

ADAPTATION TO STRESS

Preparation for parenthood through reading, attending classes, or caring for infants probably increases the prospective parent's feelings of preparedness and self-confidence, but no amount of preparation and rehearsal can fully simulate the constant and immediate needs of an infant. The sometimes overwhelming demands of new parenthood usually result in some degree of personal and marital stress (Sollie & Miller 1980). So, the question of how new parents cope is especially appropriate. . . .

Although the parents in this study were not directly asked to identify coping behaviors that they used, they were asked to write an open ended response about the positive and negative aspects of having a baby in their lives. Several strategies that they relied on were evident in their replies.

Adaptability appeared as a major strategy utilized by these first-time parents in coping with the stresses they experienced. For example, a theme that appeared frequently in their comments was the change from an orderly, predictable life to a relatively disorderly and unpredictable one. As one father said, "I certainly don't try to keep rigid schedules anymore! And I'm becoming a more flexible person." A new mother wrote,

> One of the hardest adjustments for me was the unpredictableness of my day. I couldn't be sure of anything—that I would be able to take a nap after her next feeding, that I would have time to clean the house on a certain day, that I would have time to fix supper, etc.

Other coping strategies of new parents which reflect adaptability included learning patience, becoming more organized, and becoming more flexible.

Integration of the family was also evident in the responses of these first-time parents, especially in the emphasis by some respondents on parenthood as a shared responsibility. Another example of integration was the attempt to continue some activities that were engaged in before the birth of the child—that is, to maintain a sense of continuity, and to recognize the importance of the husband-wife relationship. Husband-wife discussions of feelings were utilized by some couples during this period. One wife wrote of her husband, "He's been very understanding of my feelings and doubts and because we're very open with each other I can express a lot of what I feel, which helps." Many respondents indicated that the child brought them closer together, increased their interdependence, and expanded their feelings of unity and cohesion. In this sense, integration of the family is a coping resource that may be present before the birth of the child, but which can increase afterward. . . .

Other coping strategies seemed to be directed toward strengthening individual responses to some of the stresses experienced. These included utilizing social supports and looking to the future. For example, support from neighbors and friends in the form of advice, information, and caretaking was reported as being helpful. Taking time away from the baby was also beneficial, both during the day and at night. One husband noted that a positive aspect of parenthood was "My being able to help with the baby, giving my wife time to herself—therefore giving myself personal satisfaction." This statement also reflects family integration. Just realizing that ambivalent feelings are also experienced by others can be reassuring. One mother said, "Because an infant is so demanding, there are days when one wishes the baby did not exist. Knowing these feelings are normal, however, makes coping with the day-to-day routine possible."

Looking to the future was also a personal coping strategy. One mother commented, "Most of the time I realize that she will get better as time goes on. This isn't as hard during the day, but at night I find I can't deal with her as objectively." Another mother who missed her teaching career wrote, "I have applied to do some teaching on a homebound basis and just knowing that I might soon be working has lifted my spirits." A father expressed some of his negative thoughts about the present and hopes for the future as follows: "Care of the baby has been somewhat tiring for both of us. I expect my thoughts to become positive again after the baby grows some more, becomes more predictable, and can be played with."

One aspect of motherhood that appeared to be stress-producing did not seem to have any ready solutions—the problem of balancing motherhood and a career. . . . Although only a small number of the women in this sample were strongly career-oriented, this issue is becoming increasingly salient as more and more women make career commitments outside the home. The comments of some mothers expressed their doubts and the lack of easy answers to this dilemma. One mother said,

> My baby is a new individual in my life whom I love dearly, but at this point I am not personally fulfilled in simply being a mother. I am finding it difficult to cope with the boredom and lack of intellectual stimulation in my life. I gave up my career in teaching because I felt it would be unfair to take my baby to a daycare center or babysitter. I'm very undecided as to what I should do.

Another mother wrote, "Like many new mothers I am faced with hard decisions about the future of my career since my baby was born. I am full of doubts, and I'm uncertain how to maintain my career and raise my child satisfactorily." When a mother does interrupt her career, she may experience both intellectual and social voids in her life. Additionally, she may feel tied down and find it difficult to adjust to the changes in the husband-wife roles in her marriage. Lamb (1978) noted that a change from egalitarian roles to more stereotyped roles could be a cause of stress for some couples, and it would seem especially likely to be stressful for career-minded but homebound mothers.

CONCLUSIONS AND RECOMMENDATIONS

When babies in this study were just over a month old, changes in their parents' personal and marital stress were less evident than when babies were eight months old, providing some evidence for Feldman's notion of a baby honeymoon. Perceived personal stress (feelings of being tied down and that life is hard rather than easy) increased significantly for both mothers and fathers during the transition to parenthood, but among mothers more than fathers. Marital stress remained essentially unchanged among fathers over the course of the study, but perceptions of marital stress increased among new mothers between the time when babies were one month and eight months old.

These average or typical patterns reflect relatively small changes in total scores, and they also hide the few couples for whom the transition to parenthood was a very difficult experience as well as those whose personal lives and marriages improved. The unusual couples, whose lives and marriages more markedly deteriorated or improved during the transition to parenthood, are those whom it seems especially important to learn more about, so that new parenthood problems could be prevented, better treated, or at least better understood.

Considered as a normal developmental event in the individual and family life cycle, the birth of the first child can be both a source of stress and an event to test the family's coping strategies. That is, the baby can cause certain stresses arising from lack of sleep, tiredness, less time for self and spouse, and feelings of overwhelming responsibility and being tied down. At the same time though, the baby can provide a sense of fulfillment, new meaning in life, and can strengthen the bond between husband and wife, thus contributing to a sense of family cohesiveness (Sollie & Miller, 1980). . . .

Families not only rely on their own internal resources, but they also develop coping strategies by utilizing community and social supports. In addition to relying on extended family or friends during the transition to parenthood, many new parents are taking advantage of preparenthood classes offered by local hospitals, community agencies, and other organizations. Unfortunately, most of these classes are really prenatal or childbirth preparation classes which fall short in helping prospective parents *after* the child is born. New parents are probably in greater need of information and support during the months after their baby is born than during the months leading up to delivery.

Although there are logistical problems in bringing new parents together, it would seem that postparenthood classes have a relatively untapped potential for providing support systems after the birth of the child (Cowan, Cowan, Coie, & Coie, 1978). Such classes could teach basic skills, provide an opportunity for observing others with their infants, provide an outlet for expressing feelings, and an opportunity to share ideas, experiences, and problems of adjusting to parenthood. Since the negotiation and resolution of marital and parental roles may be an important factor in adjusting to parenthood (Fein, 1976), husband and wife integration might also be enhanced by discussing role expectations after the baby is born.

It is our general impression that romantic conceptions about having children are declining in our culture. People seem to be more realistic about the impacts children have on parents and marriage. This realization, in and of itself, might be another way of better coping with the stress of parenting. Knowledge about the probable effects of children, both positive and negative, and a less romantic definition of infants, might help new parents cope more easily with the usual stresses that accompany this normal life event.

REFERENCES

ALDOUS, J. *Family Careers: Developmental Change in Families.* New York: Wiley, 1978.

COWAN, C. P., P. A. COWAN, L. COIE, & J. D. COIE. Becoming a family: The impact of a first child's birth on a couple's relationship. In W. B. Miller & L. F. Newman (Eds.), *The First Child and Family Formation.* Chapel Hill, N.C.: Carolina Population Center, 1978.

FEIN, R. A. Men's entrance to parenthood. *The Family Coordinator*, 1976, **25**, 341–350.

LAMB, M. E. Influence of the child on marital quality and family interaction during the prenatal, perinatal, and infancy periods. In R. M. Lerner & G. B. Spanier (Eds.), *Child Influences on Marital and Family Interaction: A Lifespan Perspective.* New York: Academic Press, 1978.

SOLLIE, D. L., & B. C. MILLER. The transition to parenthood as a critical time for building family strengths. In N. Stinnett, B. Chesser, J. DeFrain, & P. Knaub (Eds.), *Family Strengths: Positive Models for Family Life.* Lincoln: University of Nebraska Press, 1980.

CHAPTER 42

Worlds of Pain

Lillian Breslow Rubin

ABSTRACT: The author studied fifty white working class families: both husband and wife were living together, neither husband nor wife had more than a high school education, and the husband was working at a blue-collar job. She compared her results with a sample of twenty-five professional families in which both the husband and wife had at least a college education and the husband worked in a professional occupation. This chapter concentrates on the author's findings from the working-class marriages, although she makes comparative points from time to time.

Rubin found that in the typical case the adjustment of the husband and wife to one another was complicated by the arrival of a child soon after the marriage. Usual reactions were bewilderment, anger, discontent, fear, jealousy by the husband, and a sense of loss of the past. Young working-class parents place heavy reliance on relatives for child care. A common problem was interference by the mother-in-law on behalf of a spoiled son.

[The study revealed that exacerbating] the financial problems of most of these young couples was the fact that the children were born just months after the wedding. The modal time between marriage and the birth of the first child was seven months, the average, nine months—leaving little time for the young couple to stabilize their financial position before assuming the burdens of parenthood. Unlike the professional middle-class families I met where, on the average, the first child was born three years after they were married and where most wives worked during that time, the working-class families were forced almost at once to give up the wife's earnings. The professional families thus are doubly advantaged. Their jobs pay more and offer career patterns that are more stable than those in the blue-collar world. And by deferring childbearing, young wives are able to work while the men are becoming established.

Other investigators, observing the same phenomena, have theorized that it is precisely those differences that account for professional success—that is, that putting off marriage and childbearing is a symbol of the middle-class ability to defer immediate gratifications in the interest of future rewards. Conversely, the early marriage and childbearing of the working class allegedly is symptomatic of their inability to defer gratifications and the cause of their low status in the society. If one examines the facts through a less self-righteous and self-congratulatory prism, however, we can see instead that it is those at the lower ends of our socio-economic order who are forced to delay gratifications, while those at the upper levels usually manage to have their cake and eat it. For example, among the college-educated middle class, premarital sexual behavior is not only more widely held to be legitimate but the opportunities for engaging in such behavior are more readily and comfortably available. In the last decade, even dormitories—those last bastions of parietal regulations—largely have given up the attempt to control the sexual activities of their student residents. For those young people, a bed and privacy are easily found; sex can be undertaken in leisure—a sharp contrast from the stories told by most working-class youth who still must resort to the back seat of a car or a dark corner in a park.

Similarly, for highly educated middle-class women to delay childbearing may simply be to defer one pleasurable activity in favor of another since they often do some kind of interesting and rewarding work that pays substantially more than the low-level clerical, sales, or factory work available to most high-school-educated working-class women. Most of the middle-class women I talked to, for example, worked at interesting jobs that they liked—social worker, freelance editor, writer, teacher, accountant, office manager, personnel manager, calligrapher. Those who either did not enjoy working or who had jobs they found dull and unrewarding often had their first child in considerably less than the three years cited as the average—a decision that can be made in professional families without the enormous economic costs exacted in the working class.

Indeed, children born just months after the wedding added emotional as well as economic burdens to the adjustment process. Suddenly, two young people, barely more than children themselves, found their lives irrevocably altered. Within a few months—too few to permit the integration of the behaviors required by new roles in new life stages, too few to wear comfortably even one new identity—they moved through a series of roles: from girl and boy, to wife and husband, to mother and father.

They often responded with bewilderment, filled with an uneasy and uncomprehending sense of loss for a past which, however, difficult, at least was known:

> I was so depressed and I felt so sad all the time. I felt like I'd fallen into a hole and that I could never climb out of it again. All I wanted was to be a little girl again, real little, so that somebody would take care of me.

. . . an angry and restless discontent with an uncomfortable present:

> I don't know why but I was just angry all the time. Everything she did would make me angry—crazy angry.

. . . and an enormous well of fear about an unknown future:

> All of a sudden, you couldn't tell what would happen tomorrow. I was scared out of my wits half the time; and when I wasn't scared, I was worried out of my mind.

As with all of us, however, such a welter of feelings are rarely recognized, let alone understood. At best, we are aware only that we're experiencing turmoil without knowing what it's about. One young mother expressed it well:

> All I knew was that I was churning up inside all the time.

Most immediately, both wives and husbands knew that the fun and good times that had brought them together were gone—replaced by a crying, demanding infant, and the fearsome responsibilities of parenthood. No longer were they free to run around with the old crowd, to prowl the favored haunts, to go to a movie, bowling, or partying whenever the mood struck. Both wives and husbands were shaken as it quickly became clear that the freedom they had sought in marriage was a mirage, that they had exchanged one set of constraints for another perhaps more powerful one. They felt stuck—thrust abruptly into adulthood, unexpectedly facing the fear that their youth was behind them.

The struggle to adapt simultaneously to so many new situations was complicated by young husbands who were jealous of their wives' suddenly divided time and attention. Before they had a chance to adapt to a twosome in marriage, they became a threesome, with the third member of the household a noisy, demanding, helpless infant. The young wife, anxious about her capacity to be a good mother, became absorbed in the child. Between household and baby-tending chores, both days and nights were full, leaving little time and energy for companionship or lovemaking. The young husband, until then accustomed to being the center of her life, felt excluded and deprived. Each time he made a move toward her that was rebuffed, the situation worsened. He became more hurt and jealous; she became more angry and defensive. The conflict escalated—both husband and wife acting out their frustration in painful and hurtful ways. Typical of such interactions is the story told by this couple, both twenty-nine, married ten years. The husband:

> Our first kid was born less than a year after we were married. By the time he came, it seemed like she'd either been pregnant or with the baby the whole time we were married.
>
> When we were first married, I'd come home from work and she'd be kind of dressed up and fixed up, you know, looking pretty for me. Then she kept getting bigger and bigger, and she'd be tired and complaining all the time. I could hardly wait for her to finish being pregnant. And when that was over, she was too busy and too tired to pay me any mind.
>
> I used to get mad and holler a lot. Or else I'd stay out late at night and get her worried about what I was doing. We had nothing but fights in those days because all she wanted to do was to take care of the baby, and she never had any time for me. It sounds dumb when I talk about it now—a man being jealous of a little kid, but I guess I was.

The wife:

> It felt like I was going crazy. There I was with a new baby and he was all the time nagging at me for something or other. Instead of helping me out so that I wouldn't be so tired, he'd just holler, or else he'd run out and stay out all night. Then he'd come home and expect me to be friendly and loving. Why should I? What was he doing for me? I didn't like being stuck with all those dirty diapers any more than he did, but somebody had to do it and he sure wasn't.
>
> We used to have the most terrible fights after my son was born; it was just awful. I couldn't understand how he could be jealous of a little, tiny baby, but he was. It made me so mad, I just didn't know what to do. But I sure didn't feel much like loving him.

Parents in professional middle-class families have a sense of their own success, of their ability to control their world, to provide for their children's future, whatever that might be. For them, the problem is not how to support the children through tomorrow, not *whether* they can go to college or professional school, but *which* of the prestigious alternatives available to them ought to be encouraged. For working-class parents, however, the future is seen as uncertain, problematic. For them, the question is most often *whether*, not *which*—and that "whether" more often asks *if* children will finish high school; *if* they will grow up without getting "into trouble"; *if* even with maximum vigilance, they—the parents—can retain some control over their children's future.

Complicating the matter still further, the men and women of these families are not at ease with most of the public or private institutions that share responsibility for socializing young children. They can't do much about the public schools with their mandatory attendance requirements and their "too liberal" teachers, although in recent years they have been trying. But they *can* keep their children at home with them as long as possible. Thus, where nursery school attendance is a commonplace among the children of middle-class families, it is rare among those of the working class—not primarily for financial reasons, nor because working-class parents value education less, but because they look with question and concern at the values that are propagated there:

> I think little kids belong at home with their mothers not in some nursery school that's run by a bunch of people who think they're experts and know all about what's good for kids and how they're supposed to act. I saw some of those kids in a nursey school once. They act like a bunch of wild Indians, and they're dressed terrible, and they're filthy all the time.
>
> [Twenty-seven-year-old housewife, mother of two, married seven years.]

So strong are these feelings that even in those families where mothers work part- or full-time, institutional child-care facilities are shunned in favor of arrangements with grandmothers or neighbors—arrangements that keep children close to home and in the care of people who share parental values. Typical are these comments from one young couple. The twenty-five-year-old wife, mother of two, married seven years, who works part-time as a file clerk, says:

> I don't want my kids brought up by strangers. This way it's just right. My mother-in-law comes here and stays with them and it's family. We don't have to worry about what kind of stuff some stranger is teaching them. We know they're learning right from wrong. I'd be afraid to leave them in a school or someplace like that. I'd worry that they might get too far away from the family.

Her husband, a twenty-seven-year-old refinery worker, agrees:

> I wouldn't let Ann work if we couldn't have my mother taking care of the kids. Even though it helps out for her to work, I wouldn't permit it if it meant somebody I didn't know was going to raise my kids and tell them how to act and what to think. With my mother, I know it's all okay; she teaches them the way she taught me.

Thus, both husbands and wives agree on the primacy of their parental responsibilities. But the costs to a marriage of ordering priorities thus can be heavy. For the demands of parenting often conflict with the needs of the wives and husbands who are the parents—needs for privacy, for shared adult time and leisure, for companionship, for nurturance from a husband, a wife.

Finally, these early years bring with them the inevitable in-law problems. Despite the prevalence of mother-in-law jokes that focus on the wife's mother, it is not the men but the women who complain most regularly and vociferously about mothers-in-law, especially in the beginning years of the marriage. Fully half the working-class women spoke of problems with mothers-in-law as second only to the financial ones; a few even put the in-law problems first. The primary struggle was over "who comes first"—wife or mother:

> That first year was terrible. He called her every single day when he came home from work. As soon as he'd walk through the door, he'd go to the telephone to talk to his mother. And then, a few times he went to see her before he ever even came home. That really did it. I said, "Listen buster, this has to stop. I'm not going to take that anymore. Either I'm going to come first or you can go live with your mother."
>
> [Twenty-four-year-old typist, mother of two, married five years.]

> He was so used to helping out around his mother's house that he just kept right on doing it after we were married. Can you imagine that? He'd go there and help her out with the yard work. Here our yard would need trimming, and he'd be over there helping his mother.
>
> [Thirty-eight-year-old housewife, mother of four, married twenty years.]

> He used to stop off there on his way home from work and that used to make me furious. On top of that, they eat supper earlier than we do, so a lot of times, he'd eat with them. Then he'd come home and I'd have a nice meal fixed, and he'd say he wasn't hungry. Boy, did that make me mad. We were always having these big fights over his mother at first.
>
> [Thirty-two-year-old housewife, mother of three, married thirteen years.]

This is not to suggest that conflicts around in-laws do not exist in other strata of society. But no professional middle-class wife or husband talked of these problems with the heat and intensity that I heard among the working-class women. Partly, that may be because few of the middle-class couples had families who lived close by at the time of the marriage which often took place when husbands were still in professional schools far from their hometowns. This gave these young couples a chance to negotiate the initial adjustment hurdles without interference from either family. Equally important, however, even when they live in the same city now, most of these professional couples do not have the kinds of relationships with parents that keep them actively intertwined in their lives. No grandparent in a professional family, for example, baby-sits with young children while their mother works—a common arrangement among working-class families, one which makes it difficult for the young couple to insist upon their autonomy and independence, to maintain their privacy.

Adding to the in-law problems, many of the women were aggrieved because their mothers-lin-law had spoiled their sons—waiting on them, tending their every need, always sacrificing self for the men and boys in the family—thus making the lives of their wives more difficult. For men like these expected similar "services" from their wives—services most modern young women of any class are not so willing to perform:

> His mother was like a maid in the house, and he wanted me to do the same kinds of things and be like her. I know it's my job to keep the house up, but wouldn't you think he could hang up his own clothes? Or maybe once in a while—just once in a while—help clear the table?
>
> [Twenty-eight-year-old housewife, mother of three, married ten years.]

Again, obviously, it is not only working-class mothers who spoil their sons. Still, no middle-class wife offered this complaint—a fact that, at least in part, may be because the professional men all had lived away from home for several years before they married. Without a mother or wife to do things for them, these men had to learn to care for themselves—at least minimally—in the years between leaving the parental home and getting married. In contrast, the working-class men generally moved from parental home to marriage, often simply transferring old habits and living patterns, along with their wardrobe, to a new address.

Indeed, overriding all these reasons why more working-class than professional middle-class women had complaints about mothers-in-law may be the simple fact that most working-class men lived with their families and contributed to the support of the household before they were married. Their departure from the family, therefore, probably is felt both as an emotional and an economic loss. Mothers, already experiencing some panic over the loss of maternal functions which have provided the core of their identity for so long, suffer yet another erosion of that function—a problem women in professional middle-class families deal with when children leave for college rather than when they marry. And the family economy, relying on income from all its working members, suffers the loss of his dollar contribution:

> His parents didn't accept me at all. Tim was a devoted son and his mother needed that; she couldn't bear to give him up to anyone. Then, he also helped out a lot when he was living there. They needed the money and he turned his paycheck over to his mother. They made me feel like I was taking a meal ticket from them when we got married.
>
> [Thirty-year-old file clerk, mother of four, married twelve years.]

These, then, were the beginning years—the years when illusions were shed along with childhood; the years when the first disappointments were felt, the first adjustments were made; the years of struggle for stability economically and emotionally—both so closely tied together; the years during which many marriages founder and sink. Some of these couples had already had that experience once; they were determined not to let it happen again.

CHAPTER 43

Permanent Postponement:

Childlessness as a Waiting Game

Jean E. Veevers

Abstract: By interviewing married couples who are childless by choice, Veevers found there were definite stages in becoming permanently childless: (1) postponement for a definite (specific) time; (2) postponement for an indefinite time; (3) deliberating the pros and cons; and (4) accepting permanent childlessness. Factors that accelerated commitment to permanent childlessness were pregnancy scares, aging and the possibility of adoption, and ambivalence toward achievement.

More than two-thirds of the couples interviewed remained childless as a result of a series of decisions to postpone having children until some future time, a time which never came. Rather than explicitly rejecting parenthood prior to marriage, they repeatedly deferred procreation until a more convenient time. These temporary postponements provided time during which the evaluations of parenthood were reassessed relative to other goals and possibilities. At the time of their marriages, most couples who became postponers had devoted little serious thought to the question of having children, and had no strong feelings either for or against parenthood. Typically, they simply made the conventional assumption that, like everybody else, they would probably have one or two children eventually.

The transition from wanting to not wanting children typically evolves through four separate stages, which will be described in some detail. Although it is convenient to discuss each stage separately, it must be realized that in reality the stages are not discrete and discontinuous categories, but represent overlapping foci of the marriage at various times. Movement from one stage to the next is facilitated, or in some instances retarded, by various career contingencies which will be outlined and illustrated.

Postponement for a Definite Time

The first stage in the postponement route to childlessness involves deferring childbearing for a definite period of time. At this stage, the voluntarily childless are difficult to distinguish from the conventional and conforming couples who will eventually become parents. In most groups, it is not necessarily desirable for the bride to conceive during her honeymoon. It is considered understandable that, before starting a family, a couple might want to achieve certain goals, such as graduating from school, travelling, buying a house, saving a nest egg, or simply getting adjusted to one another. The reasons for waiting vary, but there remains a clear commitment to have children as soon as conditions are right. For example, one wife had formulated very definite fertility plans very early in her marriage. It was her intention to work until her husband completed graduate school. His graduation was scheduled for a specific date, to be followed, if all went well, by a satisfactory job offer. When these two conditions had been met, her intentions were to conceive as soon as possible, to quit her job sometime in the middle of her pregnancy, and thereafter to devote herself full time to raising children.

During Stage One, childless couples practice birth control conscientiously and continuously. If the couple manage to postpone pregnancy deliberately for even a few months, they have established a necessary but not a sufficient condition to voluntary childlessness, namely the habit of effective birth control within marriage. Once this has occurred, habit and inertia tend to make them continue in the same behavior. The couple must now decide whether or not they wish to stop using birth control so as to have a child. Although for the first few months of marriage the postponement of pregnancy is widely accepted, even at this stage the permanently childless are somewhat different from their preparental counterparts. Many conventional couples, even those who approve of birth control and have access to it, do not seriously try to control their own fertility until they have had at least one child.

Postponement for an Indefinite Time

The second stage of the postponement route involves a shift from postponement for a definite period of time to an indefinite one. The couple often cannot recall exactly when they shifted into this second stage. They continue to remain committed to being parents, but become increasingly vague about when the blessed event is going to take place. It may be when they can "afford it" or when "things are going better" or when they "feel more ready." For example, one immigrant couple had recently experienced a rapid series of changes in country of residence, in cities within Canada, and in occupations, some of which were terminated involuntarily and some of which were terminated because they were unsatisfactory. They had very limited savings and felt that, without any family in Canada, there was no one on whom they could rely in an emergency. After nearly five years of marriage, they still wanted to remain childless until they felt financially and occupationally secure.

A more conventional couple postponed parenthood until they were "ready" and had "had some fun" in their adult, married lifestyle. The husband summed up their situation during this stage as follows:

> We were very happy and satisfied the way things were—our jobs, friends, new house, vacation trips—and we didn't want to change it just then. Our ambivalence about kids began to grow during this time, but we still assumed that someday we'd be parents just like everybody else.

Some couples postpone parenthood until they feel that they can give children all the things they think children should have. Under these circumstances, Stage Two of the postponement process closely parallels the reticence felt by many parents who do not want children too soon. A common concern is not having children until one is living in a "large enough" space, which might be defined as a two-bedroom apartment or as a three-bedroom house. Often, couples are concerned with being able to spend enough time with their children, a condition which may depend upon the woman's readiness to quit work, and/or the couple's readiness to manage on one salary. These kinds of reasons are generally relatively acceptable, in that they are attempts to maximize the advantages available to children, rather than to minimize the disadvantages that accrue to parents. A common consequence of such reasoning, however, is that the standards to be achieved before one is truly "ready" to have a child can escalate indefinitely, resulting in a series of successive "temporary" postponements.

Deliberating the Pros and Cons of Parenthood

Stage Three involves a qualitative change in the thinking of childless couples, in that for the first time there is an open acknowledgement of the possibility that, in the end, the couple may remain permanently childless. In this phase of the career, the only definite decision is to postpone deciding until some vague and unspecified time in the future.

For example, a nurse reported a typical progression from Stage One to Stage Three:

> When we were first married, we had long discussions about children. He wanted four and I only wanted two at the most, but it was no problem because it was still at the intellectual level because we were still discussing whether we wanted children and if we did, how many we would have. But we didn't want them then, we wanted to enjoy each other. Later on, we were trying to save to buy a house, the down-payment anyway, and we did, not this one but another we have sold since. Then my husband decided to go back to school, and he talked me into going back too. So that meant no kids for several years. We had been married I guess about three years when we really started to think that maybe we wouldn't have kids at all. We still haven't definitely decided never-never; it is a very hard decision to make, really. But a pregnancy now would just disrupt our whole way of life. Maybe later. He is thinking of a vasectomy, has been for a year or so. Maybe later; or maybe we might adopt or—I just don't know yet.

. . . [H]usbands are often less articulate about their rationale for avoiding parenthood because they have tended to think about it considerably less than have their wives. Since wives most often raise the issue of the advantages of a childfree lifestyle, the husband often ends up in the role of the devil's advocate, articulating the advantages of children in order to encourage his mate to consider both sides of the issue. One husband reported:

> It really became silly for a while there. She would give the routine that kids would tie us down, that they would be a big pain in the ass, etc. Then I chime in with all the "howevers" and "buts," supporting the notion of being parents and the joys of watching our own kid grow. I wasn't all that hip about the idea, but wanted to be sure she was seeing both sides of the issue. . . .

. . . Most couples who follow the normal moral career of parenthood cope with these questions [of the disadvantages of having children], in part by keeping them below the level of awareness. They do not have to decide to become parents because they have never questioned the inevitability of parenthood, or if they have questioned it, they have remained committed to the idealized and romanticized notions of what it will be like. A significant step in the moral career of childlessness is simply questioning the inevitability of parenthood and considering negative as well as positive aspects.

Acceptance of Permanent Childlessness

The fourth stage involves the definite conclusion that childlessness is a permanent rather than a transitory state. For most couples, there is never a direct decision made to avoid having children. Rather, after a number of years of postponing pregnancy until some future date, they become aware that an implicit decision has been made to forego parenthood. One wife reported a typical sequence:

> Our decision not to have children was a very gradual thing. When we first got married, we decided we were going to do a little bit of travelling before we had a family. We went to England first of all for a holiday. We decided we definitely wanted to do that before we settled down. And then when we came back from England, we decided we couldn't stand not having a car any longer; we wanted to be able to go out for drives and so on, so we figured we could wait another year and buy a car instead. And it kept getting postponed and the more we postponed, the less I really wanted to have children. Actually, I don't know that I ever really did want to have children; it was sort of a matter of this is what you do. I was never really wild about the idea. It was always going to be two at the most, and then it went down to one. We decided we would have one and if it was a girl, we would adopt a boy, and if it was a boy, we would adopt a girl. And then after that it went down to none and maybe adopt one. Or maybe just adopt one and we went to see the agency, like I told you. And then we just droped it altogether.

The process is one of recognizing an event which has already occured, rather than of posing a question and then searching or negotiating for an answer. At first, it was "obvious" that "of course" the couple would eventually have children; later it became equally "obvious" that "of course" they would not.

> Every couple of years we'd discuss whether to have a child or not, not because we really wanted children, but because the time seemed to be right. And then we'd look at the bank balance and put it off for another two years. After five years, we sort of stopped discussing it. We just decided let's let it ride, we're really not that keen on it anymore. If he really wanted to have a family, I'd go along with it wholeheartedly. Or the two of us, I'm the wishy-washy one. I would do it just because it wouldn't destroy any preconceived ideas I had about being married; you know, you get married and have children—that was already set. This is more of an unfamiliar terrain at this point, to say you are not going to. He was the one who made the decision. I never really disputed the preconceived notion that married people have children. I never even thought about it much one way or the other.

Two years later, at the age of thirty-six, the husband decided to get a vasectomy and the wife agreed it was a good decision. . . .

COMMITMENT TO CHILDLESSNESS

The degree of certainty attached to the acceptance of permanent childlessness varied among the respondents interviewed. All of the persons who were early articulators, and who had demanded a childlessness clause in their marriage contracts, felt that not wanting children was an immutable characteristic of themselves. Together with some persons who were involved in the postponement process, they felt that "becoming a parent is not the right thing for me." Such persons are "independents" (Cooper *et al.*, 1978) in that they make their decision to parent or not independently of the attitudes of their spouse. In discussing the extent to which childless persons were committed to childlessness, and the extent to which that commitment did or did not relate to their current marriage, respondents were asked: "What would you do if you (or if your wife) got pregnant?" Most immediately protested that such a thing could not happen accidentally, but were then persuaded to consider the consequences if, hypothetically, the "impossible" did occur. As an illustration of the extent to which some persons are committed to childlessness as an immutable personal attribute, rather than merely as a decision reflecting their current circumstances, one young husband replied concisely:

> Well, in that case, my wife could have three choices. One, she could have an abortion. I hope she would do that, but I guess I couldn't make her do it. If not, two, she could have the baby and place it for adpotion. Or three, she could have a divorce. . . .

In contrast to persons who characterize themselves as irrevocably childless by choice, more than half of our respondents related their decision not to have children to their present marriages. They acknowledged that, if they had happened to marry someone else, they might well have decided to have a child. Moreover, they often speculate that, if in the future they were to be married to someone who did want children, they might very well be persuaded to change their minds. Such persons feel that not wanting children reflects not their own nature *per se* so much as the situation in which they find themselves. After a period of negotiation, they and their mates came to agree that "becoming parents is not the right thing for us" or more likely "becoming parents is not the right thing for us right now." This does not imply a lack of consensus or a lack of satisfaction, but it does imply an openness to the potential for sometime living differently. One husband, who resisted the idea of sterilization, explained:

> Right now, I'm totally happy. We have a good marriage, we don't need kids. But who knows? Suppose we got a divorce. Suppose she got killed? I'd remarry, I know I would, and if my next wife wanted a baby, I would not automatically be opposed to it. That would be a different marriage, I'd be a different kind of husband married to a different kind of wife. If she wanted to be a mother, I'd be a father, I suppose. But now, here, for us? No way!

MOVING FROM STAGE TO STAGE: SOME FACTORS ACCELERATING COMMITMENT

Couples who know before they marry that they will never have children are not troubled by decisions, other than by choosing how they will avoid pregnancy. However, couples who remain childless through continued postponement, and who in doing so progress through four rather distinct phases, tend to have considerable variation in the ease and speed with which they move from one step to the next. Some circumstances tend to push couples rapidly on to the next stage; others tend to provide ample opportunity for continued delay.

Pregnancy Scares

One traumatic event which may serve to accelerate a couple's movement from one state of postponement to the next is a pregnancy scare. When the wife's menstrual period is late, or even worse, when a period is missed entirely, the possibility of pregnancy may serve to crystallize hitherto vague and unrecognized feelings about parenthood. Irregular periods, or even amenorrhea, may have many causes other than conception, but for sexually active woman pregnancy is the explanation which comes most readily to mind. The abstract idea of a child is quite different in its psychological impact from the concrete idea of a child's forming and growing day by day. For example, in response to the question of when she first knew she did not want children, one woman replied very emphatically and precisely: "The first moment I knew, and I was absolutely certain about it, was the first moment I knew I was pregnant." In fact, although she "knew" she was pregnant, her menstrual period was simply delayed and started spontaneously ten days later. During that time, she had been involved in an intense search for a competent abortionist, a search which she described as discouraging and humiliating. She was greatly relieved to discover that she was not pregnant after all, but by that time, the decision had been crystallized, and she and her husband were weighing the relative advantages of vasectomy versus tubal ligation.

The husband of another couple in a similar position stated:

> When we thought she was pregnant we found ourselves desperately trying to look on the positive side of it—that it will be fun being parents—but we weren't fooling ourselves, though we *thought* we were being nice guys and fooling each other. When her period came, we knew we'd made our decision never to risk pregnancy again.

Aging and the Decline of Fecundity: The Adoption Alternative

One of the problems of opting for the postponement model is the biological fact that childbirth cannot be postponed indefinitely. . . . Three interrelated problems are involved. In the first place, fecundity is known to decline with advancing age. Although it is theoretically possible for a woman to bear a child until her menopause is completed, in actuality her fecundity tends to decline with each year, as to a lesser extent does her husband's. Couples who could have had a child in their twenties but who chose to wait until their thirties may find that their fecundity has declined, or has been lost, during the intervening decade and that conception is no longer possible. In the second place, many childless couples perceive that once the wife is in her late thirties or early forties, the chances of having a defective child are much increased and that it therefore would be dangerous to do so at that late date.* Third, it must be realized that a larger part of the definition of how old is "too old" to have children is social, rather than biological in origin (Rindfuss and Bumpass, 1976). When the mother's age is too advanced, it is believed that her tolerance of young children is reduced and that the family situation would not be "good" for the child. Moreover, since couples tend to associate with persons their own age, a late birth would place them in the unusual situation of coping with toddlers while their friends were coping with teenagers.

As a consequence of these three factors, as the age of the wife approaches thirty, the decision to postpone deciding whether or not to have a child becomes less comfortable. In order to avoid the stress of having to make an imminent decision, one strategy is to redefine the maximum age at which reproduction would still be safe and desirable. Interestingly, this age seems to recede in time, depending upon the age of the woman, with a tendency to leave a margin of about two years. Thus, women of twenty-eight report they feel they must make a decision by the time they are thirty; women of thirty-four say they must do so by thirty-six; and women of thirty-eight vow to make up their minds by forty. Although such stalling defers immediate pressure, it is inevitably a temporary solution. When a forced choice appears imminent, a

*The increased medical risks associated with late pregnancies are more important relative to other women at younger ages than they are in absolute terms. For example, Down's syndrome is a congenital malformation which clearly increases in risk with advancing maternal age, especially after the age of forty. However, among births to women aged forty to forty-four, the incidence of Down's syndrome is less than one per cent (Nortman, 1974:7). In other words, a childless woman of this age has a better than 99 per cent chance of not having a Mongolian idiot. "Clearly, in the absence of a personal history to the contrary, older women run only a small risk of producing a congenitally malformed child, although their risk is much higher than that faced by younger women" (Nortman, 1974:7).

more practical solution is to include the vague possibility of adoption as a satisfactory "out" should one be needed. One wife makes a typical comment when she trails off her discussion of children by concluding: "If we've left having children too late, we might adopt one." An ex-nurse of twenty-nine, who believes that if you are going to have children, you should have them before you are thirty, suggests that: "If at fifty we decide we did miss something after all, we will adopt an Indian kid, or maybe a homeless teenager."

When we examined our childless couples closely on this subject of future adoption, however, it became clear that, in most instances, talk about adoption is unlikely to be a precursor of actually becoming adoptive parents. Although many of the childless couples referred at least once to the possibility of someday adopting a child, their discussions of this eventuality were exceedingly vague. They had apparently given no thought to the kind of child they might like to adopt, not even in terms of such obviously important traits as sex, age, or race. They had no information regarding the conditions under which adoption would be possible or what steps it would entail. It is noteworthy that it apparently never occurred to any of the couples who discussed adoption that, if they wanted to adopt, a suitable child might not be available. Nor did it occur to them that, if a child were available, he or she might not be placed with them. Although adoption is seldom a pragmatic option for voluntarily childless couples, it does have considerable symbolic importance in that it allows postponers to remain indefinitely at the third stage of debating endlessly the pros and cons of parenthood.

Ambivalence Toward Achievement

Couples in the first stage of postponement, who hold out other goals as "excuses" for not starting a family, may find themselves feeling quite ambivalent when they do finally achieve their goals. Such achievement is intrinsically desirable and presumably satisfying, but at the same time, it removes one of the most readily acceptable reasons for avoiding parenthood. Thus, one can be happy about graduating from college or about getting a good job, and at the same time be apprehensive about the attendant responsibilities that may come with it. For example, one husband reflected:

> I remember we were out celebrating the fact that we would both be finished with school and would graduate from college a full semester sooner, but when it dawned on us that now we didn't have any excuses left to postpone a family, we got a sinking feeling inside. Neither of us wanted that now. We found ourselves agreeing that it wouldn't be a good idea to have kids yet. We still acted the same way, but after that, it was a lot harder to explain. It was like our days of grace had run out, like on a mortgage or something.

Similarly, if couples have postponed having children until they are "out of debt," or until they can "afford to buy a house," their achievement of these goals necessitates a re-evaluation of their parenthood aspirations. Thus, removing the once-perceived obstacles to "being ready" for parenthood accelerates the couples more quickly toward a resolution of their dilemma and their inevitable entrance into either parenthood or a childfree lifestyle. . . .

REFERENCES

COOPER, PAMELA E., BARBARA CUMBER, and ROBIN HARTNER, 1978. "Decision-making patterns and postdecision adjustment of childfree husbands and wives," *Alternative Lifestyles*, 1 (February): 71–94.

NORTMAN, DOROTHY, 1974, "Parental age as a factor in pregnancy outcome and child development," *Reports on Population/Family Planning*, 16 (August): 1–51.

RINDFUSS, RONALD R., and LARRY L. BUMPASS, 1976. "How old is too old? Age and the sociology of fertility," *Family Planning Perspectives*, 8 (September/October):226–230.

PART IV

Endings and New Beginnings

DEATH AND TAXES used to be the two unavoidable facts of life. While those two still plague mankind, and are unavoidable, a third fact is rapidly gaining ground. Although it is not as common as death and taxes, divorce is on its way to joining the other two as an unavoidable fact of American life.

This is said somewhat tongue-in-cheek, for most marriages end not in divorce, but with the death of one or the other partner. Yet the divorce rate in our country has been increasing steadily for the past hundred years or so, and if it continues its increase it does appear that one day it will catch up with death and tie it for first cause of marital terminations.

Consider the following figures. It is estimated that in the late 1800s there was about one divorce for every twenty-one marriages. As the century turned, this figure had jumped to one divorce for every twelve marriages. By World War I it was up to one divorce for every ten marriages. The increase in the divorce rate continued unabated, and by 1940 it stood about one divorce for every five marriages. By 1950 for every four couples getting married, another couple was being officially unmarried. This ratio held for 1960, but during the 1970s it climbed to one divorce for every three marriages. At the present time for every two couples saying their vows, another couple is disavowing—not so blissfully untying the loosened marital knot.

Just as marriage brings with it a set of circumstances that demands adjusting to, so does divorce. Divorce also propels the formerly married into a new world. It poses new sets of expectations and problems, a whole new reality to which the individual must adapt. After entering this world, too, nothing can ever be quite the same again. One is no longer married, but one is really no longer entirely single, either. The former marriage cannot be entirely blocked out of existence as though it never happened. One was in fact married, and the substantial changes that marriage created are still carried about in the self, directly affecting the way the person looks at the world.

With the failure of a marriage, inevitably there are scars. They make a sometimes not-so-tough covering for deep wounds and for some, especially immediately after divorce, it does not take much to bruise those scars and expose the wounds. The hurting begins again, even in areas that the individual thought he or she had worked through. The adjustment comes slowly. For some it never comes at all. For most, the former marital partner, while divorced in a legal sense and gone in a legal sense, continues to be an ongoing part of life.

Some make a clean break. They terminate the marriage and put the other out of mind—at least mostly, depending on how many feelings are still unresolved and how many recordings the mind insists on playing back. Those without children appear able to make the cleanest break. They have fewer ties to their former marital partner, fewer times that they need be reminded that their world, so carefully constructed but so fragile, has come crumbling down around them to lie in ruin at their feet.

It is out of the heap of rubble that was once his or her life that the divorced person must build a new world, one that deliberately excludes the person who once was so important that they were going to spend the rest of their lives together. Separation. Attorneys. The striking gavel of the judge. And it is all over.

Only it is not. It is precisely at this point that the individual appears most liable to make serious mistakes in judging relationships. He or she has a deep void calling for satisfaction by ongoing, deep intimacy with a warm, receptive, and understanding member of the opposite sex. This yearning makes it easy to err by reaching out and grabbing what is real only in the imagination. The straw grasped in hopeful expectation is often a misjudged relationship that results in further wounds. In the unfortunate case it yields the tragedy of an ill-advised second marriage that results in yet another divorce.

To prevent further hurts, some build thick walls around the self, carefully constructing them to protect the self from imagined and expected onslaughts from the enemy, the opposite sex.

Most divorced people, however, through a painful and yet inadequately understood process, make the adjustment. They come out of it fairly whole, establish new significant relationships that bring meaning to their lives, and construct for themselves a new life. The painful events slowly recede, finally becoming hazy memories of a distant past. The nights become easier, as the capacity for openness, trust, and giving more fully of the self is reestablished as part of the individual's approach to life.

For a large majority, to put the pieces back together means a new marital partner. Few of the divorced (in spite of what they commonly say during the divorce process) are really soured on either marriage or the opposite sex. Needs that can be satisfied only by an intimate relationship do not cease with a bad marriage or with divorce. And, gradually (and not so gradually) the divorced are propelled into lasting relationships with the opposite sex. Within a few years, indeed, most of the divorced remarry (and many who do not would like to), trying once again, perhaps this time somewhat more soberly, to attain the happiness that they found so elusive in the first marriage.

It is divorce and remarriage, then, that we explore in this fourth part. Like all other complicated and multidimensional events that people experience—along with the multiplicity of feelings they evoke—words can describe only bits and pieces of it. Just as love must ultimately remain undefined, as it can only be fully grasped in its experiencing, so it is with divorce and remarriage. But through sociological research we can attain meaningful insight and understanding of these events that have taken on such significance in contemporary society.

SECTION 12

Divorce

WITH DIVORCE SUCH A COMMON EXPERIENCE in our society, it is fitting that we also explore it in this book. Because all of us experience divorce, if only indirectly through the divorces of relatives, friends, and associates, it is worthwhile to understand this aspect of life. We shall especially stress the sociological reasons for divorce and the processes by which people experience divorce and adjust to it afterward.

In the first chapter James M. Henslin delineates eight major reasons that divorce has become so common in our society. Besides becoming aware of these primary social causes of divorce, this chapter should also give you an understanding of how factors are *built into society* to either increase or decrease the likelihood of divorce.

In the second chapter, Diane Vaughan looks at the divorce process, the stages through which people go as they experience what she calls uncoupling. Note that the initial stages involve only the self, and from there they expand to the marital partner and others. As she analyzes the matter, it becomes clear that central to this process is finding new ways of looking at the self in terms of the spouse and others.

Divorce, of course, affects more than the husband and wife. Often, indeed, children become the unwilling victims of divorce, and it is on this topic that Judith S. Wallerstein and Joan B. Kelly focus. They analyze major problems that children aged six to twelve go through when they discover that their parents are going to divorce. Wallerstein and Kelly also stress how the children cope with those problems.

In a roundabout way, the children of divorce are also the topic of the last chapter in this section. Kristine M. Rosenthal and Harry F. Keshet turn the primary focus, however, onto divorced fathers. They look especially at how divorced fathers cope with the problems they encounter as they attempt to maintain a relationship with their children. They also examine the means by which divorced fathers try to maintain an identity apart from that of divorce, and their common attempts to insulate themselves from intimate relationships.

To apply the information in this section, you might try to put yourself in the situation of a divorced person. Imagine yourself having been married six months and getting a divorce. Then try three years, five years, and ten years. Then think about divorce with and without children, with and without your college degree. What differences do you think such factors would make for your process of adjustment? Who do you think has it easier in divorce, men or women? Why? Why do you think so many divorced persons get remarried? Do you think the high remarriage rate of the divorced supports the following statement: The divorced have not given up on marriage, they have just given up on marriage to a particular person? Similarly, do you think that our high rate of divorce signifies that marriage in our society is in trouble? Or do you think it means that marriage is healthier than ever because people are leaving undesirable situations and beginning other relationships in the attempt to find happiness? Why do you take that position?

CHAPTER 44

Why So Much Divorce?

James M. Henslin

ABSTRACT: Why, in spite of a married couple's best intentions, do so many marriages end in divorce? The author indicates that eight major factors underlie our high divorce rate: (1) incompatible sex roles; (2) the separateness of the sex worlds, (3) the demands of life; (4) the routines of married life; (5) changes in the functions of marriage; (6) an emphasis on personality fulfillment; (7) increased institutional support for divorce; and (8) the social roles of husband and wife.

Most newlyweds typically enter marriage with positive emotions (or love) accompanied by sincere desires for success. The best of intentions, however, often become waylaid by the pressing realities of married life. The adjustment from being single to being married usually turns out to be much more difficult than people anticipate. The positive feelings with which they begin marriage often are replaced by feelings of vague dissatisfaction, sometimes expressed as, "Something is wrong, but I can't put my finger on it." In a great number of cases the married partners can put their fingers precisely on it, however, and in doing so they usually point directly at the other. They know that *they* are trying about as hard as they can, so the problem must lie with the one they married. Frustrations build up. Each blames the other. Quarreling begins. The quarrels intensify. When the point comes at which almost all their interaction is negative, the couple begins to wonder what they ever saw in the other in the first place.

This scenario, with its many variations, is played out in marriage after marriage. The best of intentions do not make marriage a success. Beginning marriage with positive feelings toward the other does not guarantee marital happiness. If such feelings and intentions did ensure it, almost every marriage would be a success, for they characterize most brides and grooms at the wedding ceremony.

But something goes wrong in a lot of marriages and about a third or so end in divorce. Keep in mind that this figure does not include those people who live in various degrees of unhappiness, regret, and downright misery and despair, but who for one reason or another do not divorce. Add these together and one can see that the promise so blissfully held out by the ideal of marriage is difficult to fulfill.

Why? What goes wrong?

It is not just a single thing, of course. There are many contributing factors, each of which takes its toll, and all of which increase marital risk.

While we could begin in a number of places to locate the components from which divorce is constructed, it is useful to start with incompatible sex roles. Many of the essential factors that the male learns in his early socialization as part of his masculine orientation toward the world, and his "proper" place within it, conflict with the feminine orientation and presumed proper place. Consequently, for almost all couples the adjustment to marriage comes with a great deal of difficulty.

For many who divorce, there does not have to be a single other factor. Sex-role incompatibility—and the requisite self-realignment that marriage imposes—can be enough to signal the destruction of marital hopes.

Other social conditions, however, are also at work to contribute their share to the dissolution of marital dreams. The second, highly related to the first, is the separateness of the sex worlds in our society. Males and females are placed in different corners of life, with each corner representing a unique world of experience. What this separateness means is that even as adults both husbands and wives undergo a continuing socialization process during which each learns a somewhat different way of handling problems, of evaluating what is important and what is irrelevant, and, in general, of approaching life. Since the husband and wife share the same time/space/relational/income/sexual/emotional dimensions of life-space, it is almost inevitable that these differences will produce a clash.

The third contributing factor might be called the demands of life. It consists of those pressures to which adults in our culture are exposed, those things that demand satisfaction. This especially includes bills: those the couple run up when they go on their honeymoon; rent an apartment or buy a house; buy furniture to decorate it properly, including colored appliances to match the decor; buy a car, buy gasoline to run it, and pay mechanic's bills to keep it running; buy life and auto and home and accident and health insurance; pay for entertainment; buy clothing; pay for their alcohol and cigarettes; pay medical bills, taxes and social security; and, of course, buy some food somewhere in between all the other demands made on their limited income.

This third factor also includes the demands made on the time and energy of the couple. The house or apartment must be cleaned; so must the car. Their own bodies must be washed and groomed. The television set demands that it be turned on. The dog insists on being walked and, when the litter box gets to the point that the cat refuses to be seen near it, it also must be taken care of.

And so go a thousand and one items, each of which saps its share of the couple's energy, enthusiasm, and interest. Of course, if after all the above they have any spirit left, they must give at least a little to their boss, who expects something in return for signing a paycheck.

Each of these aspects of modern-day life helps account for the emotional exhaustion so many feel. The malaise has a major victim, however, one ordinarily not thought of in this context, and that is marriage With so great and exhausting and endless demands on the self, there often is not much time or energy left to direct toward the spouse. It is often the spouse who suffers and, often as a consequence, the marriage.

The fourth major factor contributing to marital difficulties can be called the routines of married life. The couple gets used to each other The newness wears off as they live with each other day after day. Before marriage, they were together because they wanted to be. They overcame whatever obstacles they faced in order to be together. After several years of marriage (for many, much less than this), some couples come to see their marriage in terms of a monotonous routine.

What happens? After marriage, the husband and wife see each other daily, no longer out of an emotional or rational choice but out of the necessity to share the same living quarters and the demands of the roles thrust upon them by marriage itself. As they are together day in and day out, they soon come to know each other extremely well. What was at first pleasant discovery eventually becomes predictability of what the other will do—including the other's words, mannerisms, gestures, and even facial expressions. In general, one knows in detail how the other will react to a myriad of circumstances.

While this factor of marriage can be used creatively to build security and dependable constancy into one's relationship, it often serves to create boredom. Boredom demands to be relieved, and some couples manage this by quarreling (and not knowing why they are quarreling), adultery (and not knowing why that other person is so appealing), and countless other ways that are destructive to the marital relationship.

The fifth major factor producing high divorce rates in our society is changes in the functions of marriage and family. As traditional functions have shrunk, taken over by other social institutions, the forces that keep a couple together *in spite of* problems have been weakened.

Consider, for example, the many bonds that used to tie a couple to one another. In the typical American farming family at the turn of the century, and common through the 1920s and 1930s, the husband and wife (and the children as well) shared a large number of *mutually interrelated and beneficial* tasks or functions. Each performed jobs that were *essential* to the support, existence, and welfare of the other. As the husband's tasks of farming the fields and managing the farm are perhaps the better known, I shall not delineate them. But what was his wife doing while he was in the fields? In addition to the usual cooking, cleaning, and child care, she made bread and most of the family's clothing, and raised a large garden, chickens, and a calf or lamb for the family's table. She also made butter, canned vegetables and meat, put up preserves, and joined in milking the cows. In addition, she sold eggs and butter in order to provide the money that was necessary to buy the little food that she and her husband did not produce themselves.

If one did not feel "emotionally satisfied" from the other, well, in general that was simply something that one had to put up with. One married a husband or wife so *each could be a provider for the other*, and with life itself precarious, one was primarily concerned about producing for survival, not about feeling good.

Now, however, with the "functions that bind" so greatly diminished, the couple splinters much more easily when problems arise.

The sixth major factor is the replacement of diminished functions with a heavy emphasis on personality or emotional fulfillment. It has increasingly become an expectation in American marriage that each spouse is to fulfill the personality needs of the other. (This is an especially onerous expectation, for our personality needs are highly complicated and ever changing.) When one spouse feels "unfulfilled," he or she tends to place blame on the marital partner for not meeting this newly basic expectation.

Depending primarily on one person to satisfy one's needs creates great pressures. It is the husband or wife who is the major adult with whom a spouse is expected to interact, and placing on him or her the burden of satisfying one's personality needs in and of itself could be imposing a full-time job. These include needs of security, being comforted, knowing you belong, knowing that the goals you are working for are right and worthwhile, knowing that you are on the right course in life, being loved, being comforted in sadness, being taken care of in sickness, and so on ad infinitum.

Who can satisfy the long list of needs that are basic to everyone's deep personality structure? Can any single person do it? And when the one on whom such need satisfactions are lodged is himself or herself so furiously busy meeting the pressing demands of life, and in addition has his or her own long list of needs, is it any wonder that contemporary husbands and wives often feel that the other is somehow letting them down?

The seventh major factor is the increased institutional support for divorced women. (This applies to men also, but its primary effects are felt by women.) Three principal elements are involved: the lessened stigma attached to divorce in our culture; the greater economic independence of women, that is, their greater employability; and a greatly expanded welfare system, the likes of which were unknown only two or three decades ago. Succinctly put, this increased institutional support means that a woman experiences less necessity for staying in a marriage with which she is unhappy.

The eighth major factor, one that many would place at the head of the list, is the social roles of husband and wife. For many, to assume the role of husband or wife is to force automatic, unthinking demands on the other, which, in turn, creates resentment. This is captured in the not uncommon refrain of the wife who laments, "Before marriage he treated me like someone special. Now he treats me like a *wife*!"

Admittedly, this last factor overlaps with and is difficult to conceptually distinguish from some of the preceding components, especially the first four. At the same time, however, it pinpoints a feature of marital roles that underlies many problems in contemporary marriage and deserves to be separately stressed.

To understand divorce in our society, then, is far from a simple matter. The above eight factors represent only one way of computing the components of our divorce rate. While other sociologists would stress these components differently, and even add or subtract from this listing, these factors make it evident that divorce is certainly due to much more than "personality problems" or a loosening of morality. Rather, our rate of divorce is directly related to the social structure of American society. From our social institutions comes a basic approach to marriage—including roles and expectations—that is played out on the individual level. On this personal level of experiences, the couple perceives the problems that result from these various alignments and misalignments as personality problems (or "mismatches" of various sorts), for the *social* roots that underlie their difficulties remain largely invisible to them.

CHAPTER 45

Uncoupling:

The Social Construction of Divorce

Diane Vaughan

ABSTRACT: The author focues on the process (stages) by which an individual moves from a coupled (married) to an uncoupled (single) identity. The process begins when one (the initiator), not receiving self-validation, questions the coupled identity. The initiator then begins to redefine the relationship, using two forms of "accompanying reconstructions." As the initiator attempts to seek self-validation (autonomy) outside the relationship, he or she experiences a heightened sense of exclusion. The next stages in the process of uncoupling are trying, separation, divorce, and continuities. Divorce is not the end of the uncoupling process, but one of the stages on the way.

[In our society social] relationships . . . are seldom static. Not only do we move in and out of relationships, but the nature of a particular relationship, though enduring, varies over time. . . . [H]*ow do individuals move from a mutual identity, as in marriage, to assume separate, autonomous identities again?* What is the process by which new definitions are created and become validated? . . .

The dimensions of sorrow, anger, personal disorganization, fear, loneliness, and ambiguity that intermingle every separation are well known.[1] Their familiarity does not diminish their importance. Though in real life these cannot be ignored, the researcher has the luxury of selectivity. Here, it is not the pain and disorganization that are to be explored, but the existence of an underlying orderliness. . . .

The formal basis from which this paper developed was in-depth, exploratory interviews. The interviews, ranging from two to six hours, were taped and later analyzed. All of the interviewees were at different stages in the uncoupling process. Most were divorced, though some were still in stages of consideration of divorce. . . .

[T]he declared purpose here is to abstract the essential features of the process of uncoupling. . . . Occasionally . . . the uncoupling process is initiated by both. More frequently, however, one partner still finds the marriage a major source of stability and identity, while the other finds it inadequate. In this form, one participant takes the role of initiator of the uncoupling process. However, this role may not consistently be held by one partner, but instead may alternate between them, due to the difficulty of uncoupling in the face of external constraints, social pressure not to be the one responsible for the demise of the marriage, and the variability in the self-validating function of the union over time. For the purpose of this study, the form of uncoupling under consideration is that which results when one partner, no longer finding the coupled identity self-validating, takes the role of initiator in the uncoupling process. The other partner, [here called] the significant other, still finds the marriage a major source of stability and identity.

UNCOUPLING: THE INITIATION OF THE PROCESS

> I was never psychologically married. I always felt strained by attempts that coupled me into a marital unit. I was just never comfortable as "Mrs." I never got used to my last name. I never wanted it. The day after my marriage was probably the most depressed day of my life, because I had lost my singularity. The difference between marriage and a deep relationship, living together, is that you have this ritual, and you achieve a very definite status, and it was *that* that produced my reactions—because I became in the eyes of the world a man's wife. And I was never comfortable and happy with it. It didn't make any difference who the man was.

An early phase in the uncoupling process occurs as one or the other of the partners begins to question the coupled identity. At first internal, the challenging of the created world remains for a time as a doubt within one of the partners in the coupling. Though there is a definition of coupledness, subjectively the coupledness may be experienced differently by each partner. . . . [T]he initial recognition of the coupling as problematic may be internal and unarticulated, held as a secret. The subworld that has been constructed, for some reason, doesn't "fit."

A process of definition negotiation is begun, initiated by the one who finds the mutual identity an inadequate definition of self. Attempts to negotiate the definition of the coupledness are likely to result in the subjective meaning becoming articulated for the first time, thus moving the redefinition process toward objectivation. The secret, held by the initiator, is shared with the significant other. When this occurs, it allows both participants to engage in the definitional process. . . . Perhaps for the significant other, the marriage as it is still provides important self-validation. If so, the initiator must bring the other to the point of sharing a common definition of the marriage as "troubled."

ACCOMPANYING RECONSTRUCTIONS

Though this shared definition is being sought, the fact remains that, for the initiator, the coupled identity fails to provide self-validation. In order to meet this need, the initiator engages in other attempts at redefining the nature of the relationship. Called "accompanying reconstructions," these *may* or *may not* be shared with the significant other. . . .

The first form of accompanying reconstruction to be considered is the initiator's redefinition of the coupledness itself. One way of redefining the coupledness is by an unarticulated conversion of the agreed-upon norms of the relationship.

> I had reconceptualized what marriage was. I decided sexual fidelity was not essential for marriage. I never told her that. And I didn't even have anyone I was interested in having that intimate a relationship with—I just did a philosophical thing. I just decided it was O.K. for me to have whatever of what quality of other relationships I needed to have. Something like that—of that caliber—was something I could never talk to her about. So I did it all by myself. I read things and decided it. I was at peace with me. I knew that we could stay married, whatever that meant. . . .

A second form of accompanying reconstruction occurs when the initiator attempts to redefine the significant other in a way that is more compatible with his own self-validation needs. The initiator may direct efforts toward specific behaviors, such as drinking habits, temper, sexual incompatibilities, or finance management. Or, the redefinition attempt may be of a broader scope.

> I was aware of his dependence on the marriage to provide all his happiness, and it wasn't providing it. I wanted him to go to graduate school, but he postponed it, against my wishes. I wanted him to pursue his own life. I didn't want him to sacrifice for me. I wanted him to become more exciting to me in the process. I was aware that I was trying to persuade him to be a different person.

Redefinition of the significant other may either be directed toward maintaining the coupledness, as above, or moving away from it, as is the case following.

> The way I defined being a good wife and the way John defined being a good wife were two different quantities. He wanted the house to look like a hotel and I didn't see it that way. He couldn't see why I couldn't meet his needs. . . . When he first asked for a divorce and I refused, he suggested I go back to school. I remembered a man who worked with John who had sent his wife back to school so she could support herself, so he could divorce her. I asked John if he was trying to get rid of me. He didn't answer that. He insisted I go, and I finally went. . . .

SELF-VALIDATION OUTSIDE THE MARRIAGE

What was at first internally experienced and recognized as self-minimizing takes a more concrete form and becomes externally expressed in a search for self-maximization. Through investment of self in career, in a cause requiring commitment, in a relationship with a new significant other, in family, in education, or in activities and hobbies, the initiator develops new sources of self-realization. These alternative sources of self-realization confirm not the coupled identity but the singularity of the initiator.

Furthermore, in the move toward a distinct biography . . . the initiator finds confirmation for a belief in *self* as a first priority [as opposed to the nuclear family].

> I now see my break with religion as a part of my developing individuality. At the time I was close friends with priests and nuns, most of whom have since left the church. I felt a bitterness toward the church for its definition of marriage. I felt constrained toward a type of marriage that was not best for me. . . .

The initiator moves toward construction of a separate subworld wherein significant conversation comes from circles which no longer overlap with those of the significant other. And, the significant other is excluded from that separate subworld.

> I shared important things with the children that I didn't share with him. It's almost as if I purposefully punished him by not telling him. Some good thing would happen and I'd come home and tell them and wouldn't tell him.

The initiator's autonomy is further reinforced as the secret of the troubled marriage is shared with others in the separate subworld the initiator is constructing. It may be directly expressed as a confidence exchanged with a close friend, family member, or children, or it may be that the sharing is indirect. Rather than being expressed in significant conversation, the definition of the marriage as troubled is created for others by a variety of mechanisms that relay the message that the initiator is not happily married. The definition of the marriage as problematic becomes further objectivated as the secret, once held only by the initiator, then shared with the significant other, moves to a sphere beyond the couple themselves. . . .

These movements away by the initiator heighten a sense of exclusion for the significant other. Deep commitment to other than the coupled identity—to a career, to a cause, to education, to a hobby, to another person—reflects a lessened commitment to the marriage. The initiator's search for self-validation outside the marriage even may be demonstrated symbolically to the significant other by the removal of the wedding ring or by the desire, if the initiator is a woman, to revert to her maiden name. If the initiator's lessened commitment to the coupled identity is reflected in a lessened desire for sexual intimacy, the challenge to the identity of the significant other and the coupledness becomes undeniable. As the significant other recognizes the growing autonomy of the initiator, he, too, comes to accept the definition of the marriage as "troubled." . . .

[While] the initiator has found other sources of self-realization outside the marriage, usually the significant other has not. The marriage still performs the major self-validating function. . . . The challenge to the identity of the significant other and to the coupledness posed by the initiator may result in increased commitment to the coupled identity for the significant other. With the joint biography already separated in these ways, the couple enters into a period of "trying."

TRYING

Trying is a stage of intense definition negotiation by the partners. Now both share a definition of the marriage as troubled. However, each partner may seek to construct a new reality that is in opposition to that of the other. The significant other tries to negotiate a shared definition of the marriage as savable, whereas the initiator negotiates toward a shared definition that marks the marriage as unsavable.[2]

For the initiator, the uncoupling process is well underway. At some point the partner who originally perceived the coupled identity to be problematic and sought self-validation outside the coupled identity has experienced "psychological divorce." . . .

The initiator tries subtly to prepare the significant other to live alone. By encouraging the other to make new friends, find a job, get involved in outside activities, or seek additional education, the initiator hopes to decrease the other's commitment to and dependence upon the coupled identity for self-validation and move the other toward autonomy. This stage of preparation is not simply one of cold expediency for the benefit of the initiator, but is based on concern for the significant other and serves to mitigate the pain of the uncoupling process for both the initiator and the other.

For both, there is a hesitancy to sever the ties. In many cases, neither party is fully certain about the termination of the marriage. Mutual uncertainty may be more characteristic of the process. The relationship may weave back and forth between cycles of active trying and passive acceptance of the status quo due to the failure of each to pull the other to a common definition and the inability of either to make the break.

> I didn't want to hurt him. I didn't want to be responsible for the demise of a marriage I no longer wanted. . . .

> I didn't want to be the villain—the one to push her out into the big bad world. I wanted to make sure she was at the same point I was. . . .

Frequently, in the trying stage, the partners turn to outside help for formal negotiation of the coupled identity. Counseling, though entered into with apparent common purpose, becomes another arena in which the partners attempt to negotiate a shared definition from their separately held definitions of the marriage as savable or unsavable. For the initiator, the counseling may serve as a step in the preparation of the significant other to live alone. . . .

At some point during this period of trying, the initiator may suggest separation. Yet, separation is not suggested as a formal leave-taking but as a *temporary* separation meant to clarify the relationship for both partners. . . . [T]he temporary separation is encouraged as a further means of bringing the other to accept a definition of the marriage as unsavable, to increase reliance of the other on outside resources of self-realization, and to initiate the physical breach gently.

> Even at that point, a initial separation, I wasn't being honest. I knew fairly certainly that when we separated, it was for good. I let her believe that it was a means for us first finding out what was happening and then eventually possibly getting back together.

Should the initiator be hesitant to suggest a separation, the significant other may finally tire of the ambiguity of the relationship. No longer finding the coupling as it exists self-validating, the significant other may be the one to suggest a separation. . . .

OBJECTIVATION: RESTRUCTURING OF THE PRIVATE SPHERE

The separation is a transitional state in which everything needs definition, yet very little is capable of being defined. Economic status, friendship networks, personal habits, and sex life are all patterns of the past which need simultaneous reorganization. However, reorganization is hindered by the ambiguity of the relationship. The off-again, on-again wearing of the wedding rings is symbolic of the indecision in this stage. Each of the partners searches for new roles, without yet being free of the old.

For the initiator who has developed outside resources, the impact of this uncertainty is partially mitigated. For the significant other, who has not spent time in preparation for individual existence, the major self-validating function of the marriage is gone and nothing has emerged as a substitute.

> I had lost my identity somewhere along the way. And I kept losing my identity. I kept letting him make all the decisions. I couldn't work. I wasn't able to be myself. I was letting someone else take over. I didn't have any control over it. I didn't know how to stop it. I was unsure that if anything really happened I could actually make it on my own or not.

The separation precipitates a redefinition of self for the significant other. Without other resources for self-validation, and with the coupled identity now publicly challenged, the significant other begins a restructuring of the private sphere.

This restructuring occurs not only in the social realm but also entails a form of restructuring that is physical, tangible, and symbolic of the break in the coupled identity. For instance, if the initiator has been the one to leave, at some point the significant other begins reordering the residence they shared to suit the needs of one adult rather than two. Furniture is rearranged or thrown out. Closets and drawers are reorganized. A thorough house-cleaning may be undertaken. As the initiator has moved to a new location that reinforces his singularity, the significant other transforms the home that validated the coupling into one that likewise objectivates the new definition. Changes in the physical appearance of either or both partners may be a part of the symbolic restructuring of the private sphere. Weight losses, changes of hair style, or changes in clothing preferences further symbolize the yielding of the mutual identity and the move toward autonomy.

Should the significant other be the one to leave, the move into a new location aids in the redefinition of self as an autonomous individual. For example, the necessity of surviving in a new environment, the eventual emergence of a new set of friends that define and relate to the significant other as a separate being instead of as half of a couple, and the creation of a new residence without the other person are all mechanisms which reinforce autonomy and a definition of singularity. . . .

OBJECTIVATION: THE PUBLIC SPHERE

The uncoupling is further objectivated for the participants as the new definition is legitimized in the public sphere. Two separate households demand public identification as separate identities. New telephone listings, changes of mailing address, separate checking accounts, and charge accounts, for example, all are mechanisms by which the new reality becomes publicly reconstructed.

The decision to initiate legal proceedings confirms the uncoupling. . . . The adversary process supporting separate identities, custody proceedings, the formal separation of the material base, the final removal of the rings all act as means of moving the new definition from the private to the public sphere. The uncoupling now becomes objectivated not only for the participants and their close intimates, but for casual acquaintances and strangers. . . .

DIVORCE: A STAGE IN THE PROCESS

[U]ncoupling involves [a] redefinition of self as the participants move from mutual identity toward autonomy. It is this redefinition of self, for each participant, that completes the uncoupling. Divorce, then, may not be the final stage. . . . In other words, the uncoupling process might be viewed as a status transformation which is complete when the individual defines his salient status as "single" rather than "divorced." When the individual's newly constructed separate subworld . . . creates for the individual a sort of order in which he can experience his life as making sense—the uncoupling process is completed.

The completion of uncoupling does not occur at the same moment for each participant. For either or both of the participants, it may not occur until after the other has created a coupled identity with another person. With that step, the tentativeness is gone.

> When I learned of his intention to remarry, I did not realize how devastated I would be. It was just awful. I remember crying and crying. It was really a very bad thing that I did not know or expect. You really aren't divorced while that other person is still free. You still have a lot of your psychological marriage going—in fact, I'm still in that a little bit because I'm still single.

For some, the uncoupling may never be completed. One or both of the participants may never be able to construct a new and separate subworld that becomes self-validating. Witness, for example, the widow who continues to call herself "Mrs. John Doe," who associates with the same circle of friends, who continues to wear her wedding ring and observes wedding anniversaries. For her, the coupled identity is still a major mechanism for self-validation, even though the partner is gone.

In fact, death as a form of uncoupling may be easier for the significant other to handle than divorce. There exist ritual techniques for dealing with it, and there is no ambiguity. The relationship is gone. There will be no further interaction between the partners. With divorce, or any uncoupling that occurs through the volition of one or both of the partners, the interaction may continue long after the relationship has been formally terminated. For the significant other—the one left behind, without resources for self-validation—the continuing interaction between the partners presents obstacles to autonomy.

> There's a point at which it's over. If your wife dies, you're a lot luckier, I think, because it's over. You either live with it, you kill yourself, or you make your own bed of misery. Unlike losing a wife through death, in divorce, she doesn't die. She keeps resurrecting it. I can't get over it, she won't die. I mean, she won't go away.

CONTINUITIES

Continuities are linkages between the partners that exist despite the formal termination of the coupled identity. Most important of these is the existence of shared loved ones—children, in-laws, and so on. Though in-laws may of necessity be excluded from the separately constructed subworlds, children can rarely be and, in their very existence, present continued substantiation of the coupled identity.

In many cases continuities are actively constructed by one or both of the participants after the formal termination of the relationship. . . . They may be constructed as a temporary bridge between the separated subworlds, or they may come to be a permanent interaction pattern. Symbolically, they seem to indicate caring on the part of either or both of the participants.

> The wife moves out. The husband spends his weekend helping her get settled—hanging pictures, moving furniture. . . .

> The husband moves out. Once a week he comes to the house to visit with the children on an evening when the wife is away. When she gets home, the two of them occasionally go out to dinner. . . .

> The holidays during the first year of separation are celebrated as they always had been—with the whole family together. . . .

In this paper . . . the stages that mark the movement from a coupled identity to separate autonomous identities are characterized, using divorce for an ideal-type analysis. Yet, there is no intent to portray uncoupling as a compelling linear process from which there is no turning back. . . .

Each stage of objectivation acts as the closing of a door. Yet at any stage the process may be interrupted. The initiator may not find mechanisms of self-validation outside the coupling that reinforce his autonomy. Or the self-validation found outside the coupling may be the very stuff that allows the initiator to stay *in* the relationship. Or continuities may intervene and reconstruction of the coupled identity may occur, despite the degree of objectivation, as in the following case.

> Ellen met Jack in college. They fell in love and married. Jack had been blind since birth. He had pursued a college career in education and was also a musician. Both admired the independence of the other. In the marriage, she subordinated her career to his and helped him pursue a master's degree, as well as his musical interests. Her time was consumed by his needs—for transportation and the taping and transcribing of music for the musicians in his group. He was teaching at a school for the blind by day and performing as a musician at night. They had a son, and her life, instead of turning outward, as his, revolved around family responsibilities. She gained weight. Jack, after twelve years of marriage, left Ellen for his high school sweetheart. Ellen grieved for a while, then began patching up her life. She got a job, established her own credit, went back to college, and lost weight. She saw a lawyer, filed for divorce, joined Parents Without Partners, and began searching out singles groups. She dated. Throughout, Jack and Ellen saw each other occasionally and maintained a sexual relationship. The night before the divorce was final, they reconciled.

The uncoupling never was completed, though all stages of the process occurred including the public objectivation that results from the initiation of the legal process. Ellen, in constructing an autonomous identity, became again the independent person Jack had first loved.[3] This, together with the continuities that existed between the two, created the basis for a common definition of the coupling as savable.

DISCUSSION

Berger and Kellner describe the process by which two individuals create a coupled identity for themselves. Here, we have started from the point of the coupled identity and examined the process by which people move out of such relationships. Using interview data, we have found that, although the renegotiation of separate realities is a complex web of subtle modifications, clear stages emerge which mark the uncoupling process. The emergent stages are like benchmarks which indicate the increasing objectivation of the changing definitions of reality, as these definitions move from the realm of the private to the public. . . .

[T]he interviewees were all at various stages in the uncoupling process—some at the "secret" stage and some five years hence. Yet, the stages which are discussed here appeared without fail in every case. . . .

Generally, uncoupling is thought of as a conflict-ridden experience that ends as a bitter battle between two adversaries intent on doing each other in. Frequently, this is the case. Yet, the interviews for this study showed that in all cases, even the most emotion generating, again and again the concern of each of the participants for the other revealed itself. Apparently, the patterns of caring and responsibility that emerge between the partners in a coupling are not easily dispelled and in many cases persist throughout the uncoupling process and after, as suggested by the concept of continuities. . . .

NOTES

1. For a sensitive and thought-provoking examination of these as integral components of divorce, see Willard Waller's beautiful qualitative study, *The Old Love and the New*.
2. This statement must be qualified. There are instances when the partners enter a stage of trying with shared definitions of the marriage as savable. The conditions under which the coupling can be preserved have to be negotiated. If they can arrive at a common definition of the coupling that is agreeable to both, the uncoupling process is terminated. But this analysis is of uncoupling, and there are two alternatives: (1) that they enter with common definitions of the marriage as savable but are not able to negotiate the conditions of the coupling so that the self-validation function is preserved or (2) that they enter the period of trying with opposing definitions, as stated here.
3. Waller interprets this phenomenon by using Jung's conceptualization of the container and the contained, analogous to the roles of initiator and significant other, respectively, in the present discussion. Notes Waller, "Or the contained, complicated by the process of divorcing, may develop those qualities whose lack the container previously deplored" (Waller:163–168).

REFERENCE

Berger, Peter L. and Hansfried Kellner, 1964. "Marriage and the Construction of Reality," *Diogenes*, 46:1–23.

CHAPTER 46

Effects of Parental Divorce

Judith S. Wallerstein / Joan B. Kelly

ABSTRACT: When children between the ages six and twelve learn of their parents' decision to divorce, they use a variety of mechanisms to master feelings of loss and rejection, helplessness and loneliness, and they initially cover (layer) their feelings and fears quite well. Some of the older children attempt to master their feelings by organized activity and play. But after the initial reactions children commonly experience intense anger, fears and phobias, a shaken sense of identity, loneliness, and loyalty conflicts. Some children will even align themselves with one of the parents to the exclusion of the other.

[T]he decision of divorce frequently ushers in an extended several year period marked by uncertainty and sharp discontinuity which has the potential to move the psychological and social functioning of the latency child* into profound disequilibrium and painfully altered parent-child relationships. Alternatively, these changes can bear the potential for promoting development and maturation, as well as the possibility of more gratifying relationships within the post-divorce family structure.

Our data for this paper are drawn from [a] sample [Kelly and Wallerstein, 1976] of 57 latency aged children from 47 families, here focused

*Latency is a psychoanalytic concept referring to school age, around six to twelve, when sexuality is considered "latent" compared to the developmental stages immediately preceding or following.

on the experiences of the 31 children from 28 families who were between nine and ten years old at the time that they were initially seen by us. As elaborated elsewhere [Kelly and Wallerstein, 1976; Wallerstein and Kelly, 1974; Wallerstein and Kelly, 1975], these 31 children from 28 families represent part of a cohort of 131 children from 60 divorcing families referred for anticipatory guidance and planning for their children around the separation, and then seen by us again approximately a year later for the first of two planned follow-up studies.

THE INITIAL RESPONSES

How They Looked When They Came

Many of these children had presence, poise, and courage when they came to their initial interviews. They perceived the realities of their families' disruption and the parental turbulence with a soberness and clarity which we at first found startling, particularly when compared with the younger children who so frequently appeared disorganized and immobilized by their worry and grief. These youngsters were, by contrast, actively struggling to master a host of intense conflicting feelings and fears and trying to give coherence and continuity to the baffling disorder which they now experienced in their lives.

> Robert said, "I have to calm myself down. Everything is happening too fast."

> Katherine told us that a long time ago, when she was little, she thought everything was fine, that her parents really loved each other, and that, "Nothing would happen to them until they got real, real old." She added with the fine perceptions of a latency age child, "Mom and Dad married 12½ years ago. They met 17½ years ago. I always thought love would last if they stayed together that long."

Some children came prepared with an agenda.

> Anna, after a few general comments from the interviewer, designed to put her at ease, interrupted with a brisk, "Down to business," and went on immediately to describe the diffuse feelings of anxiety with which she suffered these days and which made her feel "sick to her stomach."

> Mary volunteered that she was "so glad" her mother brought her to talk about the divorce because, "If I don't talk about it soon I'll fall apart."

For others the opportunity to be with a concerned adult had considerable significance seemingly unrelated to specific content. Some of these children tried in many ways to continue the relationship.

> Janet begged to return the following week. She offered, "I like to talk about my troubles," and drew a heart on the blackboard, writing under it, "I like Miss X."

> Mary tried to extend her interview time, saying that her mother had not yet returned to fetch her, and then confessing that she had just lied.

Still others among these children found these interviews threatening and painful, and barely kept their anxiety controlled by keeping themselves or their extremities in continual motion, the rhythm of which motion correlated with the subject discussed.

> Thus, legs moved much faster when Daddy was mentioned to Jim, who was bravely trying to maintain his calm and referred with some disdain to "Mother's divorce problem," adding, "I wonder who she's got now?"

Others maintained their composure by denial and distancing.

> Jack stated, "I keep my cool. It's difficult to know what I'm thinking."

> David said darkly, "I don't try to think about it."

The Layering of Response

These various efforts to manage—by seeking coherence, by denial, by courage, by bravado, by seeking support from others, by keeping in motion, by conscious avoidance—all emerged as age-available ways of coping with the profound underlying feelings of loss and rejection, of helplessness and loneliness that pervaded these children and that, in most of them, only gradually became visible within the context of the several successive interviews. Actually, testament of the resourcefulness of so many of these children is just this capacity to function simultaneously on these two widely discrepant levels, not always discernible to the outside observer. At times, only information from collateral sources revealed their simultaneous involvement in the mastery efforts of the coping stance and the succumbing to the anguish of their psychic pain. This at times conscious layering of psychological functioning is a specific finding in this age group. It is profoundly useful in muting and encapsulating the suffering, making it tolerable and enabling the child to move developmentally. But it does not overcome the hurt, which is still there and takes its toll.

> After his father left the home, Bob sat for many hours sobbing in his darkened room. The father visited infrequently. When seen by our project, Bob offered smilingly, "I have a grand time on his visits," and added unsolicited and cheerily, "I see him enough." Only later would he shamefacedly admit that he missed his father intensely and longed to see him daily.

A few children were able to express their suffering more directly to their parents, as well as to us. This is the more poignant if one bears in mind Bornstein's [1951] admonition that the latency child is *normally* engaged developmentally in a powerful battle against painful feelings.

> Jane's father left his wife angrily after discovering her infidelity, and ceased visiting the children. He moved in with a woman who had children approximately the age of his own children. Jane cried on the telephone in speaking with her father "I want to see you. I want to see you. I miss you. Alice [referring to the child of the other woman] sees you every day. We only see you once a month. That's not enough."

A very few children succumbed more totally and regressively.

> Paul responded to his father's departure by lying curled up sobbing inside a closet. He alternated this behavior, which lasted intermittently for several weeks, with telephone calls to his father, imploring him to return.

The suffering of these children was governed not only by the immediate pain of the family rupture, but expressed as well their grief over the loss of the family structure they had until then known, as well as their fears for the uncertain future that lay ahead for their newly diminished family. . . .

Finally, efforts to master inner distress were conjoined at times with efforts to conceal from the outside observer because of an acute sense of shame. Feelings of shame did not appear in the younger children in our study, but emerged specifically with this age group. These children were ashamed of the divorce and disruption in their family, despite their awareness of the commonness of divorce; they were ashamed of their parents and their behaviors, and they lied loyally to cover these up; and they were ashamed of the implied rejection of themselves in the father's departure, marking them, in their own eyes, as unlovable. . . .

Attempted Mastery by Activity and by Play

Unlike the younger latency children, so many of whom were immobilized by the family disruption, the pain which the children in this age group suffered often galvanized them into organized activity. This was usually a multidetermined response geared to overcome their sense of powerlessness in the face of the divorce, to overcome their humiliation at the rejection which they experienced, and to actively—and as energetically as possible—reverse the passively suffered family disruption. In some, this was a direct effort to undo the parental separation.

> Marian, with considerable encouragement at long distance from the paternal grandfather, embarked on a frenzied sequence of activities designed to

intimidate her mother and force her to return to the marriage. Marian scolded, yelled, demanded, and berated her mother, often making it impossible for her mother to have dates, and indeed almost succeeding in reversing the divorce decision by mobilizing all her mother's guilt in relation to herself and the other children. In one such episode, the child screamed in anger for several hours and then came quietly and tearfully to her mother, saying softly, "Mom, I'm so unhappy," confessing that she felt "all alone in the world." Following this, the harassment ceased.

Several children in this older latency group energetically developed a variety of new, exciting, and intrinsically pleasurable mastery activities which combined play action with reality adaptation. Many of these activities required not only fantasy production but the enterprise, organization, and skill of the later latency child.

Ann, whose father was a successful advertising and public relations man, designed and issued a magazine with articles and drawings, announcing the impending divorce of her parents, together with other interesting happenings, which she distributed and sold in her school and community.

In her role identification with her public media father, Ann not only overcame the loss of his ongoing presence, at the very same time, through her newspaper publication, she proclaimed her acceptance of the reality of this loss. But central to this maneuver is the psychic gratification in it—Ann transformed pain into the pleasure of achievement, and recaptured the center stage of interest. . . .

Anger

The single feeling that most clearly distinguished this group from all the younger children was their conscious intense anger. It had many sources, but clearly a major determinant was its role in temporarily obliterating or at least obscuring the other even more painful affective responses we have described. Although we have reported elsewhere [Wallerstein and Kelly, 1975] a rise in aggression and irritability in the pre-school child following parental separation, the anger experienced by these older latency children was different in being both well organized and clearly object-directed; indeed, their capacity directly to articulate this anger was striking.

John volunteered that most of the families of the kids on his block were getting a divorce. When asked how the children felt, he said, "They're so angry they're almost going crazy."

Approximately half of the children in this group were angry at their mothers, the other half at their fathers, and a goodly number were angry at both. Many of the children were angry at the parent whom they thought initiated the divorce, and their perception of this was usually accurate.

> Amy said she was angry at Mom for kicking Dad out and ruining their lives. "She's acting just like a college student, at age 31—dancing and dating and having to be with her friends."

> Ben accused his mother, saying, "You told me it would be better after the divorce, and it isn't."

> One adopted child screamed at his mother, "If you knew you were going to divorce, why did you adopt us?"

Interestingly, despite detailed and often very personal knowledge of the serious causes underlying the divorce decision, including repeated scenes of violence between the parents, most of these children were unable at the time of the initial counseling to see any justification for the parental decision to divorce. (By follow-up, many had come more soberly to terms with this.) Although one father had held his wife on the floor and put bobbie pins in her nose while their two children cried and begged him to stop, both children initially strongly opposed the mother's decision to divorce.

For some anger against the parents was wedded to a sense of moral indignation and outrage that the parent who had been correcting their conduct was behaving in what they considered to be an immoral and irresponsible fashion.

> Mark said that "three days before my dad left he was telling me all these things about 'be good.' That hurt the most," he said, to think that his father did that and knew he was going to leave all the time. . . .

The intense anger of these children was variously expressed. Parents reported a rise in temper tantrums, in scolding, in diffuse demandingness, and in dictatorial attitudes. Sometimes the anger was expressed in organized crescendos to provide a calculated nuisance when the mother's dates arrived.

> Shortly after the divorce, Joe's abusive, erratic, and rejecting father disappeared, leaving no address. The mother reported that now she had to ask the boy for permission to go out on dates, was reproached by him if she drank, and had her telephone calls monitored by him; when she bought something for herself, he screamingly demanded that the same amount of money be spent on him. Joe used his sessions with us primarily to express his anger at his mother for not purchasing a gun for him. . . .

Other children showed the obverse of all this—namely, an increased compliance and decreased assertiveness following the divorce.

Janet's behavior shifted in the direction of becoming mother's helper and shadow, and showing unquestioning obedience to her mother's orders. She became known throughout the neighborhood as an excellent and reliable baby-sitter despite her very young age (nine years). She was, however, not able to say anything even mildly critical of her rejecting father, and was one of the few children who openly blamed herself for the divorce. When initially seen by us, she was preoccupied with her feelings of inadequacy and her low self-esteem.

Fears and Phobias

Unlike the pre-school children and the younger latency group, the children of this sample were not worried about actual starvation, and references to hunger in response to the parental separation were rare. Their fears, however, were nonetheless pervasive. Some, while not entirely realistic, were still tied to reality considerations; others approached phobic proportions. In fact, among this group it was often difficult for us to separate out the reality bases, including their sensitivity to the unspoken wishes of their parents, from the phobic elaboration. Thus, approximately one-quarter of these children were worried about being forgotten or abandoned by both parents. . . .

Martha said to her mother, "If you don't love Daddy, maybe I'm next."

Some of their responses related to their accurate perception of parental feelings that children represent an unwelcome burden at this time in their lives.

Peggy reported that her mother had said to her, "If you're not good I'm going to leave." Although Peggy knew that her mother had said this in anger, she still worried about it.

Ann opined, "If Daddy marries Mrs. S., she has two daughters of her own, and I'll be Cinderella."

Some expressed the not wholly unrealistic concern that reliance on one rather than two parents was considerably less secure, and therefore the child's position in the world had become more vulnerable.

Katherine told us, "If my mother smokes and gets cancer, where would I live?" She repeatedly begged her mother to stop smoking, and worried intensely whenever her mother was late in arriving home.

Some worried, not unrealistically, about emotionally ill parents.

Ann stated about her mother, "I love her very much, but I have feelings. I'm afraid when Mom takes a long time to come home. She once tried to commit suicide. One day she ate a whole bottle of pills. I think of someone dying. . . .

how I'll be when I'm alone. Mom tried to commit suicide because of my father. It wasn't until after the divorce that she stopped crying. I think of her jumping over the Golden Gate Bridge. Mom thinks no one worries about her, but I do."

Many of these children experienced the additional concern that their specific needs were likely to be overlooked or forgotten.

Wendy referred several times through her interviews to the fact that her mother insisted on buying Fig Newtons, when she perfectly well knew that Wendy hated them.

Shaken Sense of Identity

Many of these children experienced a sense of a shaken world in which the usual indicators had changed place or disappeared. For several children, these changed markers were particularly related to their sense of who they were and who they would become in the future. . . . Specifically, the self-image and identity which in latency is still organized around, "I am the son of John and Mary Smith," is profoundly shaken by the severance of the parental relationship. Some children expressed this confusion and sense of ruptured identity with anxious questions, comparing physical characteristics of their parents and themselves, as if trying in this manner to reassemble the broken pieces into a whole.

Jack, unsolicited, volunteered a long discussion of his physical features. "My eyes change colors, just like my Mom's. My hair is going to change to light brown, just like my Dad's. Other people say I'm like my Dad. My Dad says I'm like my Mom. I say I'm like a combination." . . .

Loneliness and Loyalty Conflicts

Children in this older latency group described their loneliness, their sense of having been left outside, and their sad recognition of their powerlessness and peripheral role in major family decisions.

Betty said, "We were sitting in the dark with candles. Then they [her parents] told us suddenly about the divorce. We didn't have anything to say, and so then we watched TV."

These feelings of loneliness, not observed in this way in the younger age groups, reflect not only the greater maturational achievement of these children but also their more grown-up expectation of mutuality, as well as reciprocal support, in their relationships with parents and other adults. They thus felt more hurt, humiliated, and pushed aside by the events visited upon them, over which they had so little leverage.

It should be noted that these children, in their wrestling with this loneliness, realistically perceived the very real parental withdrawal of interest in children which so often occurs at the time of divorce. In addition to the departure of one parent, both parents understandably at such times become preoccupied with their own needs; their emotional availability, their attention span, and even the time spent with the children are often sharply reduced. Moreover, the families in our study were, by and large, nuclear families, unconnected to wider extended families or support systems of any enduring significance to the children. In this sense the children's feelings of loneliness and of loss reflected their realization that the central connecting structures they had known were dissolving.

Perhaps, however, the central ingredient in the loneliness and sense of isolation these children reported was related to their perception of the divorce as a battle between the parents, in which the child is called upon to take sides [Kelly and Wallerstein, 1976]. By this logic, a step in the direction of the one parent was experienced by the child (and of course, sometimes by the parent) as a betrayal of the other parent, likely to evoke real anger and further rejection, in addition to the intrapsychic conflicts mobilized. Thus, paralyzed by their own conflicting loyalties and the severe psychic or real penalties which attach to choice, many children refrained from choice and felt alone and desolate, with no place to turn for comfort or parenting. In a true sense, their conflict placed them in a solitary position at midpoint in the marital struggle. . . .

CHANGES IN PARENT-CHILD RELATIONSHIPS

We turn now to a necessarily abbreviated discussion of some of the new parent child configurations that emerged as a response to the marital strife and parental separation. These changed relationships constitute a significant component of the total response of children in this age group. The divorce-triggered changes in the parent-child relationship may propel the child forward into a variety of precocious, adolescent, or, more accurately, pseudoadolescent behaviors. They can, on the other hand, catalyze the development of true empathic responsiveness and increased responsibility in the child. And they can also result, as in the case of alignment with one parent against the other, in a lessening of the age-appropriate distance between parent and child. . . .

Alignment

One of the attributes of the parent-child relationship at this particular age is the peculiar interdependence of parent and child, which can become enhanced at the time of the divorce, and which accords the child a significant role in restoring or further diminishing the self-esteem of the parent. Thus the child in late latency, by his attitude, his stance, and his behavior has independent power to hurt, to reject, to confront, to forgive, to comfort, and to affirm. He also has the capacity to be an unswervingly loyal friend, ally, and "team member," exceeding in reliability his sometimes more fickle and capricious adolescent sibling.

Among the 31 children in this cohort, eight (or 26%) formed a relationship with one parent following the separation which was specifically aimed at the exclusion or active rejection of the other. These alignments were usually initiated and always fueled by the embattled parent, most often by the parent who felt aggrieved, deserted, exploited, or betrayed by the divorcing spouse. The angers which the parent and child shared soon became the basis for complexly organized strategies aimed at hurting and harassing the former spouse, sometimes with the intent of shaming him or her into returning to the marriage. More often the aim was vengence. For many of these parents, these anger-driven campaigns served additionally to ward off depressions, and their intensity remained undiminished for a long time following parental separation. It should be noted that none of these children who participated, many of them as ingenious and mischievous allies, had previously rejected the parent who, subsequent to the alignment, became the target of their angers. Therefore, their provocative behavior was extremely painful and their rejection bewildering and humiliating to the excluded parent.

Our data indicate that, although the fight for allegiance may be initiated by the embattled parent, these alignments strike a responsive chord in the children within this specific age group. . . . A central part of the dynamic of this behavior is the splitting of the ambivalent relationship to the parents into that with the good parent and the bad parent. Moreover, in our findings, these alignments have the hurtful potential for consolidation and perpetuation long past the initial post-separation period, especially in those families where the child is aligned with the custodial parent.

> Paul's father was referred to us informally by the court to which the father had gone to complain of his wife's vindictive blocking of his visits with his three children. The father, a successful chemical engineer, expressed sadness and longing for his children, and concern that his children were being systematically turned against him by their mother's unremitting attacks and falsehoods. For example, the children were told by the mother that they had to give up their dog because the father was refusing to purchase food for it, although at that time the family was receiving well over $16,000 a year in support. Paul's mother expressed astonishment and bitterness at his father for the unilateral divorce decision, describing her many years of devoted love and hard work to support the father's graduate education.
>
> Paul's initial response to the parental separation was his regression to

> sobbing in a dark closet, which we have earlier described, alternating with telephone pleas to his father to return. Later, in recalling this time, the child said to us, "I felt that I was being torn into two pieces." By the time we saw Paul, several months following the separation, he had consolidated an unshakable alignment with his mother. He extolled her as small and powerful, possessed of ESP, and knowledgeable in six languages. Of his father, he stated, "He'll never find another family like us." . . .
>
> Among Paul's activities during the year following our initial contact was his continuing reporting to his mother, and eventually to her attorney, about his father's "lurid" social life and presumed delinquencies, and his continued rejections of his father's increasingly desperate overtures, including gifts and wishes to maintain visitation. Paul also maintained a coercive control over his younger sisters, who were eager to see their father, and he made sure by his monitoring of them that they would not respond with affection in his presence. At follow-up he told us, "We are a team now. We used to have an extra guy, and he broke us up into little pieces." His anger and his mother's anger seemed undiminished at this time. . . .

FOLLOW-UP AT ONE YEAR

A first follow-up on these youngsters took place a year after the initial consultation. By and large, as with the younger latency children, the turbulent responses to the divorce itself had mostly become muted with the passage of the intervening year. In about half the children (15 of the 29 available at follow-up) the disequilibrium created by the family disruption—the suffering, the sense of shame; the fears of being forgotten, lost, or actively abandoned; and the many intense worries associated with their new sense of vulnerability and dependence on a more fragile family structure—had almost entirely subsided. But even these children with apparent better outcomes, who seemed relatively content with their new family life and circle of friends, including step-parents, were not without backward glances of bitterness and nostalgia. In fact, the anger and hostility aroused around the divorce events lingered longer and more tenaciously than did any of the other affective responses. Of the total group, ten (or one-third) of the children maintained an unremitted anger directed at the non-custodial parent; of these, four did so in alignment with the custodial mother, the other six on their own.

> Edward, who was doing splendidly in school and in new friendship relationships with his mother and with an admired male teacher, nonetheless said bitterly of his father, "I'm not going to speak to him any more. My dad is off my list now." (This was a father who, prior to the divorce, had had a very warm relationship with his son.)

Although some of these children who were doing well continued to harbor reconciliation wishes, most had come to accept the divorce with sad finality. Some seemed to be unconsciously extrapolating from these reconciliation wishes to plan future careers as repairmen, as bridge builders, as architects, as lawyers. Others, like Jane, were perhaps extending their protective attitudes toward their disturbed parents.

> Asked what she might like to do when she grows up, Jane responded. "You might laugh. A child psychiatrist. You're one, aren't you?" She talked movingly of working someday "with blind children, or mentally retarded children, or children who cannot speak."

By contrast, the other half (14 of the 29 seen at follow-up) gave evidence of consolidation into troubled and conflicted depressive behavior patterns, with, in half of these, *more* open distress and disturbance than at the initial visit. A significant component in this now chronic maladjustment was a continuing depression of low self-esteem, combined with frequent school and peer difficulties. One such child was described by his teacher at follow-up as, "A little old man who worries all the time and rarely laughs." In this group, symptoms that had emerged had generally persisted and even worsened. For instance, phobic reactions had in one instance worsened and spread; delinquent behavior such as truancy and petty thievery remained relatively unchanged; and some who had become isolated and withdrawn were even more so. One new behavior configuration that emerged during the first post-divorce year in these nine- and ten-year-olds was a precocious thrust into adolescent preoccupation with sexuality and assertiveness, with all the detrimental potential of such phase-inappropriate unfoldings. And amongst all the children, both in the groups with better and with poorer outcomes, relatively few were able to maintain good relationships with both parents. . . .

[W]e would like to close with the remarks of a ten-year-old sage from our study, whose words capture the salient mood of these children at the first follow-up—their clear-eyed perception of reality, their pragmatism, their courage, and their muted disappointment and sadness. In summarizing the entire scene, she said, "Knowing my parents, no one is going to change his mind. We'll just all have to get used to the situation and to them."

REFERENCES

BECKER, T., 1974. "On Latency." *Psychoanal. Study of Child*, 29:3–11.

BORNSTEIN, B. 1951. "On Latency." *Psychoanal. Study of Child*, 6:279–285.

ERIKSON, E., 1959. "Identity and the Life Cycle." *Psychological Issues*, Vol. 1.

ERIKSON, E., 1963. *Childhood and Society*. Norton, New York.

HARRIS, I., 1959. *Normal Children and Mothers*. Free Press, Glencoe, Ill.

KAPLAN, S. (Reporter), 1957. "Panel: The Latency Period." *JAPA*, 5:525–538.

KELLY, J. and J. WALLERSTEIN, 1976. "The Effects of Parental Divorce: Experiences of the Child in Early Latency." *Amer. J. Orthopsychiat.* 46(1):20–32.

SARNOFF, C. 1971. "Ego Structure in Latency." *Psychoanal. Quart.*, 40:387–414.

WALLERSTEIN, J. and J. KELLY, 1974. "The Effects of Parental Divorce: the Adolescent Experience." In *The Child in His Family: Children at Psychiatric Risk*, J. Anthony and C. Koupernik, eds. John Wiley, New York.

WALLERSTEIN, J., and J. KELLY, 1975. "The Effects of Parental Divorce: Experiences of the Preschool Child." *J. Amer. Acad. Child Psychiat.*, 14(4)

CHAPTER 47

Part-Time and Single Fathers

Kristine M. Rosenthal / Harry F. Keshet

ABSTRACT: Divorced fathers who maintain ongoing relationships with their children experience conflict between work and child care; feelings of inadequacy in their new roles, especially in doing "women's work"; changed feelings about the self; and feelings of depression, apathy, and being burdened. They are wary of commitment to another woman, and common ways to protect their independence are either by relationships of short duration or through multiple dating. Their dating patterns also show an attempt to establish an identity independent of that of the father role.

[Statistics show that the] number of children who live with a divorced father has tripled in the past ten years, although that still represents only one-tenth of the number of children who live with their divorced mother. Joint custody and informal sharing of childcare are becoming more common among young divorced couples with children. Unlike the once-or-twice-a-month visiting fathers whose parenting role diminishes over time, involved fathers, like single mothers, find themselves with a role overload. They must learn to coordinate work obligations, social life needs, and attempts to create a new family for themselves with the continuing daily responsibilities of childcare (Keshet and Rosenthal, 1978).

The present study was designed to determine the effects of childcare involvement on the lifestyles of young fathers. One hundred and twenty-seven separated or divorced fathers were interviewed about their childcare responsibilities. Each man had at least one child aged three to seven. Twenty-eight of the fathers saw their children at least every other weekend, for a total of six or less days each month—these we have called the "occasional" fathers; 21 of the fathers spent no less then seven days a month, and no more than 13 days with their children—they are the "quartertime" fathers. Twenty-nine of the fathers in the sample spent half of each month with their children, and the remaining 49 are full-time fathers. All respondents live in the Greater Boston Area. They represent a highly educated urban population, close to half of the sample having completed, or about to complete, graduate or professional training. The majority are in professional or semiprofessional occupations (40 percent and 16 percent), another 20 percent are in business, and 16 percent have blue-collar jobs or work in crafts. . . .

The conflicts between work and childcare experienced by these fathers are similar to those reported frequently by single mothers. Men who during their married lives expected their family to adjust to the demands of their work suddenly find themselves having to coordinate and juggle the schedules of work and childcare. Here accepted standards of nine-to-five duties begin to seem unreasonable. As one father employed by a large engineering firm told us:

> My boss is old-fashioned, he does not care what work I actually do, but he must see me there from nine to five. It is very inconvenient for me, and I knew I could get as much or more work done on a more flexible schedule, but he would not hear of it.

Other fathers who had more work independence found that it was their own expectations they had to overcome:

> I had to give up this image of being a scholar, sitting in the library till all hours of the night. Others in my department did that and they were family men too. But pretty soon I only came in to teach and did some extra work when [son] was not with me. I started to enjoy being at home. After all he would grow up and I might have missed all that, the library would always be there.

The fathers report passing up promotions that might mean a move away from the children, reducing their work hours, and choosing work for its compatibility with the demands of childcare. We must not underestimate the importance of this change for highly achieving professional men. Socialization for career performance is one of the outstanding features of male identity (Pleck, 1975). Much has been written about the general importance of work as a source of well-being for men—work as a source of life purpose (Morse & Weiss, 1955), as a prized self-image (Wilensky, 1966), and as a validating experience (Rainwater, 1974).

The reduction of work involvement has two sources. On one hand, it is a practical response to the overload of demands on the father's time. Even with daycare services, babysitters, and the help of the extended family, although the last is rare for middle-class men, much time and energy are absorbed by the child's needs. On the other hand, as indicated later, eventually childcare becomes defined as another job for which the father has contracted. When this happens the rewards of doing that job well and feeling competent in it begin to compete with work satisfaction, thus reducing the salience of occupational role for the men. . . .

[T]he initial feelings of inadequacy which many fathers experience when doing "women's work" can be more easily overcome when the childcare tasks are seen as a legitimate new assignment to be "worked on." New definitions of fathering have to be developed. "Getting a divorce really made me pause and think what is my role as a father; am I any good at raising the children? I often found myself lacking." But only at first. With additional experience comes competence and self-assurance.

For men, the issue of parenting by themselves is the issue of competence and the ways in which they understand competent performance in caring for and relating to children. Women evaluate parenting more often through their feeling relationship with the child.

The issue of competence and efficacy dominates the self-image of males. The cultural image of competence is cold and impersonal, but it also can be a way to think about feelings and to begin to learn how to function interpersonally. A man who begins to parent and who can meet the purely practical needs of children—bathing, feeding, getting them to school on time—begins to feel more effective. This sense of effectiveness translates into good feelings about the children and good feelings which he learns that the children have about him. The crisis often comes when the needs to be satisfied are purely emotional—the temper tantrum is the most trying event for a newly independent father.

> It's when she cried and I didn't know what to do for her, I didn't understand it. So I would try to figure it out by trial and error. Did I do something bad? I go through a series of hypotheses. It took a while but I finally learned how to figure out what's bothering her. I feel a lot better now. I can get an idea what's upsetting her now. I also can get her to tell me what's wrong and I can generally do something about it. . . .

Once the feelings of competence begin to be introduced into the area of dealing with children's emotions, reinforced by the child's well-being, the whole area of emotions becomes less threatening for men. Each father can develop his own criteria for doing a good job as a father in the way he relates to the children.

For men socialized to believe that feelings must be kept hidden and are a barrier to effective functioning, experiencing competency in this area can be a source of positive self-regard.

> Suddenly I found I could really do it. I saw that I could take care of the girls and respond to their emotional needs as well as run the house.

Bringing the perimeters and criteria of work performance, familiar to men, to the parenting role appears to make men at ease with their new obligations. It also gives the parenting role an external legitimacy and internal satisfaction which undermines the impact of work socialization for men, and frees them to develop a more individually determined balance of work and family commitment.

What remains to be seen is whether these individual adjustments can be maintained over time against the pressures of employees' expectations, especially when new relationships with women may reduce the father's family obligations.

THE CHANGING PATTERNS OF INTIMACY

Freud has been widely quoted as having said the two components of mental health are the ability to work and the ability to love. Both these functions are disrupted by marital breakup. At the time of separation it is difficult for many men to imagine that they could ever again feel closeness with a woman and plan a future with her. Even men who are involved with another sexual partner at the time of separation are wary of commitment. In the case of men who did not desire or initiate the divorce proceedings the process of psychological separation is even slower. These men often have hopes and expectations of reconciliation which to an objective observer appear clearly unrealistic. While the legal separation or divorce decree entitles a man to take up his single life, many are unaware that the psychological divorce may take much longer. Bohannan (1970), in describing the "six stations" of divorce, places psychic divorce at the very last, defining it as a slow process of regaining individual autonomy. Waller (1967) also describes final estrangement between the ex-spouses as complete only some time after the partners have entered new social worlds.

The divorced men themselves describe this time as one of depression or apathy. They may be tired or rushed, transient in their living arrangements, or burdened with childcare. All these become reasons to defend against an immediate involvement with a new partner. Somehow, however, new relationships do get established. We know that approximately 50 percent of the people who get divorced remarry within three years (Glick and Norton, 1977), so that not long after the separation—needing to reassert themselves as attractive males—men begin "dating." The term "dating" is used self-consciously and evokes all the insecurities, hesitations, and posturing that are part of its adolescent origins. It is a time of "trying out" a new self, even though most divorced people do not really enter the world of single people, but that of the formerly married (Hunt, 1966; Cox, 1978).

The relationships retain the status for as long as the dating couple avoids the formation of any mutual ties or obligations, even though at any given moment in time the date might fulfill all the functions of a temporary marriage mate. It is important to the partners that they maintain separate residences and have separate friends and activities. The purpose of the separateness is to underlie the "casual" nature of the relationship. The man is reestablishing his *independence*, which might be easily threatened. It is understood that the relationship could be easily terminated if either party so desired. There should be no mutual property, no need to explain to the children why "she" is not there on Sundays anymore—in other words, as little as possible which might be reminiscent of the marital breakup.

It is difficult if not impossible to adhere to such a definition of dating for a long time with one person. Deliberately or not, communalities develop, friends and children begin to expect the presence of the date, comfortable habits set in. Men who explicitly and determinably wish to prevent such a development, find themselves in the peculiar, and often hard to explain, situation of wanting to break off a relationship precisely because it feels comfortable, and because they are beginning to depend on it for both emotional sustenance and real help around the house. The experience leaves the woman bewildered and bitter. "What went wrong?"

> He wants to break off just when everything is going so well, the children have finally gotten to like me, and we've been so comfortable together, why just last week he said he does not know how he would have managed without me.

It is not often that she can get a satisfactory explanation. "I am just not ready," the man is likely to say obliquely, or else he disagrees over some small matter to create an opportunity to divest himself of the encroaching commitment. . . .

DATING PATTERNS

Relationships of short duration, or multiple dating, serve to enforce the barrier between new potential partners. All the men interviewed had, shortly after separation, dated more than one woman at a time. The pattern, which appears to repeat, begins with a fairly intense involvement immediately after separation which has the quality of a "port in a storm." The woman in question is often more a confidante than a lover: she listens to complaints against the ex-spouse, the legal system, and whatever other forces seem to conspire against the newly divorced man. She is a witness to his insecurities and a focus in gropings for a new identity. When that first stage is past, however, and some sort of emotional equilibrium is reached, this is rarely the relationship that lasts. For men anxious to try out new powers, the woman who has witnessed his setbacks is not the ideal partner. The time of quiet recuperation with one sympathetic and supportive woman is often followed by frequent and varied dating. After the first year, relationships become more exclusive and of longer duration and may lead to a more serious partnership or cohabitation. . . .

CHARACTERISTICS OF NEW PARTNERS

It was common for the men we interviewed to date women with certain social characteristics. They were frequently considerably younger than the men, of similar social class, and, whether single, divorced, or separated, were unlikely to have children of their own. Only a third of the respondents reported forming "serious relationships" with women who had children. Although such relationships were more common for men in the early stages of separation and seem to represent a desire to reconstruct the marriage configuration, they generally did not last. Whatever the attraction of the ready-made family—the woman whose life is set up for childcare, who can usually include the children of the separated father in the weekly activities, and who has a child-equipped house—it does not last. In the long run, such relationships present difficulties in coordination and planning for the two partners. . . .

Dating women of similar social class characteristics, often of similar work interests or professional concerns, increases the opportunity to separate a sense of oneself as a single adult from that of a part-time parent. This is true both emotionally and in terms of time flexibility. Many of the fathers needed the support of this love relationship immediately after delivering the children to the ex-spouse—a time of more than ordinary stress.

Dating women who did not have children of their own allowed for more time flexibility. Since most fathers take their children on the weekend, dating a woman without children of her own made it easier to plan the time alone on the weekdays when neither had other obligations. It also made it possible for the woman to be of company and assistance to the father when the children were with him and to sleep over on the nights when the children were not there. Divorced women with similar childcare arrangements were likely to resent having to spend time with someone's else's children on the weekends when they themselves were free from childcare. . . .

REFERENCES

BOHANNAN, P. (1970). *Divorce and After*. Garden City, NY: Doubleday.

COX, F. D. (1978). *Human Intimacy: Marriage, the Family and its Meaning*. St. Paul, MN: West.

GLICK, P. C., and A. NORTON (1977). "Marrying, Divorcing and Living Together in the U.S. Today." *Population Bull.* 32 (October).

HUNT, M. (1966). *The World of the Formerly Married*. New York: McGraw-Hill.

KESHET, H., and K. ROSENTHAL (1978). "Fathering after Marital Separation." *Social Work* 23 (January): 11–18.

MORSE, N. C., and R. S. WEISS (1955). "The Function and Meaning of Work and the Job." *Amer. Soc. Rev.* 20: 191–198.

PLECK J. (1975). "Work and Family Roles: From Sex-Patterned Segregation to Integration." Paper presented at the annual American Sociological Association meetings. San Francisco, August.

RAINWATER, L. (1974). "Work, Well-Being and Family Life," in J. O'Toole (ed.) *Work and the Quality of LIfe*. Cambridge, MA: MIT Press.

WALLER, W. (1967). *The Old Love and the New*. Carbondale, IL: Southern Illinois University Press.

WILENSKY, H. L. (1966). "Work as a Social Problem," in H. S. Becker (ed.) *Social Problems: a Modern Approach*. New York: John Wiley.

SECTION 13

Remarriage

NOT ONLY HAS DIVORCE BECOME COMMON IN AMERICAN SOCIETY, but so has remarriage. Of those who divorce few remain single for very long. But since some do not remarry, we can ask if there are any patterns that differentiate those who remarry from those who do not. For example, who is more likely to remarry, a divorced man or a divorced woman? Is remarriage more common for younger or for older women? Are women who are successful in their careers more or less likely to remarry than those who are not so successful? Philip Blumstein and Pepper Schwartz answer these questions in the first chapter as they present an overview of remarriage in the United States.

In Chapter 5 the concept of the family life cycle was presented; here Monica McGoldrick and Elizabeth A. Carter apply that concept to remarriage. They indicate that divorce creates dislocations in the usual life cycle of the family, and that remarriage is not simply a continuation of the family life cycle but it also contributes its own unique properties to that cycle.

As Ann Goetting emphasizes in the next chapter, the process of remarriage involves much more than merely a one-time ceremony. It is useful, she says, to view a remarried person as passing through several stations or areas of transition. Thinking of remarriage in this manner, we can say that to become fully remarried an individual must successfully traverse each of these stations, for each contributes to the coupled identity that is in process of taking shape.

You might think that those who have remarried would be less likely to divorce than those who are in their first marriages—after all, they have experienced marital problems, and they certainly should have learned from those experiences. It only makes sense that they should be able to make changes that improve their chances the second time around. But the facts belie this logic, for the divorce rate of the remarried is higher than for those who have married only once.

Andrew Cherlin wrestles with this question in the concluding chapter. He suggests that the higher rate of divorce among the remarried is due to the fact that remarriage is an incomplete institution. By this he means that society offers few firm guidelines for dealing with the difficulties that remarriage imposes, especially for handling the complicated roles and relationships it usually brings.

To apply this material, you might talk to someone who is remarried. You might ask him or her (or the couple) what difficulties they have experienced because of the remarriage. Try to locate the disruptions that the divorce created in their family life cycle, as well as the changes in this cycle that the remarriage ushered in. You might apply Goetting's six stations to the couple and try to locate the developmental problems the couple is facing. Finally, it may be beneficial to identify how the lack of institutionalized support for remarriage has created problems, as well as how the couple is solving those problems.

CHAPTER 48

The Current Situation

Philip Blumstein / Pepper Schwartz

ABSTRACT: The authors summarize select characteristics of remarriage and divorce in the United States and look at the impediments of remarriage faced by women whose chances of remarriage decreases with age, success at work, and having custody of children. They note that increases in the divorce rate, outpacing increases in the marriage rate, are uneven by age grouping, and that the divorce rate has regularities associated with age and length of marriage. It is also shown that second marriages are more likely to end in divorce.

[It is an undeniable fact that age] is a particularly strong impediment to remarriage for women. If a woman is divorced in her twenties, she has a 76 percent chance of remarriage. In her thirties her chances drop to 56 percent, and in her forties, they plunge to 32 percent. If she is in her fifties or older she has less than a 12 percent chance of remarriage. Men fare better, particularly if they are well-off, educated, and in a prestigious profession. Such men are often described as "catches," and the evidence shows that they do indeed get caught. Data from 1970 indicate that more than 90 percent of these men (both white and black) were currently married. Only 2 percent of high-achieving white men and 5 percent of similar black men had never married. And the highest earners among divorced men remarry most quickly; they are not on the market very long.[1]

Age, however, is not the only impediment. Another factor that diminishes a woman's chance of remarrying is success at work: The more she achieves in her job, the greater her chance of divorce and the smaller her chance of remarriage. For example, in 1977 women between the ages of thirty-five and forty-four with postgraduate degrees and personal incomes above $20,000 had four times the divorce rate of women with lower achievement. They also had a 20 percent greater chance of never remarrying. This was especially true if the woman had a relatively late first marriage. Let us consider men in the same category. They do just fine: A man with a postgraduate degree is half as likely as his female counterpart to get divorced.[2]

Children complicate the situation. While awards of custody are changing a bit, a single-parent household is still most likely to be headed by a woman. In 1981, 24 percent of all children were living with only one parent, and 90 percent of these children were living with their mothers.[3] At present, relatively few fathers go to court to get custody, and courts still show a pronounced tendency to award custody to the mother. The major exception to this is the concept of joint custody which is becoming more common and gives *each* parent an equal voice in major decisions affecting their children. Even here, however, the child tends to live with the mother.[4]

While we are supposed to be a nation that loves its children, remarriage statistics indicate that the financial and emotional tasks that accompany child rearing may deter many suitors. A woman with no children has a 73 percent chance of remarriage. With two children her chances dip to 63 percent, and with three they drop to 56 percent. It is interesting, however, that her age has a stronger impact on her remarriageability than the number of children she has. If she has three children but is still in her twenties, she has a 72 percent likelihood of marrying again. If she is childless, but in her thirties, her chance of remarrying is only 60 percent.[5]

This may mean that youth and beauty outweigh the man's fear of taking on additional dependents. Or it may have something to do with the age of the children. Younger women are more likely to have younger children, and a man may be more interested if the children are young enough to accept him in a parental role. Or it may be that thirty-year-old women are more established in careers and therefore less willing to marry after having tasted independence. The woman in her twenties with children may not have developed a career or found a job with a great deal of security. With several children, she probably cannot afford the luxury of being choosy about her next husband. Being the head of a large household is very demanding and without the support of a sizeable income, a woman may consider men she would not have looked at before her first marriage. Thus, she and a thirty-year-old divorcée without children may have completely different needs and therefore completely different romantic interests.

Marriages *are* increasing but perhaps not everyone still has the same chance to make that commitment. In 1982, there were 2 percent more marriages than in 1981 and 16 percent more than in 1975. We have reached a new national record.[6] But this is not necessarily a comforting statistic because the divorce rate is almost three times what it was in the 1960's. Demographers project that half of first marriages now taking place will end in divorce and that, nationwide, 41 percent of all people now of marriageable age will at some time experience a divorce.[7] There seems to be some connection to geography. In 1971, the divorce rate was lowest in the Northeast (3.6 per 1,000 people), increasing through the North Central States (6.0 per 1,000) and the South (6.1 per 1,000) and becoming highest (at 6.6 per 1,000) on the West Coast.[8] It prompts one to wonder if a couple could save their marriage by moving from California to Maine.

This kind of divorce rate terrifies people who are trying to plan a lifetime relationship and distresses those who have a durable marriage and want the same kind of permanence for their children. No one is immune from the fear that a divorce may befall someone in his or her extended family or circle of friends. Even the elderly do not seem to be totally free from risk. While it is true that the highest probability of divorce falls between the second and sixth years of marriage (and between the first and fourth years in second marriages), the rate is still quite high throughout the entire life cycle.[9] Comparing 1978 statistics with those for 1968, the greatest *increase* in the rate of divorce is in people between the ages of twenty-five and thirty-nine, where it has risen 65 percent. People under twenty-five have experienced an increase of 50 percent, as have people between forty and sixty-five. Divorce has even risen by 35 percent among men and women over sixty-five.[10] It is commonly believed that second marriages are safer, on the assumption that people must necessarily learn something from their first ventures. But actually the divorce rate for second marriages is even higher than for first marriages.[11] Even though the latest available national statistics finally showed a slowdown in divorce in 1982 (for the first time since 1962), it is hard for people to feel safe. Three percent fewer people divorced in 1982 than in 1981, but the rate is still very high.[12]

This change in the permanence of marriage must also be considered in connection with its impact on the entire family. The number of children involved in divorces is now more than 1 million a year. The number of children below the age of eighteen in households headed by women increased from 8.7 million in 1970 to 9.4 million in 1976 and 10.3 million in 1980. This represents one quarter of all American children. While the average number of children in each divorce is declining, this is still a distressing figure. Many children these days stand a good chance of becoming part of a "broken" family. Andrew Cherlin believes that if current rates of divorce continue, one third of all white children and three fifths of all black children born between 1970 and 1973 will be in a household affected by divorce by the time the child is sixteen years of age.[13]. . .

NOTES

1. Hugh Carter and Paul C. Glick, *Marriage and Divorce: A Social and Economic Study*, rev. ed. (Cambridge, Mass.: Harvard University Press, 1976). These authors have shown that black women are more likely to marry men of a lower educational level than themselves. This is one of the outcomes of a "marriage squeeze" for black men and women which the authors feel may make marital instability more likely.
2. U.S. Bureau of the Census, *Statistical Abstract of the United States* (1978), tables 114, 118, 119. See also Andrew Hacker, "Divorce a la Mode," *The New York Review of Books* (May 3, 1979).
3. U.S. Bureau of the Census, *Current Population Reports*, series P-20 (1981, 1982) and series P-23 (1981, 1982).
4. Joseph Goldstein, Anna Freud, and Albert J. Solnit, *Beyond the Best Interests of the Child* (New York: The Free Press, 1973). See also Lenore Weitzman, *The Marriage Contract: Spouses, Lovers and the Law* (New York: The Free Press, 1981), pp. 98–120. Also, Andrew Cherlin, *Marriage, Divorce and Remarriage* (Cambridge, Mass.: Harvard University Press, 1981), pp. 26–27.
5. U.S. Bureau of the Census, *Current Population Reports*, series P-20 No. 312 (June 1975) and No. 323 (March 1977), (Washington, D.C.: U.S. Government Printing Office).
6. U.S. National Center for Health Statistics, *Monthly Vital Statistics Report*, Vol. 31, No. 12 (March 14, 1983).
7. Paul C. Glick and Arthur J. Norton, "Marrying, Divorcing and Living Together in the U.S. Today," *Population Bulletin*, Vol. 32, No.5 (Washington, D.C.: Population Reference Bureau, Inc., October 1977), pp. 36–37. Another measure of divorce trends is the divorce ratio (the number of persons currently divorced per 1,000 persons currently married). The divorce ratio increased, from 47 in 1970, to 100 in 1980, and 109 in 1981. Note that the divorce ratio is not a measure of the incidence or frequency of divorce but rather of the prevalence of divorce (i.e., a measure of the previously married persons whose marriages have ended in divorce). See U.S. Bureau of the Census, *Current Population Reports*, series P-20 and series P-23 especially "Population Profile of the United States: 1981."
8. U.S. Bureau of the Census, *Statistical Abstract of the United States*, No. 122 (1977), (Washington, D.C.: U.S. Government Printing Office), p. 84.
9. U.S. Bureau of the Census, *Statistical Abstract of the United States* (1978), tables 114, 118, 119.

10. Carter and Glick, *Marriage and Divorce.* Also Arthur J. Norton, "Family Life Cycle; 1980," *Journal of Marriage and the Family*, Vol. 45, No. 2 (May 1983), pp. 267–275. Also, Arthur J. Norton and Paul C. Glick, "Marital Instability in America: Past, Present and Future," *Journal of Social Issues*,, Vol. 32, No. 1 (1976), pp.5–20.
11. Cherlin, *Marriage, Divorce and Remarriage.* Also, Norton, "Family Life Cycle: 1980."
12. U.S. National Center for Health Statistics, *Monthly Vital Statistics Report*, Vol. 31, No. 12 (March 14, 1983).
13. Cherlin, *Marriage, Divorce and Remarriage*, p. 26.

CHAPTER 49

Remarriage and the Family Life Cycle

Monica McGoldrick / Elizabeth A. Carter

ABSTRACT: The authors summarize the dislocations that divorce brings to the ordinary family life cycle; they stress the event of emotional divorce (retrieving the self from the marriage) and identify the emotional peaks that occur in the divorce process. They also outline a developmental model of the remarried family.

While the statistical majority of the American middle and upper classes still go through the traditional family life cycle stages as outlined [in Chapter 5] the largest variation from that norm consists of families in which divorce has occurred. With the divorce rate currently at 38% and the rate of redivorce at 44% (Glick & Norton, 1976), divorce in the American family is close to the point at which it will occur in the majority of families and will thus be thought of more and more as a normative event.

In our experience as clinicians and teachers, we have found it useful to conceptualize divorce as an interruption or dislocation of the traditional family life cycle, which produces the kind of profound disequilibrium that is associated throughout the entire family life cycle with shifts, gains, and losses in family membership. As in other life cycle phases, there are crucial shifts in relationship status and important emotional tasks that must be completed by the members of divorcing families in order for them to proceed developmentally. As in other phases, emotional issues not resolved at this phase will be carried along as hindrances in future relationships.

Therefore, in this view, we conceptualize the need for families in which divorce occurs to go through one or two additional phases of the family life cycle in order to restabilize and go forward developmentally again at a more complex level. Of women who divorce, 25% do not remarry. These families go through one additional phase and can restabilize permanently as divorced families. The other 75% of women who divorce remarry, and these families can be said to require negotiation of two additional phases of the family life cycle before permanent restabilization.

Our concept of divorce and postdivorce family emotional process can be visualized as a roller-coaster graph, with peaks of emotional tension at all of the transition points.

In divorcing families, emotional tension peaks predictably at these points:

1. at the time of the *decision* to separate or divorce;
2. when this decision is announced to family and friends;
3. when money and custody–visitation arrangements are discussed;
4. when the physical separation takes place;
5. when the actual legal divorce takes place;
6. when separated spouses or ex-spouses have contact about money or children and at life cycle transition points of all family members;
7. as each spouse is making the initial adjustments to rebuilding a new life.

These emotional pressure peaks occur in all divorcing families—not necessarily in the above order—and many of them occur over and over again, for months or years. A more detailed depiction of the process appears in [Table 49.1].

The emotions released during the process of divorce relate primarily to the work of *emotional* divorce—that is, the retrieval of self from the marriage. Each partner must retrieve the hopes, dreams, plans, and expectations that were invested in *this* spouse and in *this* marriage. This requires mourning what is lost and dealing with hurt, anger, blame, guilt, shame, and loss in oneself, in the spouse, in the children, and in the extended family.

In our clinical work with divorcing families, we subscribe to the basic systems view that cutoffs are emotionally harmful, and we work to help divorcing spouses continue to relate as cooperative parents and to permit maximum feasible contact between children and natural parents and grandparents. Our experience supports that of others (Hetherington, Cox, & Cox, 1977), who have found that it takes a minimum of 2 years and a great deal of effort after divorce for a family to readjust to its new structure and proceed to the next developmental stage.

TABLE 49.1 Dislocations of the Family Life Cycle Requiring Additional Steps to Restabilize and Proceed Developmentally

Phase	Emotional Process of Transition: Prerequisite Attitude	Developmental Issues
	Divorce	
1. The decision to divorce	Acceptance of inability to resolve marital tensions sufficiently to continue relationship	Acceptance of one's own part in the failure of the marriage
2. Planning the breakup of the system	Supporting viable arrangements for all parts of the system	a. Working cooperatively on problems of custody, visitation, finances b. Dealing with extended family about the divorce
3. Separation	a. Willingness to continue cooperative coparental relationship b. Work on resolution of attachment to spouse	a. Mourning loss of intact family b. Restructuring marital and parent-child relationships; adaptation to living apart c. Realignment of relationships with extended family; staying connected with spouse's extended family
4. The divorce	More work on emotional divorce: overcoming hurt, anger, guilt, etc.	a. Mourning loss of intact family: giving up fantasies of reunion b. Retrieval of hopes, dreams, expectations from the marriage c. Staying connected with extended families
	Postdivorce Family	
A. Single-parent family	Willingness to maintain parental contact with ex-spouse and support contact of children with ex-spouse and his or her family	a. Making flexible visitation arrangements with ex-spouse and his or her family b. Rebuilding own social network
B. Single-parent (noncustodial)	Willingness to maintain parental contact with ex-spouse and support custodial parent's relationship with children	a. Finding ways to continue effective parenting relationship with children b. Rebuilding own social network

TABLE 49.2 Remarried Family Formation: A Developmental Outline

Steps	Prerequisite Attitude	Developmental Issues
1. Entering the new relationship	Recovery from loss of first marriage (adequate "emotional divorce")	Recommitment to marriage and to forming a family with readiness to deal with the complexity and ambiguity
2. Conceptualizing and planning new marriage and family	Accepting one's own fears and those of new spouse and children about remarriage and forming a stepfamily Accepting need for time and patience for adjustment to complexity and ambiguity of the following: 1. Multiple new roles 2. Boundaries: space, time, membership, and authority 3. Affective issues: guilt, loyalty conflicts, desire for mutuality, unresolvable past hurts	a. Work on openness in the new relationships to avoid pseudomutuality b. Plan for maintenance of cooperative coparental relationships with ex-spouses c. Plan to help children deal with fears, loyalty conflicts, and membership in two systems d. Realignment of relationships with extended family to include new spouse and children e. Plan maintenance of connections for children with extended family of ex-spouse(s)
3. Remarriage and reconstitution of family	Final resolution of attachment to previous spouse and ideal of "intact" family; acceptance of a different model of family with permeable boundaries	a. Restructuring family boundaries to allow for inclusion of new spouse-stepparent b. Realignment of relationships throughout subsystems to permit interweaving of several systems c. Making room for relationships of all children with biological (noncustodial) parents, grandparents, and other extended family d. Sharing memories and histories to enhance stepfamily integration

NOTE: Variation on a developmental schema presented by Ransom, Schlesinger, and Derdeyn (1979).

Families in which the emotional issues of divorce are not adequately resolved can remain stuck emotionally for years if not for generations.

At the transition into remarriage, the predictable peaks of emotional tension occur at the time of serious commitment to the new relationship; at the time the plan to remarry is announced to families and friends; at the time of the actual remarriage and formation of the stepfamily; and as the logistics of stepfamily life are put into practice.

The family emotional process at the transition to remarriage consists of struggling with *fears* about investment in a new marriage and a new family: one's own fears, the new spouse's fears, and the children's fears (of either or both spouses); dealing with hostile or upset reactions of the children, the extended families, and the ex-spouse; struggling with the ambiguity of the new model of family structure roles and relationships; rearousal of intense parental guilt and concerns about the welfare of children; and rearousal of the old attachment to ex-spouse (negative or positive). [Table 49.2] depicts the process in somewhat greater detail. . . .

In our experience, the residue of an angry and vengeful divorce can block stepfamily integration for years or forever. The rearousal of the old emotional attachment to an ex-spouse, which characteristically surfaces at the time of remarriage and at subsequent life cycle transitions of children, is usually not understood as a predictable process and therefore leads to denial, misinterpretation, cutoff, and assorted difficulties. As in the case of adjustment to a new family structure after divorce, stepfamily integration seems also to require a minimum of 2 years before a workable new structure permits family members to move on emotionally.

REFERENCES

Glick, P., and A. J. Norton. Number, timing, and duration of marriages and divorces in the U.S.: June 1975. In *Current Population Reports*. Washington, D. C.: U.S. Government Printing Office, October 1976.

Hetherington, E. M., M. Cox, and R. Cox. The aftermath of divorce. In J. J. Stevens, Jr., and M. Matthews (Eds.), *Mother-Child, Father-Child Relations*. Washington, D.C.: National Association for the Education of Young Children, 1977.

Ransom, W., S. Schlesinger, and A. P. Derdeyn. A stepfamily in formation. *American Journal of Orthopsychiatry*, 1979, 49, 36–43.

CHAPTER 50

The Six Stations of Remarriage

Ann Goetting

Abstract: The remarriage process, complicated by a lack of guidelines from society, involves what might be called six stations (major areas of transition). These are: (1) emotional remarriage; (2) psychic remarriage; (3) community remarriage, (4) parental remarriage; (5) economic remarriage; and (6) legal remarriage. At each station the individual confronts major transitions, which, if dealt with successfully, contributes to the remarriage—that is, to the commitment to a new coupled identity.

While there are clear factors favoring remarriage after divorce such as experience and maturity, it remains a trying experience for most who pursue it. . . . [A] great portion of the problems associated with remarriage are related to the complexities introduced by children from former marriages. The complexity of an institution in itself need not present problems, but if society fails to provide guidelines for the relationships involved, the outcome may be one of chaos and conflict. For lack of such guidelines in Western culture, the remarried pair is often expected to function in the same way as does a first married pair, despite the fact that in addition to the new husband and wife there may be two former spouses, two sets of children, four sets of grandparents, and numerous other relatives and friends associated with a former marriage. In addition, there may be many unresolved feelings carried over into the new marriage.

Undoubtedly, remarriage after divorce is a complex process with several interrelated components. That process is described here through use of Bohannan's (1970) model outlining developmental tasks of divorce. His six "stations" of divorce consist of those tasks which must be mastered in order to exit successfully from an existing marriage. They include the emotional, legal, economic, coparental, community and psychic divorces. Those stations are revisited here in the course of moving from divorce to remarriage. As Furstenberg (1979) pointed out, a successful remarriage must involve undoing or refashioning many of the adaptions made to a successful divorce. As is true of the divorce stations, all six stations of remarriage need not necessarily occur to all remarrying people with the same intensity and in the same order. In fact, some individuals may avoid some stations altogether. The six stations of remarriage are ordered here in such a way that the first three can occur independent of the existence of children from a former marriage, while the last three assume the involvement of such children.

EMOTIONAL REMARRIAGE

Typically the remarriage process begins with the emotional remarriage. This is the often slow process by which a divorced person reestablishes a bond of attraction, commitment and trust with a member of the opposite sex. After having experienced severe disappointment in a previous relationship, the divorcee learns to release emotions in an effort to once again secure comfort and love. Often this process is wrought with the fear that this emotional investment will lead to loss and rejection. Such fears may justifiably be intense because an additional failure at relationships threatens not only to leave the individual once again disappointed and alone, but also to damage identity and self-concept. Another divorce could strongly suggest to others as well as self a deficiency in those skills, whatever they may be, which are necessary to sustain a marriage. While there is always ambiguity in terms of cause and fault with one divorce—possibly it was at least partially the fault of the other spouse, or maybe the divorce could be blamed on a situation which surrounded that particular marriage—additional failures begin to single out an individual as a "loser." Due to the loss, rejection and failure that are typically associated with divorce, the emotional remarriage is a unique and often arduous and volatile process which is not satisfactorily completed by all who attempt it.

PSYCHIC REMARRIAGE

Psychic remarriage is the process of changing one's conjugal identity from individual to couple. It involves relinquishing the personal freedom and autonomy established by the psychic divorce, and resuming a lifestyle in which a person is expected to be viewed as one component of a partnership. . . .

Since the role of adult males in our society dictates a primary identity with occupational status thereby deemphasizing conjugal identity, men are likely to experience a relatively mild identity shift as they pass from the status of single person to that of mate. In other words, since the social status and therefore personal identity of a man is relatively independent of his marital status, a shift in his marital status would not represent an extreme alteration in personal identity. But the situation may be very different for women, who in accordance with traditional gender roles, identify strongly with their marital status. While the occupational sphere tends to be the domain of the man, the conjugal sphere is seen as the domain of the woman. It is the woman, then, who is faced with the more extreme identity shift when there is an alteration in marital status.

But the shift is not of equal intensity among all women. The traditional women would suffer a great loss with psychic divorce, a true identity crisis. But upon remarriage these women would adjust easily in the psychic realm. For them psychic remarriage represents the recovery of their valued identity as wife. Non-traditional women, on the other hand, are likely to view the psychic divorce in positive terms as a period of growth into autonomous identity, an opportunity to do away with the restraints of couple identity. It is these women who are likely to have adjustment problems associated with psychic remarriage. To them the wife role is less important, and psychic remarriage represents loss of the more highly valued independence and freedom. . . .

COMMUNITY REMARRIAGE

The community remarriage like the community divorce represents an alteration which a person often must make in relationships with a community of friends. Where the community divorce involves breaking away from the world of couples, entering what Hunt (1966) called "the world of the formerly married," the community remarriage involves reentrance into the couple's world. Like the community divorce, the community remarriage may be a turbulent process. Unmarried friends are typically lost for lack of a common lifestyle, especially friends of the opposite sex. These friends are replaced by married couples, often remarried couples with whom remarrieds share important aspects of biography.

In some ways the process of community remarriage has potential for being more strenuous than does the process of community divorce because it can result in the loss of closer friends. With the community divorce one must give up couples, that is *pairs* of friends who were shared with a spouse. Often the friendships had not been intimate. Instead, they were secondary to, convenient to, and dependent upon, the marital relationship. They were not one's own friends, selected as a reflection of one's interests and needs. They were relationships based on the combined interests and needs of the spouses. But with the community remarriage, one may be put in a position of severing the close personally tailored ties established while divorced, and replacing them with less intimate, couple-oriented relationships. Furthermore, those bonds of friendship established during that period of time when one was divorced may be particularly valuable because they lent support at a time of personal crisis. These were the friends who were there to help the individual through the typically devastating experiences associated with the divorce process.

So the community remarriage, while representing reentrance into the "normality" of the couples' world, also may mean the eventual loss of valuable friendship bonds. Married life is often intolerant of relationships with unmarried friends. Its structure discourages those connections with the past, those ties with the world of the formerly married.

PARENTAL REMARRIAGE

The parental remarriage is necessary if there are children. It is the union of an individual with the children of this new spouse. Parental remarriage . . . has received the most attention in the literature as is indicated by the fact that a series of bibliographies on steprelationships, the product of parental remarriage, is periodically compiled and distributed for the use of social scientists (Sell, 1977). Unprecedented numbers of people find themselves living with other peoples' children, and many view the process of combining with them to form a family unit as challenging at best.

Fast and Cain (1966) suggested that the problems of stepparenthood are based on the fact that the role definition of stepparent in this society is poorly articulated, and implies contradictory expectations as "parent," "stepparent" and "nonparent." The stepparent cannot fully assume any of these roles, and therefore must individually work out behavior patterns for interacting with one's spouse's children. Folk tradition describes the stepmother as wicked and cruel—in a word, unparentlike—so to enact that role would be socially unacceptable. Instead, the stepparent is encouraged to assume the role of parent, for which there is legal support in the explication of the rights and duties entailed by the "in loco parentis" relationship. But the stepparent cannot totally assume the role of father or mother. The natural parent is typically still active in the parental role, which requires that the stepparent gracefully accede to the parental rights of another and behave as nonparent. The stepparent and the natural parent are placed in a position of sharing the residential, education, financial, health, and moral decisions incumbent on the parental role. Society provides no guidelines for this sharing of rights and responsibilities which can easily lead to confusion, frustration and resentment.

Another explanation for the difficulties associated with parental remarriage and the associated steprelationships is that marital role expectations between husband and wife are not worked out prior to the assumption of parental roles. Spouses are not allowed the opportunity to develop workable and comfortable marital relationships and to establish a primary husband-wife bond prior to the birth of children. Marital and parental adjustment must be confronted simultaneously which could encourage the inappropriate involvement of children in marital dissention. Marital and parental problems could easily confound one another. The natural parent's prior relationship to his child can serve as a threat to the establishment of a primary husband-wife bond. In that way it may detract from the integration of the new family unit.

One problem relating to stepparenthood that appears often in the literature is discipline. The stepparent is often reluctant to provide discipline because the clear authority vested in a natural parent is lacking. If the stepparent does actually attempt to discipline, such action may not be well-received by the child or may not be interpreted as acceptable by the spouse. This problem of discipline would seemingly be more common for stepfathers than stepmothers, since children typically stay with their mothers after divorce. It is the stepfather who most often enters a formerly single-parent family unit and who, therefore, actually experiences daily interactions with his stepchildren. The stepmother, on the other hand, usually spends limited time with her visiting stepchildren.

Another specific problem associated with parental remarriage concerns children as a link to the former marriage, and was expressed by Messinger's (1976) subjects. Some felt that continued ties through the children with previous family members made it more difficult for the new spouse to integrate into the new family unit. In this way they saw the children as a source of marital disruption. New mates frequently felt that such continued ties made them feel as though they were outsiders.

ECONOMIC REMARRIAGE

The economic remarriage is the re-establishment after divorce of a marital household as a unit of economic productivity and consumption. Like the parental remarriage, it is a particularly difficult developmental task of remarriage, as evidenced by the Messinger study, which suggested that the problem of finances in remarriage was surpassed in severity only by problems associated with children. The economic remarriage as a developmental task can be considered as being an extension of the parental remarriage in that its main difficulties stem from the existence of children from a former marriage. When there are such children involved, the economic remarriage becomes complex in that it emerges as an open system, dependent on or at least interrelated with the economic behavior of individuals other than the two spouses.

Typically the standard of living increases at remarriage due to the simple fact that financial resources which had formerly maintained two residences are combined to support only one. So the problem is not so much one of insufficient funds as it is one of financial instability and resource distribution. One source of instability stems from the sporadic nature on incoming child support payments, especially after the mother has remarried. Many reconstituted families are simply unable to predict how much money will be available from month to month because of the uncertainty associated with the arrival of child support payments. . . .

A second source of economic instability lies in the unpredictable nature of the needs of the husband's children, who typically reside with their mother. While outgoing child support payments may be constant, the possibility of unexpected needs requiring extra financial cost (medical, educational, etc.) can loom as a dark cloud over the remarriage. It can bring the same kind of uncertainty and consequent inconvenience into the remarriage household as lack of continuity associated with incoming child support payments.

The problem of *resource distribution* refers to the issue of how the money should be spent; who should get how much of what is available? For example, if *his* daughter is given ballet lessons, should not *her* son be allowed tennis lessons, even though the sources of support for the two children are quite different? If the resources available to her son from her ex-spouse preclude such tennis lessons should the stepfather finance such lessons for the sake of equity? Messinger (1976) reported frequent statements of discomfort and embarrassment on the part of mothers over the financial cost incurred for her new husband on behalf of her children. Society fails to provide guidelines for these kinds of situations, which can lead to stress in the remarital relationship.

The economic remarriage unites individuals from two different family systems and two different generations who have learned different and possibly opposing earning and spending habits. The problems involved in integrating such persons into a smooth functioning economic unit may provide a true challenge for all involved.

LEGAL REMARRIAGE

Remarriage as a form of marriage is a creature of the law. Since it is such a relatively newly recognized way of life, its legal ramifications are only beginning to be explored. By the time a remarriage takes place, alimony, child support, and the division of property have already been set regarding the former marriage. The new marriage may cause additional legal considerations concerning responsibility toward relationships from the former marriage. The complexity of what Bohannan (1970) referred to as the pseudokinship system created by remarriage after divorce requires decisions regarding his and her financial resources, his and her former spouses, and his, her, and their children. . . .

Remarriage after divorce does not mean that a person exchanges one family for another; instead it means that the individual takes on an additional family. Since legal responsibilities associated with this action have not been clearly charted, individuals are left to base legal decisions on their own moral guidelines. For some this can be a difficult process because it involves assigning weights of importance to members of their complicated pseudokinship networks. Such questions arise as to which wife deserves the life and accident insurance, medical coverage, retirement benefits, pension rights and property rights. Is it the former wife who played a major role in building the estate or is it the current wife who has contributed less but is currently in his "good graces"? Also, to which children should he lend support for college education—his children, her children or their children. Since state inheritance laws typically favor a person's current spouse and natural children, inheritance rights need to be clearly defined at the point of legal remarriage if the person wishes to will benefits to a former spouse or to stepchildren.

Until the time that state legal codes respond to the needs to the remarried, individuals will continue to be left to work out the legal problems and decisions of remarriage after divorce. The imposition of structure by the state in this area not only would make the legal remarriage logistically simpler, but might contribute to increased affability for the relationships involved. The implementation of a standard procedure for the distribution of resources, for example, would eliminate the sense of competition and jealousy which is now encouraged by the lack of guidelines. If, for example, it was predetermined by the state that the resources of remarried persons would be divided among all of their surviving spouses in proportions corresponding to the length of each marriage, bitterness on the part of any of those spouses toward one another before or after death regarding equity in inheritance rights might be reduced. The burden of responsibility for distribution of resources would have been lifted from the individual by the state. Such legal structure could relieve tension among spouses, former spouses, parent-child relationships and steprelationships, and therefore contribute to the maintenance of the complex pseudokinship structure created by remarriage after divorce.

CONCLUDING STATEMENT

As divorce and subsequent remarriage become increasingly common, adjustment to their developmental tasks becomes a greater concern for family practitioners. While individuals face different tasks in varying orders, it has been suggested here that the six developmental tasks of divorce outlined by Bohannan are also important developmental tasks of remarriage. Remarriage can be a complex process, and its adjustment accordingly difficult. The problems associated with remarital adjustment are often heightened by the fact that partners in remarriage may still be adjusting to their divorces. At remarriage, a person may be compelled to commence the stations of remarriage while having not yet completed the stations of divorce. For example, as an individual struggles with establishing bonds of affection, commitment and trust with a new partner, he or she may still be contending with the severance of emotional ties with the former spouse. . . .

REFERENCES

Bohannan, P. The Six Stations of Divorce. I.P. Bohannan (Ed.), *Divorce and After*. New York: Doubleday and Co., Inc., 1970.

Fast, I., and A.C. Cain, The Stepparent Role: Potential for Disturbances in Family Functioning. *American Journal of Orthopsychiatry*, 1966, *36*, 485–491.

Furstenberg, F.F. Recycling the Family. *Marriage and Family Review*, 1979, 2(3), 1, 12–22.

Hunt, M.M. *The World of the Formerly Married*. New York: McGraw-Hill Book Co., 1966.

MESSINGER, L. Remarriage between Divorced People with Children from Previous Marriages: A Proposal for Preparation for Remarriage. *Journal of Marriage and Family Counseling*, 1976, *38*, 193–200.

SELL, K. D. *Divorce in the 1970s*. Salisbury, N.C.: Department of Sociology, Catawba College, 1977.

CHAPTER 51

Remarriage as an Incomplete Institution

Andrew Cherlin

ABSTRACT: Why is the divorce rate for remarriages higher than for first marriages? Previous explanations include greater likelihood of personality disorders, a greater willingness to abandon a marriage, and the idea that remarried men are less economically successful. Feeling that these explanations are inadequate, Cherlin proposes *lack of institutional support* as the major reason. By referring to remarriage as an incomplete institution, the author means that society offers inadequate guidelines to traverse the complicated roles and relationships of remarriage. He illustrates how remarriage is an incomplete institution by relational terms, legal regulations, and customs concerning the disciplining of stepchildren.

[This chapter argues my theory] that the higher divorce rate for remarriages after divorce is a consequence of the incomplete institutionalization of remarriage after divorce in our society. The institution of the family in the United States has developed in response to the needs of families of first marriages and families of remarriages after widowhood. But because of the complex structure, families of remarriages after divorce that include children from previous marriages must solve problems unknown to other types of families. For many of these problems, such as proper kinship terms, authority to discipline stepchildren, and legal relationships, no institutionalized solutions have emerged. As a result, there is more opportunity for disagreements and divisions among family members and more strain in many remarriages after divorce.

The incomplete institutionalization of remarriage after divorce reveals, by way of contrast, the high degree of institutionalization still present in first marriages. Family members, especially those in first marriages, rely on a wide range of habitualized behaviors to assist them in solving the common problems of family life. We take these behavioral patterns for granted until their absence forces us to create solutions of our own. Only then do we see the continuing importance of institutionalized patterns of family behavior for maintaining family unity.

THE PROBLEM OF FAMILY UNITY

Remarriages have been common in the United States since its beginnings, but until this century almost all remarriages followed widowhood. In the Plymouth Colony, for instance, about one-third of all men and one-quarter of all women who lived full lifetimes remarried after the death of a spouse, but there was little divorce (Demos 1970). Even as late as the 1920s, more brides and grooms were remarrying after widowhood than after divorce, according to estimates by Jacobson (1959). Since then, however, a continued increase in divorce (Norton and Glick 1976) has altered this pattern. By 1975, 84% of all brides who were remarrying were previously divorced, and 16% were widowed. For grooms who were remarrying in 1975, 86% were previously divorced (U.S. National Center for Health Statistics 1977). Thus, it is only recently that remarriage after divorce has become the predominant form of remarriage. . . .

Can these families of remarriages after divorce, many of which include children from previous marriages, maintain unity as well as do families of first marriages? Not according to the divorce rate. A number of studies have shown a greater risk of separation and divorce for remarriages after divorce (Becker, Landes, and Michael 1976; Bumpass and Sweet 1972; Cherlin 1977; Monahan 1958). Remarriages after widowhood appear, in contrast, to have a lower divorce rate than first marriages (Monahan 1958). A Bureau of the Census report (U.S. Bureau of the Census 1976) estimated that about 33% of all first marriages among people 25–35 may end in divorce, while about 40% of remarriages after divorce among people this age may end in divorce. . . .

Conventional wisdom, however, seems to be that remarriages are more successful than first marriages. In a small, nonrandom sample of family counselors and remarried couples, I found most to be surprised at the news that divorce was more prevalent in remarriages. There are some plausible reasons for this popular misconception. Those who remarry are older, on the average, than those marrying for the first time and are presumably more mature. They have had more time to search the marriage market and to determine their own needs and preferences. In addition, divorced men may be in a better financial position and command greater work skills than younger, never-married men. (Divorced women who are supporting children, however, are often in a worse financial position—see Hoffman [1977].)

But despite these advantages, the divorce rate is higher in remarriages after divorce. The reported differences are often modest, but they appear consistently throughout 20 years of research. . . . We must ask why families of remarriages after divorce seem to have more difficulty maintaining family unity than do families of first marriages. Several explanations have been proposed, and we will now assess the available evidence for each.

PREVIOUS EXPLANATIONS

One explanation, favored until recently by many psychiatrists, is that the problems of remarried people arise from personality disorders which preceded their marriages (see Bergler 1948). People in troubled marriages, according to this view, have unresolved personal conflicts which must be treated before a successful marriage can be achieved. Their problems lead them to marry second spouses who may be superficially quite different from their first spouse but are characterologically quite similar. As a result, this theory states, remarried people repeat the problems of their first marriages.

If this explanation were correct, one would expect that people in remarriages would show higher levels of psychiatric symptomatology than people in first marriages. But there is little evidence of this. On the contrary, Overall (1971) reported that in a sample of 2,000 clients seeking help for psychiatric problems, currently remarried people showed lower levels of psychopathology on a general rating scale than persons in first marriages and currently divorced persons. These findings, of course, apply only to people who sought psychiatric help. And it may be, as Overall noted, that the differences emerged because remarried people are more likely to seek help for less serious problems. The findings, nevertheless, weaken the psychoanalytic interpretation of the problems of remarried life.

On the other hand, Monahan (1958) and Cherlin (1977) reported that the divorce rate was considerably higher for people in their third marriages who had divorced twice than for people in their second marriages. Perhaps personality disorders among some of those who marry several times prevent them from achieving a successful marriage. But even with the currently high rates of divorce and remarriage, only a small proportion of all adults marry more than twice. About 10% of all adults in 1975 had married twice, but less than 2% had married three or more times (U.S. Bureau of the Census 1976).

Most remarried people, then, are in a second marriage. And the large number of people now divorcing and entering a second marriage also undercuts the psychoanalytic interpretation. If current rates hold, about one-third of all young married people will become divorced, and about four-fifths of these will remarry. It is hard to believe that the recent increases in divorce and remarriage are due to the sudden spread of marriage-threatening personality disorders to a large part of the young adult population. I conclude, instead, that the psychoanalytic explanation for the rise in divorce and the difficulties of remarried spouses and their children is at best incomplete.*

A second possible explanation is that once a person has divorced he or she is less hesitant to do so again. Having divorced once, a person knows how to get divorced and what to expect from family members, friends, and the courts. This explanation is plausible and probably accounts for some of the difference in divorce rates. But it does not account for all of the research findings on remarriage, such as the finding of Becker et al. (1976) that the presence of children from a previous marriage increased the probability of divorce for women in remarriages, while the presence of children from the new marriage reduced the probability of divorce. I will discuss the implications of this study below, but let me note here that a general decrease in the reluctance of remarried persons to divorce would not explain this finding. Moreover, the previously divorced may be more hesitant to divorce again because of the stigma attached to divorcing twice. Several remarried people I interviewed expressed great reluctance to divorce a second time. They reasoned that friends and relatives excused one divorce but would judge them incompetent at marriage after two divorces.

Yet another explanation for the higher divorce rate is the belief that many remarried men are deficient at fulfilling their economic responsibilities. We know that divorce is more likely in families where the husband has low earnings (Goode 1956). Some remarried men, therefore, may be unable to earn a sufficient amount of money to support a family.

*Despite the lack of convincing evidence, I am reluctant to discount this explanation completely. Clinical psychologists and psychiatrists with whom I have talked insist that many troubled married persons they have treated had made the same mistakes twice and were in need of therapy to resolve long-standing problems. Their clinical experience should not be ignored, but this "divorce-proness" syndrome seems inadequate as a complete explanation for the greater problems of remarried people.

It is conceivable that this inability to be a successful breadwinner could account for all of the divorce rate differential, but statistical studies of divorce suggest otherwise. Three recent multivariate analyses of survey data on divorce have shown that remarried persons still had a higher probability of divorce or separation, independent of controls for such socioeconomic variables as husband's earnings (Becker et at. 1976), husband's educational attainment (Bumpass and Sweet 1972), and husband's and wife's earnings, employment status, and savings (Cherlin 1977). These analyses show that controlling for low earnings can reduce the difference in divorce probabilities, but they also show that low earnings cannot fully explain the difference. It is possible, nevertheless, that a given amount of income must be spread thinner in many remarriages, because of child-support or alimony payments (although the remarried couple also may be receiving these payments). But this type of financial strain must be distinguished from the questionable notion that many remarried husbands are inherently unable to provide for a wife and children.

INSTITUTIONAL SUPPORT

The unsatisfactory nature of all these explanations leads us to consider one more interpretation. I hypothesize that the difficulties of couples in remarriages after divorce stem from a lack of institutionalized guidelines for solving many common problems of their remarried life. The lack of institutional support is less serious when neither spouse has a child from a previous marriage. In this case, the family of remarriage closely resembles families of first marriages, and most of the norms for first marriages apply. But when at least one spouse has children from a previous marriage, family life often differs sharply from first marriages. Frequently, as I will show, family members face problems quite unlike those in first marriages—problems for which institutionalized solutions do not exist. And without accepted solutions to their problems, families of remarriages must resolve difficult issues by themselves. As a result, solving everyday problems is sometimes impossible without engendering conflict and confusion among family members.

The complex structure of families of remarriages after divorce which include children from a previous marriage has been noted by others (Bernard 1956; Bohannan 1970; Duberman 1975). These families are expanded in the number of social roles and relationships they possess and also are expanded in space over more than one household. The additional social roles include stepparents, stepchildren, stepsiblings, and the new spouses of noncustodial parents, among others. And the links between the households are the children in previous marriages.

These children are commonly in the custody of one parent—usually the mother—but they normally visit the noncustodial parent regularly. Thus they promote communication among the divorced parents, the new stepparent, and the noncustodial parent's new spouse.

Family relationships can be quite complex, because the new kin in a remarriage after divorce do not, in general, replace the kin from the first marriage as they do in a remarriage after widowhood. Rather, they add to the existing kin (Fast and Cain 1966). But this complexity alone does not necessarily imply that problems of family unity will develop. While families of remarriages may appear complicated to Americans, there are many societies in which complicated kinship rules and family patterns coexist with a functioning, stable family system (Bohannan 1963, Fox 1967).

In most of these societies, however, familial roles and relationships are well defined. Family life may seem complex to Westerners, but activity is regulated by established patterns of behavior. The central difference, then, between families of remarriages in the United States and complicated family situations in other societies is the lack of institutionalized social regulation of remarried life in this country. Our society, oriented toward first marriages, provides little guidance on problems peculiar to remarriages, especially remarriages after divorce.

In order to illustrate the incomplete institutionalization of remarriage and its consequences for family life, let us examine two of the major institutions in society: language and the law. "Language," Gerth and Mills (1953, p. 305) wrote, "is necessary to the operations of institutions. For the symbols used in institutions coordinate the roles that compose them, and justify the enactment of these roles by the members of the institution." Where no adequate terms exist for an important social role, the institutional support for this role is deficient, and general acceptance of the role as a legitimate pattern of activity is questionable.

Consider English terms for the roles peculiar to remarriage after divorce. The term "stepparent," as Bohannan (1970) has observed, originally meant a person who replaced a dead parent, not a person who was an additional parent. And the negative connotations of the "stepparent," especially the "stepmother," are well known (Bernard 1956; Smith 1953). Yet there are no other terms in use. In some situations, no term exists for a child to use in addressing a stepparent. If the child calls her mother "mom," for example, what should she call her stepmother? This lack of appropriate terms for parents in remarriages after divorce can have negative consequences for family functioning. In one family I interviewed, the wife's children wanted to call their stepfather "dad," but the stepfather's own children, who also lived in the household, refused to allow this usage. To them, sharing the term "dad" represented a threat to their claim on their father's attention and affection.

The dispute caused bad feelings, and it impaired the father's ability to act as a parent to all the children in the household.

For more extended relationships, the lack of appropriate terms is even more acute. At least the word "stepparent," however inadequate, has a widely accepted meaning. But there is no term a child living with his mother can use to describe his relationship to the woman his father remarried after he divorced the child's mother. And, not surprisingly, the rights and duties of the child and this woman toward each other are unclear. Nor is the problem limited to kinship terms. Suppose a child's parents both remarry and he alternates between their households under a joint custody arrangement. Where, then, is his "home"? And who are the members of his "family"? These linguistic inadequacies correspond to the absence of widely accepted definitions for many of the roles and relationships in families of remarriage. The absence of proper terms is both a symptom and a cause of some of the problems of remarried life.

As for the law, it is both a means of social control and an indicator of accepted patterns of behavior. It was to the law, for instance, that Durkheim turned for evidence on the forms of social solidarity. When we examine family law, we find a set of traditional guidelines, based on precedent, which define the rights and duties of family members. But as Weitzman (1974) has shown, implicit in the precedents is the assumption that the marriage is question is a first marriage. For example, Weitzman found no provisions for several problems of remarriage, such as balancing the financial obligations of husbands to their spouses and children from current and previous marriages, defining the wife's obligations to husbands and children from the new and the old marriages, and reconciling the competing claims of current and ex-spouses for shares of the estate of a decreased spouse.

Legal regulations concerning incest and consanguineal marriage are also inadequate for families of remarriages. In all states marriage and sexual relations are prohibited between persons closely related by blood, but in many states these restrictions do not cover sexual relations or marriage between other family members in a remarriage—between a stepmother and a stepson, for example, or between two stepchildren (Goldstein and Katz 1965). . . . Families of remarriages after divorce, consequently, often must deal with problems such as financial obligations or sexual relations without legal regulations or clear legal precedent. The law, like the language, offers incomplete institutional support to families of remarriages.

In addition, other customs and conventions of family life are deficient when applied to remarriages after divorce. Stepparents, for example, have difficulty determining their proper disciplinary relationship to stepchildren. One woman I interviewed, determined not to show favoritism toward her own children, disciplined them more harshly than her stepchildren. Other couples who had children from the wife's previous marriage reported that the stepfather had difficulty establishing himself as a disciplinarian in the household. Fast and Cain (1966), in a study of about 50 case records from child-guidance settings, noted many uncertainties among stepparents about appropriate role behavior. They theorized that the uncertainties derived from the sharing of the role of parent between the stepparent and the noncustodial, biological parent. Years ago, when most remarriages took place after widowhood, this sharing did not exist. Now, even though most remarriages follow divorce, generally accepted guidelines for sharing parenthood still have not emerged.

There is other evidence consistent with the idea that the incomplete institutionalization of remarriage after divorce may underlie the difficulties of families of remarriages. Becker et al. (1976) analyzed the Survey of Economic Opportunity, a nationwide study of approximately 30,000 households. As I mentioned above, they found that the presence of children from a previous marriage increased the probability of divorce for women in remarriages, while the presence of children from the new marriage reduced the probability of divorce. This is as we would expect, since children from a previous marriage expand the family across households and complicate the structure of family roles and relationships. But children born into the new marriage bring none of these complications. Consequently, only children from a previous marriage should add to the special problems of families of remarriages.

In addition, Goetting (1978*a*, 1978*b*) studied the attitudes of remarried people toward relationships among adults who are associated by broken marital ties, such as ex-spouses and the people ex-spouses remarry. Bohannan (1970) has called these people "quasi-kin." Goetting presented hypothetical situations involving the behavior of quasi-kin to 90 remarried men and 90 remarried women who were white, previously divorced, and who had children from previous marriages. The subjects were asked to approve, disapprove, or express indifference about the behavior in each situation. Goetting then arbitrarily decided that the respondents reached "consensus" on a given situation if any of the three possible response categories received more than half of all responses. But even by this lenient definition, consensus was not reached on the proper behavior in most of the hypothetical situations. For example, in situations involving conversations between a person's present spouse and his or her ex-spouse, the only consensus of the respondents was that the pair should say "hello." Beyond that, there was no consensus on whether they should engage in polite conversation in public places or on the telephone or whether the ex-spouse should be invited into the new spouse's home while waiting to pick up his or her children. Since meetings of various quasi-kin must occur regularly in the lives of most respondents, their disagreement is indicative of their own confusion about how to act in common family situations.

Still, there are many aspects of remarried life which are similar to life in first marriages, and these are subject to established rules of behavior. Even some of the unique aspects of remarriage may be regulated by social norms—such as the norms concerning the size and nature of wedding ceremonies in remarriages (Hollingshead 1952). Furthermore, as Goode (1956) noted, remarriage is itself an institutional solution to the ambiguous status of the divorced (and not remarried) parent. But the day-to-day life of remarried adults and their children also includes many problems for which there are no institutionalized solutions. And since members of a household of remarriage often have competing or conflicting interests (Bernard 1956), the lack of consensual solutions can make these problems more serious than they otherwise would be. One anthropologist, noting the lack of relevant social norms, wrote, "the present situation approaches chaos, with each individual set of families having to work out its own destiny without any realistic guidelines" (Bohannan 1970, p. 137).

REFERENCES

Becker, G., E. Landes, and R. Michael. 1976, "Economics of Marital Instability." Working Paper no. 153. Stanford, Calif.: National Bureau of Economic Research.

Bergler, Edmund. 1948. *Divorce Won't Help*. New York: Harper & Bros.

Bernard, Jessie. 1956. *Remarriage*. New York: Dryden.

Bohannan, Paul. 1963. *Social Anthropology*. New York: Holt, Rinehart & Winston.

———. 1970. "Divorce Chains, Households of Remarriage, and Multiple Divorces." Pp. 127–39 in *Divorce and After*, edited by Paul Bohannan. New York: Doubleday.

Bumpass, L. L., and A. Sweet. 1972. "Differentials in Marital Instability: 1970." *American Sociological Review* 37 (December): 754–66.

Cherlin, A. 1977. "The Effects of Children on Marital Dissolution." *Demography* 14 (August): 265–72.

Demos, John. 1970. *A Little Commonwealth: Family Life in Plymouth Colony*. New York: Oxford University Press.

Duberman, Lucile. 1975. *The Reconstructed Family*. Chicago: Nelson-Hall.

Fast, I., and A. C. Cain. 1966. "The Stepparent Role: Potential for Disturbances in Family Functioning," *American Journal of Orthopsychiatry* 36 (April): 485–91.

Fox, Robin. 1967. *Kinship and Marriage*. Baltimore: Penguin.

Gerth, Hans, and C. Wright Mills. 1953. *Character and Social Structure*. New York: Harcourt, Brace & Co.

Goetting, Ann. 1978*a*. "The Normative Integration of the Former Spouse Relationship." Paper presented at the annual meeting of the American Sociological Association, San Francisco, September 4–8.

______. 1978*b*. "The Normative Integration of Two Divorce Chain Relationships." Paper presented at the annual meeting of the Southwestern Sociological Association, Houston, April 12–15.

Goldstein, Joseph, and Jay Katz. 1965. *The Family and the Law*. New York: Free Press.

Goode, William J. 1956. *Women in Divorce*. New York: Free Press.

Hoffman, S. 1977. "Marital Instability and the Economic Status of Women." *Demography* 14 (February): 67–76.

Hollingshead, A. B. 1952. "Marital Status and Wedding Behavior." *Marriage and Family Living* (November), pp. 308–11.

Jacobson, Paul H. 1959. *American Marriage and Divorce*. New York: Rinehart.

Monahan, T. P. 1958. "The Changing Nature and Instability of Remarriages." *Eugenics Quarterly* 5: 73–85.

Norton, A. J., and P. C. Glick. 1976. "Marital Instability: Past, Present, and Future." *Journal of Social Issues* 32 (Winter): 5–20.

Overall, J. E. 1971. "Associations between Marital History and the Nature of Manifest Psychopathology." *Journal of Abnormal Psychology* 78 (2): 213–21.

Smith, William C. 1953. *The Stepchild*. Chicago: University of Chicago Press.

U.S. Bureau of the Census. 1976. *Number, Timing, and Duration of Marriages and Divorces in the United States: June 1975*. Current Population Reports, Series P-20, No. 297. Washington, D.C.: Government Printing Office.

U.S. National Center for Health Statistics. 1977. *Vital Statistic Report. Advance Report. Final Marriage Statistics, 1975* Washington, D.C.: Government Printing Office.

Weitzman, L. J. 1974. "Legal Regulation of Marriage: Tradition and Change." *California Law Review* 62: 1169–1288.

PART V

Social Policy and the Future

JUST WHAT IS SOCIAL OR GOVERNMENT POLICY FOR THE FAMILY (referred to simply as family policy)? At first the idea seems clear–there is much talk about family policy, most people seem to support it, and the government seems to pass a lot of legislation under the general heading of it. Indeed, family policy can be construed as any government action, or even inaction, that has an effect on the family. But as Gilbert Y. Steiner analyzes the matter, defining family policy is far from that simple.

To what end should family policy be aimed? This, too, seems so clear at first: "To the improvement of the family and family life, of course!" one would say. But, as Steiner points out, family policy carries no inherent meaning. So long as the term "family policy" is left vague, politicians can use it to score points with the public—even groups that represent conflicting viewpoints will give their support, for everyone wants a politician who is in favor of family policy. As soon as a politician suggests a specific program, however, the matter changes abruptly. Based on their particular viewpoints, groups align themselves on both (or more) sides of the issue and spar with one another. Instead of promoting unity, then, family policy ultimately creates divisions—ergo the need to leave the term fuzzy and undefined.

Certainly we all want what is best for our families. But just what is "best"? How do we go about getting the "best"? And how do we guard ourselves against unanticipated, even perverse, consequences of well-intentioned family policy programs? Steiner suggests a solution to handle this problem, but you have to read his "bottom line" carefully and evaluate it in terms of the criticisms that he himself raises.

In the second chapter in this section we turn the focus to a specific problem that has many people upset. To many it seems that only a few years ago spouse and child abuse were rare, incest was the act of some deranged monster, and no man raped his wife. Seemingly overnight such acts have become so commonplace that it is now rare to look at a newspaper without reading about some act of family abuse.

What has happened? Have Americans suddenly been transformed into strange creatures who do horrible things to those closest to them? What causes such abuse? Are they really common? It is to such questions as these that David Finkelhor addresses himself as he examines these forms of family abuse, looking for any common features that may be running through them.

And this brings us back to family policy. How can family policy be designed to prevent or diminish family abuse? And at the same time, how do we direct the government toward the family, yet keep it from destroying family privacy?

In the concluding chapter we take a brief look at the possible futures of the family. No one knows what the future will bring, of course, but as Edward Cornish indicates, it is worthwhile to let our imaginations soar for a moment to try to abstract from current trends what the future might hold. These glimpses, whether right, wrong, or even close, are startling. And, as you will see, some of them depend upon government instituted family policy, for current government action has a strong effect on the future. The problem, of course, is that no one can say for certain just what those effects will ultimately be.

It is fitting that we close the book with an imaginative look at family policy and the possible futures of the family. Perhaps by looking beyond the present we can in some way ensure the future. After all, as the future unfolds it will engulf us along with it—and we shall inherit the consequences of our present trends.

CHAPTER 52

The Futility of Family Policy

Gilbert Y. Steiner

Abstract: Family policy is a fuzzy concept that means different, even opposite, things to different people. Like the concept of peace, everyone has a different definition. Various groups, all supporting the idea of family policy, often vigorously oppose one another when specific goals are proposed. As the way out of this dilemma, the author suggests that we acknowledge that the crisis of the family is actually the crisis of poor families and dysfunctional families. We should then define family policy as public programs to aid parents and children in poor or dysfunctional families.

Family policy too quickly became a fad in American social policy, enthusiastically embraced without attention to the difficulties of developing, enacting, and implementing a public program. One of these difficulties involves spelling out objectives without losing support. Votaries of many of the separate causes massed behind the pro-family banner are each persuaded of the singular importance of their particular cause. Economic assistance to poor families preoccupies some. For those who see family policy as a way to preclude unwanted family formation, population control, family planning, and abortion as a right are all-consuming goals. Their antitheses are all-consuming for those who argue that family policy should both protect the rights of the unborn fetus and preserve adequate freedom for individual couples to conceive and support whatever number of children they desire. For feminists and their sympathizers, the family policy ideal is equality of employment opportunity, equal sharing of parental responsibilities, and preschool child care. But mother-in-the-home as "every child's birthright" is also argued as family policy. Although families with physically, mentally, or emotionally handicapped members divide over public support of high-quality institutional care and public support of home care, each position is rooted in a perception of family policy as government help to special families.

Since family policy is viewed differently from each of these perspectives—by no means the full range of perspectives—it is clear that the transformation from concept to program can be troublesome. History is not reassuring: the modern precursors of family policy—the war on poverty, welfare reform, child development—each generated internecine warfare as each impeccable theme was advanced to the messy and divisive stage of specific proposals. Some critical questions of family policy like abortion, income support, and foster care have already produced their own controversies.

A FLEXIBLE AND FUZZY CONCEPT

[Like many,] I am impatient with the entrepreneurs of family policy, finding it a concept without a clear content; suspicious of politicians, bureaucrats, or scholars who participate in the movement without pinpointing its objectives; and doubtful whether family policy, no matter if described as comprehensive or partial, implicit or explicit, is a useful or practical theme. Its sloganeers might more profitably concentrate on health, education, and welfare programs to serve children in need or older Americans. In those programs the tools available to government are better suited to the job to be done.

Attention has been focused on family policy because of the belief that public programs to strengthen families would mitigate the social disruption apparent since the mid-1960s. But there can be unanticipated consequences of public policy designed to achieve an objective like stronger families—an objective with many intangible and emotional components. For example, recall the unanticipated, troublesome effects on marital stability of the negative income tax experiment. Touted as family-strengthening, income guarantees to poor families appear to increase family dissolution. . . .

Clearly, too, family policy is a complicated problem because families are neither monolithic nor unchanging. . . . [T]he four-person family composed of father, mother, and two children with the father as sole earner—often referred to as "typical"—described only 7 percent of husband-wife families in the late 1970s. What is generally overlooked is that at some point in their lives a majority of Americans do live in a family with those characteristics. Thus no family policy is realistic if it is based on that kind of four-person group as the typical beneficiary, nor is it realistic if it fails to recognize the sometime typicality of that grouping. Family policy that begins with a perception of two adults sharing responsibility for one or more children will reflect the situation in which almost five-sixths of children under eighteen live. It will not reflect the living arrangements of 11 million children living with only one parent. So it becomes necessary to invent ways of strengthening different family structures. A flexible work schedule, for example, that permits one working parent to leave relatively later in the morning and the second to arrive home relatively earlier in the day is irrelevant for the single-parent family. By the same token, an afterschool group-care facility may be invaluable to the single parent—and of no value to the nonworking mother in a two-parent household.

There is no sure-fire policy prescription to strengthen families. Although elegant social science analysis might provide some surprises, rational thinking would posit that peace, full employment, income support, ready access to health care, convenient transportation, decent, safe, and sanitary housing, clean air and water, and good schools are more conducive to strengthening family life than their opposites. But families dissolve notwithstanding all these and myriad other exemplary public achievements, and families hold together—providing for their members, maintaining Lasch's haven in a heartless world—under conditions of war, economic depression, slum living, environmental pollution, and educational jungles.

Idiosyncratic and even perverse effects on family stability characterize sundry other public policies, including some public action first designed and perceived to be pro-family. . . .

[I]n half the states, public assistance to dependent children requires absence of the father from the home. Common sense says that an informed, rational, desperate father unable to provide for his family will desert in order to qualify the family for assistance. But after a decade of preoccupation with welfare reform issues, there are still no research findings to sustain that hypothesis. So some politicians and some analysts worry about the possible desertion-incentive effects of the absence-from-the-home proviso, and others worry about the possible work-disincentive effects if the proviso were eliminated. Which position is pro-family and which antifamily is far from certain.

The idea of public policy to strengthen the family gives rise to exhortation on behalf of imprecise goals. To espouse "the principle of supporting family vitality" provides little help to the public official or concerned citizen who might like to do just that. To ask that the nation develop a family policy as comprehensive as its defense policy leaves unresolved the question whether some family policy equivalent of the B-1 bomber, enclosed within the comprehensive package, is critically necessary to the country or an unnecessary and undesirable extravagance. No evidence suggests that a comprehensive family policy will endow its components with greater independent validity than they otherwise might enjoy. A child care program is the leading example. It can be argued that public child care is pro-family because it offers women an opportunity to combine family and work, or antifamily because it invites second-class child rearing. Both positions were taken before family policy became a fashionable topic. Either position could be accommodated by a comprehensive family policy, and either could be correct or incorrect. In effect, there is no way to turn a pro-family ideal into legislation or administrative regulation without making some judgments about specifics. Making those judgments means benefiting some families while implicitly asking others to wait in the queue, meeting some families' needs, disappointing others. What starts as comprehensive family policy inevitably becomes selective policy after all.

Since family policy has no consistent, accepted meaning, there can be no valid way for either true believers or skeptics to distinguish the accomplishment of family policy from its absence. . . .

Since everyone is, was, or will be part of a family, and all government activity bears on at least some of the population, the . . . definition of family policy as everything that government does to and for the family comes close to including all government action.

Delineating components invites disaster. Assume, for example, that family policy advocates delineate one-high-priority component as federal subsidies to child care facilities that are available on demand, at nominal cost. Some who think of family policy as a way to minimize, not facilitate, out-of-home child care will line up in opposition. Some others, for whom family policy means above all a program that will depopulate institutions and try to put all children in permanent family settings, will give the child care component of family policy only casual support. And still others, for whom family policy means improved opportunities for three-generational housing arrangements, will simply be indifferent to child care. . . .

This explains why family policy is irresistible in the abstract and impossible in the particular, at once unifying and divisive. . . .

The persistent issues of family dysfunction have little to do with whether the family is suddenly in trouble as an institution or whether it is here to stay. A thoughtful, scholarly inquiry leading to the here-to-stay conclusion and a politician's assertion that "the American family is in trouble" may not represent incompatible positions as much as different preoccupations.

On the one hand, it can be persuasively argued that instead of declining, the extended family never existed; that instead of increasing, family disruption has only changed in character; that instead of indicating a less stable family life for children, the growth of single-parent families indicates the reverse, because it means that single mothers are keeping their children rather than farming them out; that instead of harming children, changes in maternal work habits are mostly without effect. On the other hand, there is cause for anxiety about he percentage of children who live in poverty, about the helplessness of some victims of domestic violence, about the child support problems resulting from unmarried motherhood, desertion, separation, and divorce. Family policy would be everything. But given the tradition of family privacy and the division of power in the federal system, a more limited definition encompassing only actions expressly intended to affect families in general or specific ways would mean that precious little federal policy would fall in the net. . . .

One way to avoid the everything-or-nothing dilemma is to acknowledge that the crisis of the family is actually the crisis of poor families and dysfunctional families, and to define family policy as public programs to aid parents and children in poor or dysfunctional families. Sensitive to the tradition of family privacy, this definition is also the one most likely to be taken seriously by policymakers because it focuses on identifiable problems. In the Alva Myrdal tradition, it would make income maintenance the first-order concern of family policy, then add to that concern both parental dysfunction and child dysfunction because they are impediments to the parental nurturing of children. . . .

But no detailed prospectus on family policy as a public issue has been written. Ultimately, however, a prospectus should explain exactly what is asked of government in the name of family policy. A public issue depends for its continued existence on the mobilization of groups seeking a benefit for themselves or for others that is within the power of government to award by legislation, administrative order, or court decree. Whether the benefit is money, regulation of individual or official behavior, or special assistance to a particular class, it must be translatable into the output of government—statute law, administrative interpretation, or judicial determination. In this sense, kindness, compassion, and happiness, for example, are not public issues. Good health care is a public issue, but good health is not. Nor are strong families. They cannot be mandated by a governmental entity. Groups do not mobilize to request or demand them as formal products of governmental activity.

Social causes with measurable goals do become public issues. Equal employment opportunity for women and for blacks and Hispanics, for example, can be measured, though imprecisely; can be both legislated and adjudicated; and is a public issue. Universal access to health care involves a measurable goal and is a public issue. So is the protection of a woman's right to abort a fetus or of a fetus' right to protection against abortion. In each case, groups mobilize in support or opposition, and the public issue remains on the agenda as the effort goes on to achieve passage of a bill, or persuade a court, or influence an administrative interpretation. A loss in one arena invites a shift to another. The substantive goal of group activity is specific, and the process involved in achieving it is identifiable.

UNIFYING THEME, DIVISIVE SPECIFIC

Unless family policy is broken into component parts, it is only an abstract theme that neither blesses nor damns, neither rewards nor punishes. Only the components of family policy are susceptible to legislative action or administrative order. Mobilizing groups on behalf of family policy is a code for mobilizing groups on behalf of a particular approach to some component that is reducible to government action. At that point, however, family policy begins to bite.

The choice is not between pollyannaism and alarmism. The family can be both here to stay and in trouble. That some families survive domestic violence is no justification for the failure to develop a shelter program. Out-of-wedlock births and consequent single-parent households may be a workable family form that is preferable to out-of-wedlock births and institutional care, but to be workable is not necessarily to be best. Varieties of life-styles, changes in family form, and changes in family function, in short, should be separately examined for what they are rather than collectively deplored or accepted. . . .

Whatever the definition of a workable family, the conception and birth of an unwanted child is an undesirable event rendered no less so by an awareness that there have always been unwanted pregnancies and births. The same can be said of adolescent pregnancies, wanted or unwanted, in that the health risks to mother and child are substantial and adolescents are not likely to be ready emotionally to care for an infant. Without belaboring the illustrations, let it be acknowledged that the institution of the family has adapted to these events and continues to do so. But it should also be acknowledged that the pregnancy rate of young teenagers is evidence of trouble. For some, it will appear to be a health problem, because of the high risk of morbidity. Others will see an economic problem, because of the unlikelihood that the parents can support themselves, let alone a child. To categorize it as a family problem is surely not unreasonable, because "family" conjures up images of maternal and child health, self-support, emotional interdependence, and intergenerational relationships, all of which are involved. . . .

Identifying the appropriate issues and applying the appropriate remedy should be the essence of family policy. . . . [But family] policy is not a coherent program awaiting formal approval. Organizing on behalf of family policy is not feasible, because it is more like peace, justice, equality, and freedom than it is like higher welfare benefits, or school busing, or medical care for the aged.

Family policy is unifying only so long as the details are avoided. When the details are confronted, family policy splits into innumerable components. It is many causes with many votaries.

CHAPTER 53

Common Features of Family Abuse

David Finkelhor

ABSTRACT: Do the various forms of family abuse share common features? Although marital rape, spouse beating, child abuse, and incest seem quite unlike one another, the author identifies several features that they have in common. Among these common characteristics is that abuse tends to gravitate toward the relationships of greatest power differential, but is related to the abuser's perception of lack of or loss of power. Common features of the victims are their psychological manipulation, often accompanied by allegiance to the abuser, and their feelings of shame, humiliation, and entrapment. In addition, victims share long-term effects. The families in which abuse occurs also exhibit similar characteristics, as does the process by which the various forms of abuse came to be defined as social problems.

[T]his introductory chapter will attempt to point out some of the insights to be found from examining the commonalities among forms of family violence and abuse.

ABUSE AS ABUSE OF POWER

One commonality among forms of family abuse lies in the power dynamics of these situations. What we call abuse within the family is not simply aggression or injury committed by one family member against another. Family abuse is more precisely the abuse of power.

In part, this is the way abuse is defined. We do not classify as abuse the young child's lashing out at his mother when she deprives him of something he wants. We consider abuse to be a situation where a more powerful person takes advantage of a less powerful one.

Simple abuse of power is not even the full story. Even within the range of behaviors we define as abuse, the most common patterns in family abuse are not merely for the more powerful to abuse the less powerful, but for the most powerful to abuse the least. This is an interesting commonality: Abuse tends to gravitate toward the relationships of *greatest power differential*.

This principle is clearest in sexual abuse of children. The most widespread form of reported sexual abuse consists of abusers who are both male and in authority positions within family victimizing girls in subordinate positions (Finkelhor, 1979, 1982). This is a case of abuse across the axis of both unequal sexual power (males victimizing females) and unequal generational power (the older victimizing the younger). Abuse of boys by males appears to be much less common, and abuse of either boys or girls by female family members is extremely rare in comparison.

In physical child abuse a similar principle of the strongest victimizing the weakest operates. First, statistics show that the greatest volume of abuse is directed against the most powerless children, those under the age of six (Gil, 1979; Maden and Wrench, 1977; Straus, Gelles, and Steinmetz, 1980). Moreover, the statistics should also probably be interpreted to show the more common vulnerability to be at the hands of the more powerful parent—the father. Although raw statistics tend to show roughly equivalent numbers of pure incidents of physical child abuse committed by men and women (American Humane Association, 1978; Maden and Wrench, 1977), these figures are deceptive because they do not take into account the fact that women spend a great deal more time with children than do men. If we were to calculate vulnerability to abuse as a function of the amount of time spent in contact with a potential abuser, I think we would see that men and fathers are more likely to abuse.

In the case of spouse abuse, too, again the strongest are shown to victimize the weakest. Research by Straus et al. (1980), for example, shows that in families where a woman has less power by virtue of not being in the labor market, by virtue of being excluded from participation in decision making, and by virtue of having less education than her husband, she is at higher risk of abuse. Once again, abuse gravitates to the greatest power differential. . . .

ABUSE AS A RESPONSE TO PERCEIVED POWERLESSNESS

Although family abuse is behavior of the strong against the weak, some people who have clinical experience with abusers sometimes find this an ironic description. Many abusers give a sense of being pathetic and ineffectual, not always people who would be described in objective terms as socially powerful.

This is another commonality among the different kinds of abuse: Although they are acts of the strong against the weak, *they seem to be acts carried out by abusers to compensate for their perceived lack of or loss of power*. In the cases of spouse abuse and the sexual abuse of children, this attempt to compensate is often bound up in a sense of powerlessness, particularly with regard to masculine ideals in our society. Men, it has been noted, often start to beat their wives when their wives try to assert themselves in some way or establish some degree of independence (Gelles, 1974). It has also been noted that men often start to sexually abuse their children when they are unemployed or failing financially or have suffered some other setback (Meiselman, 1978). Reflecting a similar theme, it has been observed that the physical abuse of children tends to start with a feeling of parental impotence (Spinetta and Rigler, 1972). Mothers resort to violence, for example, when they sense that they have lost control of their children and of their own lives.

These are all examples of the uses of abuse to compensate for a perceived lack or loss of power. However, the abuse may not always be instrumental (i.e., intended to restore power): It may also be expressive. Abuse can be a way of venting anger against another family member who is seen in some way as responsible for that loss of power. Or it can be a way of trying to regain control by using coercion or exploitation as the resource for having one's will carried out. In either case, the abuse is a response to perceived power deficit. . . .

SHARED EFFECTS ON VICTIMS

Another important way in which all family abuse is tied together is in the effect it has on its victims. There are striking similarities in how the victims of family abuse experience their situations. These characteristic responses stem in part from the nature of families and family relationships and do not occur to such an extent in victimization that occurs outside the family.

All forms of family abuse seem to occur in the context of psychological abuse and exploitation, a process victims sometimes describe as "brainwashing." Victims are not merely exploited or physically injured: their abusers use their power and family connection to control and manipulate victims' perceptions of reality as well. Thus abused children are told that they are bad, uncontrollable, and unlovable (Herbruck, 1979). Abused wives are persuaded by their husbands that they are incompetent, hysterical, and frigid (Walker, 1979). Sexually abused children are misled to believe that their father's sexual attentions are normal and testimony of his great and genuine affection (Armstrong, 1978).

This brainwashing that accompanies family abuse is potent because families are the primary group in which most individuals construct reality. Family members often do not have enough contact with other people who can give them countervailing perceptions about themselves. The distortion of reality and self-image is generally one of the most devastating effects of family abuse.

One result of the psychological manipulation common among all types of family abuse is the tendency among victims to blame themselves. It is difficult for victims to avoid identifying with the rationalizations of the abuser in accounting for what is happening to them. They commonly see themselves as having provoked the abuse or having deserved it, no matter how severe or arbitrary the abuse seems to have been.

Thus it is not uncommon to hear abused women say things like, "I needed it," "I provoked him." "I was being a bad housekeeper and a bad mother" (Gelles, 1974). Among children one often hears, "My dad would lay into me but I needed it to keep me in line." Sexual abuse victims report thinking to themselves, "I must have been leading him on," "It was because my own needs for affection were so strong that I didn't make him stop." Although victims of violence and exploitation in other settings also blame themselves, it is particularly severe for victims in families, where the abuser is an influential person who has had a powerful effect on shaping a victim's perceptions.

One additional result of abuse in the family context is that many of the victims often maintain a rather incredible allegiance to their abusers in spite of all the damage they do. Many battered wives profess that they love their husbands, that they know their spouses really love them and that abuse is evidence of that (Gelles, 1974). Many victims of sexual abuse insist they are more angry at their mother for not protecting them than at their father who had sex with them for years despite their protestations (Herman and Hirschman, 1977). This attachment to the abuser is often combined with a belief that the abuse will stop if only the victim could reform herself. "If I could only be a better housewife," says the abused woman, "he would stop beating me" (Walker, 1979). "If I could only be a good little girl my father would stop punishing me," thinks the child.

Another common pattern among abuse victims is the extreme sense of shame and humiliation they harbor and the belief they have that other people could not possibly understand or identity with them. They often think they are the only ones who have undergone this kind of experience (Butler, 1978). They go to great lengths to keep it secret and often suffer from the sense of stigma and isolation.

In addition, there is a kind of entrapment that stymies the victims of all kinds of family abuse. The abuse often goes on over an extended period of time and the victims have difficulty either stopping it, avoiding it, or leaving entirely. This is one thing that people unfamiliar with family abuse are continually amazed by: Victims of spouse abuse, child abuse, and sexual abuse often do not try to escape their abusers. In fact, in many instances, they want to go back and go to great lengths to protect their abusers from outside intervention (Gelles, 1976).

This entrapment is connected to the unequal power balance in most abusive situations, to the lack of social supports that are available to victims of abuse, and also to our potent ideology of family dependency, which makes it difficult for victims to contemplate surviving outside their family, no matter how abusive it is. . . .

Of course, . . . there is the question of their long-term effects. Victims of the different kinds of family abuse report surprisingly similar long-term patterns: depression, suicidal feelings, self-contempt, and an inability to trust and to develop intimate relationships in later life (Herman and Hirschman, 1977; Walker, 1979). Such effects might well be the common result of the experience of being betrayed, exploited, and misused by someone on whom they were profoundly dependent. . . .

SHARED CHARACTERISTICS OF ABUSING FAMILIES

Still other things tie various forms of abuse together. Some of the available research, for example, shows that the type of family situation in which one kind of abuse occurs is also the type of family situation in which other abuse occurs. For example, all forms of abuse appear to be higher in the lower socioeconomic strata (Finkelhor, 1980; Pelton, 1981; Straus et al., 1980). All forms of abuse appear to be more common in families where unemployment and economic deprivation are serious problems (Meiselman, 1978; Straus et al., 1980). There is some evidence that all forms of abuse are more common in families that are more patriarchically organized (Gelles, 1974; Meiselman, 1978; Star, 1980; Straus et al., 1980). And all forms of abuse have been associated with families that are isolated and that have few community ties, friendships, or organizational affiliations (Finkelhor, 1978; Garbarino & Gilliam, 1980; Gelles, 1974; Straus et al. 1980). . . .

COMMONALITIES IN SOCIAL RESPONSE

One of the most interesting commonalities shared by the various forms of family abuse is the way in which they emerged as social problems. Even though each emerged separately at a somewhat different moment and in response to somewhat different political pressures, each type of family abuse has gone through a similar evolution as a social problem. For example, all of the abuses emerged as social problems from historical contexts where they had been minimized and where people believed that they did not occur frequently. It is now recognized that all of these forms of abuse occur with great frequency in the general population (Finkelhor, 1979; Straus et al., 1980).

Moreover, when these forms of abuse began first to come to public attention, in all cases they were analyzed as extremely pathological behaviors. Incest offenders were seen as backwoods degenerates and feebleminded freaks (Gebhard, Gagnon, Pomeroy & Christenson, 1965). Child beaters were seen as depraved (Gelles, 1979). Wife beaters were seen as alcoholic rogues and psychopaths and were considered to come from only extremely lower class and disorganized families (Walker, 1979). Today research sees these offenders as far less deviant than they were once viewed.

Another similarity in the popular mythology around all of these problems was the tendency to implicate the victims of the abuse as well as, or rather than, the offenders. The tendency was perhaps the strongest in the case of spouse abuse. Victims were described clinically as provoking, asking for it, women with masochistic needs for bullying spouses (Gelles, 1976). Early analyses of the problem of sexual abuse had great similarities. Abused children were seen as seductive and flirtatious to such an extent that they brought the sexual abuse on themselves (Armstrong, 1978).

Perhaps this tendency to blame the victim was weakest in the history of the concern about physical child abuse. It was harder to blame a one-, two-, or three-year-old child than an adolescent or adult woman. But even in this case one can find evidence of a belief that abused children were, in fact, extremely aggressive and provoking and if it had not been for their waywardness, they would not have been abused. In all cases these "blaming the victim" stereotypes took a long time to abate and continue to reappear from time to time in various guises.

In each of the kinds of abuse, a social movement arose which drew attention to the abuse that was occurring (Finkelhor, 1979; Pfohl, 1977). But in each case some ambiguity remained about how to define the normative boundaries of the abuse. In the case of child abuse, there remains much public ambiguity about where to draw the line between what is often referred to as strict discipline and child abuse (Straus et al., 1980). In the case of spouse abuse, there is a belief among large segments of the population and even the professional community that certain forms of violence between couples, such as slapping or pushing, is normative and should not be labeled spouse abuse. In the case of sexual abuse, there are large grey areas. Parents and even professionals are in substantial disagreement about whether bringing children into bed, parading in front of them naked, or exposing them to various kinds of explicit sexual material constitute a form of sexual abuse (Finkelhor, 1982). The ambiguity about normative boundaries is a problem common to all forms of family abuse. . . .

Editor's note: On the basis of this article, we can stress three areas of family policy:

1. How can we use Finkelhor's analysis to help develop sound family policy? Can the commonalities that run through family abuse provide guidelines for constructing family policy? If so, how can we use them as keys to diminish family abuse and help people who find themselves in abusive situations—both the abused and abusers?
2. Is it actually proper or desirable to develop government policy on family abuse in the first place? Are not the solutions to family abuse perhaps best left up to individual families to work out? Don't current laws already provide an adequate framework for families and friends and neighbors to apply to abusive situations? Granted that family abuse is undesirable, is it really the government's business?
3. If family abuse is the government's business, how can we prevent the government from going overboard and violating family privacy? For example, in the laudatory attempt to eliminate child abuse the government could ban all spanking of children (as in Sweden where it is now illegal for parents to spank their children). Or, indeed, should such a law be a proper goal?

—*J. M. H.*

REFERENCES

American Humane Association. *National Analysis of Official Child Neglect and Abuse Reporting*. Denver: AHA, 1978.

Armstrong, L. *Kiss Daddy Goodnight*. New York: Hawthorn, 1978.

Butler, S. *Conspiracy of Silence*. San Francisco: New Glide, 1978.

Finkelhor, D. Psychological, Cultural and Family Factors in Incest and Sexual Abuse. *Journal of Marriage and Family Counseling*, 1978, 4, 41–49. (Reprinted in Joanne V. Cook and Roy T. Bowles [Eds.], *Child Abuse: Commission and Omission*. Toronto: Butterworth.)

———. *Sexually Victimized Children.* New York: Free Press, 1979.

———. Risk Factors in the Sexual Victimization of Children. *Child Abuse and Neglect,* 1980, *4,* 265–273.

———. Public Definitions of Sexual Abusiveness toward Children. Unpublished paper, University of New Hampshire, 1982.

GARBARINO, J., and G. GILLIAM, *Understanding Abusive Families.* Lexington, MA: D. C. Heath, 1980.

GEBHARD, P., J. GAGNON, W. POMEROY, and C. CHRISTENSON. *Sex Offenders: An Analysis of Types.* New York: Harper & Row, 1965.

GELLES, R. *The Violent Home.* Beverly Hills, CA: Sage, 1974.

GIL, D. *Child Abuse and Violence.* New York: AMS Press, 1979.

HERBRUCK, C. *Breaking the Cycle of Child Abuse.* Minneapolis: Winston Press, 1979.

HERMAN J., and L. HIRSCHMAN. Father-Daughter Incest. *Signs,* 1977, *2,* 1–22.

MADAN, M., and D. WRENCH, Significant Findings in Child Abuse Research. *Victimology,* 1977, 11, 196–224.

MEISELMAN, K. *Incest.* San Francisco: Jossey-Bass, 1978.

PELTON, L. *Social Context of Child Abuse and Neglect.* New York: Human Sciences Press, 1981.

PFOHL, S. The Discovery of Child Abuse. *Social Problems,* 1977, *24,* 310–323.

SPINETTA, J., and D. RIGLER. The Child Abusing Parent: A Psychological Review. *Psychological Bulletin,* 1972, *77,* 296–304.

STAR, B. Patterns of Family Violence. *Social Casework,* 1980, *61,* 339–346.

STRAUS, M., R. GELLES, and S. STEINMETZ. *Behind Closed Doors: Violence in the American Family,* New York: Doubleday, 1980.

WALKER, L. *The Battered Woman.* New York: Harper & Row, 1979.

54

ture of the Family

Edward Cornish

ABSTRACT: The author develops five scenarios of possible futures of the family:

1. marriage and family decline as individuality becomes dominant
2. marriage and family are abolished as other institutions take over their functions
3. conservative factors reverse trends, strengthening marriage and family
4. government policy revitalizes the family
5. artificial families

Granted the dramatic changes ahead in all aspects of civilization, any prediction about the future of the family is highly risky if not foolhardy. But we can at least construct a few scenarios to show some possible futures for the family.

A scenario provides a useful starting point for thinking seriously about the family's future, because it moves us forcibly into the future by creating a plausible sequence of future events, starting with current trends and proposed actions. Until we really look at possible future developments, we live in a fairyland where actions may be contemplated without considering their manifold consequences—where hard choices are unnecessary, unforeseen events never happen, and dilemmas can be papered over with pretty words. . . .

SCENARIO I: A CONTINUATION OF PRESENT TRENDS

This first scenario anticipates that current trends will continue: The divorce rate will continue to rise, to the point where divorce is the "normal" way for marriages to end. The marriage and remarriage rates will continue to decline, as they have in the past decade or so, leaving more and more people in the "never-married" and "divorced and not-remarried" classes. Increasingly the traditional family—husband, wife, and children—will disappear. In its place will be people living by themselves or in groups of individuals unrelated by kinship or marriage. Women will increasingly pursue careers and shun the role of homemakers. Men will perform needed household chores for themselves. The individual rather than the family will increasingly be the "natural" unit of society.

The birthrate will drop further, reaching the point where people of the United States and other advanced nations are no longer reproducing themselves and are being replaced by surplus population from the developing countries. As a result the culture of the advanced countries may begin to shift in the direction of the culture of the immigrants from the developing world.

Most people will live alone. They will do their own thing, unhindered by family obligations. There will be a fantastic expansion of self-realization activities aimed at helping the individual to realize maximum personal happiness and self-expression. The solidarity of groups—families, neighborhoods, communities, associations, churches, etc.—will decline even more than in recent years. The individual will be supreme; the group will be tolerated only as a means of helping individuals to realize their private goals. People will increasingly resent having to pay money to state and church for the welfare of others. But they will lavish money on embellishing themselves and their surroundings and will travel constantly in search of excitement. Many will have a second home and some a third, fourth, or even a fifth home.

The suicide rate will reach incredible levels. As the French sociologist Emile Durkheim noted long ago, suicide thrives under conditions of *anomie*, where group norms have broken down and the individual is left to do his own thing. Unable to realize the perfect happiness they seek and unbound by any religious or group restrictions, people will kill themselves in record numbers, starting with children not yet into their teens. At the same time, the use or abuse of drugs will reach incredible heights. The crime rate will soar. . . .

SCENARIO II: THE ABOLITION OF THE FAMILY

If the family continues to weaken—and its egocentric, asocial offspring threaten anarchy—a point might eventually be reached where it may become *illegal* for people to marry or to bear children—and heavy penalties might be exacted on those convicted of willfully doing so. Such measures might be adopted also as a means of controlling population growth and of insuring in individual's dependence on a totalitarian state.

Other institutions would, of course, develop to provide the functions that the family once offered. For example, government agencies might collect sperm and ova from suitable donors, combine them in test-tubes, and then allow the fertilized ova to gestate under careful supervision in artificial wombs that would nourish and protect the baby until it was ready to breathe air and consume through its mouth. While the baby was developing into a child and later an adolescent and adult, he would be cared for by professionals rather than kinfolk. The child would have no family, at least not in the traditional sense. Possibly he might be trained to think of all mankind as his family. But possibly the word *family* would have such an archaic, unpleasant, and primitive connotation that it would not be used—except in discussing the bad days of the past.

In a family-less society, the individual would have no permanent ties to anyone else. He would not be responsible to any other individual nor would anyone else be responsible to him. Such responsibilities as he had would be to non-kinship, non-family groups such as a government, school, or special-interest group. Although he would be completely "alone" in that he would have none of the traditional ties of kinship to anyone else, he might not *feel* lonely because he would never have known such ties in his early life. Instead he might experience loneliness simply when he was not with someone else, whoever that person might be.

The abolition of the family might be accompanied by the elimination of interpersonal sex as well. Such a development might occur if new technology (1) made it possible for people to have bigger and better orgasms through drugs and/or electrical stimulation of the brain and (2) enabled people to reproduce through cloning or some other method that did not require people to produce sex cells. Once there is no need for sexual reproduction and no desire for the cumbersome, limited, and somewhat chancy sexual method of attaining orgasms, biologists can attack the relatively easy task of creating (through genetic engineering or simply by breeding) people without sexual organs. The creation of neuter people might lead to a far more peaceful and efficient—though perhaps duller—civilization. The industriousness and group loyalty of ants is proverbial, and much of it may arise from the fact that the workers are neuter and therefore not distracted by sex.

SCENARIO III: A REVERSAL

The third scenario begins with the premise that current trends cannot continue indefinitely and must eventually reverse. Life-styles will, therefore, eventually return to what they were in the past. For example, the divorce rate cannot continue to rise indefinitely or society would simply disintegrate. Therefore, we can anticipate that at some point in the future society will recognize the plight of the family and come to its rescue.

Reversals are hardly unknown through history. A period of growing prosperity is followed by a period of growing poverty. An era of licentiousness is followed by an era of puritanism. In the future, society might take deliberate steps to restore and strengthen the traditional family, through such measures as:

• *Resacramentalization of marriage.* More emphasis might be placed on the "sacredness" of marriage. Religion might be called upon to help devise more impressive ceremonies to insure that couples understand what they are undertaking. Ceremonies in which couples repeat their vows might become more common and deliberately encouraged.

• *The re-creation of communities.* The importance of the community to the family—and vice versa—might be generally recognized and heavy emphasis placed on improving community life in order to improve family life. To strengthen communities, automobiles might be banned or heavily taxed so as to encourage people to patronize local stores and institutions.

• *Control of television.* The importance of television in the socialization of children and inculcation of attitudes favorable to family life is generally recognized. Efforts might be made to make sure that television encourages attitudes favorable to good family functioning.

• *Reaffirmation of sex roles.* The blurring of sex roles might come to be viewed as a horrendous mistake. Instead society might encourage parents and teachers to train boys more carefully to perform the tasks expected of husbands and girls to perform the duties of wives. Sex-segregated institutions and groups would be encouraged as a means of protecting and strengthening marriage and family.

• *Renewal of sanctions against out-of-wedlock pregnancy.* Recognition of the importance of the intact family in the emotional development of children could lead to a reversal of the current sympathetic attitude toward unmarried women who bear children. Strong actions might be taken to prevent the birth of illegitimate children. These actions might range from a heavy emphasis on continence and/or effective birth control measures to tests for pregnancy and mandatory abortions.

• *Discouragement of sex outside marriage.* Government actions might range from televised "spot announcements" on the desirability of continence to jail sentences for adulterers and fornicators.

A reversal of the current trends toward highly individualistic life-styles and smaller households might well occur under such circumstances as:

• *Alarm at social disintegration.* Popular attitudes favorable to individual self-gratification might decline as people become alarmed about the disintegration of society at large.

• *A second great depression.* Some economists believe that the world will experience a major worldwide depression in the near future. If so, many of today's fragmented families might reunite: Children might move back into their parents' homes or old people might move in with their children. A couple thinking about getting divorced might decide they could not afford it and stay married, perhaps eventually becoming reconciled. Since few people could afford automobile travel, community stores might revive. Many people might turn to home gardening. People would stay home rather than travel to far-off places. Fewer wives would work in the reduced labor market.

• *Religious conversion.* The triumph of Christianity in ancient Rome and its spread through much of the world led to the imposition of an organized system of morality that changed life-styles everywhere. The later imposition of Islam on the vast area from the Iberian Peninsula across north Africa to distant parts of Asia had a similar impact. A new religion of whatever kind might lead to a reversal of current trends in life-styles.

• *World War III.* A World War fought with thermonuclear and other modern weapons would create devastation and horrors on a scale that would have no precedent in history and today can only be guessed at. In the aftermath of such destruction, individuals might find themselves scrabbling among the ruins for uneaten foodstuffs. People might form bands for self-protection and mutual aid, and these bands would provide a basis for tribes and communities. Within such frameworks, families might develop similar to those that now exist among primitive people around the world.

SCENARIO IV: A REVITALIZATION OF THE FAMILY

The family might successfully adapt itself to modern civilization, partly because improved economic conditions and new technology will enable people to concentrate on improving the family, a task that heretofore has tended to be neglected. New electronic communications networks may make it increasingly possible for people to work at home with their families. In addition, closer ties with other family members at distant locations could be maintained.

Growing recognition of the importance of the family in child-rearing and the provision of emotional and economic support for people could lead to changes in government policies that now tend to undermine family stability and to the institution of programs deliberately designed to enhance the quality of family life. Increasing uncertainty about national or world economic and political conditions might also encourage more people to focus on revitalizing their family lives.

A rationale for revitalizing the family rather than seeing it decline or disappear might go as follows:

The traditional family, based on ties of blood and marriage, is the "natural" basis of society and any departure from the natural way is risky. Not even the wisest social scientists know all the vital functions that the family fulfills in the operations of society and in the psychic life of the individual. Experience demonstrates the great strength of the ties that can develop between a mother and the child she has carried within her body and who has suckled her breast. Similarly potent is the "pleasure bond" that develops between a man and a woman. These natural ties, part of man's biological nature, are the root of most social life. All societies everywhere and at all times that we know anything about have developed on the basis of these natural ties. It would be folly to try to construct society in any other way, especially in view of the very primitive state of our current social science. Wisdom lies in working with what nature has given us: Our problems have arisen because we have opposed or ignored nature rather than working with her. Modern technological civilization has enabled man to raise his standard of living but has exacted a terrible penalty by destroying the family, the community, religion, and meaningful social relationships. Now that we have such a high standard of living, we can well afford to devote more attention to such matters as the family.

A program for revitalizing the traditional family might include:

• *Matching of prospective bride and groom.* Good marriages should begin with good dating. Computerized dating services are still in a primitive state, but suggest what might be done to match up people with compatible characteristics. Only too often nowadays, people rarely get to know those people whom they are really compatible with, because they never get to meet them. Instead, they find themselves dating—and even falling in love with—people whom they really have little in common with.

• *Training for marriage.* Schools could provide young people with more courses in marriage and parenthood, including not only sex education but money management, child training, and dealing with interpersonal disputes. Better training could help prevent teenage pregnancy, which leads often to marital failure or to the production of children who are unlikely to receive adequate emotional support in their development.

• *Stronger efforts to improve emotional development.* Many marriages fail because of the emotional immaturity of one or both of the partners. Programs could be instituted—starting perhaps in the schools—to identify people's emotional problems and assist them in overcoming them. Communities could provide psychiatric and other types of counseling to help individuals maintain good family relationships.

• *Community stability.* The instability of communities due to the high mobility of the population contributes to the failure of marriages. Mothers with children need neighbors whom they can talk to and leave their children with occasionally. A variety of techniques could be used to increase community stability including, perhaps, penalties for companies that require their personnel to make transfers.

• *Incorporation of families.* David P. Snyder, a management analyst, has suggested that families could be strengthened by allowing them to legally incorporate themselves. Such incorporation might provide a variety of tax and other benefits that would help to stabilize families. (See "The Corporate Family: A Look at a Proposed Social Invention," by David P. Snyder, *The Futurist*, December 1976.)

SCENARIO V: ARTIFICIAL FAMILIES

The argument for the creation of artificial families might go something like this: The traditional family has failed because it simply does not meet the needs of modern man. Permanent units based on blood relationships are simply a holdover from man's primitive past. The traditional family was never very good: There were endless problems—physical abuse, sibling rivalry, nagging, Oedipus and Electra complexes, incest, the subjugation of children, prodigal sons, adolescent rebellion, etc., etc. Clearly what is needed is a fresh start.

Already there are a number of developments that suggest a general movement toward the creation of artificial families: Many com... and collectives have much of the character of families. Some churches have encouraged the development of extended families by assigning individuals to a nuclear couple, which adopts them as family members. The enlarged family gets together for recreational and other activities and provides a certain amount of mutual aid to extended family members.

In the future, it would be possible to create such artificial families on the basis of common interests: There could be families composed solely of artists, lawyers, balletomanes, vegetarians, or stock car racing enthusiasts. Possibly such deeply held interests might substitute for the common religion and customs that have traditionally held families together.

One factor encouraging the development of artificial families is the disintegration of the natural family: Many people now find themselves without a natural family that they can really relate to. When family members are very widely scattered, the family can no longer function as the traditional family once did, and artificial families might be able to fill the void.

And perhaps it will not be necessary to choose between natural and artificial families: An individual might belong to both a natural family and one or more artificial families.

CONCLUSION

There is no need to select one scenario as the best either from the standpoint of desirability or likelihood of realization, and any evaluation of the scenarios will doubtless change with the passage of time. . . .

The family has endured from the Stone Age to the Space Age. Today it faces greater challenges than ever before in history, and its continued existence can no longer be taken for granted. But, civilization began with the family, and its decline might well mean the end of the civilization it created. No one knows, but the experience of the Israeli kibbutzim provides an object lesson. In the 1920s, these collective communities practiced a strict anti-familialism, proclaiming the kibbutz as a new and improved social order based on spiritual affinity rather than blood ties. So strong was the anti-family feeling that if a kibbutznik had relatives in another kibbutz, he was supposed to act as if they meant nothing special to him and to treat them coolly. Women generally maintained their "independent status" and even their maiden names after marriage. Weddings—if performed at all—were executed summarily. Any attempt to give a husband and wife the same day of rest was viewed as an anti-community act.

Today anti-familialism has disappeared from the kibbutzim. The family has not only revived but triumphed. A 1977 article in *Shdemot*, literary digest of the kibbutz movement, reports that the anti-familialism of the first kibbutzim "now seems like memories of some prehistoric age." What's more, the family has revived not just in its emaciated nuclear form, but in the sturdy extended version of by-gone years. Today, says Yehoshua Gilboa, author of the *Shdemot* article, it is common to find not only fathers and sons but even grandfathers and grandsons in close proximity, working side by side.

"Who could have dreamed," asks Gilboa, "that the kibbutz, that rebellious, super-progressive unit, would restore a model to modern society of the natural and human values forfeited during the headlong rush for development and progress?"

Appendix: Correlation Chart

IN ORDER TO MAKE THIS SECOND EDITION of *Marriage and Family in a Changing Society* more useful, I have developed the following correlation chart. Nineteen basic marriage and family texts are listed alphabetically across the top of the correlation chart. The chapters of these texts are the basic reference point for the chart: The numbers that refer to them are located in the column to the left of the boxes. The numbers within the boxes refer to the reading selections in *Marriage and Family in a Changing Society.*

Because some selections contain more than a single major theme, it is possible to correlate them with the basic texts in a number of ways. Depending upon your particular approach to teaching the course and the sociological principles that you want to abstract from the selections, you may wish to rearrange the ordering suggested in this correlation chart.

The numbers within the boxes refer to selection numbers in **Marriage and Family in a Changing Society**

The numbers directly below refer to chapters in the marriage and family texts:	Bell, *Marriage and Family Interaction* (1983)	Broderick, *Marriage and the Family* (1984)	Coleman, *Intimate Relationships, Marriage, and Family* (1984)	Cox, *Human Intimacy: Marriage, the Family and Its Meaning* (1984)	Dyer, *Courtship, Marriage, and Family* (1983)	Eshleman, *The Family: An Introduction* (1985)	Garrett, *Seasons of Marriage and Family Life* (1982)	Golanty and Harris, *Marriage and Family Life* (1982)	Lasswell and Lasswell, *Marriage and the Family* (1982)	Leslie and Korman *The Family in Social Context* (1985)
1	1, 2, 3	1, 2, 3, 4	1, 2, 3, 4, 6	1, 2, 3, 4	1, 2, 3, 4	2, 6, 7, 10	1, 2	1, 2, 3, 4, 6	1, 2, 3, 4, 10	2
2	4, 40	11, 12, 13	19	17, 18, 19, 20	14, 15, 16	1	3, 4	17, 18, 20	14, 15, 16	
3	22, 23, 24	28	22, 23	21, 22, 23, 24, 25, 26, 27	17, 18, 19, 20	3, 4	14, 15, 16	19	21	10
4	17, 18, 20	6, 7	14, 15, 16	6, 7	21, 23	14, 15, 32, 33, 34	21, 22, 23	11, 12, 13	17, 18, 19, 20, 22	11, 38
5	21, 38	14, 15, 16	21, 35, 36, 37	28, 29, 53	22, 24, 26, 27	51	19, 24	22, 24	23, 25, 26, 27	25, 26, 27
6	26, 27		17, 18, 20	14, 15, 16	6, 7, 11, 12, 13	11	17, 18, 20	21, 23, 25, 35, 36, 37	11, 12, 13, 24, 53	2, 3, 4
7	25	21, 22, 23	25, 26, 27		28, 29, 30, 31	12	7, 10, 28, 29, 30, 31	16	28, 29, 30	1
8	6, 19, 28	24, 25, 26	24	32, 33, 34	35, 36, 37	5, 13	25, 26, 32, 33, 34		5, 6, 7, 31, 53	6, 7,

9	7	17, 18, 19, 20, 27	28, 29, 30, 31	35, 36, 37	32, 33, 34	17, 18, 19, 20, 22	8, 9, 38, 39, 43	28, 32, 33, 34	38, 39, 43	12
10	5, 29	29, 30, 31, 32, 33	32, 33, 34	8, 9, 39	44, 45, 46, 47, 48, 49, 50	21, 23, 24	40, 41, 42	5, 7, 29, 30, 31, 53	8, 9, 40, 41	13
11	14, 32	34	7, 44, 45, 53	38	25	25, 26, 27	6, 27, 35, 36, 37	9, 39	42	
12	15, 33	35, 36, 37	8, 9, 38, 39, 40, 41, 42, 43	40, 41, 42, 43	8, 9, 38, 39, 41, 43	16, 35, 36, 37	44, 45, 46, 47, 48, 49, 50, 51	8, 38	32, 33, 34	14, 15, 16, 17, 18, 19, 20, 21
13	16, 34	8, 9, 38, 39	47, 49, 51	5	40, 42	28, 29, 30, 31		40, 41, 42, 43	44, 45, 46, 47	21, 22, 23, 24
14		40, 41, 42, 43	5	44, 45, 46, 47	51	8, 9, 38, 39	11, 12, 13	44, 45, 46, 47, 48, 49, 50, 51	48, 49, 50, 51	28, 29, 30, 31, 32, 33, 34, 53
15	35, 36, 37	5	46	48, 49, 50, 51	5	40, 41, 42, 43	5	14, 15		35, 36, 37
16	10	44, 45, 53	48, 50	10, 30, 31, 52, 54	10, 52, 53, 54	44, 45, 46, 47		10		8, 9, 30, 40, 41, 42, 43
17	8, 9, 39, 43	46, 47, 48, 49, 50, 51	10, 52, 54			48, 49, 50, 53	52, 53, 54	26, 27		5
18	41, 53	10				52, 54				44, 45, 46, 47
19	42*									48, 49, 50, 51

*Chapter 20 of Bell (1983) correlates with readings 30, 31, 44, and 45 of this volume; Chapter 21 with readings 46 and 47; and Chapter 22 with readings 48, 49, 50, and 51.

The numbers within the boxes refer to selection numbers in **Marriage and Family in a Changing Society**

The numbers directly below refer to chapters in the marriage and family texts:	*Levande, Koch, and Koch Mariage and the Family (1983)*	*Melville, Marriage and Family Today (1983)*	*Rice, Contemporary Marriage (1983)*	*Saxton, The Individual, Marriage, and the Family (1983)*	*Scanzoni and Scanzoni, Men, Women, and Change (1981)*	*Arlene S. Skolnick The Intimate Environment: Exploring Marriage and the Family (1983)*	*Stinnett, Walters, and Kaye, Relationships in Marriage and the Family (1984)*	*Strong, DeVault, Suid, and Reynolds, The Marriage and Family Experience (1983)*	*Wells, Choices in Marriage and Family (1984)*
1	1, 2, 3, 4, 10	1, 2, 3, 4, 6, 11, 12, 13	1, 2, 3, 4, 10	1, 4	1, 2, 3 4, 10	1	1	1, 2	1, 4, 25, 26, 27
2	17, 18, 19, 20	17, 18, 19, 20, 24	21, 22, 23, 24	14, 15	14, 15	4	17, 18, 19, 20, 22, 24, 26, 27	3, 4, 11 12, 13	2, 3
3	6, 11, 12, 13, 52, 54	22, 23, 25	25, 26, 27	16, 35, 36, 37	16	6, 7	6, 7	6, 15, 16	22, 23
4	14, 15, 35, 36, 37	21	17, 18, 20	21	17, 18 19, 20	5, 53	35	17, 18, 20	14, 15, 16
5	25, 26, 27	26	6, 7, 19	17, 18 19, 20	21	2	29, 30, 31	19, 21, 22, 23, 24, 25, 26, 27	21
6	21, 22, 23, 24	30, 31	14	22, 23, 24	22, 23, 24	3	2, 3, 4, 32, 33, 34	10, 29, 30, 31	17, 18, 19, 20
7	32, 33, 34	14, 15, 16	15	25, 26, 27		11, 12, 13, 32, 33	28	32, 33, 34	24
8	28, 29, 30, 31	29, 32, 33, 34	16	5, 29, 30, 31	25	14, 15, 21	23	8, 9	6, 29, 30, 31

9	7, 16, 53	7, 28, 53	32,33, 34	43, 48, 49 50, 51	26, 27	17, 18, 19, 20, 22, 23, 24, 26, 27	53		35, 36, 37
10	8, 9, 38, 39, 43	35, 36, 37	5, 29, 30, 31	28	6, 7, 28	25, 44, 45, 46, 47, 48, 49, 50, 51	14, 15, 16, 21, 36, 37	28	8, 43
11	40, 41, 42	5	28	44, 45, 46, 47	11, 12, 13, 32, 33, 34	16, 28, 29, 30, 31, 34, 35, 36, 37	8, 9	7	5
12	44, 45, 46, 47, 48, 49, 50, 51	8, 9, 38, 39, 40, 41, 42, 43	53	2, 3, 6, 7, 10, 11, 12, 13	35, 36, 37	8, 9, 38, 39, 43	38, 39	14	10
13		27		8, 9, 38, 39	29, 30	40, 41, 42	40, 41, 42, 43	35, 36, 37	32, 33, 34
14	5	44, 45, 46, 47, 48, 49, 50, 51		40, 41, 42, 43	31, 53	10		38, 39, 40, 41, 42, 43	7, 28, 53
15		10, 52, 54	35, 36, 37	32, 33, 34	8, 9, 38, 39, 43	52, 54	5	53	9, 38, 39, 40, 41, 42
16			44, 45, 46, 47, 48, 49, 50, 51		40, 41, 42		10	5	44, 45, 46, 47, 48, 49, 50, 51
17			8, 9, 38, 39		5		44, 45, 46, 47, 48, 49, 50, 51	44, 45, 46	52, 54
18			43		44, 45, 46, 47, 48, 49 50, 51		25	48, 49, 50, 51	
19			40, 41, 42				52, 54		

Name Index

Note: An asterisk preceding a name indicates that the individual is a contributor to this volume.

Subject Index

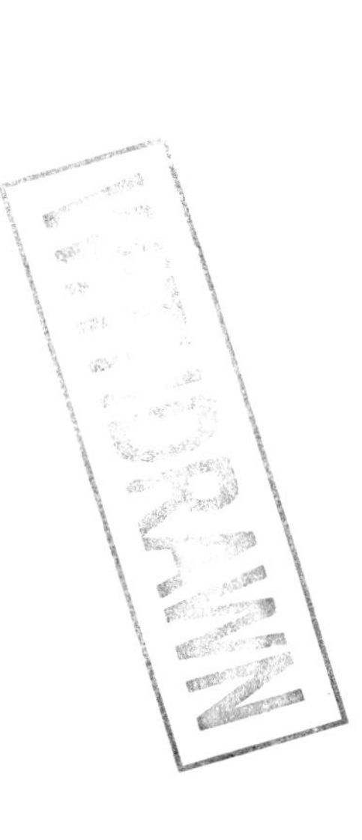